Yiddish Revolutionaries in Migration

Historical Materialism Book Series

The Historical Materialism Book Series is a major publishing initiative of the radical left. The capitalist crisis of the twenty-first century has been met by a resurgence of interest in critical Marxist theory. At the same time, the publishing institutions committed to Marxism have contracted markedly since the high point of the 1970s. The Historical Materialism Book Series is dedicated to addressing this situation by making available important works of Marxist theory. The aim of the series is to publish important theoretical contributions as the basis for vigorous intellectual debate and exchange on the left.

The peer-reviewed series publishes original monographs, translated texts, and reprints of classics across the bounds of academic disciplinary agendas and across the divisions of the left. The series is particularly concerned to encourage the internationalization of Marxist debate and aims to translate significant studies from beyond the English-speaking world.

For a full list of titles in the Historical Materialism Book Series available in paperback from Haymarket Books, visit:
https://www.haymarketbooks.org/series_collections/1-historical-materialism

Jewish socialists gather to commemorate pogrom victims, Vilnius, 1905
© YIVO INSTITUTE FOR JEWISH RESEARCH, NEW YORK

Yiddish Revolutionaries in Migration

The Transnational History of the Jewish Labour Bund

Frank Wolff

Translated by
Loren Balhorn
Jan-Peter Herrmann

Haymarket Books
Chicago, IL

First published in 2020 by Brill Academic Publishers, The Netherlands
© 2020 Koninklijke Brill NV, Leiden, The Netherlands

Published in paperback in 2021 by
Haymarket Books
P.O. Box 180165
Chicago, IL 60618
773-583-7884
www.haymarketbooks.org

ISBN: 978-1-64259-606-9

Distributed to the trade in the US through Consortium Book Sales and Distribution (www.cbsd.com) and internationally through Ingram Publisher Services International (www.ingramcontent.com).

This book was published with the generous support of Lannan Foundation and Wallace Action Fund.

Special discounts are available for bulk purchases by organizations and institutions. Please call 773-583-7884 or email info@haymarketbooks.org for more information.

Cover art and design by David Mabb. Cover art is a detail of *Two Squares, no. 7*. El Lissitzky's 'About Two Squares' on William Morris 'Daisy' wallpaper, paint and paper on canvas (2008).

Printed in the United States.

10 9 8 7 6 5 4 3 2 1

Library of Congress Cataloging-in-Publication data is available.

The 60-year history of the Bund resembles the life story of a person who lived through his most crucial phases not only at different times, but in different countries, and – in light of recent decades – on different continents.
LEON OLER, 1957

Contents

Preface XI
Editorial Note XV
List of Figures and Tables XVI
Abbreviations XVIII

Introduction 1

PART 1
The Bund as a Social Movement

1 Bundist Activism 41

2 Activism Patterns in Eastern Europe: Constituting the Transferable 55

PART 2
'Exalted Moments of Our Romantic Past': Community Building through Collective Remembrance

3 Remembrance as Activist Practice: Initial Considerations 103

4 The Bundist Press: From Agitational Publications to Transnational *Memorik* 107

5 Memories beyond 'Me' and 'Us': Bundist Autobiography as Social Formation 150

6 Preserving Collective Knowledge in Migration: Collective Biography and Questionnaires 185

7 Preliminary Conclusions 209

PART 3
Old Masses in New Streets: Transnationalising the Bund

8   Between Here and There: Bundist Gatherings Overseas   221

9   Reproduction as Creation: Worker Organisation and Secondary Bundism   250

10 Politics, Economics, *Yidishkayt*: The Tangled Web of Class Struggle and Cultural Work   284

11 Passing on *Yidishkayt*: Transfers and Limits of Bundist Educational Work   312

12 Relief Funds as Weapons: From Revolutionary Fundraising to Transnational Cultural Work   359

Conclusion, or: The Ambivalence of Bundist Modernity   408

Bibliography   425
Index   506

Preface

My search for the history of the Bund in the process of migration almost turned me into a migrant myself. Originally conceived at the University of Cologne, the project would accompany me on my move to Bielefeld and travel to Buenos Aires, Israel, and the United States on several occasions before reaching its final destination at Johns Hopkins University in Baltimore. The resulting manuscript was then completed in Berlin and Osnabrück; the translation took it back to the US (Notre Dame, Indiana) and, finally, to Berlin.

I lived out of a suitcase for several years, gathering source materials and pieces of evidence in official archives, private collections, and the dusty stacks of neglected libraries. Over the course of this search for people, memories, letters, and publications, telephones were often just as crucial as reference books – the only difference being that the latter were hardly ever forthcoming. Often enough I felt like the lyrical subject in the poem *Jacinto Chiclana*, written by Jorge Luis Borges and congenially set to music by Astor Piazolla:

Me acuerdo, fue en Balvanera,	I remember, it was in Balvanera,
en una noche lejana,	in a distant night,
que alguien dejó caer el nombre	that someone dropped the name
de un tal Jacinto Chiclana.	of one Jacinto Chiclana.
...	...
¡Quién sabe por qué razón	Who knows for what reason
me anda buscando ese nombre!	I'm driven to search for that name!
Me gustaría saber	I wish I knew
cómo habrá sido aquel hombre.	what happened to him.

My own research included quite a few such 'distant nights' in which I heard many names uttered with the greatest respect, yet whose biographies could not be found in any catalogue, encyclopaedia, or index. I often scoured the streets of Balvanera, encircling the Jewish quarter of Once where the Bundist Peretz School used to be. In these streets I found many of the archives relevant to my work, although I continued to depend on the help of sympathetic institutions and people all over the world who helped me trace vague clues, matching names with faces and sometimes even stories.

It would be impossible to list everyone who supported this effort in the limited space offered by a preface. Crucial assistance was provided in the form of a doctoral scholarship from the Friedrich Ebert Foundation, covering not only my living expenses but also a large share of the mounting travel costs. The foundation also plugged me into a scholarly network instrumental in driving my work forward. The same is true for the Bielefeld Graduate School in History and Sociology at Bielefeld University. Both institutions were solidly committed to the project and never failed to provide me with support, even in difficult periods. They consistently responded with encouragement and the necessary means to successfully and ambitiously complete my research. A subsequent year-long stay at Johns Hopkins University was invaluable, providing me with pure, undisturbed writing time. A place like Johns Hopkins inevitably leaves its mark on any historiographical project conducted within its hallowed halls. Here I encountered both stimulating intellectual exchange as well as the peace and quiet needed to assemble a coherent whole out of the work I had conducted on three continents, at three universities, with sources in five languages.

Thanks to the support of my colleagues at my current institution, the Institute for Migration Research and Intercultural Studies (IMIS)/Modern History, Dorothee Rheker-Wunsch and Patricia Simon at Böhlau Verlag, series editor Andreas Eckert, and a VG Wort publication grant, the German manuscript turned into a book in the renowned *Industrielle Welt* series. If it were not for Sebastian Budgen's and Loren Balhorn's continued interest in an English translation, the story probably would have ended there. Their encouragement and assistance paved the way for the Geisteswissenschaften International award and publication in Brill's esteemed Historical Materialism Book Series. Many surviving Bundists migrated overseas and few of them and their descendants read German. I am especially grateful that this translation makes my book available to them – for it is, after all, their story.

The groundwork for the project was laid by numerous sources. Many documents only found their way to my desk through the help of others, as they were frequently neither 'accessible' nor 'orderable'. The staffs at YIVO and the New York Public Library in New York, the IWO, the CeDInCI, and the Centro Mark Turkow in Buenos Aires, as well as the CAHJP in Jerusalem were all extremely helpful. I would like to express particular thanks to Ettie Goldwasser and the walking, talking encyclopaedia that is Leo Greenbaum at the YIVO in New York. Equally important was the work I conducted at the IWO in Buenos Aires, which still bears the scars of the 1994 AMIA bombing. At the time I conducted my research the institute lacked a functioning index system, and ordering documents often sounded something like *'Necesito todo sobre los sindicatos judíos'*. The rest was patchwork. Completing the transnational account of the history of the Bund you hold in your hands would have been impossible without the crucial assistance I received from Silvia Hansman and Debora Kacowicz, who never hesitated to fulfil even my most extravagant requests without the slightest hint of bureaucratic foot-dragging.

PREFACE   XIII

That said, working on a book involves not only research but also exchange, comments, and grant proposals. I would like to thank Regine Mehl, Manfred Alexander, Jürgen Dowe, and Christoph Schmidt for their initial advice and support. Furthermore, I am grateful to Linda Braun, Christian Alexander Bauer, Pablo Beyen, Tobias Brinkmann, Michael Bommes†, Jeffrey Brooks, Marcelo Dimentstein, Norbert Fintzsch, Heiko Haumann, Guido Hausmann, Jack Jacobs, Martin Krämer Liehn, Tony Michels, Kenneth Moss, Nick Raedburn, Christoph Rass, Dominik Schrage, Walter Sperling, Horacio Tarcus, Nerina Visacovsky, Mike Westrate, and Efraim Zadoff for conversations, opinions, and support that ensured this book's completion. I received a considerable amount of conceptual inspiration (and concrete suggestions) at numerous conferences in Germany, Great Britain, the United States, and Argentina, as well as in colloquia and discussion groups at the universities of Basel, Bochum, Bonn, Buenos Aires, Cologne, Notre Dame (Indiana), Osnabrück, Tübingen, and Bielefeld on several occasions. I thank all participants for their contributions and critical remarks. Input from the 'old Cologne crew', the other three leaves of the 'four-leaved clover' – Julia Herzberg, Alexis Hofmeister, and Alexander Kraus along with Birte Kohtz, Roland Cvetkovski, Moritz Heidkamp, and Andreas Renner – proved deeply influential from the outset. All of them, as well as my fellow 'grads' at Bielefeld and Baltimore, my colleagues at IMIS in Osnabrück, the Ibañez and Pardo families, Jean-Olivier Richard, Suzanne Werner, and Jeremy Welter, who deeply enriched my stays in Buenos Aires and Baltimore, are veritable personifications of what the Bundists called *khaverim*.

Furthermore, I owe special thanks to Thomas Welskopp for his unfailing availability and unflinching support, even during complicated times. Likewise, I thank Jochen Oltmer for numerous suggestions to embed the project more firmly in migration history. Daniel Mahla and Thomas Maier also contributed heavily, taking on the task – as the experts, colleagues, and friends they are – of reading draft versions of individual chapters and providing necessary corrections in many instances.

This list would be incomplete without five individuals who served as my bedrock throughout the project: these were, firstly, Stefanie Fischer, who as my wife and a resourceful historian in her own right helped me maintain a proper life balance. On many occasions Bundists and Jewish cattle traders came together at our dinner table for quirky yet nevertheless intriguing and inspiring conversations. Similarly invaluable was my collaboration with Gleb J. Albert. I wish anyone undertaking a major project of this kind the good fortune of having a friend and colleague like him. These two shouldered the burden of reading rough drafts of my manuscript more than once. Their annotations and questions forced me to not only apply my thoughts to paper, but to do so in a way intelligible to future readers. Lastly, I dedicate this work to my daughters Jonah Lotte, Elisabeth Maria, and Magdalena Maria, in appreciation of all the sunshine they bring to this world.

Editorial Note

One crucial element of Bundist action and thought was the oft-disdained Yiddish language. In Russia, the story of the Bund in fact began in Russian, as many of the movement's leaders and intellectuals first had to learn to speak the everyday language of those they aimed to guide and represent. Bundist history overseas was never forced down this detour, as conversations, arguments, and practical organising took place in Yiddish from the outset. To do justice to the Bund's character and the acutely significant persistence of the Yiddish language, I transliterate names, brief quotes, catchphrases, and relevant nouns according to the YIVO rules. Only in the case of Yiddish names for which an established spelling already exists in literature are these retained (e.g. Rollansky instead of Rozshansky, although you will find the Argentinian publishing house called *Yidbukh*, not *Idbuj*). I have done so to strike a balance between readability and coherence, as well as to retain the original character of the language as much as possible. Longer quotes originally in Yiddish, Spanish, Russian, or German are generally translated, as are expressions in Hebrew, or the Slavic languages. Proper nouns and established terms are introduced and explained at first mention.

This is not the case with names of organisations and publications. Although these often had translated second names, they rarely played a role in the actual work of said organisations, groups, and publications. Given the centrality of the Yiddish language in Bundist practices, in the following I speak of, for example, the journal '*Unzer tsayt*' rather than *Our Times*, of the *Yidisher sotsyalistisher farband* rather than the Jewish Socialist League, and of *yidishkayt* as a political concept characterising the Bund, in contrast to the broad possible meanings of 'Jewishness'. Furthermore, I attempt to provide clarity by writing the titles of journals in quotation marks, demarcating them from the groups and organisations surrounding them which often bore similar names. '*Der avangard*' (The Vanguard), for example, stands for the magazine published by the *Avangard* group in Buenos Aires from 1908 onwards.[1]

---

1 Citation styles of respective archives vary considerably. I used established citation styles as much as possible but encountered difficulties with both the Bund Archives as well as the IWO. In the former documents are sorted at the folder level (many of which are quite expansive) at best; in the latter the archives contained countless unsorted files and loose boxes rescued from the ruins of the AMIA building. In the interest of retaining some degree of uniformity and transparency, I have cited sources as much as possible through document descriptions.

Figures and Tables

Figures

1. Growth of the Jewish population in the US in thousands   23
2. Eastern European Jewish immigration to the US, 1881–1914   25
3. Immigration to Argentina, 1857–1924   33
4. Annual Jewish net migration to Argentina, 1900–39   34
5. Text ratios of early Bundist publications, 1899–1910   114
6. Text ratios in Bundist and secondary-Bundist periodicals on the Río de la Plata, 1908–39   118
7. Text ratio analysis of Bundist periodicals in the US, 1904–68   146
8. Regional profiles of Bundist periodicals in international comparison, 1899–1968   148
9. Trajectories of Bundist autobiographical culture   166
10. Periods and emphases of Bundist autobiographical culture   168
11. Social stratification of Bundist autobiographical culture according to writing period   175
12. Writing locations of Bundist autobiographical texts in transatlantic comparison   182
13. Reported locations in migratory Bundist autobiographical texts, pre- and post-1939   183
14. Number of entries into the Bund until 1939   199
15. Age at time of joining the Bund   205
16. Distribution of social strata at age of joining   208
17. Cover, 'Nayvelt', Buenos Aires, 2 (1927)   306
18. Communist self-depiction as the only defenders of the working class   308
19. Number and size of *Arbeter-ring* schools, 1919–39   330
20. Deceased members of the Bundist Dvinsker Branch 75 *Arbeter-ring* (*Vladimir Medem brentsh*), 1904–54   333
21. Additional memberships of TSYKO activists at time of joining, circa 1941   355
22. Schematised self-representation of the Medem Sanatorium   386

Tables

1. Schematisation of 'masses'   50
2. Bundist activism patterns in Eastern Europe   58
3. Schema of hierarchically structured text ratios in Bundist publications   113

4	Characterisation of Bundist and secondary-Bundist periodicals in Argentina, 1908–39 122	
5	'Genres' of Bundist autobiographical culture 164	
6	Distribution of Bundist autobiographical culture according to educational background 174	
7	Written languages of Bundist autobiographical texts 179	
8	Writing locations of Bundist autobiographical texts 181	
9	Autobiographical Bund questionnaires in the US 196	
10	Periodic distribution of new Bund members' educational background 206	
11	Differentiation of the Bundist activism pattern 'gathering' 249	
12	Chairmen of the *Natsyonal sotsyaler klub* of the *Arbeter-ring*, 1914–44, according to year of chairmanship 266	
13	Books published by the *Natsyonal edukeyshonal komite fun arbeter ring* 321	
14	Secular Jewish school organisations in the US before World War II 323	
15	Main currents of secular Jewish schools in Argentina, 1920s 339	
16	Secular school organisations in Argentina, 1930s 348	
17	Publicly advertised events during Barukh Shefner's campaign, June–September 1936 399	
18	Final account of Barukh Shefner's campaign, June–September 1936 405	

Abbreviations

AFL	American Federation of Labor
ACWA	Amalgamated Clothing Workers of America
AMIA	Asociación Mutual Israelita Argentina
Arbeterschulorg	Arbeter schul organisatsye
Avangard	Yidishe sotsyal-demokratishe arbeyter organisatsyon in argentina (Avangard)
DAIA	Delegación de Asociaciones Israelitas Argentinas
Emigdirect	Emigration Directorate (Paris)
Farband	Yidish natsyonaler arbeter farband
Federatsye	Yidish sotsyalistishe federatsye in Amerike, Jewish Socialist Federation – Socialist Party
FORA	Federación Obrera Regional Argentina
Gezelshaft	Gezelshaft far yidish veltlekhe shuln in Argentine
HIAS	Hebrew Immigrant Aid Society
HICEM	Fusion of HIAS, ICA, and Emigdirect in 1927
Hilfs-komitet	Hilfs komitet far yidish veltlekhe shuln in Poyln [und Argentine]; Comite de Ayuda a las escuelas laicas Israeltita de Polonia [y Argentina]
ICA	Jewish Colonization Association
IKUF	Yidisher kultur farband (also ICUF)
ILGWU	International Ladies' Garment Workers' Union
IWO	International Workers Order – Internatsyonaler arbeter ordn
IWO (Archive)	Yidisher visnshaftlekher institut, Buenos Aires (Idisher wisnshaftlejer institut)
JDC	Joint Distribution Committee
JLC	Jewish Labor Committee
NSK	Natsyonaler sotsyaler klub
Prokor	Proletarishe kolonizatsye organizatsye
RSDLP	Russian Social Democratic Labour Party
SPD	Social Democratic Party of Germany
SKIF	Sotsyalistisher kinder-farband
SLP	Socialist Labor Party
SP	Socialist Party of America
Tsenter avangard	Yidishe sotsyal demokratishe arbeyter organisatsyon Avangard – Partido Socialista [Argentina]
Tsukunft	Yugntbund 'tsukunft'
TSVYSHO	Tsentrale veltlekhe yidishe shul-organisatsye

ABBREVIATIONS

TSYKO	Tsentrale yidishe kultur-organisatsye
TSYSHO	Tsentrale yidishe shul organisatsye
UHT	United Hebrew Trades
VH	Vaad Hakhinukh
YIVO	Yidisher visnshaftlekher institut
YSF	Yidisher sotsyalistisher farband
YSFA	Yidisher sotsyalistisher farband in Argentine

Introduction

> Daniel Cohn-Bendit: *Given that I'm in Russia now, I just happened to go through my bookshelf last night – because naturally I want to learn something about Russia. By coincidence, I came across this book. It's the story of Marek Edelman, the last survivor of the Warsaw Ghetto struggle. And he, in turn, tells the story of the Bund.* [With emphatic emphasis:] *After all, who still knows the history of the Bund?*
> Laughter among the audience: *We know it, we know it …*
> – Moscow, October 2005

∴

Daniel Cohn-Bendit's Moscow lecture would go down as an affront.[1] Although the actual public controversy related to contemporary politics, his historical digression turned into an awkward blunder. The figurehead of the European Left's attempt to remind a Russian audience of this unjustly forgotten movement was met with the self-assurance of Russian political activists who considered themselves well-acquainted with the Bund and its history. Visibly moved, Cohn-Bendit continued:

> It's not a laughing matter! It's not a laughing matter. Because the memory of these people was destroyed by the Stalinists, the Zionists, by everyone. No one remembers this history … this first history … this attempt by workers to organise … They were all Jewish and spoke Yiddish, they didn't want to go to Israel, they fought here in Russia, they fought in Lithuania, they fought in Poland, and their history has been totally erased by the traditional histories of the Zionists and the Stalinists.

The audience, however, was rather put off by this attempt to segue into a genuinely oppositional topic. Discussion participant Sergei Solovyov subsequently aired his frustration: 'I am with the magazine *Skepsis*. To begin with, I would

---

1 'Kulturrevolution. Das Jahr 1968 und die Grünen', held at an event organised by *Memorial*, the Heinrich Böll Foundation, and the oppositional media platform *polit.ru*. Transcript available at www.polit.ru/article/2005/10/11/cohn_bendit/ (last accessed 23 July 2013), audio recording in the author's possession (quote lightly corrected), 18:52–20:08.

like Mr. Cohn-Bendit to understand that the people gathered here today are very familiar with the Bund and in no need of a lecture on such matters'.[2]

Unnoticed in the commotion, however, was the fact that the well-known Marek Edelman was a rather unsuitable example of the General Jewish Labour Bund (or just 'Bund') in Russia. Edelman had been a Polish Bundist and subsequently a Solidarność activist, born in either Warsaw or Gomel only after the October Revolution. His aforementioned book deals with the Warsaw Ghetto Uprising of 1943 and is therefore primarily a matter of Polish-German rather than Russian history.[3] Thus it was not the subject of the discussion itself that provoked disagreement that evening in Moscow, but rather the certainties held by the respective parties involved. When exploring the history of the Bund, neither moralising finger-wagging nor self-satisfied, all-knowing grins are particularly helpful. Instead, the Bund's historical marginalisation calls for an ongoing search for the organisation's substance and foundations. This book attempts to do so in two ways, firstly in terms of a history of social practices, and secondly by situating the Bund within broader existing research and literature on transnational social movements.

By turning to the Bund as a transnational social movement, I aim to accomplish two goals. Firstly, I agree with Daniel Cohn-Bendit to the extent that the Bund's history requires further study, as it provides insight into the activist and humanitarian responses of many twentieth-century struggles. The meaning of this troublesome yet fascinating century, I believe, can be best understood not by looking towards the centres of power, but rather the repercussions and responses along the so-called margins of power which often form the centres of social history. Secondly, in my eyes it is highly relevant today that the Bund's persistent striving for a humanitarian socialism was not confined to the specific conditions in Russia or Poland. The Bund was a transnational movement fighting for a better world wherever Jews lived. As such, it is not a story for history lessons alone.

During Bernie Sanders's first run for the Democratic presidential nomination, historian Daniel Katz pointed out that the key to understanding Sanders was not socialism as such, but rather its specific Yiddish current.[4] Like those who occupied Wall Street in 2011, those who declared they were 'undocumented and unafraid', and those who insisted that Black Lives Matter, Katz reasoned, Sanders understood oppression as an ecosystem. Yet his fight against this oppression was informed by his experiences of Yiddish socialism as a kind

---

2 Ibid., 20:08–20:51.
3 See Edelman 2002.
4 Katz 2016.

of counter-ecosystem. In this sense, the history of Yiddish socialism's development as a transnational lifeworld presented in this book sheds light on a milieu that only a few years ago appeared anachronistic, but which in fact provided a recent presidential hopeful with profound appeal among young American voters. The history of the Bund as a party may have come to an end, but the effects of its cultural and political work and their unifying humanitarian yet activist spirit described here continue to matter today.

The Bund's transnational history has its roots in late-1890s Tsarist Russia, a country already stretched to the breaking point by economic crises, state repression, and rising nationalist and revolutionary movements. Jewish workers grew increasingly predisposed to protest and revolt during this period, flocking to local illegal labour unions in large numbers.[5] Thirteen representatives of such unions founded the General Jewish Labour Bund in a small attic in Vilnius in the autumn of 1897.[6] Unlike its numerous (and significantly smaller) predecessors, the organisation was, firstly, committed to a vision of Marxism based on the activity of the masses. Secondly, it heeded the call to use Yiddish as the primary language of agitation, citing the consolidation of Yiddish as a cultural language among Russian Jews since earlier in the decade.[7] In doing so, the Bund reversed the hitherto dominant Social Democratic logic in Russia, according to which Jewish workers first had to rise to a certain 'level', expressed mainly by mastering the Russian language, before they were considered worthy of political agitation. The Bund, by contrast, elevated the slogan of 'into the streets, to the masses' to a mode of revolutionary politics, and viewed Yiddish as the Jewish national language for the simple reason that the majority of Jews already spoke it.[8] This went along with a refusal to recognise traditional Jewish authorities, arguing they had consistently protected or even aggravated class-based inequality rather than combatted it. Moreover, they were deluded by religiosity and proximity to the state.[9] That stance brought the Bund into conflict with Russian Social Democracy as well as many factions in the Jewish shtetl, as it implied abandoning both Russophilia and Hebrewism in equal measure.[10]

---

5   See Mendelsohn 1970; Bunzl 1975; Hofmeester 1990.
6   Tobias 1972 remains a foundational study. Further relevant works include G-B 1907; Mill 1946a; Aronson and Hertz et al. 1960.
7   This shift is extensively detailed in Mendelsohn 1970; see also Kurski et al. 1939.
8   A similar development took place in Galicia later on, see Kuhn 1998.
9   Among countless texts on this question, see for instance Levin 1922; Rafes 1923; Shlugleyt 1925; Epshteyn 1927; Baskin 1945.
10 On the qualitative changes to Yiddish that occurred in this context see Fishman 1981 and Trachtenberg 2008.

Here, a characteristic begins to emerge that would mark the entire history of the organisation: namely, the Bund's focus on activism. Utopian demands, draft programmes, and even organisational structures were substantiated only in and by the actions of the masses – or, as the Bund referred to them, the Jewish worker masses. Reinforced by a popularised yet revolutionary Marxist programme and ties to other Social Democratic workers' parties, on this basis the Bund became a mass movement even before the 1905 Russian Revolution. In this sense, it lived up to the label 'avantgarde of the worker's army in Russia' that Georgi Plekhanov ascribed to it.[11] The Russian Social Democratic Labour Party (RSDLP) the Bund helped to found in 1898 had roughly 5,000–8,000 members in 1905, while the Bund already claimed 30,000–35,000. Owed to its roots in the *yidishe gas*, or Jewish street, the Bund's influence extended much further than what this figure suggests.[12]

All Russian socialist movements came under renewed state pressure after the revolution was violently put down in 1907, although repression would never become an existential threat for the Bund.[13] The Bund gathered renewed strength from 1912 onwards, establishing new and extensive networks of local branches and organisations across the shtetls during World War I. These served as Bundist nuclei that would go on to flourish in Poland in the 1920s.[14] In Russia, the Bund attempted to influence the country's refashioning into a socialist state in the aftermath of the 1917 February Revolution. During that revolutionary year, the already existing tension between the Bund and the Bolsheviks reached new heights. They finally parted ways in this turmoil and competed for members, culminating in open hostility after the October Revolution that almost shattered the Bundist movement. Subsequently forced to relocate its territorial centre to interwar Poland, the Bund continued to pursue a radically left-laicist orientation towards socialist renewal of Jewish life on an anti-Zionist and anti-Communist platform.[15]

The party itself counted roughly 20,000 members in Poland, flanked by youth organisations with around 10,000 members, a network of secular schools enrolling 25,000 pupils, and various trade unions with another 100,000 members along with sports clubs, cultural associations, a national daily newspaper, publishing houses, and other institutions.[16] Put simply, the Bundist movement

---

11 Quoted in Tobias 1972, p. 61.
12 See Tobias 1965.
13 Tobias and Woodhouse 1977; Wolff 2007.
14 Foundational studies include Pickhan 2001 and Jacobs 2009.
15 Jacobs 2005.
16 Membership figures can only be estimated due to the destruction of the Bund's archives

became 'the strongest political force of Polish Jewry in the latter half of the 1930s'.[17] The strongest threads linking members together within the Bund were not electoral results or theoretical debates so much as actions. As these actions were embedded in a constantly evolving legitimising frame, they constituted more than simple acts, they formed Bundist activism.

In order to grasp this activism adequately, my book refers to the term 'movement' in a double sense: firstly in terms of social movements, and secondly in the geographical sense of migration. Both represented constitutive elements of modern Jewish history and are far more relevant to the Bund's history than hitherto acknowledged.[18] Jewish history and social movement studies are merged in this volume to present in its global dimensions, for the first time, a social history of what was once the largest Jewish social movement and one of the most important revolutionary movements in Eastern Europe.[19] Given the breadth of the Bund's spheres of activity, it goes without saying that such a social history is inconceivable without taking cultural-historical aspects into account, particularly the notion of *yidishkayt* so crucial to Bundists abroad and so heavily shaped by the Bund itself.[20] This in turn allows for the Bund to serve as an exemplary case study of 'old social movements', one that highlights the often empirically neglected links between regional work and transnational movement formation well before World War II.[21]

Actions and identities served as bridges between locality and transnationality in the Bund. This allows for an approach to a key issue in Jewish history pioneered by Shulamit Volkov: while Jewish history can be seen as essentially transnational, one should refrain from essentialising transnationalism without devoting particular attention to how it was enacted in each era and what limits it faced.[22] Therefore, this study aims to combine local detail with transnational-

---

in the flames of the Warsaw Ghetto. Gertrud Pickhan provides a rough orientation of between 9,000 and 12,000 members in 1930–5, rising to roughly 20,000 by the end of the 1930s. Membership in other Bundist organisations grew similarly in the 1930s. According to Kenneth B. Moss, the still-legal Bund had 40,000 registered supporters outside of its northwestern strongholds after the 1905 Russian Revolution. Sources for these figures, however, are disparate and hardly useful for comparison. See also the discussion in Pickhan 2001, p. 27, pp. 126–30, pp. 203–7; Jacobs 2009, p. 59 f.; Moss 2009, p. 23 f.

17 Pickhan 2001, p. 207. On electoral victories see Jacobs 2009, pp. 1–7.
18 Linfield 1933; Gitelman 2003; Klier 1996; Brinkmann 2010a.
19 See also Slucki 2009a and Wolff 2012a.
20 See for instance the outstanding Katz 2011.
21 Generally speaking, the workers' movement is by far the most prominent of the 'old' social movements, understood as distinct from the 'new' social movements mostly emerging after 1968. See Melucci 1988, p. 247; Cohen and Rai 2000. On the potential problems of this categorisation see Calhoun 1993.
22 Volkov 2006.

ity, and proposes a model of how these connections can be examined in terms of a history of social practices.[23] Numerous studies in contemporary history and sociology define transnationalism as a key factor in 'new social movements', but we lack comparable studies for many of their predecessors.[24] Classical analysis of 'old social movements' tends to emphasise rationalist and often national-economic objectives. More recent scholarship has deemed this narrative reductive.[25] The Bund's once most-prominent socialist movement issues a particular challenge to this notion, refuting Andreas Reckwitz's assertion that 'old social movements' were neither 'movements of identity' nor 'movements of subject transformation'.[26] The Bund's identificatory power came from its deep roots in the Jewish workers' movement, which itself had always been a cultural and identity-forming movement in its own right.

Being a Bundist thus became a decisive category of identity comprising both socialism and Yiddish culture. In the age of great migrations, it then travelled the world together with Bundist activists.[27] Action forged the Bund in Russia and Poland, and action would carry it into the New World as well. Transnationalism is thus essential to the history of the Bund – not only because the organisation was transpersonally connected through new means of communication, or because it was, as a socialist movement, internationalist as such. The Bund was actively formed and moulded by day-to-day practices in the era of great migrations, and thus led to new identities within 'old' social movements.[28]

1 Possibilities and Limits of Transnationalism

To move beyond the descriptive level, this study draws on a narrowly defined concept of transnationalism. As Ludger Pries observes, terms such as 'transnational' and 'transnationalism' are often used with such a lack of specificity that they run the risk of becoming '"catch-all and say nothing" terms'. Pries proposes

---

23   Hanagan 2004.
24   See esp. the prolific publications of Hanspeter Kriesi, Donatella della Porta, and Dieter Rucht (Rucht 2005; della Porta and Tarrow 2008; Risse-Kappen 1995). Empirical examples can be found in della Porta, Kriesi and Rucht 1999; della Porta and Tarrow 2008; Naples 2008.
25   Cohen and Rai 2000, p. 7 ff.; Welskopp 2000 and 2007; Wolff 2014b; Schöck-Quinteros 2007.
26   Reckwitz 2006, pp. 68–72.
27   See Wolff 2012a.
28   See esp. van der Linden 1999; McKeown 2004 and 2007; Brinkmann 2010b.

a more precise definition – a useful suggestion for historiography as well.[29] Transnationalism as an analytical approach pursued revisionist goals from the outset.[30] In one popular approach, historians utilised the new perspective to extend national histories beyond the nation-state's territorial boundaries.[31] While this fundamentally altered national historiography, the nation-state remained the centre of interest and analysis.[32] In order to include a wide array of topics, they often shied away from clearly defined methodological boundaries.[33] This prompted arguments concerning the limits of transnationalism as both perspective and phenomenon. If everything that spans or crosses a border at some point counts as 'transnational', then the perspective lacks the precision to sustainably develop what Jürgen Osterhammel calls 'historiography beyond the nation-state'.[34] For if transnational research limits itself to providing an 'empirical extension of the studied object', as Margrit Pernau has attested for many historical studies, it solidifies rather than challenges the nation, which then, in Ludger Pries's words, remains 'the allegedly natural unit of reference for the study of the relations of human life'.[35] Transnationalism's lasting capacity, Pernau suggests, lies in its ability to 'transcend the nation as ordering category'.[36] Such an assertion, however, immediately raises the question of alternative categories available to historical scholarship.

A common approach is to focus on the decentral sphere of memory or retreat into a world-historical perspective bereft of concrete historical actors.[37] Hans-Ulrich Wehler has already questioned whether this method really provides lasting insights, suggesting it may constitute little more than a welcome 'protest against musty provincialism' that gains analytical flexibility only at the cost of marginalising social inequality along with political agency and conflict.[38] Against this backdrop, leading studies argue that the provinces themselves constitute historiography's epistemological anchor. Local and re-

---

29 Pries 2008a, p. 1.
30 Schiller, Basch, Blanc 1995; Basch, Schiller, Blanc 2006.
31 See for example Conrad and Osterhammel 2004; Conrad 2006, p. 72 f.; Tyrrell 2009; Conrad 2009; Hartwich 2011; Hebel 2012.
32 Schiller 2010. For a strong critique see Lesser and Rein 2008.
33 Sometimes expressed as methodological liberty, sometimes as an enabling tool; see for instance Osterhammel 2001, p. 8 f.; Conrad and Osterhammel 2004, p. 14 f.; Pernau 2011. On the critique of labour history see van der Linden 2006.
34 Epple 2012.
35 Pernau 2011, p. 18 f.; Pries 2010b, p. 10; see also Pries 2008b, pp. 22–46.
36 Pernau 2011, p. 19.
37 Prominent examples include Manning 2005; Osterhammel 2009; Sachsenmaier 2011, esp. pp. 2–11; Zimmermann 2006; Lipphardt 2010; Kobrin 2010.
38 Wehler 2006, p. 162; Arndt, Häberlen and Reinecke 2011, p. 21 f.

gional studies in particular allow for the detection of transnational phenomena within restricted contexts.[39] Yet a lasting departure from methodological nationalism towards a transnational history rich in theory and empirical findings should not only seek an answer to the question of the capabilities of transnational historiography, but ultimately, and more importantly, of where its limits lie.[40] While most researchers agree that transnationalism constitutes 'not a method, but a research perspective', it nevertheless requires methodological reflection and tools.[41]

In recent years, research on the transnational workers' movement has made significant progress in this regard. Its traditional focus on political and structural questions and the necessity of organisational history minimises the danger of losing touch with its historical actors. The transnational workers' movement always negotiated the relation between national, ethnic, gender-based, or religious specificities connected to the overarching question of class and liberation from oppression.[42] This volume builds on that emerging line of research and similarly influential sociological debates, aiming to provide a detailed case study for these primarily theoretical considerations.

Then again, how can we apply transnationalism as a 'research perspective' without overstretching its boundaries into a fashionable but vague category? There is little use in settling for commonplace insights like confirming the existence of cross-border 'social relations', 'communication', or 'exchange of ideas'. Instead, I argue, transnationalism can benefit from one core aspect of historiography: the discipline's fundamental interest in actors and agency and how they bring about change. A consistently applicable concept of transnationalism requires actor concepts able to capture transnational modes of organisation and institutionalisation as a rule, not the exception. This agency results in the formation of what Ludger Pries calls 'transnational social spaces'[43] – analytical ordering categories that inherently transcend the nation-state. Such transnational social spaces take shape in 'relatively dense and durable configurations of transnational social practices, symbols and artefacts', namely biographies, organisations, institutions, identities, and families.[44] The identi-

---

39   See for example McKeown 2001; Shell-Weiss 2012; Huber 2012; Schiller and Çağlar 2009.
40   This also asks for a more pronounced differentiation between the oft-interchangeable use of global history, transnational history, and non-European history; see Sachsenmaier 2011, pp. 7–11; Osterhammel 2001; Arndt, Häberlen and Reinecke 2011, p. 21 f.
41   Patel 2004, p. 628.
42   Informative surveys here include van der Linden 2003; Unfried 2008; Fink 2011.
43   Pries 2008a, p. 2 f., p. 8.
44   Pries 2008a, p. 2 f., pp. 16–19; Faist 2004, p. 2 f. For a similar argument see Epple 2012, p. 168 f. Khagram and Levitt 2008 identify five separate modes.

fication of such spaces, however, cannot be the *result* of transnational history but rather must be its point of departure. Following transnationalism's rapid acceptance into historiography, there is no shortage of studies confirming transnationalism as a historical reality. Yet we still lack a more precise understanding of how certain institutions, such as a party or a social movement, shift from a local or regional initiative to a transnationally formative factor. Consequently, following the identification of persistent transnational social spaces, it would be the task of such an actor-centred transnational historiography to analyse the networks that created these spaces and account for changes to them. If we devote increased attention to the actors involved, it becomes possible to conceive of transnational social spaces as cross-border social structures resulting from concrete actions, which in turn consciously seek to stabilise themselves through institutionalisation or organisation.[45]

In contrast to a somewhat looser notion of the term, transnationalism in this sense no longer functions as an extension of a given national framework. Instead, it focuses on actors who brought about a transnational phenomenon and whose relations to one another constitute the transnational space. Actors are aware of the volatility of such 'relations' and hence seek to create institutions and networks that consolidate into more stable structures. This turns the formation of transnational social spaces into a perpetual process that in turn transforms society. For transnational social movements, this process can be observed in the dynamics of mobilisation and structural transfers, in other words primarily in the practices of activists who seek to transfer known patterns of organisation into new temporal and geographic settings. A transnational history of the General Jewish Labour Bund therefore requires a completely new survey of the Bund's social spaces constituted by human actions. It must be localisable in terms of places and actors, lest it risk slipping into the non-specific or an empty rhetoric of renewal.[46] Instead of following a traditional chronological 'party history', this volume focuses on factors through which activists created and shaped the Bund – central clusters of agency in the movement that I call activism patterns.

Bruno Latour proposes a similar approach.[47] His actor-network theory inspired the present volume in the sense that it conceives of the social not as an explanatory factor but rather as that which is to be explained.[48] Much like

---

45 Faist 2004, pp. 2–6; Abbott 2001, p. 255.
46 Pries 2008b, p. 152. Although he approaches the question entirely differently, Bruno Latour (2007, p. 179) reaches similar conclusions.
47 Latour 2007; Schimank 2007a; Schroer 2008.
48 For more a detailed reflection on actor-network-theory and historiography see Wolff 2012a.

Latour's actor-networks, social movements are unstable, sometimes even fluid. Their institutions only continue to exist if constantly 'provided with power'.[49] This provision of power and energy to an institution may at first sound somewhat esoteric, but it constitutes a social process involving actors' involvement, decisions, efforts, and struggles – and subsequently produces sources for historical study. The idea is in line with George Marcus's notion of 'following' (people, things, lives, etc.) raised as a methodological toolset for 'multi-sited' anthropological research as early as 1995. Essentially, it urges researchers to 'follow' the paths of examined actors as opposed to observing a unit (such as a party) as a stable and locally fixed unit regardless of the fluidity of social involvement.[50] In practical terms, the combination of transnational social spaces with the methodological inspirations provided by Latour and Marcus allows this study to pursue one fundamental question: how did Bundists remain Bundists after migrating to parts of the world that lacked both a Bundist organisation and the conditions to directly reproduce the movement they had known in Russia and Poland?

In the process of transatlantic migration, Bundists encountered the Americas as a condition which they nevertheless shaped through various transfers of practice and culture. This resulted in persistent relations with their former homelands. A study of this process is challenging in several respects. Bundists emigrated to the New World by the thousands, where they established numerous institutions to continue their Bundist activism. This in turn required a Bundist identity firmly tied to the centres of Jewish life in Eastern Europe. 'Following' thus means a constant shifting of perspective. There were short-lived flare-ups of transnational practices, individual attempts to mould private and yet nevertheless political social spaces, and more permanent institutions that ultimately developed into a transnational structure. Spanning the Atlantic, these Bundist transnational social spaces continued to provide an organisational and institutional harbour, shaped biographies, allowed for new identities and even a sense of family.[51] Correspondingly, the five units of transnational study Pries identifies (biographies, organisations, institutions, identities, and families) take centre stage in this history of the Bund.[52]

Accordingly, in Part I this volume identifies the practices that allowed the Bund to emerge. In Part II and III it follows their institutionalisations during

---

49 Latour 1986.
50 Marcus 1995, pp. 106–10, on Latour: p. 104 f. On implications for contemporary methodology see Gallo 2009.
51 On the longevity of this space see the impressive documentary film *Bunda'im* (Torbiner 2011).
52 Pries 2008b, p. 7.

the age of the great migration before identifying and analysing changes, transfers, and stabilisations in those new settings. The book analyses an organisation as a transnational structure through an account of its branching off into the surrounding social histories of the societies of both origin and destination. Yet because these processes of transfer did not entail creating exact copies of established institutions, but rather led to flexible adaptation of Bundist substance and content, the persistent connection to Eastern Europe also inspired changes there.

As a result, this history of the Bund proceeds from social actions and institutionalisations in Eastern Europe before following migrating Bundists to the two major destinations of Jewish overseas migration: New York and Buenos Aires. In this global history, however, Eastern Europe never recedes from view nor is the history of the Bund simply extended through the addition of overseas 'colonies'. What unfolds over the following pages is the history of the transnational Bund as a history of interdependent, heterogeneous social units facing repeated hurdles and limitations.

2   Research Approaches

The Bund is particularly suited for such a transnational movement history because, unlike its primary competitors Zionism and the Bolsheviks, it never developed a state ideology.[53] Its revolutionary utopia instead posed an experienceable and shapeable lifeworld,[54] providing Russian Jews with a secular identity 'whose manifold influence on the Polish and Russian workers' movements cannot be overestimated'.[55] Its influence did not end at the borders of the Tsarist empire, as Bundist migrants by no means jettisoned their life concepts upon boarding the transatlantic steamers. Thousand-fold emigration transnationalised the history of the Bund almost from its inception in 1897. This transfer occurred without the party's institutional support, however, and sometimes even against its explicit intentions. It essentially emerged out of activists' practices alone. Their life concepts and identities required an adaptation of Bundism into a world utterly unfit for a Bundist party. This decentral character explains why Bundist presence receives increasing attention in American Jew-

---

53   Most noteworthy here are Peled 1989 and Pickhan 2009.
54   Mendelsohn 1970, p. 158 f.
55   Haumann 2002, p. 164. The power of the Bund's lifeworld has only been taken into account for Russia and Poland in contemporary Bund research, see Mendelsohn 1970 and Gechtman 1999.

ish history, whereas traditional, party-centred historiography of the Bund fails to capture the relevance of migration for both party and movement.[56] Such a transnational approach is not altogether new to historiography of the Bund. David Slucki's book explores the history of the Bund after World War II (the 'International Jewish Labor Bund') as a transnational history, due to the organisation's strongly decentralised structure at that time. The Bund consciously responded to the global dispersion of Eastern European Jews after the Holocaust in 1947–8 with its 'transnational reorganization'.[57] The book also argues that transnationalism had been constitutive for the Bund since its initial years – a little-known and even less-studied fact. This transnationalism, however, was not the result of a decision like the one that forms the outset of Slucki's book, but of a wide array of practices.

Moreover, the subject's lack of prominence is rooted in basic conceptions of American Jewish life. Even well-conceived approaches argue that Jews emigrating to the United States from Eastern Europe were simply 'too busy to look back'.[58] While that may be true for some individuals, this book makes the case for revising such a notion. As with any migrant group, Jewish life in the Americas was fundamentally shaped by transfer and contact with the 'old home'. Based on sources from American, Argentinian, Israeli, German, Russian, and Ukrainian archives and libraries, this study demonstrates that the Bund's transnationalisation began almost immediately upon its founding. The Bund's transatlantic networks, which entered into a process of institutionalisation as early as 1903, thus represented pioneers of the modern Jewish global diaspora. At the centre of this process stood the long-term project of secular *yidishkayt* as a collective, fighting socialist identity for Jewish workers. As Gertrud Pickhan emphasises, it rested on a class-based concept of minority status within a framework of an aspirational ethnic pluralism.[59] Beyond this programmatic frame, I seek to demonstrate that *yidishkayt*, as a category in the history of social practice, defined cultural boundaries within which Bundist activism could unfold and develop in combination with other categories such as *khavershaft* (friendship, comradeship), *doikayt* ('hereness', as opposed to the 'thereness' of Zionism), and *mishpokhedikayt* as a conception of the transnational political family. *Yidishkayt* legitimated Bundist confidence while facilitating the global transfer of a positively connoted Eastern European Jewish identity.

---

56 For a more thorough discussion see Wolff 2009. Leading examples include Katz 2003; Michels 2005; Soyer 2005; Cohen and Sawyer 2006; Katz 2011.
57 Slucki 2012, p. 2.
58 Brinkmann 2010a, p. 51; Lederhendler 2009.
59 See Pickhan 2001 and 2009.

INTRODUCTION   13

Early works on the Bund focus on the party, while some even take the extent of its influence over the state as indicative of success or failure.[60] Some epigones continue this biased venture and feed the misleading impression that the Bund represented an exception in Jewish history, a strange archipelago in the millennia-old sea of the sons of Abraham united by their collective yearning for Zion.[61] Another line of research based on Henry J. Tobias's pioneering work primarily draws attention to organisational history. Such works often emphasise the Bund's impact beyond its membership.[62] Only recent studies on the party's cultural history have equipped themselves with the methodological tools to evaluate the Bund's overall efficacy beyond official membership statistics.[63] While such studies continue to argue within the conceptual framework of party history, Gertrud Pickhan's and Jack Jacobs's multiple publications in particular prompted further investigations into the Bund's broader cultural impact on Jewish society.[64] This underpinned the Bund's relevance to the traditional but ongoing debates around 'Jewish politics' in Eastern Europe.[65] Nevertheless, these studies mostly concentrate on the Bund in Poland after World War I, while a comparable study on the Bund's Russian period is yet to be written. This book can only hint at such an investigation by identifying the patterns of activism that shaped the Bund in Poland and Russia. Ultimately, the Bund emerged to become the most important Social Democratic movement of both Jewish workers and intellectuals during the first half of the twentieth century. Moreover, its activism made it one of the decisive protagonists of the modern Jewish diaspora.

In migration, the Bund's history would remain 'the history of a search and a struggle for justice, dignity, and identity'.[66] But who was doing the searching and struggling? To answer this question, I avoid the backrooms and debating clubs of the Russian intellectual milieu and instead explore the streets of the Jewish Pale of Settlement and the Jewish immigrant neighbourhoods in the largest ports of transatlantic Jewish immigration, New York and Buenos Aires. By looking at life and struggles on these streets, shops, and offices, we discover

---

60   Paretzki 1932; Johnpoll 1967. This inclination lives on today to an extent despite the proliferation of evidence to the contrary, see Gorny 2006.
61   See for instance Gorny 2006.
62   See for instance Tobias 1972; Peled 1989; Zimmermann 2004.
63   Mendelsohn 1970; Pickhan 2001, which was particularly inspiring for Jacobs 2009.
64   See for instance Jacobs 2001; Pickhan 2001b; Pickhan 2004; Jacobs 2006; Pickhan 2001a; Pickhan 2009; Jacobs 2009; Pickhan 2011.
65   Frankel 1984; Lederhendler 1989; Jacobs 1993; Mendelsohn 1993.
66   Tobias 1972, p. vii.

that the history of the Bund is found not in the implementation of a party programme but rather that the programme itself was a response to the practices and aspirations of the activists involved. These workers' visions and practices have received little attention, as scholarship often focuses on sources from leading intellectual party figures. Russian Jewish history blossomed in the wake of the post-Soviet 'archival revolution', while historiography of the Bund has yet to fully connect to this inspiring new social history of Jewish life in the Pale.[67] Unfortunately, newer Russian publications on the Bund rarely reflect this shifting paradigm and are limited to discussions of organisational aspects or programmatic debates.[68] This line of work is dominated by highly segmented source knowledge with little interest in Yiddish sources. Russian language sources, however, primarily address programmatic aspects and rarely explore the practices and experiences that constituted the Bund.[69]

In English-language scholarship, the dominant question for decades was that of the Bund's 'success'. Bernhard K. Johnpoll polemically kicked off this debate in 1965, and continues to serve as an inspiration for some contemporary studies.[70] Ultimately, however, the controversy only led to hardened fronts tending to reveal more about the authors' positions than about the Bund as a historical phenomenon. Only more in the last two decades has a thread of research on the Bund developed and indeed gained momentum in the form of pioneering works of cultural history in various fields.[71] They include not only specific studies of the Bund, but also other organisations, parties, and movements in which Bundists were active.[72] Once again, this shows how strongly Bundism and Bundist identity resonated beyond the borders of the actual party.

Another transition helped to extricate the Bund's history from that of Russian Social Democracy more generally. Prior to the publication of Gertrud Pickhan's *Gegen den Strom*, Bund historiography was dominated by the history of the organisation in Tsarist Russia, leaving the Polish period to Bundist self-descriptions.[73] Pickhan defines the Bund as a 'left-wing party' or 'class

---

67 For innovative approaches, see for instance Adler 2011; Ury 2012; Bemporad 2013. An important step in this direction was Jacob and Pickhan 2013.
68 Gusev 2000 and 2006.
69 Svalov 2007; Bund 2010. The same can be said for the Belarusian side, see Gosudarstvennyi komitet po arkhivam i deloproizvodstvu Respubliki Belarus 1997.
70 Exemplary of this proxy debate are Johnpoll 1967 and Gorny 2006.
71 Gechtman 1999; Pickhan 2001; Zimmerman 2004; Gechtman 2005; Jacobs 2005; Marten-Finnis 2005; Jacobs 2006; Denz 2009; Trębacz 2010; Mahla 2010.
72 Of particular note are Michels 2005; Moss 2009; Shtakser 2009.
73 Along with several essays, one exception was Johnpoll 1967.

party', boldly propagating the 'unity of the working class'.[74] Pickhan's study marks a break with Marxist-inspired analyses of the Bund such as John Bunzl's, which viewed class conditions as a causal force in the Bund's emergence. Pickhan instead emphasises the importance of class identity and cultural work.[75] Against this backdrop, Pickhan demonstrates the Bund's relevance to Eastern European history after the Russian Revolution far beyond the inner core of the party leadership that is usually examined.[76] Jack Jacobs underpins this notion by describing essential groups and institutions of the Polish Bund in what he coined the *Bundist Counterculture*.[77] In his description of some of the Bund's sub-organisations in Poland, Jacobs also bridges the gap to their origins in Russian times. However, such path-breaking accounts methodologically centre on organisations of or within the party rather than activists, prompting further questions of how the eponymous Polish Bundist counterculture connected to the increasingly dispersed Jewish lifeworlds and the emergence of a global Yiddish culture in the early twentieth century. This volume therefore explores Bundist cultural life from the other end, attempting to reconstruct the Bund not by adding together its different sub-groups, but by illuminating the relations and ways in which they were linked together. It entails a departure from party history and a turn towards social movement research. This shifting perspective allows us to investigate the underlying dynamics of mobilisation and community building, that is to say the formation of Bundist actors inside self-made social structures.

All substantial studies of the Bund until now chose a specific period (and thus a specific space) within which to write 'Bundist history'.[78] These studies describe how the Bund in Russia (1897–1917) became an early trailblazer of the revolutionary movement in the late Tsarist empire, simultaneously paving the way for a popular Yiddish cultural mass movement among the empire's five million Jews.[79] Furthermore, the Bund was a major protagonist in the Russian revolutionary landscape and hence a highly relevant actor to Eastern European history in general.[80] More recent studies illustrate how the Bund as a political party in interwar Poland contributed to the unique Yiddish culture forming at

---

74 Pickhan 2001, p. 27, p. 31, p. 98 f.
75 Bunzl 1975.
76 Pickhan 2001, p. 14, p. 29; with explicit reference to Kocka 1990, p. 4 f.; Peled 1989.
77 Jacobs 2009, p. 6, p. 20, p. 100 f.
78 Exceptions to this rule are partisan Bundist grand narratives as well as popular historical literature such as Hertz 1958; Arenson and Hertz et al. 1960; Minczeles 1995; Laubstein 1997.
79 Kappeler 2014, p. 396 f.
80 Especially until the 1990s, this 'Russian Bund' received most historians' attention. Path-

the time, ultimately representing a form of Jewish modernity in its own right.[81] Thirdly, the Bund continued its practice of anti-pogrom defence during World War II, despite facing an overwhelming enemy (1939–48).[82] It fought German occupation and the Holocaust in line with its 'practical philosophy' of *doikayt*, finding solutions to existing oppression in the here and now. Fourthly, the very concept of *doikayt* presented the Bund with weighty theoretical and practical challenges following the German massacre and Soviet persecution. They resulted in the scattering of its members across the globe – and yet another Bundist organisation and culture.[83] As inspiring as these individual perspectives are, the historiographical consequences thereof have been four sub-fields and four different areas of expertise.[84]

This volume represents the first academic study spanning all of the aforementioned epochs. In contrast to depictions conceiving of the Bund as a party emerging out of economic necessity and class conditions, this book calls for historicising the practices and dynamics of the transnational movement within local structures and transnational networks alike.[85] One important link within the Bund was activist memory. A specific commemorative, genre-spanning culture based on songs, poems, short and long articles, all the way to autobiographies and multi-volume histories and encyclopaedias secured the persistence of individual practices and prepared past actions for present usage aimed to inspire future repetition. This memory production constituted a pattern of activism in its own right, a subsequent secondary practice alongside primary actions such as party building, union work, demonstrations, or strikes. I call this politics of commemoration *Memorik*, a practice of collective political mobilisation fed by decentral, individual memory.[86] Leon Oler's introductory quotation above shows that Bundists thought of the Bund not only as a party or movement but also as a living being, vitalised through their actions. In

---

breaking studies include Woodhouse and Tobias 1966; Mendelsohn 1970; Bunzl 1975; Tobias and Woodhouse 1977; Frankel 1984; Peled 1989; Gitelman 2003; Trachtenberg 2008.

81 Although Johnpoll's study is controversial due to its political inclinations, the 'Polish Bund' was relegated to the backwaters of historical scholarship for many years. This has changed with Pickhan 2001; Gechtman 2005b; Jacobs 2009.

82 Blatman 2003.

83 As explored in David Slucki's innovative study (Slucki 2009b).

84 At the moment these are: Tobias 1972; Pickhan 2001; Blatman 2003; Slucki 2012b.

85 Works of German labour history conducted in a similar spirit include Welskopp 2012 and 1998.

86 Similarly, German scholarship has introduced the term *Autobiographik* to differentiate the social practice of self-commemoration from individual memoirs and the literary genre. See Frerichs 1980; Jancke 2002; Günter 2002; see esp. Herzberg 2007; Herzberg 2013.

this regard, *Memorik* was a form of collective life writing.[87] Through *Memorik* actions did not fade into the fog of the past; indeed, activists yearned to relive such experiences over and over again through narration. Over the decades the Bund increasingly and proactively built its whole presence on this feeling, an activist counter-history to the diverging memory production in the surrounding nation-states. A strike or demonstration did not lose meaning after issues were resolved or lost in this emotional landscape – the feeling of activism remained alive through *Memorik*.

The Bund soon learned how to utilise these experiences as political capital. *Memorik* spawned contacts and facilitated transfers from shtetl to shtetl, generation to generation, and across the oceans. After a few decades, however, the global transfer faced significant challenges, as the new generation shared neither the experience nor the vision of their migrant mothers and fathers. The Americas posed very different challenges to their biographies. *Memorik* as a mobilising tool lost traction less because of time than because of space. Overseas, the durability of most transferred Bundist practices was limited to the first generation of immigrants. As a response to a lifeworld left behind (and later lost), they engaged even more actively in memory production such as autobiographies, commemorative special issues, and encyclopaedic books – slowly, unwillingly transforming *Memorik* from a mobilising tool into a mourning culture. While failing to pass the Bund on to the new generation, these works now provide a unique array of sources for both Bundist and migration history from below on both sides of the Atlantic.

Beyond presenting a transnational history of the Bund, this volume also seeks to contribute to contemporary diaspora studies. I intend to demonstrate that the modern Jewish diaspora and the Jewish workers' movement not only emerged synchronously but were in fact mutually interdependent. Hence, this history of the Bund also counters the widely held notion that 'old' social movements directed their demands primarily towards the state, while 'new' social movements set their sights beyond national limitations and aimed for broader, cultural renewal.[88] The Bund combined both goals from its inception, and Bundists consequently adjusted them to new times and spaces.

This led to the formation of a distinct Bundist identity. In the Bund as a transnational social movement, being a Bundist meant more than joining a party as a rank-and-file member. A Bundist identity implied belonging realised through action and characterised by both utopian forward momentum as well

---

87 Kadar 1992; Eakin 1999; Smith and Watson 2010; Wolff 2017.
88 See Cohen and Rai 2000, pp. 6–11.

as romantic retrospection. In this regard, a Bundist identity was of course never fixed or essentialised but called for constant reconfirmation by the bearer and the identifier, that is to say emotional construction, through memory and practice.

In both the Bund's *Memorik* as well as in every activist deed, we find that, in the words of Karl Mannheim, 'not only the past but the future as well ... has virtual existence in the present'.[89] It is therefore impossible to write a 'history of the Bund' without a 'history of the Bundists'. Their reflection of individual experiences constructed the collective identity that legitimated actions, determined friendships, and rendered politics a palpable experience.[90] Grasping this historiographically requires a concept of agency that refrains from treating actors exclusively as rationally or voluntaristically motivated individuals, or as persons simply incorporated into organisations. The fundamental conceptual actors in such a social movement history, I argue, are abstract configurations – groups, networks, and institutions – that constitute the movement's transnational social space.[91]

Bruno Latour proposes the term 'actants' to differentiate this abstract level of agency from the also important but subordinate individual and human level of agency.[92] We can identify three fundamental actants for the Bund's case, which are in turn a major focus of this volume. First, the *Bundist* as an *identity-based actant* stands at the forefront of the movement's endeavour. Bundists formed the Bund via action, configured networks, transferred substance and meaning, and undertook actual physical migration. But Bundists were not only acting individuals – they also contributed to the movement psychologically, thus acquiring a personally and collectively framed identity of 'being a Bundist'. This required a point of contact for those seeking to enter said identity, provided by the second actant: the Bund as an *organisation*. While it appeared stable (anchored by name, programme, and structure), its character differed dramatically from region to region and era to era. The lifeworld the Bundists created naturally constituted much more than resolutions and party structures. The point of reference of this emerging heterogeneity was, thirdly, Bundism as an idea of political goals and practices, a *programmatic institution*. While the Bundist agenda was closely tied to the Bund as an organisation in Eastern Europe, the migration history of the Bund reveals that it must

---

89 Mannheim 1979, p. 221.
90 In this I follow Latour 1999, p. 193 ff.; Latour 2007, pp. 4–8, p. 247 f.
91 Morrow 2009.
92 On a more open actor concept see Latour 2007, primarily pp. 46–50, pp. 52–8; see also Akrich and Latour 1992; Schimank 2007.

be considered an actant in its own right. This absence of an official Bundist organisation or branch overseas inspired the rise of the powerful Jewish organisations of secondary Bundism. They relied on Bundist thought and practice while neglecting the Bund's name and structures. Bundism provided meaning as well as the necessary myths and utopias, spaces for reflection, and possibilities for identity-forming practices which then reiterated into the development of Bundism as a practical ideology.

These three actors form the foundation of Bundist history. They were interdependent but continued to overlap. This study explores this overlap while attempting to capture the shifting relations between the three actants, a vision of unity that increasingly lost its internal balance. Emigrated Bundists, for example, often found themselves in crucial positions within the American labour movement, into which they introduced Bundism (or derivatives thereof). That said, they did not draw on the Bund as an actual organisation and even proactively refrained from using the term 'Bund' for organisations closest to certain branches of the Eastern European Bund. In contrast to their nominal European counterparts, organisations bearing the Bundist label in the Americas focused on fundraising. These overseas Bundist organisations (often run by Bundists as secondary-Bundist organisations) were instrumental in transferring resources back to Eastern Europe, a function that the individual Bundists in the wider American labour movement or in Argentinian socialism would have been unable to fulfil. Observing the interaction between identity, organisation, and ideology therefore presents a particular chance to better understand the core of the Bund's transnational history.

3 *Doikayt* as Guiding Principle

The main pillar of this history was the guiding principle of *doikayt* (from the Yiddish *do*, meaning 'here', hence 'hereness') – a call to action in the 'here and now', 'with the masses and for the masses'. Within the context of a self-confident diaspora culture, *doikayt* confronted Bundists with the question of where exactly this 'here' could be found.

In Russia, the Bund's *doikayt* appeared self-explanatory, emerging from the actions of the 'masses' themselves. To make it a socialist concept, however, some Marxist concepts had to be adapted to the needs of agitating the Jewish masses.[93] An obstacle to Marxism in the multi-ethnic Russian empire grew out of Marx's observation that 'not in substance, yet in form, the struggle of

---

[93] Arkadi Kremers's 1893 pamphlet *Ob agitaci* was particularly influential in this regard, see Mendelsohn 1970, p. 187 f.

the proletariat with the bourgeoisie is at first a national struggle. The proletariat of each country must, of course, first of all settle matters with its own bourgeoisie'.[94] For the Bund, however, nation and country did not necessarily coincide. Bundist trade unions aggressively attacked Jewish factory owners (the Jewish 'bourgeoisie') but would often turn to defend them against anti-Semitic pogroms only weeks later. Neither the Jewish community nor the Tsarist empire provided the structure of the nation-state – a critical category in Marx's thought. Bundists were not the only ones confronted with this problem, sharing it with Austro-Marxists in the Habsburg empire.[95] Bundist theoreticians adapted the latter's concept of national-cultural autonomy to their own situation, viewing Jews as a nation that could rightfully claim such autonomy, and combined it with an action paradigm.[96] In doing so Bundists finally broke with the traditional Jewish notion of viewing exile as punishment. From the Hebrew *galut*, the punitive waiting for the Messiah, they established *doikayt*, the principle of fighting for better living conditions and cultivating a secular Jewish culture in the here and now. *Doikayt* thus combined a modern, contemporary notion of Jewish life and culture with a socialist utopia, while calling for individual activism to realise the goal of collective betterment without the guiding hand of the Messiah.[97]

This led to a paradox: as Bundists generally chose migration over 'making *Aliyah*', any given living environment represented a possible site of Bundist action and organising – that is, of actively practiced *yidishkayt*. *Doikayt* was thus possible across the globe; the 'here' was virtually everywhere. The Bund's political programme, by contrast, cultivated strong ties to Eastern Europe where the vast majority of Jewish workers still lived. This posited a 'here' of the masses in opposition to the 'here' of the migrated. As a result, *doikayt* necessarily remained tied to Eastern Europe throughout the migration process, leaving little room for collective Bundist experiences under the Bund's organisational roof elsewhere. In the resulting tensions between locality, delocalisation, and transnationalism, both Bund and being a Bundist, organisation and identity, began to grow apart. Bundism more generally became a double-edged sword. On the one hand, it continued to philosophically underpin the liberation struggle of the Jewish worker masses in Eastern Europe, while allow-

---

94 Marx and Engels 2010, p. 78.
95 This also led to the founding of the 'Galician Bund' in 1905, see Kuhn 1998.
96 Pinson 1945; Hertz 1969; Peled 1989; Jacobs 1993, p. 106 f., p. 119 ff.; Gechtman 2005a. This is what made *doikayt* so important to the Bund of the post-war world; see Slucki 2008.
97 Jacobs 1993; Gechtman 2005b. On high-risk activism's strong impacts on organisational cohesion see Taylor and van Dyke 2004, p. 270 f., p. 277.

ing for a modern, assimilated Jewishness overseas. Consequently, *doikayt* could mean both: the focus on a 'here' that for migrants was anchored firmly in their Russian or Polish past, alongside a focus on a 'here' that was to shape the presence of the global Jewish diaspora itself.[98] This process diminished the Bund's visibility in the destination countries and simultaneously cemented countless Bundists as *geselshaftlekhe tuer* (social activists) in the US, Argentina, and elsewhere. If *doikayt* in Eastern Europe was an expression of a proud diaspora life, then its transfer during the process of migration was an expression of a secular 'diaspora-diaspora'.[99]

This study thus on the one hand aims to untie the history of the Bund from the broader discipline of 'Eastern European History', which has monopolised virtually all discussions of its political legacy until now.[100] On the other hand, it ties the local history of Jewish migrants in New York and Argentina more closely to Eastern Europe, hopefully contributing to Jewish history's inclusion into the ongoing transnationalisation of American history.[101] As we begin to trace Bundist life trajectories and activism, we find active connections emerging between Vilnius and Warsaw, Gomel and Moscow, but also Buenos Aires, New York, Rochester, and Montevideo.[102] In this sense, this history of the transnational Bund offers a contribution to Eastern Europe history, although it took place primarily in the process of transatlantic migration. Inversely, it is also an element of the histories of Argentina and the United States – or rather, of the corresponding societies – with key concepts and patterns firmly rooted in Eastern Europe. At any rate, *doikayt* represented both a possibility and a challenge for the Bund as a transnational movement, a tension that produced a variety of largely ignored sources and is thus a fascinating opportunity for a new transnational social history.

---

98 Slucki 2010.
99 Derived from Brubaker 2005.
100 Newer case studies strongly support this broadening tendency, see Slucki 2008; Braun 2008; Mayoraz 2013; Mayoraz 2014.
101 Here migration is often reduced to a vague pre-history, a mere condition for the examined national developments. See esp. Howe 1976; Zago 1982; Levine 1993; Rutland 2001; Diner 2001; Michels 2005.
102 Foundational with regard to time-space compression as a condition of post-modernity: Harvey 1990, pp. 294–307, p. 336 f. In contrast, Karl Schlögel's approach of the historiographical 'spatial turn' renders time a mere chronology of events; see Schlögel 2016, p. xvii, p. 28.

4 Limitations and Horizons of *Doikayt* in Migration

As already indicated, Bundist transatlantic transfers not only relied on internal possibilities of transition, but depended heavily on surrounding social structures, namely cultural and economic life in the port cities and the specific character of socialism the activists encountered. It is thus necessary to first outline these structures and conditions before moving on to the history of the transnational Bund in Part I.

The US and Argentina in general and New York and Buenos Aires in particular became the most popular overseas destinations for Jewish immigrants leaving the Tsarist empire and Poland. For the Bund, conditions in these cities were about as different as could be imagined. The two port cities had one thing in common: when Bundist Abraham Brumberg's flight across the globe during a period of unimaginable persecution ended in the US in 1941, he was received by the Bundist *mishpokhe*. Although unknown in the immediate sense, the American *khaverim* were anything but strangers to him. They welcomed Brumberg and provided him with both shelter and community. He and many others at the time felt that this specific, primarily political and only secondarily ethnic immigrant community existed practically everywhere.[103] By 1941 the Bundist *mishpokhe* had spread from the Jewish Pale of Settlement in Russia across the world. At the *fin de siècle*, the onset of Bundist history, such a global dispersion of a Russian social movement was not only unexpected but also highly unlikely.

5 United States

The first Bundists who came to the US around 1900 found a Jewish community without a Bund but a very active Yiddish socialist scene nonetheless. The most important manifestation of this was the daily '*Forverts*' founded in 1897, the same year as the Bund itself. The streets of New York's Lower East Side bustled with Yiddish life and the humming of Singer sewing machines. The city was both centre and outlier of Jewish history at once. Roughly 1.4 million Russian Jews migrated to the United States between 1904 and 1914. Forty-seven percent of all American Jews lived in New York in 1907; by 1927 this figure had declined only slightly to 44 percent. Mass immigration would raise the number of Jewish

---

[103] Brumberg 1999; Slucki 2009a.

INTRODUCTION

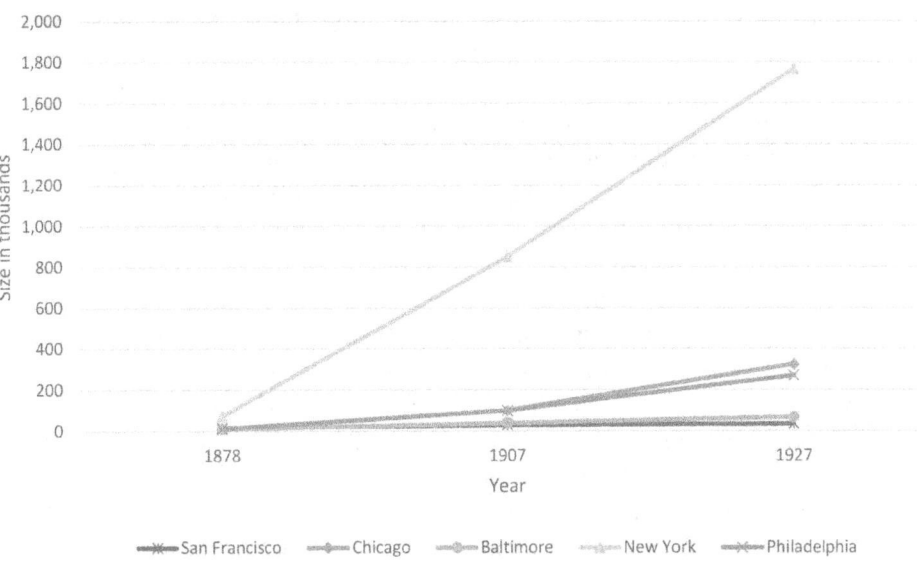

FIGURE 1　Growth of the Jewish population in the US in thousands. Beginning at a size of 10,000 in 1888, Brooklyn is counted as part of New York City
FIGURES TAKEN FROM WEISSBACH 1988, P. 84.

inhabitants in the city by about one million.[104] That may sound like an ideal breeding ground for the Bund, but the organisation faced at least one insurmountable problem.

The American labour movement was unfamiliar and often incomprehensible for many Bundists. While the trade union movement in Russia and other European states had close links to socialist parties, the American Federation of Labor (AFL) appeared to abhor any association with socialist ideas. One of its founding members, Adolph Strasser, once formulated the movement's character as follows: 'We have no ultimate ends. We are going on from day to day. We are fighting for immediate objects – objects that can be realized in a few years'.[105] The Socialist Labor Party (SLP) organised under the imperious leadership of Columbia University graduate Daniel De Leon proved similarly inept when it came to attracting the more radically inclined among European working-class immigrants. A more fitting option emerged in 1901 when American socialists around Eugene V. Debs founded the Socialist Party of America. Debs himself had grown up in a working-class milieu, and like the Bund his

---

104　Figures taken from Weisbach 1988, p. 84; Sorin 1992, p. 137.
105　Karson 1958, p. 117.

party followed the path 'from trade-unionism to socialism'.[106] The Socialist Party benefited heavily from the constant influx of immigrants and temporarily became one of the country's major political parties. Due largely to the AFL's markedly unpolitical stance, encapsulated in Samuel Gompers's slogan of demanding nothing but 'more', relations between the Socialist Party and the federation remained fraught with conflict.[107] The conflict was by no means purely organisational, it was about the critical question of whether or not socialism had a place in American society.

Numerous histories and self-descriptions of the American labour movement quote Abraham Lincoln as having said: 'All that harms labor is treason to America. ... I am glad to see a system of labor prevails under which laborers can strike when they want to'.[108] Whether authentic or not,[109] the quote's frequent use illustrates how AFL leaders viewed their proximity to the state as a strength, seeking to integrate themselves into the American national project. Their narrow economistic demands nevertheless disappointed many workers, and the AFL increasingly excluded them and their demands from day-to-day political operations.[110] In contrast to the 'House of Labor', the Socialist Party aimed to storm the temples of power[111] – an attitude that both the AFL and Theodore Roosevelt began to view as a new threat. Roosevelt for his part remarked in 1906 that the 'labor men are very ugly and no one can tell how far such discontent will spread'.[112] Before World War I, the 'thunder on the left', as Foster Rhea Dulles describes it, seized the trade unions not only from the left but also from below. Often recent arrivals from Eastern Europe, the movement's newer leaders were cause for particular alarm among polite society.[113]

One response to Jewish immigrants' exclusion from the labour market was radicalisation. During the height of nativism in the United States, its proponents frequently argued that new immigrants lacked the necessary skills to

---

106 Guérin 1979, p. 73.
107 Gompers 1986.
108 From the speeches of Abraham Lincoln (circa 1854), quoted in, for instance, Boyer and Morais 1956, p. 11.
109 Doubts are raised in, among others, Boller and George 1989, p. 77 f.
110 Foner 1977, p. 391.
111 This polarity is reflected in historiography, see the withering critique of the AFL in Shannon 1955 as compared to the praise for it found in Lens 1949. On the breadth of the party's impact, see Johnson 2008.
112 Quoted in Dubofsky and Dulles 2004, p. 195.
113 This dovetailed with growing scepticism towards the old 'labor leaders', see Lens 1949, p. 90 f.

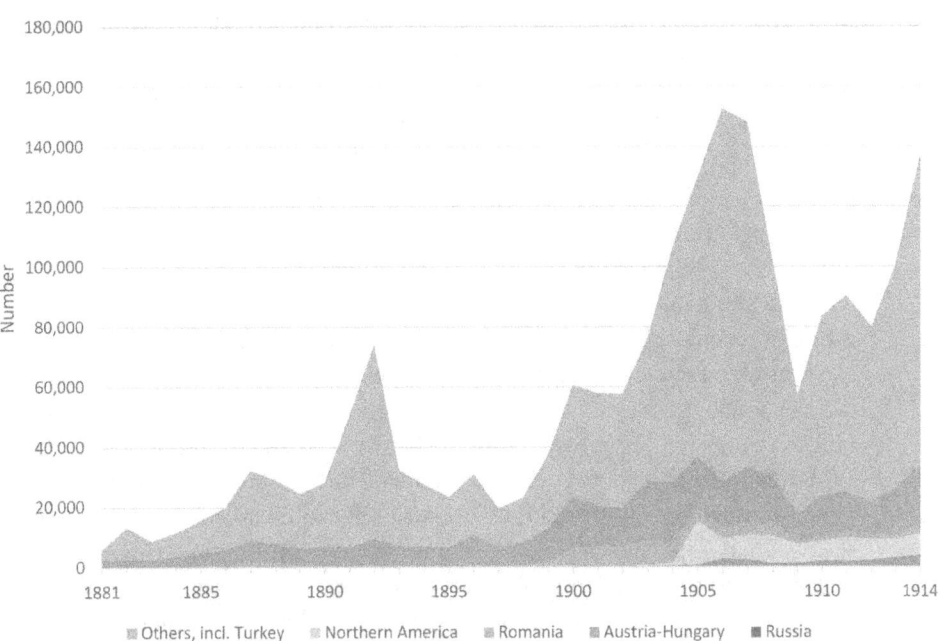

FIGURE 2   Eastern European Jewish immigration to the US, 1881–1914
FIGURES TAKEN FROM RISCHIN 1977, P. 270

work in American industry.[114] As Paul Douglass revealed, however, the statistics commonly used to prove this at the time intentionally omitted Jewish immigration. The number of skilled Jewish workers was four times higher than the average, yet the American class system condemned the newcomers to eke out a living as low-wage labourers at the very bottom of the social hierarchy.[115] Adding to this was the fact that skilled workers faced increasingly dim employment prospects. Although the proportion of qualified immigrants rose by 50 percent between 1871–82 (11.4 percent of overall immigration) and 1899–1909 (16.6 percent), their share of the total workforce declined from 22.9 to 18.1 percent over the same period.[116]

Employment often required not only skills, but also tools workers had to provide themselves and could only afford by taking out loans. Indebted workers were often compelled to become self-employed small-scale 'entrepreneurs', whose existence depended on harsh contracts forcing them to accept entre-

---

114   Jenks and Lauck 1912, esp. pp. 31–3; see also Kraut 1995; Fry 2007; Schrag 2010.
115   Joseph 1914, p. 144f.; see also Lederhendler 2009. The same was true for German and Swedish immigrants at the time, see Bodnar 1987, p. 63.
116   Douglass 1919, p. 393, p. 401f.

preneurial risk for an activity directed by their employer.[117] The contracting system thus outsourced both highly differentiated and low-skill tasks (such as sewing pockets onto clothes or bags) to contractors in addition to the associated financial burdens, risks, and responsibilities. This did not lead to the sort of 'splendid American wealth' enjoyed by 'Yankee billionaires' in other industries, but – as described by Gustavus Myers – to a situation in which '(irony upon irony!) the men, women and children who produce an infinite amount of wool ... cannot even afford adequate undergarments'.[118]

Quite frequently five, six, or even eight people would cram into one bedroom.[119] According to sociologist Charles S. Bernheimer, the average working-class family at the beginning of the twentieth century earned about 15 dollars per week.[120] Following a crisis in 1908, however, this figure declined significantly and was suppressed even further by subsequent immigration. The US Bureau of Labor noted that 90.7 percent of New York workers received a weekly wage of less than 10 dollars, while female workers earned a mere seven dollars. Only five percent of seamsters and seamstresses received the 12 dollars per week considered necessary to maintain a minimum level of subsistence.[121] Thus, in the highly differentiated American labour market of the contracting system personal networks were crucial – both to workers' survival as well as to sustaining ties among immigrant communities. These networks accordingly fostered both economic dependencies as well as political organisation.[122]

Collective socialist identity came into fierce conflict with popularly held notions of the 'American Dream' on the Lower East Side. The conservative *Saturday Evening Post* described immigrant neighbourhoods as 'hotbeds of dissent, unrest, sedition and anarchy', marked by an 'inconveniently large portion of the new immigrants float[ing] around in unsightly indigestible lumps'.[123] According to the *Chicago News*, Russian Jews were the toughest case, as they were simply 'not the kind of people to become Americanized because of their clannishness and bigotry'. As early as 1892 the renowned Commissioner of

---

117 Waldinger 1984 and 1990; Bonacich 1993. The voices of immigrants themselves can be found in, for instance, Morawska 1996, esp. p. 216.
118 Myers 1916, p. 774. Translator's note: the 1916 German translation of all three volumes of Gustavus Myers's *History of the Great American Fortunes* contains two additional chapters omitted from the original English edition.
119 Myers 1916, p. 775.
120 Bernheimer 1909.
121 Cited in Myers 1916, p. 775.
122 Wolfson 1950; Light and Bhachu 1993.
123 Simon 1997, p. 15.

Immigration Francis Walker warned in the pages of *Literary Digest* that immigrants represented 'a menace to the rate of wages and the American standard of living'. 'Living like swine', they posed 'the greatest danger that American labor has ever known'.[124] This style of rhetoric grew more frequent after the war and prompted the introduction of restrictive immigration quotas in 1924, largely closing the gates of the 'Promised Land' to Southern and Eastern European immigrants. Those Emma Lazarus once compassionately described as the 'tired', 'poor', and 'huddled masses yearning to breathe free' were now blamed for the darker sides of industrial capitalism; immigrants were reproached not only for their poverty but also for their attempts to fight against it.

In contrast to widely held belief, American socialism can neither be reduced to its alleged theoretical underdevelopment[125] nor can its existence be denied outright.[126] That said, for many Eastern European immigrants the distance between socialism and the labour movement caused it to appear as a mild and diluted version of the socialism they knew – a 'colder' variety, so to speak. As early as 1870, the American religious revolutionary socialist John Humphrey Noyes pointed out in his voluminous *History of American Socialisms* that it was precisely the experimental nature of American society that made the country 'a laboratory in which Socialisms of all kinds have been experimenting'.[127] He along with contemporary observers such as Friedrich Engels and Werner Sombart understood this as a flaw, arguing that *one* form of socialism had to be distilled from the lessons these experiments could teach the workers' movement.[128] This political demand also left its traces in historical scholarship, which often criticises a lack of unity instead of investigating and illuminating plurality.[129]

The starting point for such an investigation, however, must be the recognition of socialism as an elementary feature of American Jewish history. As Tony Michels notes, previous generations of Jewish history scholars had an interest in marginalising the Jewish immigrant majority's socialist past so as to better incorporate the former into the national grand narratives of the US and

---

124 Cited in Simon 1997, p. 17.
125 As for example in Manor 2009, p. 14 f., p. 106 ff.
126 Lipset and Marks 2000.
127 Noyes 1966, p. xix.
128 Noyes 1966, p. 671 f.; Sombart 1976, p. 3; see also Engels 2009.
129 This criticism can be found in practically any history of socialism, see for example Fried 1970. An early, theoretically oriented exception to this rule is Dumont and Mazoyer 1973; Wright 1996, p. xiv, p. 1.

Israel.[130] Yet while the 'Jewish Century', as described by Yuri Slezkine, tends to accept the Jewish revolutionary as a pioneer of liberal modernity, the complexity of Jewish immigrant experiences in America also conflicted with this liberal tale of modernity: 'The New World looked like the old country. Palestine and Petrograd did not'.[131] Indeed, in the US Jewish immigrant groups displayed varying degrees of inclination towards radical views and organisations. Many of them were drawn to the Socialist Party, a significant political actor in the country at least for a certain period of time. Despite a vicious press campaign against him, Eugene V. Debs received a remarkable 400,000 votes in the 1904 presidential elections. The figure not only exceeded the number of actual party members tenfold – evidence of a tremendously successful campaign – but simultaneously quadrupled the number of votes he received in 1900 prior to the Socialist Party's founding, already considered a sensation at the time. The party grew considerably by 1912 as did the ranks of its sympathisers, earning Debs a total of 897,000 votes or six percent of the popular vote.[132]

It would be mistaken to take this as evidence of overwhelming Socialist influence on a national scale, let alone of socialism as such. Votes were not evenly distributed, and the heavy concentrations found in urban centres were compensated by the ongoing Red Scare in other parts of the country. Consequently, under the leadership of its brilliant rhetorician the Socialist Party extended its influence beyond the boundaries of the party itself but remained a dispersed and local force.[133] It should also be noted that votes only reflect support among registered voters, whereas the party was far more popular among newly arrived immigrants who did not have voting rights. A specific type of socialism flourished among Jewish immigrants, mediating between East and West just as it did between socio-economic demands and Yiddish cultural work. This overlap defined organisations such as the *Arbeter-ring*, the *Yidisher sotsyalistisher farband*, and relevant branches of the ILGWU – all of which were shaped by Bundist immigrants. Despite their deeply American goals, their impressive success relied on transfers of Bundist practices and objectives from Russia and Poland to New York City. As they were never affiliated to the Bund, they can be considered 'secondary-Bundist organisations'.

---

130   Michels 2000; Roskies 1999. On Howe's assertion that assimilation and professionalisation made socialism superfluous see Chace 2008, p. 270.
131   Slezkine 2004, p. 210.
132   Socialists were regularly elected to the US Congress until the mid-1920s. Many American municipalities (33 in 1911) were also governed by socialist mayors, including important cities like Milwaukee, Flint, Jackson, MI, and Berkeley, CA. See Shannon 1955, p. 5.
133   Current prominent studies include Freeberg 2008 and Salvatore 2007. For a glimpse of Debs's rhetorical skills see Debs 2014 and Tussey 1970.

American historiography dates the Socialist Party's decline from 1912 onwards. Only in the wake of the Great Depression, under the leadership of the charismatic Norman Thomas, would it experience a short-lived revival. Its decline was substantiated by James Weinstein as early as 1967. One of his main indicators of the party's undeniable withering was the circulation of socialist daily newspapers, which plummeted disastrously around World War I. Yet what defined socialism in the US was not necessarily true of Yiddish socialism. The strictly Yiddish-language '*Forverts*', by contrast, soared to hitherto unknown heights during these years, reaching a maximum daily circulation of roughly 275,000 and becoming the second-largest socialist daily in the country.[134] Meyer London, the Socialist candidate for the Lower East Side, also scored sensational victories as the first Socialist congressman and was re-elected in 1920. His later ouster was only achieved through a purposeful redrawing of congressional districts. Political time ran at a different pace on the Lower East Side, where socialism sprouted from the ground as quickly as Manhattan's skyscrapers.[135] In this regard it is quite appropriate that the high-rise built as the headquarters of the *Forverts Association* in 1912 towered above all other building on the Lower East Side. Apart from the paper's editorial desk, the beautiful Forverts Building housed many other socialist groups and initiatives and symbolised how through its outspoken socialism the publication served as an important link in the migration process. Although deemed essentially un-socialist by Ehud Manor, its strong tendencies towards Americanisation were in fact a precondition for the '*Forverts*' to articulate its vision of socialism in the United States, and hence to build bridges enabling a variety of political and cultural activisms.[136]

The relevant literature generally emphasises Russian immigrants' pivotal role in the history of the American labour movement.[137] But if the Russian elements were more then mere points of origin, we have to take them into account as simultaneously occurring and intertwining facets of one story.[138] This book thus repeatedly returns to discussing the presence and relevance of the Russian workers' movement overseas and vice-versa, emphasising the transnational dimension within the functionally differentiated Jewish workers'

---

134 Weinstein 1967, pp. 84–102.
135 Glazer and Moynihan 1970, p. 137 ff.
136 Manor 2009, p. 44 f.
137 Of the many studies available see esp. Weinryb 1946; Mendelsohn 1976; Liebman 1979; Levin 1977; Sorin 1985; Enstad 1999; Bender 2004. With emphasis on *yidishkayt*: Michels 2005.
138 Michels 2009; Katz 2011.

movement in the United States such as transfers and adaptations of Russian socialist practices to American conditions. Furthermore, it relates the history of Jewish socialists in the US to their *khaverim* in Argentina, the second-most favoured destination for transatlantic immigrants.

6   Argentina

Similar to developments in the US, Jewish migration from Eastern Europe to Argentina began in the 1880s. But here it remained low until after the turn of the century. Only around 1904 did it begin to skyrocket, a fact that has prompted a rethinking of the traditionally US-centric history of Jewish migration.[139] Argentina became the second-most popular destination for transatlantic Jewish emigration after the United States, far ahead of Palestine. On a global scale it was only exceeded by closer destinations such as London, which as a hub to the New World also saw far more transmigration than the American destinations.[140] In contrast to the US, this Jewish immigration was not preceded by any significant degree of German-Jewish immigration.

So-called 'assisted migration' organised by the Jewish Colonization Association (ICA) played an important role in the early phases.[141] Founded in 1888 and based in Paris, the ICA utilised the Argentinian state's conflation of immigration and colonisation in the country's first 1876 immigration law (no. 817).[142] Around 1890 it began establishing large-scale Jewish agricultural colonies in the provinces. Prior to that, national decree no. 12,011 granted Argentinian citizen José Mariá Bustos permission to promote immigration to Argentina among Russian Jews. This 'invitation to Jewish immigrants'[143] encouraged the *agentes de inmigración en el exterior* named in law no. 817 to undertake targeted efforts to attract the Eastern European Jewish population. After receiving official support from the Argentinian state per national decree in 1892, the ICA soon

---

139   See for example Gartner 1998, p. 111. Conversely, see Elkin 1980; Moya 2004; Kobrin 2010; Lipphardt 2010.
140   Lestchinsky 1960.
141   This case was by no means unique, see Moran 2004.
142   The law explicitly stated: *'Dirigir la inmigración a los puntos que el Poder Ejecutivo, de acuerdo con la Oficina de Tierras y Colonias, designen para colonizar'* (Direct immigration to destinations which the Executive in accordance with the Office for Regions and Colonies has designated for colonisation), see República Argentina. Ministerio de Agricultura de la Nación 1920, p. 5 f. See also Winsberg 1964; Avni 1983.
143   See Yedlin 1982, p. 8.

assumed the role of such an agent.[144] The policy of settling 'white colonists' was combined with an aggressive and genocidal policy against the indigenous population.[145] In contrast to the oft-cited 'pogrom paradigm', Jewish migration to Argentina was by and large not a direct result of forced relocation, violence, and displacement but rather, in the words of Charles Tilly, 'career' or 'betterment migration'.[146] As Jochen Oltmer demonstrates, the latter distinguishes between 'area of origin and destination primarily based on economic differentials ... of individual market segments of a regional scope'.[147] This made the rising industrial nation of Argentina a compelling destination for many immigrants. For Jewish migrants in particular it gradually developed its own myth as a second 'Promised Land' alongside the United States.[148] The ICA's representative in Argentina, David Feinberg, praised his own achievements unreservedly, having completely transformed the 'lean and pitifull looking Jew' from Russia through 'free and healthy care of the country, physical labor and etc'.[149]

But these colonies were agricultural colonies. Their way of life stood in stark contrast to that of the shtetl inhabitants, who were completely untrained in farming and explicitly barred from agricultural resettlement in the Tsarist empire from 1882 onwards.[150] Many of the colonies soon failed. The fact that, when looking at Jewish Argentina before World War I, they are reflected much more extensively in Argentinian-Jewish literature than the urban life of the capital did a great deal to mystify Jewish life in Argentina. In this sense, colonies like Moisesville ought to be viewed more as an 'idea' than as structures of Jew-

---

144   Vivas Lencinas 1994, p. 103 f.; Avni 1973.
145   Of particular note here is the 'civilising mission' led by Julio Argentino Roca in Patagonia, over the course of which practically the region's entire indigenous population was murdered. Roca moreover served as Argentinian president from 1880–6 and 1898–1904, the period of the oft-glorified colonisation. Until its long overdue replacement in 2012 his portrait adorned the largest Argentinian bank note, the 100-peso bill, a decision still justified by the government as follows: 'Prepara y conduce la campaña de la Conquista del Desierto (1875–1879) que contribuyó significativamente al desenvolvimiento de la economía agropecuaria', (www.bcra.gob.ar/SistemasFinancierosYdePagos/100_Pesos_Serie_T.asp, last accessed: 4 January 2017). Scholarship views the genocide as a fundamental element of Argentinian statehood, see Trinchero 2009; Delrio and Lenton et al. 2010. Public trivialisation of the genocide also led some to draw absurd parallels to Jewish history, see for example Churchill 1997.
146   Tilly 1978; see also Solberg 1978; Klier 1992; Devoto 2003, pp. 36–42.
147   Oltmer 2009a, p. 8 f.
148   Avni 1973. This notion can be found in various autobiographies even today, particularly when life stories were closely intertwined with the ICA; see for example Aizicovich 2006.
149   Quoted in Sofer 1982, p. 2.
150   A brief depiction of the drive towards agriculturalisation can be found in Dekel-Chen 2005, pp. 1–10.

ish settlement defining Jewish Argentina.[151] Similar to the *Gaucho Judío*, they are constructions of a 'productive' Jewish origin myth, the rhetorical weight of which hardly stands up to social-historical scrutiny.[152] Against this origin myth and with his eyes soberly fixed on Buenos Aires, where the majority of immigrant Jews lived, Eugene Sofer thus observes: 'The colonies meant locusts, Indians, hostile neighbors, and disease. In the end Baron's dreams of a Jewish yeomanry foundered on the problems of Argentine rural life'.[153] In 1895 only 13.3 percent of the few Jews in Argentina lived in Buenos Aires, while by 1935 only 11 percent still remained in the countryside.[154] Buenos Aires became the only truly appealing destination, indicating that the 'assisted migration' intended to build up the country's agricultural base ultimately promoted urbanisation and proletarianisation more than anything else.[155]

With a short exception in the 1880s when the government subsidised free transatlantic passage, Argentina only entered the select circle of countries of mass immigration with over 100,000 people arriving each year in the early twentieth century.[156] By 1900 this immigration transformed the Río de la Plata region from the hitherto 'backwater of the Iberian empires' to the 'most developed region of Latin America', evidenced particularly in the expansion of Buenos Aires and the city's increased social segregation.[157] Here, 'making a living' and 'making America' went hand in hand.[158]

The exact number of Jewish immigrants necessarily remains contested. Argentinian authorities filed their migration records based on immigrants' passports, not ethnicity. Officials simply registered Jews under 'other religion', making immigration records largely useless for accurately quantifying Jewish migration to the country. The closest approximations can be deduced from the estimates of Jewish relief organisations. The chairman of the HICEM in Argentina, Simón Weill, compiled the most important study in this regard in 1935. At the time, the American Jewish Yearbook had begun requesting statistics on an annual basis, yet the data Weill provided did not (in contrast to what many, among them Marc Wishnitzer, Chaim Avni, and the American Jewish Yearbook

---

151 Yedlin 1982, p. 12. For examples of this long and international tradition see Barra 1904, p. 64f.; Avni 1973 and 1983; Lewin 1971. More critical: Schenkolewski-Kroll 2001.
152 Gerchunoff 2007; Aizenberg 1988; Schenkolewski-Kroll 2001, p. 49f. See also Berg 2002; Freidenberg 2009. On the 'agrarian myth' see Hofstadter 1956.
153 Sofer 1982, p. 3.
154 Ibid.
155 Lewis 2001; Cortés Conde 2009.
156 Ves Losada 1917, p. 36f.
157 Cited in Moya 2006, p. 11. More thorough: Moya 1998.
158 Moya 1998, pp. 205–18.

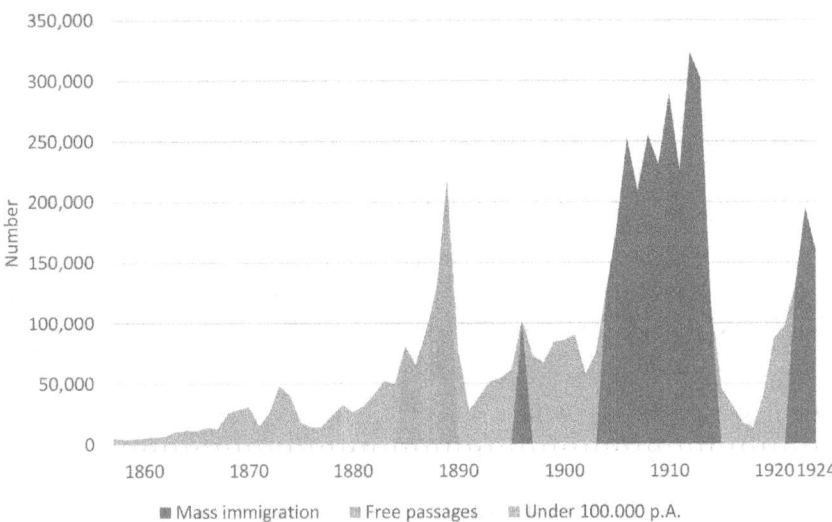

FIGURE 3   Immigration to Argentina, 1857–1924; second- and third-class tickets, transatlantic
FIGURES TAKEN FROM BEYHAUT, GOROSTEGUI AND TORRADO 1961, 'SEXO DE LOS IMMIGRANTES, 1857–1924', N.P.

itself claimed) represent actual immigration statistics, but Jewish net migration or total annual immigration less emigration. This distinction is significant in Latin America, a region characterised by transmigration.[159] Weill was only interested in the Argentinian Jewish community's net growth through migration and natural reproduction, not in transmigration through Argentina itself. From the perspective of migration history, then, his numbers represent minimum values.

Jewish immigration to Argentina remained meagre until 1903. Numbers of Jewish immigrants suddenly soared beginning with the pre-revolutionary crisis in Russia around 1904, stabilising (with the exception of the war years) around 5,000–15,000 people annually. Migration stabilised around the lower spectrum of this range in the mid-1920s due to national immigration quotas modelled on the US example, although the impact was not nearly as far-reaching as in the United States. The military junta led by General José Félix Uriburu that took power through a coup d'état in 1930 further tightened regulations on the immigration of Eastern European Jews.[160] These regulations were accompanied by growing anti-Semitic prejudice within wider Argentinian society.

---

159   Weill 1936. Compare with the annual statistics found in the *American Jewish Year Book*, 1919–39; see also Wishnitzer 1948, p. 291; Avni 1983, p. 543f.
160   Devoto 2003, pp. 353–64.

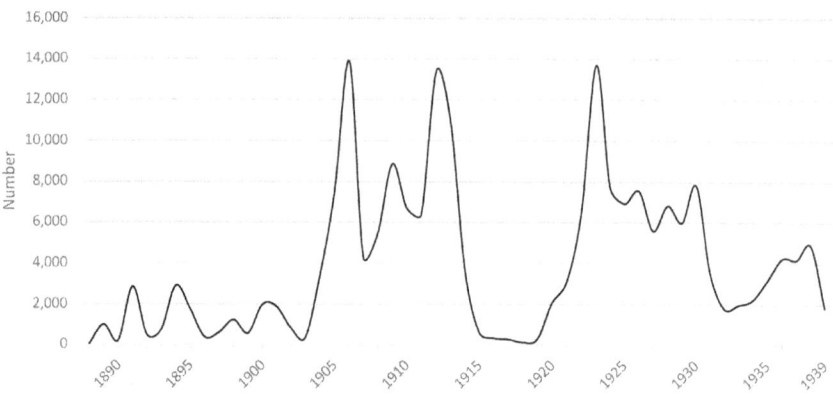

FIGURE 4   Annual Jewish net migration to Argentina, 1900–39
FIGURES TAKEN FROM WEILL 1936, P. 28 F.; LINFIELD 1945, P. 517

Coupled with sentiments surrounding the Red Scare and suspicions of revolutionary conspiracies, the dynamic directed significant amounts of public scorn towards the Bundists.[161] The renewed rise in immigration levels from the mid-1930s onwards was mostly due to German-Jewish refugees as well as a growing number of Polish immigrants who, as Efraim Zadoff notes, accounted for half of all migrants through legal and illegal routes between 1934–8, the majority of whom were Jews.[162] The Argentinian Jewish community's size increased from roughly 20,000 members in 1901 to at least 116,276 immediately prior to World War I, and more than doubled to 260,432 by 1935.[163]

The absolute majority of Jews emigrating to Argentina were of Russian origin. In the sources, the term *ruso* (Russian) thus often meant Jewish, while for a long time the term *judío* (Jewish) simultaneously meant 'from Russia'. For this reason, the migrant neighbourhoods that emerged in Buenos Aries were not Russian but rather Jewish.[164] They were situated in the city's districts no. 9 (Nueve) and 11 (Once) surrounding the Plaza Lavalle. The square became a centre of Jewish life and developed, at least according to Eugene Sofer, a characteristic social structure[165] – 'characteristic', however, not in comparison to the experience of Jewish migrants in the US, but rather with strong similarities between the socio-economic structures of Jewish life in Argentina and East-

---

161   On this phenomenon see Herbeck 2009; similar studies on the Latin American context are yet to be written.
162   Zadoff 1994, p. 43.
163   Weill 1936, p. 28 f.
164   Moya 1998, p. 158.
165   Sofer 1982, pp. 69–79.

ern Europe. In both places employment relations were often personalised and mostly unspecialised. Later Chief Rabbi of Argentina Samuel Halphon reported in 1909 while working for the ICA that he could find only 100 specialised professionals in the entire country; practically all Jews living in Argentina were craftsmen or small-scale traders.[166] Starting a business required roughly 100 pesos for the initial investment, theoretically feasible but extremely difficult for workers earning two to three pesos per day.[167]

In this regard, the boundary between workshop and commerce was as fluid in Argentina as in Eastern Europe. At the time of the 1897 census, more than half of Jewish craftsmen in the Tsarist empire worked in the textile industry. Very few Jews in either Russia or Argentina were active in the primary sector; the figure dipped below 0.6 percent of all Jews living in the Pale[168] and hardly changed during the interwar period. According to a study compiled in 1935, 47.1 percent of all Jews living in Poland in 1921 worked in the garment industry.[169] Studies conducted by Abraham Léon confirm this for the 1930s.[170] The same is true for Argentina, where most who began their working lives in the textile industry were likely to end there as well.[171] In the eyes of Bundist Pinie Vald, this created an Argentinian-Jewish *svive*, a 'communal environment' the Jewish immigrants themselves created through their economic status and practices, in turn facilitating the Bundist transfer of Jewish social movements.[172]

It was thus up to the Bundists and their fellow Jewish immigrants to devise a Jewish socialism in Argentina. The Bundists had considerable leeway in this process. When the first *khaverim* arrived from Eastern Europe in the 1900s, they found a growing city but no pre-existing patterns of socio-political Jewish community building. In comparison to the US, they also lacked both support and competition from dominant local organisations such as the '*Forverts*'. This allowed them to transfer the conceptual intentions and countless patterns of activism from the Eastern European shtetls to the Río de la Plata region more directly.[173] These new arrivals around 1905 had interpretative sovereignty over what would now be understood as Jewish life in Argentina,[174] providing fertile

---

166 Cited in Sofer 1982, p. 94, p. 112.
167 Varone 2004, p. 12.
168 Bunzl 1975, p. 33 f.
169 Radt 1935.
170 Léon 1971.
171 Sofer 1982, p. 99.
172 Vald 1942, p. 94.
173 Elazar 1983, pp. 129–46.
174 See for example Clemens 1996.

ground for Bundist activism to grow and spread. Not without reason does Ezra Mendelsohn stress in his classic study of the Bund how the organisation managed to transform the 'cultural front' found in Eastern Europe into a lifeworld that would subsequently define Bundist lives and action in Argentina.[175] If at least some facets of *doikayt* were transferrable, Buenos Aires was certainly an adequate target.

7 The Bund's Social Thread

Embedding the history of the Bund within these configurations changes our perspective on both the Bund as well as local Jewish history. A transnational perspective offers above all the opportunity to examine communities in the process of emergence and persistence. Communities in this sense are not rigid units or entities, but rather constantly shifting, erratic conglomerations of actors. It is therefore misleading to distinguish between 'authentic' and 'manufactured' communities.[176] Bundists commemorated and reimagined their community each time they sang their hymn, *Di shvue*: 'Brothers and sisters in toil and struggle / All who are dispersed far and wide / Together, together, the flag is ready ...'[177] The symbol of unity for these scattered and suffering Jews was the red flag, which extended beyond the Jewish community and allowed for new and broader coalitions and communities.

At times this combative unity and solidarity appeared as a red thread tying together a variety of disparate actors. Here, Latour's metaphorical social thread materialised into a palpable symbol of struggle. The photograph on the frontispiece of this volume shows revolutionaries in Vilnius coming together to demonstrate unity in a Bundist-led socialist memorial ceremony for the victims of the 1905 revolution. Hundreds symbolically join together, connected by a long, presumably red ribbon embroidered with the names of participating organisations and political parties. The ribbon has no visible end nor beginning, it levels and egalitarianises, creating a common performative space in which participants silently act out an expression of militant activism. Loosely linked yet united in the struggle – this was not just how many Bundist groups based in the Pale perceived themselves, but also describes the Bund's position

---

175 Mendelsohn 1970, pp. 116–25, p. 153.
176 Bauman 2009.
177 Original: '*Brider un shvester fun arbet un noyt / ale vos zaynen tsezeyt un tseshpreyt / tsuzamen, tsuzamen, di fon zi iz greyt ...*', translation by the author, based on Safran and Zipperstein 2006.

vis-à-vis other socialist parties and overseas Bundist groups. The Bund became a transnational social space in which the unifying power of *yidishkayt* gained even more momentum.

Such activism sought to carve out a set of practices allowing activists to shape Bundist history. I understand these practices as patterns of activism, as concrete manifestations of political practices. In the Bund's case these were first conceived in Eastern Europe and subsequently transferred to locations across the globe, often in highly creative ways. This demonstrates that the continued existence of a social movement can by no means be taken for granted. On the contrary, it is absolutely remarkable that the Bund survived so many ruptures and was even reborn on the Lower East Side and along the banks of the Río de la Plata. Here, a Bundist social space emerged from initiatives that implemented Bundism far removed from the actual Bund, and ultimately outlived the Eastern European Bund.

I investigate this over the course of three steps, beginning with the identification and contextualisation of modes of Bundist activism in Eastern Europe. In a second step I examine Bundist publications from a transnational and comparative perspective. As modes of expression and means of mobilisation towards community coherence, they were absolutely crucial to the transnational history of the Bund. The analysis of *Memorik* in particular sheds new light on the formation of trans- and supra-personal networks within a community. Among other things, this study is also an inquiry into the transnational commemoration practices of a socialist movement. In a third step I then turn to more localised patterns of activism. The transferred practices of assembling and organising and the creation of 'secondary Bundism' as well as equally important patterns of transnational activism around work in the trade unions, education, and fundraising take centre stage in this examination. Together they underscore the notion that transnationality cannot be complete without also accounting for locality.

The Bund's transnational and networked nature was not a product of the post-war era, dating back almost as far as the history of the Russian Bund. Nor does it represent a marginal episode in the Bund's history. Instead, the Bund is an unjustly neglected, vitally important episode in the history of both the Russian revolutionary movement and Jewish modernity. This study therefore depicts the transnational Bund as a global player of Jewish history and a remarkable but certainly not unique case of a transnational social movement. The book also seeks to once again place politically motivated practices at the centre of the Jewish diaspora. In terms of migration history, this contribution illustrates the fact that migration is characterised not only by 'movement' as such, but by concrete investigable transnational social spaces determined by network ties and countless bridge-building actors.[178] It underscores that ever since the nineteenth century, the process we call 'globalisation' – which cannot be reduced to mere intellectual or economic history – has not only spawned theoretical, macro-economic, and systemic consequences, but indeed directly influenced the lives and actions of journalists, tailors, and milliners who in turn shaped the former.

---

178 See also Brinkmann 2007. Prominent representatives of this focus on movement include Bade 2003; Hoerder 2002; Kleinschmidt 2003.

PART 1

The Bund as a Social Movement

CHAPTER 1

Bundist Activism

To explain the political and cultural activism Bundists often referred to simply as the *kamf far unzere rekht* (struggle for our rights),[1] we must look beyond theories of voluntaristic action or rationalist approaches of social movement studies.[2] Although often used as if it were, the term 'activism' remains far from self-explanatory. Despite the term's widespread usage in academic literature,[3] theoretical approaches to social movement studies rarely examine how historical actors viewed their own activism.[4]

Activism is not an anthropological constant, but rather a result of the post-Enlightenment socialist upsurge. Karl Mannheim had good reason to open his pioneering *Ideology and Utopia* by informing readers that it 'is by no means an accident that the problem of the social and activistic roots of thinking has emerged in our generation'.[5] Nevertheless, this emergence has yet to be subjected to closer investigation. As no social movement can exist without activists, the ongoing relationship between individual and movement – which in the Bund's case often spawned lifelong identities – cannot be explained with recourse to 'membership', ideology, or rational mobilisation dynamics alone. Thus, before dealing with specific manifestations of Bundist transnational activism, this study begins by hammering out a more precise definition of the term

---

1 Due to its inclusion of solidarity as a necessary element, this concept of struggle goes beyond Max Weber, who defined struggle (translated as 'conflict' in English) as 'action ... oriented intentionally to carrying out the actor's own will against the resistance of the other party or parties'. Here, emphasis is placed on unity through struggle rather than on the process of 'selection' Weber prioritised, see Weber 1978, p. 38.
2 See esp. Joas 1996; Münch 2010; Reichart 2004; Mueller 1992; Taylor and Whittier 1992; Hunt and Benford 2004.
3 Such as in Wastl-Walter's entry 'Social Movements: Environmental Movements' in the *International Encyclopedia of the Social and Behavioral Sciences* (Smelser and Baltes 2001), esp. p. 14354; also clearly the case in one of the reference articles on social movement research, see McAdam, McCarthy and Zald 1988, pp. 704–9.
4 It is not reflected in any of the relevant handbooks, not even the pioneering, 26-volume *International Encyclopedia of the Social and Behavioral Sciences* (Smelser and Baltes 2001). For further examples see Seligman and Johnson 1930; Vierkandt 1931; Sills and Merton 1968; Turner 2006; and even Ritzer 2007. One exception is Embrick 2008, although the fact that the bibliography lists only three case studies on the American civil rights movement and one National Public Radio broadcast underlines the extent of the problem.
5 Mannheim 1997, p. 5.

itself. Incidentally, the nature of Bundist activism was also the subject of lively debate among activists themselves.

When responding to a Bund Archive questionnaire about positions held in the Jewish workers' movement, Bundist veteran Abraham der Tate (Layb Blekhman) responded by reformulating the question: 'There were no posts in the Russian Bund. Rather, the question ought to be: to which bodies did you belong? In that case I can answer: mainly to the Ts. K. [Central Committee]'.[6] This response suggests that he defined his function not by an office or rank as such, but by his actions on behalf of a specific Bundist organisational unit. As leading Bundist Vladimir Medem emphasised, one did not simply *belong* to the Bund. Instead, individuals became active and in doing so brought the Bund and its organisations into being.[7]

Naturally, activity in the Yiddish workers' movement required a name. The term used was that of the *tuer* (do-er).[8] In contrast to the vagueness of the similar sounding German auxiliary verb *tun* (to do), *tuer* was applied far more specifically, never randomly, and with implications extending far beyond 'being active' or 'doing' something. The more appropriate translation in this case is thus 'activist'.[9] Activists represent the interface between individual, group, and idea within social movements. They embody the movement's continual reproduction by aligning a series of actions, endowing them with meaning, and plausibly legitimising them in a counter-cultural sense. In doing so they also open the movement to other activisms.[10] *Tuer* became both a description of activity as well as a category of honour in the Bund. Consequently, to be regarded as a *tuer* was desired not only by workers seeking to participate in the organisation, but also by intellectuals who used it to portray themselves as more grounded and in-touch with the masses.[11] The term *tuer* is thus ubi-

---

6 YIVO, Bund Archives, RG 1400, MG 2, 429, Abraham der Tate.
7 Medem 1979, p. 222. This aspect is further explored in Wolff 2014b.
8 In contrast to the explicitly left-wing term of *tuer*, the Russian term *deyatel'* was not confined to the workers' movement. Correspondingly, *deyatel' rabochego dvizheniya* (workers' movement activist) was just as common as *obshchestvenniy deyatel'* (public persona). Moreover, it was used as an honorific title for early Bund activists, such as in Tate, Frumoiskii, Gozhanskii, Kaplinski, et al. 1907. Similar to the Yiddish *tuer* was the French *militant*, which Argentinian Bundists around the publication 'Der avangard' applied ironically to rabbis in the western Tsarist Empire who took advantage of the anti-socialist reaction, see Libnyan 1909. The title was printed in Latin letters for ironic effect.
9 Weinreich (1977, p. 599) translates it as simply 'active person, leader', but the term possessed a much deeper meaning at least within the socialist milieu.
10 Latour 1986; Roßler 2008.
11 This can generally be conducted as a morally underpinning and identity-forming action; see for example M. Silver 1998.

quitous in the Bund's history as both a qualifying self-description as well as an appreciative external ascription. The term became increasingly common across the movements as time went on.[12] Its extension from the socialist milieu into newer cultural movements was often tied to references to the movement's origins, when pioneering *tuer* conquered non-territorial frontiers and secured these spaces for the activisms of subsequent *tuer* generations. The common historical project of *yidishkayt* served to unify both political and cultural *tuer* under a shared roof.[13]

The resulting counter-cultural drive distinguished activists from civil servants as revolutionaries and visionaries. In the eyes of most *tuer*, purposeful action within the state could not be regarded as activism.[14] Although civil servants could certainly be active, even in a swift and direct way, they were not regarded as activists in the proper sense. Known in the socialist movement for his talent for hunting down provocateurs, Paris émigré and Narodnik Vladimir Burcev confirmed as much with his biographical campaign, the 'Questionnaire for the Collection of Information on Participants in the Liberation Movement'. He not only sought to record the names of movement participants, but also of the 'worst enemies of the liberation movement: traitors, provocateurs, spies, police, prison guards, judges, prosecutors', arguing that it was 'also necessary to compile a biographical dictionary of such "activists" [Russian: *deyateli*]'.[15] Burcev meant what today is known as a black book, although he intentionally placed the word '*deyateli*' in quotation marks for a distancing and ironic effect. Only through this distance could the Tsarist henchmen be described as activists. They lacked utopian promise, or to paraphrase Walter Benjamin's description of the 'Angel of History', were not surrounded by the storm 'blowing from Paradise ... caught in his wings with such violence that the angel can no longer close them. This storm irresistibly propels him into the

---

12 This is evident in numerous autobiographies as well as commemorative and often glorifying anthologies on the movement's founding fathers such as Yeshurin and Hertz 1962; Hoffman 1941; Tshukhinsi 1947; Ravitch 1945; Aronson 1962. A similar state of affairs exists in Yiddish anarchism, see 'Dr. I.A. Merison [Obituary]' 1936; Tshernov 1948. On attitudes towards the founding of the autonomous Jewish Soviet republic Birobidzhan see Abramovitsh 1936, p. 11 and p. 14; or as a self-ascription in the revolutionary process Alvaysruslandishe konferents fun yidishe kultur- un bildungstuer 1931; V.Y. 1939; Rak 1958.

13 The term *tuer*, however, is only rarely found as a self-ascription, such as in the case of Socialist Revolutionary Yitsak Nakhmen Shteynberg, in YIVO, New York, Bund Archives, RG 1400, MG 2, 429, Shteynberg, Yitsak Nakhmen.

14 In any case, Social Democratic activists tended to found publications emulating the German '*Vorwärts*' all around the world, see Carreras, Tarcus and Zeller 2008; Manor 2009.

15 See questionnaire issued by the editorial board of '*Byloe*', Paris [Vladimir Burcev], annex of YIVO, New York, Bund Archives, RG 1400, MG 2, 429, Likhtenfeld, Boris.

future to which his back is turned, while the pile of debris before him grows skyward. This storm is what we call progress'.[16]

For Benjamin, the stormy wind represents historical law, while the paradise is of a worldly nature. Bundists too often resorted to religiously vocabulary when describing promise and activism. Moreover, the storm did not carry the existing culture within it but was rather the bearer of activist novelty, imbued with morally charged *potentia*. This distinguished the *tuer* from both the Tsarist authorities and the Jewish leadership, whether traditional or Chassidic. The *tuer* continued what Heiko Haumann called Judaism's maskilic 'turn towards activism', shifting messianism away from the divine and into the hands of activists once and for all.[17] Politically, the *tuer* concept emerged for the intellectual, revolutionary milieu. Workers expanded it by moving it towards the status of an 'organiser'. Both notions, however, were developed against the backdrop of a historical materialist worldview geared towards social progress.[18]

To further nuance the matter, it is important to note that this worldview was not rooted in the self-organisation of the Jewish Enlightenment personified by Max Lilienthal, which initially pursued an alliance with Russian state authorities during the 'turn towards activism'. Calls to integrate the 'Jewish street' into the movement's thinking were more important, making the young Marx's *Theses on Feuerbach* central to the genesis of modern activism.[19]

Marx's theses were so special less for the fact that they attempted to spark revolutionary action among workers than because they expanded these actions to also encompass intellectual activity. Hence the famous dictum: 'The philosophers have only *interpreted* the world in various ways; the point is to *change* it'.[20] The process of philosophical enlightenment was to be tied to a will for change – individuals were to read, think, and become activists.[21] This call became a guiding image not only for avowed Marxists like the Bundists, but also for the more distant Russian Socialist Revolutionary Party oriented towards Alexander Herzen, the Narodniks, and Pierre-Joseph Proudhon's anarchism.[22] The young Marx provided them with philosophical orientation, allowing them

---

16 Benjamin 2007, p. 257 f.
17 Haumann 2002, pp. 50 and 166 f.; Levin 1977. See also Walzer 1986; Löwy 1992.
18 On Yiddish secularism see Harshav 1990 and the classic Niger 1981.
19 Hence, what we need is not a distinction between 'political' and 'pre-political' movements, but rather a consideration of the different constitutions of activist conceptions, see Hobsbawm 1959; Hobsbawm and Rudé 1968; Thompson 1964.
20 Marx 1975, p. 5.
21 On Marx's general activist outlook and corresponding problems of coherence in his theory see Gilbert 1979.
22 See Hildermeier 2000; Häfner 1994; King 2007.

to utilise the *Theses on Feuerbach* to integrate Marx into their programme of direct action without following a strictly Marxist model of class struggle.[23] Drawing on the *Theses of Feuerbach* provided many social movements, including those with unorthodox readings of Marx, with a degree of quasi-theoretical legitimation. At least implicitly, the *Theses on Feuerbach* informed the background in every deployment of the notion of activism, making Marx the father of the *filosofia della praxis* for Narodniks, Bundists, and Antonio Gramsci's coded prison language alike.[24]

1   Activism between the Masses and the Individual

Through its focus on working towards collective aims, activisms holds the ability to de-eliticise certain social acts as long as they serve a movement's agenda. Sometimes it can even mask individual actions as elements, of the collective struggle for liberation. A shining example can be found in Vladimir Medem's reflections on activist moments in his own life, where he emphasised not only his struggle for workers' rights but also for his own rights as an author.[25]

He experienced his first activist struggle as a student in 1899 during a strike that began at Saint Petersburg Imperial University and involved 30,000 workers at its peak. According to Medem, the intelligentsia turned a student protest into a labour struggle, ultimately developing it into the political novelty of a student-led political strike, a hitherto 'generally unknown entity'.[26] For Medem, a new era had begun, one that allowed to instigate top-down processes to lead from decision to action: 'The large meeting had no sooner ended than we proceeded – the chairman leading the way – down the corridors of the university, determined to translate our resolution into action'.[27] This activism enables him

---

23   Cross 1971.
24   See Gramsci 1971. Gramsci's choice of words is owed firstly to the censorship his writings were subjected to, and secondly to informed readers' ability to decipher his coded language. On the transmission and reception of the *Theses on Feuerbach* mainly within widely influential Italian political philosophy see Roth 1972, esp. pp. 13–31.
25   Interpreting intellectual engagement with terms borrowed from the world of work is hardly limited to Medem, but is rather an expression of a broader desire for comprehensive integration. Even Bundist sociologist Moshe Kligsberg, author of *Di yidishe yugentbavegung in Poyln tsvishen beyde velt-milkhomes: A sotsyologishe shtudye* (1974), saw himself not as a 'scientist' but a 'scientific worker'. See the autobiographical questionnaire, YIVO, New York, Bund Archives, RG 1400, MG2, 429, Kligsberg, Moshe.
26   Medem 1979, p. 120.
27   Ibid.

to integrate his 'I' into the progressive 'we': 'I found myself drawn into the very hub of the movement. I had got rid of my shyness by then. ... I thus entered the circle of leaders'.[28] In his eyes this was less an individual choice so much as a calling. After the strike it 'was much self-evident: we three young expelled students ... would be entering the movement sooner or later'.[29] In his autobiographical account, being an activist entails a process of personal maturing while following one's 'destiny', albeit with the traditional division of labour intact: his task was to *lead* the struggle through his speeches and writings. This applied not only to him, of course, but to all '"professionals" under the jurisdiction of the Central Committee ... persons who devote themselves explicitly and exclusively to revolutionary activity'.[30]

Medem's activism of the pen allowed him to participate in other strikes as a mere observer, and moreover mask an entirely non-collective type of work stoppage as a strike. Numerous Russian expatriates in Switzerland earned their living as correspondents. Inspired by his comrade Moshe Olgin, who worked as a reporter for the New York-based *'Forverts'*, Medem found a similar source of income reporting for the Russian newspaper *'Den'*. The latter encountered financial difficulties at the beginning of the war in 1914 and suspended payments to foreign correspondents. Unlike Trotsky, Medem had few alternatives and soon began dispatching telegrams to Russia of a markedly different nature:

> Yet this did not stop me from becoming a striker. 'If you don't send me enough to meet my expenses', I informed them, 'I shall cease telegraphing ... !' The threat was unavailing, and I actually staged a strike, in which I persisted for a respectable period. After receiving some money I started working again. But before very long the money again stopped coming and again I struck. It was that way the whole time – one strike after another.[31]

What Medem tries to portray as a strike of course had little to do with a collective workers' struggle. He withheld his services due to a lack of remuneration, but the mental template of the strike prevented him from recognising his own isolated action as passivity resulting from unpaid wages. It allowed him to conceive of his writing as well as his abstention as activism. Both became a unified struggle bestowing his intellectual occupation with a degree of working-class flair. Reducing an act of collective solidarity such as a strike to a rhetorical figure

---

28   Medem 1979, p. 121.
29   Medem 1979, p. 146.
30   Medem 1979, p. 446.
31   Medem 1979, p. 492 f.

of speech to legitimise his own actions allowed Medem to act as an activist in his own self-interest. It is characteristic that Medem staged his only strike while in exile. Through his 'labour struggle' he subscribed to the modus operandi of those he aspired to represent and even lead from a structural and geographical distance.

Apart from such privileged individual fashioning, activism usually relates to 'the masses'. But how can we conceptualise this seminal figure? Activism is significant in the social movement context because it facilitates a de-eliticised production of meaning through actions that can be related to a receptive collective and which, through reference to a certain mass, can be seen in line with a tradition of actions.[32] This may occur *within* or *for* the collective, through which the activist is always also a driving force of the movement. The activist is more than *pars pro toto* but never the sole leader. This ongoing legitimation of actions through reference to the masses can be found across various historical periods. Be it as a socialist, an activist in the 'struggle' for new ways of living,[33] or in the extra-parliamentary political or ecological movement[34] – activism aspires to serve a collective political objective also through individual acts. At the same time, however, the individual also emancipates her- or himself through actions referring to counter-cultural patterns of interpretation.[35] As I demonstrate in Part II, that is why, at least in this context, the distinction between 'I' and 'us' often made in autobiographical research represents a false dichotomy.

That said, tensions arise due to the fact that activist communities must necessarily be exclusive (lest they not be recognisable as counter-cultural communities) while simultaneously remaining open to newcomers.[36] Hence, the term 'the masses' was not self-explanatory even in the age of mass migration and politically active 'worker masses' – its visibility had to be produced. Activist concepts of the masses must therefore be reducible to acting collectives, while at the same time they exhibit connotations that point beyond these groups. Masses were thus both a resource and a problem for transnational social move-

---

32 On the concept of 'masses' see Schrage 2006 as well as a more elaborate discussion of this topic in Part III.8.
33 From anarchist-inspired cultural sociology (Kastner 2007) to the more absurd (Craftista Crafting Circle 2009).
34 Quite expressive in this regard is Frerichs 2008.
35 The distinction between social movements and movements of subject-transformation made by Andreas Reckwitz is not tenable in this regard either, see Reckwitz 2006, pp. 68–72; Wolff 2014b.
36 All communities must be understood as processual, meaning they are subject to a constant process of association. Any reference to 'true' communities as opposed to 'constructed' ones, as emphasised by Zygmunt Bauman, therefore remains unconvincing.

ments. As Bundist activism rested on the concept of 'Jewish workers masses', a more conceptual approach will help to improve our understanding of the Bund, Bundist identity, and Bundism. In the following model I understand the term 'masses' in a purely functional sense, that is to say neither pejoratively in the sense of a polarisation between the 'mass' and 'high culture', nor teleologically charged as, say, the historical bearer of revolutionary change.[37]

As sociologist Dominik Schrage notes, given its frequent and vague application, even a purely functional use of the term is not without its problems. He suggests resolving this issue by distinguishing between affective and descriptive instances of the term. Proceeding from Schrage, it is possible to approach the substance of what may be expressed with the term 'masses' from two perspectives, by drawing on his main types of *statistical masses* and *present masses*.[38]

A statistical mass refers to any mass created through observation. It exists only on a purely argumentative basis, that is to say one that is physically non-experienceable. One initial sub-type not specifically explicated by Schrage are *argumentative masses*. These are brought into being through loose and external references and serve primarily as epistemic magnitudes and non-specifiable units of reference. In the present study, these can be 'Eastern European-Jewish immigrants', 'Jewish socialists', 'Bundists', or simply 'Jews'. Such masses stand alongside another sub-type of statistical masses, as they are formed not only in the eyes of third-party observers but also through a collective sense of self as well as indirect communication. *Communicative masses* are thus crucial formations in the construction of masses, both in mass media as well as in collective self-understanding ('we Bundists'). This communicative aspect adds an affective component to the more descriptive nature of the statistical mass, one which can be either positively or negatively charged.

Schrage identifies two forms of present masses alongside those types of statistical masses. A 'present mass' denotes a conglomeration of any larger and experienceable number of individuals who can but do not necessarily actively relate to one another. It can in turn be divided into two sub-types: *dispersed masses* such as a throng of pedestrians on a street, and *directed masses* which form in meetings and actions and thus range from a revolutionary army to stadium crowds, activist masses at strikes and demonstrations, or

---

37   The latter in particular appears to be enjoying a comeback in the wake of new emerging protest movements, see Brünzels 2013; Carlsson 2002; Köhler and Wissen 2003; and in a broader sense also Hardt and Negri 2004.
38   Schrage 2006, p. 96.

even large funeral processions.³⁹ Present masses form at a specific location and are markedly distinct from statistical masses which materialise through shared convictions, nationalism, listening to the radio, or solely by the stroke of a demographer's pen. Such a quadrinomial concept of what constitutes a mass constructively overcomes the vagueness of the term resulting from the 'modern' dichotomy between the individual and the masses that influenced Elias Canetti's conception of the mass (somewhat misleadingly translated as 'crowd' in English).⁴⁰ Although Canetti's distinction between 'closed' and 'open' masses seeks to capture intrinsic mobilisation dynamics as well as growth and reproductive processes, it nevertheless remains too abstract to actually detect the behaviour of individual actors within the larger crowd. Ultimately, for Canetti mass remains a black box.⁴¹

Schrage conceives of the relationship between present masses and communicative masses as a sequential model. In his view, different types of masses correspond to specific epochs of modernity. As the major point of division between these epochs he identifies the emergence of mass media, turning present masses into communicative masses.⁴² Considering activism, by contrast, we can make the case that the creation of activist groups requires both directed present masses as well as communicative masses. These were particularly mutually interdependent in the workers' movement, as present and communicative masses were structurally interlinked at least with regard to countercultural action. This was the case, for instance, at a May Day demonstration, where the present mass of the demonstration was flanked by leaflets and special issues of Bundist publications with the goal of forming one or rather several communicative masses (Bundists, local workers, the international working class, etc.), which in turn was followed by a retrospective evaluation of the event in Bundist media. A similar dynamic can be observed in the case of the

---

39   Schrage 2006, p. 97 f.
40   This approach also avoids the critical mass approach popular in social movement research, which argues that group formation is not determined by the largest possible mass as its resource but rather by the 'paradox of group size': both too-small as well as too-large masses can inhibit a movement's activism. Irrespective of this rather illuminating observation, I will refrain from applying this concept in the following, as it rests at least with regard to reproductive processes on a mobilisation paradigm that presupposes certain causalities which cannot be ascertained as conditions in the concept of activism analysis deployed in this study. Foundational studies include Oliver and Marwell 1988; Marwell and Oliver 1993. A more recent critical evaluation can be found in Oliver and Marwell 2011.
41   Canetti 1973, pp. 17–20, pp. 56–67.
42   Schrage 2006, p. 105 ff., p. 110 f.

TABLE 1   Schematisation of 'masses'

	Mass as observer category	Mass as object of collective self-reflection
Statistical mass	Argumentative mass	Communicative mass
Present mass	Dispersed mass	Directed mass

birzshe, where individual as well as collective self-awareness as revolutionaries was necessary for an apparent dispersed mass to become a communicative mass. Correspondingly, I propose a quadrinomial typology instead of a three-stage sequential model (Table 1).

These mass formations coalesced in various ways across distinct activism patterns within the Bund. This allowed for highly flexible construction of meaning. Medem's 'strike' at his desk in Switzerland illustrates this reality very clearly: although he suspended his writing because he was no longer being paid, it was important to him as a Bundist author to understand this stoppage as a labour conflict.[43] Retrospectively, however, he was able to successfully establish the necessary reference to the masses. Medem did not belong to the kind of present mass needed to conduct real strike action at the time of his supposed 'strike', and could only relate his own activity to the history of strike action through a communicative mass. Only in doing so did he manage to define his downing of the pen as activism and thereby portray it as an honourable act for the movement.

In this way a leader may have been able to write himself into an imagined mass, but the overwhelming majority of Bundists required (as workers generally do) other ways to shape and experience their activism. Thus, many of the Bund's activism patterns ultimately sought to form present masses.[44] In order to expand its reach beyond individual experiences, social movements require transpersonal means of communication. This is one factor explaining the relevance and importance of Bundist press work throughout its existence.[45]

---

43   Medem 1979, p. 492 f.
44   The analysis of these dynamics motivated early studies on this question, driven by fear of the socialist 'mass'. See Le Bon 2001, esp. pp. 7–12.
45   See Part II.4.

2 'Correct' Activism

The Bund's turn-of-the-century political activism rooted firmly in the masses saw the educational reformism of the Jewish Enlightenment's nineteenth-century 'turn towards activism' link up and combine with Marxist concepts and revolutionary utopias.[46] This new quality became evident primarily in the organisational and political responses to the 1903 pogroms. The renowned historian of Russian Jewry John D. Klier coined the phrase of a 'dialogue of violence' between Jews and their surrounding environment to describe this period. This dialogue was interrupted in the early twentieth century, as violence shifted from material destruction and looting to more deadly conflicts.[47]

The turning point is widely thought to have been the Kishinev Pogrom of 1903,[48] when upwards of 50 Jews were murdered in an unexpected massacre of the city's Jewish population. The Bund issued a call to arms the following summer, invoking the Kishinev Pogrom as justification.[49] When fresh rumours of another pogrom emerged in Gomel later that autumn, the Bund assembled its newly established combat units and confronted the pogromists with clubs and revolvers in a coordinated fashion for the first time in Jewish history. The outcome was not a one-sided massacre, but an armed conflict with casualties on both sides.[50] This escalation anticipated the revolution that followed in 1905.[51] The Bund's combat units were essential in equipping the 'turn towards activism' with military connotations, inscribing a newfound willingness to use violence into the Bundist conception of activism.[52] This marked a sharp rupture with Jewish tradition, which Bundists perceived as characterised by waiting for the messiah while trapped in an unbearable state of oppression, framed by a system of domination, subordination, and metaphysical utopia. The socialist movements, whether Bundism, Labour Zionism, or for its own reasons Russian Social Democracy, now pursued the salvation of the masses through and by the masses themselves, boldly proclaiming their right to slash history's Gordian Knot.

The pertinent question now, however, was how this ought to occur. Intellectual histories often suggest that differing party programmes were the basis

---

46 On the efforts of the educational reformers see esp. Dohrn 2008 and Hofmeister 2008b.
47 Klier 2002.
48 Penkover 2004; Judge 1992.
49 Schmidt 2004, p. 188 ff. and 199.
50 Summarised rather cautiously in Mikhed'ko 1998.
51 Ultimately, Bundist self-defence could offer little resistance to the violent tempest of pogroms that followed the October Manifesto, see Lambroza 1992.
52 Lambroza 1981.

of most conflicts within Russian Social Democracy. From a praxeological perspective, they can also be interpreted as epiphenomena arising from the specific constellations of power in which the respective movements developed. A significant portion of the Russian revolutionary movement at the outset of the twentieth century believed direct action would be the spark that finally ignited the spluttering revolutionary engine, most likely in the form of bombings and gunfire.[53] The Marxist groups rejected this notion as detrimental to the class struggle, arguing that a change in social being would necessarily require a change in consciousness as well. All the same, both of these views remained distinct aspects of one revolutionary movement. The Socialist Revolutionaries established their combat groups in the same year that the exiles around Lenin and the journal 'Iskra' were intensifying their polemics against direct action. The corresponding manifesto was Lenin's *What Is To Be Done?*, a political tract opposing 'limited trade-union work ... without any assistance whatever from the intellectuals', whose task was in turn to raise the 'activity of the working masses'. In Lenin's view, loosely organised movements suffered from the rigidity of spontaneity and failed to fulfil the worker's desire for leadership. The workers demanded:

> Devote more zeal to carrying out this duty and *talk less about 'raising the activity of the working masses'*. We are far more active than you think, and we are quite able to support, by open street fighting, even demands that do not promise any 'palpable results' whatever. It is not for you to 'raise' our activity, because *activity is precisely the thing you yourselves lack*. Bow less in subservience to spontaneity, and think more about raising *your own* activity, gentlemen![54]

For Lenin, the workers demanded leadership and utopias beyond economic improvements. If the intelligentsia accepted direct action as their goal of action like the Socialist Revolutionaries, the Bund, and other parties that concentrated solely on the world of work (at least in Lenin's eyes) allegedly did, then all that would remain of activism would be a sort of blind political actionism. According to Lenin, '[e]conomists and the present-day terrorists have one common root, namely, *subservience to spontaneity*'.[55] Action as such always remained

---

53 See Hilbrenner 2008.
54 Lenin 1977a, p. 416 f., emphases in original. The polemic extends far beyond the classic question of organisation to which it is often reduced, as Lars T. Lih (2006) has pointed out.
55 Lenin 1977a, p. 418.

indeterminate; meaning arose only from actions serving the overarching goal of the political struggle, that is to say 'training the masses in revolutionary activity'.[56] Instead of reading the masses as a formative resource, the 'Iskra' émigré vanguard feared that Russian socialism would 'lose its head' and steer towards its own demise.

It surely came easier to a small group of professional émigré revolutionaries to demand and theoretically implement such radically well-structured concepts from the coffee house than it would to a large and still-growing mass organisation like the Bund or the Socialist Revolutionaries. Neither of the latter developed their utopian concepts at the drafting table, but rather in direct interaction with the masses. This was accompanied by mass-based forms of organisation from which they derived origins, strength, and future alike. The kinds of problems of participation confronting illegally operating mass movements were utterly distinct from those of a group of intellectual émigrés. The situation on the ground in Russia demanded not only agitation, but resolute action if socialism was to become more than just a debating club's preferred topic.

Although it risks the danger of overstating boundaries, some basic conceptions from systems theory can help to identify a praxeological difference between the Bund and the 'Iskra'. Beyond its redemptive determinism, Lenin's thinking was also a result of the interplay between cause and effect applying to both the emergence of his conception as well as the inevitable functional differentiation of a growing world of ideas. Here, the conflict arises not from the question of organisation as such, but rather from the self-referentiality and structural arbitrariness of intra-system communication.[57] It was thus to be expected that debates between the Bund and the Bolsheviks would escalate sooner or later, albeit not only as the result of political differences (commonly asserted given the disparities between the organisations' programmes)[58] but also due to structural closures between the respective sub-systems.[59] In this sense, the primary factor was not that the groups' respective agendas were too far apart to somehow be negotiated, but rather that the communicative basis – establishing a situation allowing for communication – was not only complicated but in fact impossible over the long term due to the systematically distinct Bolshevik and Bundist conceptions of activism.

---

56   Lenin 1977a, p. 413.
57   Luhmann 2013, p. 53; Baraldi, Corsi and Esposito 2008, p. 123 ff., p. 142 f., p. 176 f.
58   A classic example of this line of argument is Keßler 1994.
59   Luhmann 1995, esp. pp. 139–43.

For similar reasons, the Bund approached the question of spontaneity in a fundamentally different manner. It was unable to yield to the secrecy of professional revolutionaries for the simple reason that it was unable, in organisational terms, to abandon present masses as the prime legitimation of its existence and activism. The Bund viewed the organisation's extensive growth in the pre-revolutionary period as confirmation of this strategy. That said, the Bund was by no means egalitarian. Its ranks were characterised by clear hierarchies and responsibilities based on differences in commitment and educational background. The term 'half-' or 'semi-intelligentsia' commonly used to denote workers rising up the Bund's internal ranks, and later willingly adopted by researchers and scholars alike, demonstrates both the desire for structure as well as the seemingly irreconcilable degree of social differentiation within the organisation.[60] The workers in question, however, often understood it as denigrating.

Given that the Bund was constituted by its members' activism, the following analysis of Bundist activism cannot limit itself to debates surrounding this issue but must go on to investigate its actual manifestations. This sort of a bottom-up model initially positions all expressions of activism next to one another without presupposing hierarchies, such as the relative importance of the written word over workers' self-organisation. Patterns of activism mutually complemented one another, whereas prerogative of interpretation and path selection were continually re-negotiated. They constituted the social movement, rendering it experienceable and transferrable for different social classes. These constructions of meaning turned worker activists into Bundists, and in the migration process transformed a loosely organised workers' movement into the transnational Bund. Correspondingly, the following exploration of Bundist activism in Eastern Europe and, building upon the former, its various transfers illustrates how the transnationalisation of social movements reached beyond the 'diffusion of ideas'. Specific practices created social movements and rendered them locally experienceable, and would in turn ultimately transnationalise them.[61]

---

60 See Mendelsohn 1970, pp. 62 and 70; Tobias 1972; Marten-Finnis 2001, p. 14; more distanced: Pickhan 2001 p. 43; similar, but addressing Russian-Jewish revolutionaries on the other side of the Atlantic: Stolberg 1944, p. 5.
61 See esp. della Porta and Kriesi 1999, pp. 3–22; Bennett 2005.

CHAPTER 2

Activism Patterns in Eastern Europe: Constituting the Transferable

> Environments are invisible. Their groundrules, pervasive structure, and overall patterns elude easy perception.
> MARSHALL MCLUHAN and QUENTIN FIORE[1]

∴

To Bundists, the Bund was the goal and cause of activism at once. Yet in memoirs and reflections, the actions constituting the latter receive far less attention than activism's social and political aims. To the extent that such reflections exist at all, they can be found in accounts of Bundists' youth sometimes contained in autobiographies, as this represented one way of turning *being a Bundist* into an identity in its own right. Biographisations, however, are subject to generational delay. What Edward P. Thompson once observed in the English workers' movement proved equally true of its Jewish counterpart: 'The working class did not rise like the sun at an appointed time. It was present in its own making'.[2] The history of the Bund did not develop along a timeline, but rather as a network encompassing distinct times and spaces. Meaning, structure, and substance were continually renegotiated as references to the history of the workers' movement and the Bund shifted, in turn providing renewed legitimation for Bundist activity.[3] In this sense the Bund only has a history because it 'was made': day by day, city by city, person by person.

1   Activism Patterns: The Foundation of a New History of the Bund

The Bund's diverse patterns of activism allowed for a continuous re-weaving of the organisation's 'social thread', generating institutions which in turn either

---

1   McLuhan and Fiore 1967, p. 84f.
2   Thompson 1964, p. 9.
3   This allowed for the development of a Bundist identity in the first place, see Wolff 2014b.

produced activists or, lacking sufficient activism, soon disappeared.[4] It was less the case that 'the labor movement offered its members a completely new way of life, a new framework within which to live and work'[5] so much as the emerging workers' movement became a lifeworld precisely because both were intentionally created in a 'daily plebiscite'.[6]

Activists are always also specialists whose sophistication grows as the social movement becomes more functionally differentiated. The Bund's *tuer* became active in distinct fields whether as agitators, authors, teachers, or printers. As these fields agglomerated and institutionalised, the emerging activism patterns formed a basis upon which we can historicise the Bund along action-theoretical lines of inquiry.

Nevertheless, the question remains as to which agglomerations, that is to say which specific activism patterns had causal effects on Bundist history. Defining such patterns constitutes the foundation of a history of Bundist social practices. Only on this basis does it become possible to ask which of these patterns are suitable or necessary for a transnational history of the Bund. This chapter first identifies distinguishable patterns of Bundist activism in Eastern Europe and localises them in the respective legal conditions under which they were conducted, before briefly evaluating their function in Bundist history.

Patterns of activism represent analytical categories, not historical units. They facilitate the classification of politically motivated action types, but only rarely lead to self-reflective source production. They are characterised not only by their spatial and temporal characteristics, but also by the retrospective ascription of meaning on the part of (former) participants. Grouped into such categories, activism patterns permeate the history of the Bund. They serve as resistors along the metaphorical circuits of history, through which the observer can detect and measure both external influences as well as voltage fluctuations within the organisation. In order to carve out these fundamental units of the Bund's history, I rely on official sources complemented by the more than 500 autobiographical questionnaires. Statistically grounded analyses can help to condense the latter into clusters, or rather activism patterns.

---

4 Following the New Institutional Economics approach, I understand 'institutions' as the entirety of distinct action patterns, norms, customs, and practices, but also organisations expressed through social conventions allowing for communication and orientation within a social movement beyond the individual; see Voigt 2009, p. 14 f.
5 Mendelsohn 1970, p. 153.
6 Renan 2000, p. 19.

At this point, the simple distinction between a 'Russian' and a 'Polish' Bund (which will be reassessed later on) shall suffice. Although the Bund was illegal in Russia with the exception of a few months after the 1905 October Manifesto, despite numerous challenges the organisation in Poland was able to develop and grow relatively freely. This process was accompanied by the disappearance of activism patterns central to illegal work, which became increasingly irrelevant under conditions of legality. The following schematisation of Bundist activism patterns is therefore not a comprehensive account of each and every Bundist-motivated activism, but instead a depiction of the qualitatively and quantitatively identifiable clusters of Bundist meaning-inducing action during different periods of shifting legal status in Eastern Europe (see Table 2).

2   Persecution and Political Identity

The Bund's rapid expansion was owed among other factors to the fact that 'the Tsarist empire was certainly not the patrimonial police state as once described by Richard Pipes'.[7] In Tsarist Russia, political action continually developed and expanded in the niches and regions, ultimately extending even into the cells of the empire's numerous prisons. Furthermore, Russia cannot be conceived of as one unified zone. As Jane Burbank shows, observers must at the very least distinguish between conditions in the East and West of the country, although based on her work on the eastern regions she considers the intelligentsia's criticisms of Russian conditions to be somewhat exaggerated.[8] Upon further differentiation, it should be noted that while the likelihood of facing state repression varied greatly between East and West, Poland and most of the Jewish Pale should be regarded as exceptions within Western Russia. This is complemented by periodic focal points in the cities of the western Tsarist empire, where both the revolutionary workers' movement as well as the Tsarist secret police focused most of their efforts. One exception to this rule were the Jewish shtetls crucial to the Bund, in which the likelihood of persecution was significantly lower even in interwar Poland.[9]

---

7   Sperling 2008, p. 19 in reference to Richard Pipes's classic *Russia Under the Old Regime* (1974).
8   Burbank 2004; on the 'intelligentsia's language' see Burbank 2008, esp. p. 99 f.
9   Compliance with the law and legal restrictions were subject to police control in the countryside far less than in the cities in both Tsarist Russia and interwar Poland, see Mahla 2010, p. 180 f.

TABLE 2 Bundist activism patterns in Eastern Europe

Activism pattern	Expression (examples)	Activism pattern in the Russian Bund	Activism pattern in the Polish Bund
Gatherings	Clandestine, cumulative (*kruzhki*, talks, meetings in forests, etc.)	+	(−)[a]
	Public conspiratorial (*birzshe*)	+	−
	Public confrontational (demonstrations)	+	+
	Commemorative, community building (memorial gatherings)	(−)	+
	Representative, community building (establishing clubs and local institutions)	(+)	+
Publishing	Material (printshops, smuggling, etc.)	+	−
	Creative (authorship)	+	+
Party work	Organisational (committees)	+	+
	Programmatic (congresses)	+	+
	Representational (elections)	−	+
Educational work	Clandestine, isolated (circles)	+	−
	Public, situational (cultural centres)	−	+
	Public with broad impact (school system)	−	+
Labour struggle	Clandestine, preparatory (plotting, *kassy*)	+	−
	Public, confrontational (strikes)	+	+
	Official, hierarchised (umbrella organisations)	−	+
	Culturalising (*yidishkayt* in the labour struggle)	+	+
Armed militancy	Situational (brawling, street fighting)	+	+
	Protective (self-defence)[b]	+	+
	Retaliatory (organised revenge)	o	−
Group-specific activism	Generational (youth)	(+)[c]	+
	Gender-specific (YAF)	−	+
Revolutionary fundraising	Membership dues	(+)	+
	Donation collection	(+)	+

a Lectures, educational work, etc. no longer clandestine but public informative.
b Did not correlate directly with legal conditions but rather with manifestations of anti-Semitism and counter-revolutionary forces.
c Existent but institutionally undesired, struggled for recognition as a Bundist activism pattern.
Legend: + tended to be present as activism; − tended not to be present as activism; (+), (−) limited tendency; o failed.

Unfortunately, historians lack conclusive micro-studies that could allow for a deeper understanding of the social interactions between the state and social movements in this regard.[10]

The intelligentsia's and its followers' fear of persecution by the structurally feeble police apparatus also contains a discursive component. One of the Russian secret police's greatest successes was appearing omnipresent in spite of its relative frailness. Its reputation in the international press was 'more overblown than accurate', yet grew into a haunting spectre repeatedly corroborated by immigrants – so much so that in 1908 it was even cited to condemn the imminent founding of the FBI in the US, which allegedly resembled the kind of state terrorism prevalent in Russia and represented 'a great blow to freedom'.[11]

Persecution was less the result of an omnipresent police state so much as dependent on whether a respective movement was targeted by the secret police and subjected to its arbitrary will. The movements possessed no reliable legal means with which to address or remedy persecution.[12] Nevertheless, it remains unclear how likely arrests really were. Frederic S. Zuckerman argues that the 5,590 individuals whose cases were processed directly by the Ministry of Justice without notification of a subordinate court in 1903 are quantitatively marginal, given Russia's population of roughly 128 million at the time.[13] The spatial distribution of these cases is of course ignored in this reasoning, along with the exceedingly harsh sentences ranging from lengthy imprisonment to fortress detention and Siberian exile. To develop a sense of what these numbers mean, we can compare them to more liberal Germany, where 10,536 individuals were tried on the basis of §153 of the *GewO*, or *Gewerbeordnung* (Trade Regulation Act) between 1903–12. Officially introduced for the 'protection of those willing to work', the paragraph was regarded as a 'special punitive

---

10   Foundational: Mishinsky 1969.
11   George E. Waldo, Republican congressman from New York, as quoted in Lowenthal 1950, p. 3 f.
12   Given that public trials could not ensure the desired verdict and were often used by revolutionaries as platforms for public propaganda, state authorities referred less and less cases to the courts as political arrests rose. According to Zuckerman, Tsarist authorities did not send a single political case to the courts between 1894 and 1902, while only 15 such cases occurred during the more tumultuous years of 1902 and 1903. At the same time, however, the number of direct sentences and people affected rose massively; see Zuckerman 1996, p. 15.
13   Zuckerman 1996, p. 16 f. The expansion of the Okhrana under Vyacheslav von Plehve also led to the creation of the pseudo-trade unionist system of provocateurs run by Sergei V. Zubatov, which in turn reinforced the isolation and aggressiveness of the revolutionary movement. See Hingley 1970, p. 89 f.

law against workers' designed to prevent them from striking.[14] According to official statistics, after the law's introduction police interference in strikes rose from 21.6 percent of strikes in 1904 to 35.9 percent in 1912, as did the extent of subsequent legal prosecution (16.6 to 22.4 percent).[15] Court rulings reveal the qualitative difference vis-à-vis Russia. In Germany, a total of 48 percent of those charged on the basis of §153 between 1903–12 were acquitted, while 40 percent received sentences lasting less than four days. Only 5.8 percent of those convicted received sentences of one to three months, while a paltry 0.5 percent were sentenced to longer than three months.[16] The discrepancy to Russia, where harsh sentences and even exile were the rule, can be explained by the fact that defendants enjoyed no right to due process in the Tsarist empire. For the most part, executive state authorities even intentionally prevented proper trials to avoid the risk of acquittals.[17] In the western provinces this was accompanied by the oppressive measures enacted in the wake of the 1863 January Uprising. The 'May Laws' introduced after the assassination of Tsar Alexander II explicitly targeted the Jewish population[18] and resulted in a concentration of political prisoners in specifically reserved sections of the Tsarist prisons. This kept the 'dangerous' political prisoners apart from the 'ordinary' criminals, yet was perfect for political gatherings.

For many Bundist workers, imprisonment was thus not only a tool of persecution, but also a major factor in their politicisation as well as a kind of political accolade bestowed by the enemy. Quite frequently, people were arrested for trivial offences only to leave prison as highly politicised individuals.[19] For example, inmates agreed to relieve Vladimir Medem, who suffered from chronic kidney disease, from his work duties if he agreed to hold lectures and political education inside the prison instead. As his former cellmate Stanislav Dvorak recalls, Medem gave talks and agitated large prison audiences on many occasions.[20] The recollections of knowledge-hungry workers in particular illus-

---

14 Kittner 2005, pp. 294–8.
15 Kittner 2005, p. 362.
16 Kittner 2005, p. 301.
17 Zuckerman 1996, p. 15.
18 These laws were intended both as punitive measures against the allegedly guilty Jews as well as a way of curbing pogroms, but only the former was achieved; see Klier and Lambroza 1992, pp. 39–134. In his classic study, Aronson (1990) demonstrates that the pogroms were less an 'initiative from above' than they were determined by a whole range of factors, primarily local dynamics.
19 About 50 percent of the questionnaire campaign type IV indicate periods of imprisonment in Russia and/or Poland. Bund Archives, New York, RG 1400, MG2-429, on the campaign see Part II.6.
20 His memoirs are printed in Dvorak 1979.

trate quite clearly that the Russian system of political detention served to politicise many if not most prisoners who walked through its gates, while prison cells offered plenty of opportunities to build revolutionary community.

The danger of arrest was not only a factor in Russian times, however, but also during the Bund's Polish period. A quarter of respondents to the autobiographical questionnaires (type IV) indicate a period of detention in interwar Poland – nearly as many as for the Russian period. When explicated in more detail, it is almost always related to preceding political meetings.[21] But periods of detention were significantly shorter in Poland. In Russia they could easily last a few months and involve immediate banishment to Siberia.[22] That said, these figures should be taken with a grain of salt. It is highly unlikely that a quarter of all activists fell into the hands of either the Tsarist or Polish police. Rather, imprisonment tended to draw activists closer to the Bund. For the state, the system of political imprisonment proved counter-productive in a double sense: firstly, many rebels became revolutionaries in their cells. Secondly, inmates' public removal from their original social context cultivated and hardened counter-cultural identities. While the fear of arrest sometimes functioned as a deterrent, imprisonment itself had a community-building effect and prepared the ground for further activism. This may be one reason why many respondents refer to their stays in concentration camps as 'imprisonment', helping to normalise and process the extraordinary experiences of the Holocaust and persecution in Stalinist Russia in Bundist terminology.[23]

3   Gathering: The Foundation of Activism

The Bund's meetings and assemblies were the starting point for further politicisation. Despite its (late-)Enlightenment roots and extensive publishing oper-

---

21   Bund Archives, New York, RG 1400, MG-2, 429.
22   Ascertained from Bund Archives, New York, RG 1400, MG-2, 429; such banishment was cast in a heroic light in one of the first autobiographies found in the Bundist party press and indeed in the first Bundist worker autobiography: A farshikter arbeyter 1904, pp. 2–7. Particularly after emigration, however, this could also be understood as suffering that allowed for further situational activism at best, such as distributing leaflets during banishment. See Pressman 1995, p. 29 f. and p. 55 f.
23   Bund Archives, New York, RG 1400, MG2, 429 – In contrast to type IV, type III did not ask about camps but rather in a more traditional terminology inquired as to when respondents were 'farhaftet un farshikt' (arrested and exiled). Roughly 20 percent of respondents used this opportunity to categorise their camp experience in the levelling manner described above, sometimes in combination with previous political arrests.

ation, the Bund was by no means a *république des belles lettres*. It drew its strength and vitality from physical gatherings. Congregating as Bundists was the most obvious and simple pattern of activism, albeit sometimes a dangerous one. The Tsarist authorities' persecution of oppositional activity forced the Russian socialist movements to hold their meetings – central to community building – in secret. These meetings were therefore exciting not only because of the propaganda and information they offered, but also because of their illegality. The sense of community required for and resulting from such meetings consolidated the group beyond the actual event. A reflection of the importance of meetings is the description of both successful and unsuccessful gatherings in all activist workers' autobiographical narratives.[24]

The threat of exposure and betrayal inspired the use of clandestine methods. Even attending a socialist meeting in the Tsarist empire represented, in the language of social movement research, a form of 'high-risk activism'.[25] Secrecy was not a goal in itself, it aimed to facilitate agitation: the step out of the backroom into the streets was the imperative. Given the danger it entailed, activists regarded mere participation in such meetings as a form of counter-hegemonic action.[26] In fact, many recall their first meeting as a kind of initial agitational spark, thus representing what Burkhard Dücker calls 'rituotopes' during which 'the socialisation of the individual occurs' in the sense that 'the objectives of the culture/formation/social become explicit and incorporated into the individual'.[27] Persons on their way to becoming Bundists contributed to both the group's and the movement's reproduction through this 'praxis form of the rituotope'.[28] The overwhelming majority of Bundist meetings held outside of prison walls can be subsumed under four different subtypes: clandestine meetings, disguised public meetings, confrontational public, and commemorative public gatherings.

---

24 Such as in YIVO, RG 102, 108, Ahron Cohen, 1942; Levine 1946; Shtern 1954. These experiences also influenced the lives of intellectuals, see Rozenthal 1942, p. 256ff.; as well as those of Zionist activists who likewise expressed their disrespect for traditional modes of community building through their gatherings, as seen in Shazar 1967.
25 See esp. McAdam 1986; Wiltfang and McAdam 1991.
26 In many depictions demonstrations are immediately followed by arrests, see Novikov 1967, p. 33.
27 Dücker 2007, p. 109.
28 Dücker 2007, p. 113.

4 Clandestine and Cumulative: Educational Meetings in Forests

Clandestine meetings refer to collective and conspiratorial gatherings held outside of public spaces. They partially occurred as direct continuities of the educational circles (Russian: *kruzhki*, later Yiddish: *kruzshki*, also *kreyslekh*, meaning circles or groups) held in backrooms, attics, and basements.[29] The most famous of these gatherings was the founding of the Bund itself in an attic in Vilnius. Attendance at these clandestine cumulative meetings was limited, as the risk of being exposed through espionage was fairly high. They primarily served as organisational and educational meetings where both institutional formation as well as workers' education took place.

Because the Bund was not a 'vanguard party' in the Leninist sense, it required the broadest possible public impact and audience.[30] The most popular meetings were thus held in public spaces and were either clandestine or cumulative. The latter included many meetings in nearby forests. Although they also risked discovery by state authorities, here secrecy as such was not the meeting's purpose so much as a condition thereof. These meetings were mainly geared towards internal community building.[31] Activists raised in the shtetls attribute particular significance to these meetings, even if, like in Berl Shtern's case, the workers' fear of getting caught caused the gathering to end in total failure.[32] These meetings were ubiquitous throughout the Pale, especially in the run up to the revolutionary year of 1905, although they remained clandestine. Carpenter Yoel Novikov recalls a 1904 celebration of the Bund's founding in Gorki as particularly noteworthy: participants imitated 'the youth, who on Tisha B'Av[33] would spend all day collecting mushrooms in the forest' to avoid suspicion. During their walk they were careful to ensure that no random or undesirable guests joined the procession. When they finally reached the envisaged location in the woods,

> a red flag reading 'Long live the Bund!' hung from a nearby tree. We spent the day listening to enthusiastic speeches while enjoying beer and

---

29 For a more elaborate portrayal of the *kruzhki* in their function as the underpinning of an emerging scientific everyday culture in Russia, see Alexandrov 1995, pp. 68–72.
30 The classic intellectual backdrop for West German research in this regard was provided by Geyer 1962. For a more specific treatment of the Bund, however, see Keßler 1994.
31 Fox 2006, p. 216; Levine 1946, p. 94.
32 Shtern 1954, p. 15 f.
33 A traditional day of fasting to commemorate the destruction of the temples in Jerusalem. In 1904 this day fell on 21 September.

snacks. In one speech, *khaver* Vilner explained that Tisha B'Av was a day of mourning from the very distant past. Among other things, he said: 'Today we celebrate the day of the future, the day of joy, freedom, and socialism'.[34]

As Daniel Mahla showed for Bundist holidays in Poland, the Bund often utilised traditional Jewish customs and holidays, as they provided days off work and good cover for such reunions, but performatively twisted their meaning into the opposite.[35] Traditional festivities thus became founding celebrations for new institutions and a new Jewish way of life embodied by the Bund, where participants mainly celebrated their own counter-culture. Ritual acts such as singing the Bundist hymn *Di shvue* served as a lived experience thereof and encouraged involvement in its shaping, thereby overwriting the old festivities with new meaning.[36]

This gregariousness and the frequent consumption of beer rather uncharacteristic of the Jewish stereotype even served to reconcile dangerous situations. Novikov impressively describes how the precarious moment of being exposed at such a meeting was turned into a revolutionary act:

> At night we suddenly hear singing coming closer and closer. We decide to stay where we are. After completing their day's work, the peasants from the surrounding area respond to our songs. They approach us carrying scythes, sickles, and rakes. They look on us with astonishment: 'Which holiday [*yom tov*] are you celebrating today?', they ask. Comrade Vilner explains: 'The youth who wish to create a world without exploitation, without oppression or poverty have gathered here. The worker should not be oppressed by the capitalist, and neither should the peasant be oppressed by the landowner. A world of freedom.' Comrade Vilner speaks clearly and enthusiastically. His explanation moved the peasants. They stayed with us for many hours, and we honoured them with beer, food, and songs. That night we returned home very late and tired, yet filled with enthusiasm and hopes for the future.[37]

---

34 Novikov 1967, p. 28 f.
35 Mahla 2010. This was of course not unique to the Bund but in fact quite common in political movements more generally, see also Goyens 2007.
36 The relevance of social life in Social Democratic gatherings was already underscored in Welskopp 2000, p. 291 f. and p. 346 f.
37 Novikov 1967, p. 28 f.

Such clandestine meetings pursued community building with popularising intent, simultaneously representing both celebration and a public expression of political allegiance. Only through gatherings outside of the state's and the Jewish community's social control was the Bundist community of renewal able to manifest in present masses, establish its initial organisations, engage in public agitation, and prepare the ground for further activism through slogans and songs.

5 Public and Conspiratorial: The *Birzshe*

A more silent exchange took place at covert meetings in public. This included especially the *birzshe* (from the Russian *birzha*, stock exchange), of which Yehuda Slutski from the shtetl of Bobruisk gave a characteristic description: 'In the evening there used to be the followers of the Bund – workers, journeymen, artisans – coming together there, walking around in the street, *shmuesn*, discussing, speaking about party meetings etc.'[38] A similar depiction of the collective and simultaneously conspiratorial walks around the Lublin *birzshe* in 1905 is provided by Bundist Nokhem Khanin, who claims that it 'buzzed like a human beehive'. According to his account, all local Bundists met there every day after work, albeit without being recognised as Bundists.[39] The *birzshe* took on the appearance of a dispersed mass, while for those on the inside it constituted a present mass held together by communication.

These collective strolls feature in almost every worker's life story. The events served to forge new contacts and bring new recruits into line, while at the same time newcomers could learn to decode and imitate Bundist behaviour, fashion, and other habitual characteristics 'on the go'. Many claim that seeing the black-clad Bundist marchers triggered a desire to participate in these only seemingly unmotivated strolls.[40] As much is stated by Bertha Fox who, following her sister's confession that '[y]es mother, I belong to the Bund and come what may I will not stop', and that very sister's explicit exclusion from the circle: 'No, and no! Such a little shrimp and she wants in on the action too', used participation in the *birzshe* to join this sought-after circle:

> Then I hit upon a plan. I spied on my sister on Yekaterinski street and saw whom she stopped to speak with. ... Without much of a thought I went

---

38 Slutski 1967, p. 161.
39 Khanin 1945, p. 64.
40 Berman 1936, p. 109; Mendel 1989, pp. 86–9; Fox 2006, p. 215.

over to the same person, tugged at his sleeve and said quietly, 'I am Rosa's sister, and I want to be a member of the Bund too'.[41]

Matters subsequently took their course, and she was later able to record her life story as that of a Bundist activist.

Beyond interaction, the *birzshe* was also a base of recruitment. As worker M.I. Shatan recalls, sewing a red banner for a May Day demonstration was a highly illegal act in Russia in 1905. Nonetheless, he was determined to do so and already knew where to find the appropriate comrades-in-arms. In a revealing, matter-of-course tone he writes: 'I went to the *birzshe* and recruited a few suitable helpers there'.[42] The same was true of militant actions. Famous Bundist organiser Grigori Aronson emphasises that the Gomel *birzshe* sometimes became a battle ground: 'Clashes between the police [armed with batons] and the workers, armed with stones, occurred on more than one occasion'.[43] Gomel's famous self-defence force had already demonstrated its willingness to engage in open confrontation during the 1903 pogrom. It now became a protective guard for the *birzshe*, which had grown into a revolutionary institution due to its importance in reproducing the workers' movement.[44] Bundist academic Yosef Lifshits's memories of Warsaw during World War I provide another indicator of the *birzshe*'s active role in organising workers. According to Lifshits, the *birzshe* reinforced, proclaimed, and popularised the work of the illegal trade committees from which the Polish Bund emerged.[45] Given the *birzshe*'s illegality, 'going for a walk' amounted to a form of activism in itself, albeit one that only served to facilitate other activism patterns. When Gertrud Pickhan concludes that the Bund in interwar Poland had 'its firm position *oyf der yidishn gas* even without a new party headquarters',[46] it should be understood quite literally with view to the *birzshe* tradition. In Russia, the *birzshe* was the local party headquarters.[47]

---

41 Fox 2006, p. 215.
42 Shatan 1970, p. 44.
43 Aronson 1968, p. 18.
44 Aronson 1968, p. 18 f. Similar to the pogrom in Kishinev, the events in Gomel are regarded as an initialising moment reflected in depth by the contemporary Bundist press and prompting a rise in the organisation's self-defence activities. See the special issue of the Bund's central publication *Di arbeyter shtime*, 36 (1903), as well as Lambroza 1981 and Shtakser 2009. On the question of violence in Gomel see Mikhed'ko 1998.
45 Lifshits 1935, p. 9.
46 Pickhan 2001, p. 177.
47 The presence of travelling speakers was frequently an occasion to hold meetings, see Vladeck 1963.

6   Public Confrontational and Public Commemorative: Expressions of Strength

One main goal at these secret gatherings was to organise large assemblies, demonstrations, and strikes, the latter of which often resulted in more demonstrations. These actions came to symbolise Bundist strength as early as 1899.[48] They were not only platforms for communicating political and social demands, but also *confrontational gatherings* which (as is true for all epochs of Bundist history) could easily turn into street battles and often resulted in arrests. Demonstrations were cultural expressions of presence with a major impact in terms of both community building as well as dissimilating participants from their environment, resulting in the formation of widely visible present masses. The impact of these demonstrations was enhanced by marching routes that frequently ran through middle-class neighbourhoods to symbolically take over these parts of town.[49] Unlike strikes, these also transcended the otherwise often strict lines of demarcation between different craft unions.[50] While the Bund's secret meetings served as the foundation of the new era to come, demonstrations sought to render palpable the sort of counter-hegemony conceived and celebrated in Bundist songs and chants. In this way, the streets became the stage for a combative new culture.[51] This was particularly true of May Day demonstrations, the international working class's annual 'day of struggle and celebration', or in the words of Rosa Luxemburg, '*our* church service'.[52] Even in the Jewish Pale, May Day demonstrations sought to move 'through the streets, and into the new world'[53] – but instead often met Cossacks' batons and mounted police. Due to the Tsarist empire's practice of isolating political prisoners, imprisonment resulting from marches often led to the aforementioned cellblock meetings and protestors' subsequent radicalisation into revolutionaries.

The Polish Bund also witnessed the emergence of another kind of public meeting: commemorative gatherings. Although precedents existed in Russian times, most were more confrontational than *commemorative* due to the organisation's illegality, and included public funerals as well as anniversaries and memorial days. The flourishing of these gatherings in the Bund's Polish phase

---

48   Tobias 1972, p. 97.
49   Mahla 2010, p. 179.
50   Tobias 1972, p. 119 and p. 140.
51   On this conversion of transportation routes into political space across the historical spectrum see Warneken 1991; Reiss 2007; Callahan 2010.
52   Luxemburg 1972, p. 18.
53   N.N. 1921.

is linked to the surge in Bundist memory during the interwar period, discussed more extensively in the following chapter. Important in this regard, however, is that these meetings of commemorative communities carried within them a progressive core.[54] May Day celebrations were hybrids in terms of their historical and international connections (even when the Julian calendar was still in use, revolutionaries set the date of their festivities according to the 'international' Gregorian calendar) in that they were acts of public commemoration that also provided space for demands and utopias. This inward-looking aspect of remembrance grew more pronounced particularly during funeral and commemorative ceremonies as well as anniversary celebrations. It is not without reason that Gertrud Pickhan's study of Polish party celebrations concentrates almost exclusively on funerals of respected veterans and Bundist anniversaries, at which 'collective mourning and jubilation' went hand in hand.[55] The past was not an end in itself, but rather the prehistory of a freedom yet to be attained.[56]

The activist character of these gatherings therefore shifted according to legal realities (see Table 2). Official party meetings were legal in interwar Poland, causing activism patterns born out of illegality to disappear relatively quickly. However, the community-building character of major gatherings in both confrontational as well as cultural and commemorative forms would remain central to the movement.

7 Representative Community Building: Places of the Bund

Under Tsarist rule, the Bund's Central Committee was forced to relocate constantly. Although this necessity disappeared with legality, other spatial challenges would continue to trouble the Bund in interwar Poland. Some important national committees and groups resided in Nowolipie 7 in Warsaw, while others could only find quarters nearby or elsewhere in the district. The Bund's dream of constructing one great Bundist house unifying all branches and functions in the city under one roof never materialised.[57] Appearances in public and in self-

---

54   On this see Part II.3.
55   Pickhan 2001, pp. 164–71.
56   Despite extolling organisational achievements, their emphasis on a *not-yet* as opposed to an *as-if* clearly distinguishes the Bund's festivities from the mass festivals of the Soviet 'staging dictatorship', see Rolf 2013, esp. p. 72 and pp. 141–6. On further important distinctions between Bundist and Soviet remembrance see Part II.3–5.
57   Pickhan 2001, pp. 175–7. I follow Detlef Ipsen in his understanding of the term 'place',

selected locations like the oft-mentioned Bundist clubs were therefore crucial to the organisation as a whole. These can be understood as a transfer of the Bund's spatial presence into actual places, and thus as the institutionalisation of the rituotope. Strength was expressed not only through the assembly of functional masses, but also through a lasting urban presence.

The first institutionalised locales were dim backrooms where the *kruzhki* met to transform average workers into 'conscious workers'. Due to the inherent risk of exposing entire circles of activists, these meetings soon grew obsolete and were replaced by the Bund's wide-ranging cultural work. Already in 1907, Noakh Portnoy spoke romantically of the *kruzhki* as a 'history from times long gone'. This was the year that Zivion participated in a meeting of more than 1,000 Bundists in Paris, and demanded the establishment of Bundist clubs in the overseas urban centres where Eastern European Jews had settled.[58]

This localisation process rarely emerged as the result of a party plan, but rather from the actions of Bundists creating community-building spaces for themselves. Many workers report with a hint of pride that they were already geared towards working under conditions of legality, although the structures in which they were socialised were illegal. When said legality briefly materialised in 1905, Bundist clubs mushroomed throughout the Pale. Yoel Novikov emphasises that these clubs also changed 'the form and substance of the Bund': 'We had to create associations, clubs, and other public legal places which could incorporate masses of people and in which it should also be pleasant to spend one's free time'.[59]

In this case, one such 'pleasant place' was a squatted house in the centre of his shtetl. While the Chassidim feared the abandoned house and believed it to be haunted, Novikov took pride in the Bund literally driving 'the ghosts' out of it. Predecessors of later cultural centres from Warsaw to Buenos Aires, these new Bundist institutions required worker activists to contribute their knowledge and expertise to establish and expand such a small cultural centre, and soon the house was filled with life and children played in the courtyard. Just as an assembly was not the ultimate goal but a means leading to further activism, neither was a gathering or meeting site an end in itself. In many cases this meant they became educational centres for workers and subsequently their children. The centres facilitated both public education through events, present-

---

arguing that places possess identity-forming characteristics but are not experienceable without the surface upon which they are located (neighbourhoods, milieus, etc.). See Ipsen 2002; this understanding of space is formulated more generally in Löw 2016.

58 Portnoy 1907; Zivion 1907.
59 Novikov 1967, p. 42.

ations, and libraries as well as the formation of a new, publicly visible performative community. Through this occupation the latter now claimed actual 'space' and hence presence in the city. Following the Bund's swift renewed illegalisation in 1907, however, the police and with them the ghosts of the past reclaimed the house.[60]

Bundists also established clubs and libraries under illegality. They were central to Jewish cultural life in Russia and drew masses of workers into the Bund.[61] Workers like Yitshok Blumenshteyn, Abraham Shuman, and Mayer Shpayzer specifically state that these contact points were seen as bearers of a secular Jewish culture satisfying the demand for self-education in Tsarist Russia.[62] Such places represented the forerunners of the many centres later created in interwar Poland. Detailed depictions of all these schools, libraries, cultural centres, and rooms of debate would exceed the scope of this study, which is why (representative for all manifest places of the Bund and its cooperative partners in Poland) I refer primarily to the Medem Sanatorium, named after Vladimir Medem and established near Warsaw as a convalescent home for destitute children afflicted with tuberculosis in 1926. It served not only as a sanatorium but also a site for secular Bundist education, with a lasting impact on the life trajectories of many children in its care.[63]

8 Publishing: Creating the Communicative Mass

The Bund's present masses needed a unifying thread, provided by the network of Bundist print shops and publishing houses. Beginning in the early twentieth century, leaflets and soon periodicals became crucial propaganda tools for the Yiddish-speaking workers' movement.[64] The Bund's publishing operations connected numerous activists to the organisation, as the written word could reach workers who lacked personal contact with Bundist agitators.[65] This was a real logistical challenge under conditions of illegality and the sheer geographic expanse of the Pale, explaining why the Bund's print shops occupy such a prominent place in historiography and Bundist remembrance. Indeed, Henry

---

60   Novikov 1967, p. 42 ff.
61   Veidlinger 2009, p. 37 f.
62   Bund Archives, MG2, 429, Blumenshteyn, Yitshok; Shuman, Abraham; Shpayzer, Mayer.
63   The recollections of some of these children can be found in Kazdan 1971. See Jacobs 2009, pp. 62–81 for a more extensive depiction.
64   See esp. N.N. 1907; Greenbaum 1991. On the hot spot of Vilnius specifically see Marten-Finnis 1999, pp. 77–84; Marten-Finnis 2000.
65   Tobias 1972, p. 97.

J. Tobias describes the Bund's first clandestine printing press as the perpetually overburdened 'heart' of the first Central Committee.[66] Due to this importance and constant pressure, Bundist publishing established strong ties to surrounding Social Democratic parties, particularly the Polish Socialist Party (PPS) and the Social Democratic Party of Germany (SPD).[67]

The Bund ran a printing press almost from its inception and soon acquired several more, operated among others by locksmith and autodidactic engineer Israel Mikhel Kaplinski. It remains one of the great paradoxes of Bundist history that this very same Kaplinski would later be exposed as a Tsarist police agent. Although he went down in Bundist history as the epitome of a provocateur, he was by no means a sort of 'Bundist Azef' who attracted nothing but scorn from his movement. Instead, his former comrades viewed him as a mystery more than anything else.[68] Even decades later, these same comrades would concede that Kaplinski had been a great help as a Bundist, but as a provocateur remained utterly perplexing.[69] Prominent veterans like Layb Berman felt compelled to defend these last shreds of the former *khaver*'s honour despite his ultimate betrayal by citing his impressive contributions to Bundist publishing.[70] The Bund's print shops would have faced persecution by the Okhrana regardless of any information Kaplinski passed on, which made working in them a highly conspiratorial undertaking.

In 1898 the early Bund learned that clandestine networks could easily lead Tsarist spies from one Bundist to the next. Once the police had succeeded in infiltrating their circles, the connections between printing presses and illegal literature distribution networks turned into traps. Following the arrest of prac-

---

66 Tobias 1972, p. 71. Commemorations of print shops thus also allowed for the construction of places of remembrance through an emphasis on their material aspects. As much is accomplished in T. 1907. Heroism was emphasised even in Communist reflections on the subject, see Yohknis 1925.
67 Tobias 1972, p. 46 and p. 83f.
68 Evgeny F. Azef (1869–1918) was a double agent of the highest rank, recruited under Zubatov to operate inside the Socialist Revolutionaries. He was repeatedly suspected of spying, but only formally accused by Vladimir L. Burcev in 1908 and subsequently exposed in 1909, see Nicolaevsky 1934. Excellently investigated in Daly 2004, pp. 81–109.
69 Zivion 1945, p. 58f.
70 Berman emphasises that Kaplinski, who was quite skilled with his hands, helped to devise among other things a special system of *skritkes*, hidden compartments in things such as desks and cupboards. They were used to store important documents and even weapons. Given that none of them were ever discovered by the secret police, Berman concludes that Kaplinski probably never revealed these structurally crucial devices to them, see Berman 1953, p. 19.

tically the Bund's entire intellectual leadership during the Okhrana's *Zubatovtshina* campaign, both the apparatus itself as well as its mouthpiece, its publishing operation, had to be rebuilt. Tobias describes the challenges facing worker activists who suddenly found themselves in positions of leadership: 'The purely technical production of literature was another major obstacle to overcome. The problems of finding a press and literate and capable workers were not solved quickly'.[71] Eventually, however, they were. The *'Arbeter shtime'*, the Bund's new central organ, its new 'Holy Scripture',[72] was produced illegally in Russia until 1904. Its influence was so great that not only Bundists[73] but later even Communist authors would praise it as an expression of the new era.[74] Well-known Russian revolutionary Vera Zasulich lamented: 'It is irksome that they [the Bundists] and not the Russians are so busy'.[75] Technical expertise was needed to run the illegal print shops, and it was here that the first workers were hired as professional revolutionaries – advancing, as in the case of Moshe Layb Paulin, up the ranks of the Bund to become agitators. Like Sholem Levin, some continued on this path even after emigration and contributed their accumulated knowledge and experience to the Jewish socialist movement in the US as political authors.[76]

Neither the microspace of a print shop nor the associated smuggling of literature possessed inherent activist value. They were materially grounded and can be subsumed under the more overarching activism pattern of the publishing operation as a whole. Neither printing, smuggling, nor working as a librarian was in itself of an activist nature, although they could become so if the content of the material produced was illegal and the actions conducted were motivated by revolutionary aspirations. The same was true for the illegal libraries, often run from an activist's closet or under his or her bed. Particularly in smaller shtetls, this storing of literature was at the same time the most promising way of obtaining at least fragments of rare revolutionary reading material.[77]

---

71 Tobias 1972, p. 90.
72 As described in Gelernt 1957.
73 Bund Archives, RG 1401, 32, 337, Recollection, manuscript, fragment. Foundational: Div 1922.
74 Yokhnis 1925.
75 Earlier: 'The Jewish Bund is a true wonder of steadfastness. Two of its printing presses and a slew of people were taken away from it ..., but they already managed to publish a small run of a newspaper in Russia using jargon. And the path across the border is working again', quoted in Bunzl 1975, p. 64.
76 Bund MG2, 429, Paulin, Moshe Layb; Levin, Sholem.
77 Shulman 1945, p. 51.

Although much Bundist literature was smuggled into Russia from abroad, smuggling plays a marginal role in most Bundist recollections. It is remembered as a highly contingent, romantic activity that tended to produce more anecdotes than actual activism.[78] The same is true for when such efforts failed.[79] Smuggling's conflicted position somewhere between contract work and high-risk activism arose not least because the Bund, like all Russian socialist movements, often resorted to professional smugglers while concentrating its own limited forces on local production and domestic distribution. International smugglers thus cannot be regarded as activists as such. Smuggling also demonstrates how misleading the notion of the 'hidden transcript' can sometimes be: although smugglers defied social rules, they by no means were interested in abolishing them, as this would have liquidated the lucrative market from which they profited.[80] According to Abraham Mutnikovitsh, the Bund kept its distance from the traffickers they employed. Few Bundists felt they truly joined their struggle, and suspected most smugglers would have raised their fees had they known what sort of contraband they were sneaking into the country.[81] As Roland Girtler elaborates, smugglers ought to be classified somewhere between free adventure-seekers, service providers, and social rebels, while coincidentally the political indeterminacy of the term 'social rebel' or 'bandit' in the Hobsbawmian sense is remarkably fitting given the political indeterminacy of the act itself.

The act of printing also changed its character as the legal situation shifted.[82] Printing was itself a form of high-risk activism under illegality. Under conditions of legality in Poland and overseas, however, it became a technical task to be hired out and with which professional party employees or even external service providers unrelated to the movement could be entrusted.[83] The printing trade, or as many Bundists explicitly emphasised in the questionnaires, 'print worker',[84] thus became a 'working-class experience' from which other activ-

---

78   YIVO, RG 102, 157 [Lena Friedman, 1942: 7–11]; 160 [Lena S. Weinberger, 1942, 5 ff.]; 196, Anonymous autobiography [1942], 25 ff.; additionally Arnold 1922.
79   Shulman 1945, p. 52.
80   The intentionality Scott claims to see so clearly in smuggling can be interpreted into it at best, see Scott 1990, p. 14 f.
81   G-B 1907. The initials stood for Abraham Mutnikovitsh, who would make this early memory the object of a later recollection. See Mutnik 1933b; see also Tobias 1972, p. 71.
82   Girtler 2006, p. 1, pp. 172–9, pp. 192–7; Hobsbawm 1959; Hobsbawm and Rudé 1968, pp. 239–49.
83   This led to new dependencies and frequently caused interruptions in the publication of certain journals such as 'Der avangard' in Argentina, see Part II.4.
84   Bund Archives, New York, RG 1400, MG2–429, Bakhrakh, Hershl; Tsuker, Mayer; Vasershtros, Alekher Zelig.

ities had to be derived in order to develop counter-hegemonic substance.[85] This situation intensified to a hitherto unknown degree in the context of Nazi occupation and repression. Smuggling and printing were again illegal, dissident clandestine activities which under conditions of totalitarianism and genocide became activism patterns worthy of commemoration themselves.[86]

In terms of activism patterns, writing for the Bund was subject to different dynamics than these material activities. Authorship remained a primary activism pattern even under legality, preserving its legitimacy irrespective of current social constellations. The less difficult printing became, however, the more it was obliged to supply counter-cultural substance. In this way both writing without fear of persecution as well as remembering were recognised as forms of activism. Still, funding remained the problem child of the Bund's ever-growing publishing wing. Fundraising will be addressed in later chapters, along with important questions of local and transnational variations in writing and printing culture.

9   Party Work: Mobilisation and Representation

None of the aforementioned nor any of the following patterns of activism could have existed without the Bund's continuously refined yet never all-encompassing core: the party. Earlier research has already investigated and depicted the party in great detail. It will only be briefly introduced here. In contrast to many other studies, however, a perspective focused on the Bund's social practices shows that party work was merely one of many ways to participate in the Bund. Its history therefore ought not to be confused with the history of the Bund itself, which as a social movement requires a much broader analytical approach.

Party work was essential for the Bund, necessitating and enabling horizontal and vertical participation and mobility to the greatest extent. Party-political activism can be understood as work in the various bodies and committees which the Bund, as one party among many, established and organised.[87] This

---

85   A Stakhanovite worker was the exception in state socialist print shops, see Koenker 2005, p. 3f. and p. 303f.
86   Tselemenski 1963b; Kling 1970.
87   As Joachim Raschke emphasised, what form a social movement chooses to adopt is of secondary importance. A movement's form, provenance, and objectives must instead be understood in relation to one another, see Raschke 1987, pp. 76–80. Drawing tight distinctions between social movement, organisation, and party is similarly over-selective in the Bund's case, see McAdam and Scott 2005.

work overlapped with other activism patterns at many points. As Joachim Raschke notes, social movements are not only 'product and producer of modernity' but 'also producer of political modernity'.[88] This was just as true for the Bund, where party work consisted of working in party committees, public appearances at congresses and conferences, and electoral campaigning.

10 Organising: Committees and 'Organisations'

Whether in local organisations or Central Committees, organisational work allowed many Bundists to participate as part of the whole and drive the Bund forward. Roughly half of respondents to autobiographical questionnaires reported activity in a committee or similar party institution, making this kind of activism the most reflected upon alongside trade-union work.[89]

For the sake of thoroughness it should be noted that despite this pattern of activism's significance, the other half of respondents made no mention of such activity whatsoever. Surely, the latter also considered themselves to be Bundists, but expressed this in other ways. Bund historiography tends to equate party work with the Bund itself, yet this simple finding alone shows that work for the Bund's party-political core must be seen as only one element of the whole.[90] Moreover, many of these committees were short-lived, emerging as the result of other activities inside and on the Bund's behalf. Only under conditions of Polish legality were some committees able to permanently establish themselves. Bundists below the leadership level found persistence in Bundist action – the fundamental prerequisite for preserving a Bundist identity – in other activism patterns.

11 Programmatic Participation: Action through Words

Better-qualified and highly educated activists stood the best chances of building a reputation through party work and ascending swiftly up the Bundist ranks. At a certain point, this also entailed having a say in programmatic and political decisions. Political debates occupy large portions of many autobio-

---

88 Raschke 1987, p. 11.
89 Bund Archives, New York, RG 1400, MG2 429, questionnaire type IV.
90 In this sense, Jack Jacobs's investigation of a few explicitly non-party political institutions represents a remarkable step, see Jacobs 2009.

graphies such as Vladimir Medem's,[91] and many subsequent historians chose to follow this programmatic focus of attention.[92] The focus was ultimately less a reflection of the Bund's history so much as the authors' personal perception of his or her career.

Published relatively early on, Medem's memoirs served as a prototype many subsequent worker-autobiographies sought to emulate. In them, we find that advances up the party hierarchy are also accompanied by a shift in narrative technique: while daily actions that could be condensed into activism were previously the dominant themes, descriptions of their rise were accompanied by a growing emphasis on the relevance of debates and congresses, and quite frequently their success as orators and thinkers.[93] Both activism itself as well as perceptions concerning the relevance of certain activism patterns shifted in relation to the activist's position in the organisational hierarchy. Nevertheless, the breadth of activism patterns remained the basic premise for the synergy of programme and action in the Bund.

12 The Parliament of the Street: Election Campaigns

The situation was somewhat different in the electoral sphere, which naturally played a major role during the Bund's Polish era. Prior to that, it had also been an important sphere of activity during the (anything but free) elections to the Duma and the Warsaw elections of 1912.

Jack Jacobs argues that Bundist electoral successes provide insights beyond the history of the elections themselves. They reveal the Bund's broad local impact and firm social base, as elections reflect broader public sympathy for political decisions and aspirations beyond the party membership itself. Yet to qualify the broader impact of Bundist activisms, we require further investigation of how the growing popularity of Bundist schools or sports associations related to Bundist electoral successes. Checking a box in an election is not a form of activism – participating in an election campaign, however, is. Then again, only six percent of respondents to the Bund Archive questionnaires indicate actively contributing to electoral efforts (preparing elections, campaigning, council membership). Three quarters were workers.[94] This

---

91 Medem 1923.
92 Gorny essentially treats the history of the Russian Bund as synonymous with the political activity of Vladimir Medem, see Gorny 2006, esp. pp. 27–47.
93 Particularly pronounced in, for example, Berman 1936; Novikov 1967; Metaloviets 1982.
94 Bund, MG2, 429, type IV. Once again we must keep in mind the effect of German massacres

low figure indicates that only few Bundists joined the electoral campaigns, while the majority viewed other activities as central to developing a Bundist identity.[95]

Given that electoral campaigning rarely had lasting identity-forming function, election results can tell us little about the Bund's social presence in any other situation than the election campaign itself. Furthermore, as Jack Jacobs notes, the Bund's electoral success in Poland was only periodic, often facing crushing defeats at the hands of its competitors.[96] Still, because the Bund mainly concentrated on elections in urban areas, at the local level it appeared much more as a workers' party than was true of its leadership.[97] Because the Bund did not send deputies to the Polish Sejm, the conditions and connections of its electoral work can only be studied from a local historical perspective – allowing for highly interesting comparative studies.[98] Whether good or bad, electoral results alone can never substantiate direct conclusions concerning the Bund's electoral work, public presence, or influence in society more generally. Reversely, neither can we afford to analytically discard the Bundist activism pattern of electoral work. Seeing as the Bund would not achieve its best electoral results until the late 1930s, however, we can only speculate as to this activism pattern's potential further developments.

13 Educational Work: Towards a New *Yidishkayt*

Bundist educational work built upon the legacy of the educational circles of nineteenth-century Russian revolutionaries. These circles provided a counter-hegemonic education beyond the Russian-Jewish Enlightenment, thereby constructing a new activist and secular form of *yidishkayt*.[99] As Verena Dohrn shows, relations with the Tsarist state marked the point of distinction between the Jewish enlighteners known as the Maskilim and the revolutionary intelligentsia.[100] The former's strategy concentrated primarily on institutions of

---

in World War II, as the Bund's major electoral successes occurred mainly in the last years of independent Poland. On source criticism in this regard see Part III.11.
95 Pickhan 2001, pp. 414–19.
96 Jacobs 2009, pp. 1–4; Abramson 1999, p. 50 ff.
97 Pickhan 2001, pp. 414–19.
98 See for example Jacobs 2013.
99 On the concept see Pickhan 2009.
100 Dohrn 2008.

integration, reforming both the state and the Jewish community through official educational institutions. This approach failed. The emancipation of the serfs in 1861 was not expanded to incorporate freedom of movement for Jews, and the May Laws following the Tsar's assassination in 1881 dramatically aggravated their already precarious state. The atmosphere of repression led to a moderate form of maskilic activism that largely avoided the conflict with the state, and thus offered the wrong tools for social improvement in such decidedly unmoderate times.

Only under conditions of secrecy and illegality would the *kruzhki* emerge as educational circles, and thus as '[t]he main form of Russian radical organization in the 1880's'.[101] First in Russian and later in Yiddish, revolutionary intellectuals provided a socialist education that soon took on the role of workers' education. During the heyday of these circles before 1905, they offered workers a general education and knowledge of the wider world while also instilling ideas of why and how to change it. Here, the transition to adulthood was just as prominent a theme as secularism and class struggle.

That said, Bundist educational endeavours were not always envisioned as mainsprings of the Bund's political history alone.[102] Educational activists like Khayim Kazdan viewed the Bund's educational network as the engine of an evolutionary process moving towards a culturally independent *yidishkayt*, to be measured more in terms of literary output than proletarian culture. This culture's structures, Kazdan suggested, were formed by authors and curricula. As the head of the TSYSHO he ascribed the Bund and its schools a leading role in this history. He praised *yidishkayt* as the Bund's greatest cultural achievement in his pivotal account, *Fun kheder un 'shkoles' biz tsysho*.[103] At the same time, his description separated the Bund's radical politics from its educational work based upon the former. Such a culturalisation of the Jewish secular education system, ignoring the fact that socialism served as the foundation of that very secularism, was necessitated by the book's origin in the US rather than by the educational activists themselves. After all, education prior to World War II operated in political and often revolutionary contexts (as did *yidishkayt* itself).

Other authors therefore strongly emphasised this overlap of cultural and revolutionary work. Moreover, they interpreted the early educational circles as

---

101   Tobias 1972, p. 13.
102   YIVO, New York, RG 102, 196. Additionally, see Dubnov-Erlich 1918a, p. 4 ff.; Dubnov-Erlich 1918b, p. 2 f.; Shlugleyt 1925; Peskin 1942, pp. 112–20; Kohen 1942; Baskin 1945; Shulman 1945; Zivion 1948a; Blekhman 1959; Sisk 1997.
103   See Kazdan 1956.

initiators who moved beyond the *kheder* system and more importantly united Jews and non-Jews in shared revolutionary efforts. The development of further educational sites began to snowball, driven by the eminent need for both analysis and action. Early worker activists in particular emphasise that their initial moment of 'awakening' occurred through reading political literature, but it was only in discussion groups or other meetings that their accumulated knowledge could develop into practicable education and political activism. Early recipients thus often went on to careers as Bundist agitators, carrying their experiences outward.[104]

Kruzhki, schools, houses of culture, and gatherings were thus intertwined in one unified counter-hegemonic system. It broke with the Jewish Enlightenment's understanding of integration while retaining its basic principle of 'education through self-education', interpreting it in an activist sense with reference to the class nature of society. Any worker could now become a *tuer* by organising new local Bund groups, holding meetings, or contributing to the organisation's educational work. Education was thus always linked to the structural formation and training of both new *khaverim* as well as corresponding branches of the movement.

Educational work was initially geared exclusively towards workers, but in time would move towards youth work over the course of a generational transition in the Bund.[105] In this sense, the emergence of the youth groups SKIF, *Tsukunft*, and the secular Bundist-Poale Zionist school association TSYSHO under Polish rule is rooted in the Bund's Russian history. Simultaneously, it represents a specific development under the conditions of legality in interwar Poland.[106] Kazdan overculturalised educational work retrospectively, as education could only become a pattern of activism and hence a substantial aspect of Bundist history if it provided *yidishkayt* with a utopian and transnationally transferrable, political, and revolutionary substance.

---

104 Workers' careers in particular depended on coming forward, trying things out, and proving oneself in such situations. See the descriptions of careers and constant return of this topos in Berman 1936; Shtern 1954; Mendel 1989; Novikov 1967; Metaloviets 1982, p. 169.
105 Dubnov-Erlich 1918b, p. 2; Baskin 1945. The decisive factor in the latter was the Bundists' youthfulness, in this regard see Part II.5.
106 While the TSYSHO still waits for a contemporary history to be written, literature on the Jewish education system in Poland is very extensive. A comprehensive account can be found in Frost 1998; Trębacz 2016.

14   Labour Struggle

Like educational work, labour struggle was equally torn between the clandestine and the public. As a pattern of activism, it was closely linked to the Bund's roots in the strike movement and trade union work. In fact, the Bund originally grew out of the *kasen* (Russian: *kassy*), strike funds maintained by local groups and movements.[107] Thirteen delegates from such funds secretly founded the Bund in 1897 in an attic in Vilnius as a response to two specific problems.

Firstly, the funds were too small and vulnerable and fluctuated heavily over time. Until then trade unions had mostly been un-institutionalised alliances limited to certain occupational groups, rising and falling according to the need for strike action and its success or failure.[108] In this context the term trade union does not refer to stable institutions, but is rather an umbrella term for the entire landscape of the *fareyne*, the associations in which workers came together to discuss and argue about improving their working and living conditions. More than 50 percent of Russia's Jewish labour force worked in the textile industry, making it one of the main battlegrounds and the bedrock for the strength of the *nadlfareyne* (needle associations).[109]

The Bund sought to forge the Jewish Pale's fragmented economic movement into one organised workers' institution. As a political umbrella organisation, it transformed the heterogeneity of the unions into a trade union movement and subsequently a politically, socially, and culturally revolutionary movement. The Bund's explicit adherence to Marxism as the sole answer to oppression set it apart from Zionism, Labour Zionism included, which in contrast to traditional Marxism not only sought to lead the workers out of their misery, but also out of Russia. The son of Bundist professor Libman Hersh stresses that his father joined the Bund precisely because of its proletarian counter-culture, although he himself had grown up in a Zionist household that harboured academic ambitions for their son. Hersh joined the Bund 'because of the reactionary attitude of the Zionists towards every socialist movement in Tsarist Russia at the time. For example, the Zionists never participated in strikes'.[110] For the Bundists, labour struggles served political purposes. Accordingly, the

---

107   RGASPI, Moscow, Fond 217, opis' 1 delo 34 [S. Gozhanski: *Perviy b'ezd bunda. Vospominanya uchastnika*]; Mendelsohn 1970, pp. 64–71; Tobias 1972, p. 58.
108   Bunzl 1975, pp. 63–7.
109   Figures according to the 1897 census: 52.2 percent textiles, 19 percent construction, 9 percent food production, 5.9 percent cultural work, 13.6 percent others. See Bunzl 1975, p. 34.
110   Hersh 1957, p. 72. This claim is probably somewhat exaggerated and only applies to the Bund's initial years. The emergence of Poale Zion provided the Bund with both a powerful competitor as well as a partner for political cooperation.

trade union movement inside the Bund never restricted itself to an economistic character, although economic demands consistently occupied a central role.

Secondly, the Bund approached the pressing problem of the 'Jewish question' as closely related to the labour question.[111] This led to major conflicts with Russian Social Democracy as early as 1903–6, and again after 1912 as the organisation began to push for greater centralisation. Lenin was particularly vehement on this question, culminating in the 1913 remark: 'Jewish national culture is the slogan of the rabbis and the bourgeoisie, the slogan of our enemies'. In a grave misjudgement of the political situation, Lenin detected revolutionary potential only among Western European Jews and those who joined the ranks of what he saw as legitimate Marxist organisations – from which he explicitly excluded the allegedly separatist Bund. He scornfully denounced everyone who 'directly or indirectly, puts forward the slogan of Jewish "national culture" ... (whatever his good intentions may be)' as 'an enemy of the proletariat'. This was an open attack on the Bund, the primary Marxist advocate of a Jewish national culture, and foreshadowed the Bolsheviks' moves against it in 1917.[112] Polemicising against his strong Bundist and Labour Zionist rivals, Lenin failed to recognise how important *yidishkayt* and specific experiences of oppression were in mobilising Jewish workers. The Bund for its part reacted to Labour Zionist competition by bolstering its claim to universal Jewish representation (which it of course never achieved).[113]

The representatives of a 'vanguard party' were naturally hardly fond of the Bund's trade unionist roots, and reduced its broad activism to accusations of economism and spontaneism. The *'Iskra'* was particularly critical of the Bund's mediating function, which Bund co-founder Dzshon Mill by contrast considered crucial to Bundist propaganda. He claimed that delegates to the 1897 founding congress rightfully decided against the 'Social Democratic' label because it would scare away too many workers.[114] He stressed the practical value of the name, claiming that the term 'socialist' was still taboo in 1897. The flexibility gained by avoiding the word allowed for the rapid foundation and growth of further committees affiliating to the Bund along occupational lines. The platform assembled under the Bund's red flag was therefore a common foundation facilitating Bundism's evolution as a philosophy that took both Jewish and proletarian aspects of oppression into account. Jewishness and proletarian identity were inextricably linked in the lived experience of Bundist

---

111 Jacobs 1993b, pp. 124–33.
112 Lenin 1977a, p. 26.
113 Jacobs 1993b, p. 127 f.
114 Mill 1946a; Tobias 1972, p. 67 ff.

activists. Particularly in the context of political agitation, the two concepts were often conceived as a unified whole and merged into a single, coherent identity in the form of *yidishkayt*. The Russian Communist Party was later forced to acknowledge this necessity, as evidenced by the foundation of the *Yevsektsiya* and various Jewish Communist cultural institutions. Nevertheless, they encountered many difficulties winning influence and recruiting competent authors in the field they had opposed for so long.[115]

The Bund's shifting legal status naturally also had an impact on its trade union work, particularly with regard to tendencies towards professionalisation. As exemplified by the radical Bershter Bund,[116] the early trade union movement inside the Bund was a strike movement that developed an increasingly political direction.[117] Long-term political goals became more important to many hitherto economistic associations in the run-up to the 1905 revolution, allowing for activism to continue beyond the immediate strike event.[118] The conspiratorial trade union strike funds (*kassy*) were just one precondition of the confrontational public strike. They alone, however, could not sustain a strike over the long term. According to John Bunzl, the 'difficulties of the strike movement' ultimately led 'to an emphasis on the *primacy of the political struggle*' from the ground-breaking fifth congress of the Bund in 1902 onwards.[119] The congress decided that political issues would be deliberated upon in a centralised manner, while economic affairs would be dealt with at the local level. Only from 1904 onwards would the two strands combine to become a single, viable politico-economic pattern of action that increasingly stressed the value of *yidishkayt* in terms of both politics and culture.[120] Therefore, although the Jewish and thus Yiddish-speaking trade unions temporarily succeeded in terms of their strike objectives, they never constituted an independent social movement. They required the Bund's material, ideological, and logistical support just as much as the Bund relied upon the labour struggle.[121]

The burgeoning Bund would force even critics like Lenin, who viewed these trade union ties with alarm and feared that such baggage would prevent them

---

115   Gitelman 1972, pp. 120–9; Moss 2009, pp. 258–62.
116   Brush Workers Union.
117   *Arbeyter shtime* 14, 1899, p. 8.
118   The problem of strike duration was two-fold: only shorter strikes enjoyed a higher success rate, and financing strike action in general was difficult. See Bunzl 1975, p. 64f.; see also the contemporary and detailed analysis from a socialist-Zionist perspective in Borochov 1984, pp. 187–90.
119   Bunzl 1975, p. 67. Emphases in original.
120   Mendelsohn 1970, p. 129 and p. 135.
121   On this mutual conditionality see also Part II.6.

from joining the clandestine class struggle, to indirectly concede that the organisation exerted a particularly strong influence over newly organising workers.[122] The Tsarist state was equally aware that the strike movement and the Bund could not be separated, and consequently subjected the trade unions to the same repression as the political movements around them. This in turn further politicised the trade unions.[123]

The Yiddish-speaking and revolutionary trade union movement that emerged from this process was specifically adapted to conditions of illegality. Like the Bund itself, it operated partially clandestine and only appeared in public by way of eruptions. The long-awaited legality the movement enjoyed in Poland after World War I brought with it a degree of functional differentiation. As leading Bundist Artur Zigelboym acknowledges, the trade unions were forced to 'lead an independent existence by necessity'.[124] What developed next was a veritable system of Polish trade unions, complete with distinct occupational and language-based branches. On the one hand, this entailed functionally differentiated components of an institutionalised hierarchy of new federations, which in turn pushed the trade unions further away from the Bund.[125] On the other hand, however, it embodied what Roni Gechtman describes as 'national-cultural autonomy in the making'.[126] After all, although the Bund's trade union wing integrated itself into the Polish federation, it retained Yiddish as the official language of spoken and written communication below the executive level handling central accounting and correspondence with the Polish central commission.[127]

Although this drew the trade union movement closer to the Bund's cultural wings, it did not imply the former's de-politicisation. In fact, the 'proletarianisation' of Jewish workers accelerated during the interwar years due to both changes in industry as well as a discursive alteration of working-class culture. The Bund now relied on an increasingly proletarianising rhetoric, in which the term 'labour' took on renewed significance by the late 1920s. Given the tripling of membership by the late 1930s, Viktor Alter was able to declare at the

---

122 Even Communist academics acknowledged this during the Cold War, see Borshchenko 1959, p. 8 f.
123 Between 1906–10 the Tsarist government banned around 500 trade unions, while 600 additional unions were denied legal recognition from the outset. Membership plummeted from 245,000 (1907) to 13,000 (1909), see Borshchenko 1959, p. 10.
124 Cited in Pickhan 2001, p. 200.
125 On trade union organisation and the relationship to the Polish national trade union federation see Pickhan 2001, pp. 200–15 ff.
126 Gechtman 2005, p. 17.
127 Pickhan 2001, p. 201.

congress of Jewish trade unions in Poland in 1939: 'The Jews are becoming more and more a people of labour!', truly turning *yidishkayt* into an expression of working-class culture.[128] The Germans invaded soon thereafter and the Bundist culture of the working class and labour struggles survived only in exile. As labour struggle depended on local conditions, however, later chapters will examine to what extent Bundist forms of labour struggle could be transferred to the US or Argentina at all.

15 Armed Militancy: Defence or Revenge?

No Bundist activism pattern was as Janus-faced as that of armed militancy. Although controversial, it was also the source of experiences and heroic stories that continued to resonate long after the events themselves. Activists' recollections therefore rarely contain reflections on the theoretical implications and problems posed by self-defence. They rather limit themselves to praxis and the often risky organisation of the combat units, which tended to be remembered as anti-pogrom defence despite actually performing a wide range of tasks.[129]

16 Arms as Argument

Armed groups formed an integral component of the Bund since its early years, constituting a two-fold counter-power: first as one specific to the workers' movement and second as a universal Jewish defence force. At their inception, embattled units served to protect Bundist party gatherings and spaces. Over time they grew into combat units increasingly engaged in the economic struggle, and building upon these experiences also fought against pogroms. With these units, the Bund repeatedly broke with Jewish history and the traditional forms of dealing with violence and protection. Rid of the notion that help might come from the state or local elites, the Bund used these units' successes to advance Jewish worker organisation and re-education as a self-confident and self-organising force.

Despite all retrospective glorification, combat units rarely consisted of an organised corps of armed militants. Their fights often tended towards a kind of

---

128 Pickhan 2001, p. 206.
129 Bund Archives, New York, RG 1333, 1, [Autobiography, untitled, undated], pp. 31–41; YIVO, New York, RG 102, 107 [A. Beitani]: 16; 173 [Samuel Carasnik]; Berman 1924; Abramovitsh 1925, p. 99 f.; Berman 1945a, p. 73; Mints 1958, p. 101 ff.; Polin 1964; Aronson 1968.

collective brawl. As Bundist bookbinder Sholem Levin recalls, members were aware that violence had hitherto reflected traditional power relations. Many saw advancing into those very hierarchies as the only way to avoid being a target of that violence: 'I realised very soon that beating the apprentice was part and parcel of the apprenticeship's "programme", that the boss did not require an excuse to deal out a blow – he beats simply because he was also beaten when he learned the trade. And the apprentice's only solace is that one day, when he is the boss, he will get to beat his own apprentices as well'.[130] This ubiquitous violence helps to explain why the Bund often required the use of force when asserting workers' interests. Given that business owners often hired 'veritable scab squads (composed of de-classed elements)', the Bund was compelled to resort to the truncheon in the economic struggle.[131] Sholem Levin succinctly and soberly describes a conflict with Rudnitski, owner of the largest local bookbindery during a strike:

> Police aside, Rudnitski also enlisted the help of professional thugs. The workers responded to this with a thrashing. One day he was intercepted at the entrance of his warehouse and received such a severe beating that he remained in bed for several weeks, and only after that did he relent.[132]

As was true for most strikes, these oft-depicted scuffles occurred locally and spontaneously, with a fine line separating violence deemed productive or harmful. Activists placed great importance on differentiating between 'conscious' and 'unconscious' workers, that is between workers organising in the strike movement underground and those who moved in the criminal underworld – two spheres of social life in close structural proximity, yet ideologically far removed.[133] To be regarded as a crook or seen as associated with criminal elements was a major insult in the workers' movement.[134]

To understand this distinction, one must take into account not only Russian revolutionary self-confidence but also the state of the trade unions at the time of writing. A large portion of Bundist activists' memoirs were penned in the 1920s, frequently in the United States, where labour racketeering, the infiltration and siphoning off of trade union funds by organised crime, posed a very real threat to trade union activists.[135] Alongside Italian immigrants, the

---

130 Levine 1946, p. 120.
131 Bunzl 1975, p. 66.
132 Levine 1946, p. 98 f.
133 Impressively demonstrated in, for example, Mendel 1989, p. 29 ff., p. 37.
134 See Berman 1945a.
135 This problem grew immensely beginning in the 1920s, and was addressed above all by the McClellan Committee hearings in the 1950s, see Jacobs 2006, pp. 76–99.

prominent role played by Jewish immigrants is often mentioned in this context as well, although primarily the second generation pursued social advancement through crime (and often quite successfully).[136] Bundist Sam Carasnik recalls the Prohibition era with mixed feelings: emigrating to the US in 1907, he struggled to make a living at first. Only after the introduction of Prohibition was he able to buy a successful grocery store that thrived mainly from the sale of raw materials for home-brewing operations.[137] In his recollections, however, he is quick to point out that he remained true to his political principles throughout, and only his duties as shop owner and father kept him from playing an active role in the workers' movement. Regardless, he was forced to give up his store in 1922 when, as he remarks quite tellingly, 'a number of things were not going in its favour'.[138] He remains noticeably vague about any further details.

From the perspective of worker activists, the distinction between underground and underworld was vital because only actions informed by political consciousness counted as activism. As Hersh Mendel recollects, this had already been the cause of 'mass-scale confrontations' in Russia, during which the strike movement and the fight against the Marxian lumpenproletariat as nuisances in the class struggle intertwined:

> That is what happened during the first great strike, in which the workers from every calling laid down their tools and streamed into the streets in order to have it out with the underworld. One of these pitched battles in the year 1905 lasted several days. That time, the workers laid waste to all the bordellos, beat the fences bloody and tracked down the underworldniks where they lived with the aid of drawn-up lists. Not seldom were pimps and thieves thrown from windows. ... At the beginning, the police stayed neutral in these battles. They thought that the workers would be beaten. When it later turned out, however, that the workers were winning, the police came out on the side of the underworld and together with them arrested the workers in droves. ... This dragged on until 1907 – that is, until the complete victory of the reaction.[139]

Mendel experienced the revolution in 1905 primarily as a series of brawls. Nevertheless, he emphasises that they compelled him to choose either 'the side of

---

136   See Seidman 1938; Landesco 1968; Rockaway 2000.
137   On the countless business opportunities during Prohibition see Welskopp 2010.
138   YIVO, New York, RG 102, 173 [Carasnik, Sam].
139   Mendel 1989, p. 36.

the workers or the side of the underworld'.[140] This extremely robust armed militancy became a source of proletarian identity and an expression of the Bund's new aspirations to dominate the public space. Proceeding from Jürgen Kocka's oft-cited three-stage model of class formation via class position, class identity, and class action, the class character of such worker autobiographies can be summed up as follows: the *becoming conscious* (of one's class position) through reading (often quite simplified) literature is followed by *choosing sides through violence* (as practiced identity), which in turn is followed by the *affirmation of this identity* via remembrance and commemoration. Because it forced workers to make a decision and choose sides, violence was a fundamental experience for activists and thus had 'conducive effects on other dimensions of processes of class formation'.[141]

17 Arms as Protection

Bundist armed militancy earned its reputation as self-defence against pogroms.[142] Following the horrific Kishinev Pogrom in 1903, the Bund re-organised existing combat units and officially called to arms in self-defence. It only approved of this, however, as a network of protective armed groups organising themselves locally, clandestinely, and under strict internal hierarchies.[143] The first organised resistance to Christian violence in Jewish history represented another step in the substantiation of the claim to power being asserted by the *tuer oyf di yidishe gas*. At the same time, it represented an attack on traditional Jewish hierarchies. The Bund refused to accept victimhood as Judaism's historical inheritance, instead calling for resistance in a secular world made and shaped by people. Despite the limited extent of its actual power, anti-pogrom defence marked a crucial high point of the Jewish 'turn towards activism' beginning in the eighteenth century.[144] The Bund openly challenged the authority of Jewish elites. Side-lining the *kehillah*, Bundist units now claimed to be the Jewish population's defensive force, often embraced by the population as a 'heroic' act or resented as the collapse of modernity.[145]

---

140 Mendel 1989, p. 37.
141 Kocka 1990, p. 5.
142 Although published 30 years apart, two essays nevertheless stand out. The first focuses on organisational history while the second addresses emotional and representational history: Lambroza 1981; Shtakser 2009.
143 Depicted in Lambroza 1981.
144 Haumann 2002, p. 50 and p. 166 f.
145 This is particularly true of Bundists, see Shazar 1967; Linden 1910, Vol. 1, pp. 383–400.

As John D. Klier points out, institutionalising resistance could potentially accelerate the dynamic of the pogroms and allow the 'dialogue of violence' between Jews and Christians to spiral out of control.[146] We should keep in mind, however, that violent institutions emerged on both sides and patrolled not only the imagined front between Christians and Jews, but the revolutionary front as well. The Bund organised the majority of combat squads, but most did not consist of committed Bundists alone. An investigatory commission convened after the 1905–6 pogroms concluded that 20 non-Jews were among the 152 self-defence fighters killed in 22 shtetls, making them the second-largest group of victims after the Bundists themselves.[147] Following the October Manifesto's publication, many pogroms were not only anti-Jewish but also anti-revolutionary. Socialist organisations thus defended both the shtetls and the revolution. In most cases, however, the Bund supplied and organised the majority of these defence units – a trait that emerged years earlier and became a constant of the Bund's organisations after the Kishinev Pogrom in 1903.[148] The Bund's dominance also triggered certain centrifugal effects. Poale Zionist A. Beitani enthusiastically joined a combat squad in the run-up to the 1905 revolution to defend the local Jewish population, but quickly left after getting caught between the ideological fault lines of Bundism and Labour Zionism, exasperated by the constant Bundist attacks on his socialist-Zionist worldview.[149]

Nevertheless, in standardised autobiography such as the Bund Archives questionnaires, self-defence appears as an integrating activity: roughly 20 percent of respondents report fighting in Eastern European self-defence squads, markedly above the historical average of actual Bundist involvement in the small and extremely conspiratorial combat units.[150] This can be explained by the identity-forming power of such an experience. Even more so than other patterns of activism, active engagement in self-defence groups generated identity that crossed any class boundaries. Although 60 percent of those involved were workers, the remaining third of higher-educated participants shows that grammar school pupils, university students, and *yeshiva-bokherim* did not consider themselves above getting their hands dirty in street fights.[151]

146 Klier 2002; Hofmeister 2008.
147 Linden 1910, Vol. 1, p. 398.
148 Tobias 1972, pp. 222–31; Mikhed'ko 1998.
149 YIVO, New York, RG 102, 107 [A. Beitani]: p. 16.
150 Bund Archives, RG 1400, MG2–429, [type IV]. Berman (1945a, p. 73) describes the honour of guarding a weapons depot.
151 Bund Archives, RG 1400, MG2–429, [type IV].

Furthermore, the formation of such defence units was not a specificity of Russian illegality. In Poland, these units served to maintain the counter-hegemonic movement and fight against the state, pogromists, and anti-revolutionaries alike.[152] As a revolutionary and anti-anti-Semitic guard, their strength did not develop in direct correlation with their legal status, but rather in response to actions by local anti-Jewish campaigners and 'lumpenproletarian' underclasses. Combat unit strength evolved independently of legislation and followed developments that occurred outside of legal strictures. This activism pattern eventually culminated in ghetto warfare against the German occupation, although these uprisings were marked by a degree of finality unknown to earlier self-defence units.[153]

18   Arms and Revenge

During World War II, the line between defence and offence was self-evident. The distinction was much more ambiguous in the period in which this activism pattern emerged, when the relationship between resistance and terror remained relatively unclear. Social Democratic forces encountered a strong rival in the Socialist Revolutionaries at least until November 1917.[154] The party's combat forces, founded in 1902 and led by Vladimir Medem's university friend Grigory Gershuni until the latter's arrest in early 1903, were highly efficient terrorist cells. They committed numerous attacks, most famously the assassination of Russian Interior Minister Plehve, a target of much scorn in the revolutionary movement, organised by the aforementioned double-agent Evgeny Azef.[155] Although the Bund distanced itself sharply from the Socialist Revolutionaries, both the relationship between Gershuni and Medem and the organ-

---

152   After all, the unconditional link between revolution and counter-revolution became evident not only in concrete revolutionary situations as depicted by Arno J. Mayer, but was in fact inscribed into all forms of activism, see Mayer 2002, p. 45 ff.

153   The Bund continued to engage in these struggles well into the war years with a clearly activist intent, see esp. Oler 1943; Pat 1944; Wiernik 1944; Pavlevski 1946; Goldstein 1947a; Blatman 2003.

154   On the proximity in which even the most radical Socialist Revolutionaries saw themselves to a romantic form of socialism, see for instance the motives of terrorist Marc Schweitzer, who accidentally blew himself up in 1905 (Nicolaevsky 1934, p. 107). On the necessity of differentiation through action due to the similarities between the organisations' respective utopias, see Hilbrenner 2008. Foundationally: Hildemeier 2000. On the radicalisation of the Socialist Revolutionaries in the context of the 1917 revolutions see Häfner 1994.

155   Nicolaevsky 1934, pp. 44–66; Medem 1923, Vol. 1, p. 151 f.

isation's politics more generally justify questioning John Bunzl's claim that the Bund categorically rejected acts of terror.[156] Or, to put it another way, at what point does resistance become vigilante justice, and at what point does the defensive struggle ultimately harm the class struggle?

As Hirsh Lekert's case shows, the Bund's position in this regard vacillated strongly, casting the Bund's allegedly unwavering steadfastness in a different light than the sympathetic interpretation Henry J. Tobias provides. In his pioneering study of this period in Bundist history, he notes that the 'Lekert case' was one of the Bund's major topoi prior to 1905. His book nevertheless only dedicates a few brief lines to the issue.[157] For this reason alone it seems worthwhile to take a closer look at the events and debates in 1902.

When the Vilnius Bundists held their 1902 May Day parade despite the unexpected absence of Christian workers and the state of siege imposed on the city, they may have anticipated that the event would end in street fighting, but they could not have known that it would mark one of the most significant episodes in Bundist history. Following a brief march, the demonstration headed straight for the rows of police and specially requested mounted Cossacks. A street battle ensued, over the course of which many Bundists were arrested.[158] Orders given by the governor of Vilnius Victor von Wahl escalated the situation. He had already gained a reputation as a fierce enemy of the revolutionary movement, and was specifically commandeered to the revolutionary city. In a departure from law and usual practice and as a humiliating gesture to the activists outside, he ordered the arrested protestors flogged.[159] Outraged, the Bund's Foreign Committee decried this anachronistic military or feudal punishment as the '*Shinderey in vilna*' (Atrocity of Vilnius). The public outcry resonated well beyond the Jewish workers' movement. Calls for targeted retaliation grew more vocal within the Bund as well, although it rejected terror in theory and regarded it as counter-productive to building the mass movement.[160] The Bund's local

---

156 Bunzl 1975, p. 66 f.
157 Tobias 1972, p. 150 ff. The only lengthy discussion composed by a Bundist author, albeit a problematic one, thus remains Hertz 1952.
158 Bund Archives, New York, RG 1400, ME-16, 29, Brochure: *Der all. yid. arb'bund in Lite, Poyln un Rus.: Hirsh Lekert un zayn protses*, Drukerey fun Bund, June 1902. Widely disseminated through various contributions in *Di arbeyter shtime*, June (1902). The case was also reported on in the US, albeit as a marginal note, before later becoming *the* Lekert case: N.N. 1902b and Valt 1904, Bund Archives, New York, RG 1400, ME-16, 28.
159 As much was stated in a leaflet by the Bund's Foreign Committee, Bund Archives, New York, ME-16, 29, *Der oyslendisher komitet fun algmeynen yidishn arbeterbund fun Lite, Poyln un Rusland: Di shinderey in Vilna*, Drukerey fun Bund, London, [1902].
160 Tobias 1972, p. 150. On the lengthy debate concerning physical punishment in Russian society see Schrader 2002; Benecke 2006, pp. 33–60.

committee was particularly faithful to a strictly Social Democratic line of argument in the ensuing debates, showing little patience for revenge or terror. When Bundist Hirsh Lekert ignored local party orders and took matters into his own hands by shooting at von Wahl shortly thereafter, deep fissures began to emerge inside the Bund. In its rather delicate role as mediator, the Vilnius committee called for compliance with party principles, for resistance via class struggle instead of the blunderbuss:

> We fight calmly, it is not our goal to spill human blood – but our patience also has limits. ... The people have taken revenge, von Wahl has been wounded by two bullets from a revolver. The social conscience has punished one of the most savage Tsarist satraps.

Yet this was no reason to elevate the action to a universal principle, because

> such a revolver [of a Social Democrat] only expresses the first cry of the wounded social conscience, so that the people do not suffocate under the pressure of their outrage. Nevertheless, we know just as well that the fight against Tsarism as a system requires other means. And we carry these means with us like our own hands – means which, in contrast to guns, daggers, or dynamite, will inevitably lead to victory.[161]

In this line of argument, the shooting would remain a singular event and was in this way reduced to the act itself, preventing it from becoming activism.

Although Lekert only inflicted minor injuries on von Wahl, he was sentenced to death by hanging in a summary trial and executed shortly thereafter. This chain of events triggered a wave of solidarity extending to the highest echelons of the movement, and confronted Bundism with the question of political revenge.[162] Party leaders struggled to find an adequate response to such 'wild acts', as even the intellectually inclined leadership of the Foreign Committee in Switzerland called for an 'avenger' to seek retribution for 'the humiliation of his brothers'.[163] The issue led to heated debates at the Bund's fifth congress in 1902, one year before the Bund adopted the organised use of arms as a means of anti-pogrom defence. The congress discussed the pressing issues of the period.

---

161   Bund Archives, New York, RG 1400, ME-16, 29, 'Khaverim arbeyter', *Der oyslendisher komitet fun algmeynen yidishn arbeterbund fun Lite, Poyln un Rusland: Di shinderey in Vilna*, Drukerey fun Bund, London, [1902], p. 4.
162   Bund Archives, New York, RG 1400, ME-16, 29, Various letters.
163   Bund Archives, New York, RG 1400, ME-16, 29, *Der oyslendisher komitet fun algmeynen yidishn arbeterbund fun Lite, Poyln un Rusland: Di shinderey in Vilna*, Drukerey fun Bund, London, [1902], pp. 1–3.

It opened with a debate on organisational structures followed by the question of 'organised revenge', before addressing party publications and, lastly, financial matters. Research on the Bund has largely concentrated on the first point. After all, this was the first party congress held after the publication of Lenin's *What Is to Be Done?*[164] Conference participants, however, would later claim unanimously that 'emphasis had been on the second point of the agenda' – not on the relationship between the Bund and '*Iskra*' so prominent in academic research, but on the question of 'organised revenge'.[165]

In the debate, the Bund (temporarily) concluded that 'organised revenge' ought to remain a tool in the Bund's activist arsenal. The Bund continued to reject terrorism as a pattern of political activism on principle, but conceded that cases like May Day in Vilnius called for 'taking organised revenge. Such acts of revenge, however, may only be organised by the Bund's Central Committee'.[166] In other words: revenge was declared a priority to satisfy the will of the masses and retain political control of the situation. It was not to develop independently, but deemed acceptable as long as it occurred in an organised manner. Party leaders sought to allow controlled individual actions but prevent the emergence of broader activism in this direction.

This change of course provoked opposition. The spokesman of the faction representing a strictly Social Democratic line, Vladimir Medem, would continue to take a rather ambivalent view of the matter even in retrospect. In his view, pre-emptive violence like in the struggle against espionage may very well have been sensible, but could not be allowed to become an end in itself. This sentiment inspired his warning at the fifth party congress that 'once embarked on, this course acquired a logic of its own and terror became a means of political struggle, a means, moreover, which gradually negated all other forms of political action'.[167] With the Socialist Revolutionaries in mind, Medem warned that the official sanctioning of 'organised revenge' could spread an inclination towards terrorism throughout the Bund. To him this was not activism but mere actionism, ultimately doing the struggle more harm than good. Many of these commentators likely also viewed it as dangerous, for the softening of the boundary between Marxists and Socialist Revolutionaries would have presented the Bund with its own problems of definition.[168] The Socialist Revolutionaries had already confirmed this suspicion with a prominent article in their

---

164   Tobias 1972, p. 155, pp. 167–70.
165   Levin 1922, p. 59.
166   Ibid.
167   Medem 1979, p. 250.
168   Mannheim 1979, p. 215.

central newspaper acknowledging Lekert's sacrifice, posthumously adopting him into to the ranks of the Socialist Revolutionaries precisely *because* of his deed and *despite* his history and party affiliation. They blamed his failure not on his actions, but on the Bund's inadequate support.[169]

The Lekert case was thus extremely delicate and partially anticipated the dilemmas surrounding the organisation of self-defence groups after the Kishinev Pogrom. For it was not the ideological ambivalence concerning terrorism, but the renewed wave of pogroms from 1903 onwards that soon ended the Bundist flirt with terror. 'Organised revenge' against the representatives of a violent state remained a volatile ideological episode and soon lost prominence in the context of broad popular violence in the Kishinev Pogrom. Now the question was how to organise counter-violence as self-defence *oyf der yidishn gas*. How could actions help form activist and combat-ready masses without allowing them to evolve into independent actors? The terror of 'organised revenge' only flared up briefly as a possible activism pattern in Bundist history, although some Bundists demanded it and others decamped to the Socialist Revolutionaries because of it. Ultimately, it was never properly integrated into Bundism nor the Bund's patterns of activism.[170] 'Organised revenge' therefore ought to be understood as a sharply contested but failed activism pattern.

19 Group-Specific Activism

All of the hitherto discussed Bundist patterns of activism were potentially open to all Bundists.[171] Two exceptions to this rule, however, were youth work and Bundist women's groups. From early on the Bund depended on a large number of very young activists, which historian Henry J. Tobias astutely grasps as an indicator of how strongly the Bund was grounded in the Jewish community.[172] These recruits often included children – activists barely 10 years of age. Against the will of the party, they even formed their own Bundist organisation, the *Kleyner bund* (Little Bund).

Former 'Little Bundist' Naythan Rozen later noted that during the Russo-Japanese War and general fear of pogroms, the mystical aura of 'incomprehens-

---

169 N.N. 1902a.
170 Tobias 1972, p. 155.
171 Another activism pattern in this category would be the Bund's athletics wing, such as its workers' sports associations under the *Morgenshtern* banner. Despite their popularity in Poland, they played no role in the Bund's migration history and are thus not discussed extensively in this volume. For a more in-depth account see Gechtman 1999; Gechtman 2005, pp. 319–55; Jacobs 2009, pp. 48–61.
172 Tobias 1972, p. 236.

ible words like "Iskraist", "Bundist", "Manifestation", "Demonstration"' proved just as magnetising as 'what [happened] in the secret *kreyslekh*'.[173] Similar to Bertha Fox, he expedited his own 'awakening' and sought to contact the Bund through his older siblings. Again, his elder brother refused to allow the young boy into the movement. Rozen, however, secretly obtained an anti-Tsarist leaflet, which he reports sent him into 'seventh heaven'.[174] The boy internalised the pamphlet's 'phrases' and in his words became a revolutionary missionary, a student agitator at his school. This activity lent him the romantic aura of a revolutionary, and 'my *khaverim* said among themselves that I was "dangerous"'.[175] Without any further reflection of the substance of the slogans, such revolutionary games developed a gravitational pull that drew further students into their wake. As a result, the *Kleyner bund* composed of '*beter-yinglekh* and pupils'[176] formed simultaneously and independently of one another in many locations throughout the Pale.

This self-organised children's movement was not a novelty in Jewish history and emerged at a very early stage of the Bund.[177] According to Tobias, the beginnings of the deeply spontaneous children's and youth movement date back to as early as 1901. Former member Yankel Levin recalls that the phenomenon was spreading by 1903. The Pale was home to growing numbers of 'truly young "activists", some only age ten or so' at the time who emulated the Bund's activism patterns in their own way.[178] Activist Sh. Shilits claims in her hitherto unpublished and unstudied memoirs that she was involved in Bundist youth organising as early as 1899, only two years after the Bund's inception.[179] In both her and Levin's cases, it becomes clear that this sort of organising was far from child's play: Levin stresses that the groups even organised their own local fighting squads, capable of violent intervention during strikes and other confrontational situations. Although these squads were activist and self-confident, they were not 'conscious', that is to say not 'class-conscious'.[180] Through tenacity and persistence the youth even managed to participate in the 1905 revolution,

---

173   Rozen 1943, p. 29.
174   It was important to him, as it was to many others, to remember his moment of awakening as an abrupt event, see for example Fox 2006; Mendel 1989, p. 27.
175   Rozen 1943, p. 29.
176   Here Rozen means both pupils of traditional religious schools as well as the state schools he attended, see Rozen 1943, p. 30 f.
177   See Jacobs 2009, p. 29 ff.
178   Levin 1924; Tobias 1972, p. 236 f.
179   Bund Archives, RG 1400, M–13, 130, [Shilits, Sh., *Zikhroynes fun a anot fun kleynen bund*], p. 2.
180   Levin 1924, pp. 15–29.

thereby inscribing themselves into the Bund as unwanted (because too young) but nevertheless extremely effective child activists. Because the Bund refused to recognise the uncontrollable *Kleyner bund*, the children – at least according to the recollections of many participants – copied the former's activism patterns[181] ranging from the *birzshe* to 'forms of economic terror'.[182] The *Kleyner bund*'s heavy reliance on direct action meant it was also subject to persecution by state authorities, which in the case of K. Roklin and Naythan Rozen led to arrest. In worse cases, like for Avremele Himelshtayn and Yankl Moyshe, it even resulted in their tragic death.[183]

As the revolutionary fervour began to subside in 1907 the *Kleyner bund* first lost its power and later its spontaneity. A Jewish Social Democratic youth organisation had emerged in Warsaw by 1911, known as *Tsukunft* from 1916 onwards. Interwar Poland thus witnessed the growth of the significant and now Bundist-led *Yugnt bund 'tsukunft'*. The integration of a major youth organisation into the ranks of the Bund reflected the movement's maturation. The Bund acknowledged Bundists' generationality and created a space for adolescent activists.[184]

Similar motives drove the Bund to launch a children's association for even younger supporters, the *Sotsyalistisher kinder-farband* (SKIF) in 1926.[185] The youth organisation exhibited major recruitment potential. This is reflected in the questionnaires, where every respondent who joined the Bund during its Polish phase reported prior affiliation to either SKIF or *Tsukunft*.[186] As we learn from 'G.W.', a young author born in 1919 who took part in an autobiographical youth competition held by the Vilnius YIVO during the interwar period, the moment of awakening shifted from mysterious private events (as earlier generations unanimously describe it) to open work and shared experience: 'In fact, I joined the movement right away; it was still in its early days. Here I discovered a new life, a life full of belief in the future'.[187] He reports with a hint of pride that he managed to persuade his older brother, a former Zionist, to join the Bund as well, and that his younger brother was now a member of the SKIF.[188] The organised youth movement turned children's and adolescents'

---

181 Ibid.; YIVO, New York, RG 102, 157, Friedman, Lena (A mitglid fun der arbeter ring mishpokhe), p. 12 f.
182 YIVO, New York, RG 102, 157 [Lena Friedman, untitled autobiography], p. 12 f.; Litvak 1925, p. 212 ff.; Levin 1924; Tobias 1972, p. 237.
183 YIVO, New York, RG 102, 209, K. Roklin, [untitled autobiography], p. 3 f.; Rozen 1943, p. 31 f.; Jacobs 2009, p. 32.
184 See Part III.11.
185 Foundational on both organisations: Jacobs 2009, pp. 8–47.
186 Bund Archives, New York, RG 1400, MG2–429, Questionnaires type IV.
187 W 2002, p. 316.
188 W 2002, p. 319.

spontaneity into recruitment. Naturally, the young activists were closely tied to the Bund's educational work and increasingly adhered to the Bund's socialist and reform-pedagogical concepts. With this work the Bund responded to spontaneous efforts to participate common among the earlier Little Bundists, and countered them with active functional differentiation. The diverse Bundist activities offered by the youth branches were an expression of this. Many *SKIFistn* and *Tsukunftistn* stayed with the youth organisations after reaching a certain age, and even took on active roles in various commissions and education offices as adults.[189] Youth work could remain a pattern of activism even after one's own youth had passed.

In contrast to the youth branches, the Bundist women's movement lacked comparable mobilising successes. Most importantly, many socialist activists felt little need for differentiation in this field. After all, the Bund claimed to treat all Jewish workers equally irrespective of gender and grant everyone the same status and opportunities in terms of rank and participation. As a logical consequence of this stance, there were no specific women's organisations in the Bund during the Russian period. In Poland, however, the Bund's differentiation progressed and was proactively driven forward. That said, the organisation emerging from this process, the YAF (*Yidishe arbeter froy*), failed to become a mass movement.[190] While certain forms of class-conscious feminism emerged to shape the agendas of many European social movements and socialist parties in the interwar years, the Bundist women's movement fell short of achieving a similar position within the Bund.[191] According to Jack Jacobs, the relative failure of the Bundist women's movement illustrates that 'Bundist counterculture had its limits, and ... that the Bund was unable to extend its reach beyond a certain point'.[192] This observation raises the question of why the Bund should have devoted more energy to establishing this group-specific pattern of activism when others already covered most of the expectable recruiting and mobilising functions – at least according to its own self-understanding, which generally demonstrated little sensitivity to gender-related questions of representation and power.

Unlike the youth organisations, the women's movement focused on political issues within the Bund that simultaneously challenged fundamental Bundist self-perceptions. Only a few women managed to develop their interest in gender politics into personal activism and contributions to the Bund. Yet as this

---

189 Bund Archives, MG2–429, Questionnaires type IV; Hertz 1946.
190 Jacobs 2009, pp. 82–97.
191 Gerhard 2001; Hyman 2006; Denz 2008.
192 Jacobs 2009, p. 82.

only led to a column in the Bund's leading daily, the *'Naye folkstsaytung'*, we might rather perceive it as a sub-form of publishing activism.[193] Moreover, only a handful of women managed to occupy important positions in the Bund – the resistance against gendered exclusion remained too weak to produce an internal counter-movement. Activism in this sphere was thus regarded as activism in its own right only to a very limited degree, due mainly to the inclusive force of other Bundist activism patterns. This is suggested by the name of the YAF itself: in the term *Yidishe arbeter froy* (Jewish worker woman), gender is only the third marker of distinction and serves as a refinement of the central two terms, 'Jewish' and 'worker'. The name *Yugnt bund 'tsukunft'* is clearly more powerful in this regard.

Above all, in the Bund being a woman generally did not count as a politically relevant sub-identity in its own right. Statistics reflect this: of the hundreds of respondents to the questionnaires contained in the Bund Archive in New York, we find only three women who indicate activity in the YAF.[194] None report pursuing such activity after migration, although four other women were active in local women's groups in their new homelands.[195]

Unlike the youth movement, the YAF was unable to assume a clearly differentiated organisational role, as non-specification was a result of the Bund's internal postulate of general equality including gender dating back to the time of illegality. This stood in stark contrast to the *Kleyner bund*, which older Bundists sought to keep outside of the Bund and whose members fought vehemently for their own integration. Work in the Bundist women's organisation may well have constituted a pattern of activism, but one unable to attain far-reaching constitutive consequences for the Bund's social and political composition.

20 Revolutionary Fundraising

All of the Bund's institutions required funds for public activity. Given that the organisation financed itself through dues and donations as opposed to expropriation, money also had to be 'mobilised'. Although *revolutionary fundraising* was hardly regarded as an activism pattern, it became clear particularly during

---

193 Clearly depicted in Denz 2008.
194 Bund Archives, New York, RG 1400, MG2, 429, Aleksandrewicz, Rosa; Hager, Libe; Kisman, Leah.
195 Bund Archives, New York, RG 1400, MG2, 429, Levental, Dukhtshe; Luksenburg-Rozen, Pale; Oler, Lanye; Yonish Rive.

the migration process that it constituted a crucial form of activism. Fundraising found not only acceptance but also legal security in migration, and became a rallying point for the transnational social movement.

As Henry J. Tobias points out, the Bund relied on funds from the US as early as 1900. The steady stream of revenue kept its operations running. Remittances were routed through and collectively registered by the Foreign Committee in Switzerland and quite frequently exceeded the total sums collected in Russia.[196] We ought to keep in mind that this was long before the overseas fundraising institutions of the 1920s and 1930s emerged. The Bund's financial need grew in proportion to the growth of its activities. Interestingly, the pivotal aspect of social movement fundraising has failed to attract deeper interest from historical researchers.[197] After all, even socialist movements need financial resources, and money thus possesses a 'social meaning' in these movements.[198] The acquisition of funds has been tacitly treated as a kind of natural precondition for all forms of socialist activism, but associated practices have not been regarded as equally essential to say the least. In my view, this is partially because a large share of the funds was raised abroad, meaning there were two reasons for its disappearance from researchers' field of vision. Because revolutionary fundraising was such a diverse and tremendously significant mode of participating in the Russian and Polish movement primarily in the US, I will address it in more detail in a separate chapter.

21   Tsuzamen, Tsuzamen

These activism patterns provided activists with numerous possibilities to shape and influence the Bund in Tsarist Russia and interwar Poland. In the process, the activists themselves devised and concretised activities as facets of the Bund's existence. In this sense they collectively defined what Bundism meant in a given moment, and what kind of activism it required for that time: 'It was present in its own making'.[199]

It is therefore futile to search for a 'basic unit' or smallest common denominator of Bundist activism as such. Neither the committees emphasised by Tobias, the organisations highlighted by Jack Jacobs, nor the libraries described

---

196   Tobias 1972, p. 130, p. 244.
197   A pioneering sociological study based on actor-network theory in this regard is Lainer-Vos 2012.
198   Zelizer 2017.
199   Thompson 1964, p. 9.

by Jeffrey Veidlinger represented the Bund's nucleus in the small towns par excellence.[200] If all Bundists held one element in common, it was activism on behalf of the Bund from which the aforementioned institutions would ultimately emerge. But the latter required clearly defined notions of the masses that would repeatedly lead to the fundamental activism pattern of 'gathering', of finding ways to mobilise groups for and representative of the Bund. That which later became known as the history of the Bund only emerged from the collective development and elaboration of these patterns and the constant search for ways to build present and communicative masses. The possibilities offered by these patterns under various conditions of legality varied across the Bund's history (see Table 2), although its fundamental premises remained remarkably constant.

That said, this is only the first part of the story. If Bundist history depended on the actions of Bundists themselves, then the history of the Bund must follow the paths of these Bundists. This turns the Bund's history into a history of migration. The Bund became a transnational social movement during the age of mass migration. The following sections investigate the trajectories of the activism patterns described above and the formation of new practices and institutions in the process of migration, while also outlining their relation to the Bund in Eastern Europe.

200   Tobias 1972, p. 66 ff.; Jacobs 2009; Veidlinger 2009, p. 37.

PART 2

'Exalted Moments of Our Romantic Past': Community Building through Collective Remembrance

∴

CHAPTER 3

Remembrance as Activist Practice: Initial Considerations

The Bund's most important ally in the struggle against oppression and traditionalism for a better tomorrow was the past. This grand Bundist utopia was built on more than just a vision of events to come; it required the active presence of all three dimensions of time – yesterday, today, and tomorrow – unified in a coherent whole.[1] Such a concept of utopia is functional in the sense of a practiced promise that guides actions and ensures its availability to experience.

Although he attached it primarily to the world of ideas, Karl Mannheim identified this functional simultaneity of temporal dimensions decades ago as a specificity of the 'socialist-communist utopia'. Utopias require actors capable of taking action. A social movement's temporal constructs cannot be defined by intellectuals alone, but must also be shaped by activists.[2] For this reason the past was integrated into the Bund's daily routines in manifold activist ways. Bundist activism combined socialism with Jewishness, which in turn were reflected and altered through a constantly modified invocation of the past. Commemorative texts were always both memorial and activist at once: they legitimised and motivated actions, forming identities which held the Bund together as a transnational social movement. The emotional-functional landscape of remembrance resting upon this foundation constitutes an essential facet of the Bund's history.

In contrast to the vast amounts of literature available on individual and national constructs of memory, its functions and dynamics in social movements have received only marginal attention.[3] Like their national counterparts, social movements are certainly also imagined communities, although their production of memory is differently nuanced to their counter-cultural character. In practice, movements place far more emphasis on that which is

---

1 In this sense it goes beyond Pierre Bourdieu's 'logic of practice', which mainly focused on the present and future but exhibited several blind spots when it came to the past. See Bourdieu 1990, p. 80 ff.
2 Mannheim 1979, p. 220 f.
3 Of particular significance in the German-speaking world are of course the works of Aleida Assmann, esp. Assmann 2007.

to be achieved than on that which tradition has handed down. Group loyalty, however, builds upon collective memory. It serves to both convey heroism as well as remind participants of the social conditions the movement seeks to change. Revolutionary groups' actions were guided by a historical legacy and sought to break with their contemporary class constellations at the same time.

The culture of remembrance found in socialist movements was distinct from that of Soviet Communists, whose acts of commemoration in the wake of the October Revolution primarily served to legitimise party leaders.[4] But here, too (and in contrast to national cultures of remembrance), the aim was to portray itself as a historical and counter-cultural social movement grounded in activism, above and beyond its individual leaders. The legitimation of Communist statehood rested on activism combating certain social conditions in need of rectification, not on the history of a national population. The Bund for its part never required this kind of legitimation, as it remained a social movement throughout its existence and never became a state power in its own right. Its *Memorik* culture was therefore directed less towards outward legitimation so much as inward, and focused on community building.

Moreover, the Bund also relied on a Jewish culture of memory that it altered through the *yidishkayt* it propagated as a modern Jewish identity. In this regard, Jewish history frequently draws on Pierre Nora's concept of *lieu de mémoire*, or 'realms of memory'.[5] Given that the concept is embedded in the idea of the modern nation-state, it cannot be directly applied to the numerous overlapping constructs of memory in Jewish history.[6] This problematic is particularly obvious in Nora's introduction to the English edition of his magnum opus. According to Nora, one important development of the post-war era was that every minority now demanded recognition of its respective memory as history: '[t]he Jewish case serves as a prime example. Hardly anyone would have spoken about a Jewish "memory" thirty years ago'. Yet in Nora's eyes, this Jewish memory was merely a mask for political aims. Not only does he claim the term 'Jewish community' was invented solely for political reasons (ignoring, for example, traditional Jewish debates around concepts like *klal*, *galut*, etc.), he even argues that said memory could now be used for purposes such as wresting an admission of France's complicity in the Holocaust from French president Jacques Chirac.[7]

---

4 See the outstanding Corney 2004. On the cult of the freedom fighter necessary for this see Figes and Kolonitskii 1999, p. 74f.
5 See for example Lipphardt 2004.
6 For a more fundamental critique see Kleist 2010.
7 Nora 2001, p. xv.

I will refrain from speculating about the implications and motivations of such arguments, but even Nora's historicisation is mistaken. The quotation marks around 'memory' are quite inappropriate. Jewish memorial practices and 'knowledge' are not post-war constructs, but much older and ever-changing constituents of Jewish history. Until the twentieth century, the national interpretation of these pasts represented a minority opinion at best. That said, various forms of memory oriented towards Jewish unity existed at all times, primarily serving the preservation of Jewish tradition in the orthoprax community. The invocation of collective suffering after God's destruction of the Second Temple and the scattering of the Jews across the world helped to create this imagined community of Judaism under the watchword 'Zakhor!' (Hebrew for 'remember').[8] Secondly, from the late eighteenth century onwards this historical invocation could be deployed in service of Judaism's renewal in the context of the 'turn towards activism'. Here, the Jewish community was understood as an educational community that could be renewed within the framework of the Russian state through its educational institutions.[9]

As this pro-state approach began to falter in the late nineteenth century, socialists from both the Bund and the Poale Zion continued the work of the Jewish enlighteners in their own way. Invoking Jewish history, they now called for the Jewish community to take collective action not just without but against the Tsarist state. It was beyond doubt to these movements, as it was to the traditional and Orthodox communities, that Judaism's renewal required a distinctly Jewish form of historical legitimation. As I intend to show in the following chapters, however, the fringes of this renewal were more open than in the religious movements' case, and promoted particular sub-identities. Realms of memory as expressions of collective national cultures of memory are thus only applicable to Jewish history to a limited extent, as both religious and social, cultural, and political currents largely took the form of movements rather than national entities.[10] Quotation marks around 'memory' in the case of Jewish history are presumptuous particularly when it comes to authors such as Moses Mendelsohn, Heinrich Graetz, Simon Dubnow, and others. In this same

---

8   Yerushalmi 1982. The term orthopraxy is distinct from orthodoxy, a somewhat misleading term commonly used to denote Jewish religious practice. In contrast to the pure doctrine central to orthodoxy, in orthopraxy correct actions ensure collective healing and liberation based on religious practices. After all, historically speaking the Jewish religion is more orthoprax than orthodox, as 'life is an expression of one's faith', see Ostheimer 2008, p. 152; quoted in Stemberger 2006, p. 9f.
9   See esp. Feiner 2002; Kleinmann 2006; Hofmeister 2008b; Dohrn 2008; Horowitz 2009.
10 See esp. Silber 1992; Ferziger 2005.

sense, the national or political functionalisation of Jewish memory represents an ahistorical oversimplification,[11] as Jewish history outside of national frames is full of debates about 'Jewishness' as a collective denominator based on a usable past. The Bund was both successor as well as innovator in this regard.

The best example of this in the Bund's history is its radical rejection of the concept of *klal*. Both traditional and Zionist readings used *klal* as a historically and religiously grounded expression of Jewish unity as a 'chosen people'. The Bund rejected this as reactionary and traditionalist, and favoured other concepts of abstract collectivity resting on notions such as *yidishe arbeter-mase*, *folks-mase*, or simply *yidn*. Such concepts always grasped class and ethno-national belonging in close relation to one another, contesting religious orthopraxy as a unifying concept.[12] The objectives of Jewish memory were manifold and only rarely oriented around national conceptions. During the social movements' heyday, Jewish identity and the historical legitimation of *yidishkayt* were not objects of a national history but of political and cultural activism.

11   As much is stated in, for example, Milman 1836, p. 117, p. 221, pp. 235–43; and prominently in Dubnow 1973, p. 757, p. 846.
12   Yosef Gorny's claim that the Polish Bund had regarded a '"world Klal Yisrael" as the bearer of Yiddish culture' and therefore conceptualised a 'proletarian klal' bears little grounding in historical fact. Although we may find individual deviations from the outright Bundist rejection of the term *klal* Jack Jacobs claims, it never served as a political concept. The term is used sporadically throughout the autobiographies surveyed in this study in a largely unreflected manner, while identities are consistently derived from concepts of the working people or the masses. Gorny's conceptual overestimation of the *klal* as an analytical link between Labour Zionism and Bundism thus serves solely to accuse the Bund of being misled by a 'tragic illusion', see Jacobs 2007; Gorny 2006, p. 2, p. 165 f., p. 266; Pickhan 2009.

CHAPTER 4

The Bundist Press: From Agitational Publications to Transnational *Memorik*

The October Revolution was not only a historical break in itself. Equally important was that it was staged as such. After the Bolsheviks took power, mass spectacles, history books, and commemorative marches represented the new authority's most important means of legitimation. As the stimulating studies by Orlando Figes and Boris Kolonitskii as well as Frederick C. Corney have shown, the new Soviet power was less concerned with opposing a 'White' interpretation of history so much as depicting the October Revolution as the history of socialism's ultimate goal.[1] This was directed primarily against rival socialists, who counterposed their own views to the notion of October 1917 as a historical linchpin and referred to other historical uprisings as their origin myth. Historical narratives as a component of the Bolsheviks' political arsenal have been analysed extensively, but neither Bundist nor other socialist practices have been submitted to similar investigations. This is quite surprising given that social movements are unable – and in fact never were able – to move forward without functional conceptions of history.[2] The following analysis of Bundist historical practice is therefore of a demonstrative character to some extent.

From the beginning, the Bund developed a distinct conception of history combining a Marxist understanding of class struggle with the cultural struggle for *yidishkayt*, elaborated primarily in Bundist publications. Consequently, questions of history's function in a Marxist movement, of the introduction of cultural work into such a movement, and the role of media in this construction process are central. It is vital to understand the Bund's deterministic historical-materialist conception of history (often subject to propagandistic reductionism) not as a misconception, but as a motivator. When inquiring about actors' motivations and reasons for behaving in certain ways, it is fairly irrelevant whether the history of class struggles really constitutes an ongoing battle between oppressors and oppressed or is just an invention of early mod-

---

1   Figes and Kolonitskii 1999; Corney 2004.
2   This was clearly recognised by Walter Benjamin, whose famous reflections on the concept of history probably represent the most lucid characterisation of the costs and benefits of historicity for socialist movements, see Benjamin 2007.

ernity. In functional terms this view of history simply made sense to young, frustrated craftsmen, painfully aware of their own exploitation and tired of the traditionalist way of life found in their Jewish environment. More importantly, it motivated and allowed them to feel the 'breath of history' even during the daily misery of the workshop. The Marxist view of history offered a past that not only explained why life seemed so unbearable, but also (and more importantly) why and how it could be changed. The ghosts of the past did not just haunt activists' minds. They also served to legitimise their own conduct, whether in the form of specific acts, a high-risk revolutionary career, or as already mentioned in the construction of a new political regime.

The past was therefore very much alive inside the Bund, and went beyond the search for a 'usable past'. As David G. Roskies notes, the latter was tremendously important to the Zionist movement in the post-war era, serving 'to cast the revolutionary past in stone, and to elevate it to a new status'.[3] To the Bund, this reshaping of history under a national-territorial banner in the post-war world served as an ahistorical beacon. As I demonstrate in the following, it contradicted both the Bund's heritage as well as its goals, and it naturally resisted the trend to the best of its abilities. The approach proved quite successful in New York during the initial post-war years, evidenced by the Bund's fiftieth anniversary celebration attended by 5,000 guests and likely the largest Bundist gathering ever. Emigrants also began publishing a new, high-quality monthly mouthpiece in 1941, '*Unzer tsayt*', that remained in circulation until 2002. The Bund's publications in this period were shaped by a strong presence of what I will call *Memorik* – expressions of a common Bundist history uttered with a commemorative function, ranging from meetings to songs and poems, autobiographies, primary sources and reprints, or the party's own historiography and the restoration of its archives in New York. The disproportionally strong presence of *Memorik* in the Bund's post-war publications and periodicals demonstrates the Bundist will to hold on to a glorious past, while also showing how remembrance grew increasingly defensive, finding its purpose in opposing the Zionist interpretation of Jewish history.[4]

This emphasis on the Bund's revolutionary history was a result of a long process in which its own *Memorik* developed in both function and form of memory. Today, the Bund's *Memorik* is probably best-known for its commemorative celebrations like the annual public gathering marking the Warsaw Ghetto Uprising still held today. Until his death, the gathering was hosted by

---

3   Roskies 1999, p. 136.
4   On post-war history see Slucki 2009a.

former ghetto fighter and Solidarność activist Mark Edelman and culminated in the collective singing of *Di shvue*, the Bund's hymn.[5] That said, gatherings to commemorate uprisings are not unique to Jewish post-war history whether in Warsaw, New York, or Buenos Aires.[6] Poignant mourning ceremonies became a significant component of *Memorik* in both the Bund and the socialist movement more generally by 1905. At that time, however, they represented explicitly activist practices, given that they gathered on-site present masses to commemorate and derive revolutionary action from their act of remembrance. *Memorik* was thus a means, not an end. Such ceremonies were also well-suited to dissemination through Bundist publications, thereby advancing the ongoing formation of the Bundist communicative mass that could in turn draw together further present masses.

Activist *Memorik* which understood memory as a call to action must therefore be distinguished from a *Memorik*, for which remembrance is largely an end in itself. While the latter preserves, the former seeks to overcome. These differences are easily demonstrated and (anticipating the conclusion of this chapter) build on one another historically. The former would ultimately lead to the latter over a process spanning more than 60 years of Bundist history. This becomes clear in the following study of Bundist publications which, as the Bund itself, were subject to ongoing transnationalisation over the course of which a cultural emphasis developed alongside the revolutionary impulse.

1 Three Bundist Regions and Three Bundist Publishing Models

The Bund's early periodicals were crucial to the emergence of a Yiddish secularism and demonstrated little ambition to establish a distinct Bundist *Memorik*.[7]

---

5 This continued after Edelman's death, and at least for the first years also included commemoration of Edelman, see Gebert 2010.
6 IWO, Buenos Aires, 1114; Bund. These celebrations were in turn used for community building within Bundist groups through, for example, mutual invitations to local activities like the annual Warsaw Ghetto Uprising memorial celebration. IWO, Buenos Aires, Gremios en proceso, Letter from A. Vilner and Sh. Shitnitski to Abraham Zak, 8 April 1961.
7 The range of Bundist periodicals is vast. Although no comprehensive academic bibliography exists, there are some scholarly depictions and contemporary lists from Bundists themselves who historicised their publishing work in as well as for their future publications. The press therefore not only became the subject of Bundist autobiography but also of the Bund's general historical narrative, see Bund Archives, New York, RG 1400, Me–18, 138, 'Amol': Die yidishe literatur in bundishe oysgabes nokh 1905. Radio Program, Shabbes, 12 September 1964 [Transcript]; N.N. 1907; Narsh 1917; Shulman 1951. Scholarly depictions of certain eras

This can be seen most clearly in a major Bundist publication called the '*Arbeter shtime*'. Founded in September 1897, it soon became the Bund's official organ after the organisation's founding later that year. It circulated illegally primarily in the Polish and Lithuanian Bundist regions until 1905 and was the early Bund's most important agitational medium alongside leaflets.[8] Accordingly, the party undertook extensive conspiratorial efforts to keep the '*Arbeter shtime*' alive despite countless arrests and targeted actions by Tsarist authorities.[9] Thanks to this activism, it appeared on a regular basis several times per year and reached the considerable size of 38 pages. Recognised as the Bund's essential periodical by both workers and intellectuals alike, it was referred to in a later writing as 'the new Holy Page' not only of the Bund but of Jewish modernity itself.[10] Unfortunately, specific analyses of Bundist press work are yet to be written. In one of the more extensive existing studies, Susanne Marten-Finnis notes that activist content was not a major factor in the significance of the '*Arbeter shtime*'. Such content instead tended to appear in local publications that were easier for workers to read. According to Marten-Finnis, the lengthy essays printed in the '*Arbeter shtime*' were primarily of interest to the Bundist intelligentsia.[11]

2   Setting the Course: '*Arbeter shtime*', '*Der avangard*', and Early American Publications

The '*Arbeter shtime*' would prepare the Bund and indeed the entire secular Jewish world for the path that lay ahead. The past, however, often received short shrift in this process. The minor presence of commemorative or historiographical texts, subsumed as *Memorik* texts in the following, distinguish the '*Arbeter shtime*' from the publications of the early Bund overseas. Bundist publications launched in emigration were a direct product of the Bundist emigrants themselves. Unlike the founders of the '*Arbeter shtime*' or the leading Bundist émigrés in Switzerland, they were often workers and their periodicals squarely

---

or aspects are found in Szajn 1983; Greenbaum 1991; Binyomen 1995; Marten-Finnis 1999, esp. pp. 77–90.
8   As in Tobias 1965, p. 394, fn. 3.
9   This in turn became the subject of numerous recollections from both the founders as well as readers of the '*Arbeter shtime*', see YIVO, Bund Archives, RG 1401, 32, 337; N.N. 1922; Gelernt 1957.
10 Gelernt 1957.
11 Marten-Finnis 2001, p. 18.

reflected the ideas, interests, and priorities of migrant workers. They benefitted from the fact that 'writing' grew in importance as a pattern of activism in emigration, where it provided opportunities to mobilise a dispersed and predominantly communicative mass. Accordingly, around one third of all respondents to the Bund Archive's questionnaires reported being active as an author following emigration – roughly 10 percent of them only turned to writing in exile, not in Eastern Europe. The increase must be granted particular weight given that many respondents referred solely to Eastern Europe and omitted activism in the New World altogether.[12]

Bundist emigrant groups' self-reliance motivated many attempts to establish a local Bundist press, some of which were path-breaking. The first Bundist periodicals for Argentinian readers in Buenos Aires simultaneously formed the beginnings of the Yiddish-language press in Latin America. In New York, by contrast, the socialist '*Forverts*' already dominated the streets. Unlike their primary-Bundist counterparts, several secondary-Bundist journals like '*Der veker*' were able to establish a foothold in certain niches.[13] This absence of official mouthpieces was due not only to the presence of other magazines, but also to the failure of their own projects. All US Bundist journals remained single issues before 1941.[14]

In order to study and compare differences and commonalities between the various press traditions, I draw on a statistically grounded media analysis referred to as a 'text ratio analysis'.[15] This procedure measures the amount of

---

12   Bund Archives, New York, RG 1400, MG2-428.
13   See Part III.9.
14   New York Bundists only founded the long-lived publication '*Unzer tsayt*' after World War II broke out.
15   This is guided by the procedure of 'hierarchical decomposition', whereby a hierarchy derived from the data is divided into distinct levels of content, encoded, and assigned a statistical value. The procedure is highly conducive to filtering out and distinguishing individual levels of meaning from the reported data. Owed to the large amount of data, I apply a rounding procedure which assigns individual items to a two-level hierarchical analytical grid (category and subtype). Each analysed item receives a definitive designation rounded from 0.1 to 0.25 pages depending on page size. This helps to detect which amount of space certain text types (in terms of category and subtype) occupy on an individual page, within a particular issue, across an entire year, etc. It represents a simplified version of the media content analysis used in communication sciences, and has the advantage of allowing for a clean and unambiguous analysis of entire bodies of text despite the undeniable expenditure of time it entails. Due to this distinction, in the following I will refrain from using the term 'media content analysis' and instead continue to refer to it as a text-ratio analysis, grasping the actual procedure more precisely. See Rössler 2005, pp. 15–23, pp. 73–76.

space occupied by different types of text in the Bund's periodicals. Each article is then assigned to a template developed on the basis of the sources themselves (mixed-method coding, see Table 3). To elaborate this classification scheme and the corresponding argument, I analysed various series of Bundist periodicals and compared them to periodicals from neighbouring movements like Labour Zionism, Jewish Communism, and anarchism. The derived categories and comparisons form the basis of the following argument.[16] My analysis focuses on selected and directly relevant Bundist periodicals in order to further specify the argument. If they ran for a longer period or even decades, I chose a number of representative years for further analysis.[17] Ultimately, Bundist media exhibits four main categories supported by various text sub-types. The first are *activist texts and reflections*, including reports and points of view from within the movement, the party, trade unions, etc. Second are *timeless texts* such as theoretical articles, visions for the future, reflections on the Yiddish language and editorial articles, as well as poetry and fiction. The third category are *contemporary texts* consisting largely of reports and news. Fourthly and finally is the category of *Memorik*, in which recollections and historiography are grouped together with obituaries, historical documents, and other texts with a commemorative focus.

Proceeding from this analysis, which applies a significantly more nuanced template than simply denoting agitational texts as 'worker texts' and theoretical texts as brain food for intellectuals, Susanne Marten-Finnis's claim that workers were less drawn to the '*Arbeter shtime*' due to its wealth of theoretical

---

16 Aside from the periodicals listed in the following footnote which are the primary focus of the analysis, the following series of journals represent the foundation of the analytical grid's development as well as the general corresponding argument. Bundist and secondary-Bundist: '*Der veker*', Vilnius, Warsaw (1905–6); '*Di hofnung*', Vilnius (1907); '*Di arbeyter shtime*', Petrograd (1917); '*Der veker*', New York (1921, 1927, 1937, 1941); '*Di naye shul*', Warsaw (1928–30); '*Kegn shtrom*', Warsaw (1930–33); '*Naye folksshtime*', Warsaw (1931, 1937); '*Labor Bund Bulletin*', New York (1947–52); '*Lebns-fragn*', Tel Aviv (1957, 1965–7). Labour Zionist: '*Der hamer*', Brăila (Romania) 1915–16; '*Unzer frayhayt*', Bialystok (1918); '*Unzer ruf*', Kaunas (1925); '*Unzer ruf*', Lviv (1927); Communist: '*Der hamer*', New York (1926–7); '*Nayvelt*', Buenos Aires (1927–9); anarchist: '*Golos trudos*', Buenos Aires (surviving issues 1926–9); '*Dos fraye vort*', Buenos Aires (1936–8). Yiddishist and Yiddish socialist: '*Dos yidishe vort*', Geneva (1915); '*Di yidishe tribune*', Paris (1915); '*Di tsykunft*', New York (1927, 1941)

17 These are, with regard to Eastern Europe: '*Di arbeter shtime*', Vilnius et al. (1899–1904). For Argentina: '*Der avangard*', Buenos Aires (1908–10, 1916–17, 1919–20); '*Argentiner veker*', Buenos Aires (1924); '*Sotsyalistishe bleter*', Buenos Aires (1930–2); '*Argentiner lebn*', Buenos Aires (1936–8); '*Tsayt-fragn*', Montevideo (1938). For the US: '*Fraynd fun bund*', New York (1904); '*Der kemfer*', New York (1906); '*Di Rotshester tsaytung*', Rochester, NY (1907); '*Unzer tsayt*', New York (1941, 1943, 1947, 1951, 1957, 1963, 1968).

TABLE 3 Schema of hierarchically structured text ratios in Bundist publications

Category	Subtypes
Category I: Activist texts and reflections	Opinion, discussion, standpoints on political parties/current affairs Socialist reports, worker issues, etc. General contemporary reflections, activist interpretations of the present Appeals, open letters, proclamations, etc.
Category II: Timeless	Fundamental questions, philosophy; Bundism, socialism, etc. Literature, poetry, fiction, stories Yiddish as spoken and literary language, reflections on Jewish secularism, theatre Editorial matters, advertising, etc. Visions of the future
Category III: Contemporary texts	Party reports, internal matters Reports and news from Poland, Russia, and other countries Miscellaneous, notes, press reports, reviews, etc.
Category IV: *Memorik*	Autobiographies, recollections Individual *Memorik* (biographies, obituaries, death notices) Substantive *Memorik* (objects, days, events) Historiography (Bund), historical documents, etc. Historiography (non-Bund) Miscellaneous, reports of *Memorik* events, reviews of historical works Specific special pages, fraternal greetings

content barely holds up. We can assume that workers generally tended to read publications more in touch with specific situations and developments on the ground, but the worker autobiographies alone tell us that exposure to pioneering texts – frequently of a commemorative or literary nature – often opened the door to Bundism. For this reason, drawing a strict distinction between theory and practice proves problematic with view to the '*Arbeter shtime*' and beyond. Not untypical for a Marxist movement, both were part of the Bund's activist complex in which theory and practice converged in multiple ways. That said, periodicals differed clearly across eras and regions. As revealed by a text ratio analysis of the Bund's early periodicals (Figure 5), these clear types represent manifestations of Bundism in each given situation.

The '*Arbeter shtime*' was clearly focused on category I, activist reflections, which at 69 percent of total page space dominated the publication's content. Texts which today are considered essential to Bundist history, by contrast – programmatic documents, utopian debates, and literary texts (categories II and III) – occupy relatively little space. *Memorik* only played a marginal role in quantitative terms, although a number of important congresses and even the first issue of a Bundist paper that explicitly described itself as an anniversary edition fall in this period. The few *Memorik* texts were thus of qualitative sig-

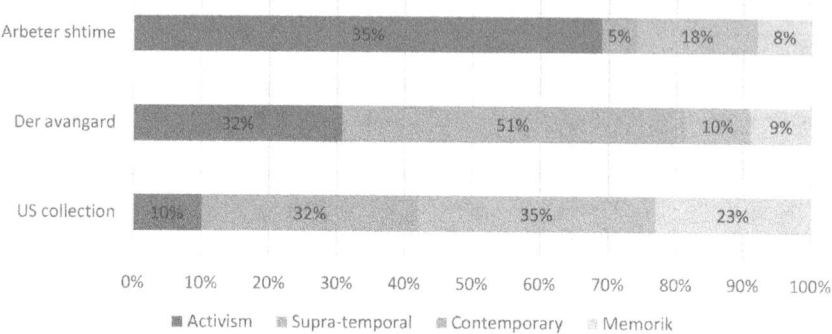

FIGURE 5   Text ratios of early Bundist publications, 1899–1910. 'Arbeiter shtime', 1899–1904; 'Der avangard', 1908–10; US total, 1904–7

nificance. Only one article is autobiographical. The rest depict past events before 1897 and thus beyond the Bund's own history, while integrating them into one unspecified narrative of historical resistance. Topics range from the Decembrists to illegal Yiddish literature in Russia prior to 1897.[18] Even the lone individual recollection published under the pseudonym of 'A Banished Worker' addresses no specific facet of the Bund, but rather recounts characteristic experiences of political exile and escape from Siberia.[19] The historical perspectives of the early Russian Bund were thus marked by strong affinities to an all-socialist and simultaneously Russian revolutionary history and historical understanding.

Contrasted to the publications produced in emigration, the differences between the three sites of Bundist history are striking. The Argentinian *Avangard* was an explicit workers' organisation in both objectives and membership. Its magazine, *'Der avangard'*, nevertheless features a high number of timeless articles (category II). This included a considerable amount of Yiddish-language prose and poetry as well as song lyrics from the outset. These were accompanied by lengthy texts on various theoretical questions, such as a regularly appearing column in which Stanislav Valski critically discussed the strand of anarchism particularly influential in Argentina at the time.[20] Once again, Marten-Finnis's assertion that workers were more attracted to simpler writing cannot be confirmed in the case of *'Der avangard'*, as the Argentinian group was closer to a workers' association than any other group in Bundist history. This is precisely why activist texts remained important in the group's publication.

---

18   N.N. 1900; N.N. 1902; N.N. 1901.
19   A farshikter arbeyter 1904.
20   First appeared in Valksi 1908.

They often dealt with the local trade unions and challenges facing socialists in Argentina. Reports from Eastern Europe, on the other hand, or articles with an explicit reference to the Bund in Eastern Europe, are rather scarce.[21]

A different orientation can be detected in the North American publications, where the dominant share was taken up by news (category III), mostly from Russia. This discrepancy between Argentina and the US was rooted in the respective publications' specific motivations. US Bundists focused less on instigating local activism targeting local conditions, but instead on raising funds for the Russian Bund. This is exemplified by differences in the use of poetry. In the US it focused on the Bund's hymn *Di shvue*, including the only rarely reproduced second stanza drawing on the struggle in the Tsarist empire for both its substance as well as its indignation.[22] In Argentina, we find numerous poems praising *yidishkayt* and rendering the production of Yiddish-language literature a transnational Bundist practice accessible from anywhere in the world. One example of this is Martin Galpern's extensive, ballad-like poem 'The Song of the Seamstress', which '*Der avangard*' printed in serialised form.[23]

These early publications carved the paths regional media would later follow. Activism was similarly emphasised in Eastern Europe, first and foremost in the Bund's official organ '*Di hofnung*' (The Hope), which circulated legally for a while beginning in 1907. Although the volume and absolute number of *Memorik* articles expanded over time (particularly during phases of legality), texts dealing with revolutionary activism always retained the strongest presence. The Bund's well-received daily newspaper the '*Folkstsuytung*' and later '*Naye folkstsaytung*' increasingly printed commemorative texts, including whole special issues. By and large, however, emphasis remained on constructive, day-to-day activism (category I), which remained the most important mode of community building in both Russia and Poland, complemented by the kind of news (category II) one would expect in a daily paper.[24]

---

21   If so then usually in letter form, such as Olgin 1909.
22   It reads: 'We swear to struggle for freedom and justice / Against all tyrants and their lackeys / We swear to defeat the dark force / Or fall with heroic bravery in the battle', 'Bund' brentsh S.P. un S.L. klub 1907b; or in the style of the sentimental poem Bundist and '*Forverts*' author A. Liesen composed for the Bund's fundraising ball (Liesin 1904).
23   Galpern 1909a; Galpern 1909b.
24   This became increasingly devoted to news of the struggle against anti-Semitism in interwar Poland, see Pickhan 2001, p. 300.

3 From Class Struggle to *Yidishkayt*: A Shift on the Río de la Plata

Bundist activists in Argentina were confronted with a number of major challenges, such as violent anti-socialist police raids in 1910 and the *Semana Trágica*, or 'Tragic Week' political pogrom in 1919. Internal conflicts over the Bund's relationship to the October Revolution ultimately triggered the collapse of '*Avangard*'. Only in 1924 would local Bundists reorganise the Argentinian movement by founding a Bund club and renew their attempts to establish a Bundist publication. This proved moderately successful in the last the pre-war decade, despite Uriburu's coup d'état and other looming obstacles like the country's partial ban on socialist activities.[25] Argentinian Bundist activism grew while the military government passed a series of special anti-socialist decrees. Attempts at repression only strengthened the resolve of the Argentinian workers' movement, growing to dominate the streets in the 1930s despite its internal strife and largely feeding into Peronism in the early 1940s.[26]

The Bund did not go along with this turn but nevertheless drew energy from the general resistance socialist groups organised. It also contributed to and benefited from growing transnational Yiddish-language activism, which found an important hub in the Yiddish culture of Buenos Aires. These priorities centred around Bundist initiatives and found expression in the movement's press: although Argentinian Bundists emphasised local issues, they simultaneously stressed that any local activism – say, for local Yiddish-speaking schools – was only conceivable in relation to transnational cultural work. The focuses of activism in the interwar period were thus unlike those of the 1900s.

Unfortunately, the history of Jewish socialism in Argentina is severely understudied. By the 1930s activists already seemed to be forgetting their past. When local Bundists pursued a renewed attempt to establish a workers' paper called '*Argentiner lebn*' in the midst of easing political tensions during the *década infama*, the editorial board proudly announced 'We're back' in large print on its front page.[27] The authors of the cover article recounted a history situating the publication as a direct descendant of the newspaper '*Argentiner veker*', published by the Argentinian Bund, as well as its immediate predecessor, '*Sotsyalis-*

---

[25] This tense relationship had an impact on the entirety of interwar Argentinian labour history, see Panettieri 2000; Matshushita 2006. It was not until 1956 that Argentinian Bundists were able to permanently establish the bi-weekly '*Unzer gedank*', appearing in Buenos Aires through the 1960s.

[26] Divided between 'old' and 'new' workers, the relationship between Perón and the socialist workers' movement was correspondingly tense, see Doyon 2006.

[27] N.N. 1936d.

tishe bleter'. The secondary-Bundist *Yidishn sotsyalistisher farband in Argentine* or YSFA published the latter. It was allegedly 'a bit luckier than its predecessors', and circulated for a full year in 1930.

Although these claims were made by 'contemporary witnesses' and *tuer* of all these periodicals in 1936, they were actually wrong. They were unable to explain how or when the *'Argentiner veker'* first appeared in the 1920s and could only vaguely indicate its founding by immigrant Bundists during the war. The paper allegedly 'muddled through for some time' before 'going down again'. They were particularly mistaken with regard to the *'Sotsyalistishe bleter'*, which circulated for at least two and a half years from April 1930 until at least October 1932.[28] Similarly, the authors claimed that the last series of *'Der avangard'* was issued from 1918 until September 1919 – an inaccurate claim, as it was not even published until 1919 and appeared until at least January 1920.

It may seem pedantic to point out these errors, but they contain a historiographical message. They are symptomatic of the role that earlier publications – that is to say, its own history – played in the present of the Argentinian Bundist press: none. At the very least they fulfilled no concrete function, apart from marking a point of reference for subsequent journals in the sense of a tradition in which newcomers could situate themselves and demonstrate they were not the first to pursue this work. The objective was to express that the struggle on the frontier had ended, but the activist deed would continue. Without much interest in details such as debates and conflicts, past publications and groups became commemorative objects designed to determine the origin of contemporary action.[29] The history of the Argentinian Bundist periodicals is both unique and remarkable, giving readers an impression of, firstly, Argentinian history's impact on Jewish immigrants, secondly internal processes of community building, thirdly local priorities, and fourthly its relationship to the Bund in Eastern Europe. The material I collected in various archives and collections allows me to reconstruct the connections between these journals in detail. A text ratio analysis of Bundist and secondary-Bundist publications between 1908 and 1938 reveals a unique 'Argentinian trajectory', placing a clear focus on timeless reflections and activist texts mainly around labour issues, while only gradually granting more space to *Memorik* (Figure 6).[30]

---

28 Copies of these issues are available. Israel Laubstein claims (unfortunately without sources) an active existence of over three years, see Laubstein 1997, p. 187.
29 Explicitly so in N.N. 1937a.
30 Complemented by a look at Montevideo, Uruguay. The small Bundist group here was closely linked to the significantly larger group in Argentina, and should be understood together with its Argentinian counterpart as a single Bund group representing the Bund in Latin America.

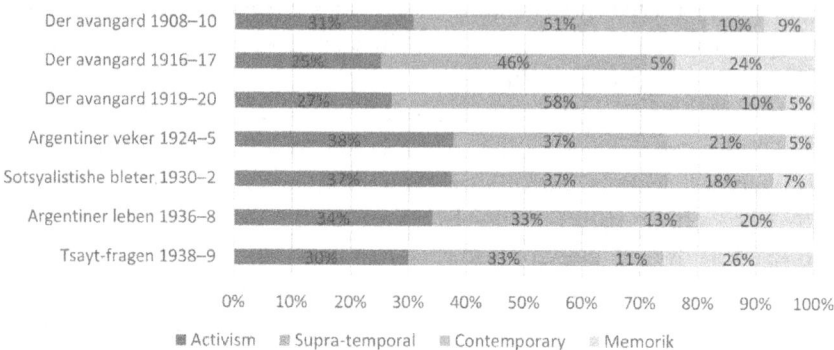

FIGURE 6   Text ratios in Bundist and secondary-Bundist periodicals on the Río de la Plata, 1908–39

Three essential points become evident here. Firstly, secondary-Bundist publications such as the bi-weekly '*Sotsyalistishe bleter*' hardly differed in profile from their Bundist counterparts like the '*Argentiner veker*', although the latter clearly identified itself as the '*Organ fun algemeynem yidishn arbeter "bund"*' on its title page. Secondly, the publications' main focus throughout the various periods was on contemporary, activist contributions and timeless reflections. '*Der avangard*' in the years 1916–17 represents a relative exception in this regard, although the statistically relevant texts mirror World War I and the trajectory of the Russian Revolution, addressing concrete current events. Thirdly, a shift in text ratios from 1930 onwards was accompanied by a rise in *Memorik*. This was around the same time that immigrants arriving in Buenos Aires in the wake of post-war turmoil, imperial decay, and US quota laws began to settle and establish roots. Demand for *Memorik* did not arise as a result of migration alone. These new immigrants had witnessed the collapse and destruction of the shtetl lifeworld, a decay depicted impressively by ethnographer, writer, and author of the Bund's hymn, An-Sky, along with many others.[31] This loss was addressed partly in *Memorik*, partly in poetry. But conditions in Argentina remained priority. Prior to 1939 activist and timeless contributions (category I and II) only ceded their dominance to *Memorik* to a limited extent, while their character changed over time.

Having focused on general reflections on class conditions and socialism in the 1920s, timeless texts shifted towards a cultural emphasis in the 1930s. New topics included the secular Jewish schools and other aspects of *yidishkayt* (see overview, Table 4). As the welcome addresses in the first issues of many

---

31   An-sky 2002; Gottesman 2003.

periodicals reflect, the substance of Yiddish-language socialism increasingly morphed into a Jewish-socialist secularism. Take for example *'Der avangard'*, where the editors' first sentence in the 1908 debut issue unwittingly and perhaps unknowingly marks the beginning of Yiddish-language periodicals in Latin America. It proclaimed the group's missionary intent and its active historical role: 'In publishing the *"Avangard"*, we seek to fulfil the great task demanded from us by history of disseminating the ideas of socialism among the Jewish population'.[32] This course was maintained by the *'Argentiner veker'* appearing in 1924, although community building came to replace proactive missionary objectives. It found expression above all in many texts on community banquets, Bundist celebrations, and in the section designed to promote community building known as 'From Party Life'. The latter also contained a list of Bundist contacts in Argentina to facilitate 'closer contact between party members'. Thus, post-immigration community building relied primarily on networks of previous affiliation while political affiliations were of only secondary importance.[33]

This became more pronounced in the 1930s. The opening passage of the 1936 *'Argentiner lebn'* makes it clear that the periodical's legitimation arose not from its pioneering character, its mission, or some general claim to a prerogative of interpretation, but rather from a gap to be filled with honourable actors who sought not to educate but to bond with their readers:

> We really cannot complain about a lack of Yiddish press in Argentina, as there are numerous press publications of various tendencies and shades today. Yet, at the same time, an authentic, sincere, candid Yiddish socialist press which speaks a clear language and thinks in socialist terms has so far been lacking. ... For only a socialist can represent the standpoint of a true socialist. ... We sincerely declare that we will raise our word, freely and unrestrictedly, without regard for our opponents. In veneration of personal, ideological [*ideyishe*] and social dignity, we will respond to ideologies, principles, directions, systems, and stories, but we will keep our weapons, our word, pure.[34]

This was seen as a specifically local task: 'We have returned to fill the gap in Argentinian Jewish life'.[35] The publication *'Tsayt-fragn'* later continued this

---

32 Der avangard 1908.
33 N.N. 1924.
34 N.N. 1936d.
35 Ibid.

shift towards a socialist but primarily Yiddish-secular lifestyle in South America in the years before World War II. Its very first sentence expressed the force of the new cultural *yidishkayt*, launching not with the usual call for socialism but instead:

> Keenly aware of the responsibility it entails, we assume the heavy burden of publishing a monthly magazine – a journal on social and cultural problems. [It will address] the historical process which the Jewish masses endure on a daily basis – the quotidian struggle for the right to live and work – the right to be free to build and shape our culture and education according to the countries from which we all come.[36]

Socialist publications increasingly became medias of cultural work, which was particularly strong in the secular Jewish schools.[37] The self-imposed educational mandate in favour of a secular Jewish modernity is also reflected in the distribution of texts: the number of timeless texts on theories and practices of revolutionary movements was virtually zero in the 1930s. Bundist institutionalised self-assurance had been realised and the unanswered questions revolved around the shape of Yiddish culture. While the latter were initially addressed only in the context of Yiddish-language theatre in the country's major cities, transnational aspects now began to emerge. Their weight grew significantly during a campaign to support the TSYSHO schools in Poland, and even more so after the visit of renowned journalist and Polish TSYSHO envoy Barukh Shefner.[38]

Interestingly, this was accompanied by the retreat of two other text types: first, the share of the once-crucial prose and poetry declined. Literature changed from an agitational tool to the object of cultural-political debates. This shift was rooted in the tremendous improvements to Argentina's Yiddish cultural landscape over the years. The large influx of immigrants in the interwar period, who often brought along role models from Poland, fostered the creation of cultural centres, publishing houses, and the Association of Jew-

---

36   N.N. 1938.
37   See Part III.12.
38   IWO, Buenos Aires, 1103 [Campagna de Ayuda – Shefner]; Escuelas Laicas en Argentine, Escuelas Laicas en Argentine y Polonia. On the 1931 campaign: IWO, Buenos Aires, Comite de Ayuda a las escuelas laicas Israeltita de Polonia y Argentina, 17, Hilfs komitet far di yidish veltlikhe shuln in Poyln: Barikht fun der aktsye durkhgefirt in Argentine fun sof may bis sof november 1931. For a more elaborate discussion see Part III.11 and III.12.

ish Authors founded by H.D. Nomberg. These new institutions were rooted in an older Yiddish culture in the city, which the *Avangard* group had fought to defend against trends towards Hispanisation. Their emergence, however, came with the decline of proletarian prerogatives. The workers' journals now largely retreated from using literature and arts as mere means of agitation and viewed this culture as a worthwhile point of departure for a new Yiddish working-class culture. The revolutionary substance of *doikayt* increasingly shifted to inner-Jewish topics (see Table 4). This was by no means merely a constriction of the Bund's perspective, but was grounded in the broadening of regional cultural work through transnational networks. Still, periodicals lacked news reports from around the world. Editors now subsumed the once-numerous brief reports on the global Yiddish workers' movement under larger sections which often focused on the situation in Spain, the global emergence of fascism, or growing anti-Semitism. The papers of course remained aware of international news, but the many short and timely reports made way for cultural questions as the new Bundist challenge.

Looking at Table 4, two mutually dependent developments deserve closer inspection. Firstly, the worker was not understood simply as a Yiddish-speaking class fighter but also a bearer of a secular, Jewish culture, although this conception by no means stripped workers of their economic or political interests. The Bund did not in any way become a pragmatic and culturalist association increasingly distanced from its own roots and past action patterns, as Daniel Blatman suggests.[39] Instead it expanded its role, seeking to represent not only the worker masses but the *yidishe folksmasn* (as opposed to Jewish elites) more generally – a term whose use would soar in the 1930s.

Secondly, both form and substance of *Memorik* changed. It referred less to the history of class struggles or pre-Bundist developments as the Bund began to discover a historicity in its own right, tying it and later many Bundists tightly to modern Jewish history. This shift, which also suggests some conclusions regarding other socialist movements, is analysed in more detail in the following.

---

39 Blatman 2003, p. xviii.

TABLE 4 Characterisation of Bundist and secondary-Bundist periodicals in Argentina, 1908–39

Publication	*'Der avangard'*, 1908–10	*'Der avangard'*, 1916–17	*'Der avangard'*, 1919–20
Subheading, editor	Organ fun di yidishe sotsyal demokratishe arbeyter organisatsyon in argentina 'avangard'	Organ fun der yud. s. d. arb. org. 'avangard'	Organ fun der yidisher sotsyalistisher arbeyter organisatsye avangard
Objectives	Promotion of Jewish socialism in theory and practice	Promotion of the idea of national-cultural autonomy, reflections on Jewish socialism	Continuation of Avangar under difficult condition
Community building	Community building around the *Biblioteca rusa* in Argentina, explicit reference to the *Partido Socialista*	Revolutionary community building based on Eastern European origin	Continuation of what ha been started
Memorik	*Memorik* as self-reflection and history of class struggle	History of Polish Jews, the Russian revolutionary movement and *Memorik* relating to important persons	*Memorik* hardly relevant
Relation to workers	Workers' organisations in Argentina, consolidation through class struggle	Discussion of worker issues and contemporary Jewry in Argentina	Brief information on current events
Role of Yiddish	Reflected mode of community building, promotion of a class-conscious Yiddish theatre	Emphasis above all on literature and poetry	Only language used, with exception of some poetry
Characterisation	Sophisticated, strictly socialist and focused on Argentina, mainly local authors, Bundist without party affiliation	Sophisticated journal with many renowned Bundist authors from around the world, Bundist without party affiliation	Slim, large-format paper with a large share of advertisements, Bundist without party affiliation

...entiner veker, 1924	Sotsyalistishe bleter, 1930–2	Argentiner lebn, 1936–8	Tsayt-fragn, 1938–9
...gan fun algemeynem ...ishn arbeter 'bund'	Tsveyvokhnshrift fun yidish-sotsyalistishn farband in Argentine	None [YSFA, editors almost identical to '*Sotsyalistishe bleter*']	Monatsshrift far gezelshaftlekhe kultur-fragen (Montevideo)
...istinct Bundist voice ...the Río de la Plata	Strengthening of Yiddish-socialist culture in Argentina, particularly with reference to the Bund and Bundism	Representation of a Yiddish, socialist voice, continuation of the tradition and extensive reflections	Reflection on and strengthening of the relation between Yiddish culture, worker issues, and Bundism worldwide
...flection on Bundist migration and sub...quent community ...ilding	Appeals for integration into pro-Yiddish-speaking socialism, explicit reference to the *Partido Socialista*	Struggle for Yiddish, against fascism and anti-Semitism	Local emphasis on Yiddish workers' community, transnational networking
...w-scale, related to ...dividuals and the Rus...n Revolution	Education and commemoration of socialist and Bundist personalities worldwide	Commitment to the Bund consistently increased, last issues exclusive special editions on Pinie Vald and the Bund	Very close to the Bund, primarily commemoration of deceased leaders
...ain addressee primar... newly arrived immig...nts to be activated and ...formed about global ...ents	Fight for workers' rights in Argentina, information on comrades in struggle worldwide	Activist integration into a growing cultural field, worldwide reports, key topic: the Spanish Civil War as class struggle	Workers as bearers of a secular Yiddish culture, information about and reflection on the state of the global workers' movement
...imarily as language ...ed	Cultural language, special emphasis on Yiddish working-class schools	Strengthening the secular Yiddish school system	Manifestation of a specific, popular culture expressed through schools and literature
...ternationally report...g and connected ...urnal of a small but ...nfident group, openly ...undist	Explicitly non-Communist, sophisticated workers' publication, secondary-Bundist	Socialist workers' paper with an emphasis on Yiddish culture, secondary-Bundist	Yiddish cultural publication for a working-class audience, secondary-Bundist

4 From a History *for* the Bund Towards a History *of* the Bund: The Five Nodes of Bundist Past

Overseas Bundist publications were forced to mediate between distinct spaces and times. The past was both heroised as well as a lost space. The present demanded critical intervention while the future motivated utopian activism. Five nodes of Bundist *Memorik* emerged in this process. The first of these was constituted by the significance of class struggles for the early Bund, the second by the rise of self-historicisation, and the third by the changing role of individual *Memorik*. A fourth node emerged around community-building processes on festive holidays, and a fifth in the founding and content of the periodical '*Unzer tsayt*' around which the new, non-Eastern European Bund formed from 1941 onwards.

4.1 First Node: The History of Class Struggles

In its early years, the Russian Bund primarily relied on the history of class struggles as its legitimatory framework. In line with Walter Benjamin, within the Bund dwelled 'both its hatred and its spirit of sacrifice ... nourished by the image of enslaved ancestors rather than that of liberated grandchildren'.[40] Frequent reference is made to Russian and German Social Democracy in the Bund's early periodicals. Numerous struggles of the 'forefathers' were a common theme, particularly in the organs of the Central Committee and Foreign Committee. Jewish history was only featured when it contained a revolutionary component.[41] Other common themes included the French Revolution, the Revolution of 1848, the Decembrists, major international figures, or stories of oppression. A substantial number of those texts were Yiddish translations from Russian and Western European journals.[42] The aim was to integrate the Bund among the political leading lights of revolutionary history.[43] This was not only an act of ideological and historical self-situating. It also served to raise political awareness, as reports of strikes and other forms of struggle were supplemented with explanations of their historical context.

The act of 'becoming conscious' repeatedly mentioned in worker autobiographies, i.e. learning to understand the social situation through a Marxist

---

40 Benjamin 2007, p. 260 (Thesis XII).
41 Such as in N.N. 1901; P. 1907.
42 Such as N.N. 1900; N.N. 1902c; N.N. 1906b. Well-known guest authors included Karl Kautsky (1906) and Franz Mehring (1906).
43 This also took place outside of *Memorik*, such as a lengthy report on the SPD's 1907 party congress spanning several issues: *Di hofnung*, Vilnius 4 (20 September 1907)–10 (3 October 1907).

framework, required a counter-hegemonic historiography. Only the combination of history, action, and utopia could 'blast open the continuum of history'.[44] This history of course diverged from hegemonic interpretations of history, whether Tsarist Russian, traditional Jewish, or Polish nationalist in terms of subject matter, language, and message. Bundist ideology's deviant utopian implications also ensured political persecution, pairing the organisation's historically conscious belief in progress with the looming danger of being discovered by authorities. The awareness of belonging to a historical process in turn reinforced internal discipline, a crucial aspect of the movement's conspiratorial work.

Initially roles were clearly defined, albeit not for very long: writers were mediating intellectuals, while workers in the shtetls were the masses to first 'be made conscious' before they could act as secondary intermediaries, as occurred in countless 'circles'.[45] This political training of workers by workers led to a formation in its own right that can be classified as the workers' movement inside the Bund. Their activism reflected a Jewish socialisation far more strongly than was the case with the often 'Russified', i.e. Russian-educated and socialised intellectuals.[46] The interplay between the two forces inside the Jewish workers' movement complemented by influences from, for example, Switzerland, Austria, and Germany fostered the development of a counter-hegemonic socialist consensus in which workers' interests, political objectives, and the creation of a Jewish secularism converged into one giant challenge. *Doikayt* emerged at this intersection.

Individuals play an insignificant role in the *Memorlk* of early publications. In this interpretation of history, the Bund was preceded by a primordial period of revolutionary movements whose heritage it now continued. In this sense the Bund styled itself as a mere mediator of history, rather than the subject of historical narratives as such. From this one could deduce that a movement first requires a longer history to be able to historicise itself. Looking at the Bund, however, this is misleading. Firstly, the Bund carried on ideas and practices from a specifically Jewish but dispersed workers' movement in Russia, yet rarely mentioned this legacy in its early publications. This must have been an active decision to favour a universalist Marxist past over concrete experiences and struggles of its predecessors. Secondly, the Bundist group *Avangard* in Argentina represents a Bundist counter-example. It began historicising itself from

---

44 Benjamin 2007, p. 261f. (Theses XV, XVI).
45 See Part I.2.
46 Mendelsohn 1965.

its publication's very first issue, only a few months after its founding.[47] Similar endeavours emerged only very tentatively in Eastern Europe.

4.2 Second Node: The Primordial Period – Creating a Founding Myth

The first step in this regard was the twenty-fifth issue of the *'Arbeter shtime'*, the Bund Central Committee's official publication. In 1901 this issue celebrated the journal's anniversary (it had by then appeared illegally for five years in Russia, despite many arrests) and its political orientation based on its heroic origins. Publishing this first purely commemorative issue of a Bundist periodical was not a matter of course, but in fact required a favourable resolution from the Bund's fourth congress. The resolution stipulated that, firstly, a special issue was to be produced marking the anniversary of the *'Arbeter shtime'* and that, secondly, it would be published in both Yiddish and Russian.[48]

Fraternal greetings from socialists across the globe take up large parts of the issue. Authors include Karl Kautsky, August Bebel, various RSDLP and Bund groups at home and abroad including a New York branch, *'Di tsukunft'*, smaller local associations, and a number of individuals. All messages praise the achievements and great future prospects for the Bund and *'Arbeter shtime'*. The paper's educational aspect can also be seen, as the editors introduce authors like Karl Kautsky in short paragraphs next to their messages. They evidently assumed that internationally known luminaries of Social Democracy would not be familiar to readers. This issue also demonstrated to its readers how deeply connected the young Bund already was to the world of Social Democracy. In stylistic terms, the issue did not yet seem to follow any identifiable routines. Party directives are printed indiscriminately next to international greetings and historical texts such as the history of the illegal Jewish press in Russia.[49] Both language and layout of the greetings appear 'raw', which is refreshing in linguistic terms but makes a challenging read due to the complete absence of accentuation. Nevertheless, this *'Arbeter shtime'* issue can be understood as the Bund's first self-historicisation, while simultaneously serving as a report on networking and other activities.

This aspect receded into the background somewhat around the 1905 revolution, only to be exceeded in issue 14 of *'Di hofnung'* in 1907, when the trailblazing Bundist publication briefly appeared legally in Russia for the first time. The issue celebrated the Bund's tenth anniversary, a demonstrative act in times

---

47   Vald 1908a.
48   *Arbeter shtime* 5, no. 25 (1901), p. 1, p. 37.
49   Ibid., party directions: p. 1, p. 37; fraternal greetings: pp. 3–10, pp. 33–7.

of increasing repression. Communal rhetoric and gestures of ongoing resistance against the Tsarist regime dominate the issue. An edited list of the Bund's earlier journals underscored the expression of a continuing struggle. Historicisation of the Bund's own publications and periodicals for the first time created a mode of participation through remembrance for authors and readers alike.[50] After all, one must keep in mind that the magazine was not read at home in a rocking chair but mostly in clubs and at illegal meetings, where collective discussion and now commemoration of the battles of 1905 occurred simultaneously. Fraternal greetings from Social Democrats abroad also provided assurance that Bundists were not alone.[51]

Periodicals featuring *Memorik* more prominently later became objects of recollections themselves, including reports of identity-forming experiences of reading and writing.[52] The commemoration of *Memorik* bridged a gap of several decades, rendering erstwhile consumers the new producers of the past. This turned the publications of the early days into living history and repeatedly reintegrated them and the risk-fraught experiences of reading them into the Bund. It fostered the notion of a distinct period in the Bund's primordial history spanning from its foundation in 1897 to its first historical apex, the revolution of 1905. This primordial phase came to an end with the banning of '*Di hofnung*' under prime minister Stolypin in 1907. Subsequent Bundist *Memorik* regularly cited these early days as the organisation's central origin myth, becoming one of the leitmotifs of Bundist identity.[53] This also led to the departure from *Memorik* as a means to integrate the Bund into a general history of class struggles towards a focus on developments and experiences within the movement itself. These 'primordial ties' created a sense of the Bund's own temporality circulating around the revolution of 1905, and either began in 1897 or appeared as a seemingly natural development from a primordial history prior to that year.[54]

---

50   T. 1907; N.N. 1907b.
51   *Di hofnung*, Vilnius 14 (1907); among them August Bebel, Paul Singer, and Karl Kautsky as well as many local and international Bundist groups.
52   Such as in T. 1907; N.N. 1922; Litvak and Salutski 1917; Medem 1948. Only '*Unzer tsayt*' would subsequently acquire a comparably significant role: Grosman 1945; Tenenboym 1968.
53   Interviews with older Bundists or even their sons revealed they were more able to relate to the early days of the Bund, which none of them had actually experienced, in far more detail than their own activity after the Holocaust. The contemporary periodisation of the Bund was similar, such as in N.N. 1907a; N.N. 1907c. The latter text constructed a concise yet comprehensive history of the Bund and was thus reprinted in the US: 'Bund' brentsh S.P. un S.L. klub 1907c.
54   Woodhouse and Tobias 1966.

4.3 Third Node: The Power of Individuals – Creating Origin Myths

The situation called for new heroes and myths. This led to a 'cult' around specific individuals that differed dramatically from later socialist or Communist cults of personality. Due to the aforementioned dearth of studies on socialist *Memorik*, historiography tends to graft certain aspects of Bolshevik history onto the history of the Russian workers' movement as a whole. Correspondingly, Orlando Figes and Boris Kolonitskii argue in their study of the freedom-fighter cult that the underground political culture of Tsarist Russia was primarily responsible for the emergence of leader figures:

> The cult of the fallen hero was essential to that underground, as each successive generation of recruits looked at them as model 'fighters for the people's cause'. As in pre-revolutionary France, there was a huge illegal literature of hagiographies, histories and legends, broadsides and prints, celebrating the exploits of Pugachev and Razin, the Decembrists, Nechaev, the SR terrorists and other martyrs of the revolutionary underground in Tsarist Russia. ... He or she was a symbol of 'the cause' – an embodiment of the courage and self-sacrifice demanded of its leaders – from which people derived inspiration and support.[55]

This brief synopsis of 125 years of revolutionary history is enticing, but as always the devil is in the details. As depicted in the following, *Memorik* was by no means tied to illegality in the Bund, the largest Social Democratic movement in the Tsarist empire. On the contrary: it proved particularly successful under conditions of legality. Moreover, Bundist presentation of martyrs made no clear distinction between leaders and ordinary activists, instead serving to obscure this distinction. *Memorik* increasingly became a cross-class mode of participation formed not in clear channels of sender and recipient but rather in a network.

The past was more than a tool of those craving power. The workers openly demanded a better understanding of it in their struggles to improve their living conditions. This can be observed, firstly, in the many worker autobiographies stressing how the authors' conversion to 'class-conscious' workers occurred while reading. Other activists' actions and memories so deeply formed Bundist self-consciousness that even in the United States, where the usual Bundist periodicals from Poland sold tepidly at best, *Memorik* issues became veritable

---

55   Figes and Kolonitskii 1999, p. 74.

bestsellers.⁵⁶ Particularly prior to 1917, these texts showed little interest in the experiences or the memories of Bundist leaders. They aimed at readers' feelings, allowing literary martyrs to have the same effect as real ones. This blurring of reality and fiction into functional and 'moving' literature was embraced by workers and intellectuals alike. Shoemaker Hersh Mendel, for example, recapitulated his youth: 'I read a great deal of belletristic and scientific literature at the time. The writers whom I loved most of all were those who placed their talents at the service of the struggle for freedom, above all the Russian writers'. Well-educated readers had similar experiences. Take Viktor Shulman, who emphasises that Plekhanov's political writings had just as much impact on him as Stenyak's novels (the alias of nineteenth-century revolutionary terrorist Sergey M. Kravchinsky), which 'nurtured [Shulman's] revolutionary romanticism'.⁵⁷ Decisive for the reader was, firstly, palpable authenticity, and secondly the potential for identification provided by the individual being 'remembered'.⁵⁸ As a major means of Bundist mobilisation, the personalisation of *Memorik* connected the printed word more to the emotionality of recipients than to the factuality of events. This blurred the distinction between factual and fictional experiential literature. The latter became increasingly important after the 1905 revolution. It ranged from early narratives and the fictional autobiography of a cigarette maker to the American Yiddish-language children's book *Berele*, in which N. Khanin tells the fictional story of a Bundist working-class child in biographical style.⁵⁹

This construction of identificatory figures of course did not rely on fiction alone, but required real, specific individuals. One possibility of doing so was through a slowly developing revolutionary obituary culture. Its own fallen played only a marginal role in the Bund's earliest publications, but as soon as the organisation began writing its own history it also began to include its dead. From 1901 onwards, a massive increase in obituaries can be observed in the Bundist press. The victims were often young workers who died in street battles or from starvation. They were neither forefathers nor leaders of movements or revolutions, but rather 'Bundists from next door'. Their biographisation became a specific genre that we can call 'proletarian short hagiography'.⁶⁰ Obituaries

---

56 Bund Archives, New York, RG 1400, ME-18, 23; 28.
57 Mendel 1989, p. 63; Shulman 1945, p. 51.
58 I thank Jeffrey Brooks for several inspiring conversations on the significance of these easily accessible heroes in newly literate Russia. On this aspect see Brooks 2003.
59 Der evig yunger 1906; Nin 1907; Gozhansky 1927; Khanin 1938.
60 The Soviets took this quasi-religious narrative mode to unprecedented levels, but it is not true that they invented it (as is often claimed), see Halfin 2000, p. 118; Corney 2004, p. 41 f.

such as that of rank-and-file Bundist Nathan Leyvik who died in Southern Russia in 1901 at age 23, or the later famous Hirsh Lekert who was executed in Vilnius in 1902, provided great potential for identification precisely because the victims had not been famous movement veterans.[61] Apart from Hirsh Lekert, none of them would acquire posthumous glory. Generally active only at the local level, the young worker victims were unknown to readers. Yet this is precisely what provided the possibility of identifying with the dead, for in death – and through formulations along the lines of 'our *khaver*', killed as a result of certain generally known conditions demanding opposition and resistance – they could be reintegrated into the community and the common sense of belonging. Language made it possible to abstract from the distant individual case and render it identifiable with the reader's own experience. This turned a comrade's death into a call to arms. Owed precisely to these texts' partial pomposity, it is rather unfair to insinuate a linguistic anachronism on the part of the Bund as Susanne Marten-Finnis does. On the contrary, the texts exhibited significant activation potential and directly addressed the heart of the matter. Their language was far from a remnant of the past and evoked the latter in an emotionally charged way, actively drawing the reader into the mourning process and the associated outrage.[62] This connects the tiny, melodramatic and nowadays forgotten obituaries of rank-and-file victims to the great narrative traditions which, as Walter Benjamin noted, are guided not by life but by death:

> Death is the sanction for everything that the storyteller can tell. He has borrowed his authority from death. In other words, his stories refer back to natural history.[63]

The Bund harnessed this pathos while simultaneously rejecting its ultimate point of reference, stating that its young fallen were robbed of their lives not by the ineluctable course of natural history, but as a result of changeable social conditions.

Around 1905–7 in Russia and almost simultaneously overseas, a new participative culture of (most likely) paid obituaries written by readers for readers

---

61   *Arbeter shtime* 6, (1901), p. 17. Obituaries only began to grow in prominence in '*Der veker*' and '*Di hofnung*' around 1905. For Lekert, this possibility of anonymous abstraction applies only to his early period before he became a hero to various movements. At first, the Lekert case was even noticed – with indignation, but in an experienced manner – in distant New York, see N.N. 1902b.

62   Susanne Marten-Finnis ascribes an anachronistic language to the Bund and a more adequate form to the Zionist movements. Membership mobilisations in pre-revolutionary Russia, however, suggest otherwise. See Marten-Finnis 2001, p. 25 ff.

63   Benjamin 2006, p. 151.

soon emerged from those short obituaries by the editorial staff of given periodicals. As with the growth of advertisements, such obituaries were rare at first. The *'Arbeter shtime'*, for example, could afford to dispense with advertising altogether. As an illegal paper it relied on donations and party resources, not an independent budget. This marked a clear distinction between the legal publications on every continent. The latter not only mobilised for the class struggle, but also praised the merits of consumption – whether through advertisements for tailors, shoemakers, and doctors, oversized promotions for modern gramophones, or even full-page ads for Quilmes, a popular Argentinian brewery.[64] Periodicals in emigration depended on financial self-reliance. As for *'Der avangard'* in Argentina, the journal was not the mouthpiece of a party but rather the hub of an emerging movement. Following several fits and starts advertisements became increasingly important, constituting more than one quarter of the entire (relatively short) third issue of *'Der avangard'*.

That said, advertisements were by no means exclusively of a commercial nature. They also facilitated indirect public communication among *khaverim* who lent each other support in good times and bad. Obituaries were particularly crucial to community building from below via inclusion of the deceased. They spurred the formation of networks within the Bund. In form and function, such obituaries had little in common with official extra pages or even special issues honouring deceased leaders. They differed qualitatively in that famous personalities were honoured and acknowledged as representing the Bund as a whole. Unknown individuals, on the other hand, posthumously became at least temporarily publicly visible Bundists through obituaries. This served to reinforce the Bund's sense of community in emigration, as all kinds of bridges and links expressed both empathy and *khavershaft*. Correspondingly, an announcement framed in black in a 1925 issue of the *'Argentiner veker'* reads: 'In deep mourning, we remember our mother Khay Sarah Kristal, who died so young. Instead of flowers, we will give 5 $ to the *Argentiner veker*'.[65] The deceased, who is not identified as a Bundist at any point, is honoured and remembered through the act of financial support to the local Bundist community that found expression in institutions such as the *'Argentiner veker'*.

Such announcements naturally also articulated emotions, sympathies, and condolences. These feelings did not count as mere private matters, but rather were part and parcel of *khavershaft*. Accordingly, we find three separate announcements in the 1936 *'Argentiner lebn'* – one from the YSFA, one from the

---

64   *Di hofnung*, Vilnius 1 (1907), p. 4; *Der avangard*, 2, no. 1 (1909), p. 36.
65   *Argentiner veker* 2, no. 4? (1925), p. 8.

publication's editors and administrators, and one from several *khaverim* along with family members – publicly mourning the death of renowned Bundist Yosef Horn's mother. Similarly, the following issue printed a note of sympathy from the *Abteylung parke tshakabuka*, the TSVISHO's kindergarten, expressing its condolences to 'the teacher Vasershpring for the death of your father'.[66] The self-referentiality of this form of local *Memorik* is made particularly clear by a line appearing in the aforementioned issue of '*Argentiner veker*' in 1925: 'We express our deepest sympathies with our mother in Warsaw on the death of her sister *Hanah Mandelmild*'. How exactly this message was to reach Warsaw remains a mystery, as the '*Argentiner veker*' was distributed and read exclusively in Argentina. Global interconnectivity therefore relied on the agency of the sympathisers themselves, while emotions always also referred to the larger association of the transnational Bundist community.

The ongoing process of building a community both of the dead as well as with reference to the dead even increased in *Memorik* referring to deceased leaders of the Bund. As depicted above, early Bundist *Memorik* spoke about individual persons only as parts of the movement. It also integrated non-human Bundist actors such as major periodicals into this biographical logic. That the latter were viewed as comrades-in-arms is illustrated best by none other than Vladimir Medem. He did not seek to compile a 'history' of the '*Lebnsfragn*' he founded after World War I, but rather a 'biography'. Its introduction opens with the following passage:

> A newspaper can also have a biography. For it is not only a piece of paper covered with black characters. A newspaper is a living being. It has its childhood just as it has more mature years. It has its own face and character ... there is a particular imprint on its entire 'self': that mysterious 'something' with which every individual, every single being [*yokhed*] distinguishes itself from the next.[67]

This individualisation of a publication – a veritable hybridisation – was necessary to attribute agency to the paper within the Bund. It contributed to the growing biographisation of Bundist *Memorik* after World War I. Among other factors, the ageing of the membership facilitated this trend. It reflected the increased popularity of evoking the Bund's primordial freedom struggles. In turn, the anonymous victims of the class struggle receded from the Bund's *Memorik*. Following World War I, special issues and inserts honoured the old and sometimes deceased heroes on a hitherto unknown scale. The Bund's his-

---

66   *Argentiner lebn* 1, no. 9 (1936), p. 7; *Argentiner lebn* 1, no. 10 (1936), p. 7.
67   Medem 1948, p. 10.

tory was depicted as a history of Bundists, finding its most pronounced expression in the bulky and portrait-filled special issue of the 'Naye folkstsaytung' commemorating the Bund's fortieth anniversary. Throughout November 1937 the Polish Bund's daily paper was filled with countless remembrances, historiographic texts, announcements, and reports covering the celebratory congress in Warsaw that commenced on 13 November – presumably the largest Bundist gathering ever held in Eastern Europe.[68] Yet at the heart of these texts and speeches lay the *singular* history of the Bund. As soon as this history needed stories and examples, the editors relied on certain figures and well-known faces. This found an epochal expression in a unique special edition of the 'Naye folkstsaytung' that featured seemingly endless photographs of deceased Bundist leaders in an iconic style.[69]

This issue marked the pinnacle of a tendency beginning in 1922 towards increasing heroisation and glorification of leading Bundist personalities.[70] The tendency was not least owed to the fact that well-known veterans were growing quite old by this time, such as Vladimir Medem who died in 1923 and Beynish Mikhalevitsh in 1928. Special texts commemorated them after their passing, first on the immediate occasion of their deaths and later on each anniversary – an honour later bestowed on other important Bundists' birthdays.[71] Here we find a significant distinction between overseas and Eastern European Bundist publications. The aforementioned pattern of prioritising activist texts exemplified by the 'Arbeter shtime' was repeated in interwar Poland, particularly in the 'Naye folkstsaytung' of the 1930s. Apart from the occasional special editions, the publication features relatively little *Memorik*, nor do reflections on Yiddish life or Yiddish-language literature assume a significant role. Everyday practices also seemed to not represent a memorable factor at this point. Although several contributions addressed it, such as in reprints of excerpts by the Jewish (albeit not Bundist) socialist revolutionary Eva Broido, practice would fail to achieve any particular significance in the editorial decisions of the Polish Bund's main publications.[72]

The situation in emigration, however, was altogether different. 'Der avangard' began discussing its own history in its very first issue, although it gave

---

68 See numerous issues of the 'Naye folkstsaytung'. On the celebrations themselves see Pickhan 2001, p. 170.
69 Naye folkstsaytung, 19 November 1937.
70 A particular milestone is *Arbeter luakh*, 3 (Warsaw: Farlag Lebns-fragn, 1922).
71 Both were commemorated extensively, such as in Kossovski 1928.
72 Broido 1931a; Broido 1931b. Broido's Russian-language memoirs were widely popular, appearing in English as *Memoirs of a Revolutionary* (Broido 1967).

organisations rather than individual activists primary focus.[73] It was not until the mid-1920s that Argentinian Bundist authors discovered the early Argentinian period as an origin story in its own right. The most illustrative example is probably Pinie Vald's memoirs. Shaped by his own experiences, he presents the early history of Buenos Aires Bundism solely through the narratives of individual, prototypical activists, whom he depicts – fully in the style of proletarian short hagiography – as simultaneously heroic and tragic miniature biographies.[74]

In Argentina it was only in the mid-1930s that texts would shift towards histories of noteworthy Bundists. Several consecutive issues of *'Argentiner lebn'* established the new genre in the Argentinian Bundist press, although *Memorik* occupied no significant role whatsoever in the periodical's first three issues.[75] In the fourth issue, the *'Argentiner lebn'* commemorated the first death anniversary of the famous Polish Bundist *Khmurner* (Yosef Lestshinsky). The editors printed a portrait alongside the piece – quite remarkable given that these sorts of periodicals featured very few images for financial reasons.[76] The theme was revisited in the following issue, albeit not in the form of a text about a distant Bundist but instead marking the approaching birthday of Argentinian *khaver* Yitskhok Blind. The article again featured a photograph, although the occasion for the piece was not even the day itself but merely the announcement of a public banquet.[77] We can assume that the importance of the banquet lay in honouring Blind as much as in the fundraising that usually took place at such events. These kinds of personalised honorifics increasingly served Bundist community-building efforts in Argentina, and received a significant boost during the visit of Polish TSYSHO representative Barukh Shefner.

Like Benjamin Tabachinsky before him, Shefner was on a fundraising tour for the network of Bundist schools in Poland.[78] Along with a second announcement of the festivities commemorating Yitskhok Blind, this visit occupied much of issue 6, taking up roughly the same amount of space as the detailed

---

73 Vald 1908a; Vald 1908b.
74 Vald 1929a.
75 The only exceptions are two autobiographical reports on the school system in Poland by TSYSHO representative Barukh Shefner, explained by the fact that Shefner was conducting a much-noticed fundraising tour across Argentina at the time, see Shefner 1936a.
76 Bigelmeyer 1936b. This important Bundist thinker and translator of socialist classics into the Yiddish language would later receive his own honours from the New York Bundists in the *Khmurner bukh* (1958).
77 B. 1936.
78 N.N. 1936a; N.N. 1936e.

reports on the Spanish Civil War in the following issue.[79] Published after Blind's honorary banquet, issue 7 was dominated by reports of the celebration and featured several illustrated articles. Together these reports on what was essentially a festive dinner occupied noticeably more space than a lengthy article on celebrations of the Bund's thirty-ninth anniversary – which, of course, occurred not least through reference to personalised histories.[80] This emphasis seems to have been to readers' liking and would henceforth shape the local Bundist press. The most conspicuous example appeared a year later with an entire issue commemorating Pinie Vald's fiftieth birthday.[81] It contains numerous photographs, advertisements, acknowledgements, and fraternal greetings from across the Bundist world. No other topic is mentioned. The subsequent issue would continue and amplify this trend. Now twice as large, it celebrated the Bund's fortieth anniversary in similar fashion by devoting the whole issue to one occasion and personalising memory.[82]

With the formation of an official Bundist club in Argentina in the early 1920s, the journals also began personalising the history of the Eastern European Bund. Following the October Revolution and later the Bund's twenty-fifth anniversary, the 'Argentiner veker' as the messenger of this new era of remembrance now addressed the Bund's Russian origins with an autobiographical account of the dispute between the Bund and the RSDLP by Bundist Zelenski.[83] The 'Argentiner veker' did not survive for very long, however, thus robbing the Argentinian Bundists of an essential platform for articulating their interpretation of history. Confronted with Bundists' growing hunger for collective remembrance, the organisation responded in style: although Bundists failed to establish another Argentinian periodical in the 1920s, a bulletin appeared in 1928 marking the death of Beynish Mikhalevitsh which, resembling the New York 'Rotshester tsaytung' in 1907, had the appearance of a periodical complete with date and issue number, but explicitly stated its character as a special issue 'in memory of the deceased *khaver* Beynish Mikhalevitsh' in the subheading. The piece not only supplied a biography of the late comrade, but also featured excerpts from the eulogy given by Polish Bund leader Henryk Erlich, as well as numerous condolence notes from Argentinian Bundists. The issue thus symbolised transna-

---

79 Geni 1936.
80 Horn 1936. On Blind see Bigelmeyer 1936, p. 4 as well as two additional articles on p. 5 and p. 7, among them an impressive 16 fraternal greetings from various institutions and individuals.
81 *Argentiner lebn* 15 (11 September 1937).
82 *Argentiner lebn* 16 (October 1937), pp. 1–16.
83 Zelenski 1924.

tional interconnectedness through collective grieving, underlining the extent to which the Bund had become (among other things) a transnational community of feeling.[84]

We can see similar tendencies in the United States, with the important difference that the even stronger personalisation of Bundist history occurring here tended to ignore the history of the Bundists in the US itself. Important actors of the early Bund such as Abraham Caspe or Israel Bergman never received the honours of Bundist *Memorik*, whereas Eastern European Bundist leaders found recognition far beyond tightly knit Bundist circles. Most importantly, the New York '*Forverts*' first serialised Vladimir Medem's famous autobiography even before it appeared as a popular book.[85]

Generally speaking, the personalised history of the Bund contained something Thomas Goetz calls the 'poetry of the necrology':

> The linguistic-symbolic practice of necrology is understood as the paradigmatic core of a specific form of cultural work that derives significance and meaning from a person's death by securing their identity beyond death, restructuring the community, alleviating existential anxieties, and thereby helping to stabilise the continued existence of the community.[86]

Goetz's enlightening analysis refers primarily to public personalities and laments a lack of sources on obituaries of figures not tied to a specific national public.[87] Looking at the countless obituaries and the general culture of personalised *Memorik*, we can expand this notion. Here obituaries served the same symbolic community-building function he identifies, and endowed lesser-known Bundists with collective meaning through public commemoration. The large number of obituaries also facilitated international contacts.

We can therefore identify three distinct fields of this poetic Bundist necrology: firstly, that of proletarian short hagiography pertaining mainly to activism and underground struggle contexts, secondly personal and emphatic messages of condolence both in texts and announcements facilitating community building beyond the actual arena of struggle, and thirdly commemorations of Bundist luminaries whose obituaries, as bearers of a Bundist past, forged a his-

---

84 *Byuletin tsum shalushim fun farshtorbenem khaver Beynish Mikhalevitsh* 1, November 1928, IWO, Buenos Aires, Fondo Escuela Sholem Aleykhem shulbibliotek.
85 For a more extensive analysis of Medem's autobiography see Wolff 2007.
86 Goetz 2008, p. 12.
87 Goetz 2008, p. 15.

tory of the Bund through its members' memory. These grew slowly at first, but would eventually become the main theme of Bundist *Memorik*.

The idea that every Bundist was at the same time bearer of a part of Bundist history stands in stark contrast to the construction of freedom fighters in the style Figes and Kolonistkii describe. In fact, this may well have constituted the central difference between Communist and socialist *Memorik*. The Bund understood remembrance as a form of activism rather than a staged production in support of those in power.[88] The dead were first and foremost the dead – reintegrated into the Bundist activist complex through constant recollection. From there they accompanied the Bund on its journey. In Bruno Latour's words, the commemorated were on the one hand objects of action (remembrance). On the other hand, they became Bundist actors in the sense that they embodied Bundist histories. They were quasi-objects, 'hybrids, composites of the spoken and the real. Those are the things that weave and stabilise the social thread'.[89] In the Bund's case this social thread was a network, not a pyramid of hierarchical power.

4.4 Fourth Node: Festivals and Memorials

Biographisation was accompanied by an emphasis on specific days of remembrance and the publication of special editions marking the occasion. The role model in this undertaking was the aforementioned 1907 issue of '*Di hofnung*'. This emphasis on events became popular only after the October Revolution, as distinct wings of Marxism argued over interpretations of the movement's history. The Bund recognised the mobilising potential of such memorial holidays and special issues relatively late. It first had to overcome its existential crisis after Red October. An important step was a bulky issue of the *Arbeter luakh* (Workers' Calendar), published in Poland in 1922 to commemorate the twenty-fifth anniversary of the whole Yiddish workers' movement. Upon closer inspection, however, it is actually a history of the 25-year-old Bund.

1922 was indeed a milestone for Jewish-socialist *Memorik*, for both the fifth anniversary of the 1917 revolutions as well as the twenty-fifth anniversary of the Bund's founding took place in this year. Cultural activists in Moscow clearly recognised the opportunities this presented for Bundists-turned-Bolsheviks. Political festivals had accrued tremendous significance even in the early Soviet Union, attracting the attention of the highest authorities and thereby contributing to their increasing bureaucratisation. In 1922 the Central Office of

---

88 Figes and Kolonitskii 1999.
89 Roßler 2008.

the Jewish section of the Communist Party (*Yevsektsiya*) launched an initiative to appropriate the Bund's anniversary for its own purposes. At a meeting held on 22 July 1922, the leaders of the *Yevsektsiya* decided to publish an anthology 'to win over old party members through a collection for the twenty-fifth anniversary of the Bund'.[90] They obediently asked the Communist Party's Department of Agitation and Propaganda to assemble an editorial team, proposing ex-Bundists Esther Frumkin and Moshe Rafes from their own ranks as experts on the matter.[91]

But recruiting old members through remembrance and reflection would not be so easy. The party's higher ranks were suspicious of the project's potential, and chose to determine the general thrust of the book in advance. The Secretariat of the RCP(b) rejected the *Yevsektsiya*'s request on 9 August 1922. The centre of power in the RCP(b), the Central Committee, backed this rejection two days later. Instead, the responsible ranks proposed that the Agitprop Department and the *Yevsektsiya* central office 'publish an anthology with critical articles about the "Bund" without tying it to the twenty-fifth anniversary'.[92] These alterations to the publication's content and timing infuriated the secretary of the Central Office, Avrom Merezhin, who immediately objected in a letter to the secretary of the RCP(b) Central Committee, Valerian Kuybyshev, on 14 August 1922:

> The formulation of the Orgburo resolution of 9/VIII on the anthology marking the twenty-fifth anniversary of the Bund gives the impression that the Central Office had proposed a celebratory volume and the Orgburo decided that a collected volume containing critical articles was necessary. But the Central Office resolution from 2 July on attracting old party members[93] already makes it evident that the *Yevsektsiya* Central Office expects an anthology of critical articles. This was also reiterated by Comrade Merezhin in his contribution at the Orgburo meeting of 9/VIII. He also pointed out that the Central Office is currently publishing the article 'Marxism and the National Question' by Com. STALIN in Yiddish, which sharply criticises the position of the Bund. The only difference between what the Central Office proposed and what the Orgburo

---

90 On the Bolsheviks' initial difficulties winning over Jewish cultural workers see Moss 2009, esp. pp. 26–33.
91 RGASPI, Fond 17, opis' 84, delo 165, l. 51.
92 RGASPI, Fond 17, opis' 84, delo 165, l. 50.
93 Refers to RGASPI, Fond 17, opis' 84, delo 165, l. 51.

resolved is that the former suggested publishing the volume on the day of the Bund's twenty-fifth anniversary, whereas the latter resolved not to tie the anthology to the anniversary.[94]

By 1922 the Bolsheviks openly opposed the Bund as an allegedly counter-revolutionary force. This meant that accusations of printing a celebratory publication could indeed prove dangerous for the members of the Central Office. Merezhin sought to defend himself, rather than the project. As the Central Office never intended to celebrate the Bund in the first place, following long internal debates he finally attached a draft resolution requesting the anthology be separated from the Bund's twenty-fifth anniversary.[95]

This episode demonstrates not only the hopes and anxieties former Bundists attached to a historicisation of the Bund in the early Soviet Union, but also the pitfalls awaiting those who sought to initiate it. Mistrust towards these Jewish activists would grow over the years, as the biographies of the two aforementioned appointees Moshe Rafes and Esther Frumkin demonstrate. They stand for both the successful recruitment of former Bundists to the Bolshevik cause, as well as the associated tragedy.

Esther Frumkin was an eminent authority in the Bund and enjoyed the honour of being one of the first Bundist women to publish her personal memoirs.[96] She also participated in the first, pioneering Yiddish language conference held in Czernowitz in 1908. There, Frumkin opposed other conference attendees who regarded the Jewish population as a nation and instead demanded that the Bundist *doikayt* policy be extended into Yiddish literature.[97] Like Moshe Rafes shortly thereafter, after 1917 she chose the 'left' path while simultaneously seeking a balance between both parties. Although Frumkin joined the *Kombund* as early as 1917, in 1921 she continued to insist that the Bund would exist as long as a Jewish proletariat did.[98] Nevertheless, she became a leading figure of the *Yevsektsiya* together with Rafes. Rafes for his part can be considered a successful recruitment case. As an old Bundist and member of the Bund's Central Committee between 1912–19, he initially opposed the October Revolution (very much to the perplexity of Hersh Mendel), even fighting against the Bolsheviks

---

94 RGASPI, Fond 17, opis' 84, delo 165, l. 49.
95 RGASPI, Fond 17, opis' 84, delo 165, l. 49.
96 The first appeared in a far-left Bundist publication she continued to publish in: Esther [Frumkin], 'Fun mayn togbk', *Unzer shtime*, Vilinus 2, 3 (1918), p. 2.
97 ERF 1908.
98 Gechtman 2012.

in Ukraine as 'leader of the Bund in Southern Russia'.[99] He ultimately converted and joined the RCP(b) in 1919, recruiting many former party members as a fierce critic of the Bund.[100]

None of this could protect them from the terror. At Trotsky's side Rafes first emerged as an important figure in the Comintern and vice-chairman of Agitprop, before ultimately falling victim to Stalin. Rafes was expelled from the party in 1927 and imprisoned two years later, before facing a show trial in 1937 and dying in detention in 1942.[101] Esther Frumkin's fate was similar: accused of belonging to the 'unreconstructed Bundists', she was put on trial in 1938 and died in an internment camp in Karaganda, Kazakhstan.[102] Like many other former Bundists, these two were tragically murdered by the Stalinist regime while their turn to Communism ensured their exclusion from Bundist *Memorik* at the same time.[103]

The situation in 1922, however, was quite different. Ex-Bundists proved particularly useful to Bolshevik recruitment policies, as their reputations ensured intrinsic credibility. It is quite likely that the Central Office initiative under Rafes's leadership led to the publication of the (still frequently and uncritically cited) volume *Ocherki po istorii 'Bunda'*, which appeared shortly thereafter but not in time for the Bund's twenty-fifth anniversary.[104] Similarly, Frumkin's near-forgotten book on the great Bundist worker martyr Hirsh Lekert must be seen in this context.[105]

In the year of its twenty-fifth anniversary, the Bund in Poland was still reconstructing itself. The rift caused by the October Revolution and more specifically its activists' continuing shifts in allegiance ran deep into the organisation's structure. The festive holiday served to reassure Bundists of a common past and develop perspectives for the Bund's work in independent Poland. But the Bund's banner only fostered unity to a limited extent. This might also explain why the aforementioned issue of the '*Arbeter luakh*' was nominally dedicated to the Jewish workers' movement as a whole, when it in fact only looked at the Bund. The past rather than the present offered hope of reunification under the Bund's comforting roof.

---

99 Gelbard 1982, p. 108; Riddell 1991, p. 1086.
100 See esp. Rafes 1920.
101 Orla-Bukowska 2004, p. 202; Riddell 1991, p. 1086.
102 Kaplan Appel 2005; Schwarz 1951, p. 128.
103 Although they were undeniably tremendously important Bundists, the *Doyres bundistn* contains no corresponding entries on them.
104 Rafes 1923.
105 Frumkin 1922.

Many overseas Bundist groups had also split by then. The local Bund committee in New York organised a relatively small celebration that leaves little trace in the organisation's archives. A first step had nevertheless been taken, and commemorative events grew in number together with the Bund's overall revitalisation. This process came to an initial head around the organisation's thirtieth anniversary in 1927. Surely, it was partially motivated by the Communist Party's increasingly successful attempts to rewrite movement history. New York Bundists thus consciously celebrated the Bund's thirtieth anniversary as the history of a leading Social Democratic and Marxist party both at meetings as well as in specific publications.[106] Such a holiday was also perfectly suited to bringing together present and communicative masses, coinciding with a redefinition of the Bund's historical presence. Whereas the Bund was still very much seen as a remnant of the Tsarist-era Jewish workers' movement in 1922, by 1927 it represented the Jewish workers' movement as a whole. In a way, the Bund's success in Poland also brought back its confidence from Tsarist times.

This even resonated overseas. In New York success could be measured by both the venues of the festivities as well as the associations involved: organised by the YSF, the *Arbeter-ring*, the United Hebrew Trades, the ILGWU, the Capmakers Joint Convention, the *Forverts Association*, and even the New York-based *Organisatsye fun bund*, the Bund's thirtieth anniversary was no longer hosted in the Forverts Building on the Lower East Side where Bundist events were usually held. This time they moved the celebration to the city's largest venue, the Mecca Center (later renamed the New York City Center).[107] The event was a success, and in 1937 a specially appointed organising committee decided to return to the grand venue. The celebration taking place here did more than foster Bundist community in New York. It also brought significant sums into the New York Bund's coffers.[108]

Bundist community building was also a primary focus in Argentina. In Buenos Aires *khaverim* even organised a people's academy for Bundist history.[109] Anniversary editions of Bundist publications circulated throughout the diaspora, ranging from the aforementioned commemorative editions of the 'Naye folkstsaytung' to special issues in the US all the way to Uruguay.[110] In

---

106   Bund Archives, New York, RG 1400, ME-14B, 7, *30 yor bund, 1897–1927* (Riga: Bund in letland, 1927). It was also the subject of former militants' critical reflections such as Epshteyn 1927.
107   Bund Archives, New York, RG 1400, ME-14B, 7, *Der 30 yoriger yubileum fun 'bund'*.
108   *Bund 40 yor. Barikht, bashlus*, Bund Archives, New York, RG 1400, ME-18, 13; detailed calculations in ibid., ME-18, 11.
109   Bundishe grupe in Montevideo 1937; Bund Archives, New York, RG 1400, ME-18, 151.
110   *Naye folkstsaytung*, 19 November 1937; Bund Archives, New York, RG 1400, ME-18, 151, *40 yor bund* (Montevideo).

New York a small booklet featuring fraternal greetings stands out, celebrating the Eastern European Bund while simultaneously calling for donations to the American Bund for the first time on record.[111] Such commemorative events' success amplified American Bundist confidence. A pioneering group in this period was the New York-based Bund Club, founded in 1923 and gaining renewed importance in the 1930s. Using freshly acquired funds, a group of authors associated with the Club published a *Zamlheft* right after the fortieth anniversary. It historicised the group and American Bundism for the first time, and naturally referred mainly to its own leading members in doing so.[112] This booklet marked a paradigm shift, as it was the first time that an American Bundist group asserted itself as a historical actor. We can only guess as to how this development would have proceeded, as the German invasion of Poland soon threw the previous order into chaos. A large number of Bundist refugees arrived in New York, while several leading figures who visited the US on a fundraising assignment in 1939 chose to remain in the city. They relied on the Bund Club while, as described below, simultaneously restructuring it entirely.

Development towards a festive *Memorik* dated back to 1907, but evolved only slowly until the outbreak of the October Revolution. Following hesitant beginnings in 1922, success came to the Bund from 1927 onwards, culminating in countless gatherings and special issues across the globe in 1937. This allowed members to refer back to the local Bund, further refining the Bund's *Memorik* culture. The decade between the thirtieth and fortieth anniversaries witnessed the institutionalisation of a movement *Memorik*. Now it referred almost exclusively to its own history as the one true and democratic Jewish socialist past. With this demonstration of self-confidence against both Labour Zionism as well as Jewish Communism, the Bund could use the compelling nature of important biographies in particular to build bridges across boundaries and generations, thereby reinforcing transnational Bundist identity with a sense of pride and honour.[113]

111　Bund Archives, New York, RG 1400, ME14B, 4, *40 yor 'bund'* (New York, 1937).
112　Bundisher Klub in Nyu York 1938; 'Brief AR and Blumin', 16 February 1938, RG 1400, ME-18, 13, Bund Archives, New York.
113　Celebrations were not limited to worldwide publications on the topic, but also included celebratory banquets facilitating local community building for the Bund. More elaborate documentation can be found in several stocks of the Bund Archives, New York, RG 1400, ME-14B, 4; ME-18, 11; 13; 14.

4.5 Fifth Node: Memorik as Culmination – 'Unzer tsayt' in New York, 1941 and Beyond

The longest-lived Bundist publication began in New York in 1941 and was named *'Unzer tsayt'* (Our Time) in honour of its Eastern European forbearers. But which temporality formed this Bundist 'us'? Did *'Unzer tsayt'* refer to collective experiences of the Eastern European past, the American immigrant present, or perhaps to an aspired to, yet-to-be-realised utopian future of brotherhood and classlessness? The attentive reader may have already guessed that these levels overlapped in *'Unzer tsayt'*, although unlike in the Argentinian publications depicted above, past events took up more and more space (Figure 7).

This common past connected publication and readers. Previously none of the overseas journals had been formal 'party publications', that is to say neither Bundist nor secondary-Bundist publications overseas were subject to the Central Committee's direct control. These publications nevertheless represented the movement, often functioning as the mouthpiece of local groups and thus a kind of 'readers' paper' in which text production and reception often overlapped. Authors, readers, and parent organisations acted in concert as an actor-network often forming around certain periodicals. The secretary of the Bundist associations in America, Israel Bergman, was thus rather one-sided in 1905 when he blamed the failure of the publication *'Der kemfer'* in the US on its literary shortcomings.[114] The rise and fall of any periodical can only be accounted for in terms of its social constellation and not the publication alone.[115]

Here we find why *'Unzer tsayt'* fared better than the *'kemfer'*: it was founded in 1941, influenced by the mass migration of World War II, and moreover aware of the situation in Poland, where the Bund was forced into an underground existence in the Jewish ghettos. The Polish Bund lost its leading role and two integral luminaries, Noakh Portnoy and Vladimir Kossovski, passed away around the same time. The Polish Bund's paramount leaders, Henryk Erlich and Viktor Alter, would be murdered in Stalin's prisons only one year later. In 1943, merely another year later, the Bund's representative to the Polish exile government in London, Szmul Zygielbojm, committed suicide in a staggering combination of protest and despair.[116] Unlike in earlier periods, the party could no longer recruit new leaders from the activist reservoir in Eastern Europe. In 1898, for instance, the Bund lost most of its leadership to repression, exile, and imprisonment in the span of a single year due to Zubatov's Tsarist secret police raids. But the Bund lived up to its reputation as a workers' movement and was

---

114 Bund Archives, New York, RG 1400, ME-18, 4, *Referat* (1906), p. 10.
115 Ibid.
116 Pickhan 1994; Zigelboym 1947; Zigelboym 1948.

'taken over' by well-prepared workers.[117] German occupation and previously unimaginable levels of violence rendered such recruitment impossible, forcing the Polish Bund to draw on outside support in its struggle for survival against National Socialism. In this sense, a process that began prior to the war now intensified: the new centre of action had to be adapted to the new living environment. As *doikayt* meant being active wherever one resided, New York quickly rose in importance. Although the Bund refused to admit this until 1947, when it re-established itself in Brussels as the International Jewish Labour Bund (or World Bund), the process already began in 1941 with the founding of '*Unzer tsayt*'.[118]

Newly arrived in the US and perhaps anticipating this new journal's historical significance, Noakh Portnoy wrote in an almost apologetic tone in the first issue of '*Unzer tsayt*' that the publication was an expression of the need for socialist parties to 'retain their independence' despite the common struggle against 'fascism and Hitlerism'. In his view, the well-known socialist path was to be continued, for

> Poland is dark these days, the Hitlerite beast is showing its horrifically shameless face to the Jewish population. The bitter truth of today, however, cannot block our view of the vibrant future that lies ahead ... We in our country, just like the working masses all over the world, will joyfully continue the struggle for our liberation, for a new social order, for socialism.[119]

Remembrance was essential to this endeavour, as is hinted at by both the use of the word 'continue' as well as the numerous texts concerning 'heroes and martyrs' that appeared in '*Unzer tsayt*' from the very first issue. Despite the failures of previous American publications, the magazine enjoyed success with these tactics and established itself as the most important Bundist medium. It retained this role until its last issue in 2002, which can also be seen as representing Bundism's last gasp in the United States.

Despite its leading role, '*Unzer tsayt*' was not simply a means of control from above. It strongly reflected the will of the publication's readers. An exemplary case of this dynamic can be observed in the 1941 deaths of leading Bundists Noakh Portnoy and Vladimir Kossovski. Not only had they been charismatic

---

117   Kossovski 1942; Shvarts 1968.
118   This period of Bundist history has only gradually received scholarly attention. Pivotal on this aspect is Slucki 2012.
119   Noakh 1941.

and credible public faces of the Bund since its earliest years, but their theoretical contributions influenced the organisation significantly. *'Unzer tsayt'* commemorated Noakh Portnoy with a special issue featuring his portrait on the cover as well as numerous articles about him in issue 9 in October, and would do the same for Kossovski in the subsequent issue 10 in November. Commemorations such as these established the publication's emerging function as the new leading and globally relevant Bundist journal. It appears, however, that these issues never found their way to Argentina. Local Bundist leader Yekum Pat dispatched a message to his New York *khaver* Emanuel Szerer in early 1942 informing him of supply issues, claiming that outstanding balances were currently being settled and that, thirdly, he heard the sad news of the two veterans' deaths.[120] He explicitly requested an elaborate obituary of the two deceased – precisely what he would have found in the issues that failed to reach him in Argentina. Remarkably, Pat worked on the editorial board of *'Tsayt-fragn'* and easily could have written such texts himself.[121] He did not want to write them, however, but *read* them. In the process of international community building, it was not enough to produce memory individually. That memory also had to be reflected by the outside world.

This episode demonstrates that the Argentinian Bundists accepted *'Unzer tsayt'* as the new leading Bundist medium as early as 1941, ascribing to it the responsibility of writing the central commemorative texts for readers regardless of whether they lived in New York, Shanghai, Kobe, or Buenos Aires.[122] Among other texts, the published editorials, calendars, obituaries, and autobiographies show that *'Unzer tsayt'* ultimately accepted this role.[123] Particularly in light of the ongoing destruction of Jewish life in Europe, it amplified the tendency towards *Memorik* already noticeable in the Bund's early American publications (see Figure 7).[124] Texts on activism (Category I) rose to the fore only temporarily in the immediate war years, but never managed to surpass *Memorik* (Category IV). Activist texts mostly consisted of commentaries on the war's progress and the struggle against the Nazis. The many commemorative texts in these early *'Unzer tsayt'* issues, however, rarely refer to this contemporary context but instead almost exclusively depict the history of the Bund

---

120 Bund Archives, New York, RG 1400, ME-14B, 32, Letter, 17 January 1942.
121 He authored a number of *Memorik* texts, such as Pat 1930.
122 An impressive account is found in Grosman 1945.
123 Bund Archives, New York, RG 1400, O, 35; 36; 39.
124 Selective albeit representative range of volumes analysed; key years (founding year 1941, anniversary series 1947 and 1957) are juxtaposed with 'inconspicuous' years in which the prominence of *Memorik* was not necessarily related to the respective year of publication.

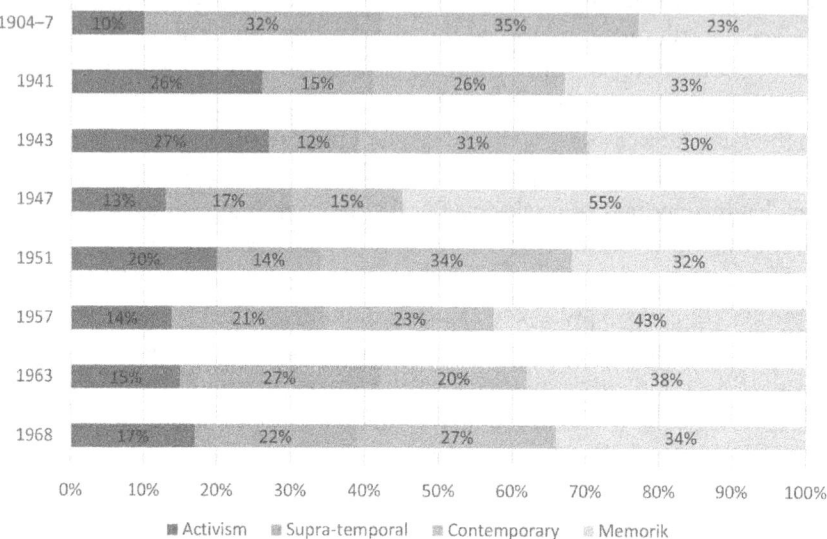

FIGURE 7   Text ratio analysis of Bundist periodicals in the US, 1904–68, representatively selected volumes. Complete collection 1904–7, representatively selected volumes of '*Unser tsayt*', 1941–68

prior to 1939. By 1947 *Memorik* took up the better part of the entire volume. This year would prove to be a turning point in several aspects. To begin with, two years after the war's end it was now clear that the German massacre had eradicated the basis for a mass movement of Jewish workers in Poland. The founding of the World Bund was a consequence of this bitter realisation. Furthermore, remaining Bund groups in Soviet-occupied Poland faced an increasingly hostile political climate. The Polish Bund was forcibly integrated into the Communist Party in 1948, against the helpless protests of the youth section in particular.[125]

This marked the end of the Bund's history on Eastern European soil. The Bund organised itself increasingly less like a party in the subsequent period, instead explicitly describing itself as a transnational network. Nevertheless, the Bund still derived its legitimacy from the workers' struggles in Eastern Europe. Now more than ever, it invoked past struggles through recourse to *Memorik*. That theme would become the common denominator of every Bundist group worldwide and also left its mark on '*Unzer tsayt*'.

---

125 The indignant initial report in 'From Our Movement. Poland' in the *Jewish Labor Bund Bulletin*, no. 4, 1948, p. 7.

After years of regular publication, it temporarily ceased appearing in mid-1947. The Bund's restructuring required every resource available. In November–December, number 3–4 appeared as a special double issue over 200 pages in length to mark the Bund's fiftieth anniversary. The issue was filled with *Memorik* and far exceeded the publications around the fortieth anniversary in this respect. Moreover, a new focal point of *Memorik* emerged: the Warsaw Ghetto Uprising. Remembrance of the Holocaust and the resistance had already filled countless pages of '*Unzer tsayt*' on previous occasions. From 1947 onwards, the period of Nazi persecution began to occupy a status comparable to Bundism's primordial years. This of course gained particular momentum in the run-up to the uprising's tenth anniversary in 1953. Commemorating the Ghetto Uprising, Bundist *Memorik* partially opened up beyond the movement's past. It integrated a more general Jewish history and re-interpreted it into the Bund's historical perspective. In other words: the Bund sought to insert itself into Jewish history more forcefully than socialist history, particularly during the years it put up its fiercest opposition to Zionism. This may well have been an attempt, similar to the aftermath of 1917, to combat undesired historical interpretations from rival movements and thereby ensure the Bund's own historical importance.

5   Regional Comparisons

Despite common trends, the Bund's commemorative culture differed significantly from region to region. A comparison on the basis of the Bund's publishing work reveals distinct regional profiles mirroring individual regions' respective emphases of Bundist activism and community building dynamics.

In Eastern Europe, activism determined the modes of community building around workers' issues and later the development of working-class culture. In both the Bund's legal and illegal periods, the practice was entirely compatible with that of *doikayt*, a principle the Bund had treated as its defining characteristic since the 1900s. Argentinian Bundists valued local activism, highly in line with their Eastern European *khaverim*. In this regard they penned numerous timeless texts articulating positions on theoretical questions rooted in their respective region, such as initial engagements with anarchism, and from the 1920s onwards with Yiddish Communism. Because these currents represented the Bund's major political rivals in Argentina, theoretical texts focused very specifically on the Bund's local practices. In contrast to the Eastern European Bundists, Argentinian Bundists had no access to printing presses of their own throughout the period studied here, and competing viewpoints were com-

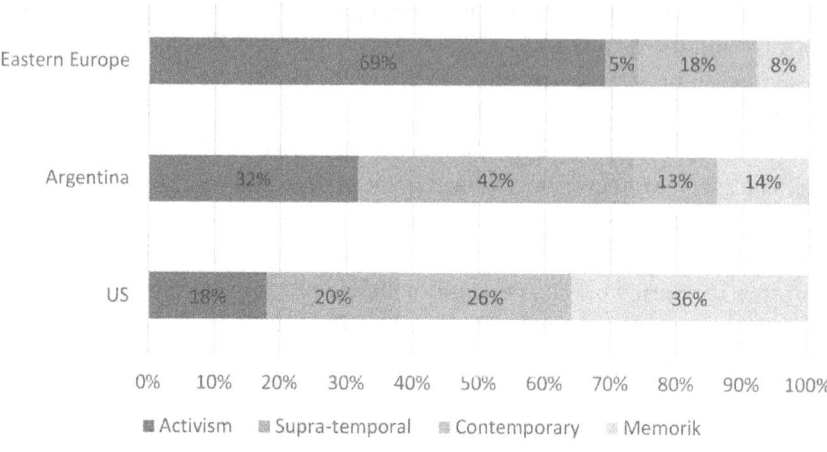

FIGURE 8   Regional profiles of Bundist periodicals in international comparison, 1899–1968

municated through self-published periodicals appearing only sporadically.[126] Interestingly, these publications rarely addressed Zionism, although post-war literature and theoretical debates among leading Eastern European and American intellectuals stylised it as the Bund's main opponent at the time. Bundists in 1920s and 1930s Argentina were aware of differences with Labour Zionism but frequently sought alliances with Poale Zionists. They also struggled with Communist splits, ultimately facilitating partial cooperation between the Bund and Poale Zion.[127] Bundist immigrants were certainly crucial to shaping a local version of *doikayt* in the US, but the Bund as such played no significant role. Apart from the *Forverts Association*, much stronger secondary-Bundist organisations like the *Arbeter-ring* took on this task as early as the 1900s. Above all, *Memorik* allowed for the preservation of Bundist identity even before World War II, and would do so even more afterwards. Remembrance embodied a collective longing for a bygone world and facilitated the establishment of persistent activism patterns through the constant translation of the past into the present. *Memorik* kept the Bund alive in the minds of many while revitalising its role in the workers' movement. This process centred on New York City, turning the American Bund into the central nexus of the Bund's transnational network. The relevance of the past after World War II centralised the Bund's network,

---

126   This shows that 'printing' as such did not become a pattern of activism in Argentina either, posing a problem. The Bundist publishing house *Yidbukh* only managed to fill this gap in the country after World War II, Bund Archives, New York, RG 1400, ME-18, 155.

127   This was particularly pronounced in the schools movement, analysed in more detail later on. IWO, Buenos Aires, 1111.

but as a downside effectively isolated the US Bund from the political activism that continued in Argentina and emerged in Australia. Now, as David Slucki notes, many émigrés considered the Melbourne Bund to be the Polish Bund's true successor.[128]

---

128   Slucki 2009a, p. 111 f.

CHAPTER 5

Memories beyond 'Me' and 'Us': Bundist Autobiography as Social Formation

Leon Oler's statement cited in the introduction to this volume, that the 60-year history of the Bund 'resembles the life story of a person who lived' through different eras on different continents, ascribed to the Bund a humanness that facilitated its biographisation. It provided the Bund with subject status and agency, both of which are strictly human characteristics in the classical sense.[1] Oler thereby questions a consensus of modernity – the distinction between humans and things, between object and subject.[2] He was not alone in doing so. Dzshon Mill also wrote of the 'birth of the Bund', and even Vladimir Medem emphasised the agency of non-human actors inside the Bund when composing a 'biography of the *"Lebns-fragn"'*, the publication he founded in Warsaw during World War I.[3] Medem's biographisation of the *'Lebns-fragn'*, however, was also an autobiographical text blending self- and external biography.

1 Worker Biographies as Collective Act

The most popular terms in historical autobiographical research over the past decade were probably 'I' or 'self'. These allegedly stand in antagonistic relation to 'us' or 'context', and remain clearly identifiable and distinctively addressable units.[4] In this view, 'I' stands for a discursively constructed 'self' marking the goal of modern autobiography. Through individualising writing, it seeks to both emancipate the author from and inscribe him or her into the 'us' at the same

---

1 This language is related to the biologisation of abstract structures, observed most prominently in proclamations of the 'awakening of nations', see Gellner 1964, p. 169; Anderson 1983, p. 6, p. 195.
2 And while representing a movement that proudly hoisted the banner of modernity! This is not necessarily a contradiction, but rather an expression of modernity as an idea rather than ineluctable praxis. See Latour 1993, p. 10 ff.
3 Mill 1952; Medem 1948.
4 For an overview see Herzberg 2007, p. 26 f.; Rutz 2002. Particularly inspiring in this regard is above all Volker Depkat's study distinguishing between context and individual, although he subsequently blurs the distinction and detects an 'event of social communication' in the text. See Depkat 2006, p. 63, pp. 65–127.

time.[5] Eva Kormann calls this the 'discovery of readers and society' in modern autobiographical research, freeing autobiography from its reduction to textual immanence and 'socialising' it in terms of both production and reception.[6] Analytically speaking, however, historical autobiography studies rarely bridge the gap between self and society. On the contrary, 'society' is often treated as synonymous with 'context', while generalising theoretical conclusions tend to be drawn from highly selective empirical evidence. The meaning of 'us' is often reduced to the concept of an author 'inscribing' himself into the collective context. This essentialisation of 'external' context can be very misleading and leads to surprising conclusions. Markus Malo, for instance, examines the emergence of the 'modern individual' in Jewish personal memoirs. Based on an assumed dichotomy between the Jewish population and the workers' movement and a conceptual division between internal 'self' and external 'context', he more or less in passing identifies an 'impossibility of socialist-Jewish autobiography'.[7] The mere existence of the Bundist autobiographies analysed in this study demonstrates the untenability of his claim. Secularism by no means precluded Jewish identity, but rather, given autobiography's social function, provoked reflections upon one's own life and biography. Bundist autobiographies did not affirm traditions and society but instead adopted a productive stance towards their own community, seeking to reform Jewish life altogether. It is thus impossible to infer 'society' on the basis of a large corpus. What we can investigate, however, are processes of community building which can in turn be situated in societies.

In doing so we should question the distinction between the literary personification of the self and the collective and external 'us'. Oler's quote again allows us to develop this approach. It introduces memories of the Bund in Poland in which the life of an individual (the protagonist author) is brought into line with that of a group (the protagonist collective). It invents a new body in order to accomplish this: the anthropomorphised Bund. Referring to the significance of *Memorik* (and its personalisation in particular) as discussed in the previ-

---

5   Leading representatives of the context method with view to Russian autobiographies include Halfin 2000; Halfin 2001; Halfin 2003; Hellbeck 1996; Hellbeck and Heller 2004. For an intriguing comparative approach see Herzberg 2010. Studies of Jewish autobiography, by contrast, place a stronger emphasis on the author's 'identity' and the textuality of the world of the 'People of the Book', see Schwarz 1998; Soyer 1999; Stanislawski 2004; Moseley 2005; Moseley 2006; Cohen and Soyer 2006. This discovery of the world through text often refers to studies of autobiographies in the Early Modern Age, see esp. Jancke 2002; Kormann 2004. Similar, arguing on the basis of a *longue durée*: Hahn 2000.
6   Kormann 2004, p. 51.
7   See Malo 2009, pp. 7–23, p. 177 ff.

ous chapter, I will demonstrate that Bundist autobiography can be understood neither as a process of 'inscribing' oneself into a context nor as a means of individual 'emancipation' from it. Rather, it represented an activist means of reproducing the social movement and Bundist identity associated with it. Autobiographical practices were an activity that co-produced the social.

Due to the relevance of *Memorik* for the social movement, the following discussion does focus not on autobiographers as movement representatives but rather on Bundist autobiography as a social formation. *Memorik* retrospectively legitimised the movement while autobiography served to bolster mobilisation. The distinctive Bundist view of history did not rest on personalisation alone. As illustrated in the previous chapter, first and foremost it required 'authentic' voices. The generational shift occurring in the Bund meant that later-born activists lacked experiential reference to the Bund's historical roots. As the organisation devoted more efforts to developing its own historical perspective – first in the wake of 1917 and once again after 1947 – legitimising experiences had to be transmitted from communicative memory to the movement's cultural memory without shedding its 'authenticity' in the process. Autobiography facilitated this transfer. Through individualisation, autobiography came to represent both counter-cultural practice as well as the sense of community conveyed by Bundist identity. Questions concerning the self remain important, but in this setting we must first determine the function of worker autobiographies in the community building process before we can address their actual form and individual content. Moreover, the latter found its relevance not only in the reference to the group (emancipation or inscription), but primarily in the construction of group and identity.

Obviously, analyses of autobiography with a focus on the collective where autobiography is commonly viewed as a barometer of group relations, moods, and perceptions are nothing new.[8] This is particularly true of labour history. A more dated school emerging in the 1970s combed worker autobiographies for 'true testimonials' of workers' lives.[9] From the 1990s onwards, more theoretically sophisticated studies of subjectification strategies pursued similar questions, but opposed the inherent positivism of earlier worker studies.[10] Grasping both approaches as complementary allows us to think of worker autobiographies as far too social to be viewed as mere texts, yet far too narrative

---

8   Group-related approaches can be found in, among others, Möller 2001; Depkat 2006; Malo 2009.
9   Münchow 1973; Burnett 1974; Bollenbeck 1976; Vincent 1981; Kuhn 1982. Inspired more by literary criticism but exhibiting a similar bias: Frerichs 1980; Vogtmeier 1984.
10   Pioneering: Maynes 1995; Hetmeier 1996; Steinberg 2002.

to realistically and immediately depict the social.¹¹ Maria Hetmeier understands this well in her study of French worker autobiographies by detecting (very much in contrast to Schmidt and Herzberg) a shift from 'I' to 'we'. In her view, this constitutes an independent step within the constitution of worker authors as subjects who pursued the aim of 'depicting the relationship between public and private experiences', expressed in the shift from '*je*' to '*nous*'.¹²

Most autobiography studies nevertheless focus on strategies of emancipation. Discussions of collective aspects beyond the exceptional cases of Stalinist biographies produced under political duress remain rather rare. A publication worth mentioning in this regard is Silke Möller's research on socialisation processes in German student fraternities. She presents the reader with a particularly dense group portrait based on a larger corpus of autobiographies.¹³ Practically, however, she mostly interprets individual memories in relation to the greater context, and thus searches for a 'lifeworld' in the 155 autobiographies she surveys. While bringing even more life to an already vivid subject, the approach underestimates the activist element of this community-building form of writing (and reception). Her concluding remarks that 'the "I" often receded in favour of "us"' at the linguistic level is hardly surprising in such a group context, given that Möller herself regards the universities and fraternities of imperial Germany primarily as 'socialisation agencies'.¹⁴ This favouring of 'us' only appears odd if one searches for a kind of 'I' the autobiographies fail to provide in its desired pure form.

This search for the 'I' is rooted in the idea of 'negative liberty', treating individual emancipation and the reduction of external resistance as synonymous. Accordingly, the 'I' is portrayed as an accomplishment.¹⁵ But as philosopher

---

11   As argued in Latour 1993, p. 6. This double relation is often ignored. James Stephen Amelang explains the silence of worker autobiographers with respect to the labour issue through the separation of working in the daytime and writing at night. One could reply that this was by no means a specificity of nightly self-discovery but rather owed to the routines of work, which were just as difficult to verbalise for steel workers in the second half of the twentieth century as they were for early modern workers. As Thomas Welskopp shows, it is precisely the absence of language that allows for routinised, collective labour. See Amelang 2009, p. 96f.; Welskopp 2014.
12   Hetmeier 1996, p. 329; Herzberg and Schmidt 2007.
13   Möller 2001, esp. pp. 166–91. Autobiography functions in a similarly group-producing fashion with similarly problematic results in Maria Kłanska's study, see Kłanska 1994.
14   Möller 2001, p. 42, p. 58f., p. 106f., p. 167.
15   Eastern European Studies unfortunately largely concentrates on the special case of autobiographies revolving around 'totalitarian' conditions, see the special issue on 'Russian Subjectivity' in *Russian Review*, particularly Halfin 2001. Herzberg and Schmidt's volume

Charles Taylor demonstrated over 30 years ago, the self which emerges through the independence of the individual is nothing more than a fiction of liberalism. Taylor counterposes to liberalism philosophies that situate freedoms in the collective, stating that 'freedom resides at least in part in collective control over the common life'.[16] Marx and Rousseau were paradoxically the latter theory's most vehement proponents, and Rousseau's *Confessions* is widely regarded as the template for modern autobiography. The modes of individualisation presented therein set new standards for modern autobiographical writing.[17] Although autobiography scholarship's fundamental critique of memory as a credible source disrupted earlier historians' inclination to reproduce the 'autobiographical pact', it tends to emphasise 'perception' or subjectification strategy as if they were virtually unrelated to the history taking place around the author. This perspective often marginalises autobiography's community-building and mobilising effects.

As depicted in the previous chapter, Bundist sense of community relied on personalisation as much as subjectification strategies depended on their group context. This is evidenced quite impressively by shoemaker Hersh Mendel's search for the '-ism' that suited him best. The turmoil of World War I stirred doubts in the once-staunch Bundist. He found it increasingly difficult to align himself with one of the many socialist movements. Various contacts throughout his migration brought him to vacillate between Bundism, Communism, anarchism, Trotskyism, and even Poale Zionism. He attests: 'Once I had weathered the storms of my ideological struggle, I again felt the ground beneath my feet'.[18] This never lasted long. His search continued in accordance with social changes and the rise and fall of various socialist groups and associated movements. Although Mendel is undoubtedly of Bundist provenance, the recurrent theme of his autobiography remains the search for congruency between his own activism and a fitting political and social movement.

---

rejects this limited view of Stalinist self-testimonials under the pretence of 'Russian' history, albeit by once again fixating on individualisation. My participation in this volume should not go unmentioned, however, as the preparatory work helped to develop my ideas for the research findings presented here. A slight unease with the volume's general orientation found expression in the fact that my contribution is the only one that does not discuss a single author, but instead compares two exemplary autobiographies, see Wolff 2007.

16   Taylor 1985, p. 211.
17   As Eva Korman establishes, the production of the 'I' did not occur independently of the outside world but was in fact profoundly influenced by it, see Kormann 2004.
18   Mendel 1989, p. 150.

Existing scholarship's focus on the search for a worker-self pushed worker autobiography's community-building function and the simultaneous creation of counter-culture into the analytical background.[19] The interrelation between self and group suggests that searching for the relationship of 'I' to 'us' is not necessarily wrong, but misleading. They stand not in relation *to* one another but rather are embedded *in* one another. I would like to both demonstrate and explain this argument based on 532 autobiographical texts retrieved from around the world, all of which can be reliably attributed to Bundist authors. They constitute a representative sample which I refer to as 'Bundist autobiography'. All Bundist autobiographies use the term 'I', but this does not imply the absence of an (albeit non-verbalised) collective 'us', the strong presence of which is commonly viewed as a distinguishing feature setting them apart from conventional bourgeois memoirs.[20] 'Us' is neither a point of departure nor a goal, but rather object of discussion and purpose. Like 'I', it is one of many co-present levels.

2 Modes of Integration

Due to autobiographies' central role in the development of Bundist identity, the editors of autobiographical texts in journals almost always decided to underline this character with certain signifiers, whether specific emphasis or by adding corresponding additional titles. This marked them as 'subjective' and simultaneously integrated them into the framework of the respective publication and the movement itself. This embedding via layout was not possible in the case of books, which readers encountered as stand-alone publications. Only prominent authors could be sure that readers would perceive their written memories as valuable expressions of collective experiences. Worker authors lacked this recognition. Although they represented the Bund's 'most authentic' voices, they nevertheless required the support of more prominent voices to establish a degree of authority. The monographs themselves were thus not enough to be integrated into Bundist *Memorik*. This was achieved through their equally important prefaces written by well-known Bundists, who vouched for the 'authenticity' of a worker author's experiences.

We can observe this dynamic in Layb Berman's '*In loyf fun yorn*', the first monographic autobiography of a Bundist worker ever published. Berman be-

---

19 As much is stated in Ebert 2004.
20 Quatemer 1988, p. 329 f.

gan writing the manuscript in the 1920s. It was eventually published in Warsaw in 1936 with support from Bundists from the New York-based *Arbeter-ring*.[21] One of the few workers among the leadership, Berman was one of the most popular Bundist personalities of the Polish period. His is the only memoir written by a Bundist worker to re-appear in an edited version after World War II.[22] Even the first printing received the honour of an introduction by famous exile-Bundist and Menshevik Raphael Abramovitch, complemented by a preface from the renowned Noakh Portnoy. His preface symptomatically formulated the inseparability of 'I' from 'us' and the factual from the emotional.[23] In an attempt to boost the status of this autobiography within Bundist *Memorik*, Portnoy feigns annoyance. He states that the request had 'flustered' him. He certainly enjoyed reading recollections, but 'what could surprise me in a new memoir enough that I would feel moved to write a preface?' His words, after all, were 'a kind of passport, a kind of recommendation, which introduces [the book] into the greater literary world – one must be very careful when issuing such a passport'.

Portnoy was fully aware of his role as a leading Bundist. His preface emphasises that quality rather than his friendship with an old comrade motivated his decision. By 'quality' he meant new insights into the history of the Bund, not of the author himself.[24] Yet this game Portnoy plays with the reader, who of course holds the proverbial 'passport' in his hand as he scans these lines, does not last. It was 'not long before my agitation disappeared entirely, no trace remained of my scepticism. I do not seek to put myself in the position of a "know-it-all", I do not claim to have already known all the facts the author presents so beautifully and so modestly'. Portnoy advertises the book through a two-fold gesture of admiration: firstly, by referring to the 'modest' author of the recollections. Secondly, Portnoy intentionally introduces himself as knowledgeable on the Bund's history only to emphasise his curiosity in Berman's recollections. This culminates in an emotional integration: 'For the first time I learned of many, many things in this book, of exalted moments of our romantic past, and read them with a trembling in my heart'. In this sense the book aroused Portnoy's emotions precisely *because* he did not experience the episodes himself. He relates this force emanating from someone else's *Memorik* directly to his own physicality, for not only did he hold those papers 'in his hands' and did his

---

21   Berman 1936.
22   Berman 1945b.
23   Similarly, the editors of the first monographic Bundist autobiography already emphasised the historical 'value' of individual perspectives, see N.N. 1921b, p. 2; Cahan 1923.
24   On their long friendship and shared experiences in the underground see Berman 1953.

heart 'tremble', but he even experienced the tension of that time once again: 'I read with bated breath, as I believe everyone who reads the story of the Dvinkser B.O. [Russian: *boevye otriady*], the combat units [Yiddish: *kamf-druzshine*] will experience'. Like Leon Oler before him, Portnoy can only envision the result of this story in both physical and historicising terms at once:

> A new generation of Jewish workers is growing up under the influence of the revolutionary movement and the 'Bund'. The 'pariah among the pariahs' is taking its fate into its own hands. A new, more balanced, prouder fighter is emerging who bravely and boldly leads the historical struggle for his class and defends his personal dignity to the death. The 'Bund' called a whole *mentsh* into being and raised him, an uncompromising Jewish proletarian fighter with a highly developed revolutionary self-consciousness.[25]

Emancipation was not only a matter of writing, but rather a collective challenge in which writing represented one activist practice among many. This activism of the text was realised less by the book's 'facts' – stressed as the reader's primary interest – so much as in the emotionality of community spirit they conveyed.

> But the factual side, which by itself is interesting and exciting to read, is not the only thing I want to emphasise in my preface. In my eyes the book has a very particular value. We have before us a simple, modest and thus beautiful depiction of the life of a *mentsh* – a life of a worker who in clear, unpretentious words describes his poor, bitter childhood years [in a world] in which the spiritual essence of a Jewish worker-socialist, a Bundist, was formed. Facts [are the] revolutionary vestments of the living *mentsh*, they grow in type and significance together with the growth and maturing of the carrier of these vestments, of the author of this memoir. This person is not separated [*obgerisn*] from that which he imparts to us. When you read this book to the end you will feel that you have before you not only an interesting tale, but a human document.

Portnoy's initial motivation for reading emphasised facts but ended with the true significance of Berman's account: the text's emotionality and humanness.

---

25   An allusion to Georgi Plekhanov's famous praise for the Jewish workers' movement as the 'pariah' of Russian socialism and the 'avantgarde of the workers' army in Russia' at the Second International's 1896 London congress, as cited in Tobias 1972, p. 61.

In conclusion, he distils the memoir's mobilising power from this combination: 'These remembrances are a wonderful chapter in our history, from which we draw courage and enthusiasm in our revolutionary struggle for socialism'.[26]

Prominent leading Bundists were not the only ones to revert to the Bund as the crucial nexus of identity. We can also find this reversion in less prominent autobiographies, unpublished manuscripts, and some texts not even composed in a Bundist context to begin with. Most significantly we find a number of such testimonies written for the autobiographical contest hosted by the YIVO in New York in 1941–2.[27] Seeking to collect Jewish immigrants' life stories for the archives, the YIVO placed several calls for submissions in numerous Yiddish periodicals, particularly in North America, under the title 'Why I left the old world and what I accomplished in America'.[28] A number of former Bundists seized the opportunity to tell their own life stories. None of them played a significant role in the Bund's primary autobiography, whether published or unpublished.[29] Despite its vast *Memorik*, the Bund thus never opened a broad enough space for remembrance to include these activists' desires to publicly recall their own pasts. Nevertheless, personal experiences within the Bund and actions on its behalf occupy a large portion of these autobiographies. Often they dominate the whole account, yet without diminishing the 'emancipation' of the narrator and actually doing quite the opposite.[30]

The Bund's crucial role in such a vast number of heterogeneous life stories, published and unpublished, as well as depictions thereof allows us to examine Bundist autobiography as a social formation in its own right.

3 The Topography of Bundist Autobiography

Two main source types allow us to better understand the integration of Bundists' individually experienced pasts into the greater collective: firstly Bundist autobiographies, and secondly, as further analysed below, biographical questionnaires the Bund used in various campaigns. In combination this produces a comprehensive, differentiated social history of the Bund's collective memory and of those creating it in their writing. In this context, we must take into

---

26 All quotes taken from Portnoy 1936.
27 This includes first and foremost Novikov 1967; Metaloviets 1982; Mendel 1989.
28 On this see Soyer 1999; Cohen and Soyer 2006.
29 YIVO, New York: RG 102, 28; 44; 47; 55; 76; 81; 83; 107; 108; 15; 142; 157; 158; 160; 171; 173; 178; 180; 191; 196; 200; 209; 222.
30 As much can be found in Fox 2006.

account that autobiographies always represent both the words of an individual Bundist as well as elements in the broader Bundist memorial culture.[31] This duality created a social space that provided the Bund with its past through *Memorik* more generally and autobiography in particular. Like the English working class before it, the Bund was 'present at its own making'.[32] This reverses the perspective and urges us to no longer search for practices within a pre-existing social formation, but rather to examine the constitution of social space through practices.

The need for a more in-depth analysis of Bundist autobiography is derived from existing Bundist research. Not a single study of the Bund can afford to ignore autobiography. Activists' words and thoughts always inform the most important parts of those studies, but they are often reduced to their spoken content and serve as sources of factual information. The social content of autobiographical texts is usually neglected. Reading these sources as individual expressions of collective experiences also leads us to look for autobiographical texts beyond a certain canon of leading Bundists' memoirs that seems to implicitly guide research. Hundreds of shorter and longer Bundist autobiographies exist beyond the work of a few, oft-cited Bundists.

4   Mapping the Autobiographical Network

I understand 'autobiography' as memorial texts of varying length in which the reader can plausibly identify the author as the first-person narrator. What Phillippe Lejeune calls an 'autobiographical pact' constitutes a major component of the 'authenticity' the reader expects to find in a memoir, and forms the implicit agreement that the reader accepts and recognises the identity of the author as protagonist.[33] I verified biographical backgrounds through various sources to distinguish the accounts analysed in the following sample from fiction written in the first person. I understand Bundist autobiographies as works composed by individuals at least temporarily affiliated to the Bund, i.e. who explicitly recollect their (former) relationship with the Bund (often as the life story of a Bundist) or recount memories with plausible reference to the Bund. Through such connections of individual and movement, activists used their

---

31   This is not intended to negate subjectivity, but rather emphasise its collective bonds more strongly. Subjective perceptions are discussed more extensively in other sections of this study.
32   Thompson 1964, p. 64.
33   See Lejeune 2005. The aspect of staging is emphasised in Kormann 2004, p. 53 ff.

commemorative writing to reflect on their (temporal) Bundist identity. The study builds on a data set of 532 autobiographies categorised as Bundist autobiography, 'filtered out' of a far greater number of Jewish (oftentimes Yiddish) autobiographies.[34] In this analysis I included only first editions of such publications without reprints or translations.[35] If the author re-edited an autobiography and re-published it, say, in a significantly extended version, I count this as a new publication.[36] I developed a specific analytic database to collect, group, and analyse the texts, allowing for both statistical evaluation and content analysis. Through such an analysis I hope to both contribute to the social history of the Bund, as well as propose a methodological approach to evaluating autobiography in a combined quantitative and qualitative analysis.

This sample constitutes a meticulously collected albeit inevitably incomplete record of Bundist autobiography. It is based on years of wide-ranging research into relevant documents in German, US, Argentinian, Russian, and Israeli libraries and archives. The lack of a defined base population to measure against caused methodological difficulties when drawing up a representative sample. For this reason the documents were not divided into sample groups, but rather analysed in full. In collecting relevant autobiographies I placed an emphasis on completeness with respect to the earlier years, but the almost exponential rise in autobiography from the interwar years onwards made this neither feasible nor necessary. After reviewing roughly one hundred autobiographies, several focal points emerged at all levels of analysis. They continued

---

34   Apart from two exceptions they all have individual authors. These include two collections of recollections composed by leading Bundists, each of which was published – or rather compiled – collectively. These are Tate, Frumoiskii, Gozhanskii and Kaplinski 1907; N.N. 1922. Autobiographies appearing in Bundist publications but written by authors who were obviously not Bundists were not included. Likewise, no secondary-Bundist authors nor intellectuals limited to the Bund's periphery were included – with the exception of Bernard Weinstein's and Abraham Kotik's autobiographies. These two are crucially important to Bundist autobiography not least because they appeared in the beginnings of monographic autobiography, and must be considered part of the Bundist autobiographical culture, although their trajectories are not confined to it. This is especially the case for Weinstein, who, as founder of the United Hebrew Trades and important member of the secondary-Bundist YSF (whose publishing house published his autobiographies), cultivated close political relations to the Bund in the US. See Weinstein 1924; Kotik 1925.

35   These would merit an investigation as a form of reproduction in their own right. Whenever 'first editions' were unavailable or irretrievable, I worked with re-prints and carefully avoided double entries.

36   Likewise, serialised editions of autobiographies eventually published in book form, as was the case with the autobiographies of Vladimir Medem and Layb Berman, were only entered once.

to stabilise, and after about 250 autobiographies the analytical grid proved saturated, i.e. further collection no longer changed but only confirmed established typologies and statistical agglomerations – and thus the database's structure. In order to retain the resulting structure, I continued the increasingly tedious search for autobiographical texts with the objective of drawing on more than twice the 250 autobiographies required to reliably establish an adequate qualitative evaluation grid.[37]

5   Basic Coordinates

The database contains both published (436) and unpublished (96) documents to guarantee the greatest heterogeneity possible. The former appeared in periodicals, as edited volumes, and as monographs published by the Bund and other institutions. The latter are primarily from the Bund Archives, although the YIVO's 1942 autobiographical contest also proved to be a rich source of information.[38]

As a first result, we find that Bundist autobiography took place largely in the public sphere or at least targeted it, as embodied by the YIVO autobiographical contest's first prize: the chance to publish a book. They enjoyed wide readership and were filled with intertextual references. As Bundist *Memorik* underwent a process of personalisation during World War II, autobiography became one of the main focal points of Bundist publications in the US. American publications like '*Unzer tsayt*' thus earned a global audience. That said, Bundists worldwide showed great interest in American Yiddish press prior to that. The Argentinian *Biblioteca rusa*, for example, began offering the American '*Forverts*' alongside Russian publications in 1907.[39] American Bundist publications only reached this far after consolidating their existence through their sensitivity to the demand for autobiography.

---

37   A particularly thorough effort was made with regard to monographs with recorded publication dates. Contributions to periodicals were meticulously researched up until the year 1947, especially in the US and Argentina. Numerous issues of important publications into the 1960s were researched extensively, as were collected volumes. Daily newspapers such as the '*Forverts*' or the '*Naye folkstsaytung*' were included to a limited extent, as were stronger secondary-Bundist papers such as '*Der veker*'. A comprehensive compilation was unjustifiable in this context, owed not least to the significantly more challenging biographical research on the authors. Moreover, extensive samples only showed confirmation of existing trends. See the complete bibliography of this volume.
38   YIVO, New York, RG 102. On this see Soyer 1999; Cohen and Soyer 2006.
39   Regularly advertised in the first issues of '*Der avangard*', Buenos Aires 1908 f.

As already noted with regard to the Bundist press, the Bund's autobiographical culture also exhibited major regional differences. This is particularly true of the unpublished sources, of which I found only few in the Argentinian archives despite intensive research. The only larger autobiographical collection resulted from an interview campaign sponsored by the Centro Marc Turkow in Buenos Aires. After the military dictatorship ended, the institution conducted lengthy interviews with more than 200 Argentinian Jews in an attempt to document Jewish life in Buenos Aires. However, many of those interviews demonstrate a strong inclination towards the interviewers' personal interests and style.[40] I identified five Bundists among the interviewees. Their recollections added a further temporal layer to the memoirs published by leading members of the *Avangard* or Bundist groups of the interwar period.[41]

In the US, by contrast, the wave of memoirs began to rise sharply by the 1920s at the latest. This led to a number of monographs totalling 67 in the sample, representing a much larger and more heterogeneous group than the at most one or two dozen historiography usually draws on. Almost all authors wrote one or several supplementary autobiographical articles commemorating specific events alongside these monographs. This followed the motto the *Lebns-fragn* publishing house formulated when introducing the first monographic Bundist autobiography, Beynish Mikhalevitsh's 1921 memoir:

> The history of a movement, of a party, consists not only of events and decisions of a general nature. It also consists of a great wealth of experiences and episodes concerning individual people that convey a plausible vision of the epoch, a vivid picture of the environment in which party work occurred as reflected in the attitudes and feelings of the militants, and allows us to hear not only the marching of the masses but the heartbeat of the marchers.[42]

---

40 The difference becomes clear in a comparison of two interviews with Bundist Hershl Goldmints. The interview conducted by historian Ephraim Zadoff in 1986 (Centro Mark Turkow, Archivo de la palabra, 22) largely follows the historian's expectations and lacks the insights into Bundist activism historian Marcelo Dimentstein's interview provides. Dimentstein relied on a narrative interview rather than fixed questions (copy in the author's possession). Interviews I conducted, such as with Israel Laubstein, were not included in the database.

41 Centro Mark Turkow, Archivo de la palabra, 11; 14; 22; 32; 53. I was able to conduct intensive research in Argentina in the stocks of the IWO, the CeDInCI, the Centro Marc Turkow, and in the archive of the Communist School I.L. Perez, Villa Lynch, located at the Universidad General San Martin UNSAM. I am grateful to Nerina Visacovsky for her support in the latter case.

42 N.N. 1921b.

More and more authors sought to convey such a 'plausible vision'. Numerous unknown Bundists composed short autobiographical texts. They focused on special experiences that appeared noteworthy for Bundist activism and could be retrieved through autobiography. Because authors intended for these articles to flow into one image, they represent the main type of Bundist autobiography. *Yidishkayt*'s broad cultural concept also provided space for autobiographical poetry. Of those, Dovid Eynhorn's *'Mayn heym'* is one example well-known beyond narrow Bundist circles.[43] Like existing research on life writing suggests, the heterogeneity of the autobiographical literature makes it more appropriate to speak of a 'mode' of autobiography rather than a genre. This mode, however, oriented itself towards emotions stemming from actions within the Bund itself.[44]

Although all authors acted within the Bund and wrote for their fellow activists, Bundist autobiography should not be understood as mere party literature. I distinguish between three levels in order to reach a more differentiated analysis. Primary Bundist autobiography is characterised by its emergence in direct relation to the Bund's official organs, such as publication in its periodicals or publishing houses. The production of secondary-Bundist autobiography took place in spaces close to but not or not fully dominated by the Bund, such as publishing houses or journals of secondary-Bundist organisations (like *'Der veker'*) or publishers not run by Bundists alone (*Farlag di velt*, Warsaw). Tertiary-Bundist autobiography, produced fully outside of the Bund by other left-wing publishers or even privately, complemented them.

When comparing the bibliographies of the most important books on the Bund, one notices a shared focus on only nine major monographs, all of which are primary-Bundist autobiographies. Several well-known Bundists who published in the secondary-Bundist milieu partially complement these sources. Books belonging to the group of tertiary-Bundist autobiographical publications mostly composed by workers and lesser-known Bundists are given far less attention. Yet these works depict the trait that made the Bund so significant in the first place: its influence beyond the leadership. Workers usually only gained a degree of prominence after advancing into the higher party ranks. Testimonies of worker activists have thus received little attention as primary sources. Researchers in the heterogeneous field of Bundist autobiography thus often found what they were looking for: leaders and unequivocal statements on the Bund's organisational characteristics. This specific selection of sources

---

43   Eynhorn 1974.
44   On the distinction see Arroyo 2001.

TABLE 5   'Genres' of Bundist autobiographical culture

Genre	Total	Type of Bundist autobiography (primary / secondary / tertiary / undefined)
Article	356	250 / 62 / 43 / 1
Manuscript (unpublished)	96	64 / – / 32 / –
Book	67	9 / 21 / 37 / –
Interview	6	– / – / 6 / –
Letter (published)	4	– / 1 / 3 / –
Other	3	1 / – / 2 / –
Total	532	324 / 84 / 123 / 1

obscured the true breadth of participation and the ambivalences of workers' everyday lives as Bundists from the outset. It was not the result of a proactive marginalisation of workers, but rather derived from epistemological interest and the lack of an analysis of Bundist autobiography as a social-historical primary source. In order to explore this in more detail, we must first inspect the ups and downs of Bundist autobiography and the stratifications within the Bund that can be deduced from them.

6   Periodisation

Most historians divide Bundist history into four distinct periods: the Russian Bund of the Tsarist era, the Polish Bund of the interwar period, the history of the Bund in its resistance to Nazi occupation, and the post-war history of the Bund that only recently received scholarly attention. No reputable academic study has managed to break through these internal delineations. The periodisation is quite reasonable in terms of the Bund's organisational history. Bundists faced distinct legal conditions and frameworks in each period, alternating between phases of persecution and illegality and legal existence and electoral campaigning. These frameworks determined organisational options and thus objectives.

In terms of a social history, however, the aforementioned eras serve as rough points of orientation. As shown above, countless practices survived the Bund's various social ruptures (albeit often in modified form). The Bund often revived patterns of activism from previous eras. Practices are tied to human actors; as the latter survived social upheavals and transformations, they produced continuities – or, in the words of Andrew Abbott, social structures – through such practices.[45] These tend to overlap in *Memorik*. Nevertheless, we can identify periodisations for a history of social practices defined by organisational forms, but also by generational configurations, experiences, and shifting priorities.

Given that autobiographical writing could represent an activist practice that reflected other practices, the texts allow for the development of an even more refined periodisation derived from Bundist action itself. There are two ways of doing so (see Figure 9). In terms of the literary epochs of Bundist autobiography, it is possible to draft a periodisation based on the time of writing. Grouping the authorship dates of the 532 autobiographies in distinct epochs helps to identify cycles in Bundist autobiographical text production. Based on this approach, we can identify five epochs: firstly, the period from the Bund's foundation in 1897 up to the revolutionary year of 1917, which would play a minor role in Bundist autobiography. Secondly, a transitional period with a growing autobiographical culture between 1917 and 1921–2 followed, thirdly, by the established, legal Polish Bund from 1921–39. The subsequent fourth period from the beginning of World War II, and particularly the fifth after the founding of the World Bund in 1947, demonstrate that autobiography in the Bund by no means declined during and after the migration process.[46]

A *written-activist* periodisation curve mirrors the periods covered by the autobiographies. Whereas the first curve depicts writing as a form of activism in a given period, this curve shows the periods writers deemed most important to their individual and collective Bundist commemorative culture. As autobiographies in the database often depict events spanning several 'epochs', and in contrast to the first periodisation, multiple indications (a total of 891 entries) are possible. Taking this focus of the texts into account, a slightly modified periodisation refined in eight additional levels emerges. The main differences here are that, firstly, the period prior to the Bund's 1897 foundation receives a great deal of attention, and secondly that the decade after its foundation is the most extensively recalled period of all. Thirdly, the texts recall World War I, although the Bund was not particularly politically visible during this time, whereas the period of intensive memory production post-1945 is the least remembered. When comparing the two periodisations it is striking that

---

45 Abbott 2001, p. 255, p. 258.
46 The latter certainly deserves more differentiation but is not the subject of this study.

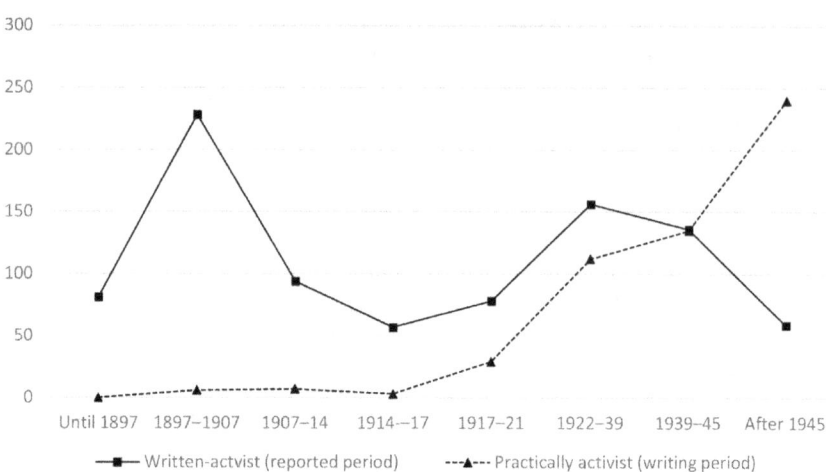
FIGURE 9   Trajectories of Bundist autobiographical culture

both timelines converge after the Bund's founding, only to run parallel during the interwar period. This suggests that the production of remembrance and the production of actions worth remembering actually coincided during this phase. In this sense Bundist culture was able to develop coherently in this period, but the German massacre and mass exile subsequently eliminated the basis for that development. The relationship between activism and remembrance was reversed, the Bund's activist complex collapsed.

Equally evident is that Bundist autobiography did not proceed along some kind of 'moving wall', that is to say the past did not somehow become more worthy of remembering after passing a certain cut-off date. Authors unequivocally emphasise the phases in which the Bund was able to win major victories while simultaneously overcoming tremendous obstacles. The latter include first and foremost the earliest and most remembered period of the Bund from 1897–1907, followed by the interwar period. Autobiographies covering the Holocaust rank only third in absolute numbers, despite the large number of postwar texts studied. It is also remarkable that Bundist autobiography in its entirety sought a kind of 'blanket coverage', meaning it attempted to address the entire history of the Bund in a comprehensive manner and therefore intensively commemorated phases in which the Bund was not a mass movement, such as 1907–21. After all, the uniqueness of this period lay in surviving it as a Bundist organisation based on individually experienced Bundist history.

In this sense, 1917 fails to appear as much of an 'epochal break'.[47] It is not commemorated to any greater extent (a major distinction vis-à-vis Bolshevik

---

47   This does not imply that 1917 was not a historical caesura, but suggests that the common

memorial culture), nor did the year kick off a wave of autobiographies.[48] But a tendency in this direction began to intensify from 1917 onwards, and the Bund's autobiography would continue to grow henceforth. As shown above, *Memorik* already played an important role in the Bund prior to 1917, but autobiography only emerged to any greater degree afterwards and eventually dominated the latter entirely. If anything resembled an epochal year in the Bund's history then it was 1922, in which the fifth anniversary of the revolution and the twenty-fifth anniversary of the Bund's founding coincided. While the years 1917 and 1918 saw the publication of a mere 10 Bundist autobiographies, 19 appeared in 1922 alone.

7   The Persistence of the Past

This study represents the first analysis of the autobiography of a political group decisive in Jewish history before and after the Holocaust.[49] The results are remarkable: the Bund's post-World War II autobiography cannot in any way be reduced to a strategy for coping with the Holocaust. In fact, we do not find any clear emphasis on dealing with it, as a breakdown of writing periods into distinct sub-periods shows (see Figure 10).[50]

The shock of World War II hit Bundists who had already opposed all forms of anti-Semitism for ages hard. Although the Bund was among the first organisations to draw attention to the persecution of Jews during the war, it did so without abandoning a sense of Bundist identity. During the war a large portion of activist texts in the Bundist press were dedicated to current affairs. The immediate past was extensively reflected in autobiography between 1939–47.[51]

It nevertheless accounted for no more than one quarter of that epoch's total autobiography. The relatively small share, which is at the same time the largest share of this period in any of the Bund's writing epochs, can be explained by two factors: firstly, Bundist autobiography was directed inward towards the interior

---

fixation on the year, as Karl Schlögel presciently observes, is 'something like a zero hour, a hiatus, a before and after', ultimately nothing more than a 'simplification' with which 'we seek to order the chaos of history', Schlögel 2002, p. 11f.
48   On Bolshevik politics of remembrance see Corney 2004.
49   See for example Malo 2009, pp. 38–42.
50   Focus is placed mostly on individual authors or attempts to address the Holocaust as narrative strategy; very inspiring in this regard is Brecheisen 1993.
51   See Part III.9.

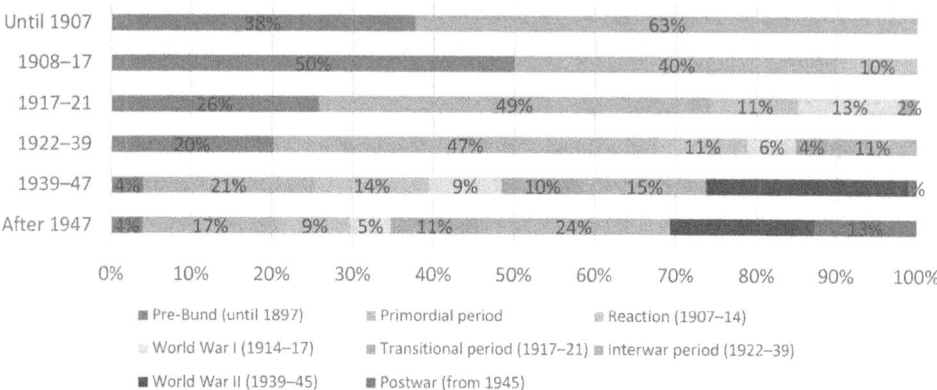

FIGURE 10 Periods and emphases of Bundist autobiographical culture. Distribution of 899 reported periods among 532 autobiographical texts

of the community, but the Bundist interior had been suddenly and thoroughly hollowed out. It is for this reason that the movement's perspective had to focus on the Bund itself, as it otherwise would have lacked the necessary energy to move forward. The Holocaust was a uniquely gruesome aspect of Bundist history, intentionally counteracted by featuring success stories from the more distant past. Autobiography now as never before stood for a stolen lifeworld. Looking back at the past was less a matter of personal introspection so much as a rebellion against the abnormality of the era.

Post-war autobiography built upon this. Bundist autobiographies by no means assumed a special status in Jewish autobiographical writing. Many survivors' reports appeared relating individual stories between invasion and liberation as a way of coping with trauma. They deal with what Dan Diner once described as 'compressed time', an experience of time that decouples from any anterior and posterior temporality and leaves behind a continuum in which beginning and end are ineluctably united as one.[52] Bundists also experienced this 'compressed time' in Stalin's Soviet Union. Both the Holocaust as well as Stalinist persecution had a strong impact on the Bundist perception of 1939–47.

Contrary to common assumptions that Jewish post-war autobiography increasingly emphasised the horror of the period, remembrances of World War II declined from one third to only 18 percent after the Holocaust.[53] Memories of

---

52 Diner 1996, p. 5 f.
53 See for example Günter 2002; McGlothlin 2003; Eichenberg 2004; Ibsch 2004; Münz 2004; Segler-Messner 2005; Brown 2008; Cohler 2009; Kangisser Cohen 2010; Werle 2010.

the interwar period overtook the war. Even the period spanning the beginnings of the Bund to 1907 amounts to a similar share, despite the fact that increasingly few 'veterans' were alive to tell the story. This corroborates more recent approaches that understand post-Holocaust Jewish autobiography less as an individual or collective method of coping with trauma so much as a public negotiation of identity in which life before the war assumes a crucial role.[54] Post-war autobiography did not break with the long-standing tradition of Jewish autobiography either.[55] Transnational Bundist community building after 1947 increasingly relied on depictions of everyday life and activism. Attempting to be as colourful as pre-war Jewish life itself, the heterogeneity of remembrance persisted and made greater efforts to remember this world precisely *because* of its disappearance.

For this reason Bundist autobiography did not become an individualised survival literature even after the Holocaust, but remained embedded in the history of the Bund more generally. The best example of this is probably famous Bundist Bernard Goldstein's autobiography. Born in 1889, his book *'Finf yor in varshever geto'* was published as early as 1947 as one of the first books from Bundist publisher *Unzer tsayt* in New York, and at the same time one of the earliest Holocaust memoirs. Goldstein also published a number of short survivor's reports in *'Unzer tsayt'*.[56] An English translation appeared in 1949, but received scant attention due to the low level of international interest in such reports.[57] This changed in the 1960s when it was also translated into German. Interest in this commemorative text has persisted ever since, as the numerous reprints of the Warsaw Ghetto Uprising classic demonstrate.

Goldstein himself, however, regarded its popularity as something of a limitation. In response, he composed an equally unique account of Jewish life in interwar Warsaw to commemorate his activism for the Warsaw Bund, and thus Polish Jewish life during the interwar period as a whole. 'Jews, remember! Jews, write down! – is the call that pervades the present Jewish post-war epoch', as Emanuel Szerer summarises Bundists' feelings in the introduction to the book:

> But this should not be understood too narrowly, it must not be reduced exclusively to the destruction [*khurbn*] and resistance during World War

---

54 Freadman 2004; Freadman 2007.
55 See esp. Moseley 2006.
56 Goldstein 1947c; Goldstein 1947b; Goldstein 1953.
57 Goldstein 1949.

11. The unprecedented genocide committed by the Nazis against more than six million Jews with the Polish population in the front row of the murdered will become more real in the eyes of the world and exhibit its true magnitude for future Jewish generations if Jewish life is depicted accurately – and to a large extent this means precisely a Jewish working-class life – that in the midst of its stormy rise was cut down so brutally and totally. ... The book by *khaver* Bernard Goldstein is devoted to that scantly described epoch. For that reason alone, it fulfils an important task.[58]

Yet the book exhibited the same weaknesses: it was hardly read outside of the Bund, nor was it translated.[59] Despite this fact, it proved significant to community building within the Bund and can be seen as belonging to the sort of interwar literature that became the main focus of Bundist autobiography after 1948. We can therefore conclude that post-war Bundist autobiography focused on all epochs almost equally – not despite, but precisely because of the horrors of the Holocaust. While more than two thirds of all reported periods covered the prehistory and beginnings of the Bund before 1939, we can identify a pronounced juxtaposition of various periods of Bundist history after the cataclysm of the war.

Depictions became increasingly redundant. This is particularly true of personal autobiographies, which assumed the function of necrologies with a large number of anecdotes in the style of 'how I came to meet late *khaver* XY for the first time'. World War I, the period Catherine Merridale identifies as the hallmark of non-Soviet autobiography, receded noticeably into the background. Unlike Merridale's conclusion concerning the Soviet Union, it retained its stable albeit marginal status.[60] The Bund opposed the war and supported a moderate Zimmerwald line. Although this contributed to the Bund's public profile, it was insignificant in its political and cultural work.[61]

The broad scope of periods surveyed demonstrates that Bundist community building emerged not from ground-breaking decisions, but from participation. The activity in which activists engaged became worthy of remembrance. Focal points included the organisation's beginnings, especially around 1905 and later

---

58 Sherer 1969, pp. x–xi.
59 This changed with the recent publication of Marvin S. Zuckerman's English translation (Goldstein 2016).
60 Merridale 2002, p. 96 ff. See also Cohen 2003.
61 Despite a great deal of agreement, the Bund did not send delegates to the 1915 Zimmer-

the interwar period. Bundist autobiography by no means dealt with emancipation or subject constitution alone, but was first and foremost a form of activism within and on behalf of the movement.

8 Stratification

The Bund saw itself as *the* Jewish workers' movement, which it justified by citing its strong presence among the Jewish worker masses.[62] But intellectuals' leading role was not ignored. The latter's organisational and programmatic achievements influenced the Bund to a large degree, which in times of crisis, however, could be run by workers alone. As Ezra Mendelsohn notes, this helped the Bund survive the first wave of arrests targeting Bundist leaders from 1898 onwards.[63] The Bund emerged stronger than before as greater numbers of workers now occupied key positions in the movement.[64] Activism and utopia subsequently appeared to balance out the differences between workers and intellectuals. However, a closer look at more subtle distinctions in the depictions of Bundist life (and their activities in particular) reveals that the Bund was a socially differentiated movement. Relevant research on the Bund emphasises this social heterogeneity, but we lack studies investigating these differences.[65] This leaves the question of the relationship between workers and the better-educated unanswered. Gertrud Pickhan's very legitimate question of 'where are the women?' therefore ought to

---

wald Conference, as the gathering declined to recognise its demand for Jewish national self-determination. The old conflict between the Bund and the 'Russian internationalists' around Lenin and Trotsky rose to the fore once again, see Eley 2002, p. 130.

62 This claim to representation provoked conflicts within the Jewish workers' movement. We must be careful not to assume a majority party from the fact that the Bund was a mass organisation. That would have been impossible under Tsarist rule at any rate, and the Bund held electoral majorities in interwar Poland in only a few cases, see Jacobs 2009, pp. 1–7; Shapiro 1994. Historiography not directly related to the Bund also confirms its mass character, such as Haumann 2002, pp. 162–75.

63 This had its roots in Sergei Zubatov's 'police socialism', which sought to form trade unions loyal to the Tsar as a tool against the revolutionary movements. While some research has interpreted this as a (failed) attempt at Russian modernisation, Bundists viewed it primarily as a threat to the workers' movement and support for the elites, see Daly 1988, p. 89, pp. 104–8; Murphy 2005, pp. 3–15. For the Bundist perspective see Mutnik 1993a, 1993b; Kossovski 1942; Shvarts 1968.

64 Mendelsohn 1970.

65 'Strata' were identified by the editor of the *Doyres bundistn*, although he referred to stages of membership and forms of activism within the Bund, see Hertz 1956, p. 9.

be preceded by a question even more central to the Bundist workers' movement: 'where are the workers?'⁶⁶

How to identify workers in a workers' movement? I propose a biography-oriented approach. After all, being a worker in the Bund resulted more from one's education and training than actual economic situation. In this sense, I do not conceive of all wage-earners or those employed in certain industries as workers, but instead those whose educational experience allowed for biographical identification as workers. This was founded on access to the written word, which played an immensely important role in processes of activist community building, and of course came far easier to Bundists with a higher level of secular or religious education than Bundists who merely spent a few years in the *kheder*. The latter acquired their knowledge of the world not through the pen or the Mishnah, but through the hammer, the needle, or the workbench. Exploitation and fraternisation at work shaped their understanding of *khavershaft* rather than group study sessions at the Talmudic school. Because access to education was also regulated economically, a biography-oriented approach keeps class-based exclusions in mind without placing them centre stage.

This produces a three-tiered model of Bundist activists. *Workers* are at the centre of it. This majority, which is often silent in the relevant literature, generally only attended the *kheder* or other primary schools and found their way into working life mostly through their parents' workbench or other craftsmen.⁶⁷ This should not be confused with 'working': a grammar school pupil could later spend a few years as a shoemaker, and the path of *yeshiva* students often took them from the classroom back to the workbench. Alienation, hunger, and wage dependency threatened even the educated classes. An improved relationship to the written word, however, remained the main distinguishing trait influencing lives and professional careers in many ways.⁶⁸ Workers generally stood less chances of advancing into the movement's upper ranks. The Bund was aware of this ambivalence, and took up workers' education as a central task. Due to this intrinsic motivation, the Bund became one of the most important actors in Jewish education: a hint that it emerged not exclusively from the trade unions of the Jewish Pale, but also from the renowned 'circles' – the sites of illegal knowledge dissemination in the backrooms of Tsarist Russia, where educa-

---

66 Pickhan 2004.
67 An approach utilising social statistics was attempted by Bunzl 1975; a narrative approach is found in Mendelsohn 1970.
68 This is true not only for the Bund but also for the PPS, see Shtern 1954.

tion and consciousness-raising in the Marxist sense went hand in hand.[69] This tradition evolved across many institutions extending into the period of legality and the TSYSHO.[70] As shown by Jeffrey Veidlinger, the emergence of a secular Jewish identity in the late Tsarist empire relied on the availability of secular, often Russian-language literature.[71] The latter had to be complemented by what I consider the far more essential Yiddish socialist literature, not available in Russia's official libraries but instead passed on the street from person to person.

Access to the written word is understood not as mere literacy, but rather as a familiarity with working with texts as both reader and author, building on basic skills and growing with continuing education. Writing was an essential precondition for later activities within the Bund as they came to rely more and more on the written word. The other two strata – Bundists with *higher secular education* and *higher religious education* – were less relevant in quantitative terms but better prepared qualitatively. Bundists pursued higher education in secondary educational institutions, which in the secular world included *Gymnasium*, college, and university, while the *yeshiva* constituted the dominant religious institution. From this arises an unbiased tiered model that also reflects biographical developments. Purely functionally and in line with the Bund's conception, secular education is deemed as the 'highest' form of education, while workers represent the basic level and higher religious education occupies the middle tier. In this model, the respective higher education 'overwrites' previous levels of education through knowledge acquisition, as education brings the actor into new associations that significantly alter his or her agency. Categorisation in the database occurred (wherever possible) on the basis of the highest level of education during the investigated period (for instance, at the time of joining the Bund or while composing the autobiography in question).

In order to investigate the impact of these stratifications on Bundist autobiography, it was necessary to reconstruct the life trajectories of the respective autobiographers. That said, it is often extremely difficult to determine their educational background, firstly because the naming of authors varies wildly in terms of names and pseudonyms depending on particular legal situations and migration patterns, secondly because many authors only used initials,

---

69   A rich depository is Kurski et al. 1939. For further examples see Novok 1957; Hofman 1948a. On the role of the educational circles even for the daughters of academic households see Dubnov-Erlich 1918a and Dubnov-Erlich 1918b.
70   Kazdan 1956. On individual personalities see Kazdan 1952.
71   Veidlinger 2009, pp. 89–113.

TABLE 6   Distribution of Bundist autobiographical culture according to educational background

Education	Confirmed	Likely	Total[a]
Worker	147	34	181
Higher religious education	32	–	32
Higher secular education	198	15	213
Undefined	106	–	106

a I refer to this figure in the following (unless stated otherwise).

thirdly because Bundist autobiography was somewhat dominated by episodic memories which make inferring an author's entire educational background difficult, and fourthly because authors of Holocaust autobiographies were often 'one-time authors' who never appeared elsewhere. Assigning authors to a certain educational background was further complicated by, fifthly, the fact that a strong tendency to conceal this status pervaded the Bund, as all Bundists whether scholar or tailor were supposedly fighting for the same cause against the same enemy. Hiding one's educational background can often be read as an indicator of an author's higher level of education, as was usually confirmed by further research. I managed to reconstruct the educational background of 80 percent of the autobiographies' authors, with Holocaust survivor testimonials constituting more than one third of those unaccounted for. Memories pertaining to the core 1897–1939 period of this study, i.e. those which were either composed during or contained memories from this time, were generally classifiable and often included extensive personal information about the author.

On this basis we can conclude that the Bund's autobiography was composed by workers and intellectuals in almost equal measure (Table 6). Workers certainly produced a significant amount of the Bund's autobiographical works and made a major contribution to writing their movement's history. The decades-long marginalisation of their perspective thus appears all the more puzzling. The number of highly educated authors is slightly higher – hardly surprising given these authors' relationship to the written word – while 30 of the 67 autobiographical monographs were written by workers, meaning no relative difference in the distribution of long-term and short-term memories can be identified.

There is also another striking tendency: although the Bund claimed that worker members' 'great wealth of experiences and episodes' constituted the essence of Bundist history, it took the organisation quite some time to dis-

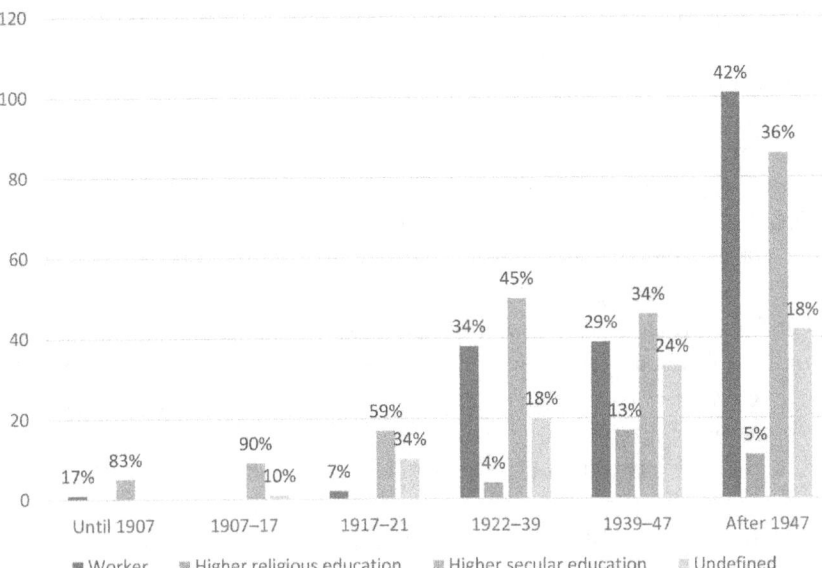

FIGURE 11 Social stratification of Bundist autobiographical culture according to writing period

cover their capacities as authors.[72] Likewise, workers only began to recognise the relevance of their own experiences to Bundist history at a very late stage (Figure 11).

Worker autobiographies only began to form a substantial portion of Bundist autobiography around 1922. At the same time, more and more Bundists who never held a party post but represented the 'mass' in the mass movement were publicly commemorated. This is apparent in the growing number of non-classifiable autobiographies, the relative share of which (except for the outlier around the October Revolution) remained almost the same. Workers increasingly became authors invigorated by the fact that there were fewer 'repeat offenders' among them compared to those with higher education of both kinds, a significant percentage of whom were journalists and to a lesser degree doctors and professors.

This data calls two proud traits of the Bund into question: firstly, the characterisation of the Bund as a workers' movement must be qualified. The Bund was a worker-mobilising movement – it attracted workers, represented their interests, and was able, over the course of its existence, not only to have an

---

72 N.N. 1921b.

impact in terms of education, but indeed to harness this education for its own reproduction. Workers were thus increasingly granted the power of interpretation, yet this occurred only – and this is eminently important – after intellectual authors had established substance and emphases worthy of remembrance, as well as modes of commemorating these episodes. In social movement research terminology, Bundist remembrance culture was framed in a way that did not officially regulate worker autobiographies, but nevertheless prescribed a certain style of remembrance and made the depiction of 'new episodes' more difficult. This framing would continue to have an impact on worker authors well after World War II, as demonstrated in the autobiographies of lathe operator Hershl Metaloviets or joiner Yoel Novikov: the passages depicting the time before their 'rise' inside the Bund are suspenseful and unconventionally recount personal aspects of life as a prospective Bundist.

As soon as the two authors begin to talk of their later positions in the organisation, substance and priorities of remembrance change as a shift towards collective events in telling the Bund's history becomes evident. Language and tone change as well, growing more formal or even bureaucratic. It is worth noting that neither of these authors enjoyed major advances up the ranks of the Bund, but 'only' engaged in regional activities with limited reach albeit strong local impact. Ultimately, these sorts of memoirs increasingly reflect the tone struck by Vladimir Medem's autobiography, the most widely read Bundist autobiography and the role model for what an intellectual author should look like, along with the autobiography of Layb Berman, a model worker who successfully climbed the party ranks. Given that they were all men, the second trait to be discussed will be the role of gender inside the Bund.

9 Gender

The Bund saw itself as an egalitarian movement not only between workers and intellectuals, but between men and women. It thus promised women equal rights within its ranks – something that many Bundists regarded as self-evident. As activist Tsirl Shtayngart correspondingly remarked in 1975, it was 'no coincidence that women played an important role in all those years of struggle led by the Bund'.[73] But what exactly was this 'important role'? Gertrud Pickhan argues that the Bund's uncritical stance towards its own self-understanding obscured women's position in the Bund for quite some time.[74] This question is

---

73 Shtayngart 1975.
74 Pickhan 2004.

particularly relevant to Bundist autography, for if women constituted up to 30 percent of active membership at one point, then their experiences and stories ought to play an important role in the Bund's activist *Memorik*.

In reality, however, as authors women Bundists are almost completely marginalised. Only 50 of the surveyed autobiographical texts (less than 10 percent) can be matched with women authors, of which only 13 were written by women workers and only three of which before World War II. Although these three texts consists of recollections, they do not depict life as a Bundist woman. In fact, they were only printed in the first place because they explicitly avoided recounting women's stories and were instead dedicated to Bundist hero Hirsch Lekert. Stronger emphasis on the Bund in these three texts would be surprising, given that they were published in the context of the Moscow *Yevsektsiya*'s mobilisation efforts.[75] Educated Bundist women appeared more frequently, although early autobiographies are limited to three leading and highly educated Bundists: Sophia Dubnova Erlich, Esther Frumkin, and Anna Rozenthal.[76]

This is not to say, however, that no need for Bundist women worker autobiographies existed. *Memoirs of a Female Cigarette Maker*, popular in Tsarist Russia, proves the opposite. This relatively long commemorative narrative (roughly 30 pages) depicts the difficulties confronting a late nineteenth-century working woman in great detail, along with the improvements Bundist activism brings to her life. Here she found not only struggle but also community, encouraging her fervent praise for the Bund. These memoirs were distributed among Jewish workers as propaganda – an excellent example of the memories of workers' movement activists serving a mobilising function. Mobilising effects were enhanced mostly by the fact that the author, much like the fallen Bundists of early Bundist proletarian short hagiography, was unknown and could therefore easily be identified with as *unzere khaverte*. The author's anonymous status was no coincidence. These memoirs were actually written by a man who himself was anything but a worker: Samuel Gozhansky, the author of *Memoirs of a Female Cigarette Maker*, worked as a well-educated teacher in Russian state schools during the Tsarist era and was one of the great teachers in

---

75   Reytshuk 1922; Grinshteyn 1922; Reytshuk 1927. A more specific search for autobiographies written by female authors in a larger source corpus would surely reveal a number of additional standalone works (such as the special supplements of the '*Naye folkstsaytung*' directly targeting women, which would also raise the total number). But it would ultimately do little to change the overall picture.

76   Dubnova 1916; Dubnov-Erlich 1918a; Dubnov-Erlich 1918b; Frumkin 1918a; Frumkin 1918b; Frumkin 1919a; Frumkin 1919b; Rozental 1939.

the illegal 'circles'. Moreover, he belonged to the first Bundist generation.[77] In contrast to the dead in the Bundist press, this cigarette maker was not only unknown but indeed non-existent. The memoirs would only be reprinted as an historical document in 1927, thereby ensuring their survival. It is unknown whether such texts were produced in the Tsarist period.[78]

Unfortunately, we find little indication as to what exactly motivated Gozhansky to write these memoirs and why the Bund did not rely on the many women active in the Bund instead. It is safe to assume that a certain dual paternalism played a role as both an intellectual and a man, although at least the former was not specific to the workers' movement in Tsarist Russia. The *Diary of a Shirtwaist Striker* published in New York in 1911, which 'created a legend about "girls" who became both heroines and pioneers of socialist ideals', also purported to be authored by a young seamstress who participated in the famous Shirtwaist Strike of 1909–10. The true author, however, was the well-educated and anything but youthful Theresa Serber Malkiel, who the publisher in turn identified as closely linked to 'Bund-type radical activism'. This kind of Bundist activity sought to break away from the 'male-centered culture' of American socialism, but only had a marginal impact on female Bundist authorship.[79] A general rule in the Bund continued to apply: memory was a man's world.[80]

10   Autobiography and Migration

While results in terms of distinct periods and stratification are ambivalent, findings with regard to language and spatiality of Bundist autobiography are all the more unequivocal. The migration process in particular stands out, as the 'changing of worlds' associated with it can be considered the Bund's most important generator of autobiography – even more crucial than the organisation's ongoing generationality. Only 45 percent of autobiographical texts were produced by authors older than 60. The same share was written by authors

---

77   Abramowicz 1999, p. 124 f.
78   Gozhansky 1927a; Gozhansky 1927b; Gozhansky 1927c.
79   Basch 1998, p. 3, p. 52.
80   This was also stylistically driven. Rebekka Denz's observation concerning the biographisation of women in the collected volume *Doyres bundistn*, namely that gender equality in textual depictions mainly entailed 'masculinisation' or was reduced to a peripheral matter 'in the context of describing her husband's activity on behalf of the Bund', also applies to Bundist autobiography, see Denz 2009, p. 20 f., p. 68 f.

TABLE 7 Written languages of Bundist autobiographical texts

Language	Number (percent)
Yiddish	506
Russian	11
English	9
Spanish	6
Polish	1

still of working age, while 13 were even written by children or adolescents.[81] In this sense Bundist autobiography cannot be reduced to the older generation's *Memorik*. Generationality nevertheless played a major role in the migration process, as can be seen particularly strongly in the choice of language.

Bundist autobiography spoke Yiddish (Table 7). The few autobiographical texts composed in Russian appeared sporadically across the various writing periods, while English- and Spanish-language texts arose exclusively after the outbreak of World War II.

Peter Pescher's work on 'first language attrition' as an identity-forming factor in the migration process is therefore an unsuitable point of departure for this investigation.[82] Here, first language retention actually facilitated Bundist identity. More than 95 percent of Bundist autobiographies were written in Yiddish, which increasingly became a 'group language' extremely significant in the community-building process, often surviving not only the migration process itself but also political reorientation. When former Bundist Hersh Mendel later composed his autobiography as an Israeli Labour Zionist, he proudly did so in Yiddish.[83] Although the bulk of migrants moved to the US and managed to integrate themselves economically, Bundist group identity continued to rely on the old language. Only eight (about three percent) of the autobiographical texts composed in the US were written in English, all of them during or after World War II. Their initial function was to make the Bund's shared knowledge

---

81 Figures (undefined or contradictory biographical data flagged as 'likely'): over 60 years: 244 (13 'likely'); working age: 240 (34 'likely'); adolescents: 13; undefined: 34.
82 Pescher 2007.
83 Mendel 1959; English: Mendel 1989.

of the Holocaust available to a non-Yiddish audience.[84] Bundist autobiographers would only begin to write exclusively in English at a much later stage.[85]

The language issue confronted the Bund with a dilemma in the migration process: the turn to Yiddish, the move *in die gasn tsu di masn* (into the streets to the masses) represented the linchpin of Bundist historical roots, which in turn grew in discursive importance. This helped to merge the revolutionary and trade union movements within the Bund. Under American conditions, however, language attrition began to set in, increasingly bringing *yidishkayt* into conflict with *doikayt*. During Meyer London's lifetime, Yiddish political activism had still been possible in the US. By the 1920s, however, local political action also began to entail speaking English despite many Bundists viewing it as 'assimilation'. The greater this danger became, the more Bundists relied on its grand *Memorik* heritage to preserve the movement's identity.

This became particularly pronounced after the Holocaust, albeit with renewed activist connotations. As Emanual Szerer noted, the insistence on *yidishkayt* was not least a mode of resistance against demographic reality and the killing off of *yidishkayt* by 'the intruding hands of demonic murderers'.[86] This dilemma encouraged the production of Yiddish *Memorik* not only in the Bund, but even more so in thousands of *yizker-bikher*. The use of Yiddish was always at the same time a declaration of survival, simultaneously turning emerging *Memorik* into a kind of linguistic island. This can be seen in journalist and early Holocaust autobiographer Pinkhas Shvarts's texts. He managed to escape to the US after witnessing the first days of the German occupation of Warsaw, and later published one of the first monographic testimonials about the Holocaust in his book '*Dos iz geven der onheyb*' (This Was the Beginning), written in the style of a chronicle.[87] He also composed a film script to further educate the public, excerpts of which appeared in '*Unzer tsayt*'. He argued that the 'authors [in Hollywood] ought to spend less time inventing nonsensical things and more time reading authentic depictions of the underground struggle in Europe'. He assumed 'that the Warsaw Ghetto will one day become a major topic in the film industry, but no one should confuse the truth with cheap trash. ... So listen, all you scriptwriters, here is a fragment for you, its title is: *khaver* Zigmunt'.[88] It was written entirely in Yiddish and therefore failed to attract Hollywood's attention,

---

84   Wiernik 1944; Goldsztejn 1948.
85   See for example Abramowicz 1996; Margules 1999; Brumberg 1999; Erlich 2006; Brumberg 2007.
86   Sherer 1960, pp. x–xi.
87   Shvarts 1943.
88   Shvarts 1945, cited on p. 78f.

TABLE 8   Writing locations of Bundist autobiographical texts

Location of writing	Certain	Likely	Total[a]
North America[b]	266	37	302
Eastern Europe[c]	84	14	99
Argentina[d]	31	2	32
Israel	24	6	30
Soviet Union	19	–	19
Other[e]	39	–	19
Unclear	10	–	10

a   This figure constitutes the point of departure for the following analysis.
b   Among these are a small number of autobiographies from Canada.
c   This means sites of active Bundist presence, namely the Tsarist empire and independent Poland.
d   This includes a small number of autobiographies from Uruguay.
e   Including primarily Australia (9), France (8), Belgium (7), England (6), and Mexico (2), of which only three were composed before World War II.

but was at least exposed to the readers of *'Unzer tsayt'*. The Bund's perspective was theoretically of a global nature, but practically all action was directed inward, towards the Bund and towards community building.

In the Soviet Union, the dynamic was reversed entirely. The *Yevsektsiya* sought to harness Yiddish-language autobiography as a motor of political mobilisation, subsuming Bundist *Memorik* into a proletarian 'prehistory' of Red October. As Stalinism consolidated, however, it became increasingly regulated. Bundist autobiography disappeared from the public sphere entirely. They first expunged the Bund's name and then erased the specific influence of the Jewish workers' movement, before finally many activists fell victim to the Red Terror.

Another picture emerges if we consider the United States, Argentina, and Eastern Europe triad underlying this study, understood here as the space in which the Bund was actively engaged after its periods in the Russian Tsarist empire and later independent Poland. Over 80 percent of Bundist autobiography was produced in these three regions combined (Table 8). The dominance of North America as a site of authorship was not a natural given, but rather developed over time (Figure 12). Bundist autobiography emerged slowly in Eastern Europe, complemented by a growing number of texts from the US beginning in 1917–21. Bundist autobiography consolidated as one of the movement's most important activism patterns in the period following the Bund's twenty-fifth anniversary. This was accompanied by a transnationalisation of

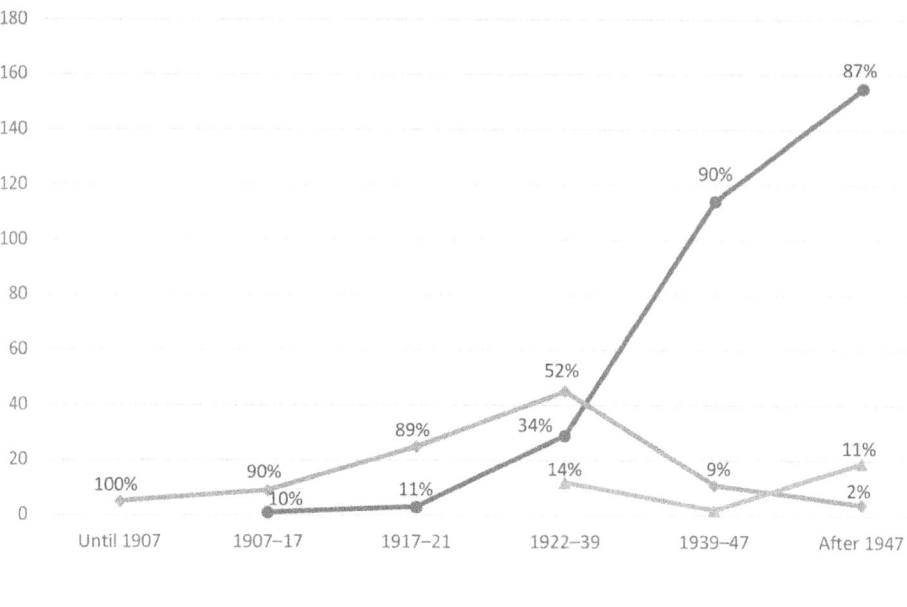

FIGURE 12   Writing locations of Bundist autobiographical texts in transatlantic comparison

Bundist *Memorik*, as almost half of the sample originated overseas from the interwar period onwards. Differences in activism between the US and Argentina also became apparent: autobiography never emerged as a central pattern of activism in the latter, even after the Holocaust.

Bundist autobiography's transnationalisation also manifested at a material level. Layb Berman's autobiography could not have been published in Poland without the financial support of the American *Arbeter-ring*.[89] Vladimir Medem's autobiography, on the other hand, appeared in the US but was also widely circulated in Poland. The already-existing transnational space of action spanning Eastern Europe and the US held together through fundraising continued to develop, and became the Bund's foundation through resource exchange in the form of financial clout and *Memorik*.[90] Because Bundist autobiography appeared not only in books but primarily in magazines and periodicals, the US would only develop into the publishing site of Bundist autobiography after the launch of '*Unzer tsayt*' in 1941. This effect was of course enhanced by the almost complete silencing of Bundist autobiographical writing in post-war Poland.

---

89   Berman 1936, p. 4.
90   See also Part III.12.

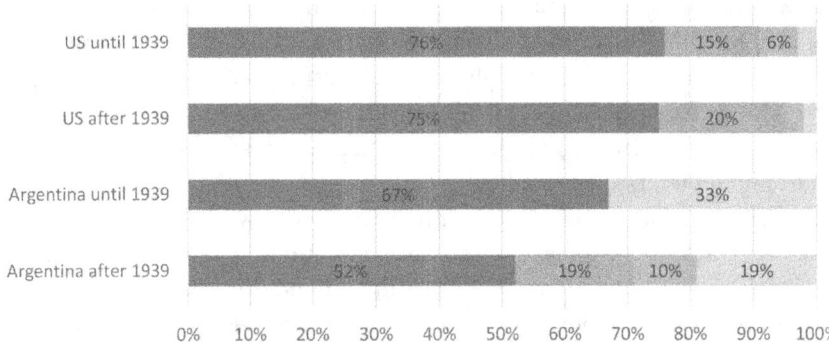

FIGURE 13   Reported locations in migratory Bundist autobiographical texts, pre- and post-1939

Argentina falls markedly behind in quantitative terms, but qualitatively differences also outweigh commonalities. The largest share of reporting addressed Eastern Europe in both North America and Argentina. In North America – which, with few exceptions, is generally understood to mean the US and in turn, again with a few exceptions, New York – around three quarters of autobiographical texts deal exclusively with Eastern Europe, whereas only a small fraction address local episodes (see Figure 13).

Representing roughly 20 percent of autobiographies, texts dealing with both the New and Old World had a relatively strong presence in the US after 1939. They include some written for the YIVO's 1942 autobiographical contest, which conflated the two spaces not out of intrinsic motivation but for the sake of meeting competition requirements.[91] Interest in the self-biographisation of the American Bund or Bundists migrating to the US remained marginal at best. This was not so in Argentina, where one third of all autobiographical texts dealt directly with Argentina even before World War II. The history of the *Avangard* group is particularly prominent. Eastern Europe and Argentina appear as two strictly divided realms of experience that overlap in Bundist biographies but not in autobiographies. This changed after 1939, especially after the founding of the Bundist publishing house *Yidbukh* in Buenos Aires that published numerous memoirs and documents of Jewish life in pre-war Poland. As the text ratio analysis indicates, ultimately a similar range of Bundist publications developed in Argentina as in the US albeit with a much more local focus, despite a numerically smaller presence of Jewish immigrants.

Autobiography was thus a crucial element to the Bund's social movement. It served to mobilise, build community, and transfer identities while in turn

91   See Soye 1999.

allowing authors to communicate them. It also separated experience from reflection, as the US was the main locus of *Memorik* but not of activism. This can be regarded as a functional differentiation lasting until the end of the interwar period. The development initially nurtured the Bund's productive transnationalisation, but Eastern Europe was lost as a point of reference after the Holocaust and remembrance could henceforth do little more than revolve around itself. This stood in contrast to groups more inclined towards activism in South America and later Australia. The transnationalisation and re-orientation of the centre after 1947 would draw the Argentinian Bund even closer to the North American Bund. Autobiography was thus a double-edged sword: it productively facilitated the retention of a social movement throughout migration over a longer period of time, but in order to be true activism as opposed to mere literature, it had to connect to the experiences of activists and articulate certain goals. The loss of the Eastern European base and the generational shift overseas posed problems irresolvable through *Memorik* alone.

CHAPTER 6

Preserving Collective Knowledge in Migration: Collective Biography and Questionnaires

Bundist *Memorik* sought to reproduce the Bund *per memoriam* on the basis of individual experiences. In the research design underlying this study, consisting of primary-, secondary-, and tertiary-Bundist autobiography combined with numerous other sources, *Memorik* also serves as the basis of a social history of the Bund, analysing the aspects of their organisation Bundists themselves deemed worthy of recording. Autobiographies were additively integrated into a total world view, most strongly expressed in promotional introductions written by third-party authors, often citing hitherto unknown aspects of Bundist history contained within the text in question. Some aspects of Bundist history were sugar-coated in the process, as can be seen in the case of gender issues. Nevertheless, this tendency only evolved to a limited degree, as ex-Bundists also composed Bundist *Memorik* and were therefore not subject to any kind of central or decentral directive. Readers also played an important role, for the texts appealed to old comrades and veterans who verified the episodes depicted through their consumption of the texts. *Memorik* texts were loaded with preconditions precisely because of their community-building function. That being said first had to be believed before it could successfully serve a mobilising function. Secondly, internal Bundist historiography reflected it. Thirdly, due to Bundist autobiography's decentral character, readers could become authors at any time.

This was increasingly true in the wake of World War II, after the Bund lost its institutional memory with the destruction of its party archive. Activists in New York made a particularly determined effort to compile a written record of their members' stories and establish a new archive as complete as possible, consisting largely of transmitted fragments, salvaged collections, and personal memoirs.[1] *Memorik* in this sense did not serve to 'recall' but rather 'make available'. As a result, historians have access to a rich source of insight not only into the functional modes of Bundist collective *Memorik*, but also the social thread of the Bund itself. Reconstructing the Bund forced Bundists to externalise, via memory, the world of the Bund – a world that until then was internalised

---

1   Pratt 1981; Web 2001.

through experience.² Correspondingly, Bundists sought not only to experience and shape Bundist community, but to explore it as well. Many of the sources produced during such attempts have yet to attract scholarly interest. This pertains especially to questionnaires the Bund compiled in an effort to survey its movement. This chapter draws on them in order to firstly investigate another central aspect of Bundist *Memorik*, and secondly analyse the Bund from a collective biographical perspective on the basis of the data retrieved.

1   Approaches to Bundist Collective Biography

Studies on social relations within the Bund are still sorely lacking. Gertrud Pickhan can be credited with expanding our perspective beyond the level of organisation and prominent individuals, although she also considers a social-historical differentiation of the Bund to be impossible.³ Subsequent cultural-historical research essentially did little more than extrapolate the Bund's social makeup from the lives of a few leading figures.⁴

Gertrud Pickhan studied this level in more detail, producing an excellent table, 'Biographical Data of Leading Bundists During the Interwar Period', bringing together the Bund's political work and collective biographical approaches for the first time.⁵ Here, the question is to what extent this reflected the actual social structure of the Bund, frequently referring to itself as 'the Jewish workers' movement'.⁶ Only three of the 30 Bundists listed can be identified as skilled workers: typesetter Lozer Klog, tailor Sara Shveber, and famous glove maker Shmuel Zigelboym. Bundists like Beynish Mikhalevitsh and Israel Lichtenstein may not have attended specific vocational training but had nevertheless, through autodidactic learning, enjoyed noteworthy and well-documented careers.⁷ This was met by 25 Bundists from the leadership with higher secu-

---

2   On problems with verbalising such inscriptions see Welskopp 2014.
3   Pickhan 2001, p. 132.
4   As much is stated in Jack Jacobs's comprehensive investigation of the Bundist youth organisation *Yugnt bund 'tsukunft'*, largely structured around leading intellectual Sofia Erlich-Dubnow's views on sexuality, see Jacobs 2009, pp. 21–7.
5   Pickhan 2001, pp. 414–19.
6   Such as in *Arbeter luakh* 3, 1922. Scholars initially accepted the Bund's claim to dominance in worker circles (Mendelsohn 1970), then categorically rejected (Frankel 1984, pp. 171–82) and eventually qualified it (Peled 1989, esp. pp. 11–121; Pickhan 2001, pp. 126–48).
7   Apart from Mikhalevitsh's autobiography, Kazdan's biography is also worth a read, see Kazdan 1962, pp. 213–52. The Jewish tradition of learning is essential in this kind of autodidactic, see Shtampfer 1999.

lar (*Gymnasium*: 19, commercial school: one, private tutor: one) or religious (*yeshiva*: four) education. The 'class party'[8] was thus not run by the working class itself.

Pickhan's table also demonstrates that biographically oriented research into the Bund cannot limit itself to Eastern Europe. Of the 30 Bundists listed, only three died as veterans in pre-World War II Eastern Europe (Khmurner in 1935, Kremer in 1935, Mikhalevitsh in 1928), as many as in the US before it entered World War II in late 1941 (Lichtenstein in 1933, Kossovski in 1941, Portnoy in 1941). More than one third (11) were murdered in Eastern Europe during the war (four by the Soviets), increasing to 12 with Zigelboym's suicide in London exile. This is exceeded, however, by the number of Bundists who survived overseas (13) – quite unrepresentative for the Eastern European Jewish population as a whole. The life trajectories of these leading Bundists are therefore closely linked to the migration process – more than 80 percent of 'leading Bundists' in interwar Poland were better or highly educated individuals who had often travelled great distances.

The refugees were not merely survivors, but wanted to join together with other emigrants to help the Bund survive. This migration is decisive in the history as well as the historiography of the Bund, for it not only saved lives but also preserved collective knowledge. These migrants were later often active in the committees of the World Bund and directed the group's political relationship to its own history from there. They also sought to reconnect the Bund to the lives of Jewish workers. From a distance the *tuer* recognised the importance of biographical factors, and would henceforth make great efforts to expand and disseminate workers' knowledge in the Bund. The cumulative outcome of this were hundreds of biographical questionnaires that are housed and accessible at the Bund Archive in New York, but ignored by most scholars.

2   Internal Lack of Knowledge

Despite the major fissures mass migration caused in Bundist networks, they persisted after 1945 in varying forms. Yet knowledge of and about each other was lost. In one instance, a 50 $ donation from a certain Manye Goldberg reached the Bund in New York in 1970 or 1971. Out of curiosity, Bundist activists were asked whether anyone knew this person. '*Khaver* Lazar' (probably Lazar

---

8 Pickhan 2001, p. 98f.

Kling), who worked for the World Bund administration, reports the episode in a letter to that same tailor, Manye Goldberg:

> A cheque worth 50 $ arrived and I was asked whether I knew who you are. I had to laugh. Whether I know who you are? An old flagbearer, an old Bundist from the early twentieth century, ... an old professional *tuer*. Is it not a disgrace that nothing in our Bund Archive is recorded on our veterans and old men [*skeynim*]? How many 90-year-old *khaverim* could we name ourselves? Whose fault is this? The archive, which does not make an effort. The old *khaverim* who have declined to register. In other words: we all deserve a good thrashing. Not only are we neglecting our own past, but the heroic deeds and *khaverim* are being forgotten.[9]

Khaver Lazar attached an elaborate biographical questionnaire to his letter, which Goldberg completed and returned immediately (type IV, see Table 9). It inquired about his background, education, training, activities, and party memberships as well as participation in specific actions, arrests, leadership positions, and many other topics. In short: the questionnaire was designed to construct a biographical profile of veteran fighters. It was developed by the mid-1950s and apparently used for the first time during a campaign in 1955. It would subsequently be distributed on sporadic occasions well into the 1980s, as in Goldberg's case. Unfortunately the majority of responses are undated, but we can deduce from the content and envelopes accompanying some of them that a large number were products of the initial 1950s campaign.

As far as an analysis of Bundist autobiography is concerned, the questionnaire as mode of autobiography can be understood as standardised autobiography.[10] This mode functioned as an information-condensing frame that many authors found too narrow. The single, question-packed page failed to provide enough space for an adequate self-biographisation. But a loophole allowed respondents to circumvent the questionnaire's standardisation: at the end of the form, respondents were given the opportunity to depict 'noteworthy events', which many used to include excerpts or even the larger part of their

---

9   The archive contains another questionnaire by Manye Goldberg. It is impossible to say whether it was completed before or after the letter was written. Both are possible, as the existence of a questionnaire by no means implies that the information contained was available while filling out the second one, see Bund Archives, New York, RG 1400, MG2, 429, Goldberg, Manye.
10 See Part II.5; Arroyo 2001.

political careers.¹¹ Some responses took the form of brief sketches, while others chose to pen lengthy, elaborate autobiographical texts. Sixty-one of the 240 returned questionnaires contained such responses, showing that more than one quarter of all respondents seized the opportunity and that the desire for self-biographisation beyond a certain limited template inside the Bund was very pronounced indeed. Information could of course be retrieved through standardised questioning, but a biography primarily rests on the production of at least a degree of meaning and coherence, which many authors found through integrating their biography into that of the Bund as a whole. Like the autobiography as such, these questionnaires also reconciled the individual with the collective. Biographisation did not aim for individuality within the functional space of the movement, which in turn depended on individual *tuer*, but rather the Bund was always implicated in the identities of individual Bundists – while from the Bund's perspective, each Bundist biography was simultaneously a partial biography of the Bund itself.

3 Central Functions: Questionnaires and the *Doyres bundistn*

Due to the positivism the Bund attached to its *Memorik*, it is impossible to discern in which specific context the questionnaires emerged.¹² We can say, however, that they fit into the major post-war waves of biographisation and historicisation.¹³ Commemorating that which had been destroyed became a fundamental collective task in the Jewish diaspora after World War II.¹⁴ While many *landsmanshaftn*, some of which already existed with Bundist participa-

---

11   This stands in stark contrast to Soviet technician Grigorii Grigor'evich Martikhin, who in a letter to Molotov *invented* and even falsified a questionnaire to underscore his request for better housing. On this specifically Soviet form of biographisation via the *anketa*, the 'basic document of Soviet life in the Stalin period', see Fitzpatrick 1997, p. 189.

12   Bund Archives, New York, RG 1400, MG2, 429. Only the questionnaires themselves can be found here. Further information concerning authors and origin can only be inferred; archivist Leo Greenbaum, who has administered the files for decades, insists that no additional materials exist. Apart from sporadic use for party purposes, these materials were largely ignored and merely alphabetised by a volunteer. Leo Greenbaum, personal conversation, New York, YIVO, 23 July 2008.

13   See Wolff 2010.

14   Indeed, while modes and extent of remembrance after the war were new, commemoration as such had its roots in both contemporary and more distant history. See the classic essay on the Jewish commandment of remembrance (Yerushalmi 1982), or the memoirs of An-sky, author of the Bundist hymn *Di shvue*, who depicts the disappearance of the shtetl in World War I (An-sky 1927; English: An-sky 2002).

tion before the Holocaust, took on this task mainly in relation to their respective shtetls of origin, the Bund focused primarily on integrating depictions of the Jewish Pale into its history.[15] The vertical, periodic remembrances of the *landsmanshaftn* and many *yizker-bikher* were complemented by the Bund's horizontal level of commemoration. The Bund's claim to represent the Jewish masses led it to conceive of its own history as a history of Jewish society, albeit not as a prehistory of the Israeli nation or state.

This historicisation was not least the legacy of an activist *Memorik* from the pre-war era, now continued to an unprecedented degree in the form of Yiddish monographs, autobiographies, and collected volumes. One of the more unique major works of collective biography is the three-volume collection of Bundist biographies, *Doyres bundistn* (Generations of Bundists), published between 1955–68 and featuring hundreds of individual biographies. The volumes were edited by Jacob Sholem Hertz, whom Erza Mendelsohn once called the 'official historian' of the interwar Bund – a title he deserved even more after World War II.[16] The collection of biographies was a representative selection intended to erect a 'modest memorial' to the 'thousands and thousands – leaders, *tuer*, and fighters – ground down by the wheel of time'.[17] According to the book's self-description, Bundists 'of various strata' had been considered, from pioneers to ghetto fighters, from leaders to individual Bundists who inscribed themselves into the Bund by committing a specific 'deed'.[18] 'Strata' here primarily denotes the individual's specific position within the Bund. One's level of education, so crucial to individual advancement inside the movement, remained unreflected, as emphasis was placed on impact in terms of individual activism on behalf of the whole. Initially organisers planned to honour more than 300 separate Bundists, but a massive increase in entries from one volume to the next would ultimately more than double that figure.[19] 'Leaders and *tuer* ... whose life stories were already published in book form', whether as biography or autobiography, were left out.[20] The positivist outlook of such a project could hardly be more obvious: the political life of the individual was subject to commemoration in a collectively interpretable context, i.e. the individual's entry into the Bund. A dominant belief in *one true* life story can be observed, yet could only be acknowledged if its temporary importance or rep-

---

15 See Soyer 1999; Lipphardt 2010; Kobrin 2010.
16 For personal data see Denz 2009, p. 16 f.
17 Hertz 1956, p. 8 f.
18 Hertz 1956, p. 9.
19 Ibid.
20 Ibid.

resentativeness for the Bund was recognised, and moreover was not marred by a subsequent crossing of party lines. Defectors to Communism or Zionism, however prominent, were omitted from the honorific volume entirely.[21] Loyalty to the Bund was considered even more important than previous activism.

This mode of selection resulted in a strong overrepresentation of highly educated activists, not as the product of a specific strategy but rather the publisher's specific interest in preservation. As Rebekka Denz demonstrates, the same is true for the privileging of men over women Bundists.[22] The Bund's gender inequality was readily ignored by most scholars for a long time, as was inequality between workers and intellectuals. In an essay that claims to present a critical perspective on gender relations, Paula Hyman euphorically emphasises that women 'seem to have been drawn particularly to the Bund', citing estimates 'that women comprised one-third of the membership of the Bund in its early years'.[23] She then stresses that the *Doyres bundistn* includes 55 women among its biographies of 320 significant activists'.[24] In Hyman's text, little is made of the fact that one third of the membership accounted for one sixth of all *Memorik* biographies – suggesting that either the *Doyres bundistn* has a representation problem, or women were in fact regarded as significantly less important than their male *khaverim*. Moreover, Hyman's figures are simply inaccurate. Rebekka Denz, by contrast, proceeds in a more detailed manner and identifies roughly 600 biographised individuals in the three volumes' roughly 570 entries, of whom 96 individuals (or 65 entries) can be identified as women.[25] Many women were active at the middle levels of Bundist organisations and seem to have been regarded as less important in retrospect, despite the organisation's emancipatory rhetoric.[26] This is also reflected in the form of their biographisation, which followed masculine patterns that posthumously inscribed women

---

21   The listed bibliographies are accordingly 'incomplete', see Hertz 1968, p. 9. See also Jacobs 2009, p. 143, fn. 33.
22   This is even more true where the categories overlap. Rebekka Denz classifies less than 20 percent of biographised women as workers, see Denz 2009, p. 143.
23   Hyman 2000, p. 48. Other research only partially confirms these numbers for the Polish period. Women presumably constituted around 20 percent of the membership, but all figures rest on estimates and highly problematic abstractions, see Pickhan 2001, p. 130 f. This decline was mainly due to changing patterns of activism under legality and illegality, see Denz 2009, p. 118 f.
24   Hyman 2000, p. 48.
25   In these collected biographies women mostly appear only as 'her husband's comrade in arms', her mention therefore often feels like an empty truism. The individual biographies are also strictly gendered. See Denz 2009, pp. 18–22, cited on p. 20.
26   Denz 2009, pp. 49–60, p. 69.

as fighters into narrative templates male comrades developed, while nevertheless treating them separately through references to their appearance or alleged motherly qualities.[27]

This special status for women was no specificity of the *Doyres bundistn* but rather characteristic of the Bund's entire *Memorik*, autobiographical questionnaires included. They were not subjected to editors' interference and yet no more than 28 of all questionnaires – less than eight percent – were verifiably completed by women. Only four female authors took the opportunity to add a supplementary biographical text (6.6 percent), none of which were subject to editorial influence. Frequently only men responded, or sometimes their children born abroad,[28] whereas women largely remained silent – although, according to the life stories provided by men, they had often been activists themselves. In short: the Bund's biographisation remained a man's world, at least for the most part.[29]

The link between *Doyres bundistn* and the questionnaires was implicit at best. Only a handful of entries are based more or less explicitly on the questionnaires,[30] although Bund historian Jacob Sholem Hertz most certainly availed himself of the included photographs, and in the case of famous Bundist Layb Berman (Abraham der Tate) forgot to return them afterwards.[31] The total number of veteran activists who willingly responded to the questionnaires in the three volumes is remarkably low.[32] The primary task of the questionnaires was therefore to fill party archives and conduct a principal acquisition of knowledge

---

27   Denz 2009, p. 21, p. 122f.
28   Bund Archives, New York, RG 1400, MG2, 429, Burshtin, Sender. He submitted an elaborate response while his son and daughter-in-law gave only brief answers, ibid., Burshtin, Dovid; Burshtin, Doris.
29   Wives were sometimes even cited as the reason for joining the Bund and lifelong political comrades. This is the case for Shaye Shikhtov and Fishl Aydlman. Nevertheless, questionnaires filled out by these women, who are still alive today, are not available. See Bund Archives, New York, RG 1400, MG2, 429, Shikhtov, Shaye; Aydlman, Fishl.
30   As much is stated in, for example, ibid., Tsalevitsh, Ben-Tsyon; Hart 1968.
31   The text on the attached note reads: 'the enclosed photo was taken by *khaver* Sholem Hertz, 26 February 1958', signed: L.Sh.; Bund Archives, New York, RG 1400, MG2, 429, Abraham der Tate.
32   Both texts and photographs from the entries were used by the editorial board of '*Unzer tsayt*', such as in the case of Russian Social Democrat Lydia Dan. See ibid., Dan, Lydia and A[leksander] Erlikh, 'Tsum Ondenk fun Lidya Dan', *Unzer tsayt*, New York, no. 5 (1963), p. 21f. They were sometimes ignored, as with Zalmen Pudlovski, who emphasises that he joined the Bund in 1913, while his obituary indicates he was active as early as 1908. It appears that the memory of commemoration 'over-wrote' that of the commemorated. Bund Archives, New York, RG 1400, MG2, 429, Pudlovski, Zalmen; *Unzer tsayt*, 7–8, 1970, p. 46.

inside the Bund. On the other hand, respondents were likely recursively influenced by the *Doyres bundistn*. This was the case for Fishl Aydlman (Philip Adelman), who submitted four questionnaires and three attached autobiographies and was not only a passionate self-biographer whose stylistic proximity to the *Doyres bundistn* was surely no coincidence, but also owned a copy of this standard reference work himself, as many surviving Bundists likely did.[33] Given the ongoing process of chain migration, which continuously reconnects and reconfigures itself, we can speak here of a kind of chain autobiography. It constantly produced new autobiographies, which in turn drew their points of emphasis from affirmation of the overarching Bundist framework and the simultaneous filling of 'knowledge gaps'.

4 Decentral Self-Exploration: The Questionnaire Mode

When approaching the Bund as a social movement, it is necessary to take the identifications of the activists themselves into account. While the *Doyres bundistn* represented an official yet unsystematic collective biography of Bundist *tuer* in both form and selection, the Bund Archive questionnaires allowed for a collective-biographical analysis of Bundist life trajectories based on a collection free from any kind of party-historical directive. Wherever authors followed the political or rhetorical emphases of official Bundist historiography, they did so as an active choice, motivated by identification with the movement and the intertextuality of activist chain autobiography.

It is therefore no coincidence that the mode of 'questionnaire' to obtain group knowledge developed particularly in the Bund's North American migration.[34] In this process, the '1955 campaign' questionnaire was unique in terms of informational density, as it both drew on previous models while also serving as a template for later forms of its kind. Although several Argentinian associations and trade unions cultivated the tradition of surveying their memberships via questionnaires, no similar campaign organised by the Bund is known to exist.[35]

---

33   Ibid., Aydlman, Fishl; Adelman, Philip. Copies of the *Doyres bundistn* complete with the ex libris of Philip Adelman are in the author's possession.

34   Gertrud Pickhan confirmed being similarly unable to retrieve any questionnaires during her work on the Polish Bund, either because they were never compiled or were lost with the party archive in the Warsaw Ghetto. In the latter case, however, some traces would have survived. Email from Gertrud Pickhan to Frank Wolff, 24 June 2010.

35   Blank forms have survived from the *Yidishe literatn un zhurnalistn fareyn, H.D. Nomberg* in Buenos Aires, founded in 1922 and closely linked to the Bund, in which information about one's life as an author and migration process were recorded. Similar is true of the

The membership forms of *Medem vinkl*, a Bundist socialist-cultural institution in late 1920s Buenos Aires linked to the YSFA, were personal forms at best, exhibiting no historical interest.[36]

In the United States, by contrast, the history of such questionnaires is tied to the emergence of the New York Bund Club in 1923, which accepted that the US would become a permanent site of Bundism and Bundist practices given the ongoing settlement of Jewish migrants. The earliest surviving questionnaire (type I, see Table 9), however, was unrelated to any specific campaign or membership application, and was printed in the programme accompanying celebrations marking the Bund's thirtieth anniversary in 1927.[37] The questions contained herein illustrate how the Bund Club grew increasingly eager to learn who had come to the US and what stories and experiences had found their way into the country with them. The novelty of such questionnaires is evidenced not least by the fact that they were not distributed as publications in their own right, but rather printed on the last page of a booklet. Gatherings thereby also became centres of Bundist knowledge acquisition; questionnaires were intended to provide information on the past as well as facilitate recruitment in the present. This is indicated by the mandatory inclusion of a return address, as the Bund did not accept anonymous questionnaires. Unfortunately, nothing is known of this campaign's outcome, but its absence in the archives suggests it was negligible.

Knowledge about other Bundists in the US was expanded and disseminated through private relationships throughout the 1920s and 1930s. An abstract mode of familiarisation through standardised questionnaires was verifiably pursued from 1941 onwards, particularly with new arrivals (type II). These questionnaires were similarly brief. As chain migration receded and gave way to a mass refugee movement, the countless new faces required a brief résumé in order to join the party's American branch. This necessitated gathering as much biographical data about the person as possible, so as to integrate the new recruit into the Bund and demonstrate his or her worthiness, particularly with regard to crucial questions such as the applicant's previous memberships. Questionnaires thus became, in the words of Sheila Fitzpatrick, a 'sociopolitical identity document' of the Bund, which now represented the gateway to

---

Jewish teachers' union, whose questionnaire inquired about working conditions in the schools in great detail. IWO, Buenos Aires, Associacion de escritores Israelitas Nomberg, Questionnaire, 1927; and ibid., Organición de maestras, 1124, 13 [undated, likely 1930s].
36 CAHJP, Jerusalem, AR, PER, 63–64, Deklaratsye (1928–9).
37 YIVO, Bund Archives, New York, ME-14B, 7, *Der 30 joriger jubileum fun 'bund', Meka-tsenter, schabbes avent, dem 15. oktober*, p. 4.

renewed affiliation necessitated by migration.[38] It grew even more necessary as the New York Bund, which began restructuring itself in 1941, became the new centre of the Bundist world. The questionnaires of the second type are still fairly short and provide little substance at least from a historiographical perspective, as they only briefly inquired about new arrivals' political background.

This practice expanded with the first wave of biographisation in 1947 – coinciding, unsurprisingly, with the Bund's refounding as the World Bund. Still in its infancy at the time, the Bund Archives in New York used questionnaires to locate Bundist Holocaust survivors all over the world (type III). This project rested on a global network: of the 45 respondents in the year 1947, only 18 percent indicated living in North America, whereas 70 percent were based in Europe (47 percent in Western Europe, 22 percent in Poland).

This stands in stark contrast to the recipients of the fourth and most elaborate type used from 1955 onwards. Here, 66 percent of respondents indicated a US or Canadian residence, two thirds of whom were in New York. Less than six percent remained in Western Europe, mostly in France and Belgium, and not a single response was returned from Eastern Europe, meaning the whole of Europe was only slightly more prominent than Australia.[39] This is an expression, firstly, of the migration process after 1945–8, and secondly of the Bund Archives' networks. Nevertheless, the network was decoupled from any spatial reference. As Manye Goldberg's example shows, a prominent *khaver* in Eastern Europe could easily be 'closer' to the Bund than a worker and 'flagbearer' in New York. The migration process clearly inscribed itself into this type IV questionnaire. Furthermore, type IV was the only questionnaire circulated over a longer period of time. This mode of questioning not only honoured respondents appropriately while simultaneously granting them a degree of space to express themselves freely, but presented the desired information in a formulated manner. The archivists had come up with a template for storing collective knowledge that satisfied their archive's specific needs.

While type IV asked direct questions about Bundists' lives – that is to say, sought to produce new sources – type II used in 1941–2 was motivated by the more pragmatic goal of evaluating the present. Type V, the last questionnaire on file used by the Bundist group in New York in 1968, proceeded from the latter and simultaneously marked the apex of inquiry into contemporary act-

---

38 Fitzpatrick 1997, p. 189.
39 Distribution, type IV: 157 US (65.4 percent), 32 Israel (13.3 percent), 23 Latin America (9.6 percent), 14 Western Europe (5.8 percent), 13 Australia (5.4 percent), 1 South Africa (0.4 percent) = 240 questionnaires (99.9 percent).

TABLE 9   Autobiographical Bund questionnaires in the US

Type	Type I[a]	Type II
Years	1927	1941–2
Initiator	New York Bundists in the context of celebrations marking the Bund's thirtieth anniversary	Bundisher klub in Nyu Yor[k]
Reach	Local	Local
Temporal/spatial focus	General past/Eastern Europe	Recent past and present/e[astern] Eastern Europe
Main themes	Name, origin Bundist? Member of Bundist organisations, committees and self-defence Participation in conferences Imprisonment Siberia Member of *Kleyner bund*? Address	Name, age Occupations Affiliation to the Bund Previous memberships Entry to the US
Number of questions	12	8
Objective	Overview of Bundists in the US and participants at the gathering	Membership application
Transmitted responses	0	60
Total, transmitted responses	378[b]	

a   Type I: Bund Archives, New York, RG 1400, ME-18; Type II: Bund Archives, New York, RG 1400, ME[...] Type III–V: Bund Archives, New York, RG 1400, MG2, 429.

b   Including another five archived responses (necrologies, press clippings, a non-Bundist question[...] which are incompatible with the grid applied here, but nevertheless were collected in the context [of] campaigns and therefore correspondingly filed.

pe III	Type I	Type V
47	1955–80s	1968
ıdefined, likely the Bund ıchive	'Bund'-arkhiv fun der yidisher arbeter bavegung o. n. Franz Kurski	Organisatsye fun 'bund' in Nyu York
orldwide	Worldwide	Local
cent past/Eastern Europe	General past/Eastern Europe extending into the New World	Present/New World
ıme, birth details	Name, age, origin	Name, family status
ccupations	Parents	Occupation
filiation to the Bund	Training	Affiliation to the Bund
rests	Occupations	Entry to the US
ımps	Affiliation to the workers' movement	Place of origin
hereabouts during the war	Arrests	Memberships in trade unions,
ıowledge of languages	Membership in other organisations	*Arbeter-ring, landsmanshaftn*
	Parents	Current engagement in commis-
	Pseudonyms	sions or similar
	Activities and locations	Reading habits
	Offices	Participation in the Bund Club
	Authorships	Remobilisation of old Bundists
	Living *khaverim*	and other activists
	Request for written accounts of experiences and episodes and photograph	
	20 (plus free text and photograph)	19
formation on surviving ındists	Gaining general historical knowledge, potentially extending into present	Acquiring information about members of the local branch
	240 (30 multiple mentions, 210 activists)	33

ivism. Type V asks for historical data rather selectively: while date of birth is ignored, date of entry into the Bund is specified. Most emphasis is placed on Bundists' actions in New York, their membership in trade unions, the *Arbeterring* and *landsmanshaftn*, reading habits, and on technical matters concerning local Bundist groups. Clearly questions were aimed less at interrogating the past, but rather evaluating the Bund group's current practices.

These questionnaires are not only an expression of Bundist interests and practices in the US, but also sources of hitherto unknown insight into social aspects of the Bund even in Eastern Europe, owed to the previously unavailable data sample they represent. Due to the substantially higher levels of standardised inquiry in comparison to freely composed autobiographies, the biographies depicted here – the number of which must be reduced to about 350, factoring in the exclusion of non-Bundist respondents and multiple responses – provide valuable information on the history of the Bund's social thread, as well as a more profound reflection on the nature and function of Bundist autobiography.

5 Periods, Not Years: Joining the Bund as Social-Historical Perceptual Phenomenon

Questionnaire type IV digs deeper into the lives of Bundists and their Eastern European past. Not all respondents were active in the Bund at the time of their response, of course, but they nevertheless saw it as it their duty to report their past to the Bund Archives. Distinct eras of the Bund overlap in these questionnaires, simultaneously charting the prehistory of the Bund, surviving the Holocaust, and the network of the post-war Bund, and represent the multiple form of temporality intrinsic to activism. In Karl Schlögel's words, they are an expression of 'the synchronicity of the non-synchronous, the coexistence and co-presence of the disparate' that allows for an analysis of distinct levels and superimpositions once the temporality of the artefact is itself viewed as an object.[40]

Time was relevant here mainly in terms of duration. Apart from the name, the most important question was the length of one's membership in the Bund. The latter was always asked and thus more important than the date of birth, which was not asked in questionnaires I and V at all.

---

40 Schlögel 2012, p. 3.

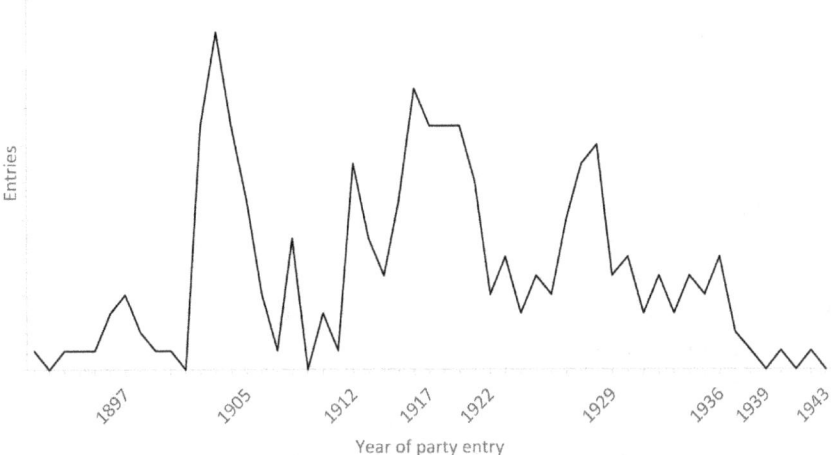

FIGURE 14   Number of entries into the Bund until 1939, questionnaire types II–V

Obvious areas of concentration emerge with respect to when respondents joined the Bund, attesting to fluctuations throughout Bundist history more generally (see Figure 14). Although the number of remaining members from the 1897 founding generation was already quite low when the questionnaires were introduced, the generation that joined from 1905 onwards was well-represented. This generation proved decisive after 1920, particularly in transmitting Bundist history in the form of *Memorik*. Moreover, as is clearly discernible, the Bund became a mass movement in this period. The steep decline in new members after 1905 can be explained by the failure of the revolution and corresponds to widely accepted opinions among historians.[41]

Whether Bundists simply faced 'defeat' after 1912, as Henry J. Tobias and Charles E. Woodhouse argue in their classic study, or whether the actual achievement consisted of enduring this period of increasingly vicious state repression[42] remains a matter of perspective. The defeat hypothesis is based on the theory of social organisations' 'inertia', slowed down by external influences.[43] The logical conclusion here is that, without these external influences, the Bund would have been able and indeed obliged to grow further. Yet if we assume that social movements do not simply 'continue to exist', but like all actors require a constant intake of energy, the surprisingly high number of new recruits around 1908 can be better explained through increased public

---

41   Tobias and Woodhouse 1977.
42   Wolff 2007.
43   Latour 1986.

support for the organisation, without which the Bund may have faced premature demise during these harsh times. From the defeat perspective, then, the high number of recruits in 1908 would constitute a statistical outlier. Yet this inference stems from an insufficiently corroborated assumption, for such statistics were simply unavailable until now. If we take the numbers seriously, this value must be related to a writing period, for most cases do not specifically address the year 1908 but rather refer to a common site of remembrance: the period of reaction. This value was based on the perception of those who completed the questionnaires in 1908 but only became active in the Bund between 1907 and the revived revolutionary fervour of 1912. It corresponds to the recollections of former New York Bund Club chairman Dovid Mayer, which he composed around the same time the type IV questionnaire circulated. He recounted that in 'roughly 1908' a group of Jewish writers received permission to found the *Yidishe literarishe gezelshaft*. The association set up a branch in Warsaw named after famous author Isaac Leib Peretz, which the Bund sought to infiltrate. Mayer became deputy secretary and used this cover to continue the illegal Bund's Yiddish-cultural project.[44] His memory is dominated by actions and problems, while exact data are ignored. The year 1908 represents nothing more than a code mediating between the need to date events and the irrelevance of exactness. Both Bundism and the Bundist organisational structure were doubtlessly forced to engage in rear-guard battles, but how the younger generation dealt with this is another question altogether. The period of membership between 1907–12 is thus a biographised code for the period of reaction. The number of entries again begins to rise significantly from 1912 onwards. This is confirmed by research on the Warsaw elections of 1912 and especially the Lena Goldmine mutiny as the end of the movement's post-1907 paralysis, if not the decisive turning point on the road to 1917.[45]

It was thus impossible for many activists to provide straightforward answers to questions like their year of joining. A conspicuous tendency towards round numbers can be detected in questionnaires that did not ask for the specific date of entry but one's duration of membership. Major inaccuracies emerge with regard to concrete years (type IV). Bundists who responded several times and in large intervals such as Avrom Byalon, Abraham Feygenboym, Naftali Gelberg, or Dovid Mayer made statements that seem plausible when considered in isolation, but prove inconsistent in comparison. They simply could not remember in what precise year they joined the Bund. Even *the* Bund historian Jacob

---

44   Mayer 1957.
45   Micgiel, Scott and Segel 1986; Singer 1996; Melancon 2006; Murphy 2005, p. 19 ff.

Sholem Hertz vacillates between 1915 and 1916, as do leading Bundists Leon Oler and Yakob Tselemenski. Important American Bundists Dovid Mayer and Dovid Boym each indicate different years prior to 1905.[46] Here once again the indication of specific years, like the duration of membership, was influenced first and foremost by memory and therefore depended on perception – a source that could provide definitive dates was available in only the rarest of cases. Individual affiliation to the Bund was instead associated with certain periods: Bundists would remember having entered the Bund *prior to 1905*, *after 1907*, *shortly after the beginning of World War I*, etc., i.e. between two watershed events. The questionnaire in this sense demanded a level of accuracy that simply could not be met.

6   Forgotten Bundist Activism in World War I

More questions are raised by the relatively high number of new members during World War I. After all, as Kevin Murphy notes, the war had brought 'working-class militancy to a virtual halt'.[47] In contrast to many other Social Democratic groups, the Bund firmly opposed war and defence of the 'fatherland'. This placed it in opposition to large parts of the Russian workers' movement.[48] Despite the split ripping through the movement at the time, new groups began to converge. Murphy demonstrates with regard to Moscow that this began even before 1915.[49]

The same can be said for the workers' movement in Warsaw, as Yosef Lipshits recounts in great detail in one of his memoirs.[50] The Bundist organisations lay in ruins in early 1915, but several illegal committees were established that same year, building on the resurgent *birzshe* movement. Despite the state of war, they were able to hold a gathering attended by more than 70 delegates and elect a nine-person Executive Committee. The prior existence of ostensibly charitable institutions like legal soup kitchens allowed meetings to take place without distinctly Bundist locales, and proved to be a crucial factor in this development. That said, they also provided the Okhrana with an excellent location to con-

---

46 All can be found in the personal records at the Bund Archives, New York, RG 1400, MG2, 429.
47 Murphy 2005, p. 27.
48 Foundational: Holquist 2002. On the scope of Jewish experiences in World War I see Schuster 2004.
49 Murphy 2005, pp. 27–37.
50 Lifshits 1935, p. 9.

duct arrests. This was the case in 1916, when 16 *khaverim* were detained and given sentences lasting several months while six were deported to Siberia. The Bund's Russian period was coming to an end – Lifshits deploys the image of an explosion detonating a bridge, evoking an association with the opening shot of the October Revolution from the battlecruiser Aurora. The corresponding decision was taken in the aforementioned soup kitchen: the Bund would abandon charity work and re-establish political craft unions. Experienced Bundists like Viktor Shulman, Yosef Lifshits, Yankl Yankelevitsh, and Hershl Metaloviets would lead the way. Apart from human actors, this required symbols and objects: 'Thus localities were organised for 10 associations, along with 10 signs and 10 stamps', complemented by three more by the end of the year. They paved the way for the great labour unions that would attract the Jewish worker masses of interwar Poland.[51]

The Warsaw Bund continued to enjoy remarkable liberties under German occupation. From 1916 onwards, the Bundist journal *'Lebns-fragn'* published by Vladimir Medem received a legal permit. Bundists now fought less against the revolution-wary Russian authorities than against paper shortages and wartime censorship.[52] The editorial board, for example, was threatened with a ban should the paper continue to 'disseminate untrue information from enemy dispatches'.[53] The board later testified they were specifically instructed to do so, which was of course strictly forbidden by Enactment III, no. 3649 of the General Governorate from 8 February 1916. Nevertheless, the *'Lebns-fragn'* continued to appear legally and soon found its way to the editing room of the New York-based *'Forverts'*, which praised the publishing role of 'famous Bundist Vladimir Medem'.[54] As the main Bundist paper of the pre-revolutionary era, it later became the object of Bundist remembrance.[55]

The relatively unrestricted scope of action available during World War I was not limited to Warsaw, but in fact prompted Lublin 'print worker' Alekher Zelig, as it did many movement-minded workers, to join the Bund after the founding

---

51   Ibid.
52   Bund Archives, New York, MG2, 504, Letter, 9 September 1916, from the press department of the chief administrator of the Warsaw Governor General, 1.a 9557 to the editorial board of *'Lebns-fragn'*, Warsaw; and Order 6991, Warsaw, 24 June 1916, Warsaw Governor General, press department.
53   Ibid., Letter, 15 July 1916, Warsaw, from the Imperial German Police President to Herr Editor-in-Chief of *'Lebns-fragn'*.
54   *Forverts*, 1 June 1916, Bund Archives, New York, MG2, 504.
55   See esp. the booklet Redaktsye 'lebns-fragn' 1919 and the memoirs of Vladimir Medem (pp. 9–13), Dovid Eynhorn (pp. 14–17), and Viktor Shulman (pp. 18–24) contained therein. See also Lifshits 1935; Shulman 1951; Bakhrakh 1952.

of a print workers' union in 1916.[56] Whether this support for the Bund occurred despite or because of its opposition to the war cannot be clarified based on the available data.

The war also caused internal migration significant for the post-war Bund. Activist Khaym Babits reports in the Israeli *Lebns-fragn* that his shtetl of Novidor was located at a strategic location, creating new war-related employment opportunities.[57] The labour migrants arriving in Novidor also included numerous Bundists, among them the 'later well-known *arbeter-tuer* Y. Rudovski'.[58] Activists like Rudovski built the Bund in Novidor during and after World War I, ensuring that it emerged as the strongest group in the 1927 elections to the Kehilla council. It also dominated the city council together with the PPS. Rudovski, who had immigrated during World War I, ultimately became the city's deputy mayor. Through lasting commitment to workers' interests, he prepared the ground upon which the Bund was able to build in the following years. In this sense the Bund resembled the Russian Socialist Revolutionary Party as it began to consolidate its bases in Moscow and Petrograd around 1915, paving the way for its own significance in the revolutionary year of 1917. That said, Rudovski's success would ultimately last longer.[59]

7 The Bund's Generational Heterogeneity

Membership statistics from subsequent years underscore the Bund's connection to the history unfolding around it: the Bund plunged into a structural and programmatic crisis after a temporary peak around the February Revolution in 1917,[60] only gradually recovering its strict left-Social Democratic profile in 1922–3. Its structures stabilised by 1929 and the Bund recorded rising recruitment in its cultural and educational work. As Jack Jacobs notes, the children and youth groups linked to the *Kleyne Bund*, namely the *Sotsyalistisher kinderfarband* (SKIF) and the *Yugnt bund 'tsukunft'* (or just *Tsukunft*), proved par-

---

56 Bund Archives, New York, 1400, MG2, 429, Vasershtros, Alekher Zelig.
57 *Lebns-fragn* was the Bund's Israeli mouthpiece, published in Tel Aviv since 1951. It not only bears the same name as Vladimir Medem's publication founded during World War I, but the cover of the special issue marking the Bund's sixtieth anniversary also featured a lengthy quote by him: *Lebns-fragn* 75–76, 1957, p. 1. The magazine continued to appear until 2016 as an online publication, see www.lebnsfragn.com (last accessed 25 May 2018).
58 Babits 1957.
59 Murphy 2005, p. 32 f.
60 Unmatched: Gelbard 1982.

ticularly decisive.[61] The questionnaires confirm this, as roughly 40 percent of respondents explicitly report membership in a youth organisation, deriving their identity from this collective socialisation.[62]

The decline in membership after 1930, and even more importantly the absence of a renewed increase after 1936 (Figure 14), merit a closer look. These were years in which the Bund enjoyed major successes in local Polish elections. Were there really so few new recruits joining the party? Newer scholarship tends to disagree, and with good reason.[63] It is likely that the calamity of the Holocaust distorted the statistics, for while earlier generations migrated in cohorts and groups, a constant stream of refugees now poured into the destinations of exile. The average age of freshly arrived refugees applying for readmission to the New York Bund Club in 1941–2 was 44 years, with the original date of membership often dating back many years. Indeed, as Sergio DellaPergola illustrates, the young generation fell victim to the Holocaust just as much as others. But because the Eastern European Jewish population was generally quite young compared to other European Jewish populations, and people generally joined the Bund for the first time in their youth, this gap in the statistics is certainly a result of the Holocaust.[64] At this stage, the Bund's social thread could no longer be reflected by the collective store of knowledge migration preserved, as it succumbed to the German invasion and mass murder of Eastern European Jews. This also helps explain why the high age of documented new registrations indicated in questionnaire type II contrasts so starkly to the age of affiliation in Eastern Europe.

Only six percent of questionnaires were returned by Bundists 26 or older at the time they joined. The larger part joined during their adolescence between 13 and 20 years (Figure 15).[65] As the highest individual values of entries are between 13 and 15 years, a significant share of the Bund must have been a kind of internal youth movement, shaping the Bund particularly in terms of its patterns of activism.

This youthfulness was not always seen as a strength, and often invited polemical attacks against it. White propaganda depicted the organisation as a movement of gun-toting, delusional revolutionary schoolchildren.[66] Another com-

---

61 Jacobs 2009, pp. 8–47. Hertz 1946 also emphasis the existence of a long tradition with regard to the *Yugnt bund 'tsukunft'*.
62 Based on questionnaire type III.
63 See generally Jacobs 2009, pp. 1–7; Pickhan 2001, p. 128f.
64 DellaPergola 1996, p. 38.
65 A number of unknown cases remain. In 52 of the questionnaires either the date of entry, birth year, or both were indiscernible or could not be ascertained through further research.
66 Budnitskii 2006, p. 320b.

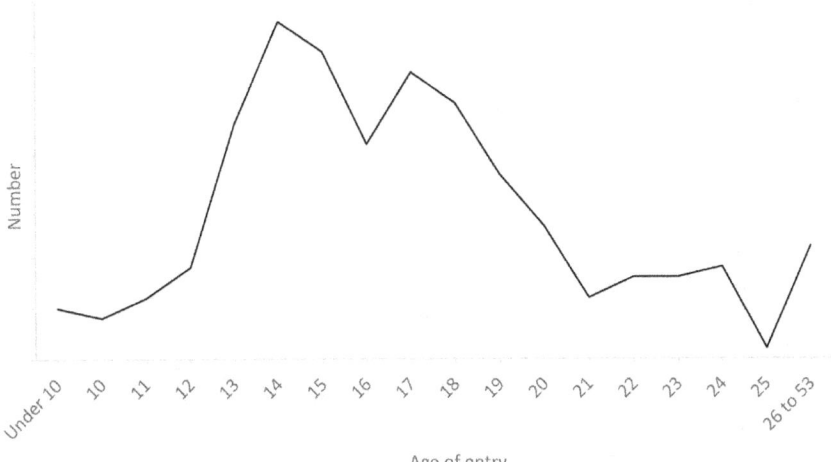

FIGURE 15   Age at time of joining the Bund, questionnaire types II–V

mon experience was the use of the derogatory term *buntovshtsikes* – in this context a Jewish *jeu de mots* combining the Bund's name with the Russian word for instigator or troublemaker. The insult was even hurled at the Bundists of the *Avangard* in Argentina.[67] Bundists returned to the word during the Holocaust, this time in dialectical inversion to describe their struggle against all forms of oppression.[68]

8   Stratification within the Bund

As in the case of autobiography, the figures above help us pinpoint 1897, 1907, 1917, 1922, 1929, and 1939 as the Bund's epoch-defining watershed years. But how did stratifications between workers and intellectuals relate to one another within these units of temporal meaning? The Bund was both a mass movement as well as a youth movement in various phases of its existence. Is its essence as a workers' movement reflected in membership figures?

Three distinct phase types can be identified from the relation between new worker members and intellectuals (Table 10): firstly, those in which intellectuals far outnumber workers such as the post-1939 period. However, as is also the case for the pre-1897 phase, in which workers outnumbered intellectuals

---

[67]   N.N. 1909c, p. 3.
[68]   Bund Archives, New York, MG2–429, Borenshteyn, Shimen *Di seks buntovshikes. Zikhroynes fun der noent fargangenheyt*, [probably *Forverts*, New York], (194?).

TABLE 10   Periodic distribution of new Bund members' educational background

First membership	Ratio of workers to Bundists with higher education[a]
Until 1897	4
1897–1907	1.14
1908–17	1.15
1917–22	3.89
1923–9	1.89
1930–9	1.38
After 1939	0.4

a   Except for questionnaire Type II, which only surveys occupation but not training or field.

four-fold, this cannot be confirmed empirically due to a low response rate and thus denotes a tendency at best – although the increase in workers is not a statistical outlier (the same is true for 1917–22). In the majority of phases (1897–07, 1908–17, 1923–9, 1930–9), a slightly higher number of new worker members over intellectuals can be derived from the questionnaires. As mentioned above, *yeshiva* students were particularly likely to earn their living as labourers, but their chances of moving up in the Bund were much better through their enhanced access to the written word.

This helped the Bund's exile groups also depicted in the chart to remain active. A staggering 47 percent of Bundists in type IV indicated they had been or were currently active as a writer or author in the New World. At first glance this is only a slight increase compared to responses regarding Eastern Europe (41 percent). On the other hand, activity overseas was generally underreported and the true figure is likely substantially higher. Moreover, questionnaire type IV primarily pursued historical interests, prompting many authors to pass over their ongoing activity in the New World while stories from Eastern Europe were often recounted in great detail. The fact that the ratios are so close is an echo of the social thread of the North American Bund in the migration process. Politics of memory set its primary focus on Eastern Europe. Nevertheless, another shift within the Bund's educational structure becomes apparent: at least immediately after the Atlantic passage, common activism patterns seem to have made remaining in the Bund overseas more attractive to those with higher education than to workers. One the one hand, we can confirm that the

Bund carried within it a workers' movement populated by workers; on the other hand, we must be careful not to miscategorise intellectuals as either a marginal group or strictly as leaders.

Subsequent history is also reflected with respect to a possible temporal dominance of workers among new members between 1917–22. The specificity of joining during this period says little about the Bund's increased appeal to workers, and is probably a reflection of the high number of young intellectuals finding their way to the Yiddish branch of the Communist Party, the *Yevsektsiya*, which attracted activists who sought to concretely combine *yidishkayt* and revolution from 1919 onwards.[69] The proportional share of former Bundists in the *Yevsektsiya* clearly exceeded that of activists from other Jewish parties. This move to a new political camp was not particularly problematic for former Bundists, as Zvi Gitelman impressionably depicts: '[t]he Jewish activists were members of the Communist family but they were illegitimate children, having been born in the Social Democracy'.[70] For this they would later fall victim to Stalinist persecution in the late 1930s, and therefore do not appear in the statistics.[71] It was another notch in the Bund's statistics, left this time by the Red Terror.

Clearly evident, however, is the relationship between the generationality of joining the Bund and the educational level of new activists (Figure 16). Workers are clearly the numerically dominant group, but their weight relies on a specific age of affiliation. An impressive 50 percent of workers indicate joining the Bund before their sixteenth birthday. Each Bundist student under 16 who attended a *Gymnasium* or similar educational institution was matched by 8.4 young workers on average. The youth movement that proved crucial to the Bund at all times was thus also dominated by a large number of working-class adolescents.

Members with higher religious education were only a small group in quantitative terms, but their backgrounds suggest that a specific experience motivated them to join the Bund: the world of work. Although students of the *yeshiva* and other religious institutions spent several more years in the classroom than workers, it is noticeable that a large number were subsequently forced or wanted to return to the *malokhe* despite their education – whether out of economic necessity or notions of active masculinity. Work experience remained a rarity among members with higher secular education. This figure may have

---

69   Gitelman 1972, p. 226f. Elaborately in Moss 2009.
70   Gitelman 1972, p. 154. On the history of persecution esp. from 1937 onwards see pp. 513–23.
71   See the depiction of a typical biography of a former Bundist and later Bolshevik who then became a victim of the Red Terror in Estraikh 2002.

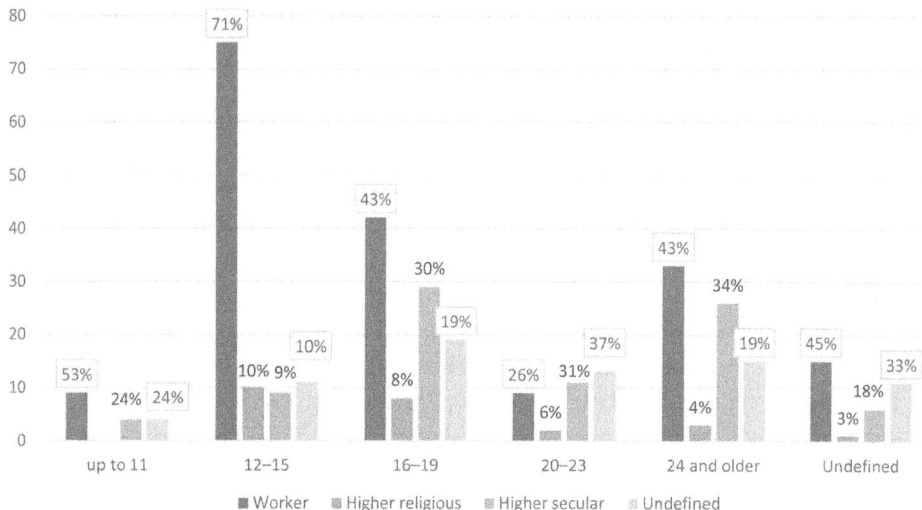

FIGURE 16   Distribution of social strata at age of joining

increased during the first post-emigration years if at all, by which point they had already found their way into the Bund after typically radicalising in Russian educational institutions.

The statistics allow us to conclude that workers and adolescents must be regarded as important actors in and on behalf of the social thread of the Bund, although they overlap considerably. They were flanked by the activism of those with higher education who mostly joined the Bund later in life, but assumed a more important role than workers in the production of memory.

CHAPTER 7

Preliminary Conclusions

> In actuality it is far from correct to assume that an individual of more or less fixed absolute capacities confronts the world and in striving for the truth constructs a world-view out of the data of his experience. Nor can we believe that he then compares his world-view with that of other individuals who have gained theirs in a similarly independent fashion, and in a sort of discussion the true worldview is brought to light and accepted by the others. In contrast to this, it is much more correct to say that knowledge is from the very beginning a co-operative process of group life, in which everyone unfolds his knowledge within the framework of a common fate, a common activity, and the overcoming of common difficulties (in which, however, each has a different share).
> KARL MANNHEIM in *Ideology and Utopia*, 1929[1]

∴

The key to activism in a social movement is commonly assumed to be the moment of affiliation, the commitment of one's identity to the movement, which in turn is understood as the framework into which new members 'inscribe' themselves.[2] But despite many new members' young age, entering the Bund was by no means synonymous with affiliating oneself to the socialist movement as such. Activists often integrated themselves into the shared identity-forming horizon of knowledge Karl Mannheim outlined long before definitively joining the party, and in many cases neglected to do so altogether. The moment of joining the movement is so strongly emphasised in Bundist biography because the Bund yielded significantly more *Memorik* than, say, the many small activist groups in the shtetls.

---

1 Mannheim 1979, p. 26.
2 Esp. Clemens 1996; Melucci 2003.

1   Moments of Conversion and Activist Practice

As Mary Joe Maynes emphasises in her pioneering study of German and French worker autobiographies, workers often tended to retrospectively view joining the workers' movement as an act of conversion.[3] In this study, we can see this in both the rhetorically charged autobiographical texts as well as the standardised autobiographies in the questionnaires. In the latter case, we can even compare data between multiple responses at different points in time. When doing so it becomes evident that this moment of conversion was not nearly as easily identified as some of the respondents may suggest. A large number of respondents appear eager to accurately tell their life story, but indications of the date they joined the Bund fluctuate heavily.

This is owed not only to the authors' aforementioned construction of meaningful epochs, but also to the widespread tendency to conflate the Bund and the Jewish workers' movement as a whole.[4] This conflation led to a temporary split between the Bund and the RSDLP in 1903 and served to demarcate the Bund, allegedly 'rooted in tradition', from the Zionist workers' movement and the Bolsheviks, who portrayed the Bund's history as a mere prologue to the October Revolution.[5]

The Bund countered with its own historical perspective based on a growing body of *Memorik* rooted in 1897 instead of 1917, and treating 1905 as the pivotal moment of the Jewish workers' movement. This development also gave the movement's *yidishkayt* a history of its own. One expression of this was the *Arbeter luakh*, a 'workers' calendar' published by the *Farlag lebns-fragn* in Warsaw. The third issue was advertised as a commemorative edition in honour of the Jewish workers' movement's twenty-fifth anniversary, although it actually dealt exclusively with the Bund.[6] The date of publication and commemorative texts contained therein suggest that the movement was born together with the Bund in that same Vilnius attic in 1897. Readers and commemorating authors of course knew the deeper roots of the Jewish workers' movement, but the Bund's foundation was increasingly depicted as the verifiable beginning of the movement in Russia.

This interpretation grew dominant within the Bund. The 1950s questionnaires (type IV) also inquire about one's date of entering 'the Jewish workers'

---

3   Maynes 1995, pp. 164–7.
4   This was of course met with criticism, especially in the context of ex-Bundist historical narratives such as Kats 1946.
5   See esp. chapters 1–3 of the foundational classic Trotsky 2008.
6   *Arbeter luakh* 3, 1922.

PRELIMINARY CONCLUSIONS   211

movement' and not 'the Bund'. Yet most respondents only indicated their entry into the Bund, as the distinction was more of a quibble than a significant historical distinction in their eyes. Worker Irshl Dubkowski declined to answer the form's direct request for his date of birth, and instead indicated the day of his entry into the Bund: 'in Zaranovits in 1918, on 17 January'.[7] Similar statements were submitted by the Lublin secretary of TSYSHO schools Abraham Feynsilber and Łodz worker-activist Herman Zshezshinski, who later commanded the city's Bundist militia.[8] The latter placed particular emphasis on the 'marches in the shtetl' he participated in before joining the Bund as his prime motivation. He became a member at age 17, but as the descriptions of his activities indicate was active in the workers' movement prior to that.[9] Respondents expected this emphasis due to the nature of the institution asking the questions, as they all knew it was an initiative of the Bund Archives. The same is true for Khaym Tabatshnik, born in 1902, who attended the *kheder* until age 12 and was later quite active in Melbourne.[10] Growing up in a shoemaker's family, he became a tailor and by his account joined the Bund in 1917. This date is preceded by an undated membership in the local tailors' union. His responses nevertheless focused exclusively on the Bundist part of his activism. The trade unions' intermediary role becomes particularly clear in the account of Lublin steel worker Moshe Vasong, who joined the *Tsukunft* at age 14 before later joining the Bund. Nevertheless, he explicitly states that he was brought to the workers' movement 'through the professional association' – the exact date of his 'entry into the workers' movement', as literally stated in the questionnaire, was identical to his indicated date of joining the Bund – the last link in a long historical chain.[11] Descriptions of such moments of conversion must therefore be seen in the context of their function in memory for the Bund. Its history hierarchized perceptions of one's own activism in different organisations.

This biography-shaping identification is especially pronounced in the case of worker Fishl Aydlman, born in 1897 in Krakow. He lived in the Hapsburg-Galician town of Domrove that was returned to Polish jurisdiction and thus the 'Bundist Pale' in the interwar period.[12] The year he joined the Bund is ambival-

---

7   Ibid., Dubkowski, Irshl.
8   Bund Archives, New York, RG 1400, MG2, 429, Feynsilber, Abraham.
9   Ibid., Zshezshinksi, Herman.
10 Ibid., Tabatshnik, Khaym.
11 Ibid., Vasong, Moshe.
12 Although a party emulating the Bund existed in Galicia, the Jewish Social Democratic Party of Galicia (also referred to as the 'Galician Bund') is only rarely considered a com-

ent, as he indicates both 1918 and 1920 in two separate instances.[13] This is quite late for a worker who would have been up to 23 years old at this point, but may be owed to the fact that he refers solely to the Bund itself. Taking into account additional information, we can reliably establish that he had been active in the workers' movement beforehand. In his enclosed autobiographies, however, he reports only of his time after joining the Bund, omitting the classical autobiographical components of childhood and adolescence as well as any phases of pre-Bundist activism entirely. He even refers to the epoch beginning after 1920 as his 'first 10 years'.[14]

This raises the question as to how exactly new members joined the workers' movement or the Bund. Given that no centrally issued membership cards existed, joining really meant affiliating to a local group. Becoming a *tuer* thus depended on activism on behalf of the Jewish workers' movement, while specific programmatic debates or currents were generally of secondary importance. This can be seen in Berl Shtern's case. As a former *yeshiva* student from a bourgeois family, the workers of his shtetl Bielsk ostracised him despite his having exchanged the Gemara for the workbench. Eventually, a poor wood carver named Mendl brought him closer to the workers:

> He introduced me to them as a new 'acquaintance'. The term 'acquaintance', however, meant – one's own person, a person of the organisation. I was quite surprised, as I had never heard of this organisation ... – because there was no organisation yet in Bielsk.[15]

Ascription to the collective emancipated him as his 'own person', which can also be understood as 'special person'. But the organisation needed to make this process visible was yet to be founded, until support eventually arrived from the nearby town of Bialystok. Programmatic issues were of secondary importance, for the support did not come from the Bund as Shtern had hoped but from the PPS:

---

       ponent of Bundist biographies. See for example, Bund Archives, New York, RG 1400, MG2, 29, Kisman, Leah; or Kreyndler, Tsharls.

13   Bund Archives, New York, RG 1400, MG2, 429, Aydlman, Fishl and Adelman, Philip. His statements made on questionnaire type III concerning the period after 1918 contradict his other answers. Central in dating his recollections was his 'feeling' of having joined the Bund immediately after Poland annexed Galicia. The same is true for Abraham Stolor, who described himself as a 'born *tuer*' and re-joined the Bund in 1915 and 1922, see Stolor, Abraham.

14   Ibid., Aydelman, Fishl, Questionnaire, 1975, Annex: Autobiography, p. 1.

15   Shtern 1954, p. 14.

Zeydl, the speaker [travelling from Bialystok], turned to me with a request – he asked me to become the chairperson of the Bielsk organisation, which would be founded under the supervision of the Bialystok committee of the PPS. I was unwilling to accept – as a Jewish worker, I am much closer to the Bund – I said, – I'm not a PPS-nik. Zeydl and Meyshke said: – let's found an organisation first, afterwards we'll see which party.[16]

He would become quite the 'PPS-nik' later on and raise funds for the party even after his emigration to New York. He only agreed to the compromise in Bielsk because he was unaware that the PPS programme contradicted his understanding of a Bundist programme at the time.[17] Only in the US, after various solidarity campaigns for the PPS failed, did he return to his old Bundist circles and become active in the *Arbeter-ring*. Organisational formation lagged behind actual activity, but was simultaneously necessary as the manifestation of utopian work in and towards the present, not least for the evolution of successful activist identities. The widely used framing approach, which conceives of organisation as a flexible framework for activists' identity formation within social movements, must at least be complemented by knowledge-producing action as the precondition of institutionalisation.[18]

Shtern also underscores the relevance of higher education in the workers' movement, along with the need to channel it into an activist direction. Like many other Bundists with a higher religious education, he successfully proletarianised his biography as a *yeshiva-bokher* through his actions, thus developing an identity as a worker-activist who only became a local worker leader because he did not receive a working-class education.

Many authors portray events prior to membership in an organisation, which in the shtetls often had to be founded first, as inevitable. This is not only true for workers or the previously cited Vladimir Medem in Swiss exile, but also for the noteworthy Bundist intellectual Benzion Hofman (Zivion). Recollecting later in life, he stresses that he discovered the Bund prior to 1897 but did not join – hardly surprising, given that the organisation did not exist yet. This statement both establishes his role as a Bundist pioneer as well as marks out his supposedly predetermined path into the Bund's ranks. His depiction of his journey into the Bund breaks off shortly after he covers the Bund's founding: 'I do not wish to go back before 1897 very far, however, for then everything would go faster and it would be a chapter of its own, I only wanted to describe how

---

16 Shtern 1954, p. 20.
17 Shtern 1954, p. 21.
18 Clemens 1996; Melucci 2003.

I came to the Bund, meaning my first acquaintance with it, although it took another few years before I joined and became a full-fledged Bundist in 1901'. His 'entry' was spurred by 'a major article' on the national question in the Swiss exile-Bundist periodical *'Der yidisher arbeter'*. When Zivion's brief explanation that 'I studied in Switzerland back then' emphasises how he became a Bundist even while abroad, he shows that intellectuals could also become Bundists there through action, albeit exclusively through the activism pattern of writing only accessible to those with higher education, if at all.[19]

2 Reducing Eastern Europe through 'Expected Expectations'

Neither in the autobiographies nor in the questionnaires can an 'I' be distinguished from 'us', nor is an 'I' dissolved through its self-inscription into 'us'. That said, respondents by all means expect a certain expectation on the part of those inquiring. These were 'expected expectations', as the archivists did not formulate any specific rules. They emerged solely out of the discursive self-positioning of the authors themselves, well aware of what was considered part of the Bund's history and what was not, but who also related 'special stories' distinguishing them from other autobiographies or historical accounts. This was not perceived as a limitation, as the Bund remained both a positive reference point and simultaneously the main engine of community building and individualisation in their self-biographisation. This made it possible to bridge oceans and later even decades, although Manye Goldberg mentioned in the previous chapter makes it clear that bank notes could be just as important here as completed questionnaires.[20]

3 Bearing Witness to Eastern Europe, Silencing North America

In contrast to many Argentinian activists, Bundists who emigrated to the US did not see themselves as witnesses of the Bund overseas, but rather as living witnesses of a *velt voz iz nishto mer* (world that is no more).[21] Questionnaire type IV asks about which 'party, organisation, and *unions*' one belonged to. Despite the

---

19 Zivion 1948a.
20 This features more prominently in the discussion of revolutionary fundraising, see Part III.12.
21 This was the title of equally influential socialist-leaning author Israel J. Singer's autobiography, *Fun a velt voz iz nishto mer* (1946); English: *Of a World That Is No More* (1971).

Anglicisation of the question (the German/Yiddish phrase contains the English word 'union' instead of the Yiddish *fareyn*), respondents only rarely mention memberships after emigration. This also applies to many Bundists who became particularly active overseas. Although they mention places in the New World in other questions about their activities, an exact description is almost only given to those in *der alten heym* (the old home).

The Eastern European Bund proves so compelling that even the forms of activity conducted most passionately in the US are pushed to the margins. Montreal activist Pinkhes Volkovitsh provides a good example. His questionnaire is completed in a very neat manner, but only mentions activities on behalf of *Tsukunft* and the Polish Bund before World War II, although he also enjoyed a reputation in North America. In fact, he was so active in the Montreal *Arbeter-ring* that he received a public funeral advertised in the local press.[22] He did not bother to mention any of these activities whatsoever. Fishl Aydlman is a similar case: he omits American activities in the questionnaire, although he concludes by stating that 'I must admit that I had the opportunity to begin my Bundist work and continue it to this day thanks to my wife'.[23] Neither his wife nor his political life in the US feature in his responses. The depiction of his 19 years in Poland occupies several pages, whereas he covers his 26 extremely active years as a Bundist in the US *Arbeter-ring* in a dozen lines – incidentally, the only lines in his three submitted autobiographical texts that even mention his life after the great voyage. Seventy-eight-year-old Fishl Aydlman concludes this last of his three submitted autobiographies[24] fully in the style of a worker autobiographer, not without a degree of self-deprecation: 'I would like to end with this, that I did not write this to receive a medal. I always did my Bundist work in silence' – a humble silence, but one that truly appears in the questionnaire when it comes to his activities in the US.[25] As for the introductions to monographic autobiographies discussed above, this sort of gesture of humility cast an activist's biography in a reputable light.

Only rarely are differences mentioned between adolescent activist life in Eastern Europe and politically informed family and work life in the US. Berl Shtern dedicates a mere eight pages of his 200-page autobiography to life

---

22 Bund Archives, New York, RG 1400, MG2, 429, Volkovitsh, Pinkhes, Questionnaires, Annex: Obituary, newspaper unclear, likely 15 March 1976.
23 Ibid., Aydlman, Fishl, Questionnaire, 1975. The fact that there is no questionnaire from his wife, who was apparently also a very active Bundist, only fits the general picture found in the records.
24 Ibid., Aydlman, Fishl, Questionnaires, likely from 1955, 1966, 1975.
25 Ibid., Aydlman, Fishl, Questionnaire, 1975, p. 2.

in North America – eight pages which he largely spends vindicating himself, pressed as he was into the 'economic yoke'. Furthermore, he explains, his family took up a lot of time in this period. Although he was still active in different areas of the *Arbeter-ring*, often until late at night, he views it all as terribly 'modest' in retrospect. Socialism seemed so remote in the US, that the only anecdote he depicts in more detail recounts an incident one night after a party committee meeting, when he was so tired he almost forgot his sleeping daughter on the subway. Not even a whiff of the 'exalted moments of our romantic past' survived into the present.[26]

The situation was very different in Argentina, where Pinie Vald was able to commemorate the heroic stories of immigrant Bundists through the group *Avangard* as early as the 1920s.[27] Yet regardless of the space being commemorated, the position of the author and his or her 'life story' was inconceivable without an increasingly and intentionally invoked symbiotic connection to the movement's past. The point was not just to create individual meaning – to produce and justify a self – but to preserve knowledge.

4 The Sound of the Bundist Symphony

This knowledge was closely emotionally tied to shared contexts of experience, representing the basis of the aestheticisation of life stories accompanying autobiographisation. The Bund's autobiography after World War II was in one sense an infinite search for new terms and metaphors of one's own. This was a highly intertextual process, used to continue the grand Bundist narrative. Noteworthy publicist Khayim S. Kazdan returned to an illustration of life in the Warsaw ghetto from Bundist author Yakob Tseleminski, who supposedly once ended a book presentation as follows:

> An old-time fiddle player walks down the street and plays his fiddle as if trying to comfort and encourage the Jewish people. The Nazis couldn't stand that and smashed his fiddle to pieces. The pieces lie on the ground, Jews pick them up and shake their heads – and still hear the sounds of the beloved songs.

In this, Kazdan sees a central metaphor for the Bund as a whole:

---

26 Noakh 1936.
27 Vald 1929a; Vald 1929b.

> Our fiddle, that of the 'General Jewish Labour Bund', also lies in ruins. It was burned together with the inhabitants of the ghetto, it lies buried under the grave mounds together with the ghetto fighters. And yet the sound of the Bundist symphony lives on in our hearts, the beautiful sounds carry on in the air and wherever there is a Bundist, he seizes it and joins in the Bundist singing.[28]

The message here was that the Bund may have been smashed, but Bundists had not been robbed of the power of memory. Remembrance became the Bund's central mode of community building, distinct from its previous function as a mobilising tool. Although it would be wrong to reduce this memory to melancholy and trauma with respect to the post-war Bund,[29] the movement's specific reference points of action had grown extremely narrow in a world shaped by migration. The Bundist publication *'Unzer tsayt'* in which the above-cited text was originally published remained an attentive observer of its times, but its provocative voice on politics, post-war socialism, and Jewish life was heard by fewer and fewer activists.[30] Bundist *doikayt* nevertheless persisted in its counter-cultural stance after the two World Wars through its rejection of Zionism and its sheer will to survive.[31]

Consequently, Bundist autobiography represents a political statement articulated over a period of multiple decades by several generations born in Eastern Europe before 1939. Memory was already a decisive connective factor in the Bund's transnational social movement long before World War II. It became necessary because the Bund's focus on Eastern Europe could not connect to a similar organisation overseas. This failed to reflect reality in the age of mass migration, and thus not the Bund itself but rather Bundists' revolutionary and simultaneously structurally conservative outlook would establish its transnational history.

---

28 Kazdan 1963.
29 See esp. Slucki 2009b.
30 This was also emphasised by Israel Laubstein, once an enthusiastic reader of *'Unzer tsayt'*. In his view, remembrance was always also a kind of admonishing of future generations, interview with Israel Laubstein, conducted by Silvia Hansmann and Frank Wolff, IWO, Buenos Aires, 8 October 2008; the author possesses a copy of the transcript.
31 This remains extremely important to surviving Bundists to this day, see Zelmanowicz 2009; Torbiner 2011.

PART 3

*Old Masses in New Streets:
Transnationalising the Bund*

CHAPTER 8

Between Here and There: Bundist Gatherings Overseas

The Bund's break with Jewish tradition was rooted in *doikayt* and its demand for activism in the 'here and now'. This 'here' in Eastern Europe was linked to the presence of the 'Jewish worker masses', from whose lives and problems an appropriate action programme could be derived. This and the subsequent activism it entailed fostered the emergence of a *bundishe mishpokhe*, the notion of one big Bundist family, and a Bundist identity with the potential to influence those who joined the organisation for the rest of their lives. This coherent action context became a paradox for Bundists in the era of mass migration. Migrant Bundists aspired to activism in the 'here' – their specific destination country – while their relation to the masses regularly dragged their perspective to Eastern Europe.

In response, Bundists developed various institutions to facilitate places of gathering and community building overseas under the Bund's auspices, linked to the organisation in Eastern Europe in manifold ways. Yet because the Eastern European side responded sluggishly to these developments, the Bund's transnationalisation occurred through its members in migration. This process required not only transfers of cultural and political practices but also adjustment and change. The movement's new institutions were interwoven into local contexts but nevertheless retained their political proximity to the Bund, which itself continued to evolve through ongoing dynamics in Russia and Poland. Their vital connection between those places depended on practiced Bundist identity in the countries of origin as well as in migration.

Based on their Bundist identities, migrants bridged the differences between their old and new lifeworlds by relying on common experiences. But migration is not a smooth experience allowing actors to seamlessly continue their old practices in a new setting. To what extent, then, did Bundists experience migration as a break or rupture? Dirk Hoerder rightfully emphasises that cooperation and community building along common cultural conventions or at least shared workplace experiences usually marked the first step towards a 'self-determined identity' among newly arrived immigrants.[1] The institutions and

---

1 Hoerder 2002, p. 439.

identities arising from them, however, were by no means 'replicas of the Old World such as the Russian empire'; instead, '[m]igrants acted within the constraints imposed by receiving societies and economic dependency, they acted outside restrictions of their cultural origin'.[2] Similarly, Eli Lederhendler argues that migration entailed a complete cultural break for immigrants from the Russian empire, as they left Russian-Jewish 'caste society' behind to join American class society.[3] Tobias Brinkmann claims that Jewish migrants in the US were 'too busy to look back'.[4] This could arguably be the case at least to the extent that identities are derived (primarily) from experiences of gainful employment. Yet if we look at culturally or socio-politically derived identities, which are constantly reshaped based on previous experiences, this can hardly be the case. Here we see how life remained strongly influenced by networks of both the lifeworld of work as well as social movements. The persistence of identities connected to one's native country is evidenced, for example, by studies comparing immigration of certain groups to the US and other destinations, as well as investigations of social relations within a given group based on common origin.[5] The latter in particular demonstrate that many Jewish migrants' origins in a certain city or shtetl continued to shape their identity even after emigration, and that a number of specific actions emerged from this conception. Studying local *landsmanshaftn*, both Lipphardt and Kobrin locate this primarily in memorial and commemorative works after the Holocaust.[6]

With regard to the Bund, however, whose identity was based not on a common place of origin but on movement participation, *Memorik* was only one pattern of activism among many. Bundists moreover forged transnational and transatlantic networks, as was generally common among socialist migrants even before World War I.[7] This raises the question as to how the overseas activists specifically practiced community building on the ground beyond remembrance, and to what extent (if at all) these practices were linked to experiences or life in Eastern Europe.

The fundamental prerequisite for any further community building in Eastern Europe as well as in emigration were *gatherings*. Their existence, however, could not be taken for granted. Buenos Aires and New York were imposing

---

2 Ibid.
3 Lederhendler 2009.
4 Brinkmann 2010a, p. 51. Elsewhere, on the other hand, he emphasises the significance of transnational relationships, see Brinkmann 2007.
5 Diner 2001; Kliger 1998; Kobrin 2006; Lipphardt 2004. For discussions outside of Jewish history see Baily 1999; McKeown 2001.
6 Kobrin 2010; Lipphardt 2010.
7 Michels 2005; Michels 2009; Wolff 2012a.

metropolises that easily overwhelmed many new arrivals through their sheer magnitude, pace of life, and complexity. Even immigrants who had seen more than just their own shtetl tended to regard Lviv, Lodz, or Bialystok as large cities.[8] New York was a completely different experience, and posed an enormous challenge to newly arriving Bundists. Their disorientation was amplified by the fact that, at least for the first waves of immigrants, no local Bundist organisation existed, forcing the *mishpokhe* to find each other through informal channels. Having arrived overseas, *a bakanter* (an acquaintance, which in the movement also meant a known activist) would often become *a griner* (greenhorn) once again, facing possible disadvantages in favour of settled immigrants.[9] As I demonstrate in the following, Bundists drew on their wealth of activist experience acquired in Russia to deal with these challenges, and in doing so introduced certain forms of Russian social grammar into their host cities.

1 Initial Points of Contact: Latency and Re-mobilisation

In the old home, the Bund's labour activism relied heavily on physical gatherings such as meetings in the Russian forests, May Day celebrations, the *birzshe*, or large demonstrations. Unsurprisingly, these gatherings would prove equally necessary for the movement's reproduction overseas. A new factor entered the equation, however, as gatherings in Eastern Europe were based on present masses recruited above all through local networks. In order to form such present masses without recourse to these networks, Bundist migrants drew on their rich organisational experience complemented by somewhat reliable information on the social and political constellations in their respective destinations.

2 Passing on the *Birzshe*

In Eastern Europe, that public and yet conspiratorial collective stroll through the shtetl streets known as the *birzshe* facilitated interaction and exchange among revolutionaries. The *birzshe* merely simulated a scattered present mass, while its true purpose was to conceal a directed present mass in public. The vigilant Russian authorities were unable to tell whether Yiddish conversations

---

8 On this immigration experience see Hödl 1991.
9 As much is stated in Friedman 1942. For the sweatshop industry more generally see esp. Bender and Greenwald 2003.

overheard in the *birzshe* pertained to jobs in the sense of a labour exchange or the planned revolution – although one was more often than not tied to the other. It represented an intermediary stage and a pattern of activism only in the sense that it enabled further activisms. While the *birzshe* finds little mention in the recollections of the intelligentsia, it is a major feature of worker memoirs, as most workers were active here, *oyf der yidishe gas*. Its secretive and yet simultaneously public character served as a gateway to the movement. In emigration the *birzshe*, or copycat versions of organisation markets on the open street, also fulfilled this orientational role, but had such a fluid character that they barely appear in the sources. Furthermore, as an accepted practice in most countries of emigration where the Tsarist secret police could not reach, it lost its conspiratorial appeal. This probably contributed to its relative absence from activist recollections, for, in the words of Max Weber, 'we often neglect to think out clearly what seems to be obvious because it is intuitively familiar'.[10]

In Argentina, labour market and point of orientation as well as organisation overlapped in a way closely resembling the *birzshe* immigrants knew from their old home. Worker intellectual and leading Argentinian Bundist Pinie Vald exemplarily remembers Mendl Maler, a *khaver* from the Bund's early Buenos Aires years.[11] To Vald, Maler embodied a prototypical Bundist in the Argentinian migration process[12] and assumes the function of a collective alter ego for Bundists in that country: born in the 'classical' 1880s, Maler actually attempted to reach the US with the aid of Jewish relief organisations but only managed to secure a ticket to the Río de la Plata, where he arrived after a 30-day passage in 1906 – the same year as Pinie Vald. He travelled alone without friends or relatives, nor did he have a specific person or point of contact at his destination.[13] Maler forewent state assistance in the *Hotel de Inmigrantes*, intrigued by news of a *birzshe* in Buenos Aires he heard about on the ship. It was located right on Plaza Lavalle in the centre of the emerging Jewish quarter.[14] Maler headed

---

10 Weber 1978, p. 44.
11 Biographical information on Pinie [Pedro] Vald (1886–1966) is found primarily in his own writings, briefly summarised in Weinstein and Toker 2004, p. 193 f.; Tarcus and Ehrlich 2007, p. 702 f. Many Bundists saw Vald as the definitive symbol of early Bundist history in Argentina. Evidence of this view is found in the first passage of an interview historian Marcelo Dimenstein conducted with Bundist Hershl Goldmints (1999). The author thanks Marcelo for making this transcript available. See also Centro 'Mark Turkow', Buenos Aires, Archivo de la Palabra, 40, Lebendiker, Moyshe [Ephraim Zadoff].
12 Vald 1929a, pp. 7–10.
13 Vald 1929a, p. 7 f.
14 On Plaza Lavalle as the centre of Buenos Aires's emerging Jewish district see Sofer 1982, p. 66 f.

straight there and made contact with other *khaverim*. In contrast to the common practice at New York's Hester Market, he was not hired on the spot for the lowest conceivable wage but instead ushered into the offices of a trade union, fully in the style Yosef Lifshits attributed to the function of Warsaw's *birzshe* during World War I.[15]

The interior of the local Yiddish-speaking trade union's offices (Vald's report is unclear whether he was also a member or simply familiar with the building) aptly symbolises the associations and references characteristic of Jewish-socialist activism in Argentina: a banner on the wall sporting Marx's famous dictum, *Di bafreyung fun der arbeter klas iz di sokh fun arbeter klas aleyn* ('the emancipation of the working classes must be conquered by the working classes themselves'), made Maler feel at home. Next to it he saw portraits of Karl Marx, Mikhail Bakunin, and South American freedom fighter San Martin.[16] While this may appear to be a somewhat surprising trinity, one would be hard-pressed to find a better expression of the sentiments among the Jewish workers' movement in Argentina at the time. Mendl Maler's connection to this particular union, Vald continues, brought him both employment as well as further personal and political contacts. He also received directions to the socialist *Biblioteca rusa* (Russian Library), where he could quench the thirst for knowledge that accompanied him on his voyage. It is no coincidence that Vald places this episode at the beginning of his memoirs of this period, as the depiction represents a common experience among Bundists immigrants to Buenos Aires in the 1900s. In the years to come, Bundists like Mendl Maler and Pinie Vald would build revolutionary life in Argentina around this *birzshe* and the immigrants congregating there.

The Argentinian *birzshe* was no copy, however, but rather a variant of the public conspiratorial *birzshe* from Russian days. Conspiratorial goals receded along the Río de la Plata in favour of gathering information. It simultaneously served to direct participants towards other patterns of activism, as a local Bund or similar organisation was yet to be founded. In fact, the character of Bundism in Argentina itself remained undefined at this point. The *birzshe* ensured that activists around Plaza Lavalle and the adjoining street of the same name were able to find one another in the first place during the key years of 1906–7. Contrary to Eugene Sofer's blanket claim, Jewish community building was not tied to a stay at the *Hotel de Inmigrantes*,[17] which some authors describe as a gov-

---

15   Lifshits 1935, p. 9; Vald 1929a, p. 8.
16   Vald 1929a, p. 8.
17   Sofer 1982, p. 66.

ernmental expression of *solidaridad humana*,[18] but which in fact primarily facilitated domestic colonisation. At least Bundist and most likely any politically or socially organised immigrants favoured transnational networks for reorientation. In their arrival practices, Bundists in Argentina maintained their faith in the Bundist *mishpokhe* and *khavershaft*.

No institution resembling the *birzshe* emerged in New York, where conditions were fundamentally different. The centres of Jewish life were well-known, accessible, and rather conspicuous in the cityscape. Yiddish-language journals were sold by paper boys on street corners and available in many trade union offices.[19] The entrepreneurial style of American capitalism also had a much stronger individualising effect.[20] In Jewish New York, the Lower East Side's Pig Market (Yiddish: *khazar mart*) represented a job market in the literal sense of the word: not as a communicative market relation, but a real place in a specific district open to both jobseekers and potential employers alike. It was also a market for everything booming American capitalism required, from tin pots and textiles to cheap labour. Irving Howe saw it as one of the harshest expressions of contemporary New York:

> One of the worst spots was 'the Pig Market', as the Jews called it, on Hester near Ludlow, where everything but pig could be bought off pushcarts ... and where greenhorns would bunch up in the morning to wait for employers looking for cheap labor.[21]

Although such places emerged in many immigrant cities from London to Baltimore and even New York, they did not assume a lasting community-building function. Central here were not workers themselves, but their labour power. Similar to the Pig Market, the *birzshe* on Plaza Lavalle also functioned as an 'informal outdoor labor exchange', but the parallels should not be exaggerated. Given the direct involvement of the trade unions on the (albeit much smaller) Plaza Lavalle, it was not remotely 'the same phenomenon'.[22] Rather, as labour economist William M. Leiserson noted in 1924, the Pig Market and the American trade unions stood in opposition to one another:

---

18 Lencinas 1994, p. 90 f.
19 On the range of Jewish cultural products available see for example Warnke 1996; Shapiro 2009.
20 General characterisations can be found in North 1990; Waldinger 1990; Dunlavy and Welskopp 2007.
21 Howe 1976, p. 69. A somewhat disdainful yet nevertheless vivid description is provided by the attentive observer and police-beat reporter Jacob Riis, see Riis 1996, pp. 93–106.
22 Sofer 1982, p. 85.

The institution arose with the first Russian Jewish immigration and came to be known as the 'Pig Market.' In Baltimore, we were told of a similar market by clothing workers, who had used it before the union established itself in the city and provided an employment bureau for its members. In those days it was common for workers to furnish their own sewing machines, and when a man was hired he lifted his machine on his back and carried it to his place of employment. One of the first demands made by the unions organized among these clothing workers was the abolition of the 'Pig Market', and the hiring of all help through the union offices.[23]

The Pig Market subverted the union's local influence, while in the *birzshe* both fostered the existence of the other. Immigrants returned to this idea when confronted with the hardships of American urban life. The *birzshe* had always been the basis for political and social transformation – making the 'unconscious' worker 'conscious', turning an insurgent crowd into a revolutionary combat unit of Bundist self-defence, or, as Bertha Fox describes, the little sister into a revolutionary, and now the new arrivals into Argentinian *khaver*.[24] Nevertheless, the *birzshe* remained a transitory space and market. As the Bundists' collective stroll lost its conspiratorial edge, it ceased to function as a place of direct activism in Argentina. Instead, it merely redirected interested parties from the dispersed present mass of jobseekers towards the trade unions – thereby aiding the establishment of the first local Russian-Jewish institutions such as the *Biblioteca rusa* and the *Avangard*. As a result, what in Russia had been a public conspiratorial pattern of activism now became public and informational, albeit still as ephemeral as its illegal predecessor.

3   Into the Woods! From Clandestine Forest Gatherings to Picnics in Liberty Park

Recalled by many workers with stirring youthful romanticism, the Bund's secret meetings in Russian forests clearly left a far stronger impression on participants than the elusive *birzshe*. At such gatherings in the woods they experienced community first-hand, often making the Bund appear palpable and comprehensible for the first time.[25] A Bundist community was forged – usually accom-

---

23   Leiserson 1969, p. 30.
24   Aronson 1968; Fox 2006, p. 215 f.
25   On this see Mendelsohn 1970, p. 152 ff.; Davis-Kram 1980; Glenn 1990, p. 35 f.

panied by red flags, fiery speeches, copious singing, and on many occasions a keg of beer – whose collective strength could then be translated into political and social confrontations.[26] The advantage of these meetings was that, in contrast to the numerous smaller meetings in backrooms, they started off from the point of a present mass and could thus sometimes be directly transformed into other mass actions like demonstrations and strikes. The conspiratorial element so essential to these meetings was absent in emigration, causing this secret cumulative activism pattern to recede into obscurity.[27]

While the pressure to retreat into nature outside of town disappeared after migration, the romantic and social components of these outdoor meetings in fact grew in relevance for the formation of Bundist groups.[28] Casual gatherings in urban parks quickly became institutions of Bundist community building in the US.[29] Yet in contrast to the *birzshe*, the form of such outdoor meetings was not a transplanted practice from Russia but rather an amalgamation. In their gatherings in city parks, Bundists drew on a practice prominent in late nineteenth-century North America: the political picnic.[30] Picnics offered not only the social component of an 'outing' but also the political group's public representation in the city,[31] and were considered one of the five most important 'campaign weapons' in electoral campaigns.[32] Canada's first prime minister John A. Macdonald allegedly won office in the 1860s with this secret populist recipe: 'Politics was entertainment. ... Put on a good show – a brass band, a hefty cold chicken and ham meal in a park, provide handshakes for the faithful and jokes for the rustics – and the town would remember for years'.[33] Picnics allowed political leaders to portray themselves as *primus inter pares* away

---

26   Novikov 1968, p. 28; Mints 1958, p. 81. This was not unique to the Bund but rather common in the Russian workers' movement more generally, see the autobiography of Bundist worker-turned-Communist Aaron Gorelik, *Shturmedike yorn* (Gorelik 1946, p. 44 f.).
27   Analogous patterns in American anarchist circles were most likely found in the specifically anarchist taverns, see Goyens 2007.
28   On the eminent significance of 'outings' for early Social Democracy see Welskopp 2000, pp. 345–8.
29   Invitations can be found, for instance, in Bund Archives, New York, RG 1400, ME-18, 3; IWO, Buenos Aires, 1114.
30   This public political act dates back to slavery, as demonstrated in Susan Merritt's painting depicting blacks and whites dining together in the countryside under the American flag and a sign reading 'Liberty', see Southgate 1999, p. 7.
31   Needless to say, picnics also occurred in the forests of Russia and Poland but were inconceivable as a lasting political institution under Tsarist rule, see Mints 1958, pp. 81–4.
32   Alongside newspapers, public gatherings, the 'campaign trail', and radio, see Nolan 1981, p. 29.
33   Donaldson 1975, p. 27.

from the glare of the formal political stage, which is why their value for political mobilisation in democratic societies should be regarded as tremendously high.[34]

Bundists overseas were not looking for support at the ballot box, but sought to establish a new community in line with their transnational interests and transferred values and practices. They blended aspects of Bundist meetings in the Russian woods with the Anglo-American tradition of the political picnic accordingly. The practice was also well-suited to the Jewish recreational culture developing on the Lower East Side. As Moses Rischin relates in his history of Jewish New York, trips and picnics became institutions of Jewish America in the 1900s. Like cycling and steamboat tours, they belonged to the 'initiatory rites that turned greenhorns into Americans'.[35] This was just as true for the Bund, whose earliest American cells hosted political picnics and 'Americanised' themselves through their adoption as a mode of community building.[36]

That said, 'Americanisation' was not the only effect of such picnics. Similar to the *birzshe*, these events also had a latent impact of soft agitation, as one-time Social Democrat and subsequent far-left screenwriter Paul Jarrico experienced at a Communist picnic in 1928. It was a gathering

> 'where Negroes and Jews laughed and laughed to see the man hit the heads off dummy Hitler, dummy Mussolini, and dummy [J.P.] Morgan with 3 balls for a ticket'. They had numerous discussions about politics, and his cousins reproached him about his 'bourgeois ideology' and raised doubts in his mind about socialism.[37]

Similar debates, albeit in the reverse direction, were likely conducted at the Bundist picnics in 1920s New York or their Argentinian counterparts. Unfortunately, the widespread nature of the picnics is also one of the reasons why few reliable first-hand accounts exist today. Picnics show up in the archives only coincidentally, such as in the form of small invitation cards – to the extent that these existed at all. One card issued by the *Nyu York brentsh fun Bund* (the New York branch of the Bund) testifies to the matter-of-course attitude with

---

34   The political picnic was deployed in a wide range of contexts, including protest movements like the abolitionist movement and mobilisations of conservative voters. For examples see Davis 2009, p. 456 ff.; Creighton and Macdonald 1955, pp. 219–25; Mitchell 1966; Nolan 1981, pp. 31–3; Southgate 2009.
35   Rischin 1977, p. 142.
36   Bund Archives, New York, RG 1400, ME-18, 3, Invitation: *Nyu yorker brentsh fun bund* (1910).
37   Ceplair 2007, p. 14.

which picnic organisers went about their business. An invitation to a 28 June 1910 picnic on the green is addressed not only to the Bund's members, but to sympathising organisations and their memberships as well. The note succinctly reads:

> The annual picnic of the Bund is well-known. This year it will take place on Shabbat, 28 June in the known Liberty Park. The Bund's New York branch decided, as in the previous year, to reduce the ticket fare for organisations, specifically: 500 tickets for 5 dollars, printed with the organisation's name. We would like to suggest your organisation take up this opportunity. Firstly, this way you can support the Bund's activities and at the same time make a good profit for your own organisation.[38]

This was a win-win-win situation benefiting Bundist community building, its fundraising campaigns, and the budgets of sympathising organisations. Invitations were distributed either via the Bund's office still located at 82 Orchard Street or through the Bundist bookseller Moyshe Gurevitsh at 202 East Broadway, whom the Bund relied on to conduct many of its early business transactions.[39] The picnics also bore an intrinsic transnational aspect, for the proclaimed support for the 'Bund's activities' not only contributed to said Americanisation, but also benefited Bundist revolutionaries in Russia. 'Americanisation' through picnics was thus not a one-way track, as political scientist Anthony King has already noted. Firstly, picnics or bazars enabled less politically active individuals to become better integrated participants in the political community, while simultaneously integrating activists into the society that granted them space for this social and political activity in the first place.[40] Thirdly, it cannot be ignored that these Bundist picnics also introduced Russian issues into American society. This transnational and politically radical component, of which all participants were well-aware, testifies to a sharp distinction between picnics hosted by politicians up for election and the recreational outings described by Rischin.[41]

---

38 Bund Archives, New York, RG 1400, ME-18, 3, Invitation: *Nyu yorker brentsh fun bund* (1910).
39 Gurevitsh was a leading Bundist in the early US years, and his bookshop was one of the most important points of contact and distributors of Bundist literature. See Bund Archives, New York, RG 1400, ME-18, 3; Mayer 1947.
40 King 1969.
41 Bund Archives, New York, RG 1400, ME-18, 3, Invitation: *Nyu yorker brentsh fun bund* (1910). More on this can be found in Part II.7.

These cheaply and widely distributed tickets (by comparison, admission to the Bund's indoor events at the time cost between 15 and 25 cents)[42] were designed not only to strengthen the Bund's position in the US as a representative of the Russian Bund, but also its ties to various left-wing Jewish organisations in the United States. The large number of tickets is striking, for even if the Bund only managed to sell a few of these packages, its influence must have extended far beyond the 3,000 members it was thought to have across the entire US in 1905.[43] As the Bund distributed the tickets in stacks of 500, we can assume that an annual mass gathering took place in New York's Liberty Park – after all, in the letter we learn that this mass ticket sale was based on previous positive experiences. Furthermore, this all occurred while the American Bund was in its infancy, as the first groups only formed around 1903. The Bund nevertheless had both the experience and the resources to legally mobilise three- to four-figure masses – something the Russian Bund was barred from doing, with the brief exception of 1905–7.

No such Bundist events are recorded for the early period in Argentina. This may be due to the relative lack of sources, as the Buenos Aires *Avangard* group issued an invitation in the summer of 1916 to a 'picnic of the Avangard' in the easily accessible and leafy district of Belgrano's Swiss Garden, scheduling the event for 3 December. This was most likely not the first of its kind.[44] It was later postponed to 17 January 1917 due to inclement weather, but the programme remained as ambitious as ever: designed as a celebration for all generations, the picnic began at 8:00 in the morning and lasted until late into the night, with common attractions like target shooting, seesaws, and ninepins just as much a part of the programme as an evening lecture by Argentinian socialist Fernando do Andreas, a film screening, and finally even fireworks. All of this took place on a Sunday, not on Shabbat, suggesting that despite their strict secularism Argentinian Bundists somehow respected religious law – even if only to facilitate their mobilisation.[45] The effort appears to have borne fruit, for although the *Avangard* group gradually disintegrated in the years after the October Revolution, it managed to host a last major picnic in January 1920.[46]

Argentina witnessed further political picnics under Bundist auspices in the 1920s.[47] These gatherings were in fact quite important, as the secular schools

---

42 See advertisements in *Der kemfer*, New York 1, no. 1 (1905), p. 7f.
43 Michels 2005, p. 156.
44 *Der avangard*, Buenos Aires 1, second run, no. 11 (1917), p. 2.
45 *Der avangard*, Buenos Aires 2, second run, no. 12 (1917), p. 2.
46 *Der avangard*, Buenos Aires 2, third run, no. 1 (1920), p. 3.
47 *Argentiner lebn* 1, no. 2 (1924), p. 6, p. 8. See also the YSFA's activities in *Sotsyalistishe bleter*, Buenos Aires 2, no. 34 (1931), p. 3.

depended on them for funding. One third of the Sholem Aleichem School's 1924 budget was raised through picnic collections.[48] It is thus hardly surprising that different organisations coordinated their picnics.[49] Even less radical organisations like the worker relief association *Yidisher arbeyterfarband far kegnzeytiger hilf* (Jewish Workers' Association for Mutual Aid) founded in Buenos Aires in the 1920s used picnics for their own purposes, as they were easily organised and required no costly accommodations, while also extending community building beyond the confines of party locales.[50] In contrast to the US, none of the Argentinian picnics claimed to benefit the Eastern European Bund. These were Argentinian gatherings with strictly local aims.

Despite this difference, they still continued to foster the Bund's transnationalisation. Participation was not only an expression of solidarity and support, but beyond opportunities for socialising also promoted the formation of Bundist directed present masses. Unlike the Bund's gatherings in Russian forests, participating in such 'outings' could not be equated with political activism. Picnics nevertheless served as Bundist recruitment pools as well as experienceable moments of the Bund's lived secularism. Primarily, however, they were sites around which collective community building could be conducted in the Yiddish language.[51]

These meetings reproduced familiar historical Bundist practices to an extent, while combining them with local structures such as the 'wild' labour market or the political picnics of the Anglo-American tradition. Given their legal status, however, they lost their independent political meaning and were redirected into other activities such as fundraising.[52] Moreover, Bundists' efforts towards a new secular culture in both the US and Argentina remained

---

48   IWO, Buenos Aires, 1111 [Educación], Collection lists; Balance of accounts, Sholem Aleichem School, 14 March 1924.
49   IWO, Buenos Aires, 1111 [Educación], Letter from the *Yidishe ratsyonalistishe gezelshaft* to Sholem Aleichem School, 17 January 1923; Letter from Prokor to Sholem Aleichem School, 18 December 1925.
50   IWO, Gremios en proceso, Yidisher Arbeyterfarband far kegnzeytiger hilf; Invitation and circular, 1927.
51   These transnationally motivated political picnics belonged to the standard arsenal of social movements and political parties at the time, including a very different New York 'Bund', the Nazi-inspired and anti-Semitic German American Bund. Its picnics around World War II were intended to firstly support the 'home front' by distributing *Mein Kampf*, and secondly to mobilise on behalf of the so-called 'Christian Front', which fuelled American anti-Semitic sentiments, see Irwin 1940, p. 18 f.
52   The same can be found in Tobias 1972, p. 130, p. 241, p. 244; Michels 2005, p. 155 f. Nora Levin on the other hand stresses the infusion of fresh energy immigrating Bundists brought with them, but does not go into detail on the matter, see Levin 1977, p. 199 f.

tied to questions emanating from the class struggle. Ultimately, although picnics were highly important, they remained starting points for other practices with a deeper political meaning, as Paul Jarrico bluntly states: 'Sad, really is, but nobody ever said the class struggle was a picnic'.[53]

4   Revolution and Soirees

Similar to the adaptation of those meetings, Bundists also reinvented another form of gatherings dating back to the nineteenth-century Russian educational circles, the *kruzhki*. Designed to raise political consciousness, these meetings in the backrooms of the Tsarist empire served as schools primarily for activists of the first generation. Gatherings could be moved from the backrooms to public spaces under legality, while mass migration made it possible to relocate to large meeting halls. The outcome was not only large *kruzhki*, as one can imagine regular public educational meetings, but rather remarkable ensembles of events with revolutionary content and bourgeois form in the style of soirees, salons, and balls. These gatherings were of course distinct due to their political content, which unlike the political picnics was programmatically inscribed into the events from the outset.[54]

Under conditions of legality, emigrated Bundists tested certain paths and modes of gathering and organising that also served as role models for reunions in Poland. The integrative force of such overseas gatherings can be deduced from their sheer quantity. Gertrud Pickhan reports that 1,000 delegates and 3,000 additional guests attended the Bund's fortieth anniversary celebrations in Warsaw in the late 1930s, which according to her marked the largest celebration in Bundist history.[55] Celebratory events in New York were equally impressive. Often enough Bundists booked the largest convention centre in town, the Mecca Center, for these purposes.[56] Moreover, at least one New York celebration was even larger, when 5,000 people gathered to celebrate the Bund's fiftieth anniversary in 1947.[57] We can safely assume this was not an isolated occasion. As with other jubilees, the anniversary was accompanied by a care-

---

53 Jarrico in a letter to Daniel Mainwaring, cited in Ceplair 2007, p. 191.
54 This alliance was not of a specifically Bundist nature but rather quite common, particularly among culturally inspired and nevertheless far-left groups, see Albert 2007.
55 Pickhan 2001, p. 170.
56 Bund Archives, New York, RG 1400, ME-18, 11; 18.
57 *Unzer tsayt*, 1–2 (1948), pp. 41–6.

fully prepared campaign across numerous publications in the tradition of commemorative or anniversary editions.[58]

New York's status as the new centre of Bundist life in 1947 was not the only reason for the gathering's size. The leading Bundists who attempted to rebuild the Bund in New York after the Holocaust drew not only on migration occurring in the war's aftermath, but also on the early experiences of mass migration beginning in the 1900s. As early as 1907, for example, the Bund's tenth anniversary was celebrated by more than 1,000 Bundist emigrants in Paris.[59] In contrast to the US, France fell well short of one million Jewish immigrants, suggesting that the Bund's celebrations must have represented a fairly concentrated gathering of the country's socialist Jews.[60] The event would even be noticed in Eastern Europe. Zivion (Benzion Hofman) attended the Paris festivities as an observer and subsequently published an enthusiastic report in the leading paper of the Russian Bund at the time, 'Di hofnung', on the front page of the Bund's tenth anniversary special edition. Zivion's report emphasised the need for the 'already half-French' Bundists to institutionalise their potential in the form of a Bundist club. A 'club will be the centre to which every Bundist can come to find what he seeks'.[61] The Eastern European Bund increasingly supported the establishment of such clubs, but only half-heartedly endorsed migrants' agency as such, refusing to grant even its largest American organisation political rights at Bundist congresses.[62] The aforementioned Paris Club was eventually founded and soon became a centre of community building among Russian political emigrants abroad, as worker Hersh Mendel recounts.[63]

Clubs organised not only the memorial meetings depicted in the previous chapter and Bundist jubilees and 'festivals', but also numerous regular meetings held on a smaller scale as 'financial resource and crowd drawer'.[64] Fundraising and organising events for that purpose became the foreign Bundist associations' main activities at least into the early 1920s. Yet fundraising was never an end in itself like it was for charity organisations, as such events were always also intended to educate and agitate the gathered Bundists and sympathisers. Whether in Paris, New York, or Buenos Aires, these countless small-scale soirees served an educational function beyond mere socialising, although precisely

---

58   Bund Archives, New York, RG 1400, O-Files, 41.
59   Zivion 1907.
60   On this see Weill 2007.
61   Zivion 1907.
62   Bund Archives, New York, RG 1400, ME 18, 4 [*referat*].
63   Mendel 1989, p. 133 f. See also Wolff 2007.
64   Welskopp 2000, p. 348.

this sociability made them attractive in the first place. The highlight of these evenings was always a highly political talk often referred to as a *referat*, an educational lecture. Topics ranged from local workers' grievances to informational events on the situation in Eastern Europe, and even wide-ranging theoretical deliberations on movement tactics.[65] On the one hand, archives and countless publications contain a flood of material on such events in the form of admission tickets, leaflets, and advertisements;[66] on the other, however, one finds an almost complete absence of information addressing what actually took place at these talks. The same is true for educational gatherings in Eastern Europe. Sporadically quoting individual *khaverim* belonged to worker autobiography etiquette, but the meetings as social events are rarely described. Because they were so common, they only seemed worth remembering when unforeseen events occurred or they were cancelled.[67]

Such unpredictability also allowed speakers to intentionally make a lasting impression. Together with other groups, *Avangard* regularly hosted large discussion meetings in Russian and Yiddish in a locale at Mexico 2070 where, for example, Jewish workers assembled to found the Yiddish-language raincoat workers' union on 14 December 1913.[68] Although these regular and presumably highly political events are not mentioned in Pinie Vald's memoirs, a certain evening in 1906 is. A peculiarly dressed man by the name of Tsheski appeared

> in a specially borrowed tailcoat, closed collar, white gloves, shaven and perfumed, to hold a lecture about ... That was precisely the question back then. The audience was unaware as to *why and what* he would speak, while the *khaverim* assured they knew just as much about his talk as the audience ... He then related, hoarsely, without addressing the audience, neither frostily nor warmly, not dryly, not bitterly ... that he had been an officer in the Tsarist army, and not just any officer. He had been successful and received a promotion, so that he signed countless death sentences for political prisoners with his own hands until ... his conscience began to torment him. After all, refusing to write any more death sentences would

---

65 These were also common opportunities for Bundist community building and fraternising in interwar Poland, as observed in Guterman 1976, p. 76.
66 See numerous documents in IWO, Buenos Aires, 1114; *Gremios en proceso*, as of 14 November 2008; Asociacion de escritores Israelitas Nomberg. See also Bund Archives, New York, RG 1400, ME-18, 3.
67 Shtern 1954, p. 27.
68 Leaflet: Yidishe S.D. Organisatsye 'avangard' in Argentine, *Tsu ale yidishe regelmantel arbeyter un arbeyterinen in Buenos Eyres*, IWO, Buenos Aires, 1114.

have bought him mistrust at best, but perhaps even a death sentence. He deserted for this reason ... That was the entire content of his lecture.[69]

Telling this story to a group of exiled Russian revolutionaries constituted the very essence of chutzpah. It ought to be noted that only his impudence rendered the meeting worthy of remembrance in the first place. Vald explains why the officer was not immediately driven from the room with fists and clubs by citing the curious circumstance that no one was quite sure whether to believe him. They returned to consensus by agreeing on how to productively exploit this confusion:

> Everyone was quite embarrassed about the organisation of this lecture, although there was one instance of solace: it was resolved to donate the 100 pesos that ended up in the coffers after the lecture to support political prisoners in Tsarist Russia.[70]

This was of course the exception, as typical meetings simply informed the audience about the Bund and its activities or hosted debates around general questions of revolutionary politics.[71]

In contrast to these content-oriented and purist meetings in Argentina, evening events in New York were often accompanied by a vibrant cultural programme. It appears that 'worker lectures' alone ceased to draw large audiences early on. By comparison, a 1906 issue of the *Forverts* sported the following announcement: 'Attention Bundists! Tomorrow night there will be a literary evening and concert rounded out by a report from the Bund congress, taking place in the clubroom at 272 East Broadway'.[72] Reports on the Bund's activities, the unique selling point in the Lower East Side's Yiddish evening calendar, only grew appealing when packaged as part of a political-cultural soiree. The same was true for a meeting not long afterwards when the New York Bund, encouraged by the renewed revolutionary hopes in Russia in 1912, advertised its presence on large posters:[73] 'A splendid literary-musical evening, including musicians from the New York Symphony Orchestra and a reading by D. Pinski

---

69 Vald 1929b, p. 23.
70 Vald 1919b, p. 24.
71 Numerous documents, IWO, Buenos Aires, 1114; Gremios en proceso.
72 Advertisement from the *Forverts*, Bund Archives, New York, RG 1400, ME-18, 3.
73 Robert E. Blobaum sees an entirely different parallel between the 'major' event, the 1905 revolution, and the 'minor' event, the Duma elections of 1912 in Warsaw, namely the extreme strain both exerted on Polish-Jewish relations. See Blobaum 2005, p. 35. On 1912 see Sujecki 1996.

and Z. Libin, will be held to support the socialist election campaign in Russia'.[74] Fully in the style of classical soirees, literature and music began accompanying most Bundist gatherings in the city's meeting halls. Yiddish cultural practice was established alongside political substance, allowing the Bund to become a cultural actor beyond the realm of class struggle even before World War I.[75]

In Argentina, by contrast, strictly political lectures continued to dominate Bundist practice well into the 1920s. When the *Yidishe sotsyalistishe organisatsye 'bund'* issued an invitation to a lecture by comrade and professor Ameriko Gioldi in Buenos Aires, the topic of the evening alone provided sufficient background music. Taking place only hours before the Aurora's historic cannon fire signalled the beginning of the October Revolution, no comment was needed beyond the meeting's modest title: 'The Revolution – and What Next?'[76] The organisers' reduction of the meeting to its political essence was rooted in their own experiences, as they had already successfully hosted a similar event on 19 June 1917, a 'mass meeting' in Salon Garibaldi on Sarmiento 2419, a Yiddish-language theatre only a few blocks from Plaza Lavalle in the heart of the Jewish district Once still popular in the 1930s.[77] Speakers included 'Mrs. Banderov, on the topic: "The role of the proletariat in the Russian Revolution and the relationship to the provisional government", Dr. Gurevitsh: "The Workers' and Soldiers' Councils in the Ongoing War", Mr. Yaroshevski: "Workers' and Soldiers' Councils and the Victory of World-Wide Democracy"' and 'Mr. Sh. Kaplinski: "The Russian Revolution and the Jews"'.[78] Unlike similar gatherings in New York, the purpose of this meeting was not fundraising but straightforward agitation. Admission was free and familiar alliances from Russia were revived, as posters often appeared in Russian and Yiddish but not in Spanish. Judging by numerous advertisements in *'Der avangard'*, the city's theatres were popular meeting places for the workers' movement even if the evening programme consisted of political education rather than entertainment.[79]

Such events were often tied to certain dates or issues, with Eastern European topics treated as themes in their own right. This continued in both Argentina and the United States well into the 1930s and 1940s, particularly at meetings on the conditions facing Jews in Europe.[80] The Bund in the US had shifted its role

---

74 Poster, Bund Archives, New York, RG 1400, ME-18, 3.
75 For context see Trachtenberg 2008.
76 Admission ticket, IWO, Buenos Aires, 1114, 62.
77 See theatre bill *Di ershte libe*, Salon Garibaldi, Buenos Aires, 27 March 1932; New York Public Library, **P (Theatre Collection, Placard no. 125), Record ID 244124, Digital ID 435166.
78 Poster, IWO, Buenos Aires, 1114.
79 In all editions up to 1910 such announcements can usually be found on the last two pages.
80 IWO, Buenos Aires, 1103; Bund Archives, New York, RG 1400, ME-18, 29.

by then. Building on its early days, many Bundist groups were able to consolidate themselves in the 1920s, accompanied by growing interaction and exchange with the Polish Bund. The groups in New York became a conduit of information between Europe and the US. In doing so they remained closely tied to local non-Bundist Yiddish organisations. Initial conflicts between the Bund and the *'Forverts'* during the 1930s were addressed in this manner, and the *'Forverts'* constructively referred back to these debates once again during World War II.[81] As part of a wider attempt to push the US into the war, the organisation issued an invitation to a 'Bund Day' complete with 'prominent speakers of the Polish Bund, including Emanuel Novogrudski, Secretary of the Bund in Poland' and Dinah Blond reporting on the situation in areas under Nazi occupation. The matter was urgent, and the *'Forverts'* restricted music to a side offering on that particular evening.[82]

Music was usually a decidedly more important component of the American Bund's events. Banquets honouring leading Bundists or the Bund itself increasingly assumed the appearance of proletarian dinner parties.[83] The Bund could charge relatively high admission fees in New York: a ticket to the banquet honouring *khaver* Noakh Portnoy, who travelled to the US in 1925, cost a handsome two dollars – roughly a day's wage for a needleworker on the Lower East Side.[84] The standard ticket price for such events was usually about one tenth of that, between 15 and 20 cents, while most Argentinian events remained free of charge.[85] Given the growing significance of *yidishkayt* for Bundist community building, such gatherings became increasingly 'cultural'. As early as 1922 advertising for the Bund's regularly occurring and increasingly sophisticated commemorative celebrations ceased to limit itself to historical or political content, but instead highlighted musical and literary elements.[86] Such evening events helped the Bund to become a local cultural institution, increasingly combining political substance with efforts to preserve immigrants' linguistic heritage. In this it followed in the footsteps of the Polish Bund, which complemented the Bund's Yiddish socialism with a Yiddish culturalism in its educational institutions.[87] This was mirrored in Argentina

---

81   On points of contention see Bundisher klub in Nyu York 1935; Mayer 1951.
82   Excerpt, Bund Archives, New York, RG 1400, ME-14B, 6.
83   Bund Archives, New York, RG 1400, ME-18, 13; 11, respectively: Various accounts of the Bund's fortieth anniversary in New York; N.N. 1932. Illustrated: N.N. 1936a.
84   Bund Archives, New York, RG 1400, ME-14B, 7, Admission ticket, 19 April 1925.
85   Bund Archives, New York, RG 1400, ME-14B, 7 Invitation, 25 December 1925.
86   Bund Archives, New York, RG 1400, ME-18, 10; Ibid., ME-14B, 7.
87   Esp. Kazdan 1956.

by Sunday matinees in the 1930s organised by the Bundist *Gezelshaft far yidishe veltlekhe shuln in Argentine*. These served as a platform for Bundist school students (accompanied by professional musicians) to present what they had learned over the previous year through Yiddish presentations, choral performances, and theatre.[88]

This professionalisation of the accompanying programme could also lead to new and unprecedented conflicts, like when later renowned violinist Samuel Antek from the NBC Symphony Orchestra turned up at the Bund's 1937 annual celebration in New York. The committee had planned the event with military precision, complete with a seating chart and a strict guest list. Although he warmed up backstage and was ready to perform, Antek would not grace the stage that evening. The festivities had already strained the Bund's budget considerably, and the organisers now insisted they had never hired the violinist. They had reached an informal verbal agreement with him at best, but never signed a written contract. He was thus neither to perform nor receive a fee. The artists' association representing Antek saw things differently, and the ensuing conflict between this representative of Jewish cultural workers and a Jewish-cultural workers' organisation went on for weeks.[89]

The specifically appointed anniversary planning committee had convened 15 times over the previous months and was sure it organised the event carefully. Evidently, some of its calculations were off. It can be assumed that the Bundists eventually reached some sort of agreement with the association, although sources remain inconclusive. Either way, that particular budget item was not the only thing preventing the committee from presenting an even balance of accounts after the event. The committee's massive efforts, from piano rental to publishing a 50-page special issue marking the event[90] (the printing of which was preceded by intense negotiations and even a conflict with the contracted printer, Chelsea Press) ate up more resources than the evening brought in.[91] The anticipated fundraising failed to materialise, but the Bund managed to drum up quite a bit of publicity. It sent out 7,500 invitation cards and 300 programmes in the run-up to the celebrations alone.[92] Numerous fraternal greetings from related organisations and just as many press reports in the event's

---

88   CAHJP, Jerusalem, AR, PER, 67–68, *Unzer arbet* 15 (November 1939), p. 1.
89   Bund Archives, New York, RG 1400, ME-18, 11, Correspondence.
90   Bund Archives, New York, RG 1400, ME-14B, 4, Brochure.
91   The celebrations earned a total of about 70 $ after deducting brochure production costs. Factoring in all other expenses, the evening ultimately lost money. A more detailed account can be found in Bund Archives, New York, RG 1400, ME-18, 11; 13.
92   Bund Archives, New York, RG 1400, ME-18, 11, Financial report.

wake underscore how much more successful the organisation was in these endeavours than in the economic sphere.[93]

As its emphasis on Yiddish cultural work grew, the Bund in New York developed from a solidary actor to a professional event organiser. Nevertheless, the form of activism that shaped the organisation locally was inherent to the Bund's gatherings overseas. The constant repetition and multi-faceted forms of integrative present mass gatherings increasingly 'directed' towards their respective destination country demonstrate how this activism pattern stimulated Bundist community building even under conditions of legality, and at great distances from its original action context. Correspondingly, *gathering* became a Bundist pattern of activism that combined progressivity and romanticism for the old home precisely *because* of the separation from Eastern Europe. In stark contrast to the early circles or forest meetings, these gatherings were sites of lived *yidishkayt* and thus focal points of Bundist *doikayt* overseas. As the social revolution appeared to recede into the background, Bundist *tuer* became cultural *tuer* for a secular Jewishness.

5   Reproduction through Confrontation? Demonstrations in the Americas

All locality aside, the Bundist gatherings depicted above always retained a transnational focus, marking a distinction to similar instances of such meetings in Eastern Europe. Conveners did not discuss specific understandings of what constituted Bundism overseas at these meetings, but rather lived it in specific local variations. This life drew on experiences from the *alte heym*. What this pattern of activism lacked were politically motivated or widely visible actions beyond community building.

There was no shortage of opportunities to do so within public confrontational activism patterns such as strikes or demonstrations. Like public gatherings, protest rallies were instrumental in raising public awareness. Depending on the issue involved, Bundist groups were in this way able to integrate themselves into surrounding contexts such as the socialist parties or the wider Jewish community. The Bund was also in great demand as a mediator between East and West, as evidenced at a mass protest on 17 October 1914 against the ongoing 'Beilis Affair' in Kiev[94] organised by the Bund's Paris section in the French

---

93   Bund Archives, New York, RG 1400, ME-14B, 4, Clippings.
94   Bernstein and AJC 1915, p. 181 f. Menahem Mendel Beilis was charged with ritual murder in

Socialist Party and the Human Rights League.⁹⁵ Both extraordinary occasions like the Beilis trial as well as annually recurring dates in the 'workers' calendar' allowed the Bund to take to the streets in specific geographical contexts without sacrificing transnational intent.

Yet the issues in question had to be transferrable, that is to say of some transnational interest to begin with (such as the Beilis case). Alternatively, the Bund could transnationalise its issues by enshrining the significance of the Bundist struggle in Russia as the essence of the Jewish workers' struggle as such. The scope of the resulting alliances was extensive and encompassed the most important personalities of Yiddish New York, including above all (apart from Abraham Cahan) the political darling of the Lower East Side: socialist congressman Meyer London, who was elected to congress three times beginning in 1914. London immigrated from Lithuania in 1891 and was already a leading member of the *Fraynd fun bund* by the early 1900s.⁹⁶ London's *yidishkayt* served as a point of interface and interaction with the Bund, and his presence seemed to electrify the crowds of the Lower East Side. As one observer recalled: 'During the campaign weeks the East Side district rocked with socialist agitation. The Socialist candidates were hailed as Messiahs. The open air meetings were monster demonstrations of public confidence and affection'.⁹⁷ Demonstrations inscribed themselves into the Jewish calendar as they began to occur more and more regularly:

> To the holidays of the Jewish calendar were added Labor Day and May Day, the Fourth of July and the exciting weeks before Election Day. With festivities and marching bands, the recitation of hymns of hope and elegies of despair, history became earnest and real. Each passing year recorded the forward march of progress, the anniversaries of the French Revolution, and Paris Commune, and the martyred assassins of Alexander II.⁹⁸

Kiev in 1913. Although he was acquitted following a tedious trial, it served as the perfect stage for a new wave of anti-Semitism and was covered by the Tsarist empire's right-wing press extensively, while international media watched on in disbelief. See esp. Rogger 1966; Lindemann 1991.

95   The Section Française de l'Internationale Ouvriere (SFIO) emerged from the 1905 fusion of the Parti socialiste français and the Parti ouvrier socialiste révolutionnaire. As a member of the Second International, it resembled the socialist parties in Argentina and the US with whom local Bundists cooperated (at least in terms of objectives and programme).

96   See Rogoff 1930, pp. 24–7.

97   Quoted in Goren 1970, p. 190.

98   Rischin 1977, p. 167.

Striking here is that these new Jewish holidays were secular and of at least socialist if not revolutionary origin. The prominent status enjoyed by the 'martyrs' after their attempt on the life of Alexander II shows once more how Bundist activity in New York relied on constant evocation of the organisation's Eastern European roots, and thereby transcended boundaries defining the party in Eastern Europe.

In this, the protagonists of the local movements (who like many rank-and-file activists had Bundist backgrounds) frequently drew on terms from the Russian era to describe conflicts in the US. When violence against African-Americans reached a peak in 1908 in Springfield, Illinois – Abraham Lincoln's former home, of all places – the Yiddish dailies carried headlines coded in familiar categories describing a 'pogrom in Springfield'. They not only appealed for donations, but also urged their readers to take to the streets.[99] The template for this response came from the Russian immigrant community, where anti-Jewish pogroms in Russia outraged the inhabitants of the Lower East Side as early as 1905 and sparked a demonstration bringing 150,000 people onto the streets, supported by just about every Jewish group in the city.[100] The votes for Meyer London must in this sense be seen not only as support for an American socialist, but also as votes for the 'first Congressman of Russian birth' who seemingly intuitively fought for socialist values.[101]

6 Unity in Action: Celebrating May Day

The most important date in the new Jewish workers' calendar was of course May Day. Dating back to labour protests in Chicago, it functioned as both a call to arms for the eight-hour day and a memorial gathering for the victims of the 1886 Haymarket Affair.[102] Interestingly enough, this tremendously important aspect of national history faded into obscurity in the US. It appears as if the fact that the definitive international labour holiday had its roots in Chicago clashed with the country's self-image in the twentieth century. A unique example of this historical amnesia can be found in a 1955 letter from the publisher of a New England magazine to the chief editor of the *Daily Worker*, the official paper of the Communist Party USA:

---

99   Leonard 1917; Miller 1971, p. 223; Lumpkins 2008, p. 118.
100 Rischin 1977, p. 167.
101 Rischin 1977, p. 235.
102 Among the veritably countless depictions see the still excellent Avrich 1984, esp. pp. 186–90.

> I am at present trying to collect details of the history about May Day. I was told somewhere that May Day, as a workers' celebration and demonstration, originated in the United States. However, I can't seem to find out the origin in any encyclopedia. Many Americans look upon May Day as some importation from Russia. We would like in our issue to dispel that notion, if it is a false notion.[103]

This search for May Day's distant origin is an expression of the abandonment of the 'Chicago Idea' in wider American society. At the same time, it testifies to how hastily the presence of a radical American workers' movement was externalised onto Russian immigrants. Although the latter surely played a part in the social upheavals of the 1900s, they were not responsible for them.[104]

Mass migration post-1905 carried the stirring and often violent demonstration experiences from Russia to America along with the migrants, and many Bundists continued to emphasise demonstrations as a special moment of their activism even long after emigration.[105] Adding to this was the fact that American Jewish institutions and the Bund both deployed memories of Bundist May Day demonstrations for agitational purposes.[106] The experiences gained in illegality also proved constitutive for the (legal) Polish Bund. Hillel Blum's memories of May Day 1896 in Vilnius did not appear in the official daily paper of the Polish Bund, 'Naye folkstsaytung', on 30 April 1936 for historiographical reasons. Rather, they were intended to prepare readers for the upcoming May Day by evoking the pride of 1896.[107]

May Day demonstrations would remain exciting constants for Bundists of all generations. Sh. Kuvelsman, who emigrated to Montevideo, recalls a May Day demonstration in Vilnius during the German occupation of the city in World War I.[108] At 16 years old, he experienced the war mainly as a confrontation with the Zionist-dominated municipal administration attempting to close down the newly founded Bundist popular library, *Algemeynes folks-hoys*, just as the Germans began marching into the city.[109] The library was ultimately spared

---

103 Quoted in Foner 1986, p. 7.
104 Foner 1986, p. 21.
105 Bund Archives, New York, RG 1400, MG-2, 429.
106 Such as in Beker, n.d. or Motolski 1945. Similar instances in Argentina are found in Pinie Vald, 'Der ershter may in Argentine mit 68 yor tsurik', *Di prese*, Buenos Aires (16 May 1958), Bund Archives, New York, RG 1400, M-14, 311.
107 Blum 1936.
108 Kuvelsman 1937.
109 Because of the harsh repression of the Jewish population under Tsarist law, despite widespread anti-Semitic sentiment among German soldiers Jewish groups of all backgrounds

in favour of other priorities, and Kuvelsman quickly radicalised by reading the class struggle literature it offered. This culminated in the announcement of a large May Day demonstration, at which a distinguished Bund speaker was to appear and call for the founding of a new Bundist organisation. Once again, we find Bundist activities occurring before a Bundist organisation even existed – only this time in the city of its founding and where the first Bundist leaflet was published.[110] Struggling to control his excitement and against the advice of his fellow *khaverim*, Kuvelsman planned to 'scatter red flowers across the city' – albeit with the German military authorities' approval just to be safe. He recalls the soldiers responding with a verbal 'thunderstorm' (written in Latin script) that shook the entire building, and rather than scatter flowers or meet his *khaverim* in the woods, Kuvelsman found himself under arrest. He soon escaped through a fortunate coincidence and headed straight to the forest, where his comrades were already singing *Di shvue*, to finally scatter the flowers. Incidentally, this experience would also serve as his Bundist moment of conversion: 'That is when I decided that the Bund alone shows the correct path that all workers must follow to fight for freedom and justice'.[111]

Kuvelsman wrote down these memories in 1937 in Montevideo to mark the Bund's fortieth anniversary. The city's local Bundists were closely linked to their *khaverim* in Buenos Aires, essentially forming a united association. May Day celebrations remained highly political events in both Americas at this point, often linked to major strikes in cooperation with trade unions and the socialist movement, and even incorporating problems and demands from Europe.[112] The occupation of 1916 may have driven May Day celebrations into the woods, but the message was clear: the first of May, the holiday of all workers, would endure for years through ruptures and great distances and was capable of fostering Bundist activism everywhere and anytime, fully in the spirit of N. Khanin. In this sense, his article in New York's '*Der veker*', 'Eyn mol a bundist – ale mol a bundist' (Once a Bundist, always a Bundist), can be understood as an appeal to Bundists to adjust their activism patterns to new contexts.[113]

Admittedly, the way in which May Day was celebrated had changed. Participants no longer came together in the forest but rather met in the city from the

---

did not necessarily view the German occupation in exclusively negative terms, see Liulevicius 2000, p. 120. Many Jewish relief organisations emerged, particularly in Vilnius and especially during these years, see numerous documents in Shabad 1916.

110   Bund Archives, New York, RG 1400, M–14, 311; *Tsu ale Vilner arbeyter und arbeyterke* (1897).
111   Kuvelsman 1937.
112   Horowitz and Seibert 1984, pp. 275–96.
113   Khanin 1934; see also Zelmanovitsh 1948.

start. In Argentina in the 1900s and again in the 1930s, this meant sharp conflicts with state security forces. Nevertheless, actual May Day proceedings in Russia, Poland, and overseas would remain remarkably similar. Like other socialist movements, the Bund harnessed these demonstrations for its own community-building purposes beyond the protest march itself. Demonstrations were often immediately followed by receptions or group dinners in the city's restaurants, many of which were officially organised and planned.[114] This dates back to the distinction between the May Day protest march and May Day celebrations overall already established in the nineteenth-century workers' movement, whereby the relationship between the two largely depended on the movement's legal status and the extent to which May Day was already recognised as a day of rest.[115]

A glimpse at local dynamics, however, clarifies that contemporary and local issues beyond these transfers were also essential to the international May Day.[116] In his study on the Austrian 'Rebel Sunday', Harald Troch notes that although internationalism was always one of May Day's central themes, a more active focus was placed on national problems, usually the struggle for voting rights.[117] Similar holds true for Argentina, where the globality of the Jewish diaspora prompted an even stronger process of transnationalisation. The *Avangard* was particularly keen to channel political strikes into other organised protests around May Day,[118] although events were both organised and criticised. The *Avangard* excoriated a seven-day general strike in 1909, accusing Argentinian workers in general and Jewish workers in particular of poor organisation.[119]

Although the 'performative turn' in cultural studies and the humanities has helped direct more attention towards May Day's ritualistic character, a contrasting comparison in the restricted field of two Argentinian Bundist May Day campaigns suffices to demonstrate that Bundists by no means understood their participation in May Day as ritual repetition, but rather as concrete political activism.[120] Both a 1919 *Avangard* campaign and another by the

---

114 See Bund Archives, New York, RG 1400, ME-18, 3, 29.
115 Troch 1991, p. 84f.
116 As in the Soviet Union, see Rolf 2013, p. 75.
117 Troch 1991, pp. 61–80.
118 See the issues of *Avangard*, Buenos Aires, May 1909, June 1909, June 1917.
119 Vald 1909b.
120 This was due above all to a perceived emptying of May Day's meaning through both state co-optation in activist-legitimating countries like the Soviet Union as well as counter-hegemonic movements' use of violence as an end in itself. On this see Kubik 1994, pp. 207–14; Malte 2013, p. 75; Lehmann and Meyerhöfer 2003.

secondary-Bundist *Yidisher sotsyalistisher farband in Argentine* (YSFA) in 1936 exhibit how the dominance of European affairs influenced activism in Argentina. In a historical depiction of the significance of May Day since 1889, the *Avangard* argued that 'a European war must necessarily bring about a European social revolution'. This mirrors the hopes for a world revolution after World War I, and the lengthy leaflet ends on an accordingly dramatic note:

> *Khaverim*! This year's May Day must become the most powerful demonstration of workers' unity. This year, this day shall be turned into a day of mobilisation of all workers' forces for the introduction of the socialist order around the world.[121]

The events of 1917 in Russia had clearly made an impression on the Argentinian Bundists in terms of their wording and general objectives. The *Avangard* pursued the same monopolistic approach locally as the Bund in Russia when urging 'all Jewish workers' to gather in Buenos Aires under its banner on May Day,[122] underscoring the *Avangard*'s confidence as an organisation in Argentina. Emerging from its radical commitment to the *yidishe gas* in Buenos Aires and now in its twelfth year, the group had established a constant presence in Argentinian socialism as well as the local Jewish community more generally.[123] This was now accompanied by the force of Russia's February Revolution, which the Bund sought to transfer to Argentina as a 'historical mission'.[124]

Ultimately, the subsequent October Revolution would not bring the *Avangard* unity of all Jewish activists under its banner as hoped, but instead its own organisational demise.[125] Many activists tacked sharply to the left in the initial post-revolutionary years,[126] and like most socialist movements the *Avangard* split into a Social Democratic and a far-left wing that later fed into the powerful Jewish section of the Partido Comunista de la Argentina.[127] Yet the Communist Party would also split in 1928, primarily around the questions of local autonomy and cultural, language-based federations (*agrupaciónes idiomáticos*) – an issue confronting practically every left-wing movement since the 1900s. One outcome of this process was a Jewish group forming largely around veteran activ-

---

121 IWO, Buenos Aires, 1114, Leaflet, *Avangard* 1919.
122 Ibid.
123 Vald 1909b.
124 N.N. 1917, p. 131, p. 133.
125 IWO, Buenos Aires, 1114, Correspondence between various *Avangard* activists.
126 CeDInCI, Buenos Aires, AR Cavazzonni, F002, 16/26.
127 Extensively depicted in Camarero 2007.

ists like Pedro Grinfeld, M. Viner, and Serafim Kupe, who attempted to develop a Yiddish and markedly 'Argentinian' communism in their journal *'Tsum kamf'*.[128]

Beyond the Bund itself (which was officially founded in Argentina in the 1920s), the YSFA founded in 1929 was the most prominent representative of the Social Democratic side. Its paradigmatic 1936 May Day appeal illustrates the holiday's inherent flexibility. After Argentinian general José Félix Uriburu's Mussolini-inspired coup on 8 September 1930 and the fraudulent election of his successor Augustin P. Justo as president in 1932, the political situation in Argentina escalated drastically. The rise of fascism in Europe, observed closely by Argentinian-Jewish organisations, further aggravated conditions.[129] The publication of Kuvelsman's May Day 1916 recollections 20 years after the fact must thus be read in this context: not merely as an exhilarating anecdote from a young, naïve revolutionary, but as a staunch reminder that the workers' struggle had been both possible and necessary even amidst the slaughter of World War I.

By 1936 the YSFA no longer viewed May Day as an 'expression of workers' unity' alone,[130] arguing that it 'ought to be a symbolic and historical event' demonstrating 'the political and economic solidarity of Argentina's working class, as supported by the country's largest bourgeois party' instead. They were convinced of the need for cross-class resistance to 'fascist reaction', and discarded revolutionary demands taken from the Russian example in favour of defence 'of democratic freedom' and the 'right to vote'.[131] Theirs was a struggle for the 'abolition of the Law of Residence' and an 'amnesty for all political and social prisoners'.[132] While the *Avangard* before World War I justified the mass demonstrations on May Day through the historical experience of the May demonstrations, and called for direct action in the Russian style, the YSFA diverted from its well-known rhetoric for 'the imminent achievement of socialism' towards concrete political demands. Like the Bund's founding, May Day remained one of the most important dates in the Bundist activist calendar but altered its content. It nevertheless remained a public confrontational form of Bundist gathering, for what ultimately did the mobilising was not an annual ritual, but local adaptive practices of diachronic and synchronous global interconnections under recognition of democratic and non-revolutionary demands.

---

128   CeDInCI, Buenos Aires, AR Cavazzonni, F002, 16/21.
129   Häfner 2008, p. 68.
130   IWO, Buenos Aires, 1114, Leaflet, *Avangard* (1919).
131   IWO, Buenos Aires, 1114, Leaflet, YSFA (29 April 1936).
132   This is not a peculiarity of past May Day celebrations, see Uitermark 2004.

7   Differentiation Dynamics in the Formation of Bundist Present Masses

Bundist meetings overseas always contained a transnational point of reference, as European problems were often nearly identical to their own. On May Day in particular, this occurred not only in solidarity but as direct participation despite great geographical distance. In the Americas, Bundist *doikayt* was always local and transnational at once and functioned as an opportunity for migrant community building. In this sense, the act of gathering illustrates how Bundist patterns of activism not only changed throughout the migration process, but also grew increasingly differentiated (Table 11). Both the movement's legal status as well as the specific local constellations facing Bundists played an important role in this process.

The marked differentiation of the Bundist activism pattern of 'gathering' in the US, a society in which the labour movement as a whole would have exhibited the strongest comparative degree of differentiation, is particularly striking. Bundists who did not give in to the diluted American variety of socialism used it for themselves and their own purposes – but it also meant that the Bund's purpose in the US shifted in this direction over time. The Bund attempted to compensate for the relative quiet on the political front by bolstering its cultural arsenal. Similar, albeit less pronounced developments could be observed in Poland and Argentina, as here the Bund understood itself as 'comprehensive'. The attempt was far more successful in Poland than in Argentina, but a comparison of the two nevertheless demonstrates similarities between Polish and Argentinian Bundisms in terms of their action-oriented character. The Argentinian setting marked a major difference, as the Bund's *doikayt* was tailor-made for its life in Poland and had to be adapted to a country shaped by immigration. In this regard, the presence and absence of Bundist patterns of activism under varying conditions of legality described in Part 1.2 is a simplification, demonstrating that the Bund changed along with legal conditions while activism patterns for the most part persisted. Processes of transfer are not marked by binary developments of either replication or rejection, but instead by dynamic adaptation and creative reproduction. In this way, transfers and transnationally situated reproduction led not only to an amalgamation of local patterns and Bundist politics, but also to the emergence of numerous Bundist activism patterns between the formal blueprints of Bundist *doikayt*, which the Russian patterns from the Bund's 'early days' continued to provide.

TABLE 11 Differentiation of the Bundist activism pattern 'gathering'[a]

Foundation	Transfer		
Manifestation (examples), existence, illegality, Russia	Legality, independent Poland	Emerges overseas	
		US	Argentina
Public conspiratorial (*birzshe*)			
	Illegal background largely dissipates		
	Latent activism pattern: public informative and public cumulative	Latent activism pattern: public informative and public cumulative, orientation for immigrants	
			Informative (*birzshe*)
Secret cumulative (meetings in the forest, circles, discussions)			
	Integrative semi-public (festivals, balls, memorial and discussion events)		
Integrative semi-public (under intense repression)			
	Heavily culturalised (balls, memorial events, emphasis on entertainment particularly in US) Integrative public, with recourse to confrontational public semantics (May Day balls and receptions)		
Confrontational public and always political, often violent (demonstrations, possible recourse to secret cumulative manifestations)			
	Confrontational public Confrontational force highly flexible according to political conditions, despite partial ritualisation		
Confrontational public (strikes), also always political	Confrontational public (strikes), often political	*Bundists*: confrontational public (strikes), highly economic, transfer via secondary Bundism *Bund*: utilisation for fundraising for Eastern Europe	Confrontational public (strikes), often political

a On the culturalisation of the Yiddish May Day and the range of associations during strikes see Part III.10.

CHAPTER 9

Reproduction as Creation: Worker Organisation and Secondary Bundism

Bundists founded Bundist organisations wherever they settled. In 1941, for example, a scattered group of Bundists around Layb Berman and Israel Grosman managed to escape to distant Kobe, Japan by way of the Soviet Union. The group immediately established a 'commission' to serve as a 'kind of Bundist representation in Kobe' that soon became a local information hub. As a self-run Bundist unit it also took up collective concerns, such as cultivating relations with the Japanese authorities and the Polish ambassador, who facilitated American visas for the stranded refugees.[1] Apart from that, the commission served as a link to the global Bundist *mishpokhe*. In some similarity to the Jewish prisoners during the Russo-Japanese War, Kobe's Bundists had been cut off from the outside world for quite some time. The Bundist network now provided a remedy to this isolation, and the commission provided them with access to coveted Bundist and Yiddish literature imported to Japan from the newly emerging centre of Bundist life in New York.

Nevertheless, such self-organised groups were only rarely granted formal recognition as Bundist organisations by the Central Committee. Bundists frequently adapted their patterns of action and thought overseas, producing entirely new collectives still rooted in Bundism but not formally affiliated to the Bund.[2] This was particularly necessary in the US, where many of the Bundist institutions painstakingly built in Russia and Poland like unions, journals, and cultural groups already existed in similar form in New York prior to the Bundists' arrival. In the 1900s few of those institutions were as powerful as the '*Forverts*', providing Bundists with a remarkable local scope of action. In order to develop a more profound understanding of the Bund as a transnational social movement, it is thus necessary to account for associations that cultivated Bundist forms of activism but were not Bundist cells as such.

---

1 Grosman 1945.
2 Grosman 1945, p. 78; Bund Archives, New York, RG 1400, ME18, 2, *Referat fun der driter yehrlikher konventsh fun di bundistishe organisatsye in Amerika* (1906), p. 9. A more extensively documented case of war refugees arriving in the US via Japan is provided by the Bundist family of Julko and Leja Litewa, see Bund Archives, New York, RG 1400, ME18, 226.

1 Decentralisation and Marginalisation

Bundist activism in the US is often criticised for failing to create an American Bund. The reasons for this 'failure' are often said to be found in problems of transferability arising from differences between East and West. In this regard, Zygmunt Bauman makes the claim that the 'intellectual idiom as embraced in the East knew no division of labor between political and cultural leaders, between body politic and "civil society", between the rights of the legislator and the duties of spiritualized leadership'.[3] While politics tended to subsume all other concerns in Eastern Europe, the greater freedom available in the US unleashed the centrifugal force of ideas and with it a process of decentralisation that would become a causal problem for the Bund. Such a view barely represents the heterogeneous social and cultural movements of Eastern Europe. With more nuance and against the claim of a single, universal Jewish experience, ground-breaking studies of the move to America by Jonathan Frankel and Eli Lederhendler showed how Jewish immigrants were overwhelmed by the complexity of American life, and often dropped their political agendas in order to concentrate on economic integration.[4] Looking at the Bundists in migration, however, we also see another facet of integration – one that combines Eastern European political agendas with the 'self-agency of migrants'.[5] As demonstrated in Tony Michels's outstanding account of Yiddish socialism in New York, the actions of Bundists themselves best reveal the limits of oversimplified East-West dichotomies.[6] Michels examines the Bundists as part of broader Jewish politics in New York and comes to a divided conclusion. On the one hand, he emphasises the exuberant Bundist activism in New York's socialist organisations like the *Yidishn sotsyalistishn federatsye*'s Agitation Bureau, which even allowed them to take stands against the significantly more powerful '*Forverts*'. Then again, he detects limited results of such activism, which he explains by these very Bundists' exclusive focus on far-more exciting Russia, diverting their attention and activism away from the immediate US context.[7] What easily appears as a contradiction in itself was in fact a characteristic expression of the Bund's transnationalism, which never hindered but

---

3 Bauman 1987, p. 168. For a critique of this position see Moss 2009, pp. 14–22.
4 Their innovative potential ought to be acknowledged as well, countering an interpretation of Jewish history (embodied most prominently by Jacob Katz) that believed to have identified universally valid role models by focusing solely on France or Germany; see Katz 1973; Frankel 1984, p. 456; Lederhendler 2009.
5 Hoerder 2002, p. 439.
6 Michels 2005, p. 156.
7 See Michels 2005, p. 155 ff., pp. 172–6.

rather inspired new forms of activisms and allowed for Bundism's adjustment from its Eastern European origin to social life overseas.

2 Secondary Bundism in Action and Organisation

The strengths posed by Jewish and Russian immigrants' ability to remain active both inside the US and on behalf of the Russian movement alike surfaced as early as 1889, mentioned in Luy Miller's speech when representing the Jewish American trade unions at a congress of the Socialist International.[8] This was further bolstered by Bundists' arrival overseas, so much so that by 1927 *Arbeter-ring* general secretary Joseph Baskin described the organisation's thriving network of schools and ongoing cultural work as 'undoubtedly a direct outgrowth of the Bund and its position on general Jewish and cultural issues'.[9] Mitchell Silver strikes a similar tone in his depiction of Jewish secularism in the US, emphasising the strong influence Bundist immigrants had in the country: 'The flowering of socialist politics and Yiddishist culture in America was heavily indebted to Bundist-formed émigrés'.[10] To better understand this practised transnationalism, in the following I suggest a reading of Bundist activism in the Americas that integrates East and West without expecting to encounter replicas from the 'Old World'.

3 The Problem

Bundists were initially keen to recreate several of the Russian Bund's primary structures in the US. This included several attempts to launch new publications, of which *'Der kempfer'* (The Fighter) founded in New York in 1905 merits special mention. Unlike the *'Fraynd fun bund'* appearing the previous year, *'Der kempfer'* did not accompany a specific fundraising event but rather intended to function as a regularly appearing Bundist publication in the US, edited by official 'American representatives of the Jewish General Labour Bund [sic] in Lithuania, Poland and Russia'.[11] Its emergence was proudly announced in Tsarist Russia by the Central Committee's paper of record, *'Der veker'* (The Alarm Clock), citing the 'organ of the American Bundists' as the first of its kind in the

---

8   Hertz 1954, p. 46 f.
9   Quoted in Trunk 1976, p. 364.
10 Silver 1998, p. 53.
11 Tsentralfarband fun die bundistishe organisatsyonen in Amerika 1905a.

world.¹² The American *khaverim* spared no efforts and enthusiastically printed 15,000 copies – yet sold only a handful. As would be the case with all American Bundist publications before World War II, *'Der kemfer'* went out with a whimper after publishing its debut issue. The general secretary of the Bundist organisations in the US remarked at an annual meeting only a few weeks later: 'Due to the lack of capable authors and unfavourable preparation, the *"Kemfer"* was very weak in the literary sense'.¹³ Little trace remains of such self-criticism in the Vilnius *'Der veker'*, although its anniversary issue celebrating the publication of *'Der kemfer'* appeared after the large annual meeting. This can easily be explained, of course, by the delayed transmission of such information across the Atlantic. Moreover, the fact was simply of little importance to Russian Bundists. As evidenced by the special editions of *'Di arbeter shtime'* in 1901 and *'Di hofnung'* in 1907, the editors spoke proudly about the emergence of a globally ubiquitous Bund's international network, while showing little interest in how Bundism actually functioned in such remote locations.¹⁴ The publication's failure had a more severe impact in the US, as it took until 1941 to launch a second attempt at an American Bundist organ (this time successfully), the renowned *'Unzer tsayt'*.

The greatest problem facing earlier Bundist journals in the US was certainly not their quality alone, but also their general orientation. The first issue of the *'Rotshester tsaytung'* (Rochester Newspaper) in 1907 was published exclusively to commemorate the tenth anniversary of the Bund in Russia. This meant Russia and Russia alone, omitting any reference to the organisation's activities in exile. Although the issue's opening editorial, framed by the Bundist hymn *Di shvue* on the left and an article by Abraham Cahan to be discussed later on the right, spoke euphorically of the Bund's 'radiant' and 'shining' future,¹⁵ the text was lifted from the anniversary issue of the Russian *'Di hofnung'*. Activists saw themselves as those

> whom merciless fate has torn from their homeland, blown them away to a country in which the greed for power, money, and more money permeates everything: life means money, literature, science, everything, everything is sold for money. In the country in which we migrants are talked about and viewed as material to be transformed into money, in a country in which the workers truly are fully under the influence of capitalist politics,

---

12 N.N. 1906a.
13 Bund Archives, New York, RG 1400, ME-18, 2, *Referat* (1906), p. 10.
14 See Part II.4.
15 'Bund' brentsh S.P. un S.L. klub 1907c, p. 3.

in which we feel uneasy, unhappy, and undignified, where hopelessness [*yiesh*] fills our heads unwantedly, driving us to sad thoughts.[16]

Revolutionary fervour this is not. Given the actual political situation on the ground, the succinct formulation following this lamentation, distilling the lessons of the Bund into a call for a workers' uprising, comes across as sheer rhetoric.

This was also reflected in activity. The occasion for which the '*Rotshester tsaytung*' was published in the first place was not a demonstration or trade union meeting, but a ball held at the local dance hall to celebrate the Russian Bund.[17] While such gatherings already functioned as valuable opportunities for Bundists to present themselves to the American public, Bundist publications failed to produce an even remotely similar effect. The same can be said for sales of Eastern European Bundist publications in the US more generally, which hovered at a negligible level and were hardly worth the effort. Bundists imported the highly successful Polish daily '*Naye folkstsaytung*' in the 1930s, but even this second high point of Bund activity saw a mere 34 subscriptions across the entire United States, earning the Bundist coffers a measly 234.32 $ between March 1937 and February 1938. Despite activists' commitment to the Polish Bund (currently at its organisational peak), the latter's journals were of little interest to American Bundists.

The only exception to this rule were special issues commemorating their own Bundist past. Annual earnings through subscriptions were almost exceeded by a single special issue of the '*Naye folkstsaytung*' that same year, selling around 1,000 copies and raising 231.95 $.[18] While such festive issues quickly sold out, total earnings from regular sales of Eastern European papers never amounted to more than several hundred dollars per year. American Bundist groups nevertheless continued to import such publications and send them free-of-charge to important institutions and libraries across the country, where they functioned as multipliers for the Bundist cause.[19]

While the Bund in the US brought together present masses through remembrance, mutual aid appeals, elegies, and pride in one's roots, its American branches hardly made an active political contribution to the improvement of living conditions in the country. At the same time, however, the local Bund organisation *Avangard* was a leading force in Argentina due to its extremely

---

16   'Bund' brentsh S.P. un S.L. klub 1907d.
17   'Bund' brentsh S.P. un S.L. klub 1907a.
18   Bund Archives, New York, RG 1400, ME-18, 23, Receipts.
19   Bund Archives, New York, RG 1400, ME-18, 28, Accounting books 1933–9.

influential monthly publication, and played a major role in founding the larger umbrella federations of the institutionalising Jewish workers' movement.[20] Were Bundists in the US unable to achieve similar results, or simply unwilling?

4   The Solution

Bundists in the US by no means lost interest in class struggle. They mobilised class-struggle motifs and rhetoric on behalf of the Bund in Russia, while Bundist intellectuals integrated themselves into the American landscape as *'Forverts'* authors. Yet even in combination with mass migration, these developments did not lead to the founding of an independent Bund in New York, as most Bundists accepted the functional differentiation of American society and adapted it to their social movement. The group publishing the *'Rotshester tsaytung'* at the time, for instance, was also recognised as a language federation and Bundist branch of the Socialist Party of America. This integration was reasonable, after all, as no Bundist activism could have challenged the Socialist Party's overall political dominance in the relationship.[21] The same is true for the early Bund groups in New York, which cooperated closely with the party and socialist trade unions without competing with them.[22]

The situation in the US should not be generalised, however. Argentina's *Avangard* also functioned as a language federation of the Partido Socialista for some time, campaigning for the party in Yiddish and seeking to win over its readership through inspiring articles in its popular publication.[23] Similar to how the Russian Bund understood itself as a part of the RSDLP (with the exception of 1903–6), the *Avangard* defined itself as the *'Organización Social-Democratica de los Obreros Israelitas en la Rep. Argentina'*[24] (Social Democratic Organisation of Jewish Workers in the Republic of Argentina) – pointedly not

---

20   As was the case with regard to the planned workers' association funded (as in Russia) with trade union resources, see N.N. 1909b.
21   Although Yiddish-speaking branches of the socialist parties existed in the US as early as 1889, this marks a new quality of the Bund's integration into the Socialist Party, see Hertz 1954, p. 46.
22   They also sent delegates to many Bundist meetings. See for example Bund Archives, New York, RG 1400, ME-18, 2, *Referat*, pp. 2–5.
23   Evidence can be found throughout, see for example N.N. 1908a; N.N. 1908b; N.N. 1910. This support diminished somewhat over the years, but generally endured even the conflicts of World War I and the abolition of the language federations in the Partido Socialista, see Kling 1917; N.N. 1919.
24   As can be observed in the titles of *'Der avangard'*, Buenos Aires.

an overseas branch of the Russian Bund. This self-understanding and the comprehensive kinds of activism resulting from it were the primary factors making the *Avangard* an Argentinian adaptation of the Bund in its own right, complete with functional differentiation inside the organisation (e.g. through committees).

In the United States, by contrast, Bundist organisations occupied clearly defined niches as early as the 1900s, accompanied by the transfer of Bundist action patterns and experiences to American institutions, albeit without the simultaneous transfer of Bundist organisational patterns. This phenomenon – in which Bundists conveyed and transformed Bundist ideas but not the Bund itself – resulted in the establishment of new, powerful organisations rooted in Bundism but outside the formal Bund that I call 'secondary Bundism'. The trajectory of these developments is depicted in the following.

5 The American Roots of Secondary Bundism

Although Bundist publications like *'Der kemfer'* would fail, New York's Jewish working-class neighbourhoods nevertheless provided an ideal breeding ground for Bundist activism. Fuelled by major events in New York such as the 1909–10 Shirtwaist Strike and the 1911 Triangle Shirtwaist Fire, activists founded several organisations in the context of the emerging Jewish workers' movement throughout the 1900s that dropped the Bund from their title but continued to base themselves on Bundist ideas.

The growing numbers of activist immigrants had an impact on many branches of the Workmen's Circle (*Arbeter-ring*) as early as 1901. Still quite small before 1905, a form of organisational reciprocity emerged between the Bund and the *Arbeter-ring* in which the affiliation of a large number of Bundists swelled the ranks of the latter significantly. Its branches in turn played an important role in the founding of early Bundist organisations in the US. Secretary of the Bund's Central Federation in the US, Israel Bergman, proudly reported the establishment of a large number of new groups in 1906, remarking that it was 'important to him to mention that the branches of the *Arbeter-ring* had contributed a great deal to this development'.[25] Even the *'Rotshester tsaytung'*, which usually restricted itself to celebrating the Bund, featured many announcements from local *Arbeter-ring* branches inviting Bundist readers to

---

25   Bund Archives, New York, RG 1400, ME-18, 4, *Referat fun der driter yehrlikher konventshon fun di bundistishe organisatsyonen in amerika* (1906), p. 10.

their meetings.²⁶ It seems clear that participants at the time knew the two entities needed one another. Both the *Arbeter-ring* and the Bund emerged not only from similar ideas, but often enough even from the very same people, albeit in different functions.

Secondary Bundism became explicitly political with the 1912 founding of the Jewish Socialist Federation (*Yidishe sotsyalistishe federatsye*). It was long recognised as a Yiddish-speaking section of the Socialist Party that combined Bundist activism with American issues and corresponding trade union work.²⁷ Some observers viewed the *Federatsye* sceptically, seeing it as an attempt to establish an American Bund. Others, such as Bundist poet and '*Forverts*' author Abraham Liessin (Avrohm Valt), regarded it as an alternative to the dominance of the '*Forverts*' and the personality of Abraham Cahan.²⁸ A prominent writer, Liessin retained his important function within the *Forverts Association* nevertheless, even becoming the chief editor of erstwhile rival publication '*Di tsukunft*' in 1913 when the *Forverts Association* bailed out the former.²⁹ Despite the close ties between the *Federatsye* and the Socialist Party, it assumed a minor role compared to that played by the Bund in the RSDLP. Hopes, or indeed fears, that the *Federatsye* could become a Bund in the US were in this sense exaggerated, but speak to the suspected potential of an official transnationalisation of the Bund. In marked contrast to the Bund in Russia or the *Avangard* in Argentina, the *Federatsye* never claimed to be the exclusive representative of Jewish workers in all political, social, and cultural matters. It nevertheless diversified the range of voices on the American Jewish street, publishing the weekly paper '*Di naye velt*' and other periodicals under the direction of Bundist Yankef Salutsky between 1912–17.

The *Federatsye*'s strong presence in Yiddish America did not emerge overnight. Yiddish-language branches of the Socialist Party, *Arbeter-ring* branches, and Bundist organisations in Syracuse, Rochester, and Buffalo founded the *Yidishe agitatsye-byuro* (Jewish Agitation Bureau) as early as 1905. It would only begin to have a wider impact and attract members to the left of the '*Forverts*' in 1908, aided by the arrival of more radical Bundists.³⁰ Both the Agitation Bur-

---

26 Texts relating to the *Arbeter-ring* can be found on nearly every page of the '*Rotshester tsaytung*' in 1907.
27 Salutski 1913. The close ties between the Bund and the *Federatsye* are also emphasised in Epstein 1953, p. 6; Michels 2005, pp. 171–8.
28 Levin 1977, p. 199.
29 On the relationship between the *Forverts Association* and '*Di tsukunft*' as well as Liessin's role see Michels 2005, p. 151 f.
30 Hertz 1954, p. 99 f.; Michels 2005, p. 161.

eau and later the *Federatsye* were certainly closer to the Socialist Party than was the case for the *Avangard* and the Partido Socialista in Argentina. The Agitation Bureau was not conceived as integrating an external language federation, but rather as an internal umbrella organisation consisting of 80 branches which 'are in every respect similar to the ordinary party locals or branches, excepting that they use and speak the Jewish language in their meetings and to a great extent use the same in the general propaganda'.[31] This endeavour was quite successful, allowing the Agitation Bureau to boast of 320 meetings in 30 states attended by 64,000 supporters over the previous year at the Socialist Party's 1912 national convention. This was accompanied by the sale of 150,000 informational brochures and 20,000 pamphlets and books in 1911 alone.[32]

These kinds of organisations were not only established by Bundists, but also adapted the Bundist concept of *doikayt* and developed an action-based self-understanding stipulating action 'then and there'. Both the opportunities and problems this transfer to the US posed quickly became apparent. The Agitation Bureau staged successful mobilisations on the one hand, as did its successor, the *Federatsye*, which re-founded itself as an autonomous branch of the Socialist Party following changes to the latter's by-laws. Against this backdrop, leading Bundists like Zivion and Zaks increasingly contradicted or even attacked Abraham Cahan and the '*Forverts*'. The new groups further differentiated the system of American-Jewish socialism at the same time, submitting it to additional refinement by new actors in the form of the Agitation Bureau and the *Federatsye*.

In 1917, the seminal activist Zivion who emigrated in 1908 explained the *Federatsye*'s failure to become an American Bund by pointing out that it adopted the Bund's understanding of the importance of the Yiddish language, of the specific economic and spiritual living conditions and of the Jewish people as such, but failed to extend these transfers into one crucial aspect: the notion of national-cultural autonomy. This helps explain why the relevant scholarship on the Bund largely focuses on the national question, and only rarely looks at the movement's transnationality. As Zivion stated, there simply was no 'national question' in the US, rendering that particular transfer both impossible and unnecessary.[33] This means that only one of the central Bundist motifs was not transferrable in its known form, namely the goal of national-cultural autonomy, whereas all other activism patterns associated with *doikayt* most

---

31 Panken 1912, p. 244f.
32 Ibid.
33 Zivion 1917.

certainly were. The price for this transfer of Bundism without one core value was the demise of its theoretical roots and its grounding in political-economic revolutionary Marxism, making the need for secondary Bundism and cultural re-orientation all the more apparent.

The absence of a struggle for national-cultural autonomy merely meant that American Bundists' activist action required a different character. As Tony Michels noted, in some ways the *Federatsye* 'functioned as the American equivalent to the Bund'.[34] From a transnational standpoint we can further qualify this assertion, given that the *Federatsye* completely accepted and simultaneously upheld functional differentiation of the Jewish workers' movement in the US, something the Bund in Eastern Europe – with its claim to sole representation of all Jewish workers – had always opposed. To understand its position, it is helpful to consider the difference between the organisation and the ideology. The *Federatyse* never was nor sought to be a Bund in the US. Secondary Bundism, however, was a significant and vibrant expression of Bundist thought and practice within the American system, and accrued a great deal of influence among the American-Jewish community. Even before World War I, the *Federatsye* and *Arbeter-ring* were two protagonists of secondary Bundism in the US that, as branches of the Bund, did far more than merely complement the Bundist exile organisations looking to Russia. The new actors changed 'Jewish politics' as well as the overall Yiddish cultural landscape in the United States significantly.[35]

6 Cultural Workers: The *Arbeter-ring* and Secondary Bundism

Although founded in 1882, it was not until after a decisive reorganisation and mass Russian Jewish immigration post-1900 that the *Arbeter-ring* would become the most important organisation in the American Jewish workers' movement. At first it primarily served as a self-organised strike- and health insurance fund. Boasting literally hundreds of branches, it eventually went on to become the most prominent actor of Jewish secularism in the US. Its tens of thousands of members made it both a socialist and cultural association, as well as a fraternally organised mutual aid society. Parallels are evident to the *kassy* system, the strike funds from which the Russian Bund originally emerged. Nev-

---

34 Michels 2005, p. 173.
35 In its last years of its existence the *Federatsye* had 3,000 registered members in New York alone, but enjoyed a far wider reach as members often occupied key positions in the Jewish workers' movement, see Michels 2005.

ertheless, the *kassy* system was not unique to Jewish labour history, whereas the *Arbeter-ring* most certainly was.[36]

Bundists were of no special importance to the *Arbeter-ring* in the first decade of its existence. With their arrival, however, it soon became the 'mightiest fortress, which defends and protects all of our socialist conquests', as Bundist A.S. Zaks praised it in a poem as early as 1910.[37] Existing scholarship often mentions the Eastern European backgrounds of activists in the *Arbeter-ring* and similar organisations.[38] To be more precise, their background was not only Eastern European but often Bundist. The *Arbeter-ring*'s rise as the central institution of *yidishkayt* in the US not only coincided with the arrival of many overseas Bundists from 1905 onwards, but was in fact enabled by their arrival. Many immigrants viewed the *Arbeter-ring* as an opportunity to find a genuine Yiddish-speaking home, while simultaneously fighting to improve their own living and working conditions. As Abraham Liessin emphasises, the *Arbeter-ring* was thus more than just another relief or mutual aid society. In his view, no civilised nation in the world treated its workers as poorly as the 'country of benefit societies'.[39] Viewed in this light, Liessin identified the *Arbeter-ring*'s major accomplishment as its ability to channel workers' suffering into activism, rather than alleviate it somewhat through immediate charity. The *Arbeter-ring* 'did not draw off the "workers"' energy from the social movements but rather freed the membership from some of the pressures *so that they might be politically active*'.[40]

The relevance of 'Bund-type radical activism', perhaps better understood as secondary Bundism, becomes evident here.[41] Secondary Bundism's 'mightiest fortress' not only built its strength on American foundations, but also drew heavily on Eastern European experiences and actively applied lessons derived from them. In contrast to the widespread assumption that the *Arbeter-ring* was a genuinely American association gratefully absorbing Bundists into its ranks, Bundists and *Arbeter-ring* were tied together through a much more complex interrelationship. Bundist influence was so great within the *Arbeter-ring* up to the mid-1920s, when it reached its peak of 85,000 registered mem-

---

36   See Paretzki 1932, p. 58; Tobias 1972, p. 98; Hofmeester 1990, pp. 479–83.
37   Quoted in Michels 2005, p. 189.
38   See for example Dubofsky 1968a; Rischin 1977, p. 167 ff.; Brandes 1976; Frager 1992. Michels also argues against expectations of 'Americanization' yet nonetheless restricts himself to American history, see Michels 2000, pp. 531–4.
39   Cited in Shapiro 1970, p. 33.
40   See ibid.
41   Basch 1998, p. 52.

bers[42] (and in a somewhat diminished form even beyond that period), that it must be considered the most prominent and powerful expression of secondary Bundism in the US.[43] This is reflected, firstly, in political priorities and emphases, including the specifics of Yiddish-Jewish educational work,[44] the exclusion of Zionist branches into the 1920s and simultaneous toleration of Zionist members or speakers,[45] the admission of women as full members (quite extraordinary for 'fraternal orders' at that time),[46] and irreconcilable opposition to Communism even to the point of accepting internal splits if needed.[47] As a result, the *Arbeter-ring* became the largest secular Jewish organisation of its time.

Secondly, the organisation encountered a meaningful qualitative foundation upon which to build, for, as Tony Michels establishes, '[t]housands of Bundists and, to a lesser extent, Social Territorialists and socialist-Zionists formed Arbeter Ring branches',[48] or in the words of Nora Levin: 'Bundist groups agreed to join the Workmen's Circle en masse'.[49] As discussed above, Bund groups in the US were not mass organisations at that time, but the *Arbeter-ring* gave thousands of Bundists an appropriate context in which to cultivate a Yiddish immigrant culture with a socialist character.

Joining a branch of the *Arbeter-ring* was often accompanied by memberships in other secondary-Bundist organisations. More than one third of delegates to the *Arbeter-ring*'s 1914 annual congress were simultaneously *Federatsye* members.[50] The new mass organisations in the US relied on activists from the Eastern European mass movements, for whom the *Arbeter-ring* became the new centre of their activism. Most were socialised in Russia as members of various trade unions and the Bund, while in the US they would commonly join a union, a specific branch of the *Arbeter-ring*, perhaps the Socialist Party, a *lands-*

---

42 Arbeter Ring, Yeshurin and Sh. 1962, p. 425f.
43 The activists' Eastern European background is often only hinted at or vaguely acknowledged at best, but rarely ever considered in its specific implications, see for example Shapiro 1970, p. 49f.
44 See Part III.11.
45 Michels 2005, p. 193f. The scepticism and downright rejection Zionism encountered within Jewish-American socialism is often ascribed to the Bund, while the meaning of *doikayt* in the US is rarely regarded as causal, such as in Diner 2004, p. 181.
46 Michels 2005, p. 186. The *zionistische Farband* did not admit women until 1918, see Rojanski 2007, p. 335.
47 Shapiro 1970, pp. 100–19.
48 Michels 2005, p. 187, fn. 17.
49 Levin 1977, p. 169.
50 Michels 2005, p. 173.

manshaft, and maybe even a Bundist organisation. The Bund's questionnaires suggest that Bundists regarded both the trade unions and the *Arbeter-ring* as the primary sites of their activism. Apart from that, it went without saying that one was also active in the *Arbeter-ring*. Only six percent of respondents in type v were not active in the *Arbeter-ring*, whereas almost one quarter indicated no trade union-related activities.[51] Another informative source collection on the relation between the Bund and the *Arbeter-ring* is an autobiographical competition held by the YIVO in 1942 with support from other Jewish organisations, in which Jewish immigrants from every conceivable political background participated. Of the 189 entries received – almost all of which speak of Eastern Europe in far greater detail than the US – roughly one third report activity in the *Arbeter-ring*, making it the largest melting pot of Jewish activists, with trade unions occupying a close second. Of the 15 percent of respondents who were already members of the Bund in Eastern Europe, however, two thirds became active in the *Arbeter-ring*, while half of them joined a trade union and one third the Socialist Party.[52] This testifies not only to the *Arbeter-ring*'s prominence among Bundists as a whole, but also to the fact that Bundists were heavily overrepresented within the *Arbeter-ring* in comparison to Jewish and even socialist Jewish immigrants. It comes as no surprise that political rivals soon founded similar organisations, including first and foremost the Poale Zionist *Yidish natsyonaler arbeter farband* (National Jewish Workers' Alliance) in 1910, and, splitting from the *Arbeter-ring* in 1930, the Communist International Workers Order (IWO).[53]

Thirdly, this Bundist overrepresentation was also expressed in qualitative terms often overlooked by scholarship. As Tony Michels acknowledges, Bundists did not isolate themselves indefinitely, prompting the question of how these transfers turned out in practice.[54] Their membership not only led to explicit 'Bundist branches', but also affected the very heart of the *Arbeter-ring*.[55] On the one hand, numerous Bundists held ranks among the executive leadership of the *Arbeter-ring* as high as general secretary. On the other, and based on activist rank-and-file membership, the *Natsyonale sotsyale klub* (NSK) founded in 1914 became a core site of these transfers. Not without reason does *Arbeter-ring* historian Yefim Yeshurin describe his collected volume on the NSK as a

---

51   See Part III.10. Bund Archives, New York, RG 1400, MG-2, 429. The two exceptions with regard to the *Arbeter-ring* are: Stockfish, Anshl; Hofman, Yekhaskl.
52   YIVO, New York, RG 102.
53   Braun 1946, p. 13.
54   Michels 2005, p. 156.
55   Ibid.

history of the *Arbeter-ring* itself, given that 'the history of the club reflected the character of our *Arbeter-ring*'.[56] In this, he wanted 'the future historian of the *Arbeter-ring* ... to note the role which the club has played over the previous 50 years. Specifically, the tasks of the club included maintaining the unity and purity of the *Arbeter-ring* as well as its tradition and democratic and socialist leadership'. In his view, the NSK was the driving force in the struggle against Communism, a sinister force seeking to mislead the workers from the 'socialist street', as it 'sought to win the Jewish worker over to the camp of those who have enslaved half the world all too terribly'. Seeking to explain or at least somehow account for the great schism within the *Arbeter-ring*, at this point in his narrative Yeshurin refers not to the political disagreements of the present but instead – very much resembling Bundist *Memorik* – to the 'heroic moments of the past'. After all,

> these were moments in which the *Arbeter-ring* risked being surrounded by the *khaverim* who spoiled and violated the term '*khaver*', a term that was baked into our hearts and souls when we fought against the despotism of the Tsarist regime in our old homeland, when the fittest and most able sons of our Jewish masses went to the Siberian taigas, to the Katorga prison camps, to the barricades and to the scaffolds. ... While remaining loyal to this era which we all lived through, loyal to the Lekerts who bravely and heroically stepped to the scaffolds, we brought those socialist and revolutionary ideas with us, and in this way our comrades continued their influence over the Jewish workers in the United States.[57]

This declaration of war against the forces of Communism reveals just how closely interwoven the *Arbeter-ring* and Bundist prehistory really were. Even when Yeshurin wrote those lines in 1930, Jewish activist identities still drew on the Bundist struggle in the Tsarist empire as embodied by Hirsh Lekert, who already had been described as the 'First Jewish Hero in Modern Times' in 1917.[58] In the *Arbeter-ring*, activists were able to establish a cultural com-

---

56 Yeshurin 1964, p. 226.
57 Yeshurin 1964, p. 5 f.
58 This was the title of an English newspaper article published in February 1917, Bund Archives, New York, RG 1400, ME-16, 28a, Article 'The First Modern Jewish Hero in Modern Times', *The Other Way* (Spring 1917). See also the only monograph on the popular Bundist hero, Hertz 1952.

munity rooted in the Bundist imperatives of *doikayt, khavershaft, yidishkayt*, and *mishpokhedikayt*. The NSK's prominent position represented a politics of secondary Bundism and was moreover committed to keeping the *Arbeter-ring* socialist even after Red October and the Balfour Declaration.

The leading personalities of the NSK occupied key posts in the *Arbeter-ring* in the years before World War II. In this function they filled crucial offices at the regional and national levels, while regularly attaining prominent positions as envoys and in committees like the national Executive Committee. For many years and almost without interruption from 1920 to the late 1930s, either the president or the vice-president of the *Arbeter-ring* came from the ranks of the NSK – indeed, often both did. As these were all elected posts, their prominence also reflects widespread support among the general membership. The NSK's annually alternating chair was thus on the one hand an honorary role, but also a position of power from which a very influential group was led.

Praise for the *tuer* in two essential *Arbeter-ring* biographical reference books primarily emphasises their Bundist commitment, which allegedly proves the honour and *khavershaft* of political leaders in a way that no other trait can.[59] In this sense the *Arbeter-ring* appropriated and perhaps even promoted the Bund's *Memorik* modes.[60] The biographies of NSK presidents in its initial 30 years (1914–44) provide convincing evidence that Bundist experience in Eastern Europe was a veritably mandatory qualification to obtain a top post. Only five of the presidents who emigrated to the US after the Bund's founding were not party members. Of those five, two emigrated while still very young and one came from Galicia, where a smaller Bund only emerged after 1905. Fifteen of the presidents, however, had direct Bundist experience (see Table 12, highlighted in dark grey), ten were active in other secondary-Bundist organisations (light grey), and only six had no biographical link to the Bund whatsoever (white) or at least none mentioned in their short biographies. Only two of them had been in Russia after the Bund's founding. Consequently, the NSK was led by individuals of Bundist background over 23 of its initial 30 years of existence, who, as evidenced by Yeshurin's introduction cited above, were perceived as honourable representatives of the *Arbeter-ring* for precisely this reason.

---

59   These can by all means be considered representative of Bundists in the *Arbeter-ring*, see Arbeter Ring, Yeshurin and Sh. 1962.

60   The organisation also supported the printing of numerous Bundist commemorative texts such as Berman 1945b; Gross 1938; Hoffman 1941; Abramovitsh 1944.

A large share of presidents also came from a working-class background, while an even greater share at least temporarily attended a *yeshiva* prior to becoming wage-earners in Eastern Europe or the US. The biographical reference books provide little information concerning the exact nature of their occupations unless they happened to be common, low-paid work such as in New York's sweatshops. While short biographies emphasise Bundist activity in Russia whenever possible, membership in the American Bundist organisations is rarely mentioned. At least presidents such as Nokhem Khanin or Israel Feynberg were simultaneously members of them. Apart from that, many more joined or even led other secondary-Bundist organisations. Two thirds of NSK presidents were active in the Agitation Bureau, the subsequent *Federatsye*, or the YSF, and often held high-ranking positions.

Similar studies could be conducted in many branches of the *Arbeter-ring*, but none of them were in such a central position as the NSK. Both NSK and *Arbeter-ring* (and its 'Bundist branches' in particular) acted as transmission belts, conveying Bundism to North America. Bundists thus built their 'mighty fortress' while establishing secondary Bundism as a mainstay of American Jewish history.[61] Their success depended on the transfer of Bundism and Bundist identity, albeit not of a Bundist organisational framework. It made the *Arbeter-ring* a quasi-Bundist organisation that nonetheless consciously separated itself from the Bund. Directly Bundist groups as units of the functional system of the Russian and later Polish Bund nevertheless remained intact precisely because they were not obliged to relate to current events in the US. Reducing the *Arbeter-ring*'s relationship with the Bund to mere 'ideological ties', as is common in existing scholarship, is therefore an understatement.[62] Activists did not suffer under decentralisation, but rather actively utilised the diversity emerging from social differentiation by establishing new groups. They thereby consciously separated the functional spheres of the Bund and secondary Bundism in the US. In this sense, the history of the *Arbeter-ring* represents not only a historical expression of an institution established by immigrants, but also a history of adaptations and transfers throughout the migration process, and another branch of the creative transnationalisation of the Bund.

---

61 It ought to be mentioned here that the later *Arbeter-ring* in Paris also started at the initiative of several local Bundists, rather than the opening of the nearby Medem Library.
62 Rojanski 2007, pp. 335.

TABLE 12 Chairmen of the *Natsyonaler sotsyaler klub* of the *Arbeter-ring*, 1914–44, according to year of chairmanship

Chairmen, 1914–44	Bund in Eastern Europe	Bund in the US	In the US before 1897	Non-Bund, in the US after 1897	Federatsye YSF
Yosef Vaynberg			x		x
Abraham Epshteyn			x		x
Shimeon Bulgatsh			x		x
Isidor Kohen	x	x			x
Eyzik Alpert	x	x			x
Bernard Lilyenblum			x		x
Naftali Feynerman				x	x
Moyshe Levenson	x				x
Naytan Pilot			x		
Leon Arkin	x				x
Ruben Guskin	x	x			x
Mayr Dayvidov			x		x
Zalmen Volom	x	x			
Yankel Rotman				x	
Abraham S. Reyzerof			x		
Oskar (Moyshe) Stirman	x				
Dr. Semyuel Silverberg				x	
Luis Dinershteyn	x				x
Dr. Yudel Kornel	x				x
Barnet Wulf			x		x
Nokhem Khanin	x	x			x
Rafael Ginzberg	x				
Bernard Feldman			x		x
Heri Berger				x	x
Dr. Aleksander Zeldin				x	
Filip Blok	x				x
Ben-Tsyon Maymon			x		x
Yakob Roberts	x				x
Bendzshamin Kaplan	x				x
Israel Feynberg		x			
Barnet Akselrod (Barukh Layb)	x				

Legend: dark grey: Bundist experience; light grey: secondary-Bundist experience outside the Arbeter (AR); white: no proven Bundist experience

DATA ACCORDING TO YESHURIN 1964, PP. 213–84; ARBETER RING, YESHURIN AND SH. 1962

rverts, rverts Ass.	SP, SLP	Trade unions or similar	Notes
	x	x	1890s: PPS representative
	x	x	Later in the Communist organisations YKF, IKUF, IKOR
	x		
	x	x	
	x	x	
	x	x	Co-founder of *Forverts*
	x	x	
	x		Active in 'radical circles' in Eastern Europe
	x	x	Higher education, President of Arbeter-ring 1950–3
		x	Self-defence in Gomel, 1903
	x	x	Co-founder of '*Forverts*', President of Arbeter-ring 1912–13
			Vice-President of Arbeter-ring 1918–19, founder of Dvinsker Branch 75
		x	From Galicia, Vice-President of Arbeter-ring 1917–18
	x		
	x		Self-defence, in numerous cultural organisations in US
	x		Arrived in the US as a school student, President of Arbeter-ring 1927–30, 1937–9
		x	Vice-President of Arbeter-ring 1927–9
	x	x	Freed prisoners in Vilna, 1903
	x	x	Born in Paris, New York councilman 1917, Vice-President of Arbeter-ring 1924–5
			Co-founder of YSF and '*Der veker*' co-founder, General Secretary of YSF 1921–36, President of Arbeter-ring 1930–2, education director from 1935 on
		x	
	x		
	x		
	x		Emigration to US in 1905, directly after studying
			Initially a Menshevik, later Bundist, emigration to US in 1913
	x		
	x	x	Likely Bundist, arrested in Russia for political activity, Vice-President of Arbeter-ring 1921–4
	x	x	*Kleyner bund*
	x	x	Vice-President of ILGWU, SP candidate
		x	

7 Splits and Differentiation before and after Red October

Transfers and experiences proved beneficial in the case of the *Arbeter-ring*. Yet there were also downsides, as Bundist and secondary-Bundist organisations would soon grow painfully aware. These organisations all experienced their heyday after the first Russian Revolution in 1905, and again after the 1917 February Revolution. The subsequent October Revolution, however, would put all of them to the test.[63] The *Arbeter-ring* survived the Bolshevik revolution, while more politically oriented organisations like the *Federatsye* or the Argentinian *Avangard* fell apart.

8 The *Avangard* Group between *Yidishkayt* and Acculturation

In the years following the October Revolution, the *Avangard* sought to regroup itself as the definitive expression of the Jewish socialist movement in Argentina through both mutual aid campaigns and new issues of *'Der avangard'*, although they paled in both style and quality compared to the famous pre-1917 issues.[64] The group had plenty of reasons to be optimistic – after all, the *Avangard* had already survived serious splits. As early as 1908–10, the *Tsenter avangard* and the *Avangard* group faced off as two competing currents within Argentinian Jewish socialism, disputing the form in which socialism and thus Bundism would be established in the country. The relevant literature often refers to them as two fronts of the Jewish workers' movement, yet only briefly discusses these important organisations. As a starting point for a better understanding of their goals and dynamics, we can analyse their highly influential yet hard-to-find publications.[65] Although both groups fought out a hard conflict, it is misleading to characterise it as a kind of ongoing internal Jewish antagonism.[66] First of all, the two sides eventually reconciled after several months of fierce polemics. Looking at the conflict as one emerging during the first years of Jewish mass migration to Argentina, their division represents a particular development within the Jewish workers' movement in that country. Increasingly

---

63 See Salutski and Litvak 1917. On the schism within the Polish Bund see Oler 1973; Brumberg 2001; Pickhan 2001, pp. 149–57.
64 Collection lists, IWO Archives, Buenos Aires, 1114; Letter to Kohn, 16 April 1920; 1114, 45.
65 I owe thanks to Nerina Visacovsky for pointing out a remote collection of the first series of *'Der avangard'* and other older sources.
66 Early versions of this interpretation can be found in Bilsky 1987, p. 37 f.; Laubstein 1997, p. 175.

virulent from 1908 onwards, the conflict between the two groups within the *Biblioteca rusa* reached a point where the *Avangard* accused the *Tsenter avangard* of appropriating its name, the movement, and even stealing its official seal. This was prominently announced in the first issue of '*Der avangard*', which beneath a bilingual stamp read: 'Attention! As the org. stamp in its hitherto form is being used by foreign hands (namely by the "Tsenter avangard"), the Jewish Social Democratic organisation of Argentina "Avangard" hereby declares it void. Our stamp is now *Yiddish and Spanish together*: remember the form'.[67]

Although lacking access to primary sources,[68] Israel Laubstein interprets this conflict as resembling that between Bundists and Iskraists in Russia, for the *Tsenter Avangard* used its publication, '*Di shtime fun Avangard*', to promote assimilatory policies.[69] This assertion is somewhat exaggerated, as the actual argument primarily revolved around the specific wording of socialist propaganda – which would downplay the conflict between the Bund and '*Iskra*' in Russia.[70] In Argentina, questions of revolutionary tactics played no role in these debates. Two circles formed, one around the Bundists Pinie Vald, Sh. Kaplansky, M. Mas, and A. Epshteyn, who subsequently referred to themselves as the *Yidishe sotsyal-demokratishe arbeyter organisatsyon in argentina (Avangard)*, while the other group, the *Yidishe sotsyal demokratishe arbeyter organisatsyon Avangard – Partido Socialista*, consolidated around A. Bondarev und Y. Sheyner. The latter group was primarily Russophone despite publishing in Yiddish, and constituted itself as a branch of the Partido Socialista that actively encouraged Jewish workers to learn Spanish.[71] Indeed, the language question was the decisive rift between both groups. If any parallel to Eastern Europe can be drawn here, then to the so-called 'Vilnius Opposition' of the 1890s and its refusal to shift from Russian to Yiddish agitation and adopt *yidishkayt* as an essential component of Jewish-socialist identity.[72] As in Russia, the Yiddish faction clearly constituted the majority in Buenos Aires.

The differences between both groups should not be overemphasised with regard to political substance nor practices, however, for '*Di shtime fun avangard*' was not another '*Iskra*' and none of its members an Argentinian Lenin. The divisive point was whether *yidishkayt* constituted a cultural value as such. The

---

67   N.N. 1908c.
68   According to both the bibliography and Laubstein himself, he had no access to the relevant journals at the time. This is also indicated in a 2008 interview conducted by Silvia Hansman and Frank Wolff; see also Laubstein 1997, p. 215f.
69   Laubstein 1997, pp. 174–7.
70   Keßler 1994; Gusev 2006.
71   Such as in Di shtime fun avangard 1909b.
72   Mendelsohn 1970, pp. 57–60.

Tsenter avangard called for language courses to help build closer ties to the Partido Socialista. The *Avangard*, on the other hand, argued for the Partido Socialista to work harder at integrating the language federations and embracing linguistic diversity in a country of immigrants. Despite the ensuing battle over political influence, both groups retained their positions on the administrative board of the *Biblioteca rusa* located at La Paz 43, advertised the library with almost identical language, and apart from that called for very similar kinds of activism (with the exception of the language courses). Specific differences were thus of a more personal nature and found in nuanced distinctions, which may also explain the harshness of the attacks.[73] The brief confrontation between the *Avangard* and *Tsenter avangard*, or rather between the *Yidishe sotsyaldemokratishe arbeyter organisatsyon in argentina (Avangard)* and the *Yidishe sotsyal demokratishe arbeyter organisatsyon Avangard – Partido Socialista*, was therefore less reminiscent of the programmatic disputes between the Bund and 'Iskra' in Russia prior to 1905[74] – driven by the question of whether to proceed as a mass organisation or as conspiratorial professional revolutionaries – so much as the conflict between the People's Front of Judea and the Judean People's Front.

Although unaware of the future Monty Python classic, Pinie Vald nonetheless seems to have viewed matters similarly, writing about the groups' ultimate reconciliation on the first anniversary of the journal *'Der avangard'* in a notably annoyed tone:

> Life carried them away and their gaze is now fixed on those they used to turn away from in disgust. One of these organisations is the 'Tsenter avangard', as there is surely enough reason to believe that had it been like this in the past it never would have come to a split in the organisation. ... At any rate, we now see that they returned to what they previously rejected.[75]

This was largely driven by the desire to publish in Yiddish, a practice that increasingly turned the workers' movement into a worker culture.

The basis of their reconciliation, however, was the founding of the opposing publication, leading to the short-lived existence of two strikingly similar journals from May 1909 onwards. This fact alone is quite remarkable, given that the launching of *'Der avangard'* the previous year had marked the first exclusively

---

73   Mannheim 1979, p. 215.
74   See Hertz 1969; Keßler 1994; Gusev 2006.
75   Vald 1909a, p. 5.

Yiddish publication in Argentina and probably all of South America. For Jewish socialism, it appears competition was also 'good for business'.

The *Tsenter avangard* was equally disinclined to build small revolutionary cells, instead announcing the goal of 'developing the class consciousness of the Jewish masses, directing them towards general revolutionary Social Democracy'.[76] Although this also included Spanish courses, it speaks volumes about the two groups' actual practice that not a single Spanish-language article appeared in either of the two journals.[77] '*Di shtime fun Avangard*' sought to effectively respond to the growing audience for a vibrant Yiddish literary landscape, including their own publications along with Yiddish magazines available at the *Biblioteca rusa*. Among them was '*Der sotsyaldemokrat*', published by the 'Galician Bund', alongside the New York-based '*Forverts*'.

The *Avangard* envisioning itself as the Bund in Argentina on the one hand, while, on the other hand, the relatively short lifespan of '*Di shtime fun Avangard*' suggests that little demand for secondary Bundism existed in Argentina at the time. For now, the Bund's holistic claim to represent all Jewish workers still struck most activists and workers as the most effective way to assert their interests – and those interests were under threat. The police attacks on the *Biblioteca rusa* compelled all parties to put aside internal disputes in 1910.[78] Given the subsequent repression, the Argentinian case once again demonstrated that the unity of the Jewish workers' movement was more than just a hollow demand, but in fact a functional necessity to strengthen the culturally and socially driven mass movements of Jewish workers.

Any hopes of convincing workers to learn Spanish through a Yiddish paper, however, were doomed to fail. Yiddish was inevitably the language of agitation, far more than a mere medium. The language question divided the two groups, while actual linguistic practice and similar understandings of mass-based socialism united them – although Bundist *doikayt* ultimately proved more resilient than attempts at functional differentiation and use of this culture as a mere bridge towards Spanish-speaking socialism, due in turn to the growing conflation of workers' movement and worker culture by 1910.[79]

---

76 Di shtime fun avangard 1909a.
77 Surviving issues include 1–4/5, May–September/October 1909, presumably discontinued thereafter.
78 The anti-socialist police raids mostly targeting the *Biblioteca rusa* are often characterised as a pogrom, see Mirelman 2005.
79 As in Gurevitsh 1916; Vald 1917a; Vald 1917b.

9 The Centrifugal Force of the 'Great Proletarian Revolution'

This type of reconciliation through shared practices grew impossible after Red October. Reconciliation foundered not only due to concrete facts established on the ground in revolutionary Russia, but also as a result of the quantitative growth of various Jewish socialist sub-currents in Argentina brought on by prolonged immigration. The individual currents had grown strong enough that both a Social Democratic movement as well as another further to its left felt justified in viewing themselves as mass movements, without ever effectively becoming such.

This circumstance did not immediately trigger an open conflict in 1917, but rather led to widespread uncertainty and paralysis. It is telling that the small and financially precarious *Avangard* and *Tsenter avangard* groups each published their own paper in the 1900s, setting lasting standards in terms of style, content, and form. Despite the general feelings of revolutionary euphoria, the last series of the united '*Avangard*' beginning in 1919 issued on four-to-six pages of cheap news print looks more like an illegally printed Russian leaflet than the edition published before 1910. The Avangardistas were in the midst of a grave identity crisis, particularly aggravated by the seminal anti-socialist pogrom of January 1919, the *Semana Trágica*.[80]

Political positioning vis-à-vis the Bolsheviks only widened the deepening gulf inside Social Democracy between 1917–20,[81] and the common denominator of Jewish culture could no longer bridge the gap. The most illuminating expressions of this decay engulfing the '*Avangard*' are probably a series of letters written by Avangardista Kohn to his *khaver* Veber in 1920. As the younger of the two, Kohn replies to Veber's concerns about the alarming state of the *Avangard* group with proud optimism:

> As I gather from your letter, you wish to form a new socialist organisation because there is great chaos and anarchy within the current 'Avangard' group, a point I would not like to discuss with you. Rest assured that the movement has been reinvigorated despite everything we have gone through, which is why I must reject your complaints ... It required a major shift to return unity to it. Is there no danger that you leave the organisation and then quickly return afterwards nonetheless? [Because you] accomplish not a single factual deed through that work? And by the way I am no

---

[80] Fundamental in this regard are Vald 1998; Godio 1985; Mirelman 1990, pp. 67–71.
[81] As this written correspondence relates to a fundraising campaign on behalf of the Bund in revolutionary Russia, it will be discussed in more detail in Part III.12.

friend of the tactic of shying away from fighting the existing evils, for it is always better to remain a proud loser than a laughable victor.[82]

Instead, long-standing Social Democrats exited the *Avangard*, leaving the remaining organisational rump to join the Partido Comunista de la Argentina in 1921.[83] The willingness to engage in revolutionary struggle imported from Russia stipulated organisational unity, yet simultaneously placed socialism on two distinct, Communist and socialist tracks. Kohn's remarks were typical of the Communists' new, confrontational unity rhetoric, urging the new to overcome the old not only in structural terms but also generationally. Kohn sums up the situation in an appropriately dry tone: 'Having been in the organisation for so many years, it breaks my heart to see so many of the old comrades withdrawing from us so quickly, and I cannot help but think of the old proverb that states: the old must make way for the youth'.[84]

Such affiliations help explain why numerous leading members of the Jewish sections of the Communist parties, the *Yidsektsye* or *Yevsektsiya*, were former Bundists. Rarely from the 1880s generation, many such as Hersh Mendel and Hershel Metaloviets in Poland or Maxim Rozen in Argentina were politically socialised around 1905.[85] A large number of groups established to organise Yiddish support for the Bolsheviks between 1917–21 had Bundist roots at least in terms of the specific individuals involved.[86] Like Zivion, many Bundists went along with the left turn at the time only to return to the Bund disillusioned soon afterwards, or to condemn their former comrades as 'social fascists' later on.[87] Many of the Jewish sections' patterns of activism resembled their Bundist progenitors. Overseas, the Communists often managed to implement this Yiddish-language political activism with a force the small Bundist groups in the 1920s lacked. The shift is particularly visible in activists' recollections. Although the interviewers working for the Mark Turcow Documentation Centre in Buenos Aires in the 1980s repeatedly tried to inquire about notions of a common Jewish history, responding Bundists took great pains to emphasise the distinction between socialists and Communists among their ranks. In individual episodes,

---

82   IWO Archives, Buenos Aires, 1114, 44 (Letter from Kohn to Veber, 12 April 1920).
83   Contrary to Kheifets and Kheifets's depiction, the entire *Avangard* did not join the PCA. Rather, this occurred only after a series of splits, see Kheifets and Kheifets 2009, p. 139.
84   IWO Archives, Buenos Aires, 1114, 51 (Letter from Kohn to Veber, 12 April 1920).
85   Mendel 1989, p. 195 ff.; Metaloviets 1982, p. 262; Camarero 2007, p. 301 f. On Soviet Russia more generally see Gitelman 1972.
86   The socialist parties naturally experienced similar dynamics, see Hertz 1954, p. 188 ff.
87   Svarch 2010.

however, the distinction begins to soften, producing personal grey areas leading to, for instance, cooperation during the 1934–5 textile workers' strike discussed later on, or the surprising level of socialist sympathy for Birobidzhan.[88] Bundist organisations in Argentina cracked under the pressures imposed by the turmoil in Russia, yet secondary Bundism nevertheless failed to establish a foothold in Argentina. The revolutionary years took a toll on secondary-Bundist organisations in the United States, above all the *Federatsye* which split into fragments. While some members joined the emerging Communist (and also competing) groups, the socialist wing of the *Federatsye* evolved into the *Yidishe sotsyalistishe farband* (YSF), while a New York Bundist club formally affiliated to the Polish Bund was founded in 1923. The group provided the template for a similar club in Buenos Aires the following year. This explicit proximity to the now-legal Polish Bund marked a clear distinction to the pre-war organisations, which at least in the US had more resembled loose gatherings in support of an anti-Tsarist movement than a permanent form of Bundist organisation. The Bund Club in New York viewed itself as a mediator between both worlds until World War II.[89]

Its members would only develop a self-understanding as truly American Bundists at a much later stage, along with a self-historicisation constituting the basis for an independent collective identity. The documentation of *Memorik* material in North America remained oriented towards Eastern Europe for quite some time, and almost all Bundist immigrant autobiographies conclude with the author's departure from European shores.[90] Bundist memoirs would only become an American issue shortly before World War II. One expression of this new confidence was the small but ground-breaking *Zamlheft* marking the fifteenth anniversary of the New York Bund Club in 1938. To highlight the difference in self-consciousness, it should again be noted that the Argentinian *Avangard* began developing such a self-historicisation in the first two issues of *'Der avangard'* in 1908.[91]

The American Bund thereby positioned itself in the middle of the road only three decades after the *Avangard*. It sought to prove it was more than just an arm of the Polish Bund, without claiming to be a genuine American secondary-Bundist organisation either. Activists began to realise the necessity of embed-

---

88   See Centro 'Marc Turkow', Buenos Aires, Archive de la Palabra, esp. 11 [José Chiaskalevitch, 1985], pp. 24–8; 14 [José Epstein, 1985], p. 4; 22 [Hersh Goldmintz, 1985], p. 2; 32 [Guitl Kanutsky, 1985], p. 5, p. 8, p. 24 f.
89   See Bundisher klub, Nyu York 1938.
90   See Part III.10.
91   Vald 1908a; Vald 1908b.

ding themselves on both sides of the Atlantic, and when the time came did not hesitate to turn down notable Polish Bundists who neglected their obligations. Responding to a late *Zamlheft* contribution by the head of the Bundist educational wing Khayim Shloyme Kazdan, the responsible Bundist in New York, Dovid Mayer, bluntly expressed the editorial staff's deep disappointment with his inability to communicate effectively, and remarked that it would not print another issue simply because of his inability to deliver a contribution on time.[92] Such a brash rejection of a request from the highest Bundist authorities does not appear anywhere before then in the relevant sources. As much as it indicates more pronounced self-confidence on the part of the American Bund, this degree of emancipation did not signify a wider transformation in practical terms, as the Bund's fundraising machine continued to hum at full capacity in the years before World War II, nor in the sense of the construction of individual ascriptions, which remained transnationally oriented. The title of first New York Bund Club executive chairman Khanine Kromorski's memoirs (published in that very *Zamlheft*) makes this unmistakeably clear: '17 Years as a Polish Bundist in America'.[93] Members were '*do*' (here) and ultimately part of the Bund, which in turn remained Polish by its very nature.

After a few years of uncertainty, secondary Bundism quickly re-organised in the United States. In 1921, two years before the Bund Club, Bundists, and other activists from the *Federatsye* such as Salutsky, Zivion, and Litvak founded the YSF. The organisation was a direct successor to the secondary-Bundist *Federatsye*, albeit characterised by a strictly anti-Communist stance. From 1922 onwards it found itself confronted by the growing Communist factions within the *Arbeter-ring*, which constituted the explicitly Communist International Workers Order (IWO) in 1930 and were later active mainly in the IKUF (*Yidisher kultur farband*).[94] The YSF prominently represented secondary Bundism over the following decades parallel to the Bund's consolidation in Poland. As a political actor, it was situated between Bundist organisations, the *Arbeter-ring*, and the Jewish trade unions, while in a constantly shifting cooperative and competitive relationship with the '*Forverts*'. On this basis it established its monthly '*Der veker*', the first influential secondary-Bundist publication in the US that lasted for decades.[95]

---

92   Letter from Mayer to Kazdan, Bund Archives, New York, ME-14B, 7.
93   Kromorski 1938.
94   Not to be confused with the IWO, the Hispanicised transliteration of the YIVO, or the ICUF (the Hispanicised transcription of the IKUF), which also denotes the association of Independent Colleges & Universities of Florida.
95   '*Der veker*' (featuring the additional title *Ofitsyeler organ fun dem Yidishen sotsyalistishen*

Communism represented an even greater challenge for Bundists in Argentina than in the US. Rather than try to re-found the *Avangard* for the 1920s and thereby connect to the organisational roots on the Río de la Plata, the *khaverim* in Buenos Aires now pursued the American model. In 1924 they founded a Bundist club with close ties to Poland, followed in 1929 by the first-ever Argentinian secondary-Bundist organisation, the YSFA (*Yidisher sotsyalistisher farband in Argentine*). It bore more than a nominal similarity to the YSF. Like its American counterpart, it operated in conscious functional differentiation as an Argentinian organisation, with a publication of its own and alongside the Bund. The Bundist club and the YSFA complemented each other to such an extent that they were often perceived as a single organisation, as Bundist veteran and activist José Chiaskelevitz frankly explained in the 1980s: 'It referred to itself as the Jewish Socialist League, but it was the Bund, it was fully the Bund'.[96]

It was not on par with the Bund in a structural sense, reflected not least by its chairmanship, occupied for many years by the intellectual Samuel Rollansky. Although socialised in a Bundist-socialist milieu, he was much more concerned with Yiddish cultural work and simultaneously served as acting chairman of the YIVO in Argentina and later editor of one of the most important Yiddish literary series.[97]

The relationship between the Bund, Bundism, and Bundists thus became noticeably more complicated in 1920s Argentina. Israel Laubstein, an activist in the Bund and its successor organisations in Buenos Aires after 1945 (and the author of the only book on the subject to this day), notes: 'In principle the Bund was of no greater relevance here, but the Bundists were very active'.[98] This of course pertained more to his experiences in later decades, when the Argentinian Bund became quite marginal, but in general holds true for any place of Bundist emigration. In the 1920s and 1930s the Bund was an actor *oyf der yidishn gas* of Buenos Aires, where it always depended on the organisations surrounding it. The best personification of Argentina's contemporary organisational differentiation and biographical intersections was probably Samuel Rollansky. As editor of the '*Sotsyalistishn bleter*', he was committed to a 'Yiddishist' orient-

---

farband fun der sotsyalistisher parṭey in Amerike for the first five years), New York, published 1921–85.

96   Interview with José Chiaskelevitz, 15 August 1985, Centro 'Marc Turkow', Archive de la Palabra, 11.
97   IWO, Buenos Aires, 1111. He was also general secretary of the Association of Jewish Writers of Argentina, see *Associacion de escritores Israelitas Nomberg*, IWO, Buenos Aires, Associacion de escritores Israelitas Nomberg, Booklet, 1931.
98   Interview with Israel Laubstein conducted by Silvia Hansman and Frank Wolff, IWO, Buenos Aires, 20 October 2008; transcript in the author's possession.

ation in the YSFA, tied not least to his role as chairman of the YIVO in Buenos Aires which Bundists also founded.[99] He was active in the Bundist education movement, the Bundist schools, and in fact founded the very first secular Jewish kindergarten in Argentina as part of the Bundist Peretz School.[100] In the Bundist club, on the other hand, Samuel Rollansky played no role whatsoever.

10   The Bund and the 'Forverts'

It ought to be noted that, although secondary-Bundist organisations played a major role in American Jewish history, not all Jewish socialist organisations fit this category – even if they counted many Bundists among their ranks. The first deserving mention in this regard is Abraham Cahan's *'Jewish Daily Forward'*, or simply *'Forverts'*. The fate of the *'Forverts'* and the *Forverts Association* was closely tied to Cahan himself, who was far more open to assimilation and less internationalist than Bundists generally approved of, leading to repeated tensions.[101] Cahan cooperated with Bundist organisations on numerous occasions and openly supported its mutual aid organisations, as long as the Bund confined itself to Eastern European issues.[102] The *'Forverts'* was nevertheless unthinkable without Bundist authors. By the 1900s, a rhetoric accompanied strikes that could have just as well been heard in Eastern Europe or Argentina. In 1909–10 the *'Forverts'* enthusiastically covered the successful Shirtwaist Strike using the classical vocabulary of class struggle.[103] This was not some kind of generalised rhetoric deployed in the case of a strike, but rather a bridge between the *'Forverts'* and the Bund. Cahan's paper noted in 1903:

> Zionism is all about talking, whereas Bundism is about action. The Zionist response to Kishinev was Uganda, whereas the Bund reacted with self-defence. The Zionist idea rests on the past and is therefore reactionary. Bundism is synonymous with progress and looks to the future.[104]

---

99   Laubstein 1997, p. 186 ff.
100   IWO, Buenos Aires, CAEI, Testimony: Esther Rollansky; Institute of Oral History, University of Texas at El Paso, Interview no. 953, Esther Rollansky, by Sandra McGee Deutsch, 2000, p. 12 f., digitalcommons.utep.edu/interviews/958/ (last accessed 29 June 2012).
101   Manor 2009, p. 1 f., p. 45.
102   On this see Part III.12.
103   *Forverts*, 23 November 1909, p. 1; *Forverts*, 15 February 1909, p. 1. Discussed more elaborately in Dubofsky 1968b, pp. 40–58.
104   *Forverts*, 16 December 1903, p. 4.

The *'Forverts'* and the Bund were both strictly opposed to American participation in the 'imperialist war' in the years leading up to World War I. Rather than isolating the *'Forverts'*, the stance propelled its circulation to unprecedented heights at a time when the rest of the English-language socialist press in the US took heavy losses.[105] Little could be felt of the alleged 'decline of socialism in America' on the Lower East Side around 1914. On the contrary: Meyer London, a fresh, Yiddish-speaking anti-war politician, would repeatedly be sent to Washington, DC as an elected congressman.

This alliance between Bundists and the *'Forverts'* nevertheless did not evolve into secondary Bundism. Moreover, the arrival of more Bundists in the US also raised questions of hegemony, ultimately resolved by Cahan's ossified dominance over the *'Forverts'*, but also by the founding of the *Federatsye* and the *Arbeter-ring*'s growing strength.[106] This dynamic intensified, culminating in Cahan's warming to Zionism after a trip to Palestine in the 1920s. He now remarked: 'The problem with Bundism was not in the Remote East but in the Lower East Side'.[107]

The *'Forverts'* remained crucial to workers' organisation in the US, and would continue to serve as a political reservoir for Bundists arriving in the country. Many leading *'Forverts'* personalities beyond Cahan were staunch Bundists, in many cases forced to leave Russia because of their Bundist activism.[108] Although Cahan's dominance over the politics of the *'Forverts'* was often absolute, focusing on his person and his alleged 'conservatism' as Ehud Manor laments fails to acknowledge the broad range of texts found in the pages of the newspaper itself. What should be stressed is the function of the *'Forverts'* as a socialist mouthpiece covering a wide spread of Jewish socialism in the United States and beyond. This also means that for Bundists like Abraham Liessin, Barukh Charney Vladeck, Dovid Mayer, and Motl Zelmanovitsh it was more than just an employer, but an intellectual home.[109] Equally, the *'Forverts'* also needed the Bundists. They shared responsibility for both its national and international success as important authors in a large network of foreign correspondents. Bundist Zivion represented the *'Forverts'* at the fifth Zionist Congress in Basel in 1901, featuring speakers like Theodor Herzl, Martin Buber,

---

105 Weinstein 1967, p. 84, p. 103, as well as the circulation figures for socialist journals from 1912–28, pp. 94–102.
106 Levin 1977, p. 199.
107 Manor 2009, p. 37.
108 Interestingly, Manor mentions primarily (ex-)Bundists as *'Forverts'* protagonists throughout, yet seems to identify no relationship between background and activism, see Manor 2009.
109 Bund Archives, New York, RG 1400, MG2, 429, Mayer, Dovid; Zelmanovitsh, Motl.

Leo Motzkin, and Chaim Weizmann.[110] Zivion had attracted attention not long before through a widely noticed article on the national question in the Swiss Bundist exile publication, '*Di arbeyter shtime*', and was able to use these Bundist ideas as the foundation of his report in the '*Forverts*'. He continued to maintain a scathing verdict on the founder of Poale Zion as late as 1909, stating that 'Dr. Syrkin seeks to make adventurism into a principle'.[111] The '*Forverts*' was not a secondary-Bundist organisation, but it provided a space for Bundist activism while simultaneously benefiting from it. Accordingly, the '*Forverts*' was also an important medium in Bundism's struggle against Zionism for many years.

This was reflected from the outside as readers passed on their expectations and experiences to the '*Forverts*', expressing their approval every day by purchasing the publication. Bundists were also very loyal readers: as late as the 1950s, when the '*Forverts*' faced a serious crisis, 75 percent of surveyed Bundists indicated reading the publication on a daily basis. This figure was followed by about 50 percent who read the *New York Times*, and a mere fifth who read '*Der tog*' primarily as a supplement to the '*Forverts*'.[112] Even long after Cahan's death, the '*Forverts*' continued to profit from the unique position it carved out for itself over the years of mass migration.

The close relationship between many Bundists and the '*Forverts*' also had a spatial element. Not only did leading Bundists write for the '*Forverts*', but when the new Forverts Building opened its doors in 1912, the representation of the Bund in America moved from its former offices at 199 Division Street to its new address on 175 East Broadway. It resided there for decades, along with a large portion of the many Bund-related organisations of the 1920s and 1930s.[113] Many Bundist receptions were celebrated in the new skyscraper during those years.[114]

Looking at this close relation between the Bund and the '*Forverts*', one can barely approve of polemics from authors like Samuel Peskin and Moyshe Baranov who claim the Bund was at best a kind of symbol for the '*Forverts*', invoked by the latter when convenient.[115] Bundists constituted a crucial resource to the '*Forverts*' on which both the daily paper and the *Forverts Association* depended, in turn leading not least to numerous thematic overlaps. Reversely, the '*Forverts*' also represented a valuable resource to the Bund. It was

---

110   Zivion 1940, p. 8 f.
111   Cited in Frankel 1984, p. 303.
112   Bund Archives, New York, RG 1400, MG2, 429; author's calculation.
113   See countless letterheads and invitations, Bund Archives, New York, RG 1400, ME-14B, 7; 8; Ibid., ME-18, 3.
114   See the invitation to celebrations marking the Bund's thirtieth anniversary in 1927, Bund Archives, RG 1400, ME-18, 2.
115   Perlman 1960, p. 307; Frankel 1984, pp. 470–96.

able – and indeed compelled – to draw on it to stay active in the US. To Bundists it thus also marked a place where they could practice *doikayt* in the United States, which in turn had a positive effect on sales of the *'Forverts'*.

11 Activist, Not Active

This inclusion and differentiation explains why the American Bund appears marginally active on the Lower East side. It took on specific segments of activism, leaving many elements of its activism patterns to secondary-Bundist and other organisations that often depended on their Bundist members' active participation. As Vladimir Medem noted, the Eastern European Bund and the *Arbeter-ring* were similar but not identical.[116] From a transnational perspective, they shared common activists and mutually complemented one another in a functionally differentiated sense.[117] This reinforced both organisations as well as the Jewish workers' movement as a whole. Bundist organisations did not seek to establish a separate organisation in direct emulation of the Bund, but rather to mobilise support for the Bund in Russia. This marks the fundamental difference to the Argentinian Bundist groups prior to 1917.

Furthermore, it is inaccurate to say that only '"greenhorn" Yiddish-speaking immigrants' were attracted to the *'Forverts'* and secondary-Bundist organisations. Existing scholarship sometimes insinuates as much in a rather patronising tone, to the effect of '[s]ome of them managed to find places in organizations such as the Arbeiter Ring, others in the Jewish Socialist Federation (part of the larger SP), yet others in lesser institutions'.[118] As depicted above, however, this was not a question of either-or, but rather was resolved by activists holding multiple memberships at once. Immigrants not only found a new political home, but also had a strong impact on these organisations. Such differentiation inevitably prompted tensions between individual organisations and actors, with the Bund's transnational position often coming under fire for diverting its energies away from the US.[119]

---

116 Mendelsohn 1993, p. 56.
117 One element of this was mutual support through advertising or announcements. See the ads in *Der kemfer*, New York 1905, p. 3. Functional differentiation primarily had an integrative effect here, as evidenced in Schimank 2005, esp. pp. 186–90.
118 Manor 2009, p. 37. For further elaboration of the classical themes see Howe 1976, p. 292 ff.
119 See the debates on the relationship between the Bund and the socialist parties in the US, Bund Archives, New York, ME-18, 1, Liliput, 'Di S.L.P. di S.P. un der "Bund"', *Der arbeyter* (1909); Zivion, 'Di bundisten un di S.L.P.', *Der arbeyter* (1909); Ahron Kohn, 'Di bundisten

Contrary to the widely held belief that this also constituted the root conflict between the Bund and Cahan, both in fact accepted and reproduced functional differentiation.[120] Cahan became a leading supporter of the *Fraynd fun bund* group as early as the 1900s, which later moved into the Forverts Building and increasingly established itself as an active fundraising group for the Polish Bund before World War II.[121] He praised the Bund in Russia as the strongest expression of a new era in one of the organisation's 1904 publications, striking an almost heroic tone in his appeal for support. As a result of the Jewish revolutionaries' devotion and commitment in Russia, 'the number of Jewish heroes' supposedly rose 'on and on, faster and faster' in the face of arrests, banishments, and executions.[122] In Cahan's eyes, the striking difference between the Jewish revolutionaries in the *Narodnaya Volya* and the Bundists was that the latter never abandoned their *yidishkayt* nor unwittingly circulated anti-Semitic literature.[123] And unlike the former, the Bundists never confused revolutionary work with the struggle for one's homeland: 'An attitude has therefore developed among revolutionaries similar to that of the Russian government: serve as a soldier and pay your dues'.[124] The historical rupture had been the initiative of the Bund exclusively, the 'living expression of the ongoing changes' in Russia, 'and the revolution is the only solution to the Jewish question in Russia'.[125] Those living in the US were now obliged to collectively support this endeavour, for, according to Cahan, the Bund was also the unifying political thread among Jewish workers in America:

> there are dedicated Socialist Revolutionaries among us who are at the same time enthusiastic Bundists; there are Social Democrats among us who regret with all their hearts that the leaders of the '*Iskra*' forced the

---

un di amerikaner sotsyalistishe parteyn. An entfer tsu genosn Zivion', *Der yidishe arbeyter* (8 October 1909).

120   This notion is mainly a product of the later conflict between Cahan and the Polish Bundists, in which the US Bund served as an intermediary. See for example Bundisher klub in Nyu York 1935; see also Mayer 1951. Cahan's détente vis-à-vis Zionism became a source of particular conflict, as documented in Goldstein 1998.
121   Bund Archives, New York, RG 1400, ME-18, 3, Letterhead 1907; 9, Circular, Account books.
122   Cahan 1904, p. 1.
123   The *Narodnaya Volya* was known for anti-Semitic publications, but Zundelevitsh was well-aware of this fact and disagreed with the group in this regard, as Erich Haberer has demonstrated. See Tsherikover 1939, p. 172; Haberer 1992, p. 124 f.; Gerngroß 2008, pp. 150–3.
124   Cahan 1904, p. 3.
125   Ibid.

Bund to leave the party; there are Polish comrades among us who dearly hope for a closer and tighter relationship between the Bund and the Polish socialist party.[126]

Framed by the *Fraynd fun bund*'s specific fundraising objectives, Cahan joined the Bund's heroising canon. Cahan's opinion on the Bund evidently continued to shift. While he openly embraced the Bund as *the* Jewish revolutionary force in these statements, he changed his tone when it came to Bundist immigrants in America, urging them to better integrate themselves into the American style of socialism rather than transfer their aims and practices too openly along the East River. As the quote shows, in his earlier years he nevertheless openly expressed admiration for the Bund and its inclusive potential in the US, and after the February Revolution continued to work for the Bund's mutual aid organisations as the representatives of a new and better Russia on American soil.[127]

This perspective on functional differentiation in American Jewish socialism gives us the opportunity to situate the Bund, Bundists, and Bundism as different actors in a complex setting. Although 'Bund-type radical activism'[128] could certainly be observed in parts of the ILWGU and UHT alongside the *Tsukunft* and the *'Forverts'*, Bundism only had a decisive influence on the character of secondary-Bundist organisations like the *Arbeter-ring* or the Yiddish-speaking branches of the Socialist Party, which can essentially be regarded as Bundist branches of that party.[129] While the Bund did not organise strikes in the US, Bundists such as Barukh Vladeck or Y. Salutsky did so with great fervour and success. Although the Bund never called for local workers' struggle in its American publications, Abraham Liessin, Zivion, and many other Bundists in the ranks of the *'Forverts'* and *Tsukunft* did so frequently. As representatives of the Bund back home, the Bund's organisations in the US only partially integrated themselves into the American political landscape defined by socialism and Yiddish culture, while secondary-Bundist associations like the *Federatsye* or the YSF and many individual (and proud) Bundists decisively shaped that same landscape. Secondary Bundism thereby contributed to the functional differentiation of American socialism, the American labour movement, and US society more generally.

---

126 Ibid.
127 Bund Archives, New York, RG 1400, ME-18, 2, *Referat*; Ibid. ME-18, 5, Letter from Amerikaner gemeynsamer hilfs komitet farn 'bund' in Rusland (14 May 1917).
128 Basch 1998, p. 52.
129 Michels 2005, p. 172 f.

As a more abstract consequence, these findings suggest that in the overlap between labour and migration history it is necessary to not only identify organisations by their name to explore their relevance after migration, but to investigate the localised practices and decipher the self-ascriptions of the activists involved. For Bundists, this differentiation was a deliberate act to remain Bundists overseas: only by abandoning the Eastern European Bund's self-ascription as the sole representation of the Jewish workers' movement could activists transfer their Bundism to various organisations in the United States. Thus, Bundist actors did not suffer under the process of 'decentralisation', so much as they acted in circumstances that would have presented any socialist movement with considerable difficulties. The diluted brand of American socialism posed a challenge, prompting the movement to further and quite consciously differentiate in a functional and integrative manner.[130] As a result of that flexibility, Bundism won an important role in the formation of Jewish worker and Yiddish culture in the country.

---

130   Schimank 2005, p. 15 f., p. 32 f.

CHAPTER 10

Politics, Economics, *Yidishkayt*: The Tangled Web of Class Struggle and Cultural Work

> It is true that the [barbers'] union does nothing. ... And, really, when you speak with an English worker, he is quite content of his union. Of course, this cannot satisfy us [the Jewish barbers] whose attention to unionism is altogether different.
>
> Jewish barber in Toronto, 1932[1]

∴

In Eastern Europe, the Jewish trade union movement and the Bund existed in symbiosis. In the United States, on the other hand, Jewish trade unions were established long before the first Bundists arrived. In Argentina, many socialist organisations were still in their infancy in the 1890s. Here, German immigrants had an even greater impact in the early phase, when anarchism became the most influential current among the local workers' movement.[2] But the rise of Social Democracy in Argentina and the Bundists' arrival changed both the labour struggle as well as its organisations.

Research on Jewish labour history has long focused on the organisations themselves, showing little interest in labour struggle practices.[3] Yet combining activism and organisation was one of the Bund's greatest strengths in Eastern Europe.[4] Researchers accordingly discuss the Bundist role in strikes overseas rather ambivalently, emphasising the presence and leading role of numerous Bundists on the one hand, while often neglecting the consequences and broad range of Bundist provenance in particular on the other.[5] As demonstrated in the following, transnational relations within the Jewish workers' movement

---

1 *Der yidisher zshurnal*, Toronto, 18 August 1932, cited in Frager 1992, p. 42.
2 Carreras, Tarcus and Zeller 2008; Suriano 2010.
3 As evidenced in Tsherikover 1961 and Bunzl 1975.
4 Bunzl 1975, pp. 63–70; Pickhan 2001, pp. 200–15.
5 One exception is Ruth A. Frager's book on Jewish labour in Toronto that delicately reconciles activists' past and present, see Frager 1992, pp. 40–51.

were fundamental components of many local labour struggles, particularly because possibilities for transnational Yiddish culture were also negotiated in this way. As the latter was to be both secular and proletarian, it was also eminently political. Labour struggles and cultural work became ever closer intertwined through Bundist activity overseas, turning Bundists into transnational experts of a practised *yidishkayt*.

1 Strike Research and Activism

Earlier, more broadly oriented historical scholarship often interpreted strikes and strike movements in terms of their socio-economic impact,[6] or analysed them through sociologically inspired social movement research as an expression of resource-based mass mobilisation.[7] Labour Studies took longer than other historical fields to adopt the methodological approaches of the cultural turn into historical inquiry, while the latter often expressed a strong interest in the evolution of a worker culture but marginalised political and economic historical questions. As a fruitful compromise, historical scholarship has developed lines of inquiry oriented towards the history of social practice.[8] The crucial aspect of community building increasingly complemented research on ethnic and national questions in the workers' movement, allowing for a closer linking of politics and culture altogether.[9] Approaches drawing connections between cultural-historical aspects and the class struggle through the discovery of 'strike culture' nevertheless remain relatively uncommon.[10]

Proceeding from this state of affairs, the following chapter aims to place a stronger emphasis on the transnational mutual conditionality of both worker and strike culture. It focuses on relations of transnational networking within social movements, arguing that the Bund's labour struggles were tied to the history of several societies simultaneously. As described in the previous chapter, the labour struggle opened up opportunities to create new institutions as expressions of ongoing cultural, economic, and political differentiation within the workers' movement. Increasingly divided between Bundism, Zionism, and

---

6   This view enjoys a long tradition and spans from Bernstein 1906; Dubofksy 1968b; Tenfelde and Volkmann 1981; Haimson and Tilly 1989 all the way to Clasen 2008.
7   See esp. Tilly 1985a; Tilly 1985b. Discussions of both approaches can be found in Haimson and Tilly 1989.
8   Welskopp 1998; Welskopp 2000; Nathaus 2009.
9   Konrad 1994; Rutar 2004.
10 Esp. Birke 2007; Koller 2009.

Communism, the Jewish workers' movement nevertheless found temporary points of unity allowing for situational alliances, such as common adversaries, the occasional overlapping of interests, and of course *yidishkayt*. In such a setting, we can understand strikes as contingent events that may lead to consequences extending well beyond the initial, often primarily economic motives. A strike's success can therefore not be measured by economic and contractual results alone, although strikes themselves generate few sources. To counter this challenge, Christian Koller proposes concentrating on a discursive history of strikes.[11] Yet if we approach strikes as social practices in political settings, we can get closer to the actual events as well as their meaning to the activists involved. The focus of attention here is therefore rather the history of strikers' associations, strategies of legitimation, and the emergence of organisations, which were in turn local roots of an emerging transnational secular Jewish worker culture.

2 The Eastern European Legacy as 'Bund-Type Radical Activism'?

Strikes in the United States and Argentina reached a new qualitative level in the 1900s. They became a repeatable mass event tied to the socialist trade unions active in the US and emerging in Argentina, flanked by publications and agitators from the Socialist Party or the Partido Socialista.

Numerous pioneering studies emphasise the role of Russian-born Jewish immigrants as engines of collective radicalisation over the course of the 1900s. John Bodnar stresses that Jewish socialists essentially brought their political views with them to 'Milwaukee, New York and elsewhere'. After Abraham Cahan prepared the ground politically, New York soon became the place where many activists could deploy their organisational patterns and 'well-developed socialist tradition and social consciousness'.[12] This view is shared by historian Françoise Basch, who credits the explosion of socialist trade unions like the ILWGU mainly to the arrival of Jewish immigrants. These unions could easily have failed without the novel combination of trade unionism and socialism they imported, which was then constantly reinforced through migration.[13] Moreover, she credits the Bundists with shaking up masculine dominance in the process:

---

11 Koller 2009, pp. 529–32.
12 Bodnar 1987, p. 105 f.
13 Basch 1998, pp. 18–21; Kessler-Harris 2003, p. 150 f.

The years 1907–8 saw a massive influx of radical women, native-born and immigrant, into the urban sector of the [Socialist] party, which marked a significant change in its gender politics. Russian-Jewish women ... played a major part in this shift. Reacting to the male-centered culture and influenced by Bund-type radical activism, these Jewish militants turned away from Socialist party bazaars and good works and demanded full political participation.[14]

According to Basch, the hardships of proletarian life in the US and the 'Bund-type radical activism' mysteriously arriving in the US along with the Bundists had led from the picnic and charitable bazaar to strikes and more gender equality. We could call this the 'souvenir hypothesis', treating activism as an object that travelled with migrants in their suitcases to be unpacked at their respective destinations.[15]

The problem here is that, firstly, complex processes of transfer and dynamic reproductions of actions and institutions are reduced to direct transfers. Secondly, this perspective restricts its view to individuals allegedly serving as 'pioneers' and typical representatives of their era. Yet it remains unclear who exactly the bearers of these political and practical souvenirs were. Basch's protagonist Theresa Serber Malkiel emigrated to the US as early as 1891, prior to the ground-breaking 1892 May Day demonstrations and a whole six years before the Bund's founding.[16] Neither Malkiel's nor Cahan's (the latter of whom arrived in the US even earlier in the 1880s) political actions were rooted in prior Bundist experience.

That said, American practices shifted with the 1905 upheaval in Russia. Contemporary observers noted that, by then, strikers articulated more comprehensive demands, seeking to improve not just their wages but Jewish workers' lives in the US more generally.[17] Modern historians will nevertheless find little evidence of direct transfers. Most importantly, no organisations emerged resembling their storied Russian progenitors who gifted the Tsarist empire three revolutions in only 12 short years. On the contrary, Bundist organisations in the US quite pointedly chose *not* to join the local labour struggle. The decision is most clearly illustrated by their publications: reports on trade

---

14   Basch 1998, p. 52.
15   See also Glenn 1990, p. 35, p. 176; Coser 1999, p. 80; Epstein 1953, p. 6.
16   Similar: Bender 2004a, p. 125 f. On 1892 see for example Wistrich 1976, p. 82; Frankel 1997; Zimmerman 2004; Dawidowicz 1967, p. 58 f.
17   See also the description of activism as the birth of a new and simultaneously familiar pattern of action in Marot 1910.

union life and international protest movements from the 'workers' front' were common in the Russian Bund's periodicals as well as Swiss exile publications. These articles portrayed strike movements and political protests as much as they motivated them. Columns like 'From Professional Life' or 'From the Movement' were standard components of even the earliest Bundist publications, like the *'Arbeyter-shtime'* published in Swiss emigration by the Foreign Committee, *'Di hofnung'* published in Russia, and the later *'Folkstsaytung'* or *'Naye folkstsaytung'* in Poland. The militant rhetoric found in these publications was not unique to illegality. The Bund published its first daily newspaper, *'Der veker'*, in the months of Russian legality shortly after the 1905 October Manifesto.[18] The authors of its opening editorial celebrated their new-found legality, but nevertheless called on readers to continue the revolutionary struggle.[19] This was underscored even in the first issue by reflections on the Russian Revolution from authors like Karl Kautsky and Franz Mehring. Although these texts were not written for a specifically Bundist context, the Yiddish translations show that the many political actions Bundists undertook in revolutionary Russia were deeply tied to the broader global process of class struggle.[20] The smaller columns providing detailed information on the revolution's progress in their own country were likely of particular interest to readers.[21] Accordingly, more and more space was devoted to correspondence and reports on local Bundist activity, complemented by a column titled 'From Party Life' and brief appeals for organised resistance. Even today, this oeuvre provides an impressive snapshot of the economic and political activism characteristic of that period.

Transfers began to take effect in the US around the same time as the *'Forverts'* increased in importance and scope. In its rapid growth, it relied heavily on both domestic Bundist authors as well as foreign Bundist correspondents. Bundists like A. Litvak wandered between both worlds in these years, and the Bund used its new foreign contacts to obtain texts from Western Social Democrats for the Bundist press in Russia.

---

18 The stock of surviving early Bundist publications is quite fragmented. The Bund Archives store issues of the Vilnius *'Der veker'* up to no. 13, Bund Archives, New York, Microfilm no. 74-Y-1028. On Bundist criticism of the post-revolutionary phase see *'Di hofnung'*, Vilnius 1 (15 September 1907), p. 1.
19 Der veker 1906.
20 Kautsky 1906; Mehring 1906.
21 Yiddish magazines resonated well with readers. To suggest they deployed an anachronistic language alien to their audience for purely propagandistic purposes, as Susanne Marten-Finnis has, may derive from claims to Hebrewist sovereignty but is certainly unfounded in historical terms; see Marten-Finnis 2001, pp. 25–7.

3 New York Bundists and the Labour Struggle

However, although the Bund and 'Forverts' developed close ties, even the immigrants in the 1900s neglected to transfer the political mobilisation of Jewish workers and their organisations to the US. Moreover, the Bundists in Europe showed little interest in organisational efforts overseas. Although the founding of the New York-based 'Der kemfer' was enthusiastically hailed in the Bundist press in Russia,[22] its subsequent collapse left no traces in the surviving literature. The secretary of the Bund's Central Association in America, Israel Bergman, explained this failure by citing low overall literary quality owed to a lack of capable authors.[23] This seems odd for New York given the large number of Yiddish socialists in the city. The number of potential readers also grew rapidly: stable Bundist groups were established in 14 other major North American cities in 1905 alone, more than doubling their total number to 25.[24] We might therefore favour another explanation: 'Der kemfer' lacked a fighting spirit fitting the conditions of the labour struggle in the US. In its sole issue, we find no mention of events in the American workers' movement. When the journal did call for activism, it was of a peculiar character:

> Help is needed! *Khaverim*! Workers and friends! Don't stand aside! In this sacred moment, help the Jewish 'Bund' fulfil its purpose for which masses of your brothers have been slaughtered [*oysshekhten*] – save the Jewish people! The 'Central Association of the Bund' in America has issued 5 cent stamps, very pretty and neatly printed. Workers! Buy the stamp, distribute it among your friends and acquaintances, agitate on behalf of the 'Bund' and help your brothers and sisters in Russia, help an entire people to become fully free – help at the last minute, help![25]

The picture of the stamp printed below the appeal was the issue's only image. Instead of forming present masses, the typical goal of appeals to action published in Russian Bundist organs, the paper called for a highly abstract form of solidarity with the movement in Russia. Because of this focus, the numerous reports from American Bundist organisations were printed only in the paper's

---

22 N.N. 1906a.
23 Bund Archives, New York, RG 1400, ME-18, 4, *Referat fun der driter yehrlikher konventsh fun di bundistishe organisatsye in Amerike* (1906), p. 10.
24 Ibid.
25 Tsentralfarband fun di bundistishe organisatsyonen in Amerika 1905b.

margins, while information on meetings and local political work was omitted entirely.[26] The sole focus on the '*alte heym*' de-localised *doikayt*, logically leading to its failure.

Although growing more radical by the day through Bundist involvement, the labour struggle on the Lower East Side went unmentioned. '*Der kemfer*' gives the impression that its publisher, the *Tsentral farband fun die bundistishen organisatsyonen in Amerike*, viewed the labour struggle in the US as unrelated to the Bundist agenda – despite the fact that American Jewish trade unions reached out and offered their cooperation on multiple occasions. Its annual meetings were attended by prominent delegates from the United Hebrew Trades like Weinstein, Brodnik, and Berman. Delivering his official fraternal greetings, Bernard Weinstein[27] even emphasised 'with warm words' that the delegates 'had learned that the Russian movement shared many similarities with the American Trade-Unionism Movement' from Gurevitsh's report on the Bund in Russia. In conclusion, Weinstein appealed to the Bundists 'to join the union with all their Bundist energy and enthusiasm, and to aid the American proletariat in its struggle against oppression while supporting the proletariat in Russia'.[28] The report states that his speech was met 'with thunderous applause'.

Weinstein called on activists to integrate their Bundist experience into the US more strongly. He did not, however, urge the Bund to stake out a stronger organisational role in the American labour struggle. This was fully in line with the Bund's perspective, as before 1917 the organisation only supported strikes in the US when it deemed them useful for solidarity with the struggle in Russia.[29] In February 1906 alone it managed to collect 1,000 $ at the end of strike assemblies for the Bund's Foreign Committee in Geneva, from strikers who were not particularly well-off themselves. The collection of donations at non-Bundist gatherings also heightened the presence of the Russian Bund's activities in the United States, while facilitating a further institutionalisation of the Bund after the secretary of the Central Committee and the administrator of the self-defence fund became paid full-time positions.[30] Successful fundraising was often followed by reports in the '*Forverts*', although criticism also surfaced. Particularly during the interwar years, both trade unions and the '*Forverts*' deman-

---

26 As much is stated, lamentingly but nevertheless apologetically, in Goldman 1905.
27 Iconic figure of socialist Jewish labour in the United States, author of *Fertsig yohr in der yidisher arbeyter bavegung* (Weinstein 1924).
28 Bund Archives, New York, RG 1400, ME-18, 4, *Referat fun der driter yehrlikher konventsh fun di bundistishe organisatsye in Amerike* (1906), p. 7.
29 Bund Archives, New York, RG 1400, ME-18, 3, Circular (ca. 1911).
30 Bund Archives, New York, RG 1400, ME-18, 4, *Referat fun der driter yehrlikher konventsh fun di bundistishe organisatsye in Amerike* (1906), p. 9.

ded more Bundist involvement in American organising activities in increasingly resentful tones.[31]

Due to Bundist organisations' orientation towards events abroad, 'Bund-type radical activism' in New York primarily occurred outside the Bund proper. Bundists themselves were not inclined to hang back on the class struggle's fringes while gripping a donation box. Around one quarter of respondents to the aforementioned Bund questionnaires reported active involvement in trade union work overseas. This is a remarkably high figure, given that only one third indicated the same in Eastern Europe. Moreover, most respondents ignored their time in America and only gave precise answers with regard to Eastern Europe.[32] Although the Bund played no role in the American trade unions, these unions were very important to the Bundists.

Bundists also influenced the Jewish workers' movement in the US.[33] Of particular note in this regard is the ILGWU, founded in 1900 and shaped by the mass migration of subsequent years.[34] Another such organisation was the Amalgamated Clothing Workers of America (ACWA), a 1914 socialist split from the increasingly moderate AFL.[35] Although neither trade union was explicitly Jewish, both were dominated by Jewish workers. Individual sections and locals of both ACWA and ILGWU could be classified as secondary-Bundist, not only because important Bundists were part of their leadership (most prominently Barukh Charney Vladeck),[36] but also due to their historical roots in the labour struggles of the needleworkers on the Lower East Side.

Although their living conditions deteriorated rapidly, the path of newly arrived New York Jews often led directly from Ellis Island to the Lower East

---

31   *Forverts*, second section (1 November 1931), p. 2 f. The Bundist Club in New York attempted to mediate between the Bund and Abraham Cahan, publishing their debates as a written correspondence between Cahan and leading Bundists in a special volume to this end: Bundisher Klub in Nyu York 1932; Mayer 1951; Jacobs 1993b, p. 28 f.
32   Bund Archives, New York, RG 1400, MG-2, 429.
33   Often acknowledged yet rarely analysed, see for example Perlman 1922, p. 220 f.; Perlman 1960; Epstein 1953; Mendelsohn 1976.
34   Levine 1924; Seaman and Danish 1947; Wolfson 1950; Laslett 1967; Asher 1976; Berrol 1976. A more current but descriptive account is found in Wolensky, Wolensky and Wolensky 2002. Particularly brilliant: Katz 2011.
35   Asher 1976; Yellowitz 1976; Vural 1994.
36   Barukh Charney Vladeck (1886–1938), trade union leader, member of the New York City Board for several terms, general manager of the '*Forverts*', co-founder and longstanding president of the Jewish Labor Committee, brother of authors Daniel Charney and Shmuel Niger, and notable advocate for public housing in New York. A large housing complex on the Lower East Side with 238 units completed in 1940 was named after him, see Shepard and Levi 2000, p. 173. On his identity as a Bundist see Vladeck 1947.

Side.[37] The district had already become the city's most densely populated by 1890. Residents lived particularly cramped towards its centre, where the highest density of workshops and housing blocks could be found. Settlement rates rose from 523.6 inhabitants per acre to more than 700 between 1890 and 1900.[38] New York City boasted 51 apartment blocks with a capacity of over 3,000 people in 1906, 37 of which were located on the Lower East Side.[39]

Renewed wage decline after 1908 led to the 1909–10 Shirtwaist Strike, a major labour stoppage with markedly Bundist characteristics that significantly bolstered the ILGWU.[40] The 20–30,000 mostly women workers went on strike for weeks, demanding not only better wages but improved living conditions and the right to organise.[41] Their collective struggle against capitalism posed a direct challenge to local authorities. When police violence threatened to crush the strike, the workers responded with a massive demonstration of about 10,000 mostly young and female workers.[42] From the outset, the '*Forverts*' wrote that a general strike would strike 'a raw blow to the pockets of the bloodspattered capitalists ... Hand in hand, heart by heart these thousands of workers will stand up and fight'. It called for solidarity, declaring: 'we must not allow the brave strikers to go hungry or face destitution. Their struggle is our struggle'.[43]

The strike not only attracted public attention, but also swelled the ranks of the workers' organisation. Only several hundred members belonged to the main responsible ILGWU branch, Local 25, at the beginning of the Shirtwaist Strike. By the strike's end this number had skyrocketed to 10,000.[44] From here on, the ILGWU became the most important trade union among Jewish immigrants.[45] Accordingly, the '*Forverts*' celebrated the workers' success months later not only as a victory against 'hunger, suffering, and persecution', but also for 'their human rights'. The '*Forverts*' stressed that its main effect was institutional success through self-organisation, as 'the main victory is the union ... Before

---

37 Simon 1997, p. 26.
38 Accordingly, these parts of New York had a population density of roughly 21,200 people per square kilometre in 1890, rising to 30,000 by 1900. By comparison, New York's overall population density today is below 11,000 inhabitants per square kilometre, while Manhattan's is 27,000 – despite wide-ranging architectural redevelopment.
39 Rischin 1977, p. 79 f.
40 Basch 1998, p. 52.
41 The ILGWU was thus not only part of the labour movement but the women's movement as well, see Katz 2000; Bender 2004b; Ott 2004.
42 Kenneally 1973, p. 48.
43 *Forverts* (23 November 1909), p. 1.
44 Simon 1997, p. 94.
45 For qualitative arguments, see Wolfson 1950.

the strike they were mass-slaves, now we have an organisation of enlightened workers'.[46] The paper was referring to the ILGWU. The union became a major force in the American labour struggle, counting numerous Bundists among its ranks and complementing other socialist and Yiddish-speaking institutions on the Lower East Side. Despite its organisational roots in New York, the organisation's practised secondary Bundism also introduced young Jewish workers, most of whom were only now becoming acquainted with socialism, to the Bundist concepts of *yidishkayt* and *doikayt*. During these years, the corresponding branches of the ILGWU, *Arbeter-ring*, and *Federatsye* grew into nationally relevant secondary-Bundist organisations. Furthermore, in contrast to *'Der kemfer'*, the *Federatsye*'s publication *'Der yidishe sotsyalist'* regularly featured a column titled 'From Professional Life' that reported on local labour struggle in the US.

This constituted an indirect transfer of Bundism on the terrain of local activism. It was vital not only to organisations, but also to migrants' identities. Barukh Vladeck became a major figurehead in the ILGWU and other labour organisations while continuing to openly profess his adherence to Bundism. He was also a frequent guest and speaker at Bundist gatherings, such as the New York celebrations of the Bund's twenty-fifth anniversary in 1922 together with Vladimir Medem and Joseph Baskin.[47] On this occasion, Vladeck – who by then was mostly known as an American labour organiser – captured his Bundist identity in the lecture's telling title: 'Four Years in the Bund, and Stayed Forever'.[48] Vladeck also remained a Bundist agitator in the US, where he even recruited trade union leaders like Shmuel Layb Regenbogen, although the man had no prior Bundist experience from Eastern Europe.[49]

While Vladeck cleverly manoeuvred his way through the functionally differentiated landscape of the American socialist movement, many Bundists found their predicament rather frustrating. One example is former *kheder* teacher (*melamed*) Julius Baron, who migrated to the United States in 1906 to work as a tailor and subsequently a postman. Following his arrival he attempted to organise workers in various workshops and sweatshops, albeit with little success.[50] Coat maker Mayr Kushner, whose life path perfectly integrated the Bund's transnationality, had better luck. Kushner was born in Russia in 1883 and at a

---

46 *Forverts* (15 February 1909), p. 1.
47 Bund Archives, New York, RG 1400, ME-18, 1, 10, *1897–1922 – 25 yoriker yubileum fun 'bund'*, 1922.
48 Vladeck 1947.
49 Bund Archives, New York, RG 1400, MG-2, 429, Regenbogen, Shmuel Layb.
50 YIVO, RG 102, 115, [untitled autobiography], p. 21f.

young age emigrated with his family to the US, where he soon became involved in the workers' movement. He came back to Russia in 1901, immediately joined the Bund as an active member, and returned to the US as a Bundist sometime after 1905. In his own telling of the story, his later activist life (largely on behalf of the ILGWU) is directly linked to previous activism in Eastern Europe. This manifested not so much in political debates, but primarily in the form of strikes as a concrete action Bundist workers pursued in the American labour struggle.[51] For some Bundists, such activism could even be therapeutic. Encouraged by enthusiastic letters from her uncle, Bundist worker Lena Friedman emigrated to the US with her mother. Upon arrival, however, they were not only exploited as 'greenhorns' but also failed to gather enough money to finance the passage of her fiancée, who ultimately died in a Tsarist prison after attempting to desert. Reeling from shock, only a new union established in Harlem would manage to 'return the old colour' to her life.[52]

These successes represent only one side of the story. Many Bundists describe being fulfilled by their trade union work, but it is often mixed with a critique of the cold nature of American socialism. Ultimately, the ILGWU was not the Bund, and consequently the structures of American trade union life could also have the opposite effect. Silk weaver Aaron Cohen, sent to the 'treyfe Land' by his parents in a bid to survive, was an enthusiastic Bundist prior to emigration.[53] Upon arrival in the US he approached his new comrades brimming with revolutionary ideals and enthusiasm for *yidishkayt*, but was left bitterly disappointed. These settled Jewish socialists in the American 'melting pot' expected him to speak English! Despite his membership in the Socialist Party and the *Arbeter-ring*, the episode broke his heart and extinguished the revolutionary flame that once burned inside him: 'The idea that a socialist revolution would soon arrive became a foolish dream. Reality turned everyone into pragmatists'. Rather than 'fight the exploiters' he now became an 'exploiter' himself, employing several workers in the silk industry.[54] Although his recollections acknowledged that he failed to provide his children with a Jewish or Yiddish education, he took pride in the fact that he offered them a 'radical education' nonetheless.[55] Another Bundist calling himself 'Der Mohilever stolier' (The joiner from

---

51 Kushner 1960, esp. pp. 77–93.
52 YIVO, RG 102, 157, Lena Friedman, (New York 1942), pp. 16–20.
53 YIVO New York, RG 102, 108, Aaron Cohen, pp. 17–23.
54 YIVO New York, RG 102, 108, Aaron Cohen, p. 23.
55 YIVO New York, RG 102, 108, Aaron Cohen, p. 26. Likewise, for example, in the memoirs of A.B. Grins, who – writing in a leading Bundist journal and typical for many Bundists at the time – laments growing old in a society which never became his own, see Grin 1969.

Mogilev) experienced similar frustration. Fleeing Tsarist authorities, he emigrated to the US in 1903. Optimistic and hopeful during the transatlantic voyage, he soon found himself disenchanted after attempting to settle down in his new home. He was unable to pay the trade union's 25 $ membership fee. The union's subsequent decision to waive the fee hardly eased his befuddlement, as he then found himself confronted with (and utterly perplexed by) internecine squabbles between the two mass political organisations of American socialism, the Socialist Party of America and the Socialist Labor Party. Although he appreciated the American radical press and cultivated deep relationships in his surrounding Jewish environment, the socialist fire inside him gradually diminished to a flicker.[56]

This mixture of identity preservation, hope, and disappointment – the conflict between pragmatism and biographically informed revolutionary drive typical of many Jewish socialist immigrants – reflects, at least in the eyes of these writers, the relatively diluted and distant nature of American socialism. The only way to remain a Bundist was to embrace the process of functional differentiation. By doing so they further accelerated the otherwise sharply criticised centrifugal forces within American socialism. As a result, the project of an egalitarian and secular Jewish modernity dispersed from one central actor, the Bund, into many differentiated organisations. If there was one major actor in the US, it was the *Arbeter-ring* – which was much more of a cultural and educational organisation than the revolutionary Bund. Compared to Russia or Poland, where the Bund united unions or provided education through the Yiddish TSYSHO schools, this reversed the relation between politics and culture.

4 Reproducing the Bund: Buenos Aires on Strike, 1907–10

Bundists in Argentina pursued the structural and organisational transfer from Russia far more directly than in the US. Most importantly, these transfers provided points of orientation. When Pinie Vald and his *khaverim* set foot on Argentinian soil in 1906, no '*Forverts*', *Arbeter-ring*, Jewish trade unions, nor established Yiddish organisations existed in Latin America. For this reason, the new arrivals primarily sought alliances with already-present Russian workers.

From this emerged the aforementioned *birzshe* on Plaza Lavalle, which in turn was often (as in Mendl Mayer's biography) followed by visits to the *Bib-*

---

56 YIVO New York, RG 102, 83, *Der Mohilever stolier*, pp. 40–5.

lioteca rusa founded in 1906.[57] Despite its name, the *Biblioteca* was not just another library, but rather an early form of later socialist cultural centres quite similar to the illegal Jewish-Russian libraries of the Tsarist era. These developed into schools in both Poland and Argentina, while remaining centres of Yiddish community building closely tied to social movements and political parties.[58] Prior to its destruction by the police in 1910, the *Biblioteca rusa* served as a headquarters for many left-wing groups, where they jointly organised regular discussions and reading circles. These meetings were highly political and often dealt with questions of the post-migration class struggle. Despite its brief existence, the *Tsenter avangard* even planned to turn the *Biblioteca rusa* into the city's main hub for Spanish classes for Eastern European immigrants.[59] The language issue represented a constant source of conflict particularly in the early years, although Yiddish – and thus the Bundists – would ultimately prevail.[60] As one observer reflected, it became evident that, similarly to the American *Arbeter-ring*, 'this language question must rather be called the cultural question', and that workers could only shape their own culture when speaking 'their own language'.[61] The historical assessment of this focus within the *Biblioteca rusa* is best summarised in Edgardo Bilsky's and Ana E. Weinstein's classic study of the Jewish workers' movement in Argentina. While they accept Yiddish as a cultural value in its own right, they note that that the *Biblioteca rusa* failed to integrate itself into the wider trade union movement in Argentina, as its 'intensive activity' found expression 'only' in cultural work.[62] While this division makes sense in Argentinian labour history, it fails to fully reflect the centrality of language and cultural work to the Bund and its emergence – and thus of the backdrop against which activists operated and organised. The *Avangard* group regarded itself as the Bund in Argentina, and for them the *Biblioteca rusa* represented the central foundation and revolutionary cultural centre from which other branches of the movement could grow. Cultural work and workers' organisation served the same purpose: the formation of a self-confident and militant Jewish workers' movement. For the Bundist in Argentina, the necessity to create organisations and structures was a possibility to transfer their

---

57   On the *Biblioteca rusa* as a centre of the movement see Vald 1929, p. 35 f., p. 165; Laubstein 1997, pp. 171–8.
58   Centro 'Mark Turkow', Buenos Aires, Archive de la Palabra, 4 [Bitman, David]; 14 [Epstein, José]; 69 [Blitz, Zalel]; 149 [Horn, Yosef]. On the Russian libraries see esp. Brooks 2003. On differences vis-à-vis legal libraries see Veidlinger 2009.
59   Di shtime fun avangard 1909a; Di shtime fun avangard 1909b.
60   Mirelman 1990, p. 166.
61   Shneefal 1910, p. 130 f.
62   Bilsky 1987, p. 36 f.

experiences and sense of meaning from Russia to Latin America. Hence, unlike Bundist groups in the US, the *Avangard* did not seek to channel its activism into fundraisers for the Russian Bund. It saw itself as part of the strike movement in Argentina and practised radical support for workers' organisations by its own means.[63]

Most founders of the *Avangard* were freshly immigrated workers who, like the Bund in Eastern Europe, claimed to be *the* single organisation for Jewish socialists in Argentina.[64] The group's publication, 'Der avangard', was the first lasting Yiddish periodical in Argentina and probably all of South America. Firmly rooted in the local immigrant society, it proudly weathered even its gravest internal crisis, the clash over the language question, with the support of a consistently expanding audience. They received increasing support because they also brought Yiddish as a political and literary language to Argentina. Work on that new worker culture on the Río de la Plata was politically radical. The best example of how serious they took their own agenda are the circumstances surrounding the only interruption of its continuous appearance prior to the police actions of 1909–10: the journal was printed at the Tseytlin print shop, an early specialist in Yiddish publications in Buenos Aires. When the Tseytlin workers staged a walkout, the *Avangard* enthusiastically supported them, 'because we are a soc. dem. organisation that ordinarily sympathises with strikers'. Very much like the workers themselves, they were immediately 'locked out' by Mr. Tseytlin.[65] The *Avangard* group lost the work already invested in the following issue as well as a down payment. Its publication, 'Der avangard', had to find a new print shop, and the group reacted with bellicose defiance: 'Hoping to receive the sympathising support of all, "Der avangard" will continue, without interruption, to move in the same direction as in the past'.[66] The Avangardistas viewed themselves as the most important organisers in the Jewish workers' movement. Moreover, Tseytlin's pattern of behaviour was well-known from experiences in Russia: he called in police against the strikers and tried to place spies in the movement. This only strengthened the Bundists' perception that these were familiar conflicts, and that their experiences were thus not merely vague memories but continued to matter in daily practices. 'Der avangard' called for a boycott of Tseytlin 'together with the socialist workers' organisations', seeing as 'it was always a place where children performed the work of grown men' and the 'working conditions in the print shop [were]

---

63   Vald 1942.
64   Der avangard 1908.
65   Der avangard 1909, p. 1.
66   Der avangard 1909, p. 2.

unbearable'.[67] The 'lockout' of 'Der avangard' also illustrates that under legality, 'printing' no longer functioned as a Bundist pattern of activism. It could be externalised and thus carried out even by actors opposed to the Bund. Tseytlin fit this description, having already printed the programmes and statutes of the deeply Zionist and bourgeois Theodor Herzl League founded in 1899.[68]

As a 'workers' organisation',[69] the *Avangard* group sought to draw together experiences and practices of political and economic resistance under one roof, yet always under the banner of an independent Yiddish worker culture.[70] Explicit parallels between Argentina and Russia were often drawn in the process.[71] The column 'From Professional Life' became a standard feature from the sixth issue of *'Der avangard'* onwards. Already common in Russia, it also contained reports on mostly local union-related issues and events, ongoing strikes, and opportunities to build solidarity.[72] The group's appeals, reports, and actions consistently focused on Argentina. This differs not only from Bundist publications in the US around the same time, but also from the Argentinian secondary-Bundist publications emerging somewhat later, which printed content from a more internationalist perspective.

The *Avangard* therefore always considered itself a Jewish representative within the Argentinian workers' movement. When a general strike was called in the aftermath of May Day 1909, the group by no means limited itself to raising donations. Of course, such calls for financial support remained part of their activity then and also during the revolutionary year of 1917, but only as a marginal component of the group's overall activities.[73] The *Avangard* threw itself into the struggle as a labour organiser and a militant force in May 1909. One month later, its reflection on the failure of the general strike resembled what many Bundists experienced in the political strikes and revolution of 1905 in Russia: the workforce was too poorly organised, and thus 'the most important strikes were squandered'.[74] The task at hand was therefore to build their organisation further, to professionalise the strike movement and foster the kind of political consciousness that would allow the 'political struggle' to realise itself inside the strike.[75]

---

67 N.N. 1909a.
68 IWO, Buenos Aires, Gremios en proceso, Statutes of the 'Lige Theodor Hertsl' (1908).
69 Der avangard 1908; Vald 1909b; Vald 1909c; Kling 1917; Vald 1942.
70 Libman 1908.
71 N.N. 1909c.
72 *Der avangard*, Buenos Aires 2 (1 January 1909), p. 30 f.
73 IWO, Buenos Aires, 1114, Collection lists.
74 Vald 1909b, p. 14.
75 Vald 1909b, p. 15.

It had little time for such an undertaking. Much of what emerged was smashed apart in the violent police actions of 1910. *Der avangard* ceased publication, and during the following years the group and its activism patterns materialised only sporadically. The old *Avangard* flared up again in 1916, before splitting once and for all in 1920 over divisions rooted in the Russian Revolution. Nevertheless, the linking of the labour struggle to *yidishkayt* in a self-organised worker culture first transferred to Argentina by the *Avangard* group would continue to dominate Jewish life in Argentina over the years to come.

5 Organising Workers in *Yiddishland*

The *Avangard*'s demise in 1919–20 was followed by the founding of the first Bundist club in Buenos Aires. It shifted the main focus of Bundist activism to transnational networking and education work. While numerous independent Jewish trade unions would emerge over the interwar period in Buenos Aires, no Bundist organisation claimed to lead the labour struggle in the city. Unlike the Bund in Vilnius in 1897, the Bund in Argentina never intended to serve as a union of unions, although it was involved in the emergence of many new unions. As previously described with view to Warsaw, the spark was set not by the revolutionary year of 1917 but already in the middle of World War I.[76] From this process emerged a functionally differentiated public in Argentina, in which *yidishkayt* could be lived out in different ways, albeit largely on a Bundist foundation.

Many socialist trade unions, such as the *Hitl-makher arbeyter fareyn* founded in the Once district in 1916, subsequently organised not only according to occupation but also language. In the less explicitly socialist unions, on the other hand, *yidishkayt* and worker organisation were less closely linked, best demonstrated by the Jewish teachers' trade unions emerging in 1919 alongside the establishment of the secular Jewish school system.[77] The so-called *Agudat Hamorim*, also known as the *Liga de Maestros Israelitas* or *Lerer fareyn*, saw itself as a workers' association and organised in the *Yudisher arbeyter farband*.[78]

---

76 See Part II.5.
77 This was preceded by a teachers' organisation around the *Cursos Religiosos* schools founded in 1911 and run by the ICA, which launched the first teachers' strike in Argentina in 1911 or 1912. It did not survive its initial years, see Zadoff 1994, p. 54, p. 78, fn. 22.
78 IWO, Buenos Aires, Gremios en proceso, *Sindicatos*, loose collection, without box, Letter, *Hitl-makher arbeyter fareyn*, 29 July 1920; Ibid., *Organisación de Maestros*, Letter, *Agudat Hamorim* to the administrative commission of the *Yudishen arbeyter farband*, 22 July 1920;

Yet it saw itself as a Jewish – not explicitly Yiddish – union. As a non-Marxist teacher's organisation, it pursued largely economic goals and called the first and partially successful teacher strikes in the mid-1920s, albeit without placing political demands at the heart of the protest.[79] Its separation of Jewishness and *yidishkayt*, failing to reflect the trade union's practice, fostered internal tensions. Intolerable for many Bundist teachers, the union aimed to mobilise neither in an overtly political form nor in Yiddish, despite conducting internal communication and even session minutes entirely in the language.[80]

As a result of this inconsistency and the radicalisation of the Argentinian workers' movement more generally, an explicitly Yiddish-speaking teachers' union split to its left in 1929, calling itself the *Yidishe lerer organisatsye in Argentine*. It opened its office at Lavalle 2339 in the heart of the Jewish district Once and in direct proximity to the Peretz School, founded shortly thereafter at Lavalle 2238.[81] The school was open to teachers from Hebrew schools, but expected them to share the Yiddish language as a marker of common identity.[82] During strikes, it portrayed itself as socialist and radical.[83] As was typical for other secondary-Bundist organisations, Yiddish was both function and substance at once, shaping internal community building to a significant extent. Its members saw the *Yidishe lerer organisatsye in Argentine* as 'educators and cultural workers',[84] and in this context managed to negotiate a 50 percent discount on subscriptions to the Argentinian Yiddish daily '*Di prese*', akin to a moderate version of the '*Forverts*'.[85] It frequently organised press conferences in the 1930s, but only in Yiddish.[86]

The degree to which this new union's activities shifted towards cultural work can be deduced from its strike fund records. The strike fund was so small in 1938 (776 pesos) that it held only twice as much as the organisation's income from

---

Ibid., Letter, *Agudat Hamorim* to the administrative commission of the *Yudishen arbeyter farband*, 1 August 1920.

79   IWO, Buenos Aires, *Organisación de Maestros*, 5; 7; Avni, Klich and Zadoff 2007, p. 433.
80   IWO, Buenos Aires, *Organisación de Maestros*, *Protkol-bukh fun lerer-fareyn*, 1921–2.
81   IWO, Buenos Aires, *Organisación de Maestros*, 14 [Letter, invitation to the organisation's second meeting on 30 December 1933].
82   Communications contained in the records are entirely in Yiddish. One questionnaire explicitly asks union members: 'Which languages (apart from Yiddish) do you read?', IWO, Buenos Aires, *Organisación de Maestros*, 7 [*Yidishe lerer organisatsye in Argentine*, 'Frage boygn (1932)'].
83   IWO, Buenos Aires, *Organisación de Maestros*, 15 [Flyer, 24 April 1933].
84   IWO, Buenos Aires, *Organisación de Maestros*, Circular, 1935.
85   IWO, Buenos Aires, *Organisación de Maestros*, Letter, 22 September 1938.
86   IWO, Buenos Aires, *Organisación de Maestros*, 16 [Invitation to an 18 December 1935 press conference addressed to *Unzer lebn*].

membership dues (323 pesos). The largest items in the annual report were not strike costs, but mailings and paper expenses (242 pesos).[87] Over several years the *Yidishe lerer organsatsye in Argentine* had gone from a radical trade union to a public institution, and a site of Yiddish community building in its own right. Of particular note is that the largest share of the organisation's 2,498 mailings between March and December 1938 were questionnaires – an instrument for strengthening membership ties while simultaneously exploring one's own new association.[88]

The *Agudat Hamorim* harshly criticised this public relations work at first, arguing that excessive cultural work had caused the union to deprioritise the labour struggle. In continued observance of *yidishkayt*, an agreement was reached in 1938 that saw both trade unions fuse into a single organisation.[89] Both unions concentrated their work entirely on Argentina and established transnational contacts only to a very limited extent. This pattern would change in 1940. At the teachers' union's last major gathering, horrified delegates mainly discussed the outbreak of the war in Europe and its political implications.[90] Their subsequent 'philanthropic' turn put an end to the existence of a Jewish teachers' union in Argentina for the time being, while the dissolution of the free trade unions under Perón in 1943 concluded their history as actors within a transnational political worker culture.[91]

Although functional differentiation along the Río de la Plata increasingly resembled the process occurring on the East River, the Jewish workers' movement in Argentina remained notably more radical and militant. Its many branches split into various currents during the 1930s. Nevertheless, the decade was not dominated by divisive debates and letter writing so much as by labour struggles more generally. One expression of this was the 1934 textile workers' strike, which also demonstrates how trade unions interacted with each other during actions on the ground, irrespective of ideological disputes.[92] A quite informative account are the memoirs of Communist activist Simon Lewintal, who, when asked about his activity around this time, enthusiastically responded: 'Constantly. Constantly there were gatherings, meetings, the union almost vibrated, just about 24 hours ...' His Communist comrades had not run the

---

87   IWO, Buenos Aires, 1124 [*Organisación de Maestros*], 22 [*Boletin*, January 1939], p. 1.
88   IWO, Buenos Aires, 1124 [*Organisación de Maestros*], 22 [*Boletin*, January 1939], p. 2; see Part II.6.
89   IWO, Buenos Aires, 1124 [*Organisación de Maestros*], 22 [*Boletin*, January 1939], p. 2.
90   IWO, Buenos Aires, *Organisación de Maestros, Rezolutsyes* (February 1940).
91   Doyon 2006.
92   Bilsky 1987, p. 68 ff., pp. 138–43.

committee alone, however, but 'Kanutsky ... and many others; Kaminetsky and ... what was her name again? ... that woman, the wife of Kaminetsky. I don't remember anymore'.[93] Once again, women actors disappear into the murky backchannels of memory as 'wives of activists', while strikes continue to be seen as central activities with major impacts on an individual's life. His depiction of political parties' influence remains similarly vague. On the one hand, he emphasises that everything was organised 'under Kanutsky' and other old Bundists, yet also states that 'everything was conducted under the influence of the Communist Party ... However, there was no direct form of party intervention'.[94] This statement is curious, as the tailor Guitl Kanutsky, a devout Bundist who immigrated in 1924, was anything but a Communist sympathiser.[95] Bringing 70–80,000 primarily Jewish workers into the streets in 1934 was not the political utopia of any single movement, but rather the result of collective action in a greater and increasingly politicised labour struggle.[96] This unifying approach gave Bundists in leading positions in Argentina an advantage in the sense that, unlike the Communists, their action did not require a permanent organisation.

Developments nevertheless gradually began to resemble those in the US, and the Argentinian Jewish trade union movement grew increasingly sophisticated and differentiated from the 1920s onwards. In the field of labour organising, this led to a shift in focus from the erstwhile guiding star, Eastern Europe, to local activity. Even active Bundists began abandoning the idea of an all-encompassing, Bund-like organisation, and instead formed and acted in small groups committed to Yiddish as an intrinsic value, yet both close to and utterly remote from Bundism proper. Meanwhile, their direct rival Poale Zion grew stronger by the day. Uniting Bundists and Poale Zionists at this point was that *yidishkayt* changed from a precondition of the labour struggle to a value in itself for the Jewish workers' movement. In Buenos Aires much more than in Poland and New York, these cultural aspects served to facilitate contact and cooperation even if rivalries persisted in other spheres.[97]

Socialist movements were not the only ones relying on Yiddish as the language of mobilisation. Even Argentinian anarchism's most significant periodical, '*La Protesta*', summarised its texts in a regularly published Yiddish insert

---

93 Centro 'Mark Turkow', Archivo de la Palabra, 42 [Simon Lewintal], p. 16.
94 Ibid.
95 Centro 'Mark Turkow', Archivo de la Palabra, 32 [Kanutsky, Guitl], p. 1.
96 Centro 'Mark Turkow', Archivo de la Palabra, 42 [Simon Lewintal], p. 12.
97 A more extensive discussion is found in the following chapter.

during the pre-war period.[98] In contrast to the Avangardistas, however, the anarchists never treated this activity as an end in itself. Yiddish anarchist movements emerged despite Argentinian anarchism's decline from 1910 onwards, most notably the *Yidishe ratsyonalistishe gezelshaft*, active in the 1920s primarily in the educational sector.[99] As was typical for Argentina, numerous small trade unions also surfaced. Bakers formed a specifically Yiddish-speaking bakers' union as a language federation of FORA's deeply radical bakery division on 1 August 1919.[100] Anarchism was also particularly widespread among Jewish cabinetmakers, as a result of which the revolutionary-syndicalist '*Acción Obrera*', the cabinetmakers' journal put out by the anarchist trade union federation *Unión Sindical Argentina* (US), began publishing a monthly Yiddish supplement in 1927. The supplement addressed international and often commemorative aspects of the anarchist movement, such as the 1927 execution of Bartolomeo Vanzetti and Ferdinando Nicola Sacco or the Haymarket anniversary. At its heart, however, lay local matters related to the secretariat's work and the labour struggle in Argentina directly affecting the lives of Jewish activists.[101]

Both anarchism as well as Communism claimed to speak for the working class as a whole, which in turn prompted fierce ideological conflicts despite local groups' efforts to emphasise shared interests. Argentinian Yiddish anarchist groups in particular built on the tradition of anarcho-communist pre-war syndicalism, which had waged several rear-guard battles against Bolshevik ideas inside the *Unión Sindical Argentina* and was perceived by many groups as a path out of the polarising dynamic for precisely this reason. The resulting amalgamation of Communism and anarchism is reflected in a resolution passed by the *Unión Sindical Argentina* to mark the tenth anniversary of the October Revolution, printed in the Yiddish publication '*Der mebl arbeter*'. Despite its sharp, fundamental criticisms of the Soviet Union, the resolution praised the 'situation in the council federation'. '[T]he iron will of the proletarians in their successful march for their own emancipation', they wrote, had achieved 'a magnificent accomplishment in a very short amount of time', showing that it 'is [even] possible to outperform the capitalist countries in some areas, for they are extremely backward when it comes to the material and

---

98   Deutsch 2010, p. 150 ff.
99   Urales 1925.
100 IWO, Buenos Aires, Gremios en proceso, *Sindicatos*, loose collection, without box, Letter, *Unión Obreros Panaderos Israelitas*, 2 August 1920.
101 N.N. 1927b; Sulam 1928.

moral conditions of the proletariat'.[102] Slowly, the mood in the once anarchist-dominated Argentinian political landscape began to shift towards a relatively independent form of Communism. Starting during the labour conflicts of 1927 and 1929, it emerged as the dominant power on the streets (and thus the Yiddish street).[103] Leading figures like Maxim Rozen, chairman of the *Yevsektsiya*, were often former Bundists. They sought to pursue socialist activism within a Communist framework and increasingly radicalised strikes in Argentinian cities.[104]

Across from the Bundists who initially remained in the *Avangard* group before joining the PCA, however, stood those who continued to build an Argentinian Bund. They found new support from fresh waves of immigrants from Poland. This Argentinian Bund dealt relatively little with worker organisation, and was much more interested in community building within the new Bundist movement and educational work, the latter of which is discussed in more detail in the following chapter. Due to relatively small numbers of activists, organising specific committees always remained a top priority as Bundists increasingly found themselves mediating between Poland and Argentina.

In doing so the Bund declared migration a subject of the transnational workers' movement for the first time in its history. When the US finally shut its doors to Eastern European immigrants with the 1924 National Quota Act, Bundist trade union leaders in Poland realised that structuring migration internationally had to become an important component of their work. To this end, they created an emigration department for the Polish unions called the *Arbeter emigratsye biro*. They also proposed that Argentinian unions establish a counterpart on their side of the ocean. The *Arbeter emigratsye biro* would in this way 'always receive the necessary information concerning conditions in Argentina'.[105] The Argentinian trade union federation's Central Committee gave the question low priority and continuously delayed its establishment, forcing Bundists to take on the issue themselves. They raised it continuously and ultimately forced the establishment of the appropriate committee.[106] For the Bund this meant new channels of information, and allowed combining worker organisation with migration management. The federation of socialist trade unions, for its part, was not particularly cooperative. Although the committee's reorganisation was formally decided on at the federation's general assembly, no action was taken in the weeks that followed. Bundists lamented this state of

---

102 N.N. 1928b, p. 3.
103 Camarero 2007, pp. 253–7, pp. 297–311.
104 These strikes were by no means limited to Buenos Aires, see Mastrángelo 2006.
105 N.N. 1924.
106 Ibid.

affairs, but were too weak to bring about changes at the executive level. It is therefore hardly surprising that their activity increasingly focused on workers who had already settled in Argentina, devoting their efforts to questions of worker education and cultural work.[107]

The traces of the Bund within the Yiddish-speaking trade union movement in Argentina begin to grow fainter in the 1930s. Taking into account the findings from the press analysis of the Bund, both the Bund and secondary-Bundist organisations like the YSFA increasingly approached workers as bearers of a secular worker culture. The former Bundists who turned to Communism, by contrast, shifted their attention more and more to political questions. Firmly rooted in the traditions of Yiddish-speaking activism and Jewish colonies in Argentina, the Birobidzhan movement was particularly successful. Probably the best expression of the resulting – and at times quite bizarre – ideological blend is a cover of the Communist cultural journal '*Nayvelt*'. The paper demanded Jews' 'productivation' via agriculturalisation in the land of the '*Gaucho Judío*'. This call to 'move to the country', however, coincided with demands for a 'workers' and peasants' state' in Russia's distant Far East (see Figure 17).[108] The aim was to shape the 'new world' from within the 'New World' in which Jewish workers had arrived – ironically, often enough with tickets provided by the ICA intended to bring them to the struggling Jewish agricultural colonies in Argentina as farmers.

That said, the position from which Yiddish-speaking Communism in Argentina proceeded was quite paradoxical: on the one hand, *yidishkayt* as discovered by authors like Chaim Nachman Bialik, Sholem Asch, and Peretz Hirschbein was treated as a remnant of an obsolete 'Jewishness'. On the other hand, it actively contributed to the formation of the new, Communist understanding of *yidishkayt*. Yiddish linguistic practice in combination with a social movement and cultural self-confidence formed the basis of Jewish Communism in Argentina, reinforced not least by its Yiddish periodicals. As in Soviet Russia, Communist activists only realised that a radical left-wing Jewish politics could not afford to break with Yiddish culture after some time. Even influential Argentinian Communist Pinie Katz, who still ridiculed fetishising Yiddish in a 1927 article in '*Nayvelt*', accepted that the class struggle in Argentina could

---

107 Ibid.
108 Some remaining Jewish colonies experienced a more stable, yet far from secure period during these years following the introduction of cooperatives. This collective self-organisation in some areas also served as a role model for equally embattled non-Jewish colonies and agricultural settlements, see esp. Schenkolewski-Kroll 2001.

FIGURE 17
Cover, 'Nayvelt', Buenos Aires, 2 (1927)
A happily toiling peasant turns impoverished traditional Jews (*luftmentshn*) into modern tractor drivers. Inscription on the sickle: 'Establish communist life on the fields of the SSSR'. On the hammer lying below: 'Field work instead of airy *Parnose*' (from the Yiddish *parnose*, meaning work or livelihood, but also *parnes*, a Jewish community leader, in reference to the concept of *luftmentshn*).

not be separated from cultural work over the course of the 1930s.[109] He represented Argentinian Jewish Communists at the founding of the Communist *Yidisher kultur farband* (IKUF) in Paris in 1937, and subsequently founded the profoundly important Argentinian IKUF section over the following two years. During the Perón era in particular, the organisation became a reservoir of illegalised, left-wing cultural workers. As a result, Katz and his comrades could rely on a great number of followers from the left-socialist camp, who joined the IKUF's clandestine practices after the bans on free trade unions, parties, and countless cultural associations from the 1940s onwards.[110]

6 Politics and *Yidishkayt*

The IKUF was another result of Argentina's increasingly Yiddish revolutionary culture, realised mostly by Bundists and former Bundists in the Communist Party as well as anarchists. Its mobilisations grew continuously, particularly

---

109 Katz 1927.
110 Centro 'Mark Turkow', Archivo de la Palabra, 32 [Kanutsky, Guitl], p. 5; 41 [Lerner, Grigori].

in the textile industry dominated by small-scale manufacturing. Thousands of garment workers organised in radical trade unions throughout the 1930s, among them around 6,000 mostly Yiddish-speaking tailors. Accordingly, the syndicalist-Communist trade union *Obreros Cortadores, Sastres y anexos* or *Algemeyner shneyder-arbeter fareyn* published two Yiddish journals filled with strike calls, appeals, and demands to release Argentinian political prisoners.[111]

Unlike Bundist work overseas, for them Eastern Europe barely provided active relations and rather served as an ideological resource. In Stalin's Soviet Union, 'the only proletarian fatherland', it was either a rather abstract and distant role model for a 'new socialist order' or, as in Poland, proved that strike action was on the rise on a global scale, and the internationalist world revolution could no longer be stopped.[112] The usage of Yiddish differed as well. Although Communist publications also turned to *Memorik*, their articles discussed the prehistory of most activists, including former Bundists in the leadership, just as little as the use of the Yiddish language itself. In contrast to the Bundist journals of the time, Communist publications treated Yiddish exclusively as a mode to mobilise for the labour struggle and build the anti-fascist front. That said, the latter – certainly a central theme from Communism's global perspective – by all means relied on the former. The labour struggle continued to be seen an international issue. For example, an issue of the tailor union's paper features a translation of a letter from Georgi Dimitrov to (among others) French author and Nobel Prize winner Romain Rolland, concerning the latter's founding of a French mass movement to free German Communist leader Ernst Thälmann.[113] Extolling this in Yiddish in an Argentinian paper demonstrates that Communism inherited and further globalised the '"panoptic" structure of the Social Democratic interpretative cosmos' Thomas Welskopp first diagnosed.[114] Moreover, such transnationality was only communicable if complemented by the locally focused texts that usually dominated the publication.

Connected to this 'panoptic' view, however, was the claim to sole interpretive discretion on the part of Communist *yidishkayt*, which became apparent with view to the popular front strategy. For example, in May 1936 one of the few illustrations in the Yiddish Communist tailors' journal depicts a worker in socialist realist style, whose decisive grip protects the worker masses from fascism's looming blade as they fade into the image's grey background (Figure 18).

---

111   N.N. 1935b.
112   N.N. 1935a; N.N. 1935b.
113   Dimitrov 1935.
114   Welskopp 2000, p. 588.

FIGURE 18
Communist self-depiction as the only defenders of the working class. Inscription on knife: 'Fascism'
IMAGE FROM *DER KONFEKTSYON ARBETER*, 2, NO. 4 (1936), P. 1

This Communist claim to leadership motivated many Bundists in the trade unions to actively seek an alliance with the anarchists of the FORA, hoping to challenge the Communist version of the popular front with alternative coalitions of their own.[115] The attempt included their own popular front strategy: on that very May Day in 1936, the secondary-Bundist YSFA called on its supporters to fight against fascism, albeit not in alliance with Moscow but with the 'support of the country's largest bourgeois party'.[116] Communist propaganda in the Argentinian context only reacted to this provocation by bolstering its claim to universal leadership of the working class, implying it had surpassed both Bundism and anarchism in world-historical terms.

Despite notable successes achieved by the Argentinian Communist movement through its aggressive form of labour struggle, its universal claim to representation was ultimately little more than political posturing. It built on the Communist rhetoric that had driven Simon Lewintal to declare the 1934 strike an entirely Communist undertaking several years before, while at the same time revealing the action's essentially Bundist leadership.[117]

A fundamental problem here was that most Jewish tailors worked from home, whereas the Communist organisations generally appealed to industrial workers.[118] Attracting the tailors came easier to the socialist trade unions, which formed countless small groups in a flexible manner, among them the ideologically socialist but primarily economistic *Heym-shneyder un tasheristn fareyn*.[119] This fact also accounts for the quantitative strength and qualitative weaknesses of the socialist trade union movement. Similar to the aforementioned anarchist-Jewish unions, on the one hand they sought to represent a

---

115   Centro 'Mark Turkow', Archivo de la Palabra, 11 [José Chiaskelevitz], p. 8 f., p. 23.
116   IWO, Buenos Aires, 1114, Flyer, YSFA, 29 April 1936.
117   Centro 'Mark Turkow', Archivo de la Palabra, 42 [Simon Lewintal], p. 16.
118   Centro 'Mark Turkow', Archivo de la Palabra, 42 [Simon Lewintal], p. 13.
119   An extensive discussion of the trade unions and the Bund's role is found in Centro 'Mark Turkow', Archivo de la Palabra, 11 [José Chiaskelevitz].

primarily Jewish branch of industry, which inevitably entailed *yidishkayt* as a key mobilising factor. On the other hand, they were part of a national umbrella organisation that viewed *yidishkayt* as, among other things, a threat to its claim of sole ideological command. The home-based tailors' union addressed this by introducing a bilingual language policy, although its Spanish component soon shrank to little more than an afterthought. Language trends were now reversed, considering that Yiddish content had once been a mere supplement in *'La Protesta'*.

Yet this occurred in parallel to the organisation's abandonment of cultural goals, to which the Bund was more and more dedicated outside its trade union work. To the tailors' union, *yidishkayt* was no longer a simultaneously political, socialist, and cultural idea to be reflected upon or analysed, but rather pure praxis. Correspondingly, *yidishkayt*'s meaning in the class struggle was reduced to the economistic slogan, 'we want to live from our labour'.[120] By doing so, trade unions ran the risk of literally 'talking past' the Jewish tailors, specifically because *yidishkayt* underwent a veritable 'Jewish renaissance' in 1930s Argentina.[121] This may also have been a reason why the tailors' union, whose internal communication was conducted in Spanish and whose statements the country's major journals often reprinted,[122] encountered severe difficulties in the late 1930s and fell to a mere 300 dues-paying members. Worse still, around 15 percent of the latter regularly defaulted on their payments.[123] Although it was common for socialist trade unions to have no more than a few hundred members (explaining their organisation into broader national federations), in 1939 the tailors' union ran out of funds and was forced to discontinue its work.[124]

7 The Cultural Struggle within the Labour Struggle

In closing, we can establish that, across party lines, the Jewish workers' movement in Argentina relied on the concept of *yidishkayt* Bundists introduced

---

120   N.N. 1937b.
121   Although Pinie Katz derided it as a nonsensical anachronism as late as 1927, Jewish renaissance and revolutionary culture were by no means a contradiction even in the early Soviet Union, as Kenneth Moss has shown; see Moss 2009, p. 2ff., pp. 108–38.
122   IWO, Buenos Aires, *Sindicatos, Boletines de la Unión Sastres a Domicilio, Talleristas y Anexos*, 1937–40, J.B. Raszer: *Memoria de la C.D.*, 29 October 1939, p. 2f.
123   IWO, Buenos Aires, *Sindicatos, Boletines de la Unión Sastres a Domicilio, Talleristas y Anexos*, 1937–40, J.B. Raszer: *Memoria de la C.D.*, 29 October 1939, p. 2.
124   IWO, Buenos Aires, *Sindicatos, Boletines de la Unión Sastres a Domicilio, Talleristas y Anexos*, 1937–40, Hersh Tikulskier: *Informe del Tesoreo*, 29 October 1939.

before 1917. As a result, the *yidishkayt* underwent continuous differentiation during the interwar period. Following the failure of early strikes and targeted police repression, activists created more robust and durable organisations which in turn occupied increasingly specialised fields. This dynamic also affected the form of *yidishkayt* the Bund introduced into the workers' movement. The inherited antagonism between economic and political movement, which influenced practically every social movement and party polemic before World War I, now expanded along a third point: *yidishkayt* as an established worker culture, with many individual interpretations of its function.

While trade unions such as the ILGWU and others did not turn to cultural work in the United States, activists created an even larger sphere for such matters in the *Arbeter-ring*. By contrast, in Argentina *yidishkayt* was the decisive mobilising factor for any kind of community building within the Jewish workers' movement. Although rare occasions like the 1934 general strike indicate that a higher inclination towards radicalism and syndicalism continued to exist in Argentina as opposed to the US, Bundists in the workers' movement in Argentina, as in the US before them, acted as individual activists, never as representatives of the Bund as such.

John Bunzl notes with regard to the Russian Bund that 'the socio-cultural and political implications of the turn toward the Jewish masses ... best describe "Bundism" as a whole, its distinction from the Russian labour movement and its conflicts with the latter'.[125] Culture came to the fore in Argentina during the 1920s and 1930s. It was no longer necessary to approach 'the masses' through Yiddish, as the local movement recruited almost exclusively from proletarian milieus and thus had to coordinate and reconcile the relationship between distinct political and economic demands. Consequently, the cultural struggle was inherent to the economic struggle. Linguistically and politically important is that the main fault lines therein were not between Hebrew and Yiddish, but rather whether Yiddish represented mere prose or a political praxis as such.[126]

This combative Jewish worker culture defined itself through a vision of *yidishkayt* that always entailed a claim to cultural interpretation, although socialist utopias were no longer necessarily a vital component thereof. This *yidishkayt* was interwoven with globally emerging Jewish modernity, which (as was clearly visible at this point) was not the work of the Yiddish literati but a deeply proletarian praxis. The latter embedded the language in local structures and

---

125 Bunzl 1975, p. 57.
126 This was not only ongoing in Argentina itself, but also a self-perpetuating conflict between religious and secular definitions of Jewish identity since the Bund's early years, see Moss 2009, p. 23.

thus localised the transnational. This integration was of a social nature unrelated to the state, as the workers' movement remained on the other side of the barricades throughout its existence. The once-essential news from Europe and continental leaders receded into the background by the mid-1930s, only resurfacing (and most strongly so) in the Communist movement. That said, they would remain a highly abstract point of reference and thus allowed for the development of a markedly distinct form of Communism in Argentina.[127] This only changed with the rise of fascism, which Communists, similar to the Spanish Civil War and the outbreak of World War II, treated as a global event with organisational implications for Argentina.

The status of cultural work was elevated even in the face of such eminently political matters. In 1939, the *Heym-shneyder un tasheristn fareyn* announced a donation of 500 pesos to 'the members of Jewish families locked away in the concentration camps'.[128] The union leadership's annual report presented it as the most important element of the previous year's 'cultural work', and not of its solidarity or relief work as had been common in the past. This demonstrates the legitimising power of cultural understandings within the Jewish workers' movement, and testifies to the ongoing expansion of cultural work's applicability. Trade unions thus, due to their locally rooted character, also became cultural actors within the emerging transnational Yiddish community. This preserved *yidishkayt*'s left-wing, political, and movement nature, which had become a matter of debate between the socialist, Communist, Zionist, and (in Argentina) anarchist movements by the 1920s. The significance of the arguments they conducted and battles they waged to the history of the secular Jewish diaspora as a whole is best illustrated by the movements' educational work, the subject of the next chapter.

127 Foundational: Camarero 2007.
128 IWO, Buenos Aires, *Sindicatos, Boletines de la Unión Sastres a Domicilo, Talleristas y Anexos*, 1937–40, J.B. Raszer: *Memoria de la C.D.*, 29 October 1939, p. 2 f.

CHAPTER 11

Passing on *Yidishkayt*: Transfers and Limits of Bundist Educational Work

Conveying *yidishkayt* to the next generation was one of the Bund's primary concerns. The secular Jewish schools played an important role in these efforts. After World War I, the Polish Bund – and in turn Bundists around the world – devoted more and more energy to them. The transnational history of Bundist educational work demonstrates how the project of secular Jewish schools, undertaken with great enthusiasm in the US and Argentina, offered the chance to combine Bundist activism with other movements, while simultaneously revealing the limits of the Bund and Bundism within the migration process.

1   Worker Education and Worker Culture as Mediation

True to Russian Social Democratic tradition, Bundist educational work's main objective prior to 1917 was worker education. Due to the young age of its membership, the Bund also became a space for politicised coming-of-age, as the rebellious potential posed by a secular yet expressively Jewish movement proved particularly appealing to many young recruits.[1] While both the *kruzhki* and the American Jewish socialist circles from 1890 onwards understood education mainly as instruction in the natural sciences and sharpening of a historical materialist worldview, over the years Bundist education would increasingly evolve into a Yiddish-language cultural education with distinctively secular Jewish goals.

To supplement Marx, Tolstoy, and Gorky, the Bund began introducing Yiddish writers *oyf der yidishn gas*.[2] Smuggled or illegally printed novels also grew in importance, as they reflected activists' situations in simple language and thereby served to mobilise them.[3] An understanding of the 'state of the culture'

---

1   Discussed in Part I.2.
2   Pinson 1945, p. 237; Weinryb 1946, p. 226. According to Mendelsohn, Yiddish as the language of education was crucial in this regard, see Mendelsohn 1970, pp. 46–63.
3   Bund Archives, New York, RG 1400, ME-18, 226, S. Dikshteyn, *Fun vos eyner lebt* (Genf: Drukerei fun Bund, 1905). This is a popular edition of S. Dickstein's *Wovon lebt das Volk?*, printed as a stapled paper brochure (without cover, etc.) and thus well-suited to smuggling. Interest in

began to emerge from an understanding of the 'condition of the working class'. Analogous to their approach to class, Bundists sought to turn a culture 'in itself' into a culture 'for itself', linking the national-cultural utopia to a Yiddish-secular culture as a worker culture yet to be built.[4] Seeking to 'unite secularism and *yidishkayt*', Bundist activists initiated the 'evolution of a cultural movement'. It began with the education movements led by Jewish socialists in Russia, and ultimately resulted in the *Arbeter-ring* schools – at least according to Shmuel Niger's account, implicitly reflecting upon his own migration process.[5]

The history of Yiddish-speaking secular schools did not unfold in a linear manner, but rather as a network: one part of the story was the transfer of Russian, revolutionary teachings to the American-Yiddish cultural context. Closely linked to these were the emerging Bundist-run schools in Poland and Argentina, with developing mutual exchanges. The educational transfer was simultaneously a building process. As noted by Naomi Praer Kadar, migrants designed Yiddish-language school materials based on their desire 'to preserve and propagate the culture that they had brought from "the old country" for themselves, and especially their children'. This was no political or cultural 'souvenir' from the old home, but rather closely linked to 'the need to learn about and acclimate themselves to their new home'.[6]

Moreover, they understood educational work in Eastern Europe to a far greater extent as an object of remembrance worth reproducing. Firstly, activists knew that Yiddish-language educational work in Eastern Europe was only successful because it occupied a function in the here and now. Secondly, any activism including that of an educational or commemorative nature is intended to instigate further activism. A reduction to mere 'memory' is impossible in activist remembrance. Thirdly, the school activists overseas maintained close contacts with the TSYSHO in Poland. A historicisation of Yiddish educational practices therefore must also take the ideas and practices of activists on both sides of the Atlantic into consideration. Doing so opens up another transnational and generational level of this study, as it was clear from the first generational shift in 1917 onwards that Bundism as a revolutionary utopia required not only the activists 'of today', but a generation to succeed them as well. This

---

    simple literature was not unique to education-hungry Bundists. Cheaply produced stories of bandits and adventurers advanced literacy in Russia more generally. The same was true for the Jewish population, whose literacy rate may have been well above that of other groups in the Russian empire, but still amounted to only 50.1 percent of Russian Jews, quite contrary to the common stereotype of the 'people of the book'. See Brooks 2003; Kappeler 2014, p. 310.

4 Kazdan 1945; Niger 1940, p. 15.
5 Niger 1940, p. 1, p. 5.
6 Kadar 2007, p. 1.

changed the constellation of the workers' movement as a knowledge formation, while the Bund complemented its function as a cultural vehicle by also becoming an educational institution.[7]

2　The TSYSHO Model

Once legalised, Bundist educational work was no longer forced to rely on conspiracy and small-group structures. It could instead be disseminated freely and openly. As the Polish Bund increasingly transformed into a 'party', it nevertheless refrained from founding pure party schools, and addressed the issues affecting Jewish secularism in the broadest possible way. Consequently, the Bund in Poland forged alliances with other left-leaning Jewish parties, including above all the socialist wing of the equally divided Poale Zion. That union resulted in the foundation of the TSYSHO, the largest secular Jewish school network in independent Poland. The schools became a role model whose influence extended beyond the borders of Poland itself. As a reflection of the TSYSHO's success and progressive concept, it was invited to present its work at the 1937 Paris World Fair as part of the Polish pavilion.[8] Finding support within the country proved more difficult. Although the TSYSHO was founded in 1921, the state only recognised it in 1924 following a protracted legal battle, and provided financial support for only a brief period.[9]

This significant institution, which Bundists dominated by the early 1930s, can only be sketched out here. Basic statistics illustrate the efforts the Bund invested in its educational work: by 1930 the TSYSHO operated 114 comprehensive schools, 46 kindergartens, 52 evening schools, three grammar schools, one teachers' seminar, and the Medem Sanatorium.[10] The TSYSHO was able to consolidate its position over the 1930s through successful fundraising campaigns in the US in particular, despite declining support from the Joint Distribution Committee.

The schools were also closely linked to the SKIF and *Tsukunft*, the Bund's children's and youth organisations. TSYSHO and SKIF complemented one

---

7　Pickhan 2001a, pp. 236–48.
8　Pickhan 2001a, p. 242, fn. 251.
9　According to Gertrud Pickhan, the TSYSHO received no state funding whatsoever. Bundist letters from the time, however, contain hints of support of some type, albeit little more than 'a moral victory'. See Pickhan 2001a, p. 243; Bund Archives, New York, RG 1471, 5, 66, Letter to the Hilfsverein der deutschen Juden, 25 October 1928, p. 3f.
10　YIVO, New York, RG 48, 1; 8; Kazdan 1947, p. 316ff.; Pickhan 2001a, p. 240.

another in the mobilisation of the youngest Bundists, and as a cross-party institution the TSYSHO also attracted parents from Labour Zionist backgrounds. The classroom provided not only a Bundist, but more than anything a modern Jewish education, entailing Yiddish, secular, and socialist teachings at once. With branches all over Poland, the SKIF integrated children directly into the Bund, becoming a waystation for pupils from other school systems to enter the TSYSHO and the Bundist educational apparatus.[11] Around 25,000 Jewish pupils attended a TSYSHO school, representing a substantial share of the 500,000 Jewish schoolchildren in interwar Poland. That said, the overwhelming majority still attended state-run elementary schools, and the TSYSHO fell short of its goal to mobilise the entire Jewish population for a secular modernist project.[12] To expect as much was utopian to begin with, for these were modern and pedagogically very progressive movement schools.

A comprehensive historical study of the TSYSHO is unfortunately yet to be written.[13] According to available sources and literature, however, it is clear that despite its class struggle rhetoric it was not necessarily a school for hardened class warriors. Yiddish grew in importance together with cultural questions and the cultural struggle, while *yidishkayt* naturally remained a 'class-conscious' worker culture. Although education in Poland no longer worked to challenge state power directly (a central component of the Russian *kruzhki*), the TSYSHO was by no means a 'compromise school that props up the reaction and fascism'[14] like the other secular schools in Poland. Bundists perceived Yiddish culture as the most effective antidote to the former, and thus declared it the TSYSHO's prime objective. Correspondingly, Article 1 of the 1923 TSYSHO basic programme reads: 'Instruction in all public schools is to be conducted in the children's mother tongue'.[15] As stipulated by Article 5, this meant Yiddish for Jewish children.[16] While Polish grew increasingly common among working-class Jewish children in the interwar period, the programme's ethno-cultural aspect rejected tendencies towards nationalisation and 'assimilation'.

Many of the TSYSHO's ambitions were forestalled by the constantly dire state of its finances. In a bid to fund itself independently, the schools were compelled to introduce tuition fees – a considerable obstacle for those with 'nothing to

---

11 Pickhan 2001a, p. 238; Jacobs 2009, p. 39.
12 For exact figures see Kazdan 1947, pp. 183–9.
13 Important steps taken in Nishimura 2013.
14 Kazdan 1947, p. 316.
15 Kazdan 1947, p. 135.
16 Ibid. On the tense relationship between minority schools and the Polish state see the German example: Eser 2010, esp. p. 24ff., pp. 295–369.

lose but their chains'.[17] The Bund was aware of this dilemma. It decided to address it openly and highlight the TSYSHO's financial plight. Bundist fundraising efforts from the late 1920s onwards often rested on the argument that tuition was necessary, but too many parents could not afford to pay it.[18] Such calls for support emotionally depicted the TSYSHO as the essence of Bundist youth outreach. Former pupils later reiterated this as they recounted the TSYSHO's great value for their later lives.[19] Numerous accounts strike a similar tone.[20]

While the TSYSHO repeatedly struggled on the verge of financial collapse, it struggled far less with one major rift in modern Jewish history: the ideological conflict between Bundism and Zionism. Although the TSYSHO experienced internal strife in its early years, it managed to consolidate in Poland as soon as internal majorities (albeit not unanimous) were reached – Bundists had essentially taken over the organisation entirely by 1929–30. As Gertrud Pickhan notes, this did not occur through the occupation of certain offices, but rather as a result of educational leaders from other parties joining the Bund.[21] The Bund thus also rose in standing and appeal among leading educational activists.

Historians' opinions are overwhelmingly critical of the TSYSHO's impact on the Jewish population. According to Mendelsohn, the TSYSHO never managed to address the younger generation as a whole, which in his view raises the question of inherent limits to a 'Yiddishist program for Polish Jewry'.[22] Neither the Bund nor the TSYSHO were able to reform Jewry as such – and not only due to their financial weakness. Yet one must also be careful not to fall for the Bund's claim to sole representation, as such rhetoric is part and parcel of any movement's standard repertoire. As an expression of Jewish modernity, the TSYSHO prioritised actor-based functional differentiation while strengthening its character as a counter-cultural and class-based institution. This alone turned it into a structural counterpart to homogenising Jewish projects. Moreover, the TSYSHO was not only oriented towards secularism and socialism, but was also a strong advocate of pedagogical reform. This earned it international merits like public praise from progressive German pedagogy professors or its aforemen-

---

17 Jacobs 2009, p. 39.
18 Such as Bund Archives, New York, RG 1471, 66, Letter to the Hilfsverein der deutschen Juden, 25 October 1928, p. 3; Ibid, Letter from I. Lichtenstein and J. Lestschinski to the Jewish congregation in Berlin, 25 April 1930.
19 Bund Archives, New York, RG 1471, 66, Letter to the Hilfsverein der deutschen Juden, 25 October 1928, p. 1.
20 See numerous contributions in Kazdan 1952; Kazdan 1971.
21 Pickhan 2001a, p. 239f.
22 Quoted in Jacobs 2009, p. 78.

tioned participation in the 1937 Paris World Fair, but was a significant reason for pause among the largely conservative majority of Jewish parents.[23]

Its rhetoric may have called for a comprehensive renewal of Jewish education, but its actual practice represented the activist counter-culture of a progressive section of Polish Jewry.[24] Thus, historical evaluation of these schools and their attendance delivers a different verdict when taking activist factors into account. The ideological debates held among the institutions' leaderships had little influence on educational practice, nor were they particularly relevant to Polish Jews 'as a whole' to begin with. Every Jewish political movement in the interwar period constituted a minority project, albeit with the potential to become a mass movement just like the Bund. Yet the Bund was *a* movement that never became *the* movement – and precisely this made it the protagonist of modernising currents within Polish Jewish life.[25] In this sense, the TSYSHO's schools sought to develop an educational programme for the Jewish 'nation', and with this focus joined the Bundist realm of institutions to build a transnational socialist culture in the Yiddish language.[26]

3   Building Worker Education Overseas

Activists migrating across the Atlantic naturally felt obligated to pass on and further refine secular Jewishness. The *Avangard* and other Argentinian groups around 1910 understood education as worker education (primarily through the aforementioned lectures). In the US, however, the question of secular Jewish education for the next generation arose as a response to the mass arrival of Jewish socialist activists after 1905.[27] Labour Zionists and Bundists both recog-

---

23   Bund Archives, New York, RG 1471, 5; 66; Letter to the Hilfsverein der deutschen Juden, 28 March 1928, p. 2; 55 percent of Jewish pupils at non-state-run schools attended the religious and conservative oriented schools of the *Aguda*, Pickhan 2001a, p. 237, p. 242, fn. 251.
24   Former TSYSHO chairman Kazdan later recalled: 'The TSYSHO was one of the greatest creative experiments of Polish Jewry. Its establishment was a pledge that the era of chaos in the education of the generation still coming of age had come to an end, the dawning of an era of conscious national school building, a phase of active creation by the people on the terrain of schools and education', see Kazdan 1956, p. 441.
25   Here the concept of Critical Mass Theory again proves helpful, as it convincingly states that activist groups can become immobile if they exceed or fall short of a certain group size. See esp. Oliver und Marwell 1988.
26   See Pickhan 2001a, p. 236.
27   Efforts to found a Jewish secular school in Argentina can be traced back to 1906, but were marginal compared to subsequent attempts and essentially unrelated to the schools

nised the importance of such efforts around the same time. As early as 1909, the Poale Zionist Joel Entin argued in *'Di varhayt'* for the establishment of public secular Jewish schools in the US to combine education as a 'global citizen' with a 'Jewish education'.[28] He saw this as especially necessary because the 'hundreds of thousands of Jewish radicals in America' who appeared content with their 'assimilation into the Christian population' did not want their children to 'lose their *yidishkayt*'.[29] Entin was able to convince the Labour Zionist counterpart to the *Arbeter-ring*, the *Farband*, of his position, and became a protagonist of the first secular Jewish school network in the United States.[30]

4 Secondary Bundism and Secular Jewish Schools in the US

The *Arbeter-ring* undertook similar initiatives around the same time. Its tenth annual congress chose to replace the struggling *'Di tsukunft'* with the new periodical, *'Fraynd'*. The decision was an expression of a greater restructuring driven by migrant Bundists, most notable among them the paper's first editor-in-chief, Zivion. He saw the new periodical as a symbol of the reversal of the *Arbeter-ring*'s politics. It was now evident to all that the organisation was 'more than a mere insurance trust', as the matter at hand was something 'different, greater, more idealistic, that cannot be measured in dollars or cents'.[31] Integrating schools as a vital component of the wider organisation would help to establish the *Arbeter-ring* as an independent cultural actor. As convincing as this was to many, these visionaries soon faced opposition from those who insisted that the *Arbeter-ring* was 'a socialist and not a Jewish order'.[32] The proponents of this idea had already established Sunday schools, created not for the sake of propagating Jewish culture but exclusively for the socialist class struggle. Although schools were needed in the Jewish immigrant culture in New York, the approach failed to satisfy the *tuer* and parents in the long run.[33]

---

of the 1920s; see IWO, Buenos Aires, 1111 [Educación], Sociedad Amigos de la Education, Receipt for 'Senior Guillermo' (1906). Equally important were the language schools run by the group surrounding the *'Shtime fun avangard'* from 1909 onwards, see Di shtime fun avangard 1909b.

28 Entin 1960b, p. 1.
29 Entin 1960a, p. 10 f.
30 Fishman 2009, p. 71.
31 Cited in Hertz 1950, p. 110.
32 Niger 1940, p. 44 f.
33 Niger 1940, p. 44. The first school of this kind was founded in 1906 by *Arbeter-ring* branch 2 in Harlem, New York, followed by a second institution on Madison Street in downtown New York in 1907; see Hertz, 1950, p. 115.

Bundists knew from their own experience that educational movements could only be sustained if quarrels between the involved parties remained in the background. Zivion articulated this position in an article, 'The *Arbeter-ring* and its Cultural Tasks', written in the run-up to the *Arbeter-ring*'s 1910 congress. Here, he argued that it was harmful for children to be overloaded with socialist doctrine, noting that 'children's socialism' would necessarily be vulgar socialism.[34] Thus, schools ought to ensure 'that the child is permitted to develop as a free human being' – which included learning about 'Jewish history in Yiddish'. Almost in passing, Zivion stated that a little Hebrew would not hurt either. As a well-versed socialist, he considered teaching Yiddish the primary task, which could not be left to the Hebrewists 'nor the wild meshuggeners from the Sunday schools'.[35] In his view, 'Jewish children ought to learn about Jewish history and Yiddish literature just like Russian children learn about Russian history and Russian literature and German children learn about German history and German literature'.[36]

It is telling that his formulation is almost identical to the Polish TSYSHO schools' basic programme (Article 5) adopted 13 years later.[37] Yet cultural work always also implied developing class consciousness: 'I want the young worker children to grow up not only as socialists but as Jewish socialists, meaning socialists who not only preach socialism into the air, but who seek to connect it to life'.[38] Against this backdrop, it is hardly surprising that many Bundists became education activists in the United States. These battles, in which socialism and *yidishkayt* were inextricably linked, were the Bundists' home turf.

Established in 1910, the education committee became a fixed component of the *Arbeter-ring*.[39] At first it refrained from creating a centrally coordinated school system. Instead, individual *Arbeter-ring* branches opened the first independent schools with the support of the *Federatsye* in the 1910s. Conditions

---

34 Bund Archives, New York, RG 1400, Workman's Circle Collection, 15, Benzion [Zivion] Hoffman 1910, 'Der arbeter ring un zeyne kultur-oyfgabn', *Suvenir: Der tsenter yerlikher konvenshon gevidmet* (New York: Arbeter ring), p. 177.
35 All quotes taken from Bund Archives, New York, RG 1400, Workman's Circle Collection, 15, Hoffman, 'Der arbeter ring un zeyne kultur-oyfgabn'. Also quoted in Niger 1940, p. 45 f.
36 Ibid.
37 Kazdan 1947, p. 135.
38 All quotes taken from Bund Archives, New York, RG 1400, Workman's Circle Collection, 15, Hoffman, *Der arbeter ring un zeyne kultur-oyfgabn*; also quoted in Niger 1940, p. 45 f.
39 The formation of this 10-person committee was stipulated by a resolution at the eighth *Arbeter-ring* congress in 1908. The tenth congress, however, then set the committee's main focus on promoting Yiddish literacy through special courses, although this also quickly led to vibrant publishing activities. See Hertz 1950, p. 111.

were rather favourable in the US and particularly in the multi-ethnic state of New York, where Jewish schools – as ethnically or religiously oriented supplementary schools – enjoyed a considerable degree of freedom. The same applied to the secular socialist schools, of which there were already 10 with a student body of 1,500 by 1911.[40] Apart from Vladeck, Shakhne Epshteyn (still a Bundist at the time) played an important role in this network. Both adopted Zivion's argument and assumed control of the school movement, which became a hallmark of the *Arbeter-ring* in the 1920s.[41] Educational work was not confined exclusively to schools, however. Early secondary-Bundist educational work was still very much guided by the enlightenment goals of both early American socialism as well as Bundism.

In 1914 the *Arbeter-ring*'s New York-based education committee officially received the assignment to help local branches open Yiddish libraries. To this end it began publishing secular teaching materials in Yiddish. The earliest of these textbooks was titled *The World and Humanity*. Its first edition of 6,000 copies mostly went to multipliers in the Jewish community, accompanied by presentations and lectures across the country.[42] This success marked the beginning of the *Arbeter-ring* library series, which included numerous popular scientific volumes between 100–400 pages long, mostly by authors with a doctorate in their respective field. The series' areas of focus generally aligned with the themes of socialist and Bundist educational work in Russia and Poland. During these early years, the *Arbeter-ring* primarily conveyed basic secular, that is to say scientific and social knowledge to the reading worker. The approach echoed a historical materialist perspective in which the Yiddish language was more a practice than cultural goal, as underscored by the subtitle of Sol Finestone's chemistry textbook, 'For Reading and Learning'. These books rarely explicitly reflected on socialism as a theory, which instead constituted the basic worldview behind these publications and their goals. Only four books explicitly discussed socialist questions (see Table 13). Jewishness appeared as an element of world history, and was less a topic than a practice in the form of the Yiddish language in which the books were written. Only one book in the initial series was devoted to Jewish history, while the majority conveyed a general humanist education in the broadest sense. A significant change had been set in motion: while Zivion still called for Jewish children to learn Jewish history in Yiddish in 1919,

---

40   Hertz 1950, p. 115.
41   Niger 1940, p. 47 f.
42   Hertz 1950, p. 111. The book focused primarily on universal education with an emphasis on the natural sciences. It also contained contributions by Poale Zionist Nachman Syrkin and leading New York Bundist Abraham Caspe, see Terman 1913.

TABLE 13   Books published by the *Natsyonal edukeyshonal komite fun arbeter ring*

Author	Title	Years of issue	Field
Terman, Morris (ed.)	*Di velt un di menshheyt. 12 forlezungen iber der entviklung fun natur un kultur mit 44 ilustratsyonen un 18 bilder*	1913	Science, Cultural History
Krantz, Philip, and Alexander Harkavy	*Gants Amerika. Di geshikhte fun ale lender in der nayer velt*	1915	History, Geography
Merison, Y.A.	*Higyene. Di lehre vi tsu ferhiten doz gesund (mit bilder)*	1916	Medicine
Chaim Žitlovski	*Der sotsyalizm fun die sotsyalistenrevolutsyoneren*	1916, 1917	Politics, Socialism
Levin, L.	*Der treyt yunyonizm*	1916, 1917	Politics, Economics, Society
Zaks, Abraham S.	*Botanik oder dos leben fun flantsen. Mit bilder*	1916, 1917	Botany
Caspe, Abraham	*Fizik (mit bilder)*	1916, 1917	Physics
Caspe, Abraham	*Geologye*	1918	Geology
Hofman, Benzion [Zivion]	*Astronomye*	1918	Astronomy
Zaks, Abraham S.	*Politishe ekonomye. Di grund-printsipen*	1918, 1920, 1924	Political Economy
Merison, Y.A.	*Fizologye fun menshen*	1918, 1925	Biology
Burgin, Herts	*Lehr-bukh far aritmetik*	1919	Mathematics
Hofman, Benzion [Zivion]	*Dos leben fun hayes. Tsoologye*	1919	Zoology
Stolinsky, Aharon	*Di kooperative bavegung. Vos zi iz un vos zi zayn darf*	1919	Politics, Society
Salutsky, Hannah G.	*Dos kind. Fizishe dertsihung*	1920	Pedagogy
Faynstun, Sol (Finestone, Sol)	*Khemye. Tsu lezen un tsu lernen*	1920	Chemistry
Heifetz, Elias	*Pogrom geshikhte (1919–1920). Di ukrayinishe shhite in 1919*	1921	Jewish History
Evensky, Michael	*Bukhfirung far brentshes fun arbeter-ring un entlikhe organsatsye*	1922	Administration, Economics

Legend: dark grey: science, general education; medium grey: guidebook; light grey: socialism; white: Jewish history

over the following years this grew into a comprehensive interpretation of the world and world history in Yiddish for young people and workers alike. In this regard, the practice of the *Arbeter-ring* library series demonstrates how deeply the organisation's cultural work prior to 1917 was still rooted in nineteenth-century humanist socialism. Similar to Bundist *Memorik* at the time, a distinctive profile of the movement's or the organisation's 'own history' had not yet formed.

5 Institutionalising the Schools

As in the *Avangard* group, *yidishkayt* was not only a topic in lectures, library collections, or proletarian theatre. It held together a lifeworld of secular knowledge and identity along with class consciousness on both sides of the Atlantic. Nevertheless, Yiddish as an aesthetic language would only gradually emerge behind political economy and the natural sciences.

Arbeter-ring schools played a greater role in this shift than the publishing houses. In light of the second generation, it became evident that if a Yiddish culture was to survive beyond the first generation of Jewish immigrants, Yiddish could not be used as a tool for teaching but had to be taught itself. This also brought the secondary-Bundist organisations together in terms of personnel. Many *Federatsye* members were at the same time active *tuer* in the *Arbeter-ring*, and as Shmuel Niger notes had 'a great degree of influence, as did the *tuer* of the *Yidish natsyonaler arbeter farband* at their Sholem Aleichem Schools'.[43]

In return, delegates to a 1915 *Federatsye* conference resolved to give education the highest priority. Representatives at the *Arbeter-ring* annual congress in 1916 accepted this decision, leading to the ceremonious founding of the *Arbeter-ring* schools as a separate organisation and core element of the *Arbeter-ring* in 1919.[44] *Arbeter-ring* and *Federatsye* had founded schools in cooperation even prior to this event. The first such institution was established in 1915 on 104th Street, South Harlem, and the second, a Sunday school run by the *Federatsye*, in Chicago on 21 May 1916.

Three distinct currents of secular Jewish schools would subsequently develop in the US: a Labour Zionist current, a secondary-Bundist current, and a cross-party current, to which a fourth Communist current was added after the *Arbeter-ring* split in 1926 (Table 14).[45] The differences between these currents went beyond their political programmes and the language question; ultimately, the claim to secular Jewish education was the only common denominator between them. Consequently, narratives of historical legitimacy differed from school to school.[46] While Shmuel Niger, a highly influential literary critic and historian commissioned by the *Arbeter-ring*, situated their roots primarily in Russia – that is to say, in the era of the *kruzhki* and the Bund's origins – Entin,

---

43   Niger 1940, p. 50.
44   This was preceded by the *Arbeter-ring* sporadically founding schools as local initiatives between 1913–18, such as in Rock Island, Albany, Rochester, and Peterson. See Niger 1940, pp. 48–51.
45   Fishman 2009, p. 72.
46   Fishman 2009, p. 73.

TABLE 14 Secular Jewish school organisations in the US before World War II

	Farband-shuln	Sholem Aleichem Folk Institute	Arbeter-ring-shuln	IWO-shuln
Founded	1910	1913	1919, with precursors from 1913	1926, following the split of the *Arbeter-ring*
Party orientation	Associated with Poale Zion	Independent, partially influenced by Poale Zion	Secondary-Bundist, socialist	Communist, dominated by IWO from 1930 onwards
Emphases	Yiddish and Hebrew, raising interest in Palestine	No strict party orientation, Yiddish dominant, no Hebrew at the primary-school level until 1940	Socialism and Yiddish, no Hebrew at the primary-school level	Yiddish, pro-Communist values and interest in the Soviet Union
Pupils in 1934	5,598	1,976	6,013	6,800

ACCORDING TO NIGER 1940, P. 49 F.; ENTIN 1946, PP. 145–97; FISHMAN 2009, P. 72 F.

the founding father of the *Farband*'s Poale Zionist schools, traced them to Eastern European emigration.[47] He thereby shifted the schools' motivation entirely to the American context. According to Entin, Jewish modernity emerged not from the movement-oriented transnationalism of Bundist *doikayt*, but rather from an emigratory mindset fed by Zionism. Although Niger had Labour Zionist roots, he could not agree to that, as this justification marginalised the Bundist role in US secular Jewish schools.

6   The Secondary-Bundist Cultural Agenda: Linking Socialism and Jewishness in the *Arbeter-ring* Schools

The question of how *yidishkayt* could be implemented in the American English-speaking schools – that is, how culture and socialism could be combined in the curriculum – arose in all secondary-Bundist organisations. By the late 1910s it had already led to open disputes between secondary-Bundist and Labour Zionist concepts. In juxtaposition to one another, these concepts demonstrate how the broad common denominator of secular Jewish education was too vague for a common secular school system. The numerous *tuer* of the *Arbeter-ring* schools, who regarded themselves as part of an interna-

---

47   Entin 1946, p. 151.

tionalist Jewish school movement more in emulation of the Polish TSYSHO schools than the American institutions, complemented this development from the 1920s onwards.⁴⁸

The schools of the Poale Zionist *Farband* attempted to address Jewishness holistically, albeit through untraditional combinations. The focus of its initial teacher-training programme in 1917 was on Yiddish and Hebrew as equally important literary languages, accompanied by English and literature, Jewish history, mathematics, and the natural sciences along with pedagogy and psychology. The curriculum also included a supplemental course on socialism and political economy and a two-year Talmud course. Although the Talmud was to be studied from a historical and cultural perspective rather than a religious or legalist vantage point, the *Farband* managed in this way to link the history of the Jewish nation with the Jewish faith. The other secular schools opposed this interlinking with their own national-ethnic or class-based concepts of Jewish history. In the important subject of political history, the *Farband* trained its teachers in the history of modern Jewish parties and movements leading up to Poale Zion. Delegates approved this school programme unanimously at the *Farband*'s 1917 congress – overlooking the comments of a famous observer, renowned historian and cultural scholar Elias Tscherikover, who rejected the agenda as 'amateurish'.⁴⁹

The *Arbeter-ring* schools developed founding guidelines designed to combine socialism and *yidishkayt* in 1919. As David Fishman notes, this move helped place cultural aspects of Jewishness at the heart of *Arbeter-ring* educational efforts. In his opinion, it also led to the paradoxical situation that Jewish pupils were brought up in a secular culture which their parents could not live out themselves.⁵⁰ From the standpoint of movement history, however, *Arbeter-ring* secondary-Bundist *yidishkayt* cannot be reduced to a secular culturalism. In context, it represented a complex socialist and consciously Jewish working-class culture that many students' parents had wanted to live out well before emigration and now finally could.

The *Arbeter-ring* relied not only on cold, scholastic education, but primarily on emotional appeal. This was important to 'familiarise [the children] with the life of workers and the broad Jewish masses in all countries', with the 'life of the Yiddish people and episodes of its freedom struggle embedded in general history'. It was the only way that 'a sense of community, love for the oppressed, love for freedom, and respect for the freedom fighters could develop in them'. These

---

48   Bund Archives, New York, RG 1471, 74, Letter to Baskin [193?].
49   Entin 1946, p. 196.
50   Fishman 2009.

and similar guidelines established in 1919 were intended to support 'the child of the oppressed class on its further life path to a better order'.[51] In the process, *Arbeter-ring* schools followed a long-term programme set out in refined curricula from 1927 onwards.[52] In that year the *Arbeter-ring* schools also adopted a central programme: 'The children's schools of the Arbeter-ring rest on three pillars: it is a Yiddish, socialist and free-thinking [school organisation]'. Free-thinking in this context primarily meant 'developing in the child the habit of thinking with its own head'.[53] Likewise, it was fairly easy to emphasise the relevance of Yiddish by referencing a transnational focus: 'Our school seeks to connect the Jewish child in America with millions of Jews who live, fight for, enjoy and create their own culture in their own language and according to the specific national nuances – in Poland, Russia, Romania, and other countries', although Yiddish was also to be conveyed as the 'history of their stock [*stam*]'.[54] No mention is made of religion as a foundational element of Jewish identity.

The programme found expression in the simultaneously compiled curricula, which Bundist archivists interestingly viewed as pieces of Bundist history themselves and stored in a special collection at the Bund Archives. The highest priority was to 'teach the children thoroughly how to read, write and speak in the Yiddish language', combined with instruction on Yiddish literature.[55] In contrast to the politically radicalised Yiddish in Communist movements, these schools taught Yiddish as a language connected to Jewish historical roots. That, for instance, meant that Hebraisms were neither banned nor vocalised, but instead imparted to children from the outset.[56] This, however, followed a carefully designed learning curve: the elementary school's first-year curriculum stipulated a total of only 19 Hebrew terms, 99 in the second, and 131 and 156 Hebrew words over the next two years.[57] These roughly 400 words even allowed those students who did not absorb the *mame loshn* (mother tongue) from their parents to read Yiddish literature. In the United States, the number of such stu-

---

51 Niger 1940, p. 108.
52 The teacher-training curriculum that remained in effect for quite some time was worked out as early as 1925. YIVO, New York, RG 575, Unsorted items, *Eynteylung fun di lektsyes fun di A.R. lerern kursn* (1925).
53 Program fun di arbeter ring shuln 1927, p. 5.
54 Program fun di arbeter ring shuln 1927, p. 3.
55 Bund Archives, New York, RG 1400, ME-13, 281, *Elementar shul. Reshime fun verter vos shtomen fun hebreish* [1924–5?], p. 1.
56 Shneer 2004, p. 70.
57 Bund Archives, New York, RG 1400, ME-13, 281, *Elementar shul: Reshime fun verter vos shtomen fun hebreish* [1924–5?], p. 1f.

dents constantly rose. Knowledge of this literature was more than an education in the classics – it served as an emotional tie to Jewish history and tradition.

Likewise, the *Arbeter-ring* schools' relationship to socialism rested on an emotional basis, rather than training in strict historical materialism:

> Our school is a socialist school. It seeks to instil in the child a profound love for labour and the worker masses, understanding and compassion for the struggle for a better life that the masses have always waged, and for the greater struggle that the working class is fighting today for the joyous future of all humanity. At our school children develop a clear picture of the socialist ideal; they come to understand modern organisation and the daily struggle of the working class: unions, cooperatives, political parties, *Arbeter-ring*, strikes, lockouts, boycotts and the like. Our school wishes to familiarise the children with the revolutionary heroes of humanity, to enrich their socialisation with the creators, leaders, and famous *tuer* of the socialist and workers' movement; it seeks to implant an activist idealism, steadfastness and the willingness to sacrifice, *khavershaft* and a sense of the collective. We *do not teach the child* programme socialism. A child is too young for that. It would not understand it and thus have to simply believe every word we say.[58]

Zivion's Bundist approach from 1910 had in fact been implemented. Middle school pupils studied Yiddish and Yiddish literature several hours per week, combined with Jewish and general history but also the 'history of the freedom movements' and revolutionary movements, complemented in the third and final year by political economy and the relationship between the workers' movement and socialism.[59] The humanist general education of the 1910s as well as the Enlightenment-based natural sciences – both of which represented the very essence of early worker education – moved to the background of this educational programme. Exams primarily tested pupils' knowledge of Jewish culture and history, although always in a cultural or historical and never a religious sense. For instance, final exam questions in the third year included 'Describe Jewish life in a shtetl', 'Name two women whom you are familiar with through Yiddish literature', 'Describe the life of Jews under the rule of the kings', or 'Describe the life of Jews in Babel'.[60] Questions of a historical materialist nature, referred to as 'social' questions, were also a regular component: 'What

---

58   Program fun di arbeter ring shuln 1927, p. 4.
59   Bund Archives, New York, RG 1400, WC, 280, *Shul-bukh* (1927–8), p. 30.
60   Bund Archives, New York, RG 1400, WC, 281, *Inerlekhe arbet in di shuln* [1924–5?], p. 29.

are unions, strikes, general strikes ...', 'Where does unemployment come from', 'How did money originate?', 'What is paper money?', and, above all, 'How can economic inequality between people be overcome?'[61]

This shows that Jewishness was never seen as somehow opposed to being revolutionary – both were combined in one cultural context. In fact, the workers' movement was part of the exam as early as the first year, taught in the form of H. Leivick's dramatic poem 'The Chains of the Messiah',[62] composed by renowned Bundist poet (and temporary Communist) Leivik in 1918 while imprisoned in Minsk. He later described the poem as pathbreaking for all his later work.[63] In the first year of middle school, no less than 30 lessons on socialist history addressed regional differences as well as socialism's origins in more depth, from antiquity to modernity.[64] The second year focused on European modernisation, discussed and conveyed on the basis of the guiding themes 'A comparison between the struggle of the past and that of today', 'The role of the working class in the Revolution of 1830–1848 and the Revolution after the World War', or 'Challenges of the mass struggle'.

The third year of middle school taught the history of socialism since the late nineteenth century and focused entirely on the American labour movement. The curricula neither hailed the Bund as sole protagonist nor relegated it to a 'pariah' of the Jewish workers' movement, just as they did not address Zionist movements.[65] Despite the distance to the Bund as an organisation, the *Arbeter-ring* schools taught Jewish history as a history of the Jewish diaspora and thus analogous to Bundist *doikayt* – as a cultural history rich with activism and resistance in its respective environments.[66] At the same time, the schools also emphasised internal divisions between Jews, while making particular mention of the Bund's progressive character as an expression of modern Jewish history under the rubric 'Religion's struggle against secular knowledge'.[67] The Bund's pioneering role with regard to the *Arbeter-ring*'s Jewish socialism manifested rather implicitly. The first step was an introduction to 'socialists among the Jews', followed by a second session on 'Jewish socialism'. This again displays a typical characteristic of the *Arbeter-ring*: the title avoids the term 'Bund', but the

---

61 Ibid.
62 Leivick 1940.
63 Leivick 1940, p. 395. Bund Archives, New York, RG 1400, WC, 281, *Inerlekhe arbet in di shuln* [1924–5?], p. 31.
64 Bund Archives, New York, RG 1400, WC, 281, *Geshikhte fun sotsyalizm* [1924–5?].
65 Bund Archives, New York, RG 1400, WC, 281, *Geshikhte fun sotsyalizm* [1924–5?].
66 Bund Archives, New York, RG 1400, WC, 281, *Program far yidisher geshikhte* [1924–5?].
67 Bund Archives, New York, RG 1400, WC, 281, *Proyekt far a program fun nayer yidisher geshikhte far der a.r. mitlshul, klas d* [1924–5?], p. 4.

subject matter of these two lessons was quite evidently a history of the Bund from a Bundist perspective.[68] That was not lost on pupils, as Bundist Julius Baron proudly reiterates. His daughter received a 'radical Jewish upbringing' at the middle school, familiarising her with 'Jewish history, the class struggle and socialism'. As a result, the Bundist parents had successfully done everything to 'educate her according to their sacred ideals'.[69]

The greatest difference between Bundism and secondary Bundism, however, lay in how they historicised the Bund. From the schools' perspective, the Bund merely represented a historical template and was therefore no more than one, albeit fundamentally important, part of the *Arbeter-ring*'s educational programme. The Bund stood for the beginning of a self-confident present that now continued even more proudly than before. The idea did not remain confined to theory, as a school essay by Rakhel Lutik, a 1930 graduate of the *Arbeter-ring* School 2 in the Bronx, demonstrates. She emphasises that the Bund pushed forward the development of Yiddish 'from the language of the people to the national language', a process in which

> the tailor apprentice ceased to be a mark of shame on the family. ... The Bund not only created the Yiddish reading worker, but also helped ensure that this reader had something to live ... Of course, the Bund did not only pursue cultural work. Everything was connected to socialist politics. ... The 'Bund' never only fought for the well-fed worker, but also for a cultural one.

Aware of this legacy, she looked 'to the future filled with hope', as the *Arbeter-ring* now came to symbolise all this and more.[70] In this sense the *Arbeter-ring* also distorted history in its own favour. After all, the Bund's cultural work had initially been little more than a necessary supplement to the revolutionary struggle in the Tsarist empire, and only eventually became a cornerstone of the party programme and activism in itself. Nevertheless, the Bund remained the central historical pivot of both *yidishkayt* and *doikayt*.

This also explains the vehemence with which the organisation conducted its internal fight against Communism after the *Arbeter-ring* split in 1926. Second-

---

68 Bund Archives, New York, RG 1400, WC, 281, *Proyekt far a program fun nayer yidisher geshikhte far der a.r. mitlshul, klas d* [1924–5?], p. 5.
69 YIVO, New York, RG 102, 115 [Julius Baron], p. 33.
70 Bund Archives, New York, RG 1400, WC, 249, Rakhel Lutik, Rakhel 1927, 'Der "Bund" un zayne virkung oyf der yidisher sprakh und kultur', *Tsen yor arbeter ring shul 2, bronks* (New York).

ary Bundism represented a political line within the educational programme of the *Arbeter-ring* in 1927 precisely because it was not explicit: 'We do not seek to corrupt the children's hearts with fraternal hatred. We shall teach only that which unites socialists with all other righteous people, not what divides them'.[71] Socialism was to be taught 'emotionally, innocently' – in contrast to the emerging Communist schools that split off in 1926 and now agitated against the *Arbeter-ring*.[72]

Hidden behind this unity rhetoric lay the conviction that the lessons being taught represented the only acceptable understanding of Jewish-socialist culture – which in turn was always associated with the Bund. In this context, former TSYSHO chairman Kazdan published an article in the *Arbeter-ring* education committee's publication *'Unzer schul'* in 1932, rejecting Shmuel Niger's claims by referring to the Bund's current strength in Poland. Niger had previously lamented that the Yiddish-socialist education system used Yiddish merely for reasons of self-preservation, lest it eventually disappear. Kazdan replied that the Bund had already deployed Yiddish on a massive scale for progressive rather than defensive reasons in 1905.[73] Incidentally, Niger himself already declared as much in 1908 together with A. Litvak in *'Der tog'*, a journal he co-edited that supported the Bund.[74]

At the outset of the 1930s, Bundists were confronted with a rival in non-Zionist, left-radical and Yiddish cultural consciousness: Communism. When education activist B. Byalostotski attempted to explain the different currents of Yiddishism and the problem of the Yiddish Communist current's strength in the US, he managed to do so only by pointing to the positions of the Polish Bund, which did not adhere to 'pure Yiddishism' but rather socialist ideas.[75] Apparently, what distinguished the Yiddish secularism of the *Arbeter-ring* from the secularism of Yiddish Communism was a question of cultural politics inherited from overseas. Nevertheless, the battle engulfed the organisation. From the mid-1920s onwards, and based on a heightened emphasis on the Bund's history as the core of Jewish modernism, Yiddish Communists were increasingly attacked as saboteurs who kicked off the 'leftist storm' and thereby also inflicted significant damage to the school system.[76]

---

71 Program fun di arbeter ring shuln 1927, p. 4f.
72 Program fun di arbeter ring shuln 1927, p. 5.
73 Kazdan 1932, p. 3, p. 5.
74 Litvak 1908. I was made aware of this source during David Fishman's 4 November 2010 lecture at Johns Hopkins University, and would like to extend my thanks to him.
75 Byalostotski 1932, p. 9f.
76 Bund Archives, New York, RG 1400, WC, 280, *Shul-bukh* (1927–8), p. 3.

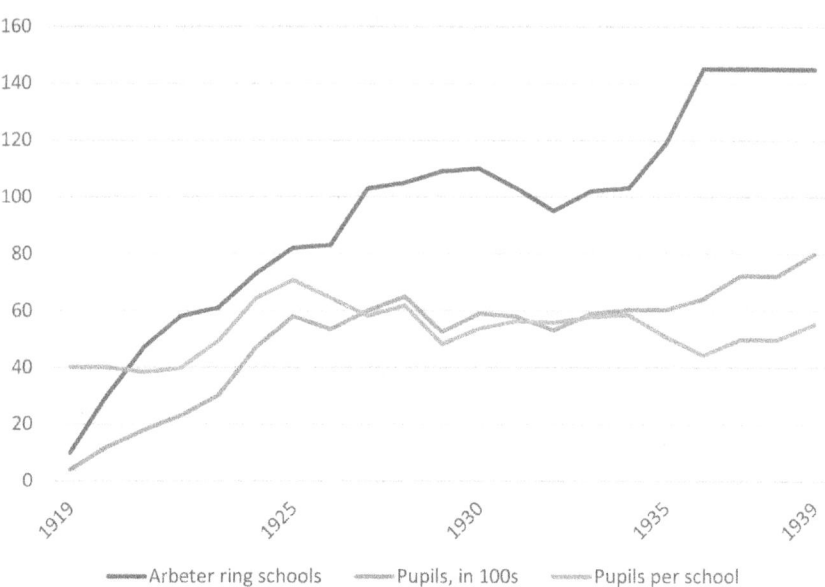

FIGURE 19   Number and size of *Arbeter-ring* schools, 1919–39

The conflict also reverberated in school life, as the *Arbeter-ring* schools stagnated following the split (see Figure 19).[77] The number of pupils rose steadily well into the mid-1920s, but the 1926 break between the *Arbeter-ring*'s Social Democratic and Communist factions led to the departure of 17 schools, preparing the ground for the *Arbeter-ordn* (IWO) schools founded in 1930.[78] The split reduced the overall size of the secondary-Bundist school movement only marginally, but robbed it of its momentum. Most importantly, many pupils' decampment to Communist schools posed a serious threat to the *Arbeter-ring*'s claim to sole representation. The organisation's claim to be the only legitimate representative of Yiddish culture proved less and less convincing, reflecting more than anything the divisions emerging between Bundist parents.

The *Arbeter-ring*'s 1935 school almanac conceded that the left, meaning the Communists, had become the strongest force in the secular school system. According to the *Arbeter-ring*'s Central Committee, in 1935 only 1,100 pupils attended the non-partisan Sholem Aleichem Schools, while 5,600 pupils attended the 56 schools of the Poale Zionist *Farband* and 6,043 pupils attended the 103 *Arbeter-ring* schools. They were all clearly outnumbered by the 8,000 pupils

---

77   Data taken from Niger 1940, p. 89f.
78   Kadar 2007, p. 90f.

enrolled at the 144 IWO schools.[79] David Fishman arrives at a somewhat lower estimate for 1934, but that changes little in the general impression that IWO schools not only engaged in an ideological struggle against the *Arbeter-ring*, but also threatened to outcompete it in quantitative terms.[80]

7 The Limits of Tradition

Another problem was that of children's 'emotional' consciousness. David Fishman makes the point that second-generation immigrants lacked life experience in traditional Jewish surroundings, and due to their unfamiliarity with the traditional way of life often failed to grasp the relevance of secular Jewishness.[81] While the schools certainly experienced returning crises, the data observed in this study, which mainly reflects the position from inside the *Arbeter-ring*, the workers' movement, and affiliated schools, cannot support this interpretation. Firstly, the figures demonstrate that the splits never led to a full-blown crisis of the secular school movement prior to 1939. Secondly, the problems emerged from within – that is to say not out of a struggle between secularism and religion, but as a result of Yiddish Communism's growing strength. IWO schools reinterpreted many Bundist symbols as their own and incorporated Bundist history as their own pre-history. A striking example is the existence of the Communist *Hirsh Lekert – Yidishe arbeter kinder shul*, where pupils were taught a heroic and simultaneously Communist-proletarianised version of the Bundist spontaneous terrorist Hirsh Lekert.[82]

Communist and socialist currents were not all that emerged from the *Arbeter-ring*'s 1926 split. Several non-partisan schools also developed under the auspices of the *Arbeter-ring*, such as the *Umparteyishe yidishe arbeter-kinder shul* in the Bronx, founded in 1926. It should be noted, however, that in these cases non-partisan did not mean non-political. They simply avoided taking sides in the debate as to how far to the left one should move, with socialist secondary Bundism marking the furthest demarcation to the right. The polit-

---

79 Vald 1935, p. 105, p. 129, p. 141, p. 161.
80 Fishman 2009, p. 72.
81 Fishman 2009. Religious activity also contained a political aspect, but a complex religious Jewishness was able to develop in the US without interference from the state, see Eisen 1998, p. 133 f.
82 YIVO, RG 575, Unsorted Material, *Serp un Hamer* (1929), numerous texts contained therein from *Kinder fun der Hirsh Lekert Yidishe Arbeter Kinder Shul*. For a Bundist reading of Lekert see Hertz 1952.

ical centre was usually further to the left, and it went without saying that any Yiddish education ought to also involve class education. The school administration was full of praise for the pupils at the children's fair marking its third anniversary in 1929: 'We have noticed that you are sensitive to all workers' problems and come together for workers' issues. We are proud of your achievements and confident that you will become class-conscious workers and people useful to society'.[83] To mark the occasion, the school published a brochure with several essays by pupils who best portrayed the school's work and agenda. Many of them were tales of love, friendship, and (perhaps metaphorically?) the winter cold. One work, from a student named Bela Khotin in her third year at the time, displays an expression of the mental and emotional awareness the school aimed to teach:

> Everybody says that the slaves are liberated and that whites and blacks are now equal. But no! I will tell you a story about how the negroes are treated. It was a cold winter day. *Dzshenki* [Yankee], a negro boy, was on the street. He heard: 'Hello, nigger!' Then he was insulted, defended himself, a brawl, then a man came who said, 'Hey, nigger, leave them in peace', and who then dragged him away from the other boys. These kinds of things happen here very often.[84]

Certainly not an individual case, Bela Khotin applied the emotional awareness from Jewish history taught in class to her American context and its pressing questions of social equality. The question of a culturally conscious working class came second, as it was evidently too vague and saturated with Eastern European experiences in both its secondary-Bundist and Communist forms to make sense to children growing up in America. Thus, the schools successfully conveyed an awareness of the condition of 'the oppressed', albeit no longer understood exclusively as the conditions facing workers. This emotional education allowed children to expand the issue of class through that of race.

While local content grounded transnational Yiddish education in concrete experiences, the change within the *Arbeter-ring* occurred mostly in generational terms. Although the school system underwent dynamic development between roughly 1905–39, it was the project of a single generation for itself. Towards the end of the 1930s, however, internal opposition to the secondary-

---

83   Bund Archives, New York, RG 1400, M-13, 255, *Dritter yerlakher kinder-kontsert*, p. 2f.
84   Bund Archives, New York, RG 1400, M-13, 255, *Dritter yerlakher kinder-kontsert*, p. 4.

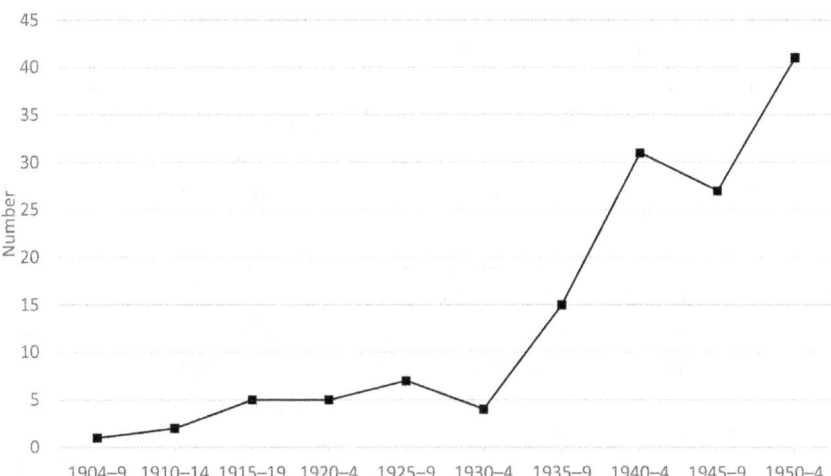

FIGURE 20 Deceased members of the Bundist Dvinsker Branch 75 *Arbeter-ring* (*Vladimir Medem brentsh*), 1904–54
AUTHOR'S CALCULATIONS BASED ON DVINSKER BUNDISTISHER BRENTSH 75 ARBETER RING 1954, N.P.

Bundist legacy began to mount. The generation that laid the foundations for the numerous secondary-Bundist organisations inevitably grew old and eventually retired or passed away. This becomes evident in the case of the once-influential Bundist Branch 75, the *Dvinsker brentsh* of the *Arbeter-ring*. The cohort's death rate began to rise rapidly from the 1930s onwards (Figure 20). Yet because the branch rested on a shared identity and experience coming from Yiddish-speaking Dvinsk, a second generation hardly joined the ranks. Similar dynamics emerged in many branches, and in logical consequence the *Arbeter-ring* sought to dissociate itself from Eastern European experiences as much as possible. This led to new paradoxes in the school context, as it drove forward 'Jewishness' as secular *yidishkayt* in a world where Yiddish was declining in significance.

Yiddish no longer mobilised the new generation. The number of children raised in Yiddish fell rapidly, and soon even Bundist elites rarely taught their offspring the *mame loshn*.[85] Likewise, what initially appeared as a blossoming of related children's literature during the interwar years turned out to be little more than a flash in the pan, so to speak, in light of the 1940s. According to education activist Yosef Mlotek, while only 34 Yiddish children's books were published in the United States during the 1910s, that figure rose to 170 over the

---

85 As evidenced in YIVO, New York, RG 102, 108 [Aaron Cohen], p. 26.

1920s–30s. During the 1940s the figure fell again to 40 books. For 1950–6 he is able to list a total of only 10 Yiddish children's books.[86]

As indicated, I consider neither the allegedly insufficiently palpable opposition to religious tradition nor the monocausally substantiated 'shift towards tradition' as the root of the secular Jewish schools' problems.[87] The youth was and remained progressive, as splits occurred over the question of how radically leftist a Jewish culture ought to be. The result was a structurally differentiated system of party schools that were popular and secular at the same time. The decline in relevance of Yiddish for one's lifeworld, particularly in the second immigrant generation, as well as the latter's unfamiliarity with the Eastern European experience, posed insurmountable obstacles for this system.

The *Arbeter-ring* was at least aware of the language problem. Following the founding of the English-language division of the *Arbeter-ring* in 1938, more and more English-language branches and alumni clubs loosely connected to the *Arbeter-ring* emerged well into the 1940s. The growth of these groups was closely linked to certain existential questions for many activists: 'It is highly desirable that the E[nglish]-S[peaking] Divisions grow in numbers; without them there is little hope for us'.[88] Proponents of an anglophone orientation in the *Arbeter-ring* came to the fore at the 1941 annual meeting of the National Organization Committee. To them, this meeting marked a major turning point, as it was the first time the committee explicitly addressed and formally recognised youth and educational work in English as a question of the group's life or death: 'It shows that [our Organization has] the Youth and English-Speaking Movement at heart. And it must be admitted that our problems are manifold and serious. Our fundamental problem is – *to be or not to be*'.[89]

This was difficult to corroborate in definitive numbers, for the English-language branches in New York amounted to a mere 1,299 members in 21 branches in 1941, joined by another 656 members in 23 branches outside the city.[90] For an organisation used to counting its membership numbers in six figures, this was troubling. Protagonists sought to accelerate the transitional

---

86   Quoted in Kadar 2007, 68.
87   Fishman 2009; Fishman 1965, p. 82 f., p. 87.
88   Bund Archives, New York, RG 1400, Workmen's Circle Collection, 1317, 6, *Report to the Annual Meeting of the National Organization Committee. Workmen's Circle*, 13 July 1941, p. 1.
89   Bund Archives, New York, RG 1400, Workmen's Circle Collection, 1317, 6, *Report to the Annual Meeting of the National Organization Committee. Workmen's Circle*, 13 July 1941, pp. 2–4 (emphasis in original).
90   Bund Archives, New York, RG 1400, Workmen's Circle Collection, 1317, 6, *Report to the Annual Meeting of the National Organization Committee. Workmen's Circle*, 13 July 1941, pp. 14 f.

process by again emphasising the *Arbeter-ring*'s insurance function and not only the cultural work, and by founding new Yiddish branches in smaller cities. As soon as these branches had grown sufficiently, they were to set up new local English-language branches as supplementary bases of recruitment.

This raised the question of these branches' mobilising goals.[91] As the Yiddish branches declined, the disappearance of Yiddish as a means of inclusion demanded an even stronger reference to ethnic Jewishness. The English-speaking branches departed not only from the language policy, but also from some political positions. They understood themselves as a 'progressive Youth movement' and identified an overemphasis of socialist internationalism in the traditional work of the *Arbeter-ring*, which allegedly had even pushed some members of the older generation close to anti-Jewish because purely internationalist positions.[92]

Not least as a result of this reorientation process, the *Arbeter-ring* underwent numerous changes over the following years without ever returning to its interwar strength. This was due not only to the migrants themselves, but to the attempted destruction of *yidishkayt* through Nazi mass murder. The National Organization Committee emphasised that a 'movement cannot be judged merely in terms of quantity. Certainly, its quality counts too', but they never again found the means to approach their old strength.[93]

What leading activists in 1941 hoped to avoid then became a reality they faced over the following years: the *Arbeter-ring* and its educational branches continued to exist, but only as a qualitative wisp of a progressive idea whose time had run out. The new generation no longer responded to their progenitors' modes of community building, the emotional and biographical connection to Eastern Europe declined, and from the late 1930s onwards socialism disappeared. First from American public life and later from public consciousness altogether.

---

91 Bund Archives, New York, RG 1400, Workmen's Circle Collection, 1317, 6, *Report to the Annual Meeting of the National Organization Committee. Workmen's Circle*, 13 July 1941, p. 6f. (emphasis in original).
92 Bund Archives, New York, RG 1400, Workmen's Circle Collection, 1317, 6, *Report to the Annual Meeting of the National Organization Committee. Workmen's Circle*, 13 July 1941, p. 4 (emphasis in original).
93 Ibid.

8   Overlapping and Centrifugal Effects: Radical Secular Jewish Schools in Argentina

Secular Jewish schools in the United States emerged from the Jewish cultural associations, while in Argentina the schools themselves functioned as centres of Yiddish culture. In contrast to the US, they represented the core of activism in which *gezelshaftlekhe tuer* sought to mould the new society they lived in. As Efraim Zadoff lays out in his detailed and still unparalleled study, the modern Jewish schools in Argentina were not an end in themselves, but rather the 'fundamental pillar of the Jewish community'.[94] As late as the 1990s, 70 percent of Jewish children in Buenos Aires still attended a Jewish supplementary school, almost all of which were secular albeit not always anti-religious.[95] Due to his primary interest in Jewish community organisation, Zadoff mainly investigates the parent organisations such as the association of Jewish schools, *Vaad Hakhinukh* (VH), most of which were not founded until the late 1930s.

Although Zadoff considers the older secular schools to be the greatest pedagogical innovators of the pre-1941 period, they remained sceptical of this umbrella association. Without going into too much detail, Zadoff mostly includes them in his history of the development of Jewish pedagogy. Apart from this, he emphasises that the Jewish schools were the mirror of the 'most important political positions on the Jewish street',[96] which was even more secular in Argentina than in the US.[97] If we follow this observation, a movement history of the Jewish schools in Argentina allows us to carve out their individual characteristics and conflicts as much as it highlights the emerging transnationalism in Yiddish activism. Far more than in the US, these schools relied on a homogenising rhetoric, yet the school system itself was torn by partisan strife across which school activists partly cooperated and partly competed.

---

94   Zadoff 1994, p. 7.
95   Zadoff 1994, p. 11.
96   Zadoff 1994, p. 12.
97   This represented the basic hypothesis guiding a wide variety of studies of Jewish history, see for example Horowitz 1962, p. 197; Rosenak 1987, p. 4; Mirelman 1990, pp. 156–9; DiAntonio 1993, p. 4; Zadoff 1994, p. 20.

9 Ideology and Reality: Schools as Political Sites from the *Avangard* to the Global Economic Crisis

The dissolution of the *Avangard* group in the years after the October Revolution marked the point of departure for a new and broad left cultural landscape, reinforced through both transfers of the Bund and socialist Zionism to Argentina as well as the second wave of Eastern European immigration from Poland. Half of all Jews living in Argentina at the beginning of World War II immigrated during the interwar years. Between 1934–8, immigrants from Poland (primarily Jews) accounted for more than half of all immigrants to the country.[98] It was accompanied by both growing population density in the Jewish districts of Buenos Aires as well as an expansion of Jewish settlement into other districts.

The 1920s must accordingly be seen, like the 1900s, as a formative period that was also extremely economically turbulent. Five currents emerged from the secular Yiddish-language schools in this decade, two of whose predecessors dated back to before World War I. These were, firstly, the schools of the anarchist *Yidishe ratsyonalistishe gezelshaft* established in 1909. Like 'La Protesta' in the pre-war era, it deployed Yiddish as a means to mobilise for the anarchist movement, which was losing its leading role among workers in Argentina.[99]

Secondly, there were the non-revolutionary secular schools of the *Folks shul rat*, or rather from 1922 onwards the *Alianza Israelita de Beneficencia y Educación*. Emerging in 1906 as a network of individual secular, often bilingual or Spanish-speaking schools, it soon became their umbrella organisation. While it worked towards a strengthening of a Yiddish-language secularism through education and charity, it omitted the radical left turn towards a specific worker culture, let alone Marxist-inspired education.[100] Its schools were often named after famous Yiddish-language writers such as Peretz or Asch.[101] They addressed their programmes to 'Jewish society' and understood their mission as a 'Jewish-

---

98 Zadoff 1994, p. 43.
99 They existed until the late 1920s and used Yiddish not only as the language of mobilisation and agitation but also for internal communication. See IWO, Buenos Aires, 1111 [Educación], Letter: Yidishe ratsyonalistishe gezelshaft to Sholem Aleikhem shul, 17 January 1923; See also CeDInCI, Buenos Aires, Collection: *La Protesta*, Buenos Aires, 1897–1910.
100 IWO, Buenos Aires, 1111 [Educación], Vouchers from the Sociedad Amigos de la Education (1906).
101 IWO, Buenos Aires, 1111 [Educación], Diverse letters and letterheads, including founding dates.

folk school' for 'Jewish-popular education'.[102] The *Alianza* schools united three strands of Jewish-Argentinian history: firstly, individual *tuer* of the *Avangard* who, secondly, increasingly dedicated themselves to Jewish cultural work. This led to, thirdly, a Yiddish-speaking secularism shorn of revolutionary aspirations that consequently would gravitate partly in the direction of a Jewish worker culture and partly towards Labour Zionism.

These schools also included the first Sholem Aleichem School, founded on 10 August 1920. It served as a role model for developments in Argentina in many respects. While politically close to political Zionism, it regarded 'work in the present' as far more important than working towards *Aliyah*.[103] Furthermore, these schools diligently collected donations mostly for their own sustenance and expansion and not for Zionist funds. Activism and community building associated with the school focused exclusively on Argentina, and, according to surviving account balances, the school was only able to stay afloat through tuition fees and additional revenues. That said, financing was left relatively unstructured for quite some time; more than one third of the Sholem Aleichem School's total income came from picnics,[104] sporadically complemented by collection lists and balls with music and drinks.[105] These served as community-building and fundraising events at which generous donors often contributed to the school.[106] None of the funds went to other Zionist endeavours, nor was that intended. In 1923 the Argentinian Zionist Federation bitterly complained that the Sholem Aleichem School had failed to pay its dues to the Zionist National Fund, allegedly unlike all other schools (which was not true). The Sholem Aleichem School in turn not only continued to decline paying the fund, but evidently even left the letters unanswered.[107] On the other hand, the Sholem Aleichem School Zadoff characterises as strictly apolitical interacted closely with far-left currents, such as the anarchist schools of the *Yidishe ratsyonalistishe*

---

102 IWO, Buenos Aires, 1111 [Educación], Letter to parents from Yidisher folks shul 'Sholem Asch', 14 March 1927.
103 On contemporary work see Blumenfield 1968, p. 27; Haumann 1997.
104 IWO, Buenos Aires, 1111 [Educación], Collection lists; Accounting books, Sholem Aleikhem shul, 14 March 1924. On the relevance of the picnics as drivers of community building see Part III.8.
105 IWO, Buenos Aires, 1111 [Educación], *Result de bailé, Sholem Aleikhem shul* [192?]; Numerous lists and entrance tickets through 1929.
106 IWO, Buenos Aires, 1111 [Educación], *Result de bailé* [192?]. The earnings alone would not have covered the ball; only individual donations turned it into a lucrative event, at the end of which some 605.50 pesos had been collected, amounting to a net profit of 352.40 pesos.
107 IWO, Buenos Aires, 1111 [Educación], Letter: Fondo Nacional Israelita/Federación Sionista Argentina to Sholem Aleikhem shul, 22 August 1923.

TABLE 15   Main currents of secular Jewish schools in Argentina, 1920s

	Yidishe rat-syonalistishe gezelshaft	Folks shul rat/ Alianza Israelita de Beneficencia y Educación	Borochow schools	Arbetershulorg	Bundist school
Founded	1909/1917	Around 1920	1920	1922	1925
Orientation	Anarchist	Yiddishist, growing tendency towards Labour Zionism	Affiliated to Poale Zion in Argentina	Increasingly Communist	Affiliated to the Bundishe organisatsye founded in 1924
Emphases	Secular, Yiddish as basis of Hispanisation	Jewish secularism, mostly Zionist, non-revolutionary but increasingly leftist	Far-left Labour Zionism	Anti-Zionist, 'proletarian', Yiddish rather as means than end	Yiddish culture, class consciousness
Maximum number of schools	3?	Several, precise figure unascertainable	5	8	1

gezelshaft or the central Communist relief committee for Jewish settlements in Soviet Russia, *Prokor*. These relations were amicable, finding expression not least in the coordination of and mutual invitations to picnics.[108]

The two organisations were counterposed by the Marxist schools, ranging from Poale Zionism and Communism to Bundism. Apart from a sole Bundist school founded in 1925, the Poale Zionist-dominated Borochov schools and the increasingly Communist-oriented *Arbeter shul organisatsye (Arbetershulorg)* were the main competitors for parents' favour.[109] Until 1930, the central conflict was clearly between the Zionist and Communist ideological poles, but would only take a full-fledged party-political expression on a widened political field at a later point.

While Zadoff attributes an identical programme to both with the exception of their stance towards Zionism, the available sources indicate that 'national' and 'proletarian' approaches to establishing a modern form of Jewishness increasingly came into conflict with one another.[110] The *Arbetershulorg* placed special emphasis on the class struggle, expecting parents to not only 'love'

---

108   IWO, Buenos Aires, 1111 [Educación], Letter: Yidishe ratsyonalistishe gezelshaft to Sholem Aleikhem shul, 17 January 1923; Letter: Prokor to Sholem Aleikhem shul, 18 December 1925.
109   More elaborate reports by leftist school activists can be found in Centro 'Mark Turkow', Buenos Aires, Archivo de la palabra, 4 [David Bitman]; 17 [Jaime Finkelstein]; 37 [Leike Kogan]; 41 [Grigorio Lerner]; 53 [Sara Novodvorsky]; 69 [Zalel Blitz]; 149 [Josef Horn].
110   See Zadoff 1994, p. 61.

their children but also 'raise [them] wisely'.[111] Former Bundist Moshe Olgin, once very active in Russia and later the US, presented his views in a central *Arbetershulorg* publication. He demanded from parents, teachers, and schoolchildren alike that they 'carry the class struggle into the classroom'.[112] Indeed, the *Arbetershulorg* advertised its 'proletarian schools' on all fronts, even mobilising pupils against the Borochov schools. One leaflet, for example, called on 'pioneers' to agitate against the 'bourgeois and chauvinist' Borochov schools of the Poale Zion. *Arbetershulorg* pupils were to become agitators and initiate an 'awareness campaign among the working-class children who attend the Borochov schools'. In full compliance with Moscow's line, the *Arbetershulorg* refused to acknowledge non-Communist schools as proletarian institutions, dismissing them as representatives of 'reaction and chauvinism'.[113]

The secular Jewish school system was riven by the conflict between socialists and Communists. Many former Avangardistas embarked on new radical political paths and corresponding school networks, yet none of the resulting organisations managed to live up to their claim to be the leading pioneer and central actor of Jewish modernity. Communist organisations' growing hostility towards others in particular drove the (at any rate merely imagined) left-Jewish community further apart, harming all parties involved. Regardless of its ambitions, each and every 1920s school organisation would remain a phenomenon of that particular decade. Their demise was a result not only of the unfavourable conditions facing the schools in Argentina, but also of problems of these organisations' own making. They included the low level of pedagogical sophistication Zadoff observed, as well as structural and financial problems deserving further study.[114]

They can best be observed at the Sholem Aleichem School, the most well-documented school in the archives. Based on its accurate accounting books written in a blend of Spanish and Yiddish, several aspects emerge that were by no means particular to the Sholem Aleichem School's experience. Tuition fees constituted the bedrock of the school's finances and were divided up between parents fairly equally until 1928, in most cases amounting to between 50 centavos and a few pesos, with the exact amount likely determined by the number

---

111 Archivo de la Escuela I.L. Peretz, Villa Lynch, Universidad Nacional de San Martín, 'A vort tsu di eltern', *Undzer shul*, Buenos Aires 1 (1929), p. 1.

112 Archivo de la Escuela I.L. Peretz, Villa Lynch, Universidad Nacional de San Martín, M[oshe] Olgin, 'Di yidishe sprokh un di arbeter shul', *Undzer shul*, Buenos Aires 1 (1929), p. 12 ff.

113 IWO, Buenos Aires, 1111 [Educación], *Arbetershulorg: Derklerung tsu der breyter arbetershaft* [192?].

114 Zadoff 1994, p. 73 f.

of children attending the school and parents' ability to pay.[115] Despite more or less stagnant enrolment, the total sum of membership payments rose from 1928 onwards. This was partially a result of growth due to increasing immigration. The main share, however, came from individual, significantly larger payments that were effectively not membership dues but donations.[116] The entire construct rested on an insurance fund run by the school, into which supporters paid dues to cross-finance its existence.[117] Periodically deployed collection lists supplemented this income.[118]

The degree of income beyond tuition fees testifies to how far beyond actual classroom occurrences the schools' relevance extended. Interest in them was no longer marginal and limited to a few activists, parents, and pupils – the schools now served as cultural facilities of Jewish secularism. Increasingly, individuals who had no children enrolled began supporting them in the form of regular dues. At the same time, the schools often served as venues for political events, just like union facilities before World War I.[119] The school received the additional function during the politicised 1920s, and the effect lasted well into the post-war era: the Jewish-Communist Peretz School in Villa Lynch, whose abandoned former location I was able to visit, accommodated classrooms and community halls, a large swimming pool, and even a bank until 1995.[120]

Such schools were therefore not merely sites of supplementary Jewish education; their centralised diversity linked them to the tradition of the religious *shul* in Eastern Europe – albeit only formally, not in terms of substance. The religious schools were also teaching facilities and social and cultural meeting places for individual religious communities within overall Jewry. No longer religiously but instead politically differentiated, the schools now served a similar function among secular Jews in Argentina. The Argentinian school's accounting books go on to reveal that, beyond political aspects, the factor of space was also quite significant. With few exceptions, members and parents lived more or less in the school's direct vicinity, Villa Crespo and Once. Only in 1937 could

---

115   IWO, Buenos Aires, Sholem Aleichem, TSVYSHO, 1, Registro de Padres (1925–28).
116   IWO, Buenos Aires, Sholem Aleichem, 2, Accounting book, Sholem Aleichem School (1928–30).
117   IWO, Buenos Aires, IIII [Educación], Membership list: Varsikherungsfond fun der folks-shule 'Sholem Aleykhem'.
118   IWO, Buenos Aires, IIII [Educación], *Zamllistn far yidishe folks-shul Sholem Aleichem* (1930).
119   IWO, Buenos Aires, Sholem Aleichem, 2, Flyer; 1114 [Bund], Flyer.
120   On this, see Visacovsky 2005a; Visacovsky 2005b; Pinkus 2008.

the TSVYSHO afford to operate a school bus.[121] Even in 1959, when school buses were quite common, roughly half of the schoolchildren still walked to school from the surrounding neighbourhoods.[122] This explains the need for so many local schools, which had to be carefully adjusted to the locality. Moreover, mass migration led to more and more Jews resettling in other cities. Accordingly, the *Arbetershulorg* maintained partnerships with associated schools in La Plata and elsewhere, while the Sholem Aleichem School attempted to found a second branch in Mataderos in southern Buenos Aires. The committee tasked with planning the construction of the school regularly convened in the late 1920s, but judging by surviving records nothing came of its efforts.[123]

Despite the energies invested, the schools were confronted with problems that would overwhelm them by the end of the decade. The global economic crisis aggravated the already tense situation in Argentina, while the Jewish population spread out across the city, forcing the school network to grow to survive. Moreover, costs for building maintenance and teacher salaries rose as a result of expansion and rising unionisation rates among teachers. The teachers' organisation itself was obviously rooted in the same political mindset that had led to the establishment the schools in the first place, but it now produced conflicts.[124] Considering the monthly balances of the Sholem Aleichem School – which still operated fairly smoothly given the circumstances – it never managed to consolidate a solid financial foundation.[125]

Neither was pure size a source of relief: towards the end of the 1920s, when the Communist *Arbetershulorg* with its eight schools had become the largest association, it found itself on the verge of bankruptcy. Apart from a 1,500 pesos debt (a quite sizeable amount given the school's annual budget of 1,000 pesos), there were no funds to pay the four full-time teachers. Although the *Arbetershulorg* counted 2,000 members and supporters, many of them were late on their payments, and, given the economic hardship of the 1920s, often simply unable to pay.[126] Under considerable strain, the *Arbetershulorg* managed to found the journal '*Unzer shul*'. Envisioned as a 'journal for parents', in 1929 it directly confronted them with the organisation's financial woes. Despite such

---

121 IWO, Buenos Aires, Sholem Aleichem, 2, Accounting book, Sholem Aleichem School (1928–30).
122 IWO, Buenos Aires, Sholem Aleichem, 2, *100 yor Sholem Aleykhem. 25 yor Sholem Aleykhem Shuln*, Buenos Aires (1959).
123 IWO, Buenos Aires, Sholem Aleichem, 2, Ticket, No. 30.
124 IWO, Buenos Aires, 1124 [Orgsanición de maetros], 10; 11; 13; 24.
125 IWO, Buenos Aires, Sholem Aleichem, 2, Accounting book, Sholem Aleichem School (1928–30).
126 IWO, Buenos Aires, 1111 [Educación], *Arbetershulorg: Tsirkular num. 1* (1928).

signals, the *Arbetershulorg* remained under tremendous pressure, compounded by the abject failure of the organisation's '100,000 Pesos Campaign'.[127]

The Borochov schools remained in existence until 1934 but fared only slightly better. Their five branches at Cangallo 2282, Guardia Vieja 3842, Planes 1180, Thames 378, and the last newly opened branch at Orán 1571 secured the school network's presence in different parts of the city. Apart from the central districts of Once and Villa Crespo, in this way the Borochov schools were able to cover the southern districts as well as the growing multi-ethnic working-class neighbourhood of La Paternal. In financial terms, however, they faced repeated crises.[128] Even their tenth anniversary celebrations were affected, as the bulletin published for the occasion confirms. In contrast to most pamphlets issued by the American *Arbeter-ring* schools on similar occasions, the issue was not a commemorative edition.[129] Instead, it was part of a campaign to secure the schools' continued existence, with the front cover featuring not a festive article but instead an 'appeal to the Jewish workers and popular masses'. The article formulated ambitious goals such as a kindergarten, a children's library, and comprehensive workers' education – albeit with the clearly stated main goal of 'securing the existence of the 5 Borochov schools'.[130] This was possible only through great sacrifice. When the schools ultimately closed in 1934, it was by no means merely the result of a temporary, extremely restrictive school policy in Argentina as a 1959 festschrift suggests, but above all a sign of deeper internal problems, financial burdens, and general incompatibility with developments in the broader school system throughout the 1930s.[131]

10 Transfer as Logistical Advantage: The Return of Bundist Influence through Exchange and Culturalisation after 1930–1

Two fundamentally contrary tendencies thus shaped the Jewish schools in Argentina towards the end of the 1920s. Firstly, the period witnessed a growing demand for secular Yiddish educational infrastructure. This emerged from

---

127 Archivo de la Escuela I.L. Peretz, Villa Lynch, Universidad Nacional de San Martín, *Unzer shul*, 2 (1929), p. 1; Y. Malamud, 'Far der vergreserung fun der mitglidershaft un ekonomisher farfestigung fun undzere shuln', *Unzer shul* 2 (1929), p. 22 f.
128 IWO, Buenos Aires, 1111 [Educación], 19.
129 YIVO, New York, RG 575, Unsorted publications.
130 IWO, Buenos Aires, 1111 [Educación], *Buyletin 10 yor Borokhov-shuln* (12 July 1930), p. 1.
131 IWO, Buenos Aires, Sholem Aleijem, Zwischo, *100 yor Sholem Aleykhem. 25 yor Sholem Aleykhem shuln* ([Buenos Aires] 1959).

a political mobilisation that, secondly, triggered fierce conflicts and scattered activists' resources. While the system grew, it also became increasingly financially unsustainable.

This changed in the 1930s, when Bundism reappeared on the stage of Jewish secularism in Argentina. The Bundist club founded in 1924 led a marginal existence over the 1920s, and was only able to boost its status by briefly establishing its own school in 1925. Although only holding out for two years, it anticipated the Bundist schools' pioneering pedagogical role. This must be credited to a large degree to headmaster Guitl Kanutsky, who originally came from the TSYSHO in Poland and would become one of the leading education activists in Argentina.[132] For the Bund, the 1920s marked the decade in which the distinction between individual activists and the organisation as a whole became most palpable: while the Bund was slow to reorganise itself after the disintegration of the *Avangard*, Bundists were highly visible and engaged as social *tuer* across Jewish cultural life and in many school organisations. They managed to establish secondary-Bundist cultural organisations in Buenos Aires in the form of the YSFA and the Argentinian branch of the YIVO (IWO). Until the 1930s, however, similar efforts in the school system failed. As demonstrated in the following, the increasing transnationalisation of *yidishkayt* now granted the well-connected Bundists a structural advantage.

Paradoxically, the Argentinian secular schools' success ultimately revealed their relative 'backwardness' compared to the secular schools in Poland. On 2 January 1930, a letter from the TSYSHO's main office in Poland arrived in the office of the Bundist school activists around Pinie Vald in Buenos Aires. A crucial document in the history of the Argentinian school system, the letter marks the shift towards a practised transnational *yidishkayt* through contacts among Bundists. It began with praise for the 'great struggle you lead for our schools', a reference to Argentinian Bundists who collected donations for the TSYSHO in Poland, albeit with negligible success. This was helpful in light of the current 'economic crisis' in Poland, the letter continued, but unfortunately insufficient. Next, the authors lamented receiving news from all over the world about the 'guardians and fighters for the liberation of the child of the Jewish masses' but no 'first-hand' information from Argentina. This spurred the decision to send a delegate to the country.[133] The relatively isolated Argentinian school system was growing in size and significance, and its reputation now extended all the

---

132   Centro 'Mark Turkow', Archivo de la palabra, 11 [José Chiaskelevitz], p. 8 f.; 32 [Guitl Kanutsky], p. 2 f.; Vald 1935.

133   IWO, Buenos Aires, 1111 [Educación], Letter, Yidishe shul-organisatsye – hoyptfarvaltung, Warsaw to Shul komitet, Buenos Aires, 2 January 1930.

way to Poland, hence the TSYSHO's bewilderment at receiving no communications from their own *khaverim*. On the Argentinian side of the Atlantic, however, this praise coincided with the system's organisational collapse, not least because funds were also scarce here. In their immediate reply, Argentinian Bundists advised against dispatching an envoy – not only due to their internal problems, but also because Argentinians found themselves 'in the hands of a military dictatorship' in the wake of General Uriburu's coup d'état. The TSYSHO ignored the advice and sent Bundist Benjamin Tabachinsky to Argentina. The *khaverim* in Buenos Aires were initially displeased, as they did not even know the man, yet as he was about to arrive they organised a major fundraising campaign throughout Argentina.[134] Despite its limited financial success, the campaign's structural effects were invaluable. Firstly, Bundists and their educational ambitions now garnered widespread attention in the local press through their visitor from the old home. Secondly, Tabachinsky was an ambassador in the best sense: although he returned to Poland with a relatively small sum, he left behind the idea of the TSYSHO, an idea that called for secular organisation with a progressive educational programme able to mobilise across party lines.

Inspired by Tabachinsky's narrative, the Argentinian-Jewish school system began to change in two decisive aspects. Firstly, an alliance formed between Bundists and Social Democrats from the 'right-wing' Poale Zion (as in Buenos Aires, there was also a relatively strong Left Poale Zion with stronger leanings towards Communism). It brought together persons such as the Labour Zionist Mordekhai Regalsky with leading Bundists like Pinie Vald and Guitl Kanutsky and devoted Yiddishists like Samuel Rollansky.[135] Impressed by the TSYSHO's example, they founded the *Gezelshaft far yidishe veltlekhe shuln in Argentine* immediately after Tabachinsky's visit. Its intention was to transfer substance and structures true to the Polish model, and 'its founders made great efforts to import the spirit of the "TSYSHO" schools from the old home'.[136] The activists were mainly the same people who had already worked on the aid campaign for Polish schools. Joining forces, they reversed some of the dominant organisational logics of the 1920s and refrained from starting with

---

134 IWO, Buenos Aires, Fondo CAEI, Pinie Vald, 'Di aktsye vos mir hobn durkhgefirt', *Barikht*, p. 3 ff.
135 Zadoff 1994, p. 95. The Social Democratic Poale Zion, or Red Poale Zion, cooperated (in contrast to the Left Poale Zion) with labour organisations and increasingly with the Bund itself across multiple fields of activity during the 1930s; see Centro 'Mark Turkow', Archive de la palabra, 11 [Chiaskelevitz, José], p. 8; 22 [Goldmitz], p. 10, pp. 15, 32 [Kanutsky, Guitl]; 1111, Circular, Letterhead.
136 Tsuker 1972, p. 5; Zadoff 1994, p. 95 ff.

expensive schools, instead developing a less-activist and better-structured financing system and finally opening the long-desired first Yiddish kindergarten. As Rollansky remarks, although the *Gezelshaft* was founded in 1931 the economic crisis delayed the opening of its first kindergarten to 1933.[137] Eighty-four children already attended only several months after its opening.[138] Proceeding from this initial base, activists developed a small but highly progressive school network later followed by the *Yiddishland* holiday camp.[139] At the heart of this network stood the I.-L.-Peretz School.[140]

Secondly, Tabachinsky's campaign – and the success of the *Gezelshaft*'s progressive approach to education – represented a test case for the Borochov schools. This may help explain why the somewhat more left-leaning Borochov schools did not support the campaign even remotely, a fact Pinie Vald noted with a degree of surprise.[141] Nevertheless, its activists – particularly those around Jaime Finkelstein, who attempted to draw clearer distinctions between the Left Poale Zion and the Communist currents – were so impressed by the TSYSHO that they eventually changed course after initial attempts to save the Borochov schools. They founded the *Tsentrale veltlekhe yidishe shul-organisatsye* or TSVYSHO, again in concert with left-leaning Bundists.[142] As had been the case with the *Avangard*, activists transferred Eastern European Bundist ideas and organisational patterns to Argentina, making them their own by placing local constellations at the heart of their work while continuously advancing and developing their transnational network.

---

137   IWO, Buenos Aires, 1111 [Educación], 21, *Unzer arbet*, 1, 2–3 (1933), p. 2, p. 4f. Additional material is stored at CAHJP, Jerusalem, AR, PER, 2.
138   Knapheyt 1972, p. 14.
139   Rozshanski 1972, p. 7.
140   Zadoff 1994, p. 389. The Peretz School example illustrates the difficulties confronting research on the Bund on the Río de la Plata: despite an intensive search and numerous enquiries directed to informed staff at the IWO, the AMIA, and other private individuals in Buenos Aires, the archives of the I.-L.-Peretz School remained untraceable. Some suspect they were lost during the military dictatorship, while others (indeed, Bundists) insist that no archive ever existed. There is reason to doubt the latter version, however, which IWO archivist Silva Hansman eminently summed up with: 'No, they were Bundists'. Eventually, a letter from 1986 in the personal archive of Bundist Hershl Goldmintz pointed towards Israel. In this letter the University of Tel Aviv affirmed its interest in the offer of the I.-L.-Peretz School's archive. Yet an inquiry at the university archive revealed that it did not hold the collection. A crucial suggestion from Efraim Zadoff, whom I thank, finally led to the Central Archive for the Jewish People in Tel Aviv, where the collection is housed. See IWO, Buenos Aires, Goldmintz, Letter: Shimen Rashen, Tel Aviv, 27 February 1986; CAHJP, Jerusalem, AR, PER, 1–84.
141   IWO, Buenos Aires, CAEI, *Barikht* (1931), p. 4.
142   IWO, Buenos Aires, Escuela Sholem Aleichem, TSVYSHO *Akt-bukh* (1934), pp. 1–3.

This restructuring led to a significant boost in school enrolment. Between 1934–8 some 40 percent of Jewish schoolchildren attended one of the three secular and politically left supplementary schools.[143] Compared internationally, this very high figure speaks volumes about the political constitution of Jewish secularism in Argentina and the political orientation of the parents. The schools of the Bundist-led *Gezelshaft* were among the more moderate in terms of proletarian education, but among the more radical when it came to secularism and *yidishkayt*. This found expression in numerous reports, episodes, and appeals published in the *Gezelshaft*'s bulletin, '*Unzer arbet*', between 1933– 42.[144]

Alongside these two school organisations, which each in their own way relied on cooperation between Bundists and Poale Zionists, a third, Communist current emerged as the *Farband fun yidishe folks shuln* (see Table 16). Its predecessor, the *Arbetershulorg*, was banned in the wake of Uriburu's coup d'état. Although activists continued to teach in illegality for two more years, resurrecting the old *Arbetershulorg* proved impossible.[145] Only a re-founding would clear a path out of the miserable situation. Former Avangardistas and Labour Zionists who had drifted quite far from their political origins played a major role, but immigration of fellow party members was the most significant factor. The *Farband fun yidishe folks shuln* became important in Argentinian Jewish history through its function as both a school organisation as well as a means of Communist agitation. During the 1930s it not only promoted Communism on a mass scale, but also advertised the Birobidzhan movement, which was widely supported in the country.[146]

Following the heterogeneity of the 1920s, three currents defined the Yiddish school movement in the 1930s. All of them boasted former Avangardistas in leading positions and two were heavily influenced, if not guided by current Bundists. While the Communist school movement isolated itself rather aggressively in the style of the *Arbetershulorg*, neither the TSVYSHO nor the *Gezelshaft* operated as 'party schools'. Under the guidance of Bundists as well as left-wing and Social Democratic Zionists, both also cooperated on a case-by-case basis. In contrast to the polarisation between Zionists and Communists common in most relevant literature, this story reveals a more complex situation

---

143 Author's own calculation; total numbers of Jewish pupils can be found in IWO, Buenos Aires, Sholem Aleijem, Zwischo, 2, *100 yor Sholem Aleykhem. 25 yor Sholem Aleykhem shuln*, ([Buenos Aires] 1959).
144 Contained in a comprehensive form in: CAHJP, Jerusalem, AR, PER, 67–68; most relevant issues in: IWO, Buenos Aires, 1114 [Bund].
145 Svarch 2010.
146 See *Nayvelt*, Buenos Aires, 11–13 (1928).

TABLE 16   Secular school organisations in Argentina, 1930s

	Gezelshaft far yidishe veltlekhe shuln in Argentine	*TSVYSHO/Sholem-Aleichem-School*	*Farband fun yidishe folks shuln*
Founded	1931/1933	1934	1934
Orientation	Similar to TSYSHO, run by Bundists and Poale Zionists, strictly socialist, anti-Communist, increasingly Yiddishist and Bundist	Similar to TSYSHO in Poland, but stronger influence by Poale Zion – including the Left Poale Zion, Bundists rather marginal, alliance between leftist and Yiddishist forces, *de facto* successor to the Borochow schools	Communist successor of the Arbeterschulorg, persecuted by the state, closed in 1937–8
Emphases	Yiddish as means and end in school and general cultural work, kindergartens, schools, summer camp, worker culture; Peretz school also served as Bundist meeting space	Yiddish, increasing turn to modern Hebrew as classroom feature; general cultural work, kindergartens, schools, later also a summer camp; pro-Zionist outlook	Yiddish incl. Spanish, focus on Communism and temporarily on Birobidzhan
Size	1934: 90 pupils 1938: 3 schools, 400 pupils, 'people's academy' and kindergarten – additionally: independent but similar – the Zalmen-Reizen-School on Avellenada: 120 pupils, affiliated and similar school (with a kindergarten) in Montevideo, Uruguay	1934: 2 schools, 4 teachers, 130 pupils 1942: 29 teachers, 770 pupils	1937: 7 schools (in Buenos Aires), 200 pupils and affiliated schools in La Plata, Rosario, Santa Fe, and Bahia Blanca, one teacher per group

DATA TAKEN FROM IWO, BUENOS AIRES, 1111 [EDUCACIÓN], 1114 [BUND]; SCHOLEM ALEIJEM, ZWISCHO, 2, 100 YOR SHOLEM ALEYKHEM. 25 YOR SHOLEM ALEYKHEM SHULN, [BUENOS AIRES] 1959, N.P.; ZADOFF 1994, P. 98

of conflict and overlap with many (current and former) Bundists in leading positions, as well as a crucial influence of transnational Bundism over the entire constellation.[147]

The relevance of Bundist activism in Buenos Aires also led to the fact that, in contrast to the IWO schools in the US and the *Arbeterschulorg* in the 1920s, in the 1930s the *Farband fun yidishe folks shuln* remained the smallest of those organisations. It first and foremost failed to provide a quality education. Activists tried to counter this by launching their own series of publications titled

---

147   See Visacovsky 2005b; Svarch 2010.

'Children's Library', featuring famous Eastern European authors like former Bundist Gina Medem.[148] The TSVYSHO schools were also forced to first improve their pedagogical standards. As Zadoff establishes, the *Gezelshaft*'s high standard emerged from educational innovation from the outset – less through local expertise and instead based on transnationality and migration, above all immigrant Bundist TSYSHO teachers ensured high pedagogical standards, which they brought with them from their work in the Polish Yiddish school system. Ties between Bundists in Argentina and Poland grew as well, and pedagogical material also began to move. However, readers should not be misled by the name 'TSVYSHO' – none of the three organisations were as closely in contact with the Polish TSYSHO as the *Gezelshaft*.[149] This was compounded by the Bundist philosophy of *doikayt*, which facilitated the development of a pedagogical conception with local impacts, rather than orienting pupils towards a far-off land, whether Palestine or the Soviet Union, Moscow or Birobidzhan. In contrast to the Polish TSYSHO, Labour Zionists were important figures in the TSVYSHO at all times, whereas the *Gezelshaft* can be understood essentially as a Bundist organisation. Although both organisations ran several schools across the city so as to remain as locally engaged as possible, two schools quickly crystallised as centres: for the *Gezelshaft* this was the I.-L.-Peretz School, while for the TSVYSHO it was the Sholem Aleichem School.[150] Both were stable institutions that weathered numerous upheavals over the course of Argentinian history. The Sholem Aleichem School exists to this day, albeit in a modified and Hebraised form. It resembled the aforementioned Sholem Aleichem School of the 1920s in some respects, but generally represented a refounding in the spirit of the TSVYSHO. As late as 1995, the Yiddish-language I.-L-.-Peretz School was fortunate enough to host Mark Edelman as an honorary guest to their Warsaw Ghetto Uprising anniversary celebrations, in the old tradition of Bundist emissaries. That said, it was forced to close its doors forever the very same year, as was the Communist Peretz School in Villa Lynch.[151]

While Bundists like Kazdan became leading figures in the Polish TSYSHO, Left Poale Zionist Jaime Finkelstein was the decisive leader in the Argentinian TSVYSHO. Although he was devoted to the 'direct social struggle against the *Yevsektsiya*', he criticised the increasingly Yiddishist culturalism of some

---

148 Medem 1936.
149 Zadoff 1994, p. 86, pp. 164–68.
150 The Bundist I.-L.-Peretz School at Lavalle 2238 should not be confused with the Communist I.-L.-Peretz-School in Villa Lynch, see Visacovsky 2005b; Pinkus 2008.
151 IWO, Buenos Aires, Escuela Sholem Aleijem; 1114 [Bund]; Archivo Goldmintz, Speech Goldmintz 1995; Photography of Marek Edelman.

Bundists.[152] Although its financial basis was more stable than before, the organisations' respective problems were far from resolved. In 1936 the TSVYSHO owed its teachers around 14 months' worth of unpaid salaries, a sum of 2,000 pesos. The first school of the workers' movement, the TSVYSHO, became the site of a teacher strike.[153] Nevertheless, the situation improved to some extent with the economic recovery of the 1930s. The *Gezelshaft* in particular was able to consolidate itself thanks to targeted acquisition and a more sophisticated organisational structure, allowing it to develop new models of Jewish education for Argentina.[154] Bundists conceived of the I.-L.-Peretz School at Lavalle 2238 as a role model institution from the outset, labelling it the 'First Model School'.[155] *Khaverim* in Montevideo, adopted this approach in explicit alignment with the TSYSHO as well as the *khaverim* in Buenos Aires. They certainly benefited from the lively exchanges among many Jewish and socialist parties between both cities. A similar alliance of Bundists and Poale Zionists also founded first a kindergarten and then a school in the city, adhering to the models put forward by the *Gezelshaft* in both cases.[156]

The kind of Bundist culturalism more radical forces so often criticised proved to be an advantage at this point. As a Marxist socialist organisation, the Bund was able to forge alliances with both radical groups as well as Yiddishists and more culturally oriented institutions. Although the socialist tradition certainly omitted a number of Jewish holidays and instead celebrated May Day, it did not seek to exclude everyone who chose to observe Jewish traditions. The main protagonist of Jewish cultural work in Argentina, chairman of the YIVO in Buenos Aires and co-founder of the YSFA Samuel Rollansky, consequently also became chairman of the *Gezelshaft*'s education committee.[157] A Yiddishist at the time, he supported the Sholem Aleichem School with a private donation of 40 pesos in 1930, but that did not stop him from also occupying a

---

152   IWO, Buenos Aires, Escuela Sholem Aleijem, 'Hakdome', *Khaym Finkelshtayn tsu zeyne 60 yor* (Montevideo, 1971), [3].

153   On the vibrant Buenos Aires teachers' union see Part III.10; Zadoff 1994, p. 167.

154   However, the problems shifted – in a way not least an outcome of the newly forming national association of Jewish schools, *Vaad Hakhinukh*. The latter was particularly significant, as it tied its support for schools to certain conditions, like the recognition of Jewish holidays and the Shabbat. Like the TSVYSHO, the Bundist *Gezelshaft* sought to maintain its distance to *Vaad Hakhinukh* through a more stable funding structure of its own, fearing excessive interference with its cultural and political work. On the changes in fundraising this necessitated see Part III.12.

155   IWO, Buenos Aires, Comite de ayuda a las escuelas laicas Israeltita de Polonia y Argentina (CAEI), Testimony of Esther Rollansky.

156   Bundishe grupe in Montevideo 1937a, pp. 38–41.

157   Zadoff 1994, p. 164.

leading position in the *Gezelshaft*. In the end, he even sent his children to the Bundist I.-L.-Peretz School.[158] Particularly in the education system, Bundists found a way to develop a culturalist version of Bundist *doikayt* that spoke to the many secular, but not always revolutionary Jews in Buenos Aires. It allowed the *Gezelshaft* to establish three kindergartens, four model schools, numerous youth classes, and even a 'people's university' in Buenos Aires by 1936.[159]

Nevertheless, the *Gezelshaft* was a Bundist and not just secondary-Bundist organisation, and thus insisted that the majority of teachers be active in the party. It imported many of its teaching materials directly from Poland, ensuring the schools' high standards as well as interaction between the Bund in Poland and Argentina. For these reasons, the *Gezelshaft*, like the TSVYSHO, rejected membership in an umbrella organisation like the *Vaad Hakhinukh* for many years. Still, there were of course personal overlaps which secured communication between both. This was true not only of prominent personalities like Rollansky and Kanutsky, but also of 'ordinary' staff such as teacher Sara Novodvorsky. She grew up as a Bundist in the *Tsukunft* in Poland and afterwards became a trained teacher at a TSYSHO school in Warsaw. She left Poland in 1933 to marry a Poale Zionist who had moved to Haifa in 1926 but by then resided in Buenos Aires. Following her arrival, she found a position at the Bundist I.-L.-Peretz School on Lavalle after attempting to work as an office secretary – a difficult undertaking given her lack of Spanish skills. Priorities were reversed at the Peretz School. Botoshansky and Rollansky conducted the job interview: 'I had three years of experience and a good command of Yiddish, so they accepted my application and I received a job in the kindergarten'.[160] Her chances were likely improved by a letter of recommendation from the Polish TSYSHO she had wisely arranged after learning about the school while still in Warsaw.[161] Nevertheless, she only worked there for six months before receiving a position at the Poale Zionist Sholem Aleichem School. This occurred due to personal rather than political motives, as she succinctly explains: 'a new kindergarten teacher arrived'.[162] She enrolled her daughter, born in 1937, in the first version of the Communist-oriented and newly founded I.-L.-Peretz School in

---

158   IWO, Buenos Aires, 1111 [Educación], Folks-Shul Sholem Alejem, Confirmation to Shmuel Rollansky; IWO, Buenos Aires, CAEI, School report card of Esther Rollansky.
159   IWO, Buenos Aires, IWO-Escuelas, 1036, 25.
160   Centro 'Marc Turkow', Buenos Aires, Archive de la palabra, 53 [Sara Novodvorsky, 1985], p. 9.
161   Ibid.
162   Centro 'Marc Turkow', Buenos Aires, Archive de la palabra, 53 [Sara Novodvorsky, 1985], p. 11f., p. 20.

Villa Lynch.[163] Regardless, she considered herself to be a Bundist in principle.[164] Sara Novodvorsky was well aware of the differences between the schools, but argued they were 'all socialists and very far-left', and that the political disagreements ought not to be overstated. Most subject matter was 'about life', which of course also included the 'culture of the fathers', for ultimately 'we are speaking about a Yiddish secular culture [*cultura laica ídish*]'.[165]

These kinds of personalised, mixed arguments are no rarity in narrative accounts. A similar case is that of Bundist José Epstein, who was born into a traditional family between 1908–10 and reached Argentina in 1927.[166] He moved further and further left over the 1920s, eventually becoming a Communist who voiced strong support for Birobidzhan, and insisted he only refrained from going himself because of his marriage.[167] He notes as an aside that he sent his son, born in 1938, to the Sholem Aleichem School, prompting his interviewer to ask: 'Why the Sholem Aleijem School and not–?', interrupted by the harsh response: 'Because the Sholem Aleichem School at the time was run by Poale Zion and because Matis Goldfarb, the owner of "*Di prese*" back then, was a close friend of mine from the times of struggle; he was also a worker and a fighter'. Friendship and personal ties in educating the second generation thus helped to build bridges where party politics had proven incapable or even sought to prevent them. At any rate, Epstein continued, his son was now 50 years old and had become profoundly religious.[168]

The long-term effects of being raised in a secular Jewish culture could thus be limited. Regardless, for activists and parents this upbringing constituted a link that not only went beyond local party politics, but ensured exchange across the Atlantic. In this sense, the strict stipulation of Yiddish as the language of instruction gave Bundists an advantage, for a nationally-culturally defined yet globally diasporic community enabled extensive transnational exchange of personnel, material, and programme without having to deal with translation

---

163 Centro 'Marc Turkow', Buenos Aires, Archive de la palabra, 53 [Sara Novodvorsky, 1985], p. 16.
164 Centro 'Marc Turkow', Buenos Aires, Archive de la palabra, 53 [Sara Novodvorsky, 1985], p. 6.
165 Centro 'Marc Turkow', Buenos Aires, Archive de la palabra, 53 [Sara Novodvorsky, 1985], p. 17.
166 Centro 'Marc Turkow', Buenos Aires, Archive de la palabra, 14 [José Epstein, 1987], p. 1. The vagueness concerning his date of birth is owed to his claim of being born in 1910 yet seven years old when war broke in 1914, and entering the *kheder* at age four-and-a-half before the war.
167 Centro 'Marc Turkow', Buenos Aires, Archive de la palabra, 14 [José Epstein, 1987], p. 8.
168 Centro 'Marc Turkow', Buenos Aires, Archive de la palabra, 14 [José Epstein, 1987], p. 11.

problems. Furthermore, most subject matter was also transferrable. As textbooks illustrate, topics like natural history, Yiddish literature, social consciousness, and a secular Jewish general education took centre stage. Similar prioritisation can also be observed in the TSYSHO and the schools of the *Arbeter-ring* in the US.[169]

In Argentina, however, the schools provided a formal education as much as they taught pupils about community building. That was mostly because these schools not only talked about the community, but fulfilled an important role in them. When the *Gezelshaft* started to develop the Peretz School as the new role model, it drew on experiences from the old Bundist school founded in 1925, the TSYSHO in Poland, and the Vladimir Medem Centre in Buenos Aires. Founded as a cultural centre in 1927, the venue secured the Bund a space for its own political and cultural events on the Río de la Plata.[170] It merged into the I.-L.-Peretz School in the 1930s, which in turn became an important Yiddish cultural club in the Jewish district. As a result, the school enjoyed the support of teachers and parents, and increasingly also of culturally and politically interested Jews without children enrolled in the school. Its appeal radiated to the opposite bank of the world's widest river: inspired by the *Gezelshaft*, *khaverim* in Montevideo pledged to intensify their work and create a school after this model. They appealed for support beyond the narrower circle of possible parents: 'our call ... is directed not only to the *tuer* and administrations of existing schools, but mainly to the countless friends and sympathisers of Yiddish schools and culture, to all those who are among the first when it comes to actions of a truly cultural character'. In contrast to previous party schools, they sought to mobilise all members of 'cultural clubs' across social strata who understood Yiddish culture as a worker culture, without necessarily being a class culture at the same time. Activists hoped to establish many new schools in this way, 'for a people's culture cannot be measured by the number of *benk* [Yiddish pun alluding to both 'banks' and 'synagogue benches'] ... but by the number of schools'.[171]

These schools subsequently became an important factor in the institutionalisation of the *kehillah* in Buenos Aires (DAIA/AMIA), which in contrast to New York did not remain a mere experiment.[172] That said, it only became a generally recognised administration of the Jewish community after trade unions were

---

169 IWO, Buenos Aires, 1111 [Educación], 6–9 [School books].
170 CAHJP, Jerusalem, AR, PER, 63–65.
171 Bundishe grupe in Montevideo 1937a, p. 41. Ironically, an advertisement for the Jewish-Polish Association's commercial bank was placed directly under the article.
172 Goren 1970; Elkin 1980, p. 186f.

forced to merge and independent socialist movements were banned (severely curtailing *yidishkayt* in the process) during the initial Peronist phase.[173] Before that, however, the closely linked trade unions, schools, and political movements in Argentina worked towards the new Jewish education system, which became an important albeit historically often underestimated element of the transnational history of modern Jewry.

Their function for Jewish community building and their symbiosis with the social movements in the city questions the remark by Judith Laikin Elkin, who notes that activists of the distinct school movements 'captured' the Jewish community's leading bodies in order to secure permanent funding.[174] This was hardly possible before 1939, when the organisation of the Jewish community in Buenos Aires was weak and at best slowly emerging. Until the arrival of Peronism, not the *kehillah* or any other ethnic or religious Jewish umbrella organisation, but the cultural and social movements defined Jewish life on the Río de la Plata. The prominently represented secular schools were tied to their political currents and continued to cultivate a distance from the community for years, even after the founding of the first umbrella organisation. They did not share the same basic understanding of Jewishness, and feared interference with their autonomy. Initial signs of rapprochement would emerge towards the late 1930s as pressure from the outside rose. The history of secular Jewish schools prior to World War II therefore should be understood not in the context of the history of community organisation, but rather of the transnational social movement and activist community building.

Had it not been for the social movements, neither a school organisation nor a national association of Jewish cultural affairs and especially the *Tsentrale yidishe kultur-organisatsye* (TSYKO) could have developed in Argentina. The TSYKO became one of the most important associations of Jewish life in Argentina over the course of the 1940s. As the first major organisation of non-partisan *yidishkayt*, it encompassed more than 80 schools and school organisations of all political currents except the now effectively banned Communist movement.[175] The TSYKO illustrates quite clearly that school activists did not 'capture' the overarching associations, but rather created them. Membership card No. 1

---

173   Mirelman 1990; Laubstein 1997, p. 195 f.; Doyon 2006.
174   Elkin 1980, p. 177.
175   Apart from Jacob Botoshansky, Bundist José Horn and Left Poale Zionist Jaime Finkelstein were important activists and vice-secretaries of the organisation in 1940. See IWO, Buenos Aires, Fondo CIKO [TSYKO], *Reshimah un adresn kalender fun di yidishe shuln, velkhe zenen ongeshlosn ...*, Entry: 43, 45; Circular, TSYKO, 22 July 1940.

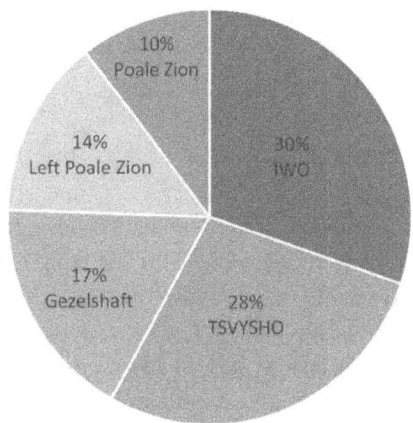

■ IWO   ■ TSVYSHO   ▪ Gezelshaft   ▪ Left Poale Zion   ■ Poale Zion

FIGURE 21   Additional memberships of TSYKO activists at time of joining, circa 1941
SURVEY: IWO, BUENOS AIRES, CIKO, DEKLARAT-
SYE, 1–136

was issued to Jacob Botoshanksy, an important Bundist and *Gezelshaft* activist who became the TSYKO's first president.[176] Beyond such Bundists, the TSYKO integrated social multipliers from various party backgrounds. The preserved documentation of the first 136 members allows a closer analysis of this alliance.[177] Firstly, TSYKO activists often held memberships in other organisations, even representing them within the TSYKO at times. Secondly, the 'Bund' is not mentioned as an organisation even once, although some TSYKO members were demonstrably active in the Argentinian Bund. Instead, reference is made exclusively to the *Gezelshaft*, which represented Bundist cultural projects in Argentina for the time being and was a central force in the evolution of Bundist community building through its school on Lavalle. Thirdly, activity in the TSYKO was almost always accompanied by IWO membership, which is why simultaneous membership in the *Gezelshaft* and the IWO is the most common combination during the first phase of group affiliation (up to roughly member No. 70). From this (unfortunately un-dateable) point onwards, hardly any other *Gezelshaft* activists joined the TSYKO. Evidently, the main actors were already on board. Fourthly, at this point a sudden influx of activists from the

---

176   IWO, Buenos Aires, *Deklaratsye Nr. 1* [Jacob Botoshansky].
177   Author's own survey according to: IWO, Buenos Aires, CIKO, *Deklaratsye*, 1–136.

Left Poale Zion and the TSVYSHO set in, which soon exceeded the number of members from other organisations, including the moderate Poale Zion. The TSYKO's political breadth expanded as a result, while Zionist forces also grew stronger.

The activists mobilised for Yiddish cultural work from within the movements, first creating the schools, unions, and ultimately a national association in the form of the TSYKO. As it united the schools that had developed into cultural centres, the TSYKO also endowed *yidishkayt* with structure and, more importantly, an organisational voice. The education movement thus largely contributed to Argentina's rise to a qualitatively and quantitatively significant site of Jewish modernity during the interwar period, a fact generally underestimated in general Jewish historiography. Like a laboratory for Jewish modernity, the development in Argentina sheds light on the greater question of which direction Jewish modern life should and could take. To answer it, the conflicts are as important as the final – and often neglected – merger between the many parties and actors for one common goal of a secular Yiddish education. Even today's Jewish community in Buenos Aires, anything but dominated by secularism, is built on these roots. The causes behind the definitive shift towards Zionism and the side-lining of any Bundist groups (like the *khavershaft* group after World War II) towards Hebrew instead of Yiddish, to modern orthodoxy instead of secularism, however, are located in the post-war decades. Their rise cannot be attributed to any alleged shortcomings of interwar *yidishkayt* either in Argentina or the US, which faced its crises but was not under the pressure of any of the forces which would later prove important. Moreover, Jewish life in Argentina was very different before and after the Holocaust. *Yidishkayt* flourished in late-1930s Argentina, and, in the sense of a cultural turn, indeed side-lined the socialist components albeit without abandoning it. The process intensified under Perón, as political opposition was now persecuted and the cultural realm constituted a safe haven for Jewish activists.

The individual schools nevertheless remained political places. In line with global trends, they now also turned towards *Memorik*. The structure of the Peretz School building at Lavalle 2238 again came in handy. Functioning as a Bundist cultural centre, it housed the *Gezelshaft*'s headquarters and provided rooms for events and meetings. In short, it provided what Bundists in New York could only access through the *Forverts* or had to rent at a high cost. Bundists hosted regular events in their own physical facilities as early as the 1930s, although these were oriented towards internal community building and hardly noticed outside the local context. Things had changed considerably by 1947, when the Peretz School hosted a festive banquet commemorating the TSYSHO in Poland (and thus also praising the successes in Buenos Aires). Attended by more than 600 guests, even the New York-based *'Forverts'* covered the celebration.[178]

11 Bundist Education: Gaining Relevance through Cultural Work

Against this backdrop, we can briefly recapitulate the differences and similarities of Bundist educational work in Argentina and the United States. For quite some time, the American *Arbeter-ring* schools provided a Bundist-inspired education embedded within the framework of a greater secular and cultural association. They functioned as transmission belts for knowledge created largely outside this frame, adapted to suit local contexts. The situation in Argentina on the other hand was quite different: here the schools themselves became the cultural centres and new points of departure for the Yiddish movement, resonating throughout Buenos Aires, the Jewish community, and beyond. The schools only stabilised due to intensified transnational exchange and enforced contacts to the Yiddish movement in Poland. This facilitated transfers of ideas, structures, and most importantly knowledge in the form of people and teaching material to Argentina.

As a result, school activists in all of those places regarded their work as part of their common struggle 'on the cultural front'.[179] Their understanding of Jewishness changed in the process. Activists no longer regarded secularism as an aspiration to be attained via rebellion, but a manifest reality to be implemented and sustained. The active relationship with Polish Bundists was more than just a source of inspiration in this undertaking, yet the question remained as to how a transnational Yiddish culture was to be locally embedded. The respective organisational responses in Poland, the US, and Argentina were each quite distinct. Local coalitions as well as transnational interaction became increasingly important as a result, an aspect underscored not least by the biographies of individuals like Zivion, Vladeck, Tabachinsky, Kazdan, Vald, Botoshansky, and Kanutsky.

That said, in many regards it also highlighted the limits to Bundism in migration. The *Arbeter-ring* schools emancipated themselves from secondary Bundism over the course of the 1930s, as did the *Arbeter-ring* as a whole. In Argentina,

---

178   IWO, Buenos Aires, 1114, Ticket; N.N. 1947a.
179   This is pointed out in many publications, while a direct link between Argentina and the US is presented in N.N. 1931.

the *Gezelshaft* achieved a different role, as it internally became far more significant for the Argentinian Bund than the TSYSHO was for the Polish Bund. Despite its comparatively small size by TSYSHO standards, this lent it decisive qualitative weight in the process of community building in Argentina. As cultural politics became an arena of greater Bundist success in the country, the Bund began to play a very different role than in Poland, where it dominated entire local parliaments.[180] This change, however, also lowered the barrier between Bundist and Zionist cooperation, whereas cooperation between these two groups and their Communist counterparts became almost impossible due to their utterly distinct conceptions of Jewishness. Apart from these political tensions, from the perspective of pupils and parents, personal motivations and networks were more important.

While the Argentinian Jewish schools under Bundist influence deserve an elevated position in the history of Jewish education, in the US the limitations of such schools became all too apparent. To begin with, until after World War II Bundists refrained from developing a distinct idea of an American Bund independent of the Polish Bund, and thus resorted to (highly successful) secondary Bundism. Yet as the second generation increasingly integrated into American society towards the end of the 1930s, their success ebbed while Bundist schools in Argentina and Poland were witnessing their heyday. Even before the Holocaust, the generational shift was accompanied by the dwindling relevance of Yiddish. Bundist activism in the US therefore found an easier field in transnational networking and commemorative practices geared towards one specific generation, but faced growing difficulties connecting with local developments. While this hindered a lasting institutionalisation of the Bund in the local culture and politics, it gave space to Bundist activism and proliferated Bundism well beyond party lines. This opened the door to active transnationalisation, which emerged most successfully in the mutual aid campaigns on behalf of the Polish Bund discussed in more detail in the following chapter.

180 Jacobs 2009, pp. 1–7.

CHAPTER 12

Relief Funds as Weapons: From Revolutionary Fundraising to Transnational Cultural Work

On Monday, 6 February 1905 the Executive Committee of the *Fraynd fun bund* (Friends of the Bund) in New York received a telegram from the Bund's Foreign Committee in Geneva. It told the New York Bundists perhaps the most exciting news prior to 1917: 'Whole Bundist Pale in revolt; many victims; great financial difficulty'.[1] These brief lines heralded nothing less than the beginning of the first Russian Revolution.

The last point concerning 'financial difficulty' deserves particular attention, given that, as Jonathan Frankel notes, '[r]evolutionary organizations depended to an extraordinary extent on the ebb and flow of fund-raising and this dependence grew as the Russian economy was undermined by the turbulence of war and internal disorder'.[2] Fundraising's ebbs and flows nevertheless require explanation. As I demonstrate in the following, fundraising did not occur automatically based on external macro-historical events, but rather through activism. The Bundists' success in this area was contingent on many factors and not only led to funding for the Bund in Eastern Europe, but also strengthened local cultural work and allowed Bundists to play a meaningful role in their societies of immigration.

Correspondingly, the *khaverim* reacted to the letter from Geneva not with actionism, but a swift inquiry as to what exactly was happening. The Foreign Committee responded more explicitly the following day: 'General Political Demonstrations by striking Workmen in Riga, Wilno, Kovno, Minsk, Dwinsk, Homel, Berdichev etc. etc. Serious conflicts in many places with Military and Police; numerous victims etc'.[3] The *Fraynd fun bund* in the US quickly understood that this was not just the mere passing on of information between comrades, but a call to action. They convened a meeting that same evening and founded an emergency fund to which 40 well-known activists made initial contributions, including Abraham Liessin (5 $), Samuel Peskin (10 $), Karl Foren-

---

1 Quoted in Bund Archives, New York, RG 1400, ME-18, 3, Circular: Dr. J. Halpern, Friends of the 'Bund', February 1905.
2 Frankel 2009, p. 68.
3 Also quoted in Bund Archives, New York, RG 1400, ME-18, 3, Circular: Dr. J. Halpern, Friends of the 'Bund', February 1905.

berg (5 $), and Morris Wintshevsky (5 $). The largest sum of 50 $ was donated by Meyer London. Like many other leading figures of Jewish New York such as Abraham Cahan, Jacob Gordin, and Abraham Caspe, the man who would later become a socialist congressman was a member of the *Fraynd fun bund* Executive Committee founded only a few months earlier. An impressive 426.50 $ was collected over the course of that single evening. The attendees resolved to increase the sum to 1,000 $ through a loan, and the money was transferred to the Bund in Geneva immediately.[4] The true value of these funds is best illustrated by the fact that the *Arbeter-ring* insured its members with a sickness benefit of 9 $ per week, corresponding to a low but common weekly wage. Measured against the Real Value Index (RV), 1,000 $ would correspond to 29,400 $ today.[5]

That such a sizeable sum was made available in just one evening indicates that the Bundists in question were not collecting pennies with a tin bucket on Hester Street. Solidarity relied on the emigrants' community-building work. Different groups close to the Bund pursued distinct ways of doing so, for the circle of organised fundraisers of course exceeded the circle of organised Bundists in the US who saw themselves as intermediaries between East and West. Fundraising earned the *Fraynd fun bund*, which had been a loosely organised association until then, a degree of recognition as members of the Bundist *mishpokhe*. The annual meeting of American Bundists in 1906 resolved that they were permitted to attend and speak at Bundist congresses, albeit without voting rights. On the other hand, they retained their organisational independence and were able to found supporter groups wherever they pleased without Bundist supervision.[6] This distinction between the Bund and Bund supporters also existed in Europe, where there were 11 'central Bundist *kreyslekh*', numerous Bundist workers' associations, and eight charity organisations in 1906.[7]

---

4 Bund Archives, New York, RG 1400, ME-18, 3, Circular: Dr. J. Halpern, Friends of the 'Bund', February 1905.
5 'RV' stands for today's real value of a historical amount of money. It is measured using the relative cost of a defined bundle of goods and services consumed by an average household in the historical year compared to 2018, the last year available at the time of writing. Measuring worth over time is complicated, while real value presents a more conservative estimate: for example, an income value of 1,000 $ in 1905 compares to roughly 181,000 $ in 2018. Further information and different calculations available at and all estimations based on Williamson 2020.
6 Bund Archives, New York, RG 1400, ME-18, 3, Referat fun der driter yehrlikher konventsh fun di bundistishe organisatsye in Amerika 1906, p. 17.
7 Bund Archives, New York, RG 1400, ME-18, 3, Excerpt from the Bund Foreign Committee's report to the sixth Bund Congress, Referat fun der driter yehrlikher konventsh fun di bundistishe organisatsye in amerika 1906, p. 8.

The loan the *khaverim* extended in 1905 also entailed the obligation to continue the fundraising effort beyond that evening. To achieve this on the widest possible basis, the *Fraynd fun bund* formulated an initial circular in English (addressed to a 'Dear Friend') – a rare exception – where they cited the cables and reported on the donations and loan. Finally, they issued an eloquently formulated call to action: 'We are certain that you will gladly contribute your share and help us not only cover the loan, but swell the fund to a greater figure than a thousand dollars'.[8] They succeeded.[9]

1   Spontaneous First Steps

This marked a sea change in financial relations between the Bund's American supporters and the Eastern European Bund (or rather its responsible representatives at the Geneva office). Only one year earlier, the Geneva Foreign Committee had asked the American *khaverim* whether a shipment of three boxes of literature reached the US, as they had not heard from them in months. Furthermore, the American comrades were urged to step up and pay their debt of 120 £ (about 584.40 $ at the time, 15,900 $ RV) that had accumulated through previous orders. Added to this were another 20 £ (97.40 $) for the latest delivery. So far, they had only once sent a meagre 10 £ (48.70 $, 1,430 RV).[10]

This means that the flow of cash from American cities into revolutionary coffers, which research takes for granted, by no means came without strings attached. As Toni Michels has already noted, the 'export of socialism' was not simply an 'eastward influence', but rather a reciprocal exchange.[11] The patterns of this exchange must be fleshed out, as it included not only literary and ideological but always also a material aspect, which eventually even moved to the centre of local activism. The 1905 initiative marks a turning point in this history, as after it the patterns of fundraising for Eastern Europe in the US changed. Until then, the 'old guard' around Abe Cahan and Max Pine had intervened only in emergency situations through solidarity campaigns, while hoping for a constant contribution to the European Bund through the sale of its publications overseas. The problem with this was less the dependence on information

---

8   Bund Archives, New York, RG 1400, ME-18, 3, Letter: Dr. J. Halpern, Friends of the 'Bund', February 1905.
9   Bund Archives, New York, RG 1400, ME-18, 3, Bergman: *Tsentral farband* report, Referat fun der driter yehrlikher konventsh fun di bundistishe organisatsye in Amerika 1906, p. 9.
10   1905 exchange rate: 1 pound = 4.87 dollars; Officer 2010.
11   Michels 2009, p. 18 f.

flows from Eastern Europe, but rather that the imported literature was eagerly consumed, while local organisations exhibited little willingness to pay.[12] This changed profoundly after the 1905 appeal, and 'paying up' would become a way of being a Bundist. From now on, Bundists pursued fundraising in a more structured and long-term fashion.[13]

2 Trouble on the Print Market

Based on numerous annual reports, albeit primarily that of the *Tsentral farband fun di bundistishen organisatyonen in amerika* in 1906 (1 January 1905–1 January 1906), we can identify three modes of flushing money into Bundist coffers and strengthening relations between Bundists on both continents: selling literature, establishing long-term funds, and support from secondary-Bundist organisations.

Selling literature remained difficult. Secretary Bergman noted that, counterintuitively, 'the stormy times ... weaken sales in this field'. In the year of its founding, 1903, the *Tsentral farband* sold literature for 1,800 $ – which with an RV of 53,000 $ was a remarkable sum. In the next year, however, it dropped to 1,000 $ and only 800 $ in 1905. The slump was reinforced by the fact that many branches owed larger sums, amounting to 450 $ in 1904 and soaring to 750 $ in the fiscal year for the national convention in 1906. The money local branches owed to the *Tsentral farband* matched the value of literature sales for the entire year.[14]

This trend would continue over the following decades, although importing Bundist literature to the US was only profitable in the early years. While it remained important for political reasons, it never generated revenue worthy of mention. Highly successful in Poland, the Bundist daily paper '*Naye folkstsaytung*' hardly sold, despite its low subscription price of only three cents per day (53 cents RV) and its network of 'permanent correspondents in London, New York, Buenos Aires, Paris, Vienna; Brussels, Madrid and Palestine'.[15] The

---

12 Bund Archives, New York, RG 1400, ME-18, 3, Bergman: *Tsentral farband* report, Referat fun der driter yehrlikher konventsh fun di bundistishe organisatsye in amerika 1906, p. 11.

13 This thought is already expressed in Epstein's classic work, yet he detects the change only after the World War I relief campaigns, which in light of this study form a second step in the transformation, see Epstein 1953, p. 63.

14 Bund Archives, New York, RG 1400, ME-18, 3, Bergman: *Tsentral farband* report, Referat fun der driter yehrlikher konventsh fun di bundistishe organisatsye in Amerika 1906, p. 11.

15 Bund Archives, New York, RG 1400, ME-18, 138, Bundisher klub fun Nju York 1937, *Vegn 'bund' in Poyln* 5, back cover.

Bund Club in New York distributed it during the 1930s along with the periodical 'Forois'. In 1937 it had only 70 subscribers in America, 40 of whom were multipliers and received the paper at least partially free-of-charge (34 'Naye folkstsaytung' and six 'Forois'). The Bund's financial records reveal that earnings from print sales totalled a mere 31.98 $ in the first quarter of 1939 (about 578.00 $ RV), and only 356.53 $ (6,450 $ RV) over the entire year. Given that a sum of 48.90 $ had to be paid to the 'Folkstsaytung' in 1939, the profit was still enough to avoid falling into debt, support writers like Josef Opatoshu (155 $) and H. Leivick (Leivik Halpern, 60 $) in 1936, and grant the Bund Club a credit of 25 $ on 12 May 1939.[16] Yet the earnings were not enough to support the Eastern European Bund. A better way of accomplishing this was through *Memorik* issues, such as the special edition of the 'Naye folkstsaytung' marking the Bund's fortieth anniversary. While the 34 paying 'Naye folkstsaytung' subscribers generated a turnover of 234.43 $ between March 1937 and February 1938, the Club earned almost the same amount (231.95 $, 4,060 $ RV) from sales of a single, heavily illustrated special issue in the autumn of 1937.[17] Overall, it can be assessed that print sales possessed a community-building effect and drew multipliers closer to the Bund, but did not contribute to successful and reliable fundraising.

3   Activism's Strength

The other two modes of early Bundist fundraising relied on situational mobilising and sought to institutionalise this model. After their success in 1905 following the aforementioned call to action, the *khaverim* continued to develop the spontaneous collection of the *Fraynd fun bund*. They founded a revolutionary fund that same year which, as treasurer Karl Fornberg reported, was able to muster 10,010 $ (295,000 $ RV) in 1905 and transferred exactly 9,006.39 $ to Geneva after deducting local costs.[18] This was amassed through many small donations from workers in the US, often collected in the context of strikes.[19] The records list only a few large individual donations (such as Meyer London's). They never stood out much, as the Bund did not gain favour among the Jewish

---

16 Bund Archives, New York, RG 1400, ME-18, 28, Account books (1933–9).
17 Bund Archives, New York, RG 1400, ME-18, 23, Bills.
18 Bund Archives, New York, RG 1400, ME-18, 3, Fornberg: Treasurer's report, Referat fun der driter yehrlikher konventsh fun di bundistishe organisatsye in Amerika 1906, p. 12.
19 Bund Archives, New York, RG 1400, ME-18, 3, Bergman: *Tsentral farband* report, Referat fun der driter yehrlikher konventsh fun di bundistishe organisatsye in Amerika 1906, p. 9.

philanthropists who sometimes provided other Jewish projects with exorbitant sums from their private assets.[20] The Bund was successful in fundraising only as a network. It not only refrained from seeking out philanthropists, but in fact denounced them as 'bourgeois' and situated them on the other side of the class struggle.[21] The revolutionary fund was able to increase its revenue in 1906, providing a total of 11,500 $ (331,000 $ RV) to the Russian Bund.[22] Such large sums exceeded the most costly item in the Russian Bund's budget, smuggling literature into the Pale, which amounted to 10,000 $ between autumn 1903 and the end of 1905, as well as the Foreign Committee's entire budget in 1903 (9,000 $).[23]

Due to the rise in incoming donations after 1903 and the looming revolution in Russia, the Bund's budget rose to 41,500 $ in the first 11 months of 1905 alone.[24] The sum was accumulated mainly through fundraising in Russia and primarily the US. It built on the storms of outrage that followed the Kishinev Pogrom in 1903. While Jews all over the world established philanthropic relief organisations for pogrom victims, the American Bundists reported that they stuck to their activist participation patterns and established self-defence units. In the US this militant response to violence could not be exercised with a Browning rifle or paramilitary training, but only through solidarity. The self-defence units explicitly formed not as a relief organisation, but as a 'self-defence fund' that saw itself, similar to the 'revolutionary fund', as a part of the battalions in Russia rather than mere supporters. Owing not least to the incoming news of more pogroms in Russia, the fund became the most important representative of this second mode of Bundist fundraising and the most successful part of the network. Commenting on the successful defence against a pogrom in Zhytomyr in 1905, chairman of the self-defence fund Abraham Caspe summarised: 'The Zhytomyr Pogrom showed to all the miracles that self-

---

20   Noteworthy examples in this regard include the classical benefactors of poor Jews, usually on behalf of the 'people' as a whole, such as the aforementioned Baron Hirsch, the Jewish Colonization Agency or ICA, the Russian-Jewish Gintsburg family, or Moses Montefiore. On this see Avni 1973; Nathans 2004, pp. 57–70; Green 2010, esp. pp. 123–7.
21   The *Forverts* supported this policy for several years, but as Ehud Manor noted, eventually moved closer to banker Jacob Schiff and upper-class lawyer Louis Marshall, largely to the same degree it distanced itself from Bundism; see Manor 2009, p. 44f.
22   Michels 2005, p. 156.
23   Bund Archives, New York, RG 1400, ME-18, 3, Excerpt from the Bund Foreign Committee's report to the sixth Bund congress, Referat fun der driter yehrlikher konventsh fun di bundistishe organisatsye in Amerika 1906, p. 8f.
24   Bund Archives, New York, RG 1400, ME-18, 3, Excerpt from the Bund Foreign Committee's report to the sixth Bund congress, Referat fun der driter yehrlikher konventsh fun di bundistishe organisatsye in Amerika 1906, p. 9.

defence can accomplish and the work became successful' – explicitly including the work of the American *khaverim*.²⁵ The fund collected some 30,363.49 $ (894,000 $ RV) in 1905 alone, exceeding the volume of the revolutionary fund almost three-fold. Caspe was thus able to transfer around 5,000 $ to the Foreign Committee in Geneva five times per year, along with additional sporadic smaller sums.²⁶ As the fund's operating costs were only 437.11 $ that year, the collection can be considered tremendously successful.²⁷

The *Tsentral farband* also had low operating costs in 1905, which compared to the previous year only rose because it now paid a full-time secretary, and temporarily even a paid treasurer. Their salaries swallowed up about two thirds of the 1,500 $ the *Tsentral farband* spent on overhead in the revolutionary year.²⁸ This was an investment to professionalise activism in the US, although these 'professional revolutionaries' were no agitators like their nominal colleagues in Eastern Europe but rather activist financial administrators.

The third mode of Bundist fundraising emerged in the branches of the secondary-Bundist organisations, above all the *Arbeter-ring* and certain branches of the ILGWU. Support from the latter depended more on individual initiatives like later chairman Vladeck, who supported the Polish Bund's children and youth work well into the 1930s.²⁹ Inside the *Arbeter-ring*, however, certain branches sought to organise secondary-Bundist institutional support. One such organisation was the *Dvinsker brentsh fun Arbeter-ring*, or Branch 75. At its founding in 1904, it adopted the bylaws of the Russian Bund and later renamed itself the *Vladimir Medem brentsh*. The branch committed itself not only to the usual solidarity among *Arbeter-ring* members, but also declared support

---

25   Bund Archives, New York, RG 1400, ME-18, 3, Referat fun der driter yehrlikher konventsh fun di bundistishe organisatsye in Amerika 1906, p. 10; on Zhytomyr in the context of the pogroms around 1905 see Lambroza 1992, p. 223 f.
26   It is unclear if and to what extent this went into the Foreign Committee's budget. If the entire sum was used for this purpose, the US *khaverim* would have raised nearly the entire 1905 budget.
27   Bund Archives, New York, RG 1400, ME-18, 3, Referat fun der driter yehrlikher konventsh fun di bundistishe organisatsye in Amerika 1906, p. 12.
28   Salaries (480 $), printing and advertising (363.50 $), mail and related (207.25 $), external rents (139 $), festivities (126 $), demonstrations (50 $), office rent (42.45 $), and miscellaneous (32.65 $) for a total of 1,440.82 $. The annual report miscalculates by 10 cents; Bund Archives, New York, RG 1400, ME-18, 3, Referat fun der driter yehrlikher konventsh fun di bundistishe organisatsye in Amerika 1906, p. 12.
29   This becomes clear above all in the film discussed in more detail below, 'Mir kumen on', in which Vladeck reads the introductory words in his function as chairman of the ILGWU. On this see also Kantorovitsh-Gilinksi 1971; Pickhan 2001a, p. 249 ff.; Jacobs 2009, p. 77 f., p. 139.

for the Bund in Russia as one of its main goals. It officially resolved that a minimum of 10 percent of all earnings would be sent there. This worked quite smoothly during the initial years, with the sums paid to the Bund often exceeding those allocated to members in need of support. They began to recede after 1908. Although the sums grew more modest, the Bundist self-understanding did not.

In the late 1920s and with the recovery of the Bund in Poland, the branch's activity again soared, allowing it to support both its 200 members as well as the Bund in Poland.[30] Over the course of 35 years until 1939, the branch transferred a total of 3,097.67 $ (around 38,000 $ RV) to the Bund back home. A relatively small sum and not remotely comparable to the donations the *Fraynd fun bund* collected, it nevertheless added to the many similar contributions flowing in from overseas.[31] That said, the *Dvinsker brentsh* should not be reduced to the money it raised. Apart from dollars, it also exchanged substance and experience. Many branch members were highly influential Bundists in the ranks of the *Arbeter-ring*.[32] It also engaged in transnational cultural work, most prominently by publishing the memoirs of important worker Bundist Layb Berman in Warsaw in 1936. To this day, these memoirs represent the most widely known recollections of a Bundist worker.[33]

4 Fundraising as Activism

Given the relevance of the American *khaverim* to the Bund in Russia, it is hardly surprising that in 1906 the American Bund office also aspired to send a delegate in good standing to the next Bund central assembly in Russia.[34] The activists understood their work as active participation in the social thread of the Russian Bund and thus also a continuation of their Bundist activism in America. While scholarship on transnational political networking mostly concentrates on the transfer of worker organisation models and ideological exchange,

---

30 See reports and accounts in Dvinsker bundistisher brentsh 75 arbeter ring 1909; Dvinsker bundistisher brentsh 75 arbeter ring 1914; Dvinsker bundistisher brentsh 75 arbeter ring 1924; Dvinsker bundisher brentsh 75 arbeter ring 1939; Dvinsker bundistisher brentsh 75 arbeter ring 1954.
31 Dvinsker bundisher brentsh 75 arbeter ring 1939.
32 This referred to educational work from very early on, see Zaks 1925, p. 505, p. 509, p. 824f.
33 Berman 1936.
34 Bund Archives, New York, RG 1400, ME-18, 3, Referat fun der driter yehrlikher konventsh fun di bundistishe organisatsye in Amerika 1906, p. 16.

fundraising also represented a crucial element in the network between Eastern European and North and South American activists.[35]

To understand this network, it is important to note that fundraising consists of more than the sums of money transferred across the ocean, which are frequently mentioned in research as contributions or support from the periphery to the centre. The central part of activist fundraising was not the transfer, but rather the collection of money. This was a transnationally oriented yet eminently local practice that, in the case of the American Bundists, also built on North American and Jewish traditions of participation through contribution. Research on these topics is largely preoccupied with the functional modes of civil societies and national welfare management.[36] As a social practice, fundraising for charity fostered social cohesion in society, as it supported and structured the emerging social system through individual integration in the anglophone democracies of the period. Geared towards national questions of social security and belonging, it helped create local institutions.[37] It was often tied to gender-specific role models, local needs, and paternalistic social relations.[38]

In this regard, the Bund linked up with the Jewish philanthropic tradition that had been politicised since the Jewish Enlightenment.[39] The turn towards the masses in Jewish politics around the turn of the century added a new activist layer. This culture of donating for political ends often pursued secular goals, but nevertheless retained the religious background of the Jewish 'culture of giving'.[40] The Bund broke with this traditional legitimation. It viewed the collection of donations as revolutionary action facilitating the creation of a new, Bundist world. While charity had been a substitute for modern diplomacy to a politically ambitious Jewish elite, and the charitably inclined middle classes mostly focused on community work, the Bund represented a transnational model of solidarity embodying the global Yiddish community on a class basis.[41] Both Bundist and secondary-Bundist organisations – the latter of which, such

---

35 Frankel 1984, p. 175 f.; Frankel 2009, p. 63, p. 68; Michels 2009.
36 Foundational: Finlayson 1994; Beito 2000, pp. 228–34; Alexander 2006, pp. 229–34; Tillotson 2008, p. 14 f., pp. 102–29, pp. 228–37. Lainer-Vos 2012 (building on actor-network theory) also emphasises its social-constructive character.
37 See esp. Beito 2000; Tillotson 2008; Morris 2009.
38 Gordon 1998; Bender 2004a.
39 Haumann 2002, p. 50, p. 163 f.; Horowitz 2009.
40 Plotinsky 1995; Sherwin 2005, p. 118 f.
41 For a rather uncritical but nevertheless foundational depiction of the personal component of political philanthropy see Green 2010, pp. 43–98, p. 155 ff., pp. 190–3.

as the ILGWU and the JLC, are discussed in the following – contributed to this, were open along their fringes, and supported *yidishkayt* across party lines.

Because Bundists took the turn to the masses seriously, they acquired the needed funds on the street. This in turn required propaganda and made the Bund visible. Their practice departed from traditional patterns of Jewish charity, while simultaneously addressing the open question of where money for the revolutionary movement in Russia actually came from. Although most research treats money as an available good in revolutionary history, this perspective argues that fundraising was a crucial transnational activism pattern. The Eastern European Bund depended on it and often enough all other activism patterns were tied to it. Moreover, the corresponding publicity caused Bundist activism and Bundism to thoroughly permeate the Jewish societies of the New World, even if the 'Bund' label gradually faded away.

This historiographical marginalisation also has a 'historical' side to it. Contrary to other activism patterns, the activists themselves neither commemorated nor heroised it. Although fundraisers exerted all their energies in pursuit of financial resources, they nevertheless dealt in 'filthy lucre' and thus lacked the grandeur of ideological debates or cultural work. In revolution, activists are seen as printing leaflets, smuggling weapons, and running schools. The history of activist transnational fundraising thus represents an initial, important step towards an economic history of the Russian revolutions yet to be written.[42]

5 Transnational Ties Further Institutionalisation

Initial fundraising initiatives were tied to special events and situations, although the American *Tsentral farband* pushed forward structures and professionalisation. These were absolutely necessary, as the Russian Bund required a reliable partner in the US. According to estimates, at least half of the Bund's income came from American donors.[43]

This is why, in 1906, Mark Liber turned to supporters in the name of the Central Committee of the Russian Bund with a letter he distributed through Abraham Caspe in New York. Untypically, it addressed 'all Jewish workers and citizens of America'. Liber's opening line included the most diverse range of supporters, who might side with the Bund not for its class politics but rather for its cultural and modernist programme. Although Liber explicitly reiterated

---

42 Wolff 2012b.
43 Michels 2009, p. 20.

the aims of the struggle, asking for support during the election campaign to the second Duma in 1906 'to settle accounts with the bloody leaders of the reaction and to take power from the ruling gang',[44] he toned down the class-struggle rhetoric and emphasised more common Jewish traits. The revolution, he stated, was not only against 'hatred and slavery', but also against anti-Semitism and for the unity of the 'Social Democratic Party', for the Bund as the 'party of the international brotherhood of the proletariat can fight against anti-Semitic agitation with much more success than all other parties'.[45] As the Bund was 'the strongest Social Democratic organisation in the Jewish Pale', only it could wage the struggle 'for the freedom and happiness of the people'. Consequently, 'everyone who cares about and values the cause of freedom must help the people in this struggle'. The letter closed with an appeal that drew on experience and duty, rather than on a recent involvement in the class struggle. Liber called on all 'Jewish workers in America' to give something back to the Bund, for the '"Bund", in which whole rows of you enjoyed their revolutionary education, expects from you the necessary material support'.[46] Secondly, he turned to those who did not previously share in this knowledge formation: 'Jewish citizens ... who want to support the Jewish people in its struggle against political, bourgeois, and national rightlessness'.[47]

The appeal ennobled the US fundraisers as supporters authorised by the Central Committee, and simultaneously extended Bundist work beyond the narrow field of socialists to include any Jews with a modern mindset. Fundraising remained radical and activist nonetheless, and abstained from allying with major Jewish financiers over the years to come. This allowed the *Tsentralfarband* to consolidate its position and become a constant presence in the transnational Bund alongside the *Fraynd fun bund* for many years.

Conditions in Argentina are more difficult to ascertain. No sources indicate any relevant flow of financial resources to the Russian Bund, and no such activities are noted in the self-historicisations of the *Avangard* or Bundist Pinie Vald. However, even the earliest sources mention fundraising on behalf of local groups.[48] Pinie Vald's memoirs in particular suggest that early funding for the *Avangard* was obtained through active workers making regular sacrifices to support the movement. This could easily lead to financial ruin or criminal activ-

---

44   Bund Archives, New York, RG 1400, MG-7, 20, Oyfruf [1906], p. 2.
45   Bund Archives, New York, RG 1400, MG-7, 20, Oyfruf [1906], p. 2 f.
46   Bund Archives, New York, RG 1400, MG-7, 20, Oyfruf [1906], p. 3.
47   Bund Archives, New York, RG 1400, MG-7, 20, Oyfruf [1906], p. 3.
48   Der avangard 1908; Vald 1908a, pp. 12–15; Vald 1908b, pp. 21–3; Vald 1942.

ity.[49] The contributions were often start-up funds before *'Der avangard'*, for example, became self-sustaining.[50]

This changed at least from the twentieth anniversary of the Bund onwards. In 1917 the *Avangard* group issued a series of postcards featuring portraits of famous Bundists including Bronislav Grosser, Noakh Portnoy, and Raphael Abramovitch.[51] The lustre of such leading figures was intended to rub off on the *Avangard*. In 1919 it published a postcard of A. Litvak, 'the radiant author of the Bund. One of its best *tuer*, leaders, and propagandists', and in March 1919 staged a play based on one of his texts 'to benefit the propaganda fund of the organisation *"Avangard"*', an event that charged 0.50 pesos for admission – contrary to the norm in Argentina, where events and lectures were usually free.[52]

Of course, this did not mean there were no relief funds for Eastern European issues in Argentina. Influential personalities of Jewish Argentina founded the *Tsentral hilfs-komite far di yidishe milkhomeleydende* (*Comité Central de Socorro a las Víctimas Israelitas de la Guerra*), the Central Relief Committee for Jewish War Victims (referred to as *Comité Central de Socorro* in the following). Over the following decades, the latter first supported any Jews affected by World War I, later pogrom victims, and eventually, during World War II, Jewish war victims and refugees. It increasingly organised itself internationally with branches in many Latin American countries and collected sums at its headquarters in Argentina, which in several years exceeded the one-million pesos mark.[53] The organisation was a modern, philanthropic institution founded for the purpose of aid, not participation in the sense of Bundist activism or even self-defence.[54] This is also reflected in the number of individual donations from wealthy community members or the Banco Israelita del Río de la Plata of up to 20,000 pesos.[55]

---

49   Various depictions can be found in Vald 1929.
50   Vald 1909a.
51   IWO, Buenos Aires, 1114, Postcard 'Tsum 20-yohriken yubiley fun "bund"', 1917.
52   IWO, Buenos Aires, 1114, Card: A. Litvak, 1919.
53   IWO, Buenos Aires, Comité Central Pro Socorro a las victimas israelitas de la guerra y refugiados, Annual reports 1918–1923, 1935; Circular [194?].
54   On this see esp. Brinkmann 2007.
55   IWO, Buenos Aires, Comité Central Pro Socorro a las victimas israelitas de la guerra y refugiados, Circular [194?]: Algunos Donantes de Sumes Desde Pesos 1000,-. The exchange rate to the US dollar was about 4:1 at the time. When directly converted, 1,000 pesos would represent about 3,630 $ RV, albeit based on purchasing power in the US. While we lack the tools for measuring the worth of pesos, it can be safely assumed that the corresponding real value would be somewhat higher than the calculated RV in dollars.

6 The Pitfalls of Institutionalisation: Relief Campaigns, Collection Lists, and the (Re-)Birth of the Argentinian Bund after 1917

Civil war and pogroms in Russia also mobilised the Avangardistas. Yet instead of setting up their own self-defence funds, they supported the *Comité contra les pogroms* [sic] *en Polonia*. In contrast to the *Comité Central de Socorro*, this committee mostly relied on its contacts with many small Zionist and socialist groups, but also Talmud schools and religious organisations.[56] While it accepted major patrons, a large share of its funds came from small-scale collections. From June 1919 onwards the *Avangard* regularly sent delegates to the committee's meetings.[57] Numerous workers' organisations adopted a similar approach, such as the Union of Jewish Tailors (*Unión Obrera des Sastres Israelitas*) or the *Biblioteca popular nueva rusia* – which naturally communicated with the committee in Yiddish, despite its Russian name.[58] The committee did not restrict its actions to raising money, and also called for symbolic collective protest. In this regard, the *Centro Sionista* from Concordia in the province of Entre Rios proudly reported that on 29 July 1919 at 12:00 all Jewish shops closed and displayed messages in their shop windows such as: 'Closed due to the Persecution of Jews in Poland'.[59] A meeting 'of delegates from all existing Jewish communities' in Buenos Aires also passed a corresponding resolution.[60] The committee's record therefore displays a certain form of activism in Argentina, although its financial results remained meagre: all together, 47 individuals and organisations from Buenos Aires donated a mere 1,515 pesos, rising to 2,229.60 pesos when donations from the interior were added. After deducting expenses, only 643.44 pesos remained in the treasury.[61] In the end, the undertaking was only profitable due to 700 pesos from the 'upper-class' *Comité Central de Socorro* – the largest individual donation. By comparison, in its first year of 1916–17 – even before outrage at the pogroms in Eastern Europe and the *Semana Trágica* in Argentina engulfed the Jewish community – the latter's skilful lobbying efforts allowed it to raise 22,230.55 pesos in the *Capital Federal* alone, amounting to a total of 60,493.33 pesos nationwide.[62]

---

56 IWO, Buenos Aires, 1036, 13; 27.
57 IWO, Buenos Aires, 1036, 1; 6.
58 IWO, Buenos Aires, 1036, 13; 19; 20; 21.
59 IWO, Buenos Aires, 1036, 32.
60 IWO, Buenos Aires, 1036, 26.
61 IWO, Buenos Aires, 1070, 16.
62 IWO, Buenos Aires, Comité Central Pro Socorro a las victimas israelitas de la guerra y refugiados, Balance General, Desde el 1. Diciembre de 1916 hasta el Noviembre de 1917 (1918).

Looking at successful modes of activist fundraising, we can conclude that the *Comité contra les pogromes en Polonia* was only mildly successful because it was too broadly oriented. Its mobilisations did not occur within the context of a specific social movement. Normally quick to offer solidarity and support, even the socialist initiatives participated with marked reluctance. The tailors' union contributed the largest share at 25 pesos, undercut by the Poale Zion (15 pesos), the *Biblioteca nueva rusia* (10 pesos), and even the *Avangard* group, which only paid the minimum of five pesos – despite the fact that Bundists usually spared no expense to fight pogroms.[63] While these sums had the character of token contributions, their participation expressed a shift: fundraising became more important and more international in Argentina, able to reach more people than just the milieu surrounding certain organisations. Nevertheless, activist fundraising organisations still had to discover a more successful operating mode in Argentina.

7 Collection Lists

The first of these organisations emerged on behalf of the Bund in Russia. Bundist and Avangardista M. Veber founded the *Hilfs komitet farn bund in freyen rusland* with several fellow activists in 1920. In March of that year, the committee sent out collection lists to many of their comrades 'to help the Bund in free Russia' by gathering donations and addresses. The procedure relied not on the network of a central organisation, but rather employed countless *tuer* as intermediaries to raise funds on behalf of the Bund in Russia. This well-documented example illustrates the successes and problems of such an approach. Some recipients responded tersely that they never asked for the lists in the first place and were, as a certain A. Pinsker wrote, utterly unfamiliar with the committee or its goals.[64] Some of Veber's letters went unanswered.[65] Others, however, threw themselves into the work and tried to raise as many pesos for the Bund as possible.[66]

Judging by the lists' sequential pagination, Veber must have distributed at least 159 lists. The archives, however, contain only a low two-digit figure, possibly reflecting the number of successful responses. Collectors took various approaches. Some used the lists as official forms and accurately recor-

---

63 IWO, Buenos Aires, 1070, 15.
64 IWO, Buenos Aires, 1114, 37.
65 IWO, Buenos Aires, 1114, 47: 48.
66 See various letter written by Bundist *tuer*: IWO, Buenos Aires, 1114, 37; 38; 40.

ded names and individual sums ranging between 50 centavos and usually one peso, sometimes even five or 10 pesos. They were mostly active in their immediate social surroundings, often their family and friends. Others added sums obtained 'at front doors'.[67] While the former built upon established networks, the latter relied on less-defined networks such as their neighbourhood. A final account is not available, but according to the existing lists (it remains unclear whether these are all returned lists) the campaign managed to collect 333 pesos from several hundred donors.[68] This means that neither approach was particularly successful in financial terms, but that the campaign reached a substantial number of supporters and brought the issue to the attention of many more.

Yet from the standpoint of Bundist fundraising, and despite some collectors' ambitions, the results were disappointing. Most activists collected between 20 and 50 pesos, stating in the attached letters that they considered the sum insufficient but it was all they were able to collect.[69] One *khaver* even insisted that 'it wasn't my fault' the collection was so meagre.[70]

This campaign not only exemplifies Bundist fundraising as such, but moreover helps to understand the *Avangard* group's demise. The strongest expression in this regard is a correspondence between the two Avangardistas A. Kohn and M. Veber. Veber not only founded the *Hilfs komitet farn bund in freyen rusland*, but tried to sustain the Bundist *khavershaft* within the *Avangard* through it. In the spring of 1920, however, the gulf between left and right finally and irreversibly tore open between him and the younger A. Kohn. On 17 March 1920 Kohn wrote to Veber, still in a friendly tone, that he whole-heartedly supported the campaign. Matters were complicated, however, as

> your statement concerning the 'Bund in free Russia' with 'I therefore also call on the youth to take the initiative' appeals to only a small section of the youth. You will be able to tell when you see the list which I hope to complete without stress. It remains to be seen, however, whether I will manage to do so. I shall not be able to fill out more than one list, because among [the youth] are those who support the Bund as well as unfortunately those who are effectively against building it there, who fail to understand that they themselves can be the root.[71]

---

67 IWO, Buenos Aires, 1114, 52.
68 Sums taken from collection lists and added together, IWO, Buenos Aires, 1114, 52.
69 See various letters, IWO, Buenos Aires, 1114, 40; 41; 45; 46; 49; 50.
70 IWO, Buenos Aires, 1114, 43 [Signature illegible, Hirsch, followed by a sketch of an octopus].
71 IWO, Buenos Aires, 1114, 39.

Kohn thus already had difficulty conveying Bundist goals to Jewish youth in Argentina, but was particularly unable to convince young Argentinian Jews that they could help found a radical left-wing Bund in Soviet Russia. Bundist solidarity was also tied to identity and experience. Kohn and Veber had agreed until then, but Kohn would subsequently address broader problems:

> But now permit me a few questions. As I read in the daily press, a Bund committee has been established. Is it really just a relief committee? Or is it acting independently? I hope you will explain all this to me very precisely, for which I thank you in advance.[72]

While Kohn notes in the first part of his letter that the activist value of fundraising for the distant Bund was very difficult to convey to the Argentinian-Jewish youth, in the second part he asks, from the perspective of a left-wing Avangardista quite capable of distinguishing between the Bund and a relief organisation in support of the Bund, whether there are really plans for an Argentinian Bund. Veber's response did not make it to the archives, but Kohn's answer only 10 days later was noticeably more uncouth:

> Received your letter. In sum, I don't understand your reasoning regarding the necessity of organising a Bund here in B. Aires. You state that the interests of the 'Bund' were once represented by the organisation 'Avangard', but why does it no longer defend it? With its latest statement?[73] In this respect, I can tell you that I myself was one of those who stood with [the *Avangard*] as long as possible, which is why it is certainly unnecessary for me to condemn it now. I'm the wrong person for this, and if you now set up a 'Bund' organisation simply to confirm the aforementioned – well, do you really believe that is necessary![74]

He changed his tone in closing, promising to collect more money and continue until reaching 100 pesos.[75] In the last letter between the initiator of the lists, Veber, and their most successful collector, Kohn, the lists were no longer relevant. The conflict over the proper organisation pushed the fundraising aspect into the background. Kohn accused Veber of being a splitter for sticking to

---

72   IWO, Buenos Aires, 1114, 39.
73   This was most likely a stance on the Russian Revolution, which later led to the remainders of the *Avangard* joining the Partido Comunista de la Argentina.
74   IWO, Buenos Aires, 1114, 42.
75   IWO, Buenos Aires, 1114, 42.

his plan of organising a Bund, since 'in the current *Avangard* group [there is] a great deal of chaos and anarchy'. This rendered Veber an opponent who endangered the movement's unity through his aspiration to become a 'preposterous victor'.[76] Ultimately, the *Avangard* split. It was driven by changes in Eastern Europe from both sides, the Communist and the Bundist, but ultimately motivated by questions rooted in Argentina. The Relief Committee for the Bund in Free Russia thus also disappeared, caught in the middle and lacking an overarching social movement. While Veber aimed to establish such a movement, Kohn disparaged this as 'splitting', not reflecting however that the alleged 'splitters' in fact continued to work as Bundists, while the remainers turned towards Communism. The relief committee was officially dissolved in late April 1920.[77]

Following this rather inglorious end of the *Avangard* and Bundist relief campaigns, fundraisers' interest during the 1920s focused primarily on Argentinian issues. Collection lists were often deployed in the process, mostly on behalf of the smaller schools.[78] Yet these lists never became 'activist questionnaires', which, as demonstrated above, acquired a deep, identity-forming meaning essential to the movement's survival.[79] The only items inquired about were name and donation sum, whereas contact information or the donor's self-reflection as part of the organisation were omitted. The lists were not about collecting information on donors and subsequently the supportive network, but rather tools to motivate collectors to gather as many individual donations as possible.

Fundraising therefore relied on activists' personal networks, a method that was too unreliable for long-term funding. Due to the ongoing financial need, the school movements in particular were eager to stabilise this income and began establishing a multi-tiered membership system in the late 1920s.[80] Collection lists as a method remained highly popular in Argentina nonetheless. No such dominance can be detected in the records pertaining to the United States, although there were of course certain campaigns marking specific occasions. After similar strike collections during the 1900s, Bundists in the US began

---

76 IWO, Buenos Aires, 1114, 44; 51.
77 IWO, Buenos Aires, 1114, 45, general comparison: Part III.8.
78 Such as IWO, Buenos Aires, 1111, various appeals and lists, esp. Donation list for 'Yidishe folks-shul Sholem Alejiem', 1930.
79 See Part III.11.
80 The first Sholem Aleichem School, for instance, changed its collection of addresses from 'parents' to 'members': IWO, Buenos Aires, Sholem Aleijem, Zwischo, Registro de Padres, 1925–8; Libro de Socios, 1928–30.

utilising their stronger base and established stable organisations that would gradually become important institutions the Bund's organisational network.

8 Institutionalising the Actors: Relief Organisations as Organs of Struggle

In the United States, the first years after the October Revolution were also a period of Bundist reconstitution that became a period of re-institutionalisation following the Bund's twenty-fifth anniversary in 1922.[81] In the process, which also included a re-orientation towards the new Bund in independent Poland, the Bundist organisations in Argentina and the US grew more similar.[82] After both the *Avangard* and the *Federatsye* broke apart, activists used the local centrifugal process to set up official Bund Clubs in New York in 1923 and Buenos Aires in 1924.[83] An organisation in Montevideo followed in 1930.[84] Membership cards of the American Bund Club in New York clearly stated its three main goals:

1. The aim of the Bund Club in NY is to support, morally and materially, the struggle of the Bund in Poland.
2. Anyone who sympathises with the ideas and principles of the Bund in Poland and is willing to support it both morally and materially can be a member of the Bundist Club in New York.
3. The members of the Club commit themselves to paying membership dues and contributions in accordance with the decisions of Club meetings.[85]

This is remarkable. Although the Bund Club was a new Bundist institution in New York, it defined all of its relevant issues with reference to the Bund in Poland. Moreover, all three points had a material aspect at their core. Contrary to the American *khaverim*'s demand for representation at the Bund's congresses around 1906, they now recognised the Polish organisation's supremacy. I

---

[81] On the celebration see Part II.4.
[82] Oler 1973; Brumberg 2001.
[83] Bund Archives, New York, RG 1400, ME 18, 10, Poster; Circular; Kromorski 1938, p. 9f.; Laubstein 1997, p. 186f.
[84] Bund Archives, New York, RG 1400, ME18, 151, Ershte derklerung vegn der grindung fun a bundisher grupe in montevideo, hoypt-shtat fun urugvay (11 July 1930).
[85] Bund Archives, New York, RG 1400, ME 18, 10, Bund Club membership card, New York [1923].

am not aware of a single source suggesting the New York Bund Club demanded representation within the Polish organisational structure. The Club declared itself a component of the Polish Bund and obliged its members to keep their attention focused eastward. This allowed the New York Bund Club to conceive of itself as a revolutionary socialist organisation just like the Bund in Poland, and thus withdraw from the certainly futile revolutionary struggle in the US during the 1920s.

The Bund Club maintained this position until 1947, officially even during World War II when the German occupation of Poland effectively destroyed the Bund as a party in that country. The exiled General Secretary of the Polish Bund, Emanuel Novogrudski, whose fundraising campaign sent him to the US in 1939 where he decided to stay after war broke out in Europe, signed off on one of the many donations from the New York Bund Club to the Bund in the Polish underground in March 1940 as follows:

> We are writing to confirm the receipt of 500 dollars [7,650 $ RV]. We are not expressing our gratitude to you because we see you not as an outsider, but rather as part of the whole, and you don't say thank you to yourself. Bundist greetings, Emanuel Novogrudski.[86]

Novogrudski was undoubtedly in a position to extend such recognition at the time, as he firstly occupied an appropriate office and secondly acted as the main administrator of the external Bund branches.[87] To him, it was clear that the exchange consisted of far more than just money, and included solidarity in the struggle – even if realities in the US and occupied Poland could hardly have been more different. In this mediating function he also issued letters of recommendation for membership in the New York Bund Club to several activists unknown in New York, thereby testifying in both directions that the Bundist *mishpokhe* provided the desired community particularly during these harsh times.[88]

Three functionally differentiated types of Bundist relief organisations emerged from this solidarity work during the interwar period. The first group

---

86 Bund Archives, New York, RG 1400, ME-18, 29, Letter: E. Novogrudski to the Bund Club, New York, (4 March 1940).
87 Goldfarb 1967. On his pivotal role in the Bund's leadership see Novogrudski 1941; Novogrudski 1951; N.N. 1968.
88 Bund Archives, New York, RG 1400, ME-18, 29, Numerous letters of recommendation from Novogrudski to the Bund Club, New York (1940). Similar experiences of a Bundist *mishpokhe* are reflected in Grosman 1945; Brumberg 1999.

supported educational work, particularly the TSYSHO schools and the Medem Sanatorium, while a second group raised funds for the political Bund in Poland. From the mid-1930s onwards, these groups were joined by a third type of relief organisation fighting fascism and National Socialism. It included major organisations like the JLC, which in some regard exhibited similarities to non-activist relief organisations such as the JDC or the HIAS, although they differed in that the JLC and similar relief organisations were rooted in class consciousness and socialist solidarity.

9 Focus: Educational Work

Fundraising developed in accordance with the growing Bundist focus on schools in the 1920s. The TSYSHO and the Medem Sanatorium primarily attracted the fundraisers' attention.[89]

Advocacy on behalf of children was not confined to emigrated Bundists overseas. After the Tsarist empire disintegrated, a small Bundist colony emerged in Berlin. It was initially linked to the Menshevik 'Foreign Delegation of the Russian Social Democratic Party', led by the ex-Bundist and now prominent Menshevik Raphael Abramovitch together with Julius Martov.[90] From the mid-1920s onwards, however, Bundists in Berlin sought to represent themselves and founded an official Bundist organisation focused on local community building, complemented from the late 1920s onwards by fundraising on behalf of the TSYSHO. To this end they founded the 'Representation of the Jewish Schools in Poland'.[91] Its activists proved flexible, and broke with activist fundraising for the first time. They appear to have relied much more on support from other Jewish relief organisations and representatives than mass actions.[92]

Despite the gulf between German Jews and 'Eastern European Jews' (*Ostjuden*) characterised by both xenophobia and social difference,[93] the Representation nevertheless turned to the Aid Organisation of German Jews (*Hilfsverein der deutschen Juden*). In this letter, the *khaverim* adjusted their rhetoric and skipped the sort of '*alte heym*' romanticism so often evoked in the US. Most

---

[89] On the Medem Sanatorium see Kozłowska 2014.
[90] On Abramovitch's time in Berlin see esp. Abramovitsh 1944, pp. 343–55.
[91] Bund Archives, New York, RG 1471, 5, 66; Invitation, agenda: meeting of the '"B"-grupe inm "Sholem Aleykhem-Klub"' (25 February 1928).
[92] A targeted search in the stocks of the Bund Archives in New York could perhaps illuminate further aspects.
[93] Aschheim 1982; Barkai 2002, p. 7 f., p. 137 ff.; Saß 2012.

importantly, they now portrayed the TSYSHO as a Jewish charitable institution rather than an activist socialist one:

> The Yiddish secular school is a home for the children in the literal sense, where they at least during the day are protected from exposure to the misery and corrupting influence of the street and the milieu. After regular class in the morning, the children remain at the school to casually socialise, engage in voluntary group work in the reading room or school workshop, and the children feel safe – this is their home, where they feel sheltered and comfortable and which they leave only reluctantly.[94]

To underline this idyllic depiction, the letter included a list of quotes from German professors attesting to the progressiveness of the TSYSHO and the Medem Sanatorium. According to them, the Bundist schools did everything to 'live up to the demands of modern pedagogy and raise the child in a new spirit', particularly through the strengthening of 'creative, artistic powers'.[95] In an attempt to convince the *Hilfsverein*, Bundists sugar-coated their relationship to the Polish state and emphasised that, although they received a small government subsidy, it was very difficult to obtain and marked a 'major moral victory', whereas 'in its effect on the school budget this support is negligible'.[96] The text avoids the terminology of class struggle, carefully navigates around references to socialism, and refrains from any discussion of the growing anti-Semitism of Polish state institutions.[97] Yet the call for help was not particularly successful, and thus in a similar tone Bundists would turn to other institutions like Berlin's Jewish congregation in 1930. The authors of this letter, Israel Lichtenstein and Jakob Lestschinsky, once again portrayed the TSYSHO as a solely Jewish organisation, omitting its socialist background altogether.[98]

Their address to Eduard Bernstein, the grey eminence of German Social Democracy's reformist wing, was quite different. In a longer letter, Bernstein

---

[94] The original document is in German and explicitly speaks of a secular Yiddish, not secular Jewish school. Bund Archives, New York, RG 1471, 5, 66, Letter to the Hilfsverein der deutschen Juden (25 October 1928), p. 2.

[95] Bund Archives, New York, RG 1471, 5, 66, Letter to the Hilfsverein der deutschen Juden (25 October 1928), p. 2.

[96] Bund Archives, New York, RG 1471, 5, 66, Letter to the Hilfsverein der deutschen Juden (25 October 1928), p. 3.

[97] See especially the numerous activist and incendiary articles in the Polish Bund's youth publications, particularly *'Yugnt veker'* and *'Khavershaft'*.

[98] Bund Archives, New York, RG 1471, 5, 66, Letter to the Jewish congregation, Berlin (25 April 1930).

praised the TSYSHO's socially conscious work to the skies and pledged his solidarity. Unfortunately, he wrote, he was unable to provide any funds nor appear at a scheduled meeting.[99] Success in the city remained limited for the Berlin group, even when they explicitly played the Social Democratic card. On the other hand, it also showed that the Bund was far from the dogmatic organisation whose programme left no space for flexibility as it is often depicted. When it came to supporting the Polish schools, the Bund pursued cooperation with a wide array of organisations including those it usually opposed ideologically, whether reformist Social Democracy or 'bourgeois' Jewish community organisations. Even in North America – where there was no TSYSHO, TSVYSHO, or *Gezelshaft*, but rather a quarrel among Bundists, Zionists, and Communists between the *Arbeter-ring*, the *Farband*, and the IWO – the division along party lines began to unravel. Building on his experience, leading New York Bundist and *tuer* of the school movements inside the *Arbeter-ring*, Philip Gelibter, soberly and tersely telegraphed his *khaver* A. Gelberg in Toronto: 'Please cooperate with the Poale Zion in the Work of the Jewish Schools in Poland'.[100]

Situational cooperation between the Bund and Poale Zion became common before World War II. The ongoing functional differentiation and subsequent emergence of new single-issue organisations and committees created new overlaps. The quest for a new Jewish education in particular served as a bridge between the two, while the conflict escalated in other areas. This at least reinforced the secular position in the Jewish *kulturkamf* (cultural struggle). Despite similar developments on the general level, its respective evolutions in the US and Argentina were quite distinct. The Bund's American organisations tried their best to truly become part of the Polish-Jewish secular school system, with clearly separated support campaigns for the schools in Poland and, to a smaller extent, the *Arbeter-ring* schools. Argentinian Bundists, by contrast, combined the two, envisioning a global school movement with Poland at its centre. As I show in the following, they would subsequently organise fundraising accordingly.

10 Priorities: Pro-Bundism and Anti-Fascism

It should first be noted that the schools were by no means the only field of Bundist fundraising. Different organisations pursued different goals to support

---

99 Bund Archives, New York, RG 1471, 5, 66, Letter from Eduard Bernstein (27 November 1928).
100 Bund Archives, New York, RG 1471, 5, 71, Telegram from Gelibter to Gelberg (5 April 1932, 17:29).

the schools, but often overlapped in terms of personnel. The boards of organisations close to the Bund often featured recurring names, among them Dovid Mayer, Joseph Baskin, A. Litvak, Nokhem Khanin, Benjamin Levine, and Barukh Vladeck and Zivion.[101] The differentiation was purely organisational, helping to turn the organisations into clearly defined points of contact for both US donors and the Polish Bund. In this fundraising network the Bund Club acted primarily as a recruitment pool and logistical switchboard, distributing work among smaller groups and committees whose addresses (hardly surprisingly) often matched that of the Club, namely the Forverts Building at 175 East Broadway, Room 418.[102]

The Medem Club stood out among these organisations. While the Bund Club had to make do with just a few hundred dollars per year through the 1930s – which is why its donations remained marginal despite low overhead costs – the Medem Club was able to generate much higher sums.[103] The Medem Club emerged from a relief committee for Jewish schools in Poland founded in New York in the 1930s, and subsequently transferred regular donations of several thousand dollars to Poland.[104] It intensified its work in 1937 for the Bund's fortieth anniversary, allowing for multiple fundraising methods. Apart from individual actions and celebratory events, the Bund published a small booklet filled with supporters' ads and fraternal greetings costing these supporters, including individuals, ILGWU and ACWA locals, and branches of the *Arbeter-ring*, between two and 15 dollars.[105] Although the bill for the large celebration at the Mecca Center in 1937 exceeded its revenue, it (re-)mobilised activists who then supported the fundraising work of other organisations.[106] The Medem Club launched a campaign of articles, lectures, and other agitation in this context, allowing it to increase its initial capital of 392 $ (6,850 $ RV) on 1 March 1937 to 46,500 $ (829,000 $ RV) by the end of 1938. This exorbitant sum went directly to the TSYSHO schools in Poland with hardly any deductions. It was requisitioned from local committees' donations in various US cities (17,030.49 $), supporting associations (7,936.77 $), trade unions (3,785.09 $), *Arbeter-ring* schools (2,227.38 $), *Arbeter-ring* branches (3,963.04 $), along with a major donation from the Jewish Labor Committee, or JLC (5,000 $).[107]

---

101 Bund Archives, New York, RG 1400, ME-14B, 6.
102 Bund Archives, New York, RG 1400, ME-14B, 8.
103 Bund Archives, New York, RG 1400, ME-18, 28, Bund Club accounting books (1933–8).
104 Bund Archives, New York, RG 1400, ME-18, 18, Letters, receipts.
105 Bund Archives, New York, RG 1400, ME-14B, 4, 40 yor bund (1937); ME-18, 18, Price list (1937).
106 Bund Archives, New York, RG 1400, ME-18, 11.
107 Bund Archives, New York, RG 1400, ME-18, 18, Income for Jewish schools in Poland from the Last Campaign, 1.3.1937 – 31.12.1938.

The latter is probably the best-known secondary-Bundist relief organisation. It was founded with the support of the AFL in 1934 in order to support European Social Democrats, and acquired fame as a Social Democratic relief organisation in the 1940s, when it assisted not only Jewish but also many German socialists in their escape to the US.[108] It leaned heavily on Bundist networks, and its founder and longstanding president Barukh Charney Vladeck represented the secondary-Bundist line within American unions.[109] The JLC largely depended on its successful integration into the wider US labour movement.[110]

Before it became a prominent relief organisation during World War II, the JLC functioned primarily as a fundraising organisation collecting large sums from American workers and intellectuals for European purposes. Already at its founding meeting it raised 150,000 $ (roughly 2.8 million $ RV), which was not immediately transferred but rather used as capital stock for further projects.[111] The JLC donated substantial sums to Social Democratic parties and movements in Europe in the years to come. The Bund also benefited, receiving 9,000 $ (160,000 $ RV) in 1937–8 alone.[112]

The JLC raised another 100,000 $ (ca. 1.79 million $ RV) in the first year of the war up to September 1940. Scholarship on the Bund takes a curious view of these numbers. Daniel Blatman, who introduced the figure, estimates that an escape from Vilnius to the US via Vladivostok and Yokohama would have cost about 518 $. He goes on to conclude that the available capital could only have helped 200 refugees due to the high cost. Blatman deduces that the 'high costs of the trip and the limited resources available' also led to major tensions in the Bund.[113] Yet if Blatman's cost estimates for escape are correct, his own figures for funds raised in that year alone indicate that the sum would have sufficed to cover the passage of almost 10 times as many refugees. Whatever the exact number, it would inevitably appear marginal given the magnitude of the Holocaust. This explains the despair Bundists felt in the US, who looked on from overseas with their hands tied.

No fundraising campaign could have adequately addressed the monstrosity of the war and the Holocaust. In this light, and in relation to surrounding fundraising history, the history of the JLC – although largely helpless when facing

---

108 Jacobs 1993a; Jacobs 2010.
109 Vladeck chaired the JLC until his death in 1938.
110 The European socialist networks became equally important during and after the war, see de Bollardière 2012.
111 See esp. Collomp 2005, p. 115 ff.
112 Pickhan 2001a, p. 220, fn. 162.
113 See Blatman 2003, p. 28 f.

the destruction of European Jewry – must be seen as a tremendous success. As the JLC was not a specifically Bundist but rather socialist relief organisation, it also supported non-Jewish and Social Democratic parties. Moreover, the JLC's funds not only went directly to Poland, but also to Bundist relief organisations in the US. During the 1930s, for instance, it funnelled several thousand dollars to the Bundist schools in Poland through the Medem Club. Intra-American cash transfers thus also benefited the European movements.

Just as fundraising has thus far received little attention in movement research, the historiography of the Bund also confines itself to brief mentions of transfers by major organisations like the JLC or JDC.[114] As important as such transfers were, major organisations were in fact either latecomers to revolutionary fundraising or, as evidenced by the JDC's declining support for the TSYSHO, unreliable partners for Bundists.[115] External support for the Bund in Poland therefore rested on the many small organisations that made it, as exemplified by the *Fraynd fun bund*, into an activist issue.[116] Not even the Medem Club restricted its activities to school-related fundraising, granting financial support to the '*Naye folkstsaytung*' or even the Bund Club in New York.[117] The various links between the organisations often converged on Levine's desk.[118] From there, the larger portion of the funds went directly to the TSYSHO and could be used at the latter's discretion. Other transfers had defined purposes, such as those from Jacob Pat, who, as chairman of the Medem Club, transferred 1,000 $ to the TSYSHO and announced another payment of 4,750 $ (ca. 86,900 $ RV) in the coming days, of which 1,250 $ was to be allocated to the schools, 500 $ to the Sanatorium, 500 $ to the trade unions, and 2,500 $ to other purposes. The JLC, which was behind the donation, likely determined this earmarking.[119]

11   Issue-Based Fundraising and the Film '*Mir kumen on*'

To gather such sums, the Medem Club and similar institutions entered the public life of New York's Yiddish cultural landscape to engage in activist fundraising among the *khaverim*. This occurred at major events and fundraisers, directly

---

114 See for example Pickhan 2001a, p. 219 ff.; Blatman 2003, pp. 21–30.
115 Pickhan 2001a, p. 243 ff.
116 Pickhan 2001a, p. 245; Blatman 2003, p. 23, p. 195.
117 Bund Archives, New York, RG 1400, ME-18, 18, Letter from M. Levin to S. Oshri (29 March 1938).
118 Bund Archives, New York, RG 1400, ME-18, 18.
119 Bund Archives, New York, RG 1400, ME-18, 18, Night Letter Pat (1938?).

contacting large organisations of the US labour movement by appealing to a combination of Jewish identity, trade union life, and socialism in a way that was quite untypical for the country. During the 1930s, however, the erstwhile smallest common denominator of socialism would increasingly become an obstacle in the pursuit of broader public impact. Recognising this fact, on 9 February 1938 Bundists founded the Medem Committee, a body designed to serve as the new interface between Bundism and Jewish-cultural fundraising with a philanthropic background.[120] Although New York Bundists led by Benjamin Levine and Dovid Mayer dominated the Committee, it avoided the rhetoric of class struggle. Its activities resembled those of the Berlin-based Representation. It organised numerous fundraising events as well as screenings of the Bundist film 'Mir kumen on', now translated into 'Children Must Laugh', accompanied by announcements which, in terms of style, fit the letter to the *Hilfsverein der deutschen Juden* cited above.

'Mir kumen on' is a scripted documentary about the Bund-operated Medem Sanatorium near Warsaw. Based on progressive education, it was a convalescent home for children of Jewish workers who stayed there for three to 12 months. Beyond that, it was also an institution of political socialisation. Produced by the Sanatorium in 1936 exclusively for fundraising purposes, the film represents a remarkable source today.[121] The English introduction to this multilingual film – mixing Yiddish, English, and Polish segments delivered by Barukh Charney Vladeck – spoke to the American immigrant audience. He was not introduced as a Bundist, however, but in his prestigious function as ILGWU chairman. Vladeck personally helped fund the film and promoted its distribution in the US as chairman of the Medem Sanatorium Committee.[122] Named after the Medem Sanatorium hymn, 'Mir kumen on' (literally: 'here we come'), the documentary introduces the Sanatorium's work in a loose narrative. Three key motifs illustrate what the producers and the fundraisers considered essential for the presentation of educational work in Poland and the mobilisation of mostly American donations.[123]

Firstly, shot only with children from the Sanatorium and no professional actors, 'Mir kumen on' portrays the Medem Sanatorium as an idyllic children's

---

120 Bund Archives, New York, RG 1400, ME-14B, 8, Medem komitet tsharter, founding charter (1938).
121 On this matter see the extensive material in Bund Archives, New York, RG 1400, ME-12, 18; 30B; 30D; additionally Kantorovitsh-Gilinksi 1971.
122 Bund Archives, New York, RG 1400, ME-14B, 8, Screening tickets; Invitations; Gilinski 1971, p. 23f.; Jacobs 2009, p. 139, fn. 82, fn. 83.
123 All subsequent scenes described with reference to Ford 2006.

refuge, created by the Jewish workers' movement in defiance of the Jewish lifeworld in Poland ravaged by capitalism, destitution, and starvation. The depiction of Poland draws on narratives and experiences that once motivated the potential donors now living in the US to join the social movements in Eastern Europe. In the Sanatorium, the film informs the audience, there is 'little talking and much eating', children learn about modern hygiene, and there is a general atmosphere of mutual understanding. In one scene, a boy who just arrived at the Sanatorium is caught stealing food. The caretaker pulls the bread roll out of the embarrassed-looking boy's pocket, garnishes it with fresh toppings, and puts it back in his pocket. The film places great emphasis on the depiction of happy children playing outdoors, portrayed in stark contrast to life in the Polish cities. Lengthy scenes depict summer and harvest festivities, including many children's song performances, poems, and plays. It culminates in an almost professionally delivered reading of a poem by a boy about the 'Schlauraffen Land', the golden land far across the sea:

> Far away, behind China / lies a praised land / where men do not toil like slaves, but rather live like earls / not tied to the classes / full of honey in the streets / one cannot wash himself with it / one can eat chocolate ... / if you want, you can leap here in no time / if you want, you can play in the band / and they have all kinds of fish / children dance on the tables / see, there you live like a king ... / if you take the long road behind China, you will see the land.

In the English subtitles, this vision of a childlike, classless utopia is shortened, politically softened, and not situated 'behind China'. They read:

> There is a land beyond the sea / Where people do not work like slaves / Where children play; where men are free / Where men not know of kings or knaves / Where one may do whate'er one please / Where honey from our fingers drips / I'd like to make the wondrous trip / If I could only sail a ship.[124]

There is reason to believe that this utopia of a 'land beyond the sea' corresponded to the motives that drove so many Jewish migrants to the US – and which were now to be translated into donations for the Medem Sanatorium.

---

124   Ford 2006, Chapter 19 f.

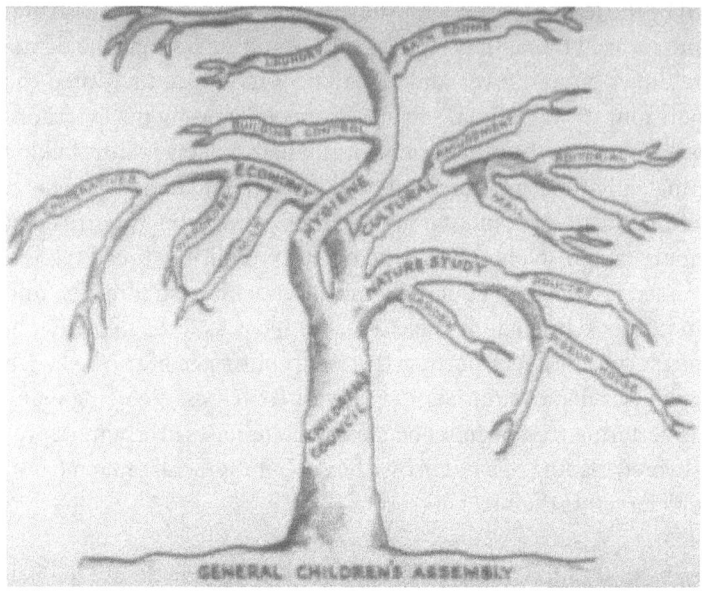

FIGURE 22 Schematised self-representation of the Medem Sanatorium. Captions from bottom to top: General children assembly; Children's council [with the four focus areas]: Nature study (garden, poultry, pigeon house); Cultural (amusement, mail, editorial); Economy (milk, wardrobe, cooperatives); Hygiene (bath rooms, building control, laundry)
IMAGE TAKEN FROM FORD 2006

This brings us to the film's second motif: solidarity. The children set an example with their behaviour, such as when resolving an argument: the boy Lazar learns after a fight with Zalmen that 'Zalmen is a *khaver* like all of us'.[125] Needless to say, the daily collective salutation is '*Khavershaft!*' Another scene shows how children 'administer' the Sanatorium through a democratic general assembly, which a diagram described as the Sanatorium's educational foundation (see Figure 22). Throughout the documentary, solidarity and children's happiness mutually determine each other, extending well beyond the circle of the Sanatorium. In another scene, a girl reads out the day's news to the other pupils: firstly, six new rabbits have been born; secondly, new children have arrived; and thirdly, the mineworkers are on strike because their children have nothing to eat. In a later scene, the children's council resolves to sacrifice a daily portion of their food to invite at least a few of the suffering miners' children to the Sanatorium. The Sanatorium's headmaster approves of this with delight.

---

125   Ford 2006, Chapter 14.

The third motif is that of secularism, which develops through the role of the small, newly arrived Orthodox boy named Zalmen. On his arrival he wears a black coat and hat in the summer temperatures, in accordance with tradition. Despite his anxiety, he is fascinated by the other boys playing volleyball. The narrator remarks: 'Zalmen in his long Orthodox coats thinks this is a pretty rough game'. When the ball flies towards him while standing on the side-lines, he heads for it but does so quite clumsily and trips, allowing another boy, dressed in shorts and a t-shirt, to snatch it from him. Zalmen then gets the ball thrown at his head in a boyish, friendly sort of way. This encourages him and he quickly joins the game, amicably welcomed by the older boys and girls in their athletic outfits. Caught up in the game, he promptly loses his hat without noticing. The hat simply vanishes in the dust between the children's feet. Next, he takes off his long black Orthodox frock and flings it into the corner, running after the ball as euphorically as the other children. The narrator remarks laconically: 'Off with the coat and Zalmen is a boy among free boys'.[126]

These three motifs – healthy and happy children, solidarity and self-help, and secularism – correspond to the focal points of Bundist fundraising and its secular educational work described in the previous chapter. The film's narrative integrated seamlessly into the rhetoric of 1930s Bundist activism. Consequently, the film proved beneficial to the Medem Committee's work as a high-end fundraising medium. Although the elaborate production had been difficult to finance and the film was banned in Poland, individual donors ultimately bridged all funding gaps. In the US, the Medem Committee even used the film's ban in Poland to drum up interest.[127]

The Committee's donation earnings quickly reached several thousand dollars, which now came from workers, worker organisations, and for the first time also from American-Jewish benefactors. Among them was New York-based financier Jacob R. Schiff, an important Jewish philanthropist to various Jewish organisations, but not the Bund. As Ehud Manor notes, it was owed not least to Schiff's influence that the 'Forverts' increasingly grew from a socialist propaganda paper to a Yiddish-language institution of Americanisation. Although Bundist groups never consciously assumed this role, their cultural turn during the interwar period ultimately allowed them to accept 'bourgeois' money. Schiff transferred 1,000 $ to the Medem Sanatorium in 10 monthly instalments immediately after the Medem Committee's founding.[128] Accord-

---

126   Ford 2006, Chapter 12.
127   Bund Archives, New York, RG 1400, ME-14B, 8, English-language invitation.
128   Bund Archives, New York, RG 1400, ME-14B, 8, Donation receipts; Letter from Jacob R. Schiff to the Medem Committee (14 February 1939).

ing to available documents, it was the largest individual donation the Bund received before World War II. The Medem Committee further advanced this new kind of fundraising among Jewish elites and multipliers by issuing special invitations to screenings for valued supporters.[129]

The film also inspired campaigns by secondary-Bundist organisations. In 1937 the *Arbeter-ring* launched a collection under the motto, 'The Jewish children in America for the Jewish children in Poland'. The *Arbeter-ring* schools alone raised 1,518.55 $ (ca. 26,600 $ RV) in a short period of time, of which about half (707.94 $) was donated by schoolchildren. As its initiators commented, the campaign fulfilled a solidary double purpose:

> The campaign already exhibits very fine [financial] results. But it also has an important educational meaning for the children, who are participating in the campaign with their class. They have connected mentally with the Jewish children, with their schools – with their suffering and their joys.[130]

'*Mir kumen on*' generated a feeling of affinity, and the *Arbeter-ring* branches continued to conduct collections. A total of 52 branches and committees participated, contributing another 2,248.31 $. In the end, the campaign yielded no less than 3,766.86 $ (ca. 65,900 RV) among workers and worker children, which went directly to the TSYSHO.[131]

The outbreak of World War II shifted everyone's priorities. Bundist fundraising now aimed at emergency relief, assistance for refugees, and supporting the armed resistance. The Medem Club and Medem Committee essentially merged in their work. Although the Medem Sanatorium continued to exist in occupied Poland, it could no longer be supported in the same way. Its 'dissolution' by the Nazis in 1942 meant the murder of its children and teachers in Treblinka. The Medem Club chaired by Dovid Mayer adjusted its priorities during this phase, and began focusing on collections for the Bund in the US and the journal '*Unzer tsayt*', founded by New York Bundists and war refugees in 1941. These constituted the first steps that would later lead to the founding of the World Bund.[132] During the war, Bundist groups returned to mainly internal movement mobilisation, organising meetings and events for members and sympathisers in the

---

129 Bund Archives, New York, RG 1400, ME-14B, 8, Invitations (1938).
130 Bund Archives, RG 1471, 76, Report: Di yidishe kinder fun Amerike far die yidishe kinder in Poyln [1937].
131 Bund Archives, RG 1471, 76, Report: Di yidishe kinder fun Amerike far die yidishe kinder in Poyln [1937]; ibid., Accounting report: Der arbeter-ring far di yidishe shuln in Poyln [1937].
132 On this see Slucki 2012.

familiar activist style, including the use of collection lists.[133] Yet this also meant that the 1943 support campaign for '*Unzer tsayt*', for example, was able to raise the sum of 1,000 $ (ca. 14,500 $ RV) only through the help of 114 activists – a sum Schiff had provided by himself only four years prior.[134]

Apart from the campaigns for party and educational institutions, in the 1930s Bundist fundraising also began supporting important individuals, in a way mirroring the trend of personalising the Bund's history. The honour of being recognised as an important person was no longer reserved for deceased Bundists. The main relief organisation herein was the *Komitet far di veteranen fun der yidisher arbeyter bavegung*, or *Veterans Fond*, led by well-known fundraisers Khanin, Pat, and Levine. Frequently supporting longstanding veteran Bundist activists in Europe from 1934–5 onwards, the fund acquired its resources in the old familiar manner, with a blend of activist fundraising, minor earnings from book and '*Naye folkstsaytung*' sales, and membership dues. Adding to this were sporadic donations from socialist organisations like the *Arbeter-ring* or *Forverts*.[135] Its annual income was usually around 1,000 $, which sufficed to provide a number of great Eastern European Bund personalities with fixed monthly sums between 20 and 30 dollars over several years. Twenty dollars in 1934 correspond to 375 $ RV in 2018, not to mention that the money likely had a higher purchasing power in Eastern Europe.[136] In other words: Bundists in the US not only helped finance the Bund and its institutions to a large extent, but also organised a kind of grant system to support the lives and activities of selected important *tuer* from the Jewish workers' movement. Among those who benefited in the long term were D. Aysenshtot and M. Blyumin-Kurski in France, as well as F. Loyzer Zelmanovitsh in Lodz and J. Portnoy in Warsaw. The system also periodically subsidised the living costs of Mendel Skutelski or Bund leader Henryk Erlich in Poland, or Bundist and leader of the Mensheviks in emigration Raphael Abramovitch in Berlin and Paris for short periods of time.[137] Between 70 $ and 110 $ were transferred to these veterans every month, amounting to at least 15,633.56 $ (ca. 273,000 $ RV) between February 1934 and February 1939.[138]

---

133 Bund Archives, New York, RG 1400, ME-18, 17, Invitations, lists (1941–3).
134 Bund Archives, New York, RG 1400, ME-18, 17, List: Beyshteyerungen far 'Unzer tsayt', New York (14 September 1943).
135 See for example Bund Archives, New York, RG 1400, ME-18, 23a, Finantsyeller Barikht fun dem komitet far di veteranen fun der yidisher arbeyter bavegung (1934).
136 Bund Archives, New York, RG 1400, M–13, 69, Finantsyeler barikht (1938); ME-18, 23, Reports, wire transfers.
137 Bund Archives, New York, RG 1400, ME-18, 23a, Money orders (13 February 1934 to 24 August 1937).
138 The archives contain the financial records of only ten months in 1937 and 11 months in 1938.

This was accompanied by frequent spontaneous campaigns, such as in early 1935 when the fund collected some 254 $ in just a few days through a press campaign 'for a sick comrade in Europe'. It included a publicly accessible annual statement of accounts published in the *Forverts*, complete with donors' names and the volume of donations.[139] The campaign and the printed names of its supporters thus honoured both the veterans as well as the donors. At the same time, it once again linked the *Forverts* to Bundist fundraising. Correspondingly, the *Forverts* proclaimed a recurring annual Bund Day as a day of action on behalf of the Polish Bund in 1938.[140]

Despite repeated conflicts between the Bund and Cahan's *Forverts*, all parties could rely on one another in these contexts. This was true for the *Veterans Fond* not least because it essentially represented a continuation of the *Fraynd fun bund* founded in 1903.[141] Both had a Bundist leadership, while the equally important advisory board included many prominent non-Bundists, or at least people whose names were associated primarily with non-Bundist organisations. While these were people like Meyer London and Abraham Cahan in the 1900s and 1910s, now socialists and trade union leaders like David Dubinsky, Vladeck, or Hillel (Harry) Rogoff came to the fore. Similar to Bundists Zivion, Basin, and Mayer, they used their prominence to draw attention to the Polish Bund.[142]

The funds raised were essential for the chronically underfunded Polish Bund. While the transnational workers' movement had still been the mobilising argument in the 1900s, now *yidishkayt* and transnational secular Jewish worker culture took centre stage. Secular Jewish schools therefore attracted most donors. Many supporters saw them as the spearhead of modern Jewish life emerging from Yiddish worker culture. As shown above, the construction of the past was essential here. Whenever there was a collection, it occurred with little reference to current political work or even the urgently required arming of the Bund. Instead, it drew on both progressive orientation as well as commemorative practices, including letters advertising the veteran fund and countless *Memorik* events.[143] In this context, it is hardly surprising

---

Bund Archives, New York, RG 1400, ME-18, 23, Geld geshikt tsu di veteranen fun yanuar 1935 biz merts 1939; 23a, Money orders 1934.
139 *Forverts* (8 June 1935).
140 Bund Archives, RG 1400, ME-14B, 6, Excerpt, *Forverts* [1938].
141 Cahan 1904; Cahan 1942, pp. 229–31.
142 Bund Archives, New York, RG 1400, ME-18, 9, Circular: Der komitet far di veteranen fun der yidisher arbeter bavegung (1936).
143 Bund Archives, New York, RG 1400, ME-18, 9, Appeal (1936); 10, Poster: 1897–1922 – 25

that the largest-ever official Bundist gathering took place in 1947 on the Bund's fiftieth anniversary in New York.[144]

This all rested on decades of established practices and evolved networks. In that regard, it was an important insight that Bundist fundraising would not lose its worker base even when expanded to include and embrace classical philanthropists. Unfortunately, the exact sum reaching Poland through this Bundist network over the course of the 1930s cannot be precisely determined. Based on the available data, we can confidently estimate that transfers between 1933–9 alone amounted to around 150,000 $, probably closer to 200,000 $. Measured by today's RV, this corresponds to between 2.7 and 3.5 million dollars through those organisations, committees, and campaigns alone. Adding to this were the substantial payments from the JLC and sums mobilised by travelling fundraisers.

12 Transnational Actors: Travellers as Ambassadors and Activists

In Argentina, fundraising and other activism patterns overlapped to a far greater extent than in the US. It peaked in the 1930s, when the Argentinian and Polish Bundist schools were conceived as elements of one transnational cultural complex. The key document in this regard is once again the TSYSHO's letter to Bundists in Buenos Aires discussed in the previous chapter, which called for fundraising on behalf of the TSYSHO and announced the visit of *khaver* Tabachinsky in his function as a school ambassador. During that trip he inspired the founding of the *Gezelshaft* and the TSVYSHO.[145] This was not only an act of reaching out from Poland to Argentina, but also a transfer of a fundraising method developed in the United States: from now on campaigns were led among émigrés, but often supported by envoys from Europe.

13 Early Travellers, Political Travellers

In the early years, fundraising in the US relied only on emigrated Bundists and their sympathisers. The Bund in Europe supported them in the form of inform-

---

yoriker yubileum fun 'bund' (1925); ibid., 11, Numerous materials for the fortieth anniversary (1937).
144 *Unzer tsayt*, 1–2, (1948), pp. 41–6.
145 IWO, Buenos Aires, 1111 [Educación], Letter from the Yidishe shul-organisatsye – hoyptfarvatltung, Warsaw to Shul komitet, Buenos Aires, 2 January 1930.

ation and appeals where possible, and from 1903 onwards also through 'manpower'. As the Bund groups' collections aided by the '*Forverts*' became more and more successful, Abraham Cahan recalls the Bund 'finally [dispatched] a delegate for the following purpose: to agitate for the Bund in America, to collect financial supports for it. One after another they came, all important leaders'.[146] Regrettably little is known about these early travellers. The first to break initial ground was no less a figure than the 'father of the Bund' himself, Arkadi Kremer. As a founding member and organiser, he impressed audiences not through theoretical acuity or rhetoric skills, but rather earned his reputation as a teacher and warm-hearted intellectual. He represented a 'charismatic leader' in the Weberian sense, although he felt at home in the *kruzhki*, not at demonstrations.[147]

Very much in the style of Bundist *Memorik*, Cahan emphasises that Kremer was the first Bundist traveller of this sort. Only in passing does he mention that Kremer's equally important wife Pati Kremer already travelled to the US a few months before him, and represented the Bund very actively there. Cahan refers to her only as 'Kremer's wife', not as one of the otherwise heroised 13 co-founders of the Bund to which she belonged. His memory circles around the 'leading man', indeed on the very first meeting of 'great men' or, literally, 'brothers' – namely that between Cahan and Kremer in Vilnius in the 1890s. With regard to fundraising (the reason for Kremer's visit), Cahan only mentions that, in contrast to the also-present Chaim Zhitlowsky or many of his Bundist successors, delegate Kremer never agitated in public. He left that to his fellow traveller and *tuer* Ezra Berg. Unlike Zhitlowsky, who acquired large sums for the Socialist Revolutionaries as a travelling fundraiser that same year and left a deep impression on US Bundists, Kremer was no socialist missionary and never even intended to 'import' Bundism to the United States.[148] Kremer was at his best in local community building and personal conversations. This was significant 'among *khaverim*', which is why not only appearances at large gatherings, but also smaller banquets and receptions were part and parcel of such trips.[149]

---

146 Cahan 1942, p. 229.
147 See Medem 1942; Milner 1942; Kohen 1942; Kossovski 1942; Pinson 1945.
148 For a more elaborate treatment of Zhitlowsky and his impact on American Jewish socialists see Michels 2009, pp. 125–49.
149 These occurred frequently in the US and Argentina well into the 1940s, see for example IWO, Buenos Aires, 1103 [Campaña de ayuda – Shefner], Invitations (1936); 1111 [Educación], Escuela Sholem Aleichem, Invitations (1936–7); Bund Archives, ME-14B, 7, Invitation to A. Litvak's appearance in the US, Nyu Yorker Klub fun 'bund' (21 December 1925); ME-18, 13, Ticket to the 'Erlich-Bankett 1937'; ME-18, 17, Invitations to the Medem Club (1941–3); see also corresponding reports in all Jewish periodicals of the time.

This mixture proved quite successful, leading to many new contacts outside the actual movement. Non-Bundist Cahan recalls that Bundists constantly asked him what he thought of 'their Arkadi'. He replied that he considered 'their' Kremer to be 'an important personality', upon which 'they walked on with a smile on their faces, as if the person in question was their father'.[150]

Solidarity, participation, and identity merged together for local activists, sometimes also prompting travel in the other direction. Among the supporters of the Russian February Revolution were many Bundists like A. Litvak, who embarked on the arduous journey during the summer of 1917 in order to contribute to the revolution personally. The leading American Bundist nevertheless continued to play an important part in local fundraising. His co-authored book, 'Dos revolutsyonere rusland' (Revolutionary Russia), was published during his absence, and sales earnings were passed on entirely to the Bundist Yiddish papers in Russia. In an expression of *khavershaft*, it celebrated the anticipated freedom: 'Through the cold ink and the dry pages of this collective volume waves a word of greetings and best wishes from us all to the brothers and comrades over there, in the old, long-enslaved, and finally free homeland'.[151]

Departing with the highest of hopes, Litvak would turn his back on the Soviet experiment in disillusionment not long after. At first he became active in the Polish Bund, and returned to the US in December 1925 for more fundraising activities. The renowned Noakh Portnoy had travelled there only a few months earlier.[152] He endured the long trip several times and was also there at the outset of World War II in 1939. This was no special occurrence, as the travels of Polish *khaverim* to the US increased steadily in the interwar period. Such trips were complemented by several American fundraisers' visits to Europe, including activists from the JLC, among them, at least in 1935 and 1936, Bundist and JLC co-founder Vladeck.[153] These travellers did not come to Europe in search of money, however, but to inspect the institutions they supported from the US and establish new contacts.

One of the many Polish Bundist travellers in the 1920s deserving special mention is Henryk Erlich, who presided over the Bund together with Viktor Alter at the time. As party leaders, Erlich and Alter embodied the Bund's renaissance

---

150 Cahan 1942, p. 232f.
151 Salutski and Litvak 1917, p. 3.
152 Bund Archives, New York, ME-14B, 7, Ticket to honorary banquet, Portnoy (19 April 1925); Ticket to honorary banquet, Litvak (21 December 1925).
153 Collomp 2005, p. 121.

in Poland. The Polish Bund achieved its first major electoral successes during nationwide local elections held in 1927.[154] A large share of the funds required for the campaign were an outcome of Erlich's trip to the US, which produced around 40,000 $ (578,000 $ RV) – almost the Bund's entire campaign budget.[155] While this personalised fundraising was largely aimed at such political purposes until the late 1920s, it subsequently followed the turn towards the secular cultural struggle.

14   Delegates as School Activists

In this development, the much-nearer yet far-weaker Berlin Bundists were the trailblazers. Berlin's networks supporting Polish Bundists dated back to the days of Vladimir Medem, and famous Polish visitors supported the TSYSHO in particular from 1930 onwards. The decisive factor in this was TSYSHO *tuer* Israel Lichtenstein, who travelled westward via Berlin on a Bundist mission in 1930, backed by famous author, social scientist, and YIVO activist Jakob Lestschinsky. Between the German capital and Paris, they turned to important local organisations such as Berlin's Jewish congregation. Their trip through Europe also enabled the Berlin-based Bund group to organise a tour around Germany.[156] The Bund group in Berlin acted as an organ of the Polish Bund in the process, and distributed the Polish Bund's orders with the following terse instructions:

> *Khaver* Lichtenstein will come to you on 8 April to conduct a relief campaign in Germany for our schools. We ask that you work out a plan and potentially also make corresponding preparations. His action also foresees work in the provinces. Perhaps you would like to make contact with a series of cities for this reason.[157]

---

154   Jacobs 2009, pp. 1–7.
155   Once again, few sources have survived. This number is based on the Poale Zion figures the Warsaw government commissariat took on. In light of the roots of Bundist fundraising and the mobilising force of charismatic leader Henryk Erlich, I consider this sum to be fairly realistic. See Pickhan 2001a, p. 94, fn. 87.
156   Bund Archives, New York, RG 1471, 5, 66, Letter from I. Lichtenstein, J. Lestschinski to the Jewish congregation, Berlin (25 April 1930); Circular of the school committee, Berlin (30 April 1930).
157   Bund Archives, New York, RG 1471, 5, 66, Letter to the school committee, Berlin (30 March 1930).

His trip served the aim of fundraising, while at the same time advancing community building in Germany, where the small Bundist groups in cities such as Karlsruhe, Cologne, and Berlin now came into contact with each other.[158]

In the US, fundraising and community building had long worked hand-in-hand. Over the course of the 1930s, Polish Bundists continuously travelled overseas and engaged in fundraising on behalf of the schools in the US, frequently appearing at *Memorik* or cultural events.[159] Organised talks and events now mostly addressed the school system, the topic of *yidishkayt*, and during the 1930s the rise of fascism in Europe and Germany, whereas local political, socialist, or trade unionist talks are hard to find in the schedules. Such events were often flanked by reports in '*Di tsukunft*' and the '*Forverts*', guaranteeing additional audiences beyond the Bundist spectrum. Eastern European visitors integrated themselves almost seamlessly into political and cultural work: publicly they were the crowd-pullers, but within Bundist circles they were treated as *primus inter pares*. They often participated in meetings of various committees and the *Arbeter-ring*. This was such a normal occurrence that it is hardly ever reflected in the sources. Apart from that, they also supervised collections, as a letter from leading Bundist Jacob Pat to the *Varshever Vladimir Medem brentsh 215* of the New York *Arbeter-ring* indicates:

> I had barely departed from the United States when I learned that you sent money for the Warsaw schools – 150 dollars.
>
> To be honest, that puzzled me. Your meeting decided that the branch would raise 1,000 dollars for the Warsaw Medem Schools. The slogan was, 'From the Medem branches to the Medem Schools'. I delightedly informed the Warsaw schools about it immediately.
>
> Surely, you can imagine how this news was received. In my report to Warsaw I also recounted how a member at the meeting stood up and pledged a full hundred dollars. And in the end only 150 dollars came.
>
> ...
>
> The whole process is a mystery to me. I would be most grateful, dear friends, if you could let me know when and how this matter can be discussed. I await your response impatiently.[160]

---

158 Bund Archives, New York, RG 1400, ME-14B, 33. A comprehensive study has yet to be undertaken; initial explorations in Braun 2008.
159 See esp. Bund Archives, ME-14B, 7, Numerous invitations; ME-18, 13, Tickets, invitations; ME-18, 17, Invitations and corresponding reports in various Yiddish periodicals from the time.
160 Bund Archives, New York, RG 1471, 76, Letter from Jacob Pat to Branch 215 (27 July 1937).

It is unclear from the available sources how this matter ended, but during times of labour racketeering the episode must have left a bitter aftertaste – not only for the Warsaw school administration.

Such distrust marked an exception, however, and often the travellers' participation in meetings simply secured these gatherings' 'palpability'. This led to ambitious travel itineraries across North America. Kazdan's 1935 trip through the United States, Canada, and Mexico was a great success, generating 20,425.71 $ (374,000 $ RV) – surely not unrelated to his rank as TSYSHO chairman. On the other hand, his trip was no exception and certainly corresponds to the tradition Erlich started in 1927 of returning with a five-digit travel surplus.[161] The trips also prompted corresponding reports in the Yiddish-language press, further bolstering their success cycle.[162]

Bundist fundraisers often also acted as cultural ambassadors from Yiddish Poland, representing both the '*alte heym*' and the 'state of the art' with regard to secular education. Whenever possible, the meetings reproduced this lived *yidishkayt* with festivities, songs, laughter, and education. Often these visiting trips included a screening of '*Mir kumen on*'.[163] This communal fundraising practice turned the events into spaces of transnational, solidary *yidishkayt* through politics, language, music, and entertainment similar to how Tom Goyens identifies New York's anarchist beer bars as 'anarchist spaces' and 'repositories of anarchist history and memory'.[164] Donating thus not only meant 'supporting' this *yidishkayt* but participating in it, for these gatherings were habitats of a secular Jewishness that understood itself as Jewish modernity.

The process was more centralised in Argentina. Although there were local organisations in the region beyond the Bundist headquarters in Buenos Aires, such as the Montevideo group, they were more or less explicitly dependent on Bundist actions and networks in the Argentinian capital. School activists began raising funds not just for local school networks but also for the Polish TSYSHO as early as the 1920s. Their focus on schools was so overwhelming that hardly any other Bundist organisations emerged.[165] One crucial factor in this was the *Hilfs-komitet far di yidish-veltlekhe shuln in Poyln* (henceforth *Hilfs-komitet*). From the second half of the 1920s onwards, its networking efforts resulted in a rise in the

---

161   Bund Archives, New York, RG 1471, 5, 75, Barikht fun Kh. Sh Kazdan vegn zayn kampeyn n Fareynigte Shtatn, Meksike un Kanade (1935).
162   For example: Bund Archives, New York, RG 1471, 73: 20 toysend dolar geshafen fun Kh Kazshdan far di yidishe shulen in Poylen, [*Forverts*?], 30 June 1935.
163   Bund Archives, RG 1471, 77, Circular: *Hilfskomitet far yidishe shuln in Poyln* (20 February 1938); also Circular: *Hilfskomitet far yidishe shuln in Poyln* (15 March 1938).
164   Goyens 2007, p. 40.
165   See the section on secular Jewish schools in Part III.11.

number of paying members and supporting organisations.[166] The early 'associated institutions' did not include the major actors of Jewish life in Argentina such as 'Di prese' or Jewish banks, but instead countless small socialist organisations – children's, language, and workers' clubs, worker libraries, small trade unions, and *landsmanshaftn*.[167]

Tabachinsky's visit in 1931 pushed the *Hilfs-komitet* towards modernisation. Over the following years it joined forces with the *Gezelshaft* and physically relocated, first to a building at Lavalle 2239 and later changing over to the Peretz School building at Lavalle 2238. The *Hilfs-komitet* may have been of Bundist origin, but it nevertheless reflected the entire range of the secular school movement. Alongside Bundists like Pinie Vald and Jacob Botoshansky, other members such as later leader of the IKUF Pinie Katz and Samuel Rollansky, who as a socialist Yiddishist was in charge of the IWO in Buenos Aires, also determined the committee's fate.[168] It was tied to the *Gezelshaft* by the fact that *Hilfs-komitet* representatives not only collected donations for the TSYSHO, but also received the latter's school materials for the Jewish schools in Argentina. These textbooks and programmes effectively ensured the *Gezelshaft*'s progressiveness and quality.[169]

Tabachinsky's trip was successful on three levels: firstly, campaigns and activism in the capital as well as countless subcommittee visits across the country raised 15,648.75 pesos.[170] Pinie Vald was less thrilled about the sum itself and much more about the fact that each peso came from poor Jewish workers. He concluded that the first campaign of this kind in Argentina expressed symbolic solidarity with the Polish Bund, and also strengthened the Bund's presence in Argentina.[171] His 'soft' interpretation can be explained by the circumstance that the action's success as such, given the political situation in the country after Uriburu's coup d'état and the turbulent aftershocks of the global economic crisis, was rather minor in financial terms. After deducting all costs

---

166 IWO, Argentina, Fondo CAEI, Letter from Hilfs-komitet to Yidishe bine (28 October 1926).
167 IWO, Argentina, Fondo CAEI, Address and note book (192?).
168 IWO, Argentina, Fondo CAEI, Letter from Hilfs-komitet an Komitet fun gevezenem yidishn folks teater (193?).
169 IWO, Argentina, Fondo CAEI, Letter from Yidishe shul organisatsye – hoyptfarvaltung, Warsaw, no. 3429/2 to Dr. Kovenski, Buenos Aires (26 October 1933), Feyerlekhe derklerung [1931].
170 IWO, Buenos Aires, CAEI, 17, Barikht far der aktsye durkhgefihrt in Argentine fun sof may bis sof november 1931, p. 11 f., pp. 14–32.
171 IWO, Buenos Aires, CAEI, 17, Barikht far der aktsye durkhgefihrt in Argentine fun sof may bis sof november 1931, p. 5 f.

some 10,077.80 pesos remained, which were wired to the TSYSHO.[172] A comparison may help to comprehend Vald's disenchantment in this regard: at the time, the sum corresponded to about 2,400 $ (39,600 $ CPI) and was a large figure, but could hardly compare to the sums transferred by the *Fraynd fun bund* and the Medem Club – especially when taking into account the journey's half-year duration and the far-more-elaborate complexity of a trip to and through Argentina.

Secondly, the visit gradually inspired the founding of the *Gezelshaft* and later the TSVYSHO, which as Argentinian organisations of the transnational secular Jewish school system increasingly moved closer to the TSYSHO both materially as well as in terms of personnel.[173] Thirdly, it helped consolidate the organisation of fundraising itself. The *Hilfs-komitet* established itself in the capital and Jewish Argentina more generally, becoming an umbrella organisation of activist fundraising on behalf of the secular schools. It would subsequently house many campaigns benefiting secular Jewish schools, elevating the *Hilfs-komitet* to a status permitting it to invite the prominent Bundist journalist and writer from Poland Barukh Shefner to Argentina in 1936.

15 Barukh Shefner in Argentina: Campaigning between *Doikayt* and Diaspora

Shefner's visit marked the high point of exchange between Polish and Argentinian Bundists, making it a worthy empirical conclusion to this volume as it aptly illustrates the central dynamics of revolutionary fundraising. While it was an important event in its time and received far more attention than any other campaign in the press and public, so far it has gone entirely unstudied in relevant historiography.

The attention emerged above all from wide-ranging press coverage: all Jewish papers and magazines in the country regularly reported on Shefner's appearances in the various regions (see Table 17).[174] Things took off rather slowly following Shefner's arrival in late June 1936. Even Executive Committee meetings increased in frequency only after he was already in Buenos Aires. As record books and internal communications from the *Hilfs-komitet* indicate, the initial weeks saw little action – followed soon after, however, by increas-

---

172 IWO, Buenos Aires, CAEI, 17, Barikht far der aktsye durkhgefihrt in Argentine fun sof may bis sof november 1931, p. 13.
173 Zadoff 1994, p. 95 f.
174 IWO, Buenos Aires, 1103, 6 [press review 1936].

TABLE 17 Publicly advertised events during Barukh Shefner's campaign, June–September 1936. IWO, Argentina, 1103 [CAEI], 2; 6; 11, each: Posters, leaflets, cards, newspaper articles, etc.

Date	Location	Announcement	Notes
30 June	Teatro Argentino, Bme. Mitre 1446 [Buenos Aires]	Conference on the topic 'Winter and Spring in Poland'	Advertised as a thematic 'lecture', several distinct leaflets, sliding-scale admission from 0.40 to 6 pesos
6 July	Teatro 'Argentine', Bme. Mitre 1448 [Buenos Aires]	'A stroll through today's Germany'	'Tickets available at low prices'
11 July	Salón Max Nordau, Murillo 661 [Buenos Aires]	Festive evening banquet	Admission 1.50 pesos
13 July	Teatro 'Argentine', Bme. Mitre 1448 [Buenos Aires]	'Second conference: "A stroll through today's Germany"'	Continuation of 6 July, widely reported in the press
19 July	5th Sholem-Aleichem-School, Castillo 351 [Buenos Aires]	Reception, visit to the school	
20 July	Teatro 'Excelsior', Corrrientes 3234 [Buenos Aires]	'First literary conference: "The Laughter of Sholem Aleichem"'	Widely reported in the press
25 July	Montevideo	Conference on the topic of 'Winter and Spring in Poland'	
26 July	'Lokal', General Cesar Rios 4575 [Buenos Aires]	'An educational act concerning the school action'	Free admission
27 July	Teatro 'Excelsior', Corrrientes 3234 [Buenos Aires]	'A tribunal on Yiddish Theatre [*Teatro Israelita*]' with Yankef Mestl, Zalmen Zilbertsvayg, B. Shefner, Jacob Botoshansky, Samuel Rollansky	Show trial, debate, various leaflets, widely reported in the press
2 August	'Lokal', General Cesar Rios 4575 [Buenos Aires]	'A conference concerning the school campaign'	Free admission
3 August	Teatro 'Excelsior', Corrrientes 3234 [Buenos Aires]	'Tribunal over the Yiddish Theatre [Teatro Israelita]' with B. Shefner, Zalmen Zilbertsvayg, Jacob Ben-Ami, Jakob Mestel, Jacob Botoshansky, Samuel Rollansky	Show trial, debate, various leaflets, sliding-scale admission between 0.50 and 8 pesos
6–21 August	Cordoba, Tukuman, Salta, Moisesville, Santa Fe	'A tour of the provinces'	Advertised locally, tight schedule[175]
23 August	Teatro 'Corrientes'	'Morning concert, featuring the envoy of the TSYSHO, B. Shefner, as well as a major artistic programme'	Presumably broadcast via radio,[176] excellent reviews

---

175 IWO, Buenos Aires, 1103 [CAEI], 2, Plan, notes: Kh. B. Shefners tur iber provints [1936].
176 IWO, Buenos Aires, 1103 [CAEI], 2, Sopran.

TABLE 17   Publicly advertised events during Barukh Shefner's campaign (*cont.*)

Date	Location	Announcement	Notes
5 September	Tailors' house [Buenos Aires]	Reception for Shefner	
6 September	Salón 'Ezrah', Arenales 132, Avellaneda [Buenos Aires]	Major banquet and conference in honour of the famous publicist and now envoy from Poland, B. Shefner, lecture on the topic of 'A stroll through today's Germany'	
8 September	Lavalle 2238	Lecture by Dr. M. Merkin on 'From the Bastille to the Thermidor. A bit of history of the French Revolution'	Free admission
19–20 September	Rosario	Visit	Appearances in the context of local fundraising
27 September	Teatro 'Excelsior', Corrrientes 3234 [Buenos Aires]	'Grandiose artistic morning concert to conclude the current school campaign'	Many preliminary and follow-up reports, programme ranging from a satirical show to tango and classical music as well as 'Gipsy melodies' at the end, many Jewish small business owners as sponsors, tickets were available at theatres, bookshops, and 'at all three school organisations', various leaflets, sliding-scale admission from 0.70 to 12 pesos
[28 September?]		Closing event	

ing bustle. The campaign's press coverage ultimately exceeded any degree of attention Bundists had received in Argentina since the *Avangard*. As a result, Shefner's presence shifted to the centre of Jewish public attention in Argentina for a few weeks. The press barely noticed his first talk about Poland, only '*Di prese*' reported on it afterwards. This most likely accrued from the close contacts between Bundists and the socialist '*Di prese*', the most influential Yiddish daily paper in Argentina at the time. Widely renowned in Poland, Shefner's first appearance had already earned him a name in Argentina, although at first he was announced simply as a famous journalist from Poland.[177] His second talk

---

177   IWO, Argentina, 1103 [CAEI]; 6, Di prese: Der ershte efntlekhe aroystrit fun B. Shefner (2 July 1936), Di prese: B. Shefners tsveyte konferents montig dem 6tn in 'Argentine' (2 July 1936).

on the situation in Germany caused a stir and excited the audience to the point that it was continued the following week.[178]

At the same time, the *Hilfs-komitet* became more active and used its networks to help put Shefner on the map.[179] Developments gathered pace quickly from there. The announcements in the three Yiddish dailies were effusive by Shefner's second presentation on Germany on 13 July. Shefner and the *Hilfs-komitet* temporarily constituted the main topic of Jewish Argentina, and the papers consistently reported on his trip from then on. Apart from meeting announcements, both short and lengthier texts explaining the campaign and its background were printed on an almost daily basis. Shefner's appearances even marginalised worker organisation, a topic that usually received top billing. On 12 July, for example, the three leading papers published the following announcement:

> Tomorrow, at Lavalle 2238, at 19:30, the meeting of the organised workers will be held in order to finally found the committee to coordinate the work among organised workers. Given that B. Shefner's presentation will take place the same evening, the *khaverim* are asked to appear on time so that the meeting can be concluded at 21:00.[180]

The *Hilfs-komitet* was able to grow, establishing many subcommittees that collected donations across the city and in other cities, and organised Shefner's tour of the country.[181] As a result the committee's chairmen, Bundists Pinie Vald and Jacob Botoshansky, also grew in prominence and importance. The *Hilfs-komitet* began to send out a regular bulletin to the press as well as supporters and interested readers, disseminating news and appeals for support and cooperation. Eventually, most organisations of Jewish life from the tailors' union to the *Banco Israelita Argentina* supported the campaign.[182]

The Teatro Argentino, a theatre well-known for its progressive Yiddish programme, was particularly helpful during the weeks of the campaign, and the *Hilfs-komitet* addressed it as a 'friend of the secular Jewish schools'. Following suit, most Yiddish theatres across the capital supported the campaign, although

---

178   IWO, Argentina, 1103 [CAEI], 4, Various announcements; ibid., 6, Ads, reports, and dispatches in '*Di Prese*', '*Morgntsaytung*', '*Di yidishe tsaytung*', 12–15 July 1936.
179   IWO, Argentina, 1103 [CAEI], 2, Letters, cover letters (1936).
180   Cited in IWO, Argentina, 1103 [CAEI], 6, Di prese: Morgn di tsvayte konferents fun B. Shefner (12 July 1936).
181   IWO, Argentina, 1103 [CAEI], 2, Circular [1936]; ibid., 6; Numerous press reports.
182   IWO, Argentina, 1103 [CAEI], 1, Correspondence (1936).

activists had to exert pressure on several more sceptical establishments.[183] They turned to the theatres' offices and noted that they had heard their admission policy was causing 'problems', because it did not permit donation collectors. Surely, the activists wrote, this had to be a mistake, as the campaign also helped to promote the Yiddish language more generally, which was why the theatre in question must have had an 'interest in the success of the action for the secular Jewish schools'.[184] Their argument proved convincing, and in the end the biggest share of the campaign's earnings came from 'collections in the theatres'. This underscored the Yiddish theatre's relevance, elevated the campaign organisers to protagonists in the public fight for Jewish secularism, and turned Shefner into a Yiddish celebrity on the Río de la Plata.[185] One noteworthy example is the 'Trial of the Yiddish Theatre', which brought figureheads of Yiddish Argentina onto the stage together with Shefner in the style of a show trial, including the corresponding roles of prosecutor, lawyer, and judge. This show trial is not to be understood as a Stalinist instrument of power. Instead, it merged the debating culture of the Russian-Jewish intelligentsia with Chassidic and Enlightenment traditions of the 'Trial of God'.[186] Famous author, ethnographer, and composer of the Bundist hymn, *Di shvue* An-Sky (alias Shloyme Zanvl Rappoport), had already staged show trials of God in Russia as early as 1908.[187] A little later, the early Soviet Union had also witnessed a culture of show trials seeking 'justice' against various objects, from abstract concepts to historical figures.[188] Its transfer to Argentina generated a large degree of publicity, and was so successful that the trial was scheduled for an immediate re-run.

The committees convened several times per week from mid-July to the end of September, the Executive Committee almost every day. The Yiddish press flanked even these organisational meetings by announcing details and dates. This publicity probably ensured that representatives of all supporting organisations participated in the meetings, rendering the *Hilfs-komitet* a point of convergence for highly distinct movements and organisations in the city. Even the Communist *Farband fun yidishe folksshuln* joined in. From August onwards it sent delegates to the meetings, provided fundraising assistance, and like the *Gezelshaft* and the TSVYSHO organised ticket sales to Shefner's events for its

---

183 IWO, Argentina, 1103 [CAEI], 1, Letter from Hilfs-komitet to Theater 'Anboy' (11 July 1936).
184 IWO, Argentina, 1103 [CAEI], 1, Letter from Hilfs-komitet (11 July 1936).
185 Of particular significance in this regard was firstly his 'first literary conference' on 20 July, and secondly the double-feature 'show trial' of Yiddish theatre on 27 July and 3 August.
186 Wood 2005, p. 23 ff.
187 Wood 2005, p. 24.
188 Wood 2005, p. 25 f., p. 49 f.

members.[189] In contrast to the 1934 general strike, now the boundaries between Bundists, Zionists, and Communists not only began to blur, but the organisations officially worked together. This unexpected coalition was of course not without disagreement. When Bundists accused the Communist representatives of 'sabotage' and 'infiltration' after only several days, the *Farband* assured it had no intention of 'controlling' or 'leading'. The responsible *khaver* Hirsch did not withdraw from the committee, but instead delivered an 'explanation' at one of the following meetings.[190] The *Farband* remained a member of the committee as a result, which in turn would ultimately benefit from its work.

As far as refusing support is concerned, the extensive archival source collection of the *Hilfs-komitet* contains a single rejection letter written in Spanish from the *Union Israelita de Galitzia*, which refused to sell tickets in very frosty tones. Yet even the *Union Israelita de Galitzia* refrained from expressing its opposition to the campaign, instead citing its own founding statutes which explicitly forbade such activities.[191]

Because a great deal of fundraising took place at the Yiddish theatres, schools, and cultural centres, it combined transnational activism with local cultural work. That said, activism literally on the Jewish street remained equally important. Despite the many cultural events and other forms of centralised acquisition through action committees, the greatest share of money was collected via collection lists.[192] Due to the accompanying press reports, this was just as true for the local committees in Rosario, Santa Fe, and elsewhere, which Shefner visited briefly at best, but nevertheless participated in the campaign for its duration. Many of the meetings there took place in Shefner's absence. Whenever he travelled the country, Shefner simultaneously acted as a cultural ambassador. Alongside the official engagements cited above, local committees organised receptions, banquets, and gatherings without public announcement or any echo in the press. These meetings were nevertheless crucial for community-building processes within Jewish secularism in Argentina.[193]

---

189 IWO, Argentina, 1103 [CAEI], 1, Letter from Y. Shlos (Farband) to Hilfs-komitet (7 August 1936); 5, Flyer for Frimorgn-kontsert, 27 September (1936).
190 IWO, Argentina, 1103 [CAEI], 1, Letter from Y. Shlos (Farband) to Hilfs-komitet (24 August 1936).
191 IWO, Argentina, 1103 [CAEI], 1, Letter from Union Israelita de Galitzia to Hilfs-komitet (31 August 1936).
192 IWO, Buenos Aires, 1103, 13, 1–8; 14, 1–5.
193 See numerous comments in the Yiddish daily press, IWO, Buenos Aires, 1103, 6; N.N. 1936a.

To reach beyond such present masses, Shefner used all available means to also address communicative masses. He gave talks on the radio and published texts about Poland and its relevance for Argentina.[194] All this strengthened Bundism locally, garnering it even more publicity. Following a few years of interruption, Bundists could now launch a new journal called '*Argentiner lebn*'. The cover page of its first issue featured two themes: the history of Bundist publishing in Argentina, and activism on behalf of the secular schools.[195]

16 Results beyond Pesos and Dollars

The effects of this relief campaign altered local cultural politics on various levels. First and foremost, the fundraisers realised that such collections for Poland also benefited Argentina.[196] One expression of this insight was that the committee subsequently changed its name from the *Hilfs-komitet far yidish veltlekhe shuln in Poyln* (Relief Committee for Yiddish Secular Schools in Poland) to the *Hilfs-komitet far yidish veltlekhe shuln in Poyln un Argentine* (Relief Committee for Yiddish Secular Schools in Poland and Argentina).[197] This represented a novelty: activists broke through fundraising's hitherto typical barrier, which drew a clear distinction between the Old World as the target and the New World as a resource. They created a transnational space of solidarity for the secular school system, in which East and West worked together towards one progressive movement. Bundist *doikayt* remained diasporic, and thereby linked different parts of the world through practices and organisations. Attention no longer focused exclusively on distant Polish schools, but on chronically underfunded Argentinian schools as well. The emphasis of the cultural value for Argentina also made it possible to win over the Partido Socialista as a supporter.[198] The mutual benefit here was by no means merely ideological, as it practically linked the highly regarded progressive Yiddish schools in Poland with their counterparts in Argentina. By the end of the campaign the *Hilfs-komitet* had become a cultural actor in Jewish Argentina, and the *khaverim* could now focus on supporting the schools of the *Gezelshaft* and the

---

194　IWO, Buenos Aires, 1103, 15; 16; 26; Shefner 1936a; Shefner 1936b.
195　N.N. 1936d; N.N. 1936c.
196　IWO, Buenos Aires, 1103, 1, Correspondence.
197　IWO, Buenos Aires, 1103, 2, Hilfs-komitet minutes book (1936), *Es ruft di yidish-veltlekhe shul in Poyln un Argentine*.
198　IWO, Buenos Aires, 1103, 1, Letter from Hilfs-komitet to Secretario General del Partido Socialista (3 August 1936).

TABLE 18   Final account of Barukh Shefner's campaign, June–September 1936. IWO, Buenos Aires, 1103, 2, Minute book, Hilfs-komitet: session minutes (22 December 1936), pp. 57–61

Revenue (in pesos)			Expenses (in pesos)				
Direct donations	Individual donations	5,661.80	Costs				2,548.20
	Theatre collections	1,579.55	Payments	Argentina	TSVYSHO	500.40	
	Collection lists	1,902.80			Farband fun folksshuln	447.65	
	Contributions	134.00			Gezelshaft	1,443.10	
Subcommittees		3,150.45			Others	146.80	2,537.95
Institutions		2,041.00		Poland	TYSYHO		9,068.25
Events		1,654.85	Retained in cash				1,970.05
Total		16,124.45					16,124.45

TSVYSHO. The basis for this local work were funds raised during Shefners's visit that remained in Argentina after his departure.[199]

The campaign brought in 16,124.45 pesos in revenues, tediously collected over a period of three months. The profit was thus only marginally above that of Tabachinsky's trip in 1931, but the organisational structure established after the 1931 campaign allowed Shefner's campaign to collect a similar amount in half the time. Of that sum, the TSYSHO in Poland received 9,068.25 pesos and Argentinian schools 2,537.95 pesos. Around 2,000 pesos remained in the account of the *Hilfs-komitet* for upcoming local work. Apart from private donations and targeted collections, the classic collection lists were the most successful fundraising methods in Buenos Aires. They were complemented by decisive donations from major institutions ranging from trade unions to banks and revenue from the campaign's many meetings and gatherings.[200] The total sum coming from the sub-committees in more distant parts of the city or other cities, most of which was collected in the form of small donations via collection lists, is equally remarkable.[201] The *Hilfs-komitet*'s fundraising was therefore 'modern' in the way that it combined work for a secular counter-culture with the Jewish

---

199   IWO, Buenos Aires, 1103, 1, Correspondence; 1114; CAEI, Accounting book (July 1936); N.N. 1947a; Rozshanski 1972; Knapheyt 1972.
200   IWO, Buenos Aires, 1103, 2, Minutes book, Hilfs-komitet: meeting minutes (22 December 1936), p. 58f.
201   IWO, Buenos Aires, 1103, 13; 14.

mainstream. At the same time, it remained 'classically activist' as it relied on a large number of *tuer* who collected or donated money for the secular schools in the theatres and streets of Argentina's cities. Both activists and donors were therefore not only 'contributing citizens' of an already-existing community, but helped create it.[202]

The financial gain was the result of many years of cultural work. The acquired funds did not come out of nowhere, and the willingness to donate in the first place relied on finding and building adequate structures and generating sufficient interest. Donors saw themselves as participating activists of a modern community that increasingly conceived of itself as society *as such*. This is illustrated by the rhetoric of the letters, the comprehensive coalitions, the variety of topics at Shefner's evening events, and the constant positive press reports. Specific schools mattered less and less, while the general theme was increasingly that of a new society characterised by a confident Yiddish culture. While this built on an activist and class-conscious *yidishkayt*, its self-understanding was no longer limited to class conditions.

Worker culture became a transnational popular culture created by the social movement. Although banks could be won over as supporters, the many donating workers remained the primary base. *Hilfs-komitet* posters and leaflets made this point quite clear in both Yiddish and Spanish: 'The Jewish workers in Poland give their last penny to keep the secular Jewish schools alive. The Jewish workers in Argentina will follow this example'.[203] This was followed by an appeal for worker solidarity from the *Komitet fun organizirte yidishe arbeter* (Committee for Organised Jewish Workers), as 'with the school action we extend our hand to our class brothers in Poland'.[204] It was no longer the revolutionary battle cry known from the first Russian Revolution, but rather the assumption of a position in the cultural struggle in favour of a Yiddish-speaking and class-conscious definition of Jewishness. This modern *yidishkayt* adjusted Bundist *doikayt* to the realities of Jewish mass migration and new Yiddish-speaking communities far from Eastern Europe, despite the ebbing of the class struggle.

The *khaverim*, for whom the collection had been 'a historic action' from the outset, also recognised the historically relevant shift. Already during the campaign's early stages, Jacob Botoshansky stated in an important '*Di prese*' article

---

202 Tillotsonn 2008, p. 21, p. 51.
203 IWO, Buenos Aires, 1103, 5, Poster: Hilfs-komitet (1936).
204 IWO, Buenos Aires, 1103, 5, Komitet fun organizirte yidishe arbeter: Far der aktsye far yidish-veltlekhe shuln in Poyln un Argentine [1936].

that it was 'not a collection, but a cultural manifestation'.²⁰⁵ Despite their differences, supporters agreed that the fundraiser never aimed only at sending money to Poland. It was a collective statement in favour of a secular Jewishness in the diaspora, lived out through the transnationally linked means of *doikayt*. Consequently, the Bund's transnational movement stood at the very heart of Jewish secularism prior to World War II. The shift in those decades was not that the transnational social movement lost its revolutionary character, but rather it partially redirected it, redefining the socio-political workers' movement as the bearer of a socialist worker culture. The activism pattern of fundraising thus targeted the collection of money only on the surface. Through alliances and new practices, the Bund's political-economic struggle had become a transnational cultural struggle. In an age of rampant nationalism, this constituted a highly political act.

205   IWO, Buenos Aires, 1103, 5, Flyer: Kampeyn-komitet: A historishe aktsye (1936), p. 1; 6, Yankev Botoshanski, 'In loyf fun tog. Bamerkungen', *Di prese*, Buenos Aires (20 July 1936).

Conclusion, or: The Ambivalence of Bundist Modernity

The Faustian 'Gretchen question' of 'Tell me, how do you stand on religion?' became a crucial question for all of Jewish life in the first half of the twentieth century. If previous debates among Eastern European Jews had centred on the forms of religiousness, now religion as an anchor of Jewish life itself was in question. Not only did the Bund position itself firmly on the radically secular side of the debate, but as a socialist representative of the Late Enlightenment became a trailblazer and protagonist of a new secular Jewish identity that resonated with the masses. It rejected the necessity of religion and its related hierarchies on the one hand, and on the other managed to inspire a 'Jewish Renaissance' through its emphasis of *doikayt* and *yidishkayt* like no other mass movement of its time. It did so by proposing new, secular modes of organisation to Jewish communities and filling them with life.[1]

Michael Brenner diagnosed a 'Jewish Renaissance' among German Jewry for the interwar years, revolving around the rediscovery of a religious Jewish identity and modern Hebrewism.[2] In line with this notion, Kenneth Moss's study of Yiddish culture in the early Soviet Union identified a 'Jewish Renaissance' in that period, but one which in his view was committed firstly to governmental revolutionary politics and secondly to absolute secularism. The problem was that many Yiddish activists reluctantly joined the Soviet path.[3] In addition to these two, my study focused on a third type of Jewish renaissance during the interwar years. In line with Michael Brenner's description, it drew on both aging intellectuals as well as a powerful youth movement. Yet rather similar to the renaissance characterised by Kenneth Moss, it was committed to radical secularism, the workers' movement, and Yiddish culture. Not despite, but rather because of global dispersion and secularisation, Jewishness became truly colourful and diverse in the interwar years. Jewish socialism transformed into a Jewish worker culture that went far beyond the primarily political associations of the pre-war era.[4] Unlike both forms of 'Jewish Renaissance' Brenner and Moss depict, the Bundist version was confidently diasporic and transnationally organised, manifesting above all in the creation of numerous 'transna-

---

1 Still worth a read on this is Mendelsohn 1970, p. 158f.
2 Brenner 1996, p. 4, p. 21ff., p. 69ff.
3 Moss 2009, p. 14, p. 38, p. 280f.
4 Michels 2005; Trachtenberg 2008.

tional social spaces'.[5] These included genuinely Bundist organisations such as Bund Clubs and corresponding schools, as well as secondary-Bundist organisations that either provided comprehensive programmes (e.g. the *Arbeter-ring*) or introduced Bundist ideas in specific niches such as trade union work, cultural associations, or the media. They all insisted that neither could Jewishness be measured by degree of religiosity, nor was Jewish life defined by the striving from *Galut* to *Eretz Israel*. For the Bundists, the struggle for Jewish life was not between cultural or political alternatives, but rather between past and present. Perceived as the *only* modern way of life, this emphasis on the secular-activist life in the diaspora allowed the Bund's transnational movement to become a major protagonist of Jewish history in the first half of the twentieth century – while leading to its utter marginalisation in the second.[6]

That trajectory was not inscribed into the programme of the Bund or any of its practices from the outset.[7] On the contrary, the expanded perspective this book adopts shows, firstly, that the Bund was the result of diverse social practices, that it was built and shaped by its *tuer*, from which in turn emerged a modern, progressive, and self-organised *yidishkayt*. These activists expanded the Bund by forming countless networks through various crises and against all odds, turning it into one of the most important political and cultural actors of Jewish modernity. Thus, the Bund's conception of national-cultural autonomy relied on its implementation in daily life. Only through practices did it become not just a concept, but a convincing concept of modern Jewish self-organisation. This requirement also made it flexible, as initially it was not bound to territory or statehood, but instead carried by activists to wherever they found responsive masses. It led from an anti-Tsarist, revolutionary mass movement into a proactive concept of a self-confident, global, Yiddish-speaking diaspora. The decisive secular organisations, from schools to workers' organisations and institutionalising forms of solidarity, developed transnationally in constant communication between the Old and New World. Developments peaked during the interwar years, when the Bund was able to claim the legacy of the 1905 revolution and subsequently develop a corresponding memorial culture on the one hand, while on the other the movement's legality in Poland and the presence of countless now well-funded Bundists overseas created a transnational social movement that radically transformed Jewish cultural life.

5   Pries 2008a.
6   On this see Slucki 2012.
7   On such lines of argument, which only function when far removed from actual Bundist practices, see works ranging from Johnpoll 1967 to Gorny 2006.

Given this diaspora's strong ties to the heart of the Bund in Russia and Poland, its equally reflective choice to use the Yiddish language, and Bundists' consistent identification as 'Eastern European', the Bundist diaspora constituted an 'Eastern Europe Abroad' – a vital component of Eastern European history, albeit outside its native territory.[8] In that sense, this volume sees itself as a further contribution to the historiography of Eastern European life outside Eastern Europe, yet with a particular addition. Other studies impressively demonstrate that the *landsmanshaftn*, which were based on a common place of origin, were not a specific expression of American Jewish life.[9] Based on a survey of emigrants from Vilnius and Bialystok, Anna Lipphardt and Rebecca Kobrin show that the *landsmanshaftn* of specific towns or cities were globally networked, and their remembrance work actually established spatial (in *Memorik* terms) and yet transnational (in practical terms) diasporic communities.[10] The emphasis on *landsmanshaftn* as a distinct ordering category of Jewish emigrants, however, tends to favour spatialised identities over the political divides between the emigrants. As the largest Jewish party in Eastern Europe, the Bund also provided such opportunities for (new) ascriptions in the transnational space, either counter to the *landsmanshaftn*, or, as was the case in the *Vilner brentsh* of the *Arbeter-ring*, by merging political and spatial identities. Like the numerous institutions of Bundism, countless Bundists also built the transnational network from below. Consequently, they sometimes aimed to reproduce local hegemonies from the 'old home' in their respective country of immigration. Now, however, the legitimacy of this claim emanated not from the uniting force of the party or a leading communal role, but rather from the Bund's transnational presence and historical legacy. To evaluate the efficiency and lasting success of this claim we would require a similar study of Poale Zion, as the one rival party and movement in the same social and political milieu with a similar set of practices. Although the latter never managed such a 'head start'[11] in the New World, its influence on Yiddish culture in the diaspora should not be underestimated.

Considering the existing literature on the Bund from this perspective, Bundist historiography's classical frame – party history divided into distinct epochs – appears too narrow to understand the global persistencies and changes in Bundist activism or Bundist identity formation. By combining movement and migration research with the Bund's history, we find that long before the Bund

---

8   Wolff 2012a.
9   See for example Soyer 1997.
10 Lipphardt 2010; Kobrin 2010.
11 Frankel 2009, p. 63.

came to institutionally accept its transnational form,[12] it had become a transnational social movement with sufficient flexibility to inspire independent foreign organisations and institutions of secondary Bundism on which the Eastern European party increasingly depended, but that could clearly demarcate itself from rival organisations when needed. A distinction between three different actors appears reasonable. The Bund as an organisation, Bundists as activists, and Bundism as both an ideology and utopia continually reciprocally shaped the history of the Bund, while each nevertheless developed its own dynamics and alliances. The result was the establishment of the transnational and functionally differentiated Bundist network as a persistent and simultaneously changing, community-forming, and cultural actor. For decades, its main source of legitimation was Bundist history and its relevance in Eastern Europe, conveyed through autobiography and other forms of *Memorik*. Then again, over the first decades the practices necessary to continue existing were successfully geared to conditions in the New World. Some of these, particularly fundraising, constituted a mainstay of the Eastern European Bund. Without the constant cash flow from overseas, the Bund in Russia and Poland would never have become the actor of Eastern European history it was practically exclusively studied as for years. The periphery carried the centre at least from a financial perspective, and surely in terms of *Memorik* practices. The Bund never recognised this fact. Although dependencies were reversed from inward to outward, hierarchies and identifications were not.

That said, these general observations require local specification, as the comparison between New York and Buenos Aires illustrates. Although quantitatively unrivalled, the history of Jewish migration to the United States – or even just New York – cannot be confused with a general history of Jewish migration. In that sense, I hope above all to inspire further comparative studies on transnational migrant agency. Although it may sound odd, despite the factually close link between Jewish history and migration history, most questions concerning social practices and transnational organisational formation have gone overlooked to this day – while countless collections languish unused in archives around the world. In this regard, I hope that my book helps to strengthen a line of research that elevates the many national histories of Jewish immigrants around the world, in order to pay more attention to the transnational treasures hidden in those histories, stories, and archives.[13]

---

12   Slucki 2012.
13   Wolff 2014a.

If we read the Bund as a transnational social movement and not merely an Eastern European class party, we see that its transnational network character was less the result of reorganising for the sake of survival after World War II[14] so much as an integral component of its history from the very outset, rooted in members' activism and the supra-territorial Bundist utopia. The transnational applicability of Bundism and *doikayt* in particular made it possible for members to shape their views on and approach to Jewish modernity in multifaceted ways, both at local hot spots and as a global phenomenon. Here the question again arises of comparable movements throughout Jewish as well as non-Jewish history – a question that only further research can answer. Based on my work thus far, I contend that the Bund does not represent an exception in this regard, but rather the transnational component was far more significant in the processes of community formation in the port cities and in numerous European social movements of the nineteenth and twentieth centuries than scholarship has hitherto acknowledged.

Correspondingly, this volume is conceived as a pioneering social- and cultural-historical study of four general aspects that should constitute a central focus of further studies of 'old' social movements. The proposed research design offers, firstly, the possibility of emancipating scholarship on socialism and the workers' movement, heavily marginalised in recent years, from its outdated three-fold isolation of party, intellectual, and national history.[15] The rather pervasive disinterest in both labour history as well as scholarship on socialism during the ongoing transnational turn in historiography is, frankly speaking, a missed opportunity.[16] For it is particularly in these networks that we find that which is markedly more difficult to detect in most contexts: committed actors of a self-defined global history, functionally differentiated institutional ties, and in many cases superb collections of unused sources in accessible archives.

My research implies, secondly, that social movement and party research should take the transnationality of its objects of study more seriously into account. This applies to both the context of contemporary possibilities as well as problems of activism. Confirming transnationality on the basis of international relations is not enough. The question of transnationalism is not that it existed, but rather *how*. Thus, we need clear and methodologically reliable identification of transnational actors and their relevance for international com-

---

14   Slucki 2012, p. 2, p. 24, p. 68, p. 144.
15   Important impulses from Welskopp 1994; van der Linden 2003.
16   In this context see also more recent research on the relation between internationalism and activism, such as Albert 2011.

munity formation.[17] This ties social movement research closely to migration history, the latter of which is increasingly challenging the dominance of immigration history and lifting the 'saltwater curtain'.[18] Even more recent and notable studies of Jewish history in the US rely on national-historical relevance. This leads to a blurring of the transnational conditions of numerous allegedly genuinely American institutions, like the Jewish-dominated trade unions or relief organisations.[19]

Thirdly, it calls for a global history that takes more than mere trade routes, actor-less transfer processes, and cultural contacts into account, and is less enthused by the existence of abstract networks but instead committed to studying the institutionalisation of individual and collective actors. Subsequently, the big picture is not the starting point, but rather the result of a more focused investigation of local specificities, meaningful alliances, and limitations of transfers. Such a global migration history would not only be a history of movement and relations, but above all a history of organisation.[20] Pursuing this perspective would not least make it possible for the discipline to link up with current sociological research on migrant organisations. The latter not only represent dynamics inherent in the integration process, but are indeed places in which persistencies, ruptures, and identities are negotiated and transnationally processed.[21] As the Bund's example demonstrates, historiography's specific merit in this context would be its emphasis on long-term developments and intergenerational dynamics and transfers. The need for organisation forced even the Bund, an organisation endowed with an extremely strong sense of its own distinctiveness, to devise various combinations of political action patterns containing elements from both the origin and immigration countries.

Finally, although they of course did not invent it, Bundists and the Bund must nonetheless be regarded as protagonists of modern Jewish life. Diaspora was reconceived and reshaped through their agency, changing from a condition to a purpose. In the process of migration to the 'new diaspora' in the Americas, Bundists transferred and transformed their practices and organisational patterns, and in the truest sense of the word implemented them in multiple forms. This posits the formation of transnational actors and political move-

---

17   Problem framing and methodological proposals in Pries 2008b, pp. 9–32, p. 73 f., pp. 95–8, pp. 147–70.
18   Thistlewaite 1960, p. 32.
19   Bender 2004a; Katz 2011.
20   The movement aspect has occupied centre stage in research thus far, see among others Bade 2003; Hoerder 2002; Moch 2003; Oltmer 2012; Hahn 2012.
21   Pries 2010a.

ments as a new potential focus of migration history. Here, actively shaped diasporas or diasporic identities can be identified as focal points of the nineteenth and twentieth centuries. In the case of Jewish history, it brings us back to the aforementioned 'Gretchen question'. More so than any other sphere the Bund had an impact on, it shows that Bundist activism was always of a counter-hegemonic nature, but could by no means guarantee the successful, permanent mobilisation of new generations.

1 The 'Two Bodies' of the Bund: A Praxeological Explanation for the Bund's 'Failure'

Despite its distance to actual practiced Bundism, the new centre emerging in New York in the 1940s (complemented by the temporary party headquarters in Brussels) proved essential in the *longue durée* of Bundist history. The Bund was compelled to undergo a double hybridisation to continue to exist as a World Bund in 1948: first, it had to coordinate Bundist groups worldwide and a changing meaning of Bundism after the Holocaust in the sense of a functional central unit. This task was attended to by the Coordinating Committee of the Bund's and Affiliated Jewish Socialist Organisations in Various Countries, and by '*Unzer tsayt*' as the movement's new mouthpiece.[22]

Secondly, the legitimacy of these new centres was rooted in the lost Eastern European Bund. It could only be maintained through *Memorik*. The Bund increasingly drew its authority not from waging street battles, but instead from its history and thus also from its dead. It allowed the American Bund to continue the American Bundist tradition as a functionally differentiated subsystem and gradually develop a new Bundist profile in its own right on this basis. In this context, Bundist *Memorik* ultimately became an end in itself, more than anything separating the group from younger generations. It overemphasised the Bund's metaphysical side.

As long as the Bund's nerve centre was located in Eastern Europe, *Memorik* and direct activism were co-present. One supported the other, making the Bund powerful in political and in cultural terms. Due to the generational shift, this activist complex began to fragment well before the Bund's relocation and resettlement after the Holocaust. Following the destruction of the European Jews, it became increasingly evident that the 'two bodies' of the Bund certainly mutually conditioned one another, but simultaneously were

---

22 Bund Archives, New York, RG 1400, ME-18, 138.

CONCLUSION, OR: THE AMBIVALENCE OF BUNDIST MODERNITY 415

growing more and more distant.[23] The *primary body* of the Bund emerged from its practical activism in accordance with Bundists' desire for community formation. Its existence depended on the actions and lives of Bundists. The *tuer* represented a practicing agent of Bundism in this process, committed to reproducing the social of the Bund through their Bundist action. This primary body continued to determine the course of Bundism in both Argentina and, after World War II, Australia.[24]

The *secondary body* by contrast was composed of reflective forms of activism, most importantly *Memorik*. It increasingly drew its strength from the dead and survivors as long as *Memorik* was produced and received. However, this tied it firmly to the generation of Bundists who were able to personally and emotionally connect to the Eastern European experience as *their* memory. This body was highly present in the US. From the outset, the very first Bundists there remained Bundists less through local Bundist activism so much as their support of practical Bundism taking place elsewhere. Such *tuer* were often Bundists 'in memoriam' and far stronger in words than deeds. Their activism through writing, however, simultaneously allowed the transfer of Bundist identity to places where Bundism as such had never possessed political weight.

Before World War II, these two bodies effectively supplemented each other despite various crises. After the war, the two bodies of the Bund effectively separated. Although that made it possible for the Bund to recognise the centre in New York in the sense of a parent organisation, being scattered across the globe simultaneously robbed the ideologically and practically unified concept of *doikayt* of its foundation. This was bound to overwhelm the Bund. Community formation required an increasing amount of *Memorik*, while less and less noteworthy deeds or actions were performed. In terms of Hans Vaihinger's 'law of the preponderance of the means over the end', the former means of *Memorik* by then preponderated over the end of political struggle and became an end in itself.[25] The secondary body of the Bund increasingly ceased to promote any concrete Bundist utopia, attempting to compensate for this more and more by keeping the past alive.[26] The more the Bund's activist engine began to sputter, the more community formation depended on *Memorik* fuel.

---

23   According to Kantorowicz 1997; Latour 2007, p. 162 f. Klenner criticises the lack of boundaries in the concept of the 'two bodies'. I, by contrast, personally consider it such a strong concept precisely because it allows for conceiving of metaphysically and rationally appearing actors both together and separate. See also Klenner 2009.
24   Slucki 2008.
25   See Vaihinger 1968.
26   The loss of the party archive in the Warsaw Ghetto represents the causal trauma in this regard, reinforced by Bundists' aging.

From this we can derive a new explanation for the Bund's 'failure' during the second half of the twentieth century. It was not, as has been alleged on various occasions, rooted in the absent drive for state power, nor a consequence of the Bund's purported inferiority to Zionism. The Bund's demise was not a result of its programme, but a practical consequence of the mass murder of Jews during the Holocaust. In their transnational constitution, both bodies formed an activist complex constituting the Bund. The Bund's transnationalisation prior to the Holocaust had a strengthening effect in this regard, as solidarity and a shared identify tied Bundist groups overseas closely to the Polish Bund. The Holocaust and Soviet persecution wiped out this European point of reference entirely. Memories certainly had an effect in terms of internal coherence, but were hardly suitable for renewed mobilisations in the present. Instead of a common goal, *experience* now stood at the heart of community formation. Naturally, this failed to appeal to new generations. Bundist *doikayt* thus lost its compatibility precisely because of the place-based focus of remembrance. Bundism could no longer get actively involved locally. Not transnationalism, but regional de-focusing put *doikayt* to the final test and ultimately became an insoluble problem.

Consequently, the Bund's failure in the second half of the twentieth century did not spring from the concept of *doikayt* itself, as an entire school of thought from Johnpoll to Gorny alleges.[27] The explanation rather lies in the dissolving of the tense relationship between the two bodies of the Bund, which could never again be brought into a viable balance due to mass murder, illegality, and subsequent migration after the Holocaust. The dissolution of Bundism was a result of the dissolution of Bundist activism into a global constellation rather than inherently 'built-in' to Bundism from the outset. The post-war Bund became so sectarian precisely because its representatives continued to fight for the recognition of Bundist modernity. That this fight represented a lost cause seems obvious. Yet in conclusion, it raises the question of the relationship between the Bund's 'unique case' and global Jewish modernity more generally. This is particularly worth noting because the continuation of the secondary body not only allowed the Bund to survive as a small party, but also led to the rescue and collection of memories, documents, and many other sources that now allow us to study this important movement of modern Jewish history.[28]

---

27   Johnpoll 1967; Gorny 2006.
28   Wolff 2020.

2 In Lieu of an Epilogue: The Legacy of Bundist *Doikayt*

This book explored in detail how global transfers between political actors were by no means limited to demonstrative role models or ideological exchange. Indeed, the relevance of the exchange of ideas is nothing new to Jewish history. Jonathan Frankel traced the roots of the Lithuanian workers' movement to American-Jewish role models.[29] Tony Michels followed the exchange of revolutionary ideas and corresponding literature between US and Russian-Jewish socialists, further corroborated by Susanne Marten-Finnis with regard to Jewish socialists in London.[30]

This volume, however, looked beyond ideas and at lives, experiences, and practices as sources of transnationalism. Whichever place or movement we address, 'national' workers' movements had highly practical transnational components that fundamentally defined them. This was due above all to two factors: firstly identity formation, which is absolutely essential to every social movement, and secondly the omnipresence of migration throughout the twentieth century, spreading these identities across the globe and necessarily entailing a search for transfers and adaptations.[31] The Bund was able to influence this process because it was able, particularly by strengthening the status of the Yiddish language, to continually (re-)create a transnational social space. This globalised all forms of Bundist activism principally through migration movements, and strengthened social ties with the Old World at the same time. Practices, experiences, and memories bound Bundists to Eastern Europe and the Americas at once. In this sense, educational work was not just the transmission of knowledge and fundraising was not simply activism on behalf of the revolution on the Old Continent – both served as examples of Bundist activism's transferability inward, i.e. into and inside the movement, as well as outward, into the world and in pursuit of improving and harnessing resources for them. As a result, the functionality of a socialist movement not only developed with local conditions, but the question of class and nation was also continually reformulated – and answered in an increasingly culturalist fashion.

Yet this by no means stripped Bundist activism of its political dimension, as some scholars claim.[32] By observing the educational sector and revolutionary fundraising but also the labour struggle, this study showed that Bundism became a highly important, active form of secular cultural politics that retained

---

29 Frankel 1984, p. 176.
30 Marten-Finnis 1999, pp. 57–77; Michels 2005, p. 125 f., p. 156; Michels 2009.
31 Gabaccia and Ottanelli 2001; Goyens 2007.
32 Blatman 1996.

its political aggressiveness, which in turn represented the very cornerstone of any kind of activist counter-culture. After establishing and developing its own view of history, the Bund was consistently able to directly connect to the cultural-revolutionary ideas of the 1900s and refer to the counter-culture through which the Bund had challenged traditionalism's or Chassidism's inner-Jewish hegemony from the outset. Partly inside the Bund and partly through secondary-Bundist organisations, Bundists had managed to institutionalise this approach and aspiration around the world by the time Germany invaded Poland. Yet it had its limits. While Red October triggered splits between socialists everywhere (which the Bundists eventually managed to overcome), the Holocaust tore up the constellations of Jewish life worldwide.

The history of the Bund before 1939 was therefore not a false path or process of decline from radicalism to reformist cultural work, but a stronger turn towards developing the concept of a class-conscious Jewishness, namely *yidishkayt*, combined with the aspiration to represent Jewish modernity. In his classic study, Ezra Mendelsohn noted that the Bund was active on two economic and cultural fronts from its very inception, although its accomplishments on the cultural front had a far more lasting impact.[33] While this remains an accurate judgement, the separation of the Bund's economic-political and cultural dimensions into two distinct segments does not correspond to the Bund's activism. Institutionally and in terms of personnel, both were tied together into one activist complex. The dichotomy thus omits that the Bund always understood its cultural work as political, or in Jack Jacobs's sense as counter-culturally activist. While the cultural relevance of Bundism for the realms of Yiddish literature has been established,[34] this study shows that the Bund's concept of culture around the world was symbiotic with its concept of *yidishkayt* as the perceived essence of Jewish life and the politically charged workers' movement. In the process, the Yiddish language increasingly changed from being a medium of class struggle to the goal of a socialist worker culture as such, and ultimately the linchpin of this modern Jewish secularism. It also suggests that the murder of millions of Yiddish-speaking Jews tore the foundations out from under the Bund's political concept, regardless of where or how it formed.

Nevertheless, the Holocaust was not the end of Jewish history, nor was Israel its only goal. It led to new forms and a new relevance of *Memorik*, including Bundist *Memorik*, a variety of modern Jewish diaspora concepts, and a new diversity of diasporic identities. Indeed, many activists and Bundists remained

---

33   Mendelsohn 1970, p. 158 f.
34   Kazdan 1945; Nath 1992; Gechtman 2005b; Cohen 2008; Michels 2009.

vocal about social consciousness and Yiddish culture even after World War II. Attempts to transfer the Bundist identity to the second immigrant generation in the New World largely failed, achieving temporary success only within the context of a secular *yidishkayt*. The separation of Jewish secularism from *yidishkayt*, not least linked to Israel's language policy favouring the exclusive use of Hebrew, robbed the Bund of its crucial points of contact with this modernisation movement.

There were still intense efforts to retain the familiar. Living in Uruguay, Bundist Noyekh Tsukerman wrote full of appreciation to his Australian *khaverim* in 1966 that, due to the persistence of active practices, Melbourne was the only place where a true Bund still existed. The youth work struck him as the 'only one that is reminiscent of the pre-war Polish Bund'.[35] Tsukerman thereby confirms for the post-war period what already applied to the period from 1897–1939 or 1947: the Bund existed and was conceived through actions for its own survival; its utopia was its own counter-culture, which required implementation through practice alone. But this increasingly became the work of disseminating the idea of Jewish secularism. To pursue this overseas was, and that is one if this study's main findings, neither a development after World War II, nor were the numerous Bundist institutions and organisations overseas marginal figures in the Bund's history. Bundists' practices and networking efforts clearly show that secular Jewish Eastern Europe and the respective centres of immigration in the Americas were bound by a symbiotic relationship. The Bund was by no means just a 'pariah' of the Russian workers' movement, but also a pioneer of transnational networking processes. It is anything but a paradox that the Bund assumed this transnational role precisely *because* it was linked so closely to Eastern Europe. On the one hand, it indissolubly tied *doikayt* to the Eastern European experience of activists, thereby excluding the following generations in the destinations of immigration by definition. On the other hand, this secured Bundism's influence until 1939. It often acquired relevance in the context of the migration process precisely because it could be transferred into many other organisations, while the Bund itself lost influence. Secondary Bundism was the essential contribution of socialist *doikayt* to the emerging, culturally legitimated Jewish diaspora.

Bundist history continued after World War II and the relocation of the Bund's centre to New York. What ensued was a stronger exchange between North and South America, inspiring fundraising campaigns by North American *khaverim* such as the representative of the World Coordinating Committee,

---

35   Quoted in Slucki 2009a, p. 111.

Emanuel Novogrudsky, who travelled through South America in the late 1950s. Argentina represented a focal point in this context, and like Shefner's trip in 1936, Novogrudsky's tour became a crowd-puller for many other activities all over the country, with a total of 10,684 $ raised.[36] Due to the long Bundist tradition on the Río de la Plata, the Bund in Buenos Aires became an important switchboard that, like all Bundist strongholds, was engaged in a vain – and increasingly sectarian – fight against the Yiddish language's declining relevance and its factual 'counter-thesis', the founding of Israel as a Hebrewist state.

The aging of the membership meant that the Bund was rapidly losing its base. Focus shifted entirely from the struggle to its commemoration. That said, this also led to the potentially unique source production and autobiography systematically evaluated for this study, and presented here in its potential for a social history of the Bund. With regard to the Bund's dynamics and growing isolation, it is significant that Bundists and the Bund dealt with the experience of migration very differently, and that they sometimes even consolidated the Bund's relevance in activists' identities. The Holocaust initiated a development that irreversibly drove a wedge between remembrance and political activism. While both had previously been interdependent and mutually complementary, feeding into the Bund's activist complex, remembrance now became a value in itself – contributing to the Bund's isolation in the post-war world.

This development occurred gradually and differently from place to place. While the secondary-Bundist schools of the *Arbeter-ring* peaked in the 1930s, the decade marked a new beginning not only in Australia but also in Argentina.[37] Over the last pre-war decade activists had built a tripartite foundation of community work, school movement, and *yidishkayt* that ensured the continued existence of a Jewish worker culture after Perón banned free trade unions. The long-term effect was a cultural advance that also helped the Argentinian Bund and the secondary-Bundist YSFA to assert themselves as independent factors in Jewish Argentina. While the period of decline until the final dissolution of the Argentinian Bund and the Peretz School in 1995 overshadows the memory of the post-war Bund in Buenos Aires, it remained a crucial part of Jewish life for decades. This is reflected, for instance, in the decades-long presence of the Bund in the AMIA and the central role of the Peretz School, which acted as a cultural centre for Yiddish-speaking Argentina well into the 1960s.[38] From this emerged new Bundist institutions, among them the bi-weekly journal

---

36 Bund Archives, New York, RG 1400, ME18, 97, Balance of accounts.
37 On Australia's relevance after 1945 see Slucki 2009a; Slucki 2009b.
38 IWO, Bund Archives, 1114, Various documents on the post-war Bund; N.N. 1947a; Knapheyt 1972. This also promptly inspired work in Montevideo, where Shefner's 1936 visit had an

CONCLUSION, OR: THE AMBIVALENCE OF BUNDIST MODERNITY 421

'Unzer gedank' launched in 1956, or the Bundist publishing house Yidbukh that published landmarks of Yiddish post-war literature, such as the series 'Dos poylishe yidntum' comprising more than 200 volumes. Considering the prehistory of Yiddish cultural work in Argentina, it is hardly surprising that not only this series was published on the Río de la Plata, but also the 'Musterverk fun der yidisher literatur'. It was edited by then-president of the Argentinian YIVO, Samuel Rollansky, whose past (as was the case for Jewish secularism in Argentina as such) was rooted in Bundism. He had been a leading member of many Bundist organisations, among them particularly the Gezelshaft, shown great commitment to the Hilfs-komitet, and as long-time chairman of the YSFA was one of the central protagonists in the formation of secondary Bundism in Argentina. He sent his daughter Esther Rollansky, today a scholar of Yiddish literature at the University of Tel Aviv, to the Bundist Peretz School on Lavalle 2238.[39]

Such transfers and the continuing Bundist drive to shape a new and just Jewish world are precisely the origins of the Bund's exemplary significance to modern history that Daniel Cohn-Bendit recognised (albeit intuitively rather than explicitly). Its activism positioned the Bund in a prominent place both qualitatively and quantitatively in modern Jewish history, which as a substantial number of scholars attest was virtually a showcase, if not engine, of pivotal developments in the twentieth century.[40] Here it becomes noticeable, however, that the road into Jewish modernity was not a 'track' on which a discernible group was transported from one condition to another.[41] Nor was modernity merely a condition of the outside world, to which Jewish people reacted in some way or another.[42] Neither was there any clarity as to what this modernity should look like, nor which language it spoke, or how 'Jewishness' was defined in the first place. On the contrary, that contingency marked the point of contention; its realisation was the very essence of modernity. We therefore should speak not only of 'multiple modernities', but indeed of 'contested modernities' as distinct visions, mutually interlocked in a complex relational structure of cooperation and conflict.[43] While overlapping in certain regards, they mutually excluded one another in others. As a result, countless networks emerged built on dis-

---

    impact similar to Tabachinsky's trip to Buenos Aires in 1931, see Bundishe grupe in Montevideo 1937a.
39   IWO, Buenos Aires, Comite de Ayuda a las escuelas laicas Israeltita de Polonia y Argentina, Report card for Esther Rollansky.
40   See for example Slezkine 2004; Brenner 2006.
41   Similarly, see esp. Cohen 1983; Katz 1987; Lederhendler 1989; Bauman 2000.
42   This precept is followed in many otherwise quite appealing works including Meyer 1995; Lederhendler 1997; Meyer 2001.
43   See esp. Eisenstadt 2000; Tambiah 2000; David-Fox 2006.

tinct spaces and places, times and notions of time, and the deeply contingent exchange of actors. The latter's primary aspiration was to channel their activism into institutions that stood for experienceable forms of 'their' modernity, and were also always counterprojects to other modernities.

3 Radicalism and Romanticism

The Bund's greatest success in this regard was achieved in Argentina. During Barukh Shefner's visit in 1936, the years in which the YSFA called for the formation of a pro-democratic 'popular front',[44] Bundists were truly shocked by their success sweeping them into the centre of Argentina's Jewish public sphere. It inspired Pinie Vald to invoke the activist spirit. In his view, the lack of opposition to Bundist relief campaigns for Jewish schools was a sign that Bundists' activism was changing from counter-culture to mainstream. The participant in the 1905 revolution and founder of the *Avangard* was certain that this would mean the movement's demise. In a long article titled 'Forward, an Enemy!' in the biggest daily Yiddish paper in Argentina at the time, '*Di prese*', he argued that 'the current action ... did not encounter an enemy', that every actor supported it, 'the workers and the employers ... all social layers ... from right and left and centre'. He took up several columns explaining why everyone would naturally support the action. In the end, it all came down to one once-divisive but now apparently rhetorical question: 'who could not be for children's schools?' But for Vald, this unifying success threatened the power of the Bundist counter-culture, precisely because this consensus was simply *too good*:

> Too good means to be satisfied, tame, difficult to motivate to activity and generosity. Weak and lazy and sloppy. Sharp interests are necessary in life, burning faith, zeal, ambition, fight, which grow out of antagonism, from rival camps, from rocky paths, from turmoil.[45]

Only this created 'the necessary struggle element [*kamfelement*] that must be fought in life'. Pinie Vald of course already had an old adversary in mind, namely 'the reaction from the Jewish street' whose 'struggle it is to disrupt every progressive movement'. Vald thus explicitly linked fundraising for the secular schools and the Bundist cultural struggle of the 1900s, in which young

---

44 IWO, Buenos Aires, 1114, Flyer, YSFA, 29 April 1936.
45 IWO, Argentina, 1103 [CAEI], 6, P. Vald, 'Foran a kegner', *Di prese*, Buenos Aires (9 July 1936).

CONCLUSION, OR: THE AMBIVALENCE OF BUNDIST MODERNITY 423

Bundist modernists aggressively took on their parents' generation's traditionalism along with corresponding institutions in the Russian *shtetl*. Vald, however, believed that conditions were greatly improved compared to those days, given that the secular schools had by then become a 'mature Jewish tradition'. This allowed Vald to pit a 'modern tradition' against 'the reaction'. He unequivocally identified religious Jews as rivals. 'For what else is the current campaign for the secular Jewish school system to the religious citizen than a direct attack?' Vald was determined to carry out this attack with full force, calling for a final showdown in the arena of the cultural struggle:

> Forward! As you can see, the enemy is a very powerful and noxious one. All institutions and supporters must recognise it as such and bear in mind: live with the reaction or for a progressive Jewish sociality and a secular Jewish educational life.[46]

A clearer summation of the alliance between political activism and cultural work can hardly be found. As the history of the twentieth century shows, ultimately neither of the two prevailed. Both contributed their specific part to the formation of modern Jewish actor-networks. The tale of success thus must be supplemented by highlighting the transfer's limitations: social movements do not follow socially entrenched developmental logics and require constant activism.[47] Only this made it possible for the Bund's 'social thread' to be rewoven time and again, and thus it was precisely that transnationality, alongside Yiddish, that established a living relationship between 'here' and 'there', between the profoundly individual experiences of 'back then' and 'today'. But it also constricted the Bund to the worlds of experience of the first immigrant generation.[48]

The second generation was unable to feel a strong presence of the '*altn heym*' in their everyday lives in the New World, or the urgency of the problems and struggles occurring there. Despite all progress in modern communications and transportation, to the Bundists' children the Atlantic Ocean appeared far more vast and Russia much more distant than had been the case for the first immigrant generation. This generation travelled back and forth in large numbers during the first decades of the twentieth century, creating numerous transnational identity-forming networks. Due to the lack of first-hand experience, fac-

---

46 Ibid.
47 Latour 1986.
48 Bund Archives, New York, RG 1400, Workmen's Circle Collection, 1317, 6, Report to the Annual Meeting of the National Organization Committee, Workmen's Circle, 13 July 1941.

tual distance, increasingly exclusionary migration regimes, the Red Scare, and of course the Cold War, such action (and movement) patterns became more and more abstract for subsequent generations. As New York-based flaneur and writer Alfred Kazin, son of a socialist Jewish emigrant, noted as early as 1947, the latter eventually shelved cultural socialism and the political networks and extinguished the revolutionary flame. To him, socialism was no longer synonymous with progressiveness and activism experienced through *khavershaft*, strikes, and arrests, but instead a yearning for distant places and romanticism. The socialist networks and communities no longer struggled against capitalism, but merely against loneliness in the New World:

> *Aleyn! Aleyn!* Did immigrant Jews, then, marry out of loneliness? Was even Socialism just a happier way of keeping us together?
>
> I trusted it to do that. Socialism would be one long Friday evening around the Samovar and the cut-glass bowl laden with nuts and fruits, all of us singing *Tsuzamen, tsuzamen, ale tsuzamen!* Then the hero of the Russian novel – *our* kind of people – would walk the world, and I – still wearing a circle-necked Russian blouse '*a la Tolstoy*' – would live forever with those I loved in that beautiful Russian country of the mind.[49]

---

49   Kazin 1979, p. 62.

Bibliography

Archives and Collections

Bund Archives, New York, US[1]

RG 1400, M 12
RG 1400, M 13
RG 1400, ME 1
RG 1400, ME 14B
RG 1400, ME 16
RG 1400, ME 18
RG 1400, ME 34
RG 1400, MG 2
RG 1400, MG 7
RG 1400, Office Files
RG 1400, American Collection
RG 1401 (Foreign Committee, 1898–1926)
RG 1471 (Schools)
Reference List (Pseudonyms)
Unsorted Collections

Yidisher viznshaftlekher Institut (YIVO), New York, US[2]

RG 48 (TSYSHO)
RG 102 (YIVO Autobiographies)
RG 575 (Workmen Circle)
RG 791 (Autobiography Contest – Announcements)
RG 1333 (Papers of Saul Shally)

New York Public Library
Theatre Collection

---

1 I owe particular thanks to Leo Greenbaum for his tireless and reliable support.
2 I thank all of the very helpful staff for their assistance in the archive, particuarlly Ettie Goldwasser, who granted me access to the unsorted collections on *Arbeter-ring* schools.

Yidisher visnshaftlekher institut (IWO), Buenos Aires, Argentina[3]

RG 236 (Escuelas laicas en Argentina)
RG 1103 (Campaña de Ayuda – Schefner)
RG 1111 (Educación)
RG 1114 (Bund)
RG 1142 (Komerts un Handl – Union Aceiteros Minoristas)
Archivo Goldmintz
Asociacion de escritores Israelitas Nomberg
CICO
Comite Central Pro Socorro a las victimas israelitas de la guerra y refugiados
Comite de Ayuda a las escuelas laicas Israeltita de Polonia y Argentina
Escuelas Laicas en Argentine
Escuela Sholem Aleijem, Zwischo
Gremios en Proceso (14 November 2008)

Centro de Documentación e información sobre juadísmo Argentino 'Marc Turkow', Buenos Aires, Argentina

Archivo de la Palabra

Centro de Documentación e Investigación de la Cultura de Izquierdas en la Argentina (CeDInCI), Buenos Aires, Argentina

Fondo Cavazzonni
La Protesta
Publicaciones de movimientos sociales de la Argentina y el mundo
Publicaciones políticas de las izquierdas argentinas

Archivo de la Universidad Nacional de San Martín, San Martín, Provincia de Buenos Aires, Argentina[4]

Escuela I.L. Peretz, Villa Lynch

---

3   In 2008 the IWO Buenos Aires was provisionally housed in the Casa Simon Dubnow, Ayacucho 583; construction of a new archival building is still unfinished. Scars of the 1994 AMIA bombing were clearly visible. A large portion of the collection was accessible, although almost entirely 'in the process' of being re-sorted. I cite sources as precisely as possible according to the ordering system in place in 2008. However, many documents were found scattered between various collections and folders listed as *'gremios en proceso'*. I extend my deepest thanks to Silvia Hansman and everyone at the IWO who helped satisfy my seemingly inexhaustible hunger for more documents.

4   I am particularly grateful to Nerina Visacovsky for recovering several documents believed to have been lost.

Rossiiskii gosudarstvennyi arkhiv sotsial'no-politicheskoi istorii (RGASPI), Moscow, Russia[5]
Collection 271 (Bund)

TSentral'nii derzhavny arkhiv hromads'kykh ob'ednan' Ukraïny[6]
Collection 41

Central Archives for the History of the Jewish People, Jerusalem, Israel[7]
RG Argentina (AR), PER

Interviews[8]
Israel Laubstein, Buenos Aires (2008, conducted by Frank Wolff, Silvia Hansman, three sessions of roughly two hours each)
Herzke Goldmintz (1999, conducted by Marcelo Dimentstein)
Melekh Fridman (2002, conducted by Marcelo Dimentstein)
Samual Posklinsky (2002, conducted by Marcelo Dimentstein)

Library Collections (Sources)[9]
YIVO, New York, US
New York Public Library, New York, US
Sheridan Libraries, Baltimore, US
Library of Congress, Washington, DC, US
IWO, Buenos Aires, Argentina
CeDInCI, Buenos Aires, Argentina
Staatsbibliothek, Berlin, Germany

---

5 Many thanks to Gleb Albert for his support and photocopying.
6 Best of thanks to Martin Krämer for providing me with hitherto unknown sources.
7 I owe thanks to Daniel Mahla for decisive bits of information and for providing me with various copies.
8 Heartfelt thanks are due to Marcelo Dimentstein for providing me with the interviews from his own research on the Bund.
9 For the collection of autobiographies I used numerous sources ordered via interlibrary loan. Not all corresponding libraries are listed here, but only those whose unique and archive-like collections were cited extensively.

Methodologically Analysed Periodicals (Series)[10]

Arbeter luakh, Warsaw (1921–4)
Argentiner lebn, Buenos Aires (1936–8)
Argentiner veker, Buenos Aires (1924)
Byuletin fun heym shneyer und mazsheristn fareyn, Buenos Aires (1937–40)
Byuletin/Boletin, Centro Cultural y Deportivo, Escuela Laica Israelita 'I.L. Peretz', Villa Lynch (1945)
Der hamer, Brăila (Romania) (1915–16)
Der hamer, New York (1926–7)
Der kemfer, New York (1905)
Der konfektsyon arbeter, Buenos Aires (1934–8)
Der mebl arbeter, Buenos Aires (1927–8)
Der shneyer arbeter, Buenos Aires (1935)
Der veker, New York (1921, 1927, 1937, 1941)
Der veker, Vilnius, Warsaw (1905–6)
Di arbeyter shtime, Petrograd (1917)
Di arbeter shtime, Vilnius et al. (1899–1904)
Der avangard, Buenos Aires (1908–10, 1916–17, 1919–20)
Di hofnung, Vilnius (1907)
Di naye shul, Warsaw (1928–30)
Di rotshester tsaytung, Rochester, NY (1907)
Di shtime fun avangard, Buenos Aires (1909)
Di sotsyalistishe shtime, New York (1936–41)
Di tsukunft, New York (1927, 1941)
Di yidishe tribune, Paris (1915)
Dos fraye vort, Buenos Aires (1936–8)
Dos yidishe vort, Geneva (1915)
Fraynd fun bund, New York (1904)
Golos trudos, Buenos Aires (surviving issues, 1926–9)
Kegn shtrom, Warsaw (1930–3)
Labor Bund Bulletin, New York (1947–52)
Lebns-fragn, Tel Aviv (1957, 1965–7)
Naye folksshtime, Warsaw (1931, 1937)
Naye velt, New York (1913–21)
Nayvelt, Buenos Aires (1927–9)
Partey-byulletin, Chicago (1913, became *Yidisher sotsyalist* after first issue)

---

10   Only periodicals methodologically fundamental to the study, i.e. analysed as a complete series, are listed in the following. Additional issues and periodicals are cited individually throughout the text.

Royter pinkes, Warsaw (1921, 1924)
Sotsyalistishe bleter, Buenos Aires (1930–2)
Tsayt-fragn, Montevideo (1938)
Unzer arbet, Buenos Aires (1933–42)
Unzer frayhayt, Bialystok (1918)
Unzer ruf, Kaunus (1925)
Unzer ruf, Lviv (1927)
Unzer shul, Buenos Aires (1929)
Unzer tsayt, New York (1941–7, 1951, 1957, 1963, 1968)
Unzer vort, Buenos Aires (1943)
Yidisher sotsyalist, Chicago, New York (1913, 1914)

Bundist Autobiographies[11]

A farshikter arbeyter 1904, 'Vi bin ikh gelofn fun sibir', *Di arbeyter shtime* 37, pp. 2–7.
Abramovitsh, [Hirsh] 1925, 'Zshitomirer pogrom un unzer kamf-druzshine', *1905 yor in Barditshev*, Kiev: Barditshever Hisport dem krayz-komitet fun K.P. (B.) An, p. 99 f.
Abramovitsh, [Hirsh] 1958, *Farshvundene geshtaltn (zikhroynes un siluetn)*, Buenos Aires: Tsentralfarband fun poylishe yidn in Argentine.
Abramovitsh, Rafael 1944, *In tsvey revolutsyes*, 2 volumes, New York: Farlag Arbeter-ring.
Abramowicz, Dina 1996, 'The World of my Parents. Reminiscences', *YIVO Annual* 23, pp. 105–55.
Afrim 1941, 'Oyb nisht nokh hekher', *Unzer tsayt*, New York 5, pp. 36–8.
Alter, Dzshon 1951, 'Lui der brokher', *Unzer tsayt*, New York 7–8, p. 8 f.
An-Man, P. 1921, 'Der bialistoker period in lebn fun tsentral-komitet fun "bund"', *Royter pinkes*, Warsaw 1, pp. 45–69.
Arbabanel, Tsvi Hirsh Borukh, n.d., untitled, Bund Archives, New York, RG 1400, MG-2, Folder 429.
Arih 1951, 'Viktor Shulman – der mentsh', *Unzer tsayt*, New York 10, pp. 20–2.
Arnold 1922, 'A nesye mit Tshemodones: An episod fun dem amolikn umlegaln literatur-transport', *Arbeter luakh*, Warsaw 3, pp. 129–42.
Aronson, Grigori 1955, untitled, Bund Archives, New York, RG 1400, MG-2, Folder 429.
Aronson, Grigori 1962, *Rusish-yidishe inteligent: Klal-tuer, shreyber, politiker, tragishe geshtaltn*, Buenos Aires: Yidbukh.

---

11   Complete listing of researched Bundist autobiographies according to the definition given in Part II.5. In order to make the list more comprehensible, autobiographies with an identifiable author are listed under their featured names (including real names, second names, pseudonyms, etc.) irrespective of the author's actual citation.

Aronson, Grigori 1968, 'Di birzshe un di zelbstshuts in Homel', *Unzer tsayt*, New York 10, pp. 18–20.

Artuksi, Israel [Oskar] 1966, untitled, Bund Archives, New York, RG 1400, MG-2, Folder 429.

Artuksi, Israel [Oskar] 1975, untitled, Bund Archives, New York, RG 1400, MG-2, Folder 429.

Artuksi, Israel [Oskar] 1976a, 'A por verter oyfklerung vegn mayn areyntrit in "bund"', *Yid. Mentsh. Sotsysalist. I. Artuski ondenk-bukh*, edited by I. Artuski Bukh-Komitet, Tel Aviv: Lebns-fragn, pp. 134–8.

Artuksi, Israel [Oskar] 1976b, 'Mayne letste bagegenish mit Viktor Alter', *Yid. Mentsh. Sotsysalist. I. Artuski ondenk-bukh*, edited by I. Artuski Bukh-Komitet, pp. 287–91.

Aydlman, Fishl, n.d., untitled, Bund Archives, New York, RG 1400, MG-2, Folder 429.

Babits, Khaym 1957, 'Mayn shtetl novidvor: A kleyn shtetl mit a groysn beyshteyer tsu der geshikhte fun "bund"', *Lebns-fragn*, Tel Aviv 70–1, p. 18.

Bakhrakh, H[arry] 1952, 'Ven bundistn shtreytn tsvishn sikh ...', *Unzer shtime*, Paris, Bund Archives, New York, RG 1400, MG-2, Folder 504, p. 2, p. 4.

Baron, Julius 1942, untitled, YIVO, RG 102, Folder 115.

Baskin, Yosef 1934, 'Tsu dem 37 yorign yubilum fun "bund"', *Der veker*, New York 528 (10 November), p. 14 f.

Baskin, Yosef 1945, 'Yeshivah, haskole un der ibergang tsum "bund". Derinerungen fun a yeshivah-bokher vegn dem baginen fun bund', *Unzer tsayt*, New York 3, pp. 68–72.

Baskin, Yosef 1947, 'Fun der yeshive tsum "bund"', *Unzer tsayt*, New York 3–4, p. 63 f., p. 74.

Beitani, A. 1942, untitled, YIVO, RG 102, Folder 107.

Beker, Sh., n.d., *An ershter may. A bletel fun der fergangenheyt o. A. 1. Mai 1911 o. A.*, Bund Archives, New York, RG 1400, ME16, Folder 28.

Berman, Layb [Laybetshke, Israel Moszwa] 1924, '"Der Dvinkser Boyevoy otryod" – B.O. (Kamf-druzshine). Zikhroynes fun yor 1905', *Arbeter luakh*, Warsaw 5, pp. 61–80.

Berman, Layb [Laybetshke, Israel Moszwa] 1936, *In loyf fun yorn. Zikhroynes fun a yidishn arbeter*, Warsaw: Memuarn komitet beym dvinsker 'bund'-brentsh 75 – Arbeter ring in Amerike.

Berman, Layb [Laybetshke, Israel Moszwa] 1943, 'Vi Henrik Erlikh is arestirt gevorn', *Unzer tsayt*, New York, pp. 24–7.

Berman, Layb [Laybetshke, Israel Moszwa] 1945a, 'Ikh ver bashuldigt a ganeyve. A kapitl zikhroynes', *Unzer tsayt*, New York 3, pp. 72–5.

Berman, Layb [Laybetshke, Israel Moszwa] 1945b, *In loyf fun yorn. Zikhroynes fun a yidishn arbeter*, New York: Unzer tsayt.

Berman, Layb [Laybetshke, Israel Moszwa] 1952a, 'A rede fun khaver Laybetshke', *Unzer tsayt*, New York 10, pp. 20–3.

Berman, Layb [Laybetshke, Israel Moszwa] 1952b, 'Der gang fun a dor', *Unzer tsayt*, New York 11, pp. 28–31.

Berman, Layb [Laybetshke, Israel Moszwa] 1953, '"Skritkes". Mayn ershte bagegenish mitn khover noakh', *Unzer tsayt*, New York 12, pp. 18–20.

Bernshteyn, Leon, n.d., untitled, Bund Archives, New York, RG 1400, MG-2, Folder 429.

Bernshteyn, Leon 1942, '"Undzer Aleksander"', *Arkadi. Zamlbukh tsum ondenk fun Arkadi Kremer*, New York: Unzer tsayt, pp. 214–28.

Bernshteyn, Leon 1954a, 'David Katz ("Taras") un der zveyte kongres fun Bund', *Unzer tsayt*, New York 10.

Bernshteyn, Leon 1954b, 'David Katz ("Taras") un der zveyte kongres fun Bund', *Unzer tsayt*, New York 11.

Bernshteyn, Leon 1954c, 'David Katz ("Taras") un der zveyte kongres fun Bund', *Unzer tsayt*, New York 12.

Bernshteyn, Leon 1956, *Ershte sprotsungen*, Buenos Aires: Yidbukh.

Bernshteyn, Mordekhay [Mardoqueo, W. Bernsztein] 1955, 'Areynfir-vort', *In labirintn fun tkufes*, Buenos Aries: Yidbukh, pp. 9–15.

Beser, Moshe 1976, 'Bagegenish mit Oskarn', *Yid. Mentsh. Sotsysalist. I. Artuski ondenkbukh*, edited by I. Artuski Bukh-Komitet, Tel Aviv: Lebns-fragn, pp. 94–8.

Blekhman, Layb [Abraham 'der tate'] 1941, 'Oyfn frishn kibur fun khaver Noakh. Etlekhe verter fun an alt bundistn', *Unzer tsayt*, New York 10, p. 12 f.

Blekhman, Layb [Abraham 'der tate'] 1959, *Bleter fun main yugent: Zikhroynos fun a Bundist*, New York: Unzer tsayt.

Blit, Lutsyan 1963, 'Di lange tsen yor', *Unzer tsayt*, New York 9, p. 8 f.

Blit, Lutsyan 1943, 'Ver fun unz vet dos fargesn …', *Unzer tsayt*, New York 6, p. 28 f.

Blum, Hillel [Kats Blum] 1936, 'Der 1-ter may in Vilne mit 40 yor tsurik. Zikhroynes fun an altn bundistn', *Naye folkstsaytung*, Warsaw (30 April).

Blum, Hillel [Kats Blum] 1940, *Zikhroynes fun a bundist. Bilder fun untererdishn leb in tsarishn rusland*, New York: Atlantik, Bildungs-komitet fun arbeter-ring.

Blum, Hillel [Kats Blum] 1942, 'Der ershter may 1896 in Vilne', *Arkadi. Zamlbukh tsum ondenk fun Arkadi Kremer*, New York: Unzer tsayt, pp. 132–44.

[Borenshteyn, Shimen?], n.d., 'Di seks buntovshikes. Zikhroynes fun der noent fargangenheyt', [*Forverts?*], Bund Archives, RG 1400, MG-2, Folder 429.

Botvinik, Kh. 1922, 'Di Vilner may-demonstratsye in 1902 yor. Zikhroynes', *Hirsh Lekert. Tsum 20-tn yortsayt fun zayn kepung*, edited by Ruslendishe komunistishe partey, Ts. K. fun R.K.P., Ts. B. fun yidsektsye, Moscow, pp. 22–34.

Botvinik, Kh. 1926, 'Lekerts khaverim', *Der emes*, Moscow (9 October).

Boym, Dovid, n.d., untitled, Bund Archives, New York, RG 1400, MG-2, Folder 429.

Brener, L. 1948, 'Der kamf mitn judenrat Tshenstokhover geto. A bisl zikhroynes fun Tshenstokhover geto-lebn', *Historisher Zamlbukh. Materialn un dokumentn tsut-*

shayer tsu der geshikhte fun Algemeyner Yidisher Arbeter-Bund, Warsaw: Ringen, pp. 105–8.

Brumberg, Abraham 1999, 'From Vilna to San Francisco. Pages from a Diary', *The Jews in Poland*, Vol. 2, edited by Sławomir Kapralski, Krakow: Judaica Foundation, pp. 75–84.

Brumberg, Abraham 2007, *Journeys through Vanishing Worlds*, Washington, DC: New Academia Publishing.

Burshtin, P. 1953, '"Ikh ken dem nisht!"', *Unzer tsayt*, New York 4, pp. 34–5.

Byalon, Avrom, n.d., untitled, Bund Archives, New York, RG 1400, MG-2, Folder 429.

Byalon, Avrom 1955, untitled, Bund Archives, New York, RG 1400, MG-2, Folder 429.

Carasnik, Sam [Nekhemie] 1942, untitled, YIVO, RG 102, Folder 173.

Chiaskelevitz, José 1905, interview, *Centro de Documentación e información sobre juadísmo Argentino 'Marc Turkow'*, Buenos Aires, Archivo de la Palabra, Nr. 11.

Cohen, Aaron 1942, *Der Lodzer fun Patterson, Nyu Dzshersey*, YIVO, New York, RG 102, Folder 108.

Davidman, Shloyme [Dovid] 1938, 'Tsu der graduiertung fun der ordn-shuln, 22. Mai 1938', *Meka tempel, N.Y. Sobvay-Bibliothek. Geshikhtn far groys un kleyn* 11.

Daykh, M. 1929, 'Vegn mayn revolutsyonerer arbet', *Royte bleter* 1.

Der bruder-kibur 1919, 'Derinerung fun redaktions-sokretar', *Unzer Grus. Zamelheft*, Warsaw: Lebens-fragn, pp. 18–24, Bund Archives, New York, RG 1400, MG-2, Folder 504.

Der evig yunger 1906, 'Gelebt – gekemft. (Strikhn)', *Der veker*, Vilnius (12 January), p. 2f.

Der Mohilever Stolier 1942, untitled, YIVO, New York, RG 102, Folder 8.

Dibriln, Kh. 1922a, 'Hirsh Lekert. Derinerungen, Bd. 1', *Unzer tsayt*, Vilnius 17 (13 May), p. 2.

Dibriln, Kh. 1922b, 'Hirsh Lekert. Derinerungen, Bd. 2', *Unzer tsayt*, Vilnius 18 (20 May), p. 2.

Dibriln, Kh. 1922c, 'Hirsh Lekert. Derinerungen, Bd. 3', *Unzer tsayt*, Vilnius 19 (28 May), p. 2f.

Dibriln, Kh. 1922d, 'Hirsh Lekert. Derinerungen, Bd. 1', *Der veker*, Warsaw (17 June), p. 6f.

Domnitz, Aaron 2006 [1942], 'Why I left my old home and what I have Accomplished in America', *My Future is in America. Autobiographies of Eastern European Jewish Immigrants*, edited by Jocelyn Cohen and Daniel Soyer, New York: NYU Press, pp. 124–88.

Droznes, B. 1922, 'Zikhroynes', *Hirsh Lekert. Tsum 20-tn yortsayt fun zayn kepung*, edited by Ruslendishe komunistishe partey, Ts. K. fun R.K.P., Ts. B. fun yidsektsye, Moscow, pp. 46–58.

Dubitski, A. 1957, 'In toytn-kamer', *Unzer tsayt*, New York 7–8, pp. 35–8.

Dubkowski, Irshl, n.d., untitled, Bund Archives, New York, RG 1400, MG-2, Folder 429.

Dubnova, Sofia [Sofia Dubnov-Erlich] 1916, ['Remembrances of Sholem Aleichem'], *Evreiskaia starina* [mentioned in Dunova 1918a and 1918b].

Dubnova, Sofia [Sofia Dubnov-Erlich] 1918a, 'Zikhroynes vegn Mendele Abramovitsh, Bd. 1', *Kharkover tsaytung* 5, pp. 4–6.

Dubnova, Sofia [Sofia Dubnov-Erlich] 1918b, 'Zikhroynes vegn Mendele Abramovitsh, Bd. 2', *Kharkover tsaytung* 6, p. 2 f.

Dubnova, Sofia [Sofia Dubnov-Erlich] 1941, 'VICTORY! Bletlekh fun togbukh', *Unzer tsayt*, New York 9, pp. 31–3.

Dubnova, Sofia [Sofia Dubnov-Erlich] 1943, 'Mentshn fun a gants yor', *Unzer tsayt*, New York 10, pp. 31–3.

Dubnova, Sofia [Sofia Dubnov-Erlich] 1948, 'Ringen. Derinerungen fun bundisher arbet tsvishn militer', *Unzer tsayt*, New York 3–4, pp. 67–70.

Dubnova, Sofia [Sofia Dubnov-Erlich] 1957, 'Dos shtetl', *Unzer tsayt*, New York 11–12, p. 71 f.

Duntov, Yosef, n.d., untitled, Bund Archives, New York, RG 1400, MG-2, Folder 429.

Dushkan, M.N. 1930, 'Minskaia konferentsiia 1895 goda (Iz vospominanii)', *Revoliutsionnoe dvizhenie sredi evreev*, edited by S. Dimanshtein, Moscow, pp. 238–43.

Dvinsker bundistisher brentsh 75 arbeter ring (ed.) 1909, *Zamelbukh. Sovenir tsum 5-yoriken yoresfest*, [New York]: Dvinsker bundistisher brentsh 75 arbeter ring.

Dvinsker bundistisher brentsh 75 arbeter ring (ed.) 1914, *Zamelbukh. Aroysgegebn tsum tsehntn yahres-fest*, New York: Dvinsker bundistisher brentsh 75 arbeter ring.

Dvinsker bundistisher brentsh 75 arbeter ring (ed.) 1924, *Zamelbukh*, New York: Dvinsker bundistisher brentsh 75 arbeter ring.

Dvinsker bundistisher brentsh 75 arbeter ring (ed.) 1954, *Zamlbukh. 50th golden jubilee celebration*, [New York]: Arbeter ring brentsh 75.

Edelberg-Shatan, Mırl 1957, 'Shmuen Htotshik. A biografishe skitse', *Unzer tsayt*, New York 10, p. 43 f.

Edelman, Marek 2002, *Der Hüter. Marek Edelman erzählt*, Munich: C.H. Beck.

Epstein, Frank 1942, untitled, YIVO, New York, RG 102, Folder 180.

Epstein, José 1987, interview, *Centro de Documentación e información sobre juadísmo Argentino 'Marc Turkow'*, Buenos Aires, Archivo de la Palabra, Nr. 14.

Erlich, Victor 2006, *Child of a Turbulent Century*, Evanston, IL: Northwestern University Press.

Erlikh, Shashke 1973, 'Dzshelne 22', *Leon Oler. Zayn lebn und tetigkayt*, New York: Unser tsayt, pp. 83–8.

Etkes, Tsvi 1956, untitled, Bund Archives, New York, RG 1400 MG-2, Folder 429.

Eynhorn, Dovid 1917, 'Fun mayn tog-bukh. In a frihlings-nakht', *Di arbeyter shtime* 42–43, p. 2 f.

Eynhorn, Dovid 1974, 'Mayn heym in', *Fun dor tsu dor. Fragmentn fun forsharbetn tsu der kharakteristik un zikhroynes*, edited by A. Veyter, David Eynhorn et al., Buenos Aires: Josef Lifshits-fond fun der literatur-geselshaft beym IWO, p. 84 f.

Fagan, L. 1942, untitled, YIVO, New York, RG 102, Folder 191.

Fefer, Shimshe, n.d., untitled, Bund Archives, New York, RG 1400, MG-2, Folder 429.

Feldman, I. 1969, 'Arest in redakstye fun der bundisher teglekher tsaytung mit 50 yor tsurik', *Unzer tsayt*, New York 4–5, p. 44f.

Feybushkevitsh, Moshe 1946, 'In oshvientshimer gehenem. Fun eynem, vos iz dort geven', *Unzer tsayt*, New York 7, pp. 26–28.

Feygl 1953, 'Mali di "loyferin"', *Unzer tsayt*, New York 4, p. 33.

Feynman, Enrike 1937, 'Vegn Pinie Vald', *Argentiner lebn*, Buenos Aires 15, p. 2.

Feynsilber, Abraham, n.d., untitled, Bund Archives, New York, RG 1400, MG-2, Folder 429.

Finklshtayn, Leo 1949, 'Inm amolikn varshe. Shloyme Mendelson – zayn lebn und shafn', *Unzer tsayt*, New York, pp. 79–99.

Fishgrund, S. 1937, 'A yor farn geto-oyfshtand in Varshe. Tsugreytungen fun "bund" tsum bavafnetn oyfshtand. A kapitl zikhroynes', *Unzer tsayt*, New York 3, pp. 19–21.

Fogel, Yakob 1957, *Zikhroynes fun mayn yugnt*, self-published.

Fox, Bertha (Brukhe) 2006 [1942], 'The Movies Pale in Comparison', *In My Future is in America. Autobiographies of Eastern European Jewish Immigrants*, edited by Jocelyn Cohen and Daniel Soyer New York: NYU Press, pp. 204–32.

Frenkel, Borvin 1972, 'In memoriam', *Unzer shtime*, Paris (January).

Friedman, Lena ['A mitglid fun der arbeter ring mishpokhe'] 1942, untitled, YIVO, New York, RG 102, Folder 157.

Frumkin, Esther [EThR, Esther] 1918a, 'Fun mayn togbukh', *Unzer shtime*, Vilnius 2 (8 December), p. 2.

Frumkin, Esther [EThR, Esther] 1918b, 'Fun mayn togbukh', *Unzer shtime*, Vilnius 3 (9 December), p. 2.

Frumkin, Esther [EThR, Esther] 1919a, 'Fun togbukh', *Unzer shtime*, Vilinius 21 (3 January), p. 2 f.

Frumkin, Esther [EThR, Esther] 1919b, 'Alte Geshtaltn', *Unzer shtime*, Vilnius 42 (19 February), p. 2 f.

Gelberg, Naftali 1958, untitled, Bund Archives, New York, RG 1400, MG-2, Folder 429.

Gelernt, H. 1957, 'Der nayer heyliker sefer. A mesieh vegn der "arbeter shtime"', *Unzer tsayt*, New York 11–12, p. 95 f.

Gilinski, M. 1942, 'Kremer der lerer', *Arkadi. Zamlbukh tsum ondenk fun Arkadi Kremer*, New York: Unzer tsayt, pp. 249–53.

Gilitski, Sh. 1943, 'Vi azoy iz arestiert gevorn Viktor Alter', *Unzer tsayt*, New York 5, pp. 27–9.

Gintsburg, M. 1938, 'An ovnt mit Virgilin', *B. Kahan-Virgili: Zamlbukh tsu zayn biografie un kharakteristik*, Vilnius: YIVO, pp. 54–66.

Ginzberg, Rafael 1941a, 'Noakh un zayn krankheyt', *Unzer tsayt*, New York 10, pp. 14–16.

Ginzberg, Rafael 1941b, 'Vladimir Kosovskis krankhayt', *Unzer tsayt*, New York 11, pp. 26–28.

Glants-Leyenlem, Ahron, n.d., untitled, Bund Archives, New York, RG 1400, MG-2, Folder 429.

Gliksmal, Mendl 1978, untitled, Bund Archives, New York, RG 1400, MG-2, Folder 429.

Goldberg, Herman [Manye Goldberg], n.d., untitled, Bund Archives, New York, RG 1400, MG-2, Folder 429.

Goldberg, Herman [Manye Goldberg] 1953, 'Bay tebentsn – in kleynem geto', *Unzer tsayt*, New York 4, p. 24f.

Goldberg, Herman [Manye Goldberg] 1971a, untitled, Bund Archives, New York, RG 1400, MG-2, Folder 429.

Goldberg, Herman [Manye Goldberg] 1971b, untitled, Bund Archives, New York, RG 1400, MG-2, Folder 429 [second draft].

Goldmintz, Herskhe 1985, interview, *Centro de Documentación e información sobre juadísmo Argentino 'Marc Turkow'*, Buenos Aires, Archivo de la Palabra, Nr. 22.

Goldmintz, Herskhe 1998, *Entrevista a Herzke Goldminz*, interview conducted by Marcelo Dimentstein, copy in possession of the author.

Goldsamer, Mordekhay 1953, 'Als mekhanik baym "kleynem shults" un bay di getobunkers', *Unzer tsayt*, New York 4, p. 20.

Goldshmidt, A.J. 1919a, 'Kalman Krapivnits (Zikhroynes), Bd. 1', *Unzer shtime*, Vilnius 51 (likely 2–3 March), p. 2f.

Goldshmidt, A.J. 1919b, 'Kalman Krapivnits (Zikhroynes), Bd. 2', *Unzer shtime*, Vilnius 52 (likely 3/4 March), p. 2f.

Goldshmidt, A.J. 1919c, 'Kalman Krapivnits (Zikhroynes), Bd. 3', *Unzer shtime*, Vilnius 53 (5 March), p. 2f.

Goldshmidt, A.J. 1919d, 'Kalman Krapivnits (Zikhroynes), Bd. 4', *Unzer shtime*, Vilnius 56 (9 March), p. 2f.

Goldshmidt, A.J. 1919e, 'Kalman Krapivnits (Zikhroynes), Bd. 5', *Unzer shtime*, Vilnius 57 (10 March), p. 2f.

Goldshmidt, A.J. 1919f., 'Kalman Krapivnits (Zikhroynes), Bd. 6', *Unzer shtime*, Vilnius 60 (14 March), p. 2f.

Goldshmidt, A.J. 1919g, 'Kalman Krapivnits (Zikhroynes), Bd. 7', *Unzer shtime*, Vilnius 61 (16 March), p. 2f.

Goldshmidt, A.J. 1919h, 'Kalman Krapivnits (Zikhroynes), Bd. 8', *Unzer shtime*, Vilnius 62 (17 March), p. 2f.

Goldstein, Bernard [Goldshtayn, Bernard] 1947a, *Finf yor in varshever geto*, New York: Unzer tsayt.

Goldstein, Bernard [Goldshtayn, Bernard] 1947b, 'Fun di zeydes – tsu di eyniklekh. Di bundishe kinder unter der natsisher beytsh', *Unzer tsayt*, New York 3–4, pp. 133–7.

Goldstein, Bernard [Goldshtayn, Bernard] 1947c, 'Tsvishn vidershtand un onmekhtigkeyt', *Unzer tsayt*, New York 1, pp. 40–2.

Goldstein, Bernard [Goldshtayn, Bernard] 1948, 'Fighting in the Ghetto', *Jewish Labor Bund Bulletin* 4, p. 3.

Goldstein, Bernard [Goldshtayn, Bernard] 1953, 'Fun dem kamf kegn geto – biz der letster geto-shlakht', *Unzer tsayt*, New York 4, pp. 8–12.

Goldstein, Bernard [Goldshtayn, Bernard] 1960, *20 yor in varshever 'Bund' 1919–1939*, New York: Unzer tsayt.

Goldstein, Bernard [Goldshtayn, Bernard] 2016 [1960], *Twenty Years with the Jewish Labor Bund: A Memoir of Interwar Poland*, translated and edited by Marvin S. Zuckerman, West Lafayette, IN: Purdue University Press.

Goldvaser, Kalman [Mordekhay] n.d., untitled, Bund Archives, New York, RG 1400, MG-2, Folder 429.

Goldvaser, Kalman [Mordekhay] 1966, 'Mayn meyster Shmile', *Lebns-fragn*, Tel Aviv 176–177, p. 14f.

Gordon, Abraham 1926, *In friling fun yidisher arbeter-bavegung. Di antstehung fun yidisher 'arbeter-opozits' in 1893 un ir literatur*, Vilnius.

Gozhansky, Samuel [Gozhanskii, S.] [ca. 1909/10], *Pervyi v"ezd bunda. Vospominania uchastnika*, RGASPI, Moscow, Fond 217, opis' 1 delo 34.

Gozhansky, Samuel [Gozhanskii, S.] 1927a [pre-1914], 'Erinerungen fun a papirosenmakherke, Bd. 1', *Unzer tsayt*, Warsaw 7, pp. 89–95.

Gozhansky, Samuel [Gozhanskii, S.] 1927b [pre-1914], 'Erinerungen fun a papirosenmakherke, Bd. 2', *Unzer tsayt*, Warsaw 8–9, pp. 110–26.

Gozhansky, Samuel [Gozhanskii, S.] 1927c [pre-1914], 'Erinerungen fun a papirosenmakherke, Bd. 3', *Unzer tsayt*, Warschau 10, pp. 85–92.

Gozhansky, Samuel [Gozhanskii, S.] 1930, 'Evreiskoe rabochee dvizhenie nachala 90-kh godov. Stenogramma vospominanii, zachitannykh na zasedaniiakh sektsii 5 i 20 ianvaria 1928 g.', *Revoliutsionnoe dvizhenie sredi evreev*, edited by S. Dimanshtein, Moscow, pp. 81–93.

Grin, A.B. 1969, 'Eyner fun milyonen. Betrakhtungen oyf di eltere yorn', *Unzer tsayt*, New York 6, pp. 25–9.

Grin, Moshe, n.d., untitled, Bund Archives, New York, RG 1400, MG-2, Folder 429.

Grin, Moshe 1989, untitled, Bund Archives, New York, RG 1400, MG-2, Folder 429.

Grinboym, Henri 1937, 'Tsum ondenk fun a lerer un fraynt', *Leon Oler. Zayn lebn und tetigkayt*, Unzer tsayt: New York, pp. 177–80.

Grinboym, Moshe 1963, 'Maydanek – Oyshvits – Alakh', *Unzer tsayt*, New York 4, pp. 13–15.

Grinshpan, Rutke 1968, 'Oyf di veg fun peyn', *Unzer tsayt*, New York 3–4, pp. 7–11.

Grinshteyn, Sheyne 1922, 'Di Vilne geshehnishn fun Lekerts tsaytn', *Hirsh Lekert. Tsum 20-tn yortsayt fun zayn kepung*, edited by Ruslendishe komunistishe partey, Ts. K. fun R.K.P., Ts. B. fun yidsektsye, Moscow, pp. 17–21.

Grosman, Y. 1945, 'Geleyent dem ershtn numer fun "unzer tsayt" in kobe', *Unzer tsayt*, New York 3, p. 77f.

Grosser, Bronislav 1921, 'Bronislav Grossers avtobiografye', *Royter pinkes*, Warsaw 1, pp. 80–91.
Gros, Shaul 1957, 'Bundistn in Shankhay', *Unzer tsayt*, New York 11–12, pp. 91–3.
Gudvin, P. 1944, 'Zikhroynes vegn Hirsh Lekert', *Fraye arbeter shtime* (26 May), p. 7.
Gummer, A. 1942, untitled, YIVO, New York, RG 102, Folder 44.
Gurevitsh, G. 1924a, 'Der protses fun A. Liberman, G. Gurevitsh un M. Aronson in berlin', pp. 107–10.
Gurevitsh, G. 1924b, 'Tsu der biografye fun L. Tsukerman. Zikhroynes', *Royter pinkes*, Warsaw 2, p. 112 ff.
Guterman, Perets 1973, 'Mit Leonen in der sovetisher tfise', *Leon Oler. Zayn lebn und tetigkayt*, Unzer tsayt: New York, pp. 67–71.
Guterman, Perets 1976, 'A muster fun oyfrikhtigkeyt', *Yid. Mentsh. Sotsysalist. I. Artuski ondenk-bukh*, edited by the I. Artuski Bukh-Komitet, Tel Aviv: Lebns-fragn, pp. 76–9.
Gutman, B.A. 1952, 'Hirsh Lekert-akademye in krake in 1903. A kapitl zikhroynes', *Forois* (August), p. 10 f.
Hartshik, A. (or no. 141078) 1953, 'Bundishe arbet in natsi-lagern' *Unzer tsayt*, New York 4, pp. 31–2.
Hart, Yosef 1931, 'Kh' Noakh un undzer yugnt', *Unzer tsayt*, New York 10, pp. 25–6.
Hart, Yosef 1943a, 'A trer oyfn kibur', *Unzer tsayt*, New York 4, pp. 26–8.
Hart, Yosef 1943b, 'Kinder', *Unzer tsayt*, New York 3, pp. 24–8.
Hersh, Libman 1953, 'Fir brider zeynen mir geven ...', *Unzer tsayt*, New York 4, pp. 40–1.
Hersh, Yosef 1957, 'Vegn politisher eynshtelung fun mayn fater. Etlikhe kurtse derinerungen', *Unzer tsayt*, New York, 11–12, p. 72 f.
Horn, Yosef 1946, *Mayn khoreve heym. A yidish shtetl in Poyln tsvishn beyde veltmilkhomes*, Buenos Aires: self-published.
Hurvits, Shual [sic.; Shaul?] 1953, 'In der malokhe fun "bund". Derinerungen', *Unzer tsayt*, New York, 12 (1953), pp. 42–43.
Infeld, Ikhyal 1997, 'A dank dem "bund"', *100 yor 'bund'. Spetsyele oysgabe fun der bundisher organisatsye in Myami-bitsh. Algemeyner yidisher arbeyter 'bund' 1897–1997. Tsum 100 yorign yubl fun 'bund'*, Miami Beach, p. 25.
Kahan, Yitsak 1976, 'I. Artuski in Melburn. Fun mayn notits-bukh', *Yid. Mentsh. Sotsysalist. I. Artuski ondenk-bukh*, edited by I. Artuski Bukh-Komitet, Tel Aviv: Lebns-fragn, pp. 99–106.
Kamashnmakher, Kalman 1924, 'Tsvey momentn, velkhe ikh vel keynmol nisht fargesn', *Arbeter luakh*, Warsaw 5, pp. 142–7.
Kanutsky, Guitl 1985, interview, *Centro de Documentación e información sobre judaísmo Argentino 'Marc Turkow'*, Buenos Aires, Archivo de la Palabra, no. 32.
Kater, A. 1941, 'In yene teg', *Unzer tsayt*, New York, 8, pp. 23–9.
Kats, Moshe 1956, *A dor voz hot farloyrn di moyre. Bleter zikhroynes fun arum 1905*, New York: Moshe Kats yubiley-komitet.

Kazdan, Khaym Sh. 1963, 'A briv tsu khaver Yakob Tselemenski', *Unzer tsayt*, New York, 10, pp. 31–3.

Khanin, N. [Nokhem] 1934, 'Eyn mol a bundist – ale mol a bundist', *Der veker*, New York, 528 (10 November), p. 16 f.

Khanin, N. 1938, 'Bundistn in Amerike', *Zamlheft fun bundishn klub in Nyu York. Aroysgegebn lekhoved dem 15 yoriken yubiley*, New York: Bundisher Klub in Nyu York, pp. 14–18.

Khanin, N. 1941, 'Noakh geshtorbn', *Unzer tsayt*, New York, 10, p. 41 f.

Khanin, N. 1945, 'Lublin', *Unzer tsayt*, New York, 3, pp. 63–8.

Khanin, N. 1952, 'A kriveshe tsu a fraynd', *Der veker*, New York (1 May), pp. 12–14.

Kharkher, Yitshok [P. Smith] 1942, untitled, YIVO, New York, RG 102, Folder 76.

Kharlash, I. 1957, 'Fun 1917 in rusland. Fragmentn', *Unzer tsayt*, New York, 3, pp. 14–18.

Khaytovisth, I.A. [A-Ki, I.] 1922a, 'Dos voz ikh veys vegn Hirsh Lekert', *Hirsh Lekert. Tsum 20-tn yortsayt fun zayn kepung*, edited by Ruslendishe komunistishe partey, Ts. K. fun R.K.P., Ts. B. fun yidsektsye, Moscow, pp. 13–16.

Khaytovisth, I.A. [A-Ki, I.] 1922b, 'Hirsh Lekert. Tsum 20ten yortsayt fun der Vilner tragedye', *Folkstsaytung*, Warsaw, 32; also in *Der veker*, New York (27 May 1922), pp. 13–15.

Kingston, Max, n.d., untitled, Bund Archives, New York, RG 1400, MG-2, Folder 429.

Kirsh Holtman, Rakhel 1948, *Mayn lebns-veg*, New York: Rakhel Holtman bukh-komitet.

Kisman, I. 1943, 'Henrik Erlikh in Tshernovits', *Unzer tsayt*, New York, 4, p. 43 f.

Kisman, Leah 1957, untitled, Bund Archives, New York, RG 1400, MG-2, Folder 429.

Kling, Lazar 1970, 'A geheymer bundisher drukerey in Brinsk', *Unzer tsayt*, New York, 11, pp. 28–31.

K., M. 1951, 'Yusef Aronovitsh in sovetisher tfise', *Unzer tsayt*, New York, 7–8, pp. 37–40.

Kohen, Yesir 1942, 'Bey aleksandern in kreyzl', *Arkadi. Zamlbukh tsum ondenk fun Arkadi Kremer*, New York: Unzer tsayt, p. 145 f.

Kolir, Olyesr 1967, 'Bletlekh zikhroynes vegn Z. Segalavitsh. Tsu zayn 19tn yortsayt', *Lebns-fragn*, Tel Aviv 184–5, p. 10.

Kolski, Fishl 1963, 'A por verter vegn kh'te Solomea Reyndorf', *Unzer tsayt*, New York 11, p. 36.

Kopelsohn, Timofei [Ts.] 1907, *Na zare evreiskogo rabochego dvizheniia*, RGASPI, Moscow, Fond 217, opis' 1 delo 315.

Kopelsohn, Timofei [Ts.] 1917, 'A provokator (erinerung)', *Dos revolutsyonere rusland*, edited by A. Litvak and J.B. Salutski, New York: Yidishe sotsyalistishe federatsye in Amerike, pp. 123–7.

Kopelsohn, Timofei [Ts.] 1922, 'Di ershte shprotsungen (zikhroynos fun di yorn 1887–1890)', *Arbeter luakh*, Warsaw 3, pp. 49–70.

Kopelsohn, Timofei [Ts.] 1930, 'Evreiskoe rabochee dvizhenie kontsa 80-kh i nachal 90-kh godov. Stenogramma vospominanii, zachitannykh na zasedaniiah sektsii 16 fevralia i 9 marta 1928g', *Revoliutsionnoe dvizhenie sredi evreev*, edited by S. Dimanshtein, Moscow, pp. 65–80.

Kossovski, Vladimir 1928, 'Dem andenk fun Vladimir Medem. Bletlekh zikhroynes', *Unzer tsayt*, Warsaw 1, pp. 30–9.

Kotik, Abraham 1961, 'How I arrived at Yiddish [originally in Yiddish]', *Zabludov yisker bukh*, edited by Sh. Tsesler et al., Buenos Aries: Zablodow bukh komitet, pp. 137–43.

Kotik, Abraham [Avraham Hersh] 1925, *Dos lebn fun a yidishn inteligent*, New York: H. Toibenshlag.

Kot, Srolke 1947, *Khurbn Białystok*, Buenos Aires: A grupe fraynd.

Kremer, Arkadi [Aleksander] 1922, 'Di grindung fun "bund"', *Arbeter luakh*, Warsaw, 3, pp. 91–100.

Kremer, Arkadi [Aleksander] 1928, 'Mit 35 yor tsurik', *Unzer Tsayt*, Warsaw, 2, pp. 83–7.

Kremer, Arkadi [Aleksander] 1939, 'Di grindung fun Bund', *Opshatsungen un zikhroynes vegn Arkadin*, Vilnius, pp. 356–66.

Kremer, Arkadi [Aleksander] 1947, 'Di grindung fun "bund"', *Unzer tsayt*, New York, 3–4, pp. 53–6.

Kremer, Pati 1942, 'Zikhroynes vegn Arkadi', *Arkadi. Zamlbukh tsum ondenk fun Arkadi Kremer*, New York: Unzer tsayt, pp. 22–72.

Kribus, Khil 1952, 'An Erlikh-Alter ovent – oyf sovjetisher erd', *Unzer tsayt*, New York, 1, p. 20f.

Krishtal-Frishdorf, Khane 1949, 'Iberlebungen beyzn oyfshtand', *Unzer tsayt*, New York, 4–5, pp. 17–20.

Kromorksi, Khonine 1938, '17 yor a poylisher bundist in Amerike', *Zamlheft fun bundishn klub in Nyu York. Aroysgegebn lekhoved dem 15 yoriken yubiley*, New York: Bundisher klub in Nyu York, pp. 8–11.

Krotoshinski, Abraham 1957, *Interesante momente fun mayn leben*, Bund Archives, New York, RG 1400, MG-2, Folder 429.

Kurski, Franz [Frants Kursky] 1928a, 'Pe und Tshe. Bletlekh zikhroynes, Bd. 1', *Unzer Tsayt*, Warsaw 7, pp. 5–28.

Kurski, Franz [Frants Kursky] 1928b, 'Pe und Tshe. Bletlekh zikhroynes, Bd. 2', *Unzer Tsayt*, Warsaw 8–9, pp. 11–31.

Kurski, Franz [Frants Kursky] 1928c, 'Pe und Tshe. Bletlekh zikhroynes, Bd. 3' *Unzer Tsayt*, Warsaw 10, pp. 32–62.

Kurski, Franz [Frants Kursky] 1937, *Bletlekh zikhroynes*, 2 volumes, New York.

Kurski, Franz [Frants Kursky] 1941, 'Khaver Dan', *Unzer tsayt*, New York 11, pp. 17–19.

Kushner, Mayr 1960, *Lebn un kamf fun a kloukmakher*, New York: A komitet fun lokal 9.

Kuvelsman, Sh 1937, 'Mit a royt bliml? Donerveter!', *40 yor 'bund'*, Montevideo: Bundishe Grupe in Montevideo, p. 51.

Lerer, Layb, n.d., untitled, Bund Archives, New York, RG 1400, MG-2, Folder 429.

Lerman, Artur 1999, *Un dokh, dem morgnroyt antkegn. Eseyen*, Tel Aviv: Farlag Y.L. Perets.
Lerman, Artur 1943, 'A balerndiker derinerung', *Unzer tsayt*, New York 8, p. 24 f.
Lev, Abraham 1971, *Bleter fun kibuts*, Tel Aviv: Farlag Y.L. Perets.
Lev, Abraham 1957a, 'Bletlekh fun mayn tog-bukh in kibuts. Bd. 1', *Lebns-fragn*, Tel Aviv 70–1, p. 17 f.
Lev, Abraham 1957b, 'Bletlekh fun mayn tog-bukh in kibuts. Bd. 2: A dermanung', *Lebns-fragn*, Tel Aviv 75–6, p. 28 f.
Levin, Bentse 1922, 'Di 5te konferents fun "bund"', *Hirsh Lekert. Tsum 20-tn yortsayt fun zayn kepung*, edited by Ruslendishe komunistishe partey, Ts. K. fun R.K.P., Ts. B. fun yidsektsye, Moscow, pp. 58–60.
Levin, Elke 1960, untitled, Bund Archives, New York, RG 1400, MG-2, Folder 429.
Levine, Sholem [Shlomo Levin] 1946, *Untererdishe kemfer*, New York: Sholem-Levine-Bukh-Komitet.
Levin, Yankel 1924, *Fun yene yorn: 'Kleyn Bund'*, Homel: Beltrespetshat.
Leyzers, Khaym 1932, 'Er iz gevorn a yevsek', *Sotsyalistishe bleter*, Buenos Aires 41, p. 2.
Liesin, Abraham 1954, *Zikhroynes un bilder*, New York: CYCO, L.M. Shteyn folks-biblyotek baym alweltlekhn yidishn kultur-kongres.
Lifshits, Yosef 1976, 'Oskar – a getreyer khaver un ibergegebener fraynd', *Yid. Mentsh. Sotsysalist. I. Artuski ondenk-bukh*, edited by I. Artuski Bukh-Komitet, Tel Aviv: Lebns-fragn, p. 83 f.
Lifshits, Yosef 1957, 'Tsvey bagegenishn. Mitn poylishn komunistishn firer un tfisekh', *Unzer tsayt*, New York 10, pp. 39–42.
Lifshits, Yosef 1935, 'A bisl zikhroynes fun far 20 yor', *Naye folkstsaytung*, Warsaw (15 November), Bund Archives, New York, RG 1400, MG-2, Folder 504.
Lilke 1947, 'Fun fargangene teg. Der Piotrkover geto', *Unzer tsayt*, New York 3–4, pp. 147–9.
Lipski, Ytsak 1976, 'Ot azoy gedenk ikh im – dem khaver Artuski ...', *Yid. Mentsh. Sotsyalist. I. Artuski ondenk-bukh*, edited by I. Artuski Bukh-Komitet, Tel Aviv: Lebns-fragn, pp. 107–14.
Litvak, A. [Khaym Yankel Helfand] 1921, 'Di "zshargonisher komitet"', *Royter pinkes*, Warsaw 1, pp. 5–30.
Litvak, A. 1925, *Vos iz geven. Etyudn un zikhroynes*, Vilnius: Vilner farlag fun B. Kletskin.
Litvak, A. 1943a, 'Mayne bagegenishn mit Pavel Akselrod (kapitlekh zikhroynes)', *Unzer tsayt*, New York 2, pp. 31–4.
Litvak, A. 1943b, 'Kapitlekh zikhroynes', *Unzer tsayt*, New York 9, pp. 31–5.
Litvak, A. 1944, 'Bletlekh zikhroynes. Bagegenish mit Karl Radek, Benzya und Trya', *Unzer tsayt*, New York 1, pp. 33–8.
Lozovski, L. 1948, 'Kh. L. Poznanski', *Historisher Zamlbukh. Materialn un dokumentn tsutshayer tsu der geshikhte fun Algemeyner Yidisher Arbeter-Bund*, Warsaw: Ringen, p. 94 f.

Mandelman, Moshe 1947, 'Di fri-farshnitene – lezikorn', *Unzer tsayt*, New York 3–4, pp. 124–8.
Margules, Lily M. 1999, *Memories, Memories ... From Vilna to New York with a Few Steps Along the Way: A Collection of Essays*, Anapolis, MD: ProStar Publications.
Marishe 1947, 'Konspirative doyres', *Unzer tsayt*, New York 3–4, pp. 139–41.
Mayapit, Abraham, n.d., untitled, Bund Archives, New York, RG 1400, MG-2, Folder 429.
Mayer 1942, untitled, YIVO, New York, RG 102, Folder 200.
Mayer, Dovid 1957, '"Yidishe literarishe geselshaft" in Varshe. A bletl zikhroynes', *Unzer tsayt*, New York, 11–12, p. 104 f.
Medem, Gina 1950, *A lebnsveg. Oytobiografishe notits*, New York: Gina Medem bukh-komitet.
Medem, Gina 1963, *Lender, felker, kamfn*, New York: Gina Medem bukh-komitet.
Medem, Vladimir 1918a, 'Turme zikhroynes', *Zikhroynes un artiklen*, Warsaw: Farlag Yudish, pp. 3–60.
Medem, Vladimir 1918b, 'Tifer in leben', *Zikhroynes un artiklen*, Warsaw: Farlag Yudish, pp. 135–60.
Medem, Vladimir 1919, 'Di Lebens-fragn', *Unzer Grus. Zamelheft*, Warsaw: Lebens-fragn, pp. 9–13; Bund Archives, New York, RG 1400, MG-2, Folder 504.
Medem, Vladimir 1920, *Fun mayn notits-bukh*, Warsaw.
Medem, Vladimir 1923, *Fun mayn leben*, 2 volumes, New York: Vladimir Medem komite.
Medem, Vladimir 1942, 'Di tsentrale figur', *Arkadi. Zamlbukh tsum ondenk fun Arkadi Kremer*, New York: Unzer tsayt, pp. 232–5.
Medem, Vladimir 1948 [1919], 'Biografi fun di "lebns-fragn"', *Historisher Zamlbukh. Materialn un dokumentn tsutshayer tsu der geshikhte fun Algemeyner Yidisher Arbeter-Bund*, Warsaw: Ringen, p. 10 f.
Mendel, Hersh 1959, *Zikhroynes fun a yidishn revolutsyoner*, Tel Aviv: Farlag Y.L. Perets.
Mendelman, Moshe [also Mandelman?] 1955, untitled, Bund Archives, New York, RG 1400, MG-2, Folder 429.
Mendzizshetska, Vladke 1946, 'Vi azoy mir hobn gegreyt gever', *Unzer tsayt*, New York 5, pp. 33–6.
Mendzizshetska, Vladke 1947, 'Derhoybene momentn oyf der "arisher" zeyt', *Unzer tsayt*, New York 3–4, pp. 137–9.
Metaloviets, Hershl [Hersh Leib Bekerkunts] 1982, *A veg in lebn. Fragmente fun an oytobiografie*, 2 volumes, Tel Aviv: Farlag Y.L. Perets.
Mićkun, R[obert?] 1927, 'Vilenskaia demonstratsiia 1902 goda', *Pravda* 97 (3629) (1 May), p. 7.
Mikhalevitsh, Beynish 1921a, *Zikhroynes fun a yidishen sotsyalist*, Vol. 1, Warsaw: Lebns-fragn.
Mikhalevitsh, Beynish 1921b, *Zikhroynes fun a yidishen sotsyalist*, Vol. 2, Warsaw: Lebns-fragn.

Mikhalevitsh, Beynish 1929, *Zikhroynes fun a yidishen sotsyalist*, Vol. 3, Warsaw: Di velt.
Mikhalevitsh, Beynish 1951, 'Mit Sholem-Aleykhem', *Unzer tsayt*, New York 7–8, p. 32 f.
Mill, Dzshon 1942a, '37 yor yung. Shtimungen', *Der veker*, New York 528 (10 November), p. 17 f.
Mill, Dzshon 1942b, 'Arkadi un der ershter tsuzamenfar', *Arkadi. Zamlbukh tsum ondenk fun Arkadi Kremer*, New York: Unzer tsayt, pp. 147–69.
Mill, Dzshon 1946a, 'Der grindungs-tsuzamenfor fun "bund"', *Unzer tsayt*, New York 3–4, pp. 35–8.
Mill, Dzshon 1946b, *Pionern un boyern. Memuarn*, Vol. 1, New York: Der veker.
Mill, Dzshon 1947, 'Mayn arbet in oyslendishn komitet', *Unzer tsayt*, New York 3–4, pp. 57–60.
Mill, Dzshon 1949a, 'Geshtaltn, bagegenishn, epizodn', *Unzer tsayt*, New York 11, pp. 25–9.
Mill, Dzshon 1949b, *Pionern un boyern. Memuarn*, Vol. 2, New York: Der veker.
Mill, Dzshon 1950a, 'Frants Kurski', *Unzer tsayt*, New York 2, p. 4 f.
Mill, Dzshon 1950b, 'Der emes vegn dem bundish arkhiv', *Unzer tsayt*, New York 4–5, pp. 52–5.
Mill, Dzshon 1952, 'Di geburt fun "bund"', *Unzer tsayt*, New York 11, p. 39 f.
Milman, Sh. 1947, 'Der "bund" in Lodzsh fun 1912 biz 1939', *Unzer tsayt*, New York 3–4, pp. 107–12.
Milman, Sh. 1948, 'Der letster Lodzsher komitet fun "bund" in 1939', *Historisher Zamlbukh. Materialn un dokumentn tsutshayer tsu der geshikhte fun Algemeyner Yidisher Arbeter-Bund*, Warsaw: Ringen, pp. 60–8.
Milman, Sh. 1957, 'Tsvishnparteyishe batsiungen in Lodzsh', *Unzer tsayt*, New York 11–12, pp. 78–81.
Milman, Sh. 1969, 'Mit 30 yor tsurik. A kapitl zikhroynes', *Unzer tsayt*, New York 10, pp. 36–8.
Mintovski, Ali 1954, 'Der bershter bund. A kapitl zikhroynes', *Unzer tsayt*, New York 7, pp. 26–9.
Mints, Pinkhas [Pinjas Minc, Aleksander] 1954, *Di geshikhte fun a falsher ilusye*, Buenos Aires: Tsentral-farband fun poylishe yidn in Argentine.
Mints, Pinkhas [Pinjas Minc, Aleksander] 1956, *In di yorn fun yidishn umkum un vidershtand in frankreykh. Perzenlekhe zikhroynes*, Buenos Aires: Yidbukh.
Mints, Pinkhas [Pinjas Minc, Aleksander] 1958, *Lodzsh in mayn zikhroyn*, Buenos Aires: Yidbukh.
Mints, Rakhel 1976, 'Oskar in tser un in likht', *Yid. Mentsh. Sotsysalist. I. Artuski ondenkbukh*, edited by I. Artuski Bukh-Komitet, Tel Aviv: Lebns-fragn, pp. 90–3.
Mitskun, Isak [Karl] 1922, 'Di Vilner organisatsye fun Bund un Lekerts onteyl', *Hirsh Lekert. Tsum 20-tn yortsayt fun zayn kepung*, edited by Ruslendishe komunistishe partey, Ts. K. fun R.K.P., Ts. B. fun yidsektsye, Moscow, pp. 42–6.

Motolski, Elye 1945, '1-ter may 1903 in varshe. A bletl zikhroynes', *Unzer tsayt*, New York 5, p. 36 f.
Mutnik, Abraham [A. Mutnikovitsh; 'Gleb', G-B] 1907, 'Der ershte zusamenfar fun bund', *Di hofnung*, Vilnius 14.
Mutnik, Abraham [A. Mutnikovitsh; 'Gleb', G-B] 1933a, 'Bletlekh fun mayn leben. Erinerungen', *Di tsukunft* 11, pp. 664–6.
Mutnik, Abraham [A. Mutnikovitsh; 'Gleb', G-B] 1933b, 'Bletlekh fun mayn leben. Erinerungen', *Di tsukunft* 12, pp. 718–20.
Mutnik, Abraham [A. Mutnikovitsh; 'Gleb', G-B] 1942, 'Der soyresdiker lamtern-salup', *Arkadi. Zamlbukh tsum ondenk fun Arkadi Kremer*, New York: Unzer tsayt, p. 170 ff.
N.N. [likely 1914], untitled [memoirs on the creation of the *Arbeter shtime*], Bund Archives, New York, RG 1401, Box 32, Folder 337.
N.N. ca. 1918, *Belostokskii period z zhizni TS.K. Bunda*, Tsentral'nii derzhavnyi arkhiv hromads'kykh ob'ednan' Ukraïny, d. 41, op. 1, spr. 11, ark. 16.
N.N. 1921, 'Der ershte may amol', *Dos fraye vort*, Vilnius 15 (1 May), p. 2.
N.N. 1922, 'Der ershter numer "arbeter-shtime". Zikhroynes fun die onteylnehmer', *Arbeter luakh*, Warsaw 3, pp. 101–9.
N.N. 1942, untitled, YIVO, New York, RG 102, Folder 196.
N.N. 1951, 'A lebendiker mentsh in a toyter velt', *Unzer tsayt*, New York 2, p. 33 f.
N.N. 1963a, 'An untergeherter shmues', *Kinder-khronik fun Varshever geto*, edited by Mordekhay V. Bernshtayn, *Unzer tsayt*, New York 4, p. 20 f.
N.N. 1963b, 'Ikh hob amol gehat a heym', *Kinder-khronik fun Varshever geto*, edited by Mordekhay V. Bernshtayn, *Unzer tsayt*, New York 4, p. 21.
N.N. 1963c, 'Efsher ken ikh krign a hemdl?', *Kinder-khronik fun Varshever geto*, edited by Mordekhay V. Bernshtayn, *Unzer tsayt*, New York 4, p. 21.
N.N. 1963d, 'Mayn shvester iz aza sheyn', *Kinder-khronik fun Varshever geto*, edited by Mordekhay V. Bernshtayn, *Unzer tsayt*, New York 4, p. 21.
N.N. 1963e, 'Ikh vil mer garni', *Kinder-khronik fun Varshever geto*, edited by Mordekhay V. Bernshtayn, *Unzer tsayt*, New York 4, p. 21.
N.N. 1963f., 'An zol men mir iberlozn khotsh a finger shmues', *Kinder-khronik fun Varshever geto*, edited by Mordekhay V. Bernshtayn, *Unzer tsayt*, New York 4, p. 22.
N.N. 1963g, 'Di poyerim hobn rakhmoynes', *Kinder-khronik fun Varshever geto*, edited by Mordekhay V. Bernshtayn, *Unzer tsayt*, New York 4, p. 22.
N.N. 1963h, 'Nokh nisht in kibur', *Kinder-khronik fun Varshever geto*, edied by Mordekhay V. Bernshtayn, *Unzer tsayt*, New York 4, p. 22.
N.N. 1963i, 'Ikh hob nokh tsvey briderlekh', *Kinder-khronik fun Varshever geto*, edited by Mordekhay V. Bernshtayn, *Unzer tsayt*, New York 4, p. 22.
N.N. 1963j, 'Tsu shpet', *Kinder-khronik fun Varshever geto*, edited by Mordekhay V. Bernshtayn, *Unzer tsayt*, New York 4, p. 22.
Nemanski, A. 1917, 'Bletlekh zikhroynes', *Di arbeyter shtime* 45, pp. 10–12.

Nirnberg, Y. 1947, 'In Lodzsher geto. Fragmentn fun a geshikhte', *Unzer tsayt*, New York 3-4, pp. 141-6.

Nisenboym, Khaym 1952, 'Viktor un Branke Ivinski. Fun mayne partisaner-iberlebungen in di veysrusishe velder', *Unzer tsayt*, New York 10, p. 39 f.

Nordon, Abraham Yitzak 195?, untitled, Bund Archives, New York, RG 1400, MG-2, Folder 429.

Novikov, Yoel 1956, untitled, Bund Archives, New York, RG 1400, MG-2, Folder 429.

Novikov, Yoel 1963, 'Bamerkungen tsu der geshikhte fun "bund"', *Unzer tsayt*, New York 11, p. 37 f.

Novikov, Yoel 1967, *Zikhroynes fun a yidishn arbeter*, Tel Aviv: Kultur-Lige.

Novodvorsky, Sara 1985, interview, *Centro de Documentación e información sobre juadísm Argentino 'Marc Turkow'*, Buenos Aires, Archivo de la Palabra, no. 53.

Novogrudski, Emanuel [E. Mus] 1941, '25 yor mit Noakhn', *Unzer tsayt*, New York 10, pp. 21-3.

Novogrudski, Emanuel [E. Mus] 1951, 'Azoy veynik zayen zey geblibn ...', *Unzer tsayt*, New York 10, pp. 18-20.

Nunberg, Artur 1946, 'Geselshaftlekhe tetigkeyt in di lagern', *Unzer tsayt*, New York 8-9, pp. 24-7.

Nunberg, Artur 1953, 'Mit a ku durkh der "grine grenets"', *Unzer tsayt*, New York 4, pp. 26-7.

Nunberg, Artur 1972a, 'From the yeshiva bench straight to the "bund" [Yiddish]', *Pinkhes Zaglembie*, edited by J. Rapaport, Melbourne: Zagłębie Society in Melbourne Tel Aviv, pp. 210-13.

Nunberg, Artur 1972b, 'Memories of the Bund in Zagłębie [Yiddish]', *Pinkhes Zaglembie*, edited by J. Rapaport, Melbourne: Zagłębie Society in Melbourne Tel Aviv, pp. 213-15.

Oler, Leon 1943, 'A por bletlekh "iberlebungen"', *Unzer tsayt*, New York 12, pp. 26-8.

Oler, Leon 1947a, 'Tsum tsvayten yortsayt fun Leon Feyner', *Unzer tsayt*, New York 1-2, pp. 6-8.

Oler, Leon 1947b, 'Momentn', *Unzer tsayt*, New York 3-4, pp. 113-15.

Oler, Leon 1947c, 'Leyvik Hodem. Tsum opshid fun a mitkemfer', *Unzer tsayt*, New York 4-5, pp. 23-7.

Oler, Leon 1973, 'In der partey un far der partey: Derinerungen vegn khaver Khaym Vaser', *Leon Oler. Zayn lebn und tetigkayt*, Unzer tsayt: New York, pp. 113-19.

Olgin, Moshe 1917, 'Nokh a pogrom (geshriben zumer 1906 in bialystok)', *Dos revolutsionere rusland*, edited by A. Litvak and J.B. Salutski, New York: Yidishe sotsyalistishe federatsye in Amerike, p. 117 ff.

Olgin, Moshe 1940a, 'Mit Lekert's fraynt um khaverim. A bletl zikhroynes', *1905*, New York: Olgin ondenk komitet, pp. 61-6.

Olgin, Moshe 1940b, 'Tsebrokhene grates', *1905*, New York: Olgin ondenk komitet, p. 15 f.

Olgin, Moshe 1951, 'Mit Hirsh Lekert's fraynd un khaverim. Zikhroynes fun der Vilner turme', *Morgn frayhayt*, New York (30 April), p. 5.

Olgin, Moshe 1962, 'Mit Hirsh Lekert's khaverim in turme', *Morgn frayhayt*, New York (24 November), p. 5, p. 11.

Oliver, Yehuda 1973, 'Der ershter may in plotsk 1936. A bletl zikhroynes', *Leon Oler. Zayn lebn und tetigkayt*, Unzer tsayt: New York, pp. 92–4.

Osipov, Shneur Zalmen 1954, *Derinerungen un iberlebungen fun a yidishn sotsyalist. In fir teyln*, Boston: Farlag 'ARK'.

Oyerberg, Rakhel 1957, 'Pan Mikolay', *Unzer tsayt*, New York 7–8, pp. 38–41.

Palevski, Samuel [Shimeon] 1946, 'Bayshpiln fun eynheyt un kamf', *Unzer tsayt*, New York 8–9, pp. 27–8.

Palevski, Samuel [Shimeon] 1963, 'Als partisan in vilner velder', *Unzer tsayt*, New York 4, pp. 30–1.

Palevski, Samuel [Shimeon] 1973, 'Leon – mayn firer, khaver un fraynt', *Leon Oler. Zayn lebn und tetigkayt*, Unzer tsayt: New York, p. 171f.

Pat, Jacob 1941, 'Kapitel Noakh', *Unzer tsayt*, New York 10, pp. 42–4.

Pat, Jacob 1943a, 'Mord un shand', *Unzer tsayt*, New York 4, pp. 31–3.

Pat, Jacob 1943b, 'Varshe oyn yidn? ...', *Unzer tsayt*, New York 5, pp. 12–14.

Pat, Jacob 1944, 'Der nes fun oyfshtand', *Geto in flamen. Zamlbukh*, New York: Amerikanishe representatsye fun 'bund' in Poyln, pp. 82–95.

Pat, Yekum 1930, 'Finf milyon hiner', *Sotsyalistishe bleter*, Buenos Aires 14, p. 5.

Pats, P. 1931, 'Khaver Groser: A trokener fakt', *Naye folkstsaytung*, Warsaw 3 (4 January), p. 7.

Peskin, Yakob 1942, 'Di vilner grupe un Arkadi Kremer', *Arkadi. Zamlbukh tsum ondenk fun Arkadi Kremer*, New York: Unzer tsayt, pp. 112–20.

P.-K., Sh. 1927a, 'Yidishe provokatorn in tshenstokhov. Abisl zikhroynes', *Tshenstokhov arbeter tsaytung* 2 (14 January), p. 2.

P.-K., Sh. 1927b, 'Yidishe provokatorn in tshenstokhov. Abisl zikhroynes', *Tshenstokhov arbeter tsaytung* 3 (21 January), p. 2.

P.-K., Sh. 1927c, 'Yidishe provokatorn in tshenstokhov. Abisl zikhroynes', *Tshenstokhov arbeter tsaytung* 4 (28 January), p. 2.

P.-K., Sh. 1927d, 'Yidishe provokatorn in tshenstokhov. Abisl zikhroynes', *Tshenstokhov arbeter tsaytung* 5 (4 February), p. 2.

P.-K., Sh. 1927e, 'Yidishe provokatorn in tshenstokhov. Abisl zikhroynes', *Tshenstokhov arbeter tsaytung* 6 (11 February), p. 2.

P.-K., Sh. 1927f., 'Yidishe provokatorn in tshenstokhov. Abisl zikhroynes', *Tshenstokhov arbeter tsaytung* 7 (18 February), p. 2.

Podell, Max 1942, *The Story of My Life*, YIVO, New York, RG 102, Folder 178.

Poeyra, Ana 1931, 'Mateatis muter in toyt. Perzenlekhe zikhroynes', *Naye folkstsaytung*, Warsaw 45 (17 February), p. 4.

Polevski, Shumke, n.d. [a], untitled, Bund Archives, New York, RG 1400, MG-2, Folder 429.
Polevski, Shumke n.d. [b], untitled, Bund Archives, New York, RG 1400, MG-2, Folder 429 [second draft].
Polin, M.L. 1957, '17 yor "fraynt fun 'bund' in shikago"', *Unzer tsayt*, New York 11–12, pp. 81–3.
Polin, M.L. 1964, 'Farzamlungen in mayn zikhroyn', *Arebeter ring in ranglenishn un dergreykhungen (1914–1964)*, edited by Yefim Yeshurin, New York: 'Natsyonaln sotsyaln klub' tsu zayn fuftsikstn yubl, pp. 301–3.
Portnoy, Noakh 1907a, 'Der ershter tsuzamenfahr fun Bund. Erinerungen', *Di hofnung*, Vilnius 14, p. 3.
Portnoy, Noakh 1907b, 'Der geheymnisfoler laterne-klub. A Maysyeh fun alte tsayten', *Di hofnung*, Vilnius 14, p. 3.
Portnoy, Noakh 1934, 'Mit 37 yor tsurik', *Der veker*, New York 528 (10 November), p. 11 f.
Poznanski, Khaym Layb 1938, *Memuarn fun a bundist. Ershter band*, Warsaw.
Pressman, Israel [A poshteter shneyder] 1942, untitled, YIVO, New York, RG 102, Folder 189.
Pressman, Israel [A poshteter shneyder] 1950, *Der durkhgegangener veg*, New York: Aroysgegebn durkh a grupe fraynd.
Pressman, Israel [A poshteter shneyder] 1995, 'Roads that Passed: Russia, My Old Home', *YIVO Annual* 22, pp. 1–80.
Pudlovski, Zalmen 1970, 'Shikt iber a grus dem khaver Zalmen Pudlovski', *Unzer tsayt*, New York 7–8, p. 47 f.
Pustau, Erna 1957, '"Nit keyn geveyntlekher iberloyfer"', *Unzer tsayt*, New York 10, pp. 37–9.
Pyura, Ahron Yosl, n.d., untitled, Bund Archives, New York, RG 1400, MG-2, Folder 429.
Rafalovski, Ahron, n.d., untitled, Bund Archives, New York, RG 1400, MG-2, Folder 429.
Rafes, Moshe 1919a, 'Hirsh Lekert un zayn heldische tat. Mit 16 yor tsurik', *Unzer shtime*, Vilnius 11 (14 January), p. 2 f.
Rafes, Moshe 1919b, 'Hirsh Lekert un zayn heldische tat. Mit 16 yor tsurik', *Unzer shtime*, Vilnius 12 (15 January), p. 2 f.
Rafes, Moshe 1922, 'In Lekerts tsaytn. Zikhroynes', *Hirsh Lekert. Tsum 20-tn yortsayt fun zayn kepung*, edited by Ruslendishe komunistishe partey, Ts. K. fun R.K.P., Ts. B. fun yidsektsye, Moscow, pp. 34–41.
Ravitsh, Melekh 1941, 'Ikh hob mir farkhenkt nor a nigen', *Unzer tsayt*, New York 3–4, pp. 25–8.
Reynharts, Manye [Morim], n.d., untitled, Bund Archives, New York, RG 1400, MG-2, Folder 429.
Reytshuk, Elye 1922, 'Hirsh Lekert', *Hirsh Lekert. Tsum 20-tn yortsayt fun zayn kepung*,

edited by Ruslendishe komunistishe partey, Ts. K. fun R.K.P., Ts. B. fun yidsektsye, Moscow, pp. 7–10.

Reytshuk, Elye 1927, 'Hirsh Lekerts onteyl in novigoroder onfal. Zikhroynes fun 1900tn-yor', *Der emes*, Moscow 129 (10 June).

Reyzen, Abram [Abraham Reisen] 1941, 'Er hot gesukht a lid. Etlekhe verter vegn umfargeslekhn Noakhn', *Unzer tsayt*, New York 10, pp. 27–9.

R.H., Sh. 1963, 'A bletl tsu der geshikhte fun "bund"', *Unzer tsayt*, New York 2–3, p. 33f.

Rogof, Hillel 1934, 'Der "bund" vi ikh hob im gezen', *Der veker*, New York 528 (10 November), p. 19.

Roklin, K. 1941, untitled, YIVO, New York, RG 102, Folder 209.

Rosten, Eydel [Rozenberg], n.d., untitled, Bund Archives, New York, RG 1400, MG-2, Folder 429.

Rotnberg, Yosef 1948, *Fun Varshe biz Shanghay. Notitsn fun a polit*, Mexico City: Shloyme Mendelson fond bay der gezelshaft far kultur un hilf.

Royel, M. 1942, *Aleph-Khaf-Shin*, YIVO, New York, RG 102, Folder 55.

Rozenberg, ThUKh 1947, 'Der bund un mayn tate', *Unzer tsayt*, New York 3–4, p. 194f.

Rozenfeld, Hersh, n.d., untitled, Bund Archives, New York, RG 1400, MG-2, Folder 429.

Rozen, Naytan 1943, 'Iberlebungen fun a "kleynem-bundist". Derinerungen fun Vilne, Vitebsk un Polotsk', *Unzer tsayt*, New York 12, pp. 29–33.

Rozental, Ana 1939, 'Bletlekh fun a lebns-geshikhte', *Historishe shriftn fun YIVO*, Warsaw 3, pp. 416–37.

Rozental, Ana 1942, 'Arkadis letste yorn', *Arkadi. Zamlbukh tsum ondenk fun Arkadi Kremer*, New York: Unzer tsayt, p. 256ff.

Salutski-Hardman, I.B. 1957, '"Zekhtsik yor" iz a lange tsayt. Notitsn vegn amol – un morgn', *Unzer tsayt*, New York 11–12, pp. 43–8.

Salzman, Mosche 1982, *Als Mosche Kommunist war*, Darmstadt: Darmstädter Blätter.

Sarah 1957, 'Mayn veg tsum "bund"', *Unzer tsayt*, New York 11–12, pp. 73–5.

Shally, Saul, n.d. [a], *A bashraybung vegn eynem vos bashraybt ale groysn yidishn persenlikhkeytn. Mayn tayern groysn landsman Isreal Ber Beylin tsu zayn 75ten yubiley banket okt. 19. Biografishe strikhn*, YIVO, New York, RG 1333, Box 1, Folder [unpaginated], sheet 7.

Shally, Saul, n.d. [b], *A yugend episod fun dem geystikn gvureydele persenlikhkeyt I.B. Beylin*, YIVO, New York, RG 1333, Box 1, Folder [unpaginated], sheet 3.

Shally, Saul, n.d. [c], 'An episod vegn a "pasirungl"', YIVO, New York, RG 1333, Box 1, Folder [unpaginated], sheet 5.

Shally, Saul, n.d. [d], untitled [1–2 missing], YIVO, New York, RG 1333, Box 1, Folder [unpaginated] sheet 65.

Shally, Saul, n.d. [e], untitled [2–5 missing], YIVO, New York, RG 1333, Box 1, Folder [unpaginated], sheet 62.

Shally, Saul, n.d. [f], *Oytobiografishe notitsn. Zikhroynes un episodn*, YIVO, New York, RG 1333, Box 2, Folder [unpaginated], ca. 500 sheets.

Shapiro, Moris 1956, untitled, Bund Archives, New York, RG 1400, MG-2, Folder 429.
Shatan, M.I. 1970, 'Di ershte bundishe fon in Kutne. A kapitl zikhroynes fun Moyshe-I. Shatan, ibergegebn fun zayn zun Dr. Khaym Shatan', *Unzer tsayt*, New York 9, p. 44 f.
Shats, Velvel 1935, 'Di blutige Vilner ershter may demonstratsye in 1902. Bashriben fun Velvel der znaken malyer, velkher hot getrogn a fohn in der demonstratsye', *Vilne. A zamlbukh gevidmet der shtot vilne*, edited by Yefim Yeshurin, New York: Vilner brentsh 367 Arbeter ring, pp. 162–6.
Shefner, Barukh 1936a, 'Betlekh un shoytfim', *Argentiner lebn*, Buenos Aires 3, p. 2 f.
Shefner, Barukh 1936b, 'Mayne forn keyn Poyln', *Argentiner lebn*, Buenos Aires 1, p. 4 f.
Shefner, Barukh 1941, 'Poylishe romantik', *Unzer tsayt*, New York 9, pp. 17–20.
Shefner, Barukh 1957, 'Etapn fun a lebn. Beym frishn kibur fun Leyvik Hodem', *Unzer tsayt*, New York 4–5, pp. 27–30.
Shefner, Helene 1970a, 'Der marsh fun "kleynem geto"', *Unzer tsayt*, New York 4, pp. 18–19.
Shefner, Helene 1970b, 'Zamoshtsh nokhn khurbn', *Unzer tsayt*, New York 1, pp. 34–6.
Sherer, Emanuel [Szerer] 1941, 'Fun Lite tsu Poyln. Tsu Noakhs ideen-veg', *Unzer tsayt*, New York 10, pp. 23–5.
Sherer, Emanuel [Szerer] 1943, 'Zayr tolerants, zayer eshoyres un unzer nalevkes', *Unzer tsayt*, New York 12, pp. 18–20.
Sherer, Emanuel [Szerer] 1951, 'Der lerer fun di lerer', *Unzer tsayt*, New York 11–12, pp. 27–9.
Shiker, Rahel, n.d., untitled, Bund Archives, New York, RG 1400, MG-2, Folder 429.
Shikhatov, Shaye, n.d., untitled, Bund Archives, New York, RG 1400, MG-2, Folder 429.
Shikhatov, Shaye 1948, 'Mayn letster tog in Kartuz-Bereze. A kapitl derinerungen', *Historisher Zamlbukh. Materialn un dokumentn tsutshayer tsu der geshikhte fun Algemeyner Yidisher Arbeter-Bund*, Warsaw: Ringen, p. 59 f.
Shikhatov, Shaye 1957, untitled, Bund Archives, New York, RG 1400, MG-2, Folder 429.
Shikhatov, Shaye 1967, 'Paviak – di geshtapo-turme in Varshe', *Lebns-fragn*, Tel Aviv 184–5, p. 19 f.
Shikhatov, Shaye 1973, *Yorn fun kamf un gerangl*, Ramat-Gan: Lior.
Shikhatov, Shaye 1976, 'I. Artuski – Der yid, der mentsh, der bundist', *Yid. Mentsh. Sotsysalist. I. Artuski ondenk-bukh*, edited by I. Artuski Bukh-Komitet, Tel Aviv: Lebns-fragn, p. 115 ff.
Shilits, Sh. 1942, *Zikhroynes fun a anot fun kleynen bund*, Bund Archives, New York, RG 1400, M-13, Folder 130.
Shlevin, B. 1976, 'Khaver Artuski – Vi ikh hob im gekent', *Yid. Mentsh. Sotsysalist. I. Artuski ondenk-bukh*, edited by I. Artuski Bukh-Komitet, Tel Aviv: Lebns-fragn, pp. 71–5.
Shlugleyt 1925, 'Bam vigele fun "bund"', *1905 yor in Barditshev*, [Kiev]: Barditshever Hisport dem krayz-komitet fun KP(B) An, p. 66 ff.

Shneyd, Herman 1957, 'Mit gever oyf beth-eulim', *Unzer tsayt*, New York 11–12, p. 87 f.
Shpayzer, Mayr, n.d., untitled, Bund Archives, New York, RG 1400, MG-2, Folder 429.
Shpigel, Kheyke 1953, 'Zibn bundistn shpringen fun a toyt-vagon. Oyfn veg keyn treblinke', *Unzer tsayt*, New York 4, pp. 21–3.
Shpigl, Yisheyhu 1966, 'Der shvartser alef', *Lebns-fragn*, Tel Aviv 174–5, p. 10 f.
Shrager, Fayvel 1976, *Oyfn rand fun tsvey tkufes*, Paris: self-published.
Shtern, Berl 1954, *Zikhroynes fun shturmishe yorn: (Bielsk 1898–1907)*, Newark, NJ: Arbeter ring komitet in nyuark.
Shteynberg, Pinkhas [Paul Steinberg], n.d., untitled, Bund Archives, New York, RG 1400, MG-2, Folder 429.
Shulman, Viktor 1945, 'Baginen. Ideyen, geshtaltn, bagenishn – bletlekh fun a leben', *Unzer tsayt*, New York 3, pp. 47–55.
Shuster, Velvel [William] 1955, untitled, Bund Archives, New York, RG 1400, MG-2, Folder 429.
Shvarts, Moshe, n.d., untitled, Bund Archives, New York, RG 1400, MG-2, Folder 429.
Shvarts, Moshe 1947, 'Fun yeshiva tsu "bund" un kidush-hashem. A basheydener yizkher – di umgekumene khaverim fun "arkadi-grupe"', *Unzer tsayt*, New York 3–4, pp. 150–2.
Shvarts, Pinkhas 1943, *Dos iz geven der onheyb*, New York: Arbeter ring.
Shvarts, Pinkhas 1945, 'Khover Zigmunt', *Unzer tsayt*, New York 3, pp. 78–83.
Sisk, Arnold 1997, 'Der "bund" in mayn shtetl Shtok', *100 yor 'bund'. Spetsyele oysgabe fun der bundisher organisatsye in Myami-bitsh. Algemeyner yidisher arbeyter 'bund' 1897–1997. Tsum 100 yorign yubl fun 'bund'*, Miami Beach, p. 20.
Slavin, L. 1942, untitled, YIVO, New York, RG 102, Folder 171.
Sobotko, Henry, n.d., untitled, Bund Archives, New York, RG 1400, MG-2, Folder 429.
Sokol, Hari [Hershl der Tanner; Aleks], n.d., untitled, Bund Archives, New York, RG 1400, MG-2, Folder 429.
Sokol, Hari [Hershl der Tanner; Aleks] 1942, untitled, YIVO, RG 102, Folder 142.
Solomon, Simon 1952, *Derinerungen fun der yidisher arbeter bavegung*, New York.
Spashevski, Moshe 1976, 'Shtrikhn tsu Oskars persenlekhkeyt', *Yid. Mentsh. Sotsyalist. I. Artuski ondenk-bukh*, edited by I. Artuski Bukh-Komitet, Tel Aviv: Lebns-fragn, p. 118 ff.
Spiegelman 1942, untitled, YIVO, New York, RG 102, Folder 222.
Steyngart, Tsirl 1963, 'Fun gele bleter un fun zikhroyn', *Unzer tsayt*, New York 4, pp. 16–18.
Steyngart, Tsirl 1997, 'Der eynflus fun "bund" oyf mayn dor', *100 yor 'bund'. Spetsyele oysgabe fun der bundisher organisatsye in Myami-bitsh. Algemeyner yidisher arbeyter 'bund' 1897–1997. Tsum 100 yorign yubl fun 'bund'*, Miami Beach, p. 17 f.
Stolor, Abraham, n.d., untitled, Bund Archives, New York, RG 1400, MG-2, Folder 429.
Tabachinsky, Benjamin 1947, untitled, Bund Archives, New York, RG 1400, MG-2, Folder 429.

Tabatshnik, Khaym 1956, untitled, Bund Archives, New York, RG 1400, MG-2, Folder 429.

Tenenboym-Beker, Nina 1973, 'Leon Oler – Der lerer un geystiker vegvayzer', *Leon Oler. Zayn lebn und tetigkayt*, Unzer tsayt: New York, pp. 72–7.

Tenenboym, Shaye [Shea] 1969, 'Mayn shtetl khaloymes beym fenster', *Unzer tsayt*, New York 10, pp. 43–6.

Tenenboym, Shaye [Shea] 1970a, 'Leyener fun der "folkstsaytung"', *Unzer tsayt*, New York 10, pp. 24–7.

Tenenboym, Shaye [Shea] 1970b, 'Mayne ershtn literarishn kritiker', *Unzer tsayt*, New York 7–8, pp. 51–6.

Tratsh, Shaye, n.d., untitled, Bund Archives, New York, RG 1400, MG-2, Folder 429.

Trunk, Israel I. 1947, 'Kenigin fun der Lodzsher nokht', *Unzer tsayt*, New York 3–4, pp. 182–4, p. 187.

Tsalevisth, Ben-Tsyion [Bentsl], n.d., *Tsugab tsu der ankete*, Bund Archives, New York, RG 1400, MG-2, Folder 429.

Tselemenski, Yakob 1951, 'Der ershter may in di Vishkover velder', *Unzer tsayt*, New York 5, pp. 45–7.

Tselemenski, Yakob 1963a, 'Der varshever geto-oyfshtand', *Unzer tsayt*, New York 4, pp. 7–9.

Tselemenski, Yakob 1963b, *Mitn farshnitenem folk. A kuryer fun bund dertseylt vegn yidishn khurbn un vidershtand unter di deytshe natsim*, New York: Unzer Tsayt.

Tsholkosh, Adam 1944, 'September derinerungen', *Unzer tsayt*, New York, 2, p. 26f.

Tsholkosh, Adam 1957, 'Torne – Kroke – London', *Unzer tsayt*, New York 11–12, pp. 75–8.

TSoglin, V. 1930, 'Mezhdu pervym i tret'im s"ezdami Bunda. Pererabotannaia stenogramma vospominanii, zachitannyh na zasedianiiah sektsii 23 dekabria 1927g. – 5 ianvaria 1928', *Revoliutionnoe dvizhenie sredi evreev*, edited by S. Dimanshtein, Moscow, p. 166.

Tsukerman, Noakh 1967, 'Der 30-ster yubl fun "bund" in Tel-Aviv', *Lebns-fragn*, Tel Aviv, 188–9, p. 10.

Tsuker, Mayer 1987, untitled, Bund Archives, New York, RG 1400, MG-2, Folder 429.

Tsudiker, Yankl 1928, 'In a yidisher kolonye', *Di Presse*, Buenos Aires, Suplemento, pp. 159–72.

Vald, Pinie [Pedro Wald] 1929, *Bletlekh. [Hojas. Semblanzas de mi ambiente]*, Buenos Aires: Yidisher literatn un zshurnalistn fareyn in Argentine.

Vald, Pinie [Pedro Wald] 1936, 'Mayne yidishe bagegenishn in Shpanye', *Argentiner lebn*, Buenos Aires, 10, p. 4f.

Vald, Pinie [Pedro Wald] 1937, 'Heroishe tsaytn', *40 yor 'bund'*, Montevideo: Bundishe Grupe in Montevideo, pp. 44–8.

Vald, Pinie [Pedro Wald] 1952, 'Dos Hirsh Lekert-Lid. Derinerung tsum fuftsigstn yortsayt fun Hirsh Lekerts martirer-toyt', *Undzer gedank*, Buenos Aires, 1 (61) (June), p. 10.

Vald, Pinie [Pedro Wald] 1966, *Argentine. Yidn in der republik. Fun mayne reyzes*, Buenos Aires: Yidbukh.
Vapner-Levin, Paye 1999, *Mayne flikht tsu dersteyln. Derinerungen fun a leereren in Vilner geto*, Buenos Aires: Acervo Cultural.
Vasershtros, Alekher Zelig, n.d., untitled, Bund Archives, New York, RG 1400, MG-2, Folder 429.
Vaver, Abraham 1981, untitled letter, Bund Archives, New York, RG 1400, MG-2, Folder 429.
Vaynberg, I. 1952, 'Fun dem altn kval', *Der veker*, New York (1 May), p. 11.
Vayzlits, Y., n.d., untitled, Bund Archives, New York, MG-2, Folder 429.
Velner, Pinkhas, n.d., untitled, Bund Archives, New York, RG 1400, MG-2, Folder 429.
Vernitski, Berl 1968, untitled, Bund Archives, New York, RG 1400, MG-2, Folder 429.
Veynopel, Mikhal I. 1976, 'Artuski – in mayn zikhroyn', *Yid. Mentsh. Sotsysalist. I. Artuski ondenk-bukh*, edited by I. Artuski Bukh-Komitet, Tel Aviv: Lebns-fragn, pp. 80–4.
Veysman, Gabryel I. 1976, 'Artuski – Der Idelogist un folks-mentsh', *Yid. Mentsh. Sotsysalist. I. Artuski ondenk-bukh*, edited by I. Artuski Bukh-Komitet, Tel Aviv: Lebns-fragn, pp. 66–70.
Vigurski, Yekov 1925, 'Lekerts toyt. A bletl zikhroynes', *Yidishe vilne in vort un bild. Ilustrirter almanakh*, edited by M. Grosman, Vilnius: H. Mats, p. 20f.
Vintshevski, Modim 1922, 'Tsum bunds 25-tn geburtstog', *Arbeter luakh*, Warsaw 3, pp. 124–8.
Vintshevski, Modim 1927a, 'Erinerungen, 1. Bd', *Gezamelte verk*, Vol. 9, New York: Frayhayt.
Vintshevski, Modim 1927b, 'Erinerungen, 2. Bd', *Gezamelte verk*, Vol. 10. New York: Frayhayt.
Vinyecki, Yosef [Yosele Kessler] 1942, untitled, YIVO, New York, RG 102, Folder 28.
Vladeck, Barukh Tsharney [Baruch Charney Vladeck] 1917, 'Unlegal ... (shtrikhn)', *Dos revolutsionere rusland*, edited by A. Litvak and J.B. Salutski, New York: Yidishe sotsyalistishe federatsye, p. 111f.
Vladeck, Barukh Tsharney [Baruch Charney Vladeck] 1947, 'Fir yor in "bund" un geblibn oyf stendik', *Unzer tsayt*, New York 3–4, p. 83f.
Vladeck, Barukh Tsharney [Baruch Charney Vladeck] 1963, 'A farzamlung oyfm betheulum', *Unzer tsayt*, New York 11, pp. 21–3.
Vladke 1948, '"Selektsye" in Varshever geto', *Unzer tsayt*, New York 4–5, pp. 20–4, p. 31.
Vladke 1953, 'Eyner fun fil ...', *Unzer tsayt*, New York 4, pp. 15–17.
W., G. 2002, 'My Autobiography', *Awakening Lives. Autobiographies of Jewish Youth in Poland Before the Holocaust*, edited by Jeffrey Shandler, New Haven and London: YIVO, pp. 297–320.
Weinberger, Lena S. 1942, untitled, YIVO, New York, RG 102, Folder 160.
Weiner, Frieda [Vikhotshnik] 1942, untitled, YIVO, New York, RG 102, Folder 158.

Weinstein Bernard 1924, *Fertsig yor in der yidisher arbeter bavegung. Bletlekh erinerungen*, New York: Der veker.

Wiernik, Yankel [1944?], *A Year in Treblinka. An Inmate Who Escaped Tells the Day-To-Day Facts of One Year of His Torturous Experience*, New York: The American Representation of the General Jewish Workers Union of Poland.

Yanushkevitsh, Tsheslov 1957, 'Mit kh Erlikh in a sovetisher tsife', *Unzer tsayt*, New York 2, pp. 20–2.

Yeshurin, Yefim 1939, 'Viliam Bakst der grinder fun undzer klub', *Khavershaft*, New York, p. 4; Bund Archives, RG 1400, ME-14B, Folder 5.

Yokhnis [Peysi] 1925, 'Vegn der drukerey fun ts. k. fun "bund" un vegn dem tayern khaver Yoyne (Fishl Kogan)', *1905 yor in Barditshev*, [Kiev]: Barditshever Hisport dem krayzkomitet fun K.P. (B.) An., pp. 76–80.

Yosef, Ben 1942, untitled, YIVO, New York, RG 102, Folder 47.

Yosh 1945, 'Vos zelner dertseylt', *Unzer tsayt*, New York 3, pp. 75–7.

Yoysef, A. Ben 1942, untitled, YIVO, New York, RG 102, Folder 81.

Yudl 2002, untitled, *Awakening Lives. Autobiographies of Jewish Youth in Poland Before the Holocaust*, edited by Jeffrey Shandler, New Haven and London: YIVO, pp. 391–403.

Zakhariash, Yosef Yehuda 1957, 'A bundisher yom-tof mit 55 yor tsurik. A kapitl zikhroynes', *Unzer tsayt*, New York 7–8, pp. 31–3.

Zakhariash, Yosef Yehuda 1969, 'Zikhroynes fun mayn leben', *Unzer tsayt*, New York 2, pp. 21–5.

Zalevitsh, Bentsl 1957, 'Mayne 35 yor in Israel. Mayne ranglenish far yidish un far bundism' *Lebns-fragn*, Tel Aviv 75–6, pp. 13–17.

Zalevitsh, Bentsl 1948, 'Der bagin fun der Byalistoker yidisher arbeyter-bavegung. A kapitl zikhroynes', *Historisher Zamlbukh. Materialn un dokumentn tsutshayer tsu der geshikhte fun Algemeyner Yidisher Arbeter-Bund*, Warsaw: Ringen, p. 46 ff.

Zelenski 1924, 'A bisl zikhroynes', *Argentiner veker* 2, p. 4.

Zelmanovitsh, Efrim-Lozer [A.L.] 1947, 'Episodn fun partey-lebn in Lodzsh', *Unzer tsayt*, New York 3–4, pp. 117–119.

Zelmanovitsh, Efrim-Lozer [A.L.] 1948, 'Mayn baheft sikh mitn "bund"', *Historisher Zamlbukh. Materialn un dokumentn tsutshayer tsu der geshikhte fun Algemeyner Yidisher Arbeter-Bund*, Warsaw: Ringen, pp. 49–53.

Zelmanovitsh, Efrim-Lozer [A.L.] 1952, 'Tsvey arestn', *Unzer tsayt*, New York 10, pp. 36–8.

Zelmanovitsh, Motl Khaym 1973, 'Leon Oler in partey-reyen', *Leon Oler. Zayn lebn und tetigkayt*, New York: Unzer tsayt, pp. 78–82.

Zigelboym, Shmuel [Szmuel Zygielbojm, Artur] 1944a [1940], 'Mayn opfor fun varshe, 1. Bd.' *Unzer tsayt*, New York, 5, pp. 30–5.

Zigelboym, Shmuel [Szmuel Zygielbojm, Artur] 1944b [1940], 'Mayn opfor fun varshe, 2. Bd.', *Unzer tsayt*, New York 11, pp. 38–41.

Zigelboym, Shmuel [Szmuel Zygielbojm, Artur] 1944c, 'Mayn rayze in natsi-deytshland', *Unzer tsayt*, New York 9, pp. 28–31.

Zigelboym, Shmuel [Szmuel Zygielbojm, Artur] 1944d [pre-1943], 'Mayn rayze-zikhroyn natsishn gihnum', *Geto in flamen. Zamlbukh*, New York: Amerikanishe representatsye fun 'bund' in Poyln, pp. 140–55.

Zigelboym, Shmuel [Szmuel Zygielbojm, Artur] 1949 [pre-1943], 'Der farbrekhn – un di shtrof', *Unzer tsayt*, New York 4–5, p. 26f.

Zivion [Benzion Hofman] 1937, 'Fun mayne amolike bundishe yorn', *Argentiner lebn*, Buenos Aires 16, p. 10.

Zivion [Benzion Hofman] 1940, 'A bisl zikhroynes vegn khaver Hillels zikhroynes', *Hillel Katz (Blum). Zikhroynes fun a bundist. Bilder fun untererdishn leb in tsarishn rusland*, New York: Atlantik, pp. 7–10.

Zivion [Benzion Hofman] 1941, 'Noakh in der redaktsye fun der vilner "folkstsaytung". An erinerung', *Unzer tsayt*, New York 10, pp. 30–2.

Zivion [Benzion Hofman] 1945, 'Vi azoy ikh bin gekumen tsum "bund"', *Unzer tsayt*, New York 3, pp. 55–63.

Zivion [Benzion Hofman] 1948a, 'Vi azoy ikh bin gekumen tsum "bund". A kapitl erinerungen', *Far 50 yor: Geklibene shriften*, New York: A. Laub, pp. 118–31.

Zivion [Benzion Hofman] 1948b, 'Groyse mentshn un groyse firer. Tsum toyt fun Nikolai Lenin', *Far 50 yor: Geklibene shriften*, New York: A. Laub, pp. 249–56.

Zivion [Benzion Hofman] 1948c, 'Der tate fun "bund"', *Far 50 yor: Geklibene shriften*, New York: A. Laub, pp. 275–8.

Zivion [Benzion Hofman] 1952, 'Mayn fraynd un khaver Franz Kurski', *Franz Kurski. Gezamelte shriftn*, New York: Der veker.

Zshelenikov, Abraham 1950a, 'Di letstn yor mit khaverte Pati', *Unzer shtime*, Paris (23 September).

Zshelenikov, Abraham 1950b, 'Vilner geto – 1-ter may 1943', *Unzer tsayt*, New York 4–5, pp. 31–3.

Zshelenikov, Abraham 1953, 'Der vey-geshrey oyf geto-vent', *Unzer tsayt*, New York 4, pp. 28–9.

Zshelenikov, Abraham 1956, 'Dos lid geshribn iz mit blut', *Yugnt-veker* 3, p. 4f.

Zsheleznikov, Y. 1948, 'In yene teg. Kuriosn in shturmishn yor 1905', *Historisher Zamlbukh. Materialn un dokumentn tsutshayer tsu der geshikhte fun Algemeyner Yidisher Arbeter-Bund*, Warsaw: Ringen, pp. 54–8.

Literature and Other Published Sources

Abbott, Andrew 2001, *Time Matters. On Theory and Method*, Chicago, IL: University of Chicago Press.

Abramovitsh, H. 1936, 'Vos toronter yidish klal-tuer zogn vegn Birobidzhan', *Kanader 'Icor'*.

Abramowicz, Hirsh 1999 [1958], *Profiles of a Lost World. Memoirs of East European Jewish Life Before World War II*, edited by Dina Abramowicz, New York: YIVO Institute for Jewish Research.

Abramson, Henry 1999, *A Prayer for the Government: Ukrainians and Jews in Revolutionary Times, 1917–1920*. Cambridge, MA: Harvard University Press, Harvard Ukrainian Research Institute and Center for Jewish Studies.

Adler, Eliyana R. 2011, *In Her Hands: The Education of Jewish Girls in Tsarist Russia*, Detroit: Wayne State University Press.

Aizenberg, Edna 1988, 'Translating Gerchunoff', *Judaica latinoamericana: estudios histórico-sociales* 4, pp. 403–9.

Aizicovich, Samuel 2006, *Viaje Al País De La Esperanza*, Buenos Aires: Editorial Mila.

Akrich, Madeleine and Bruno Latour 1992, 'A Summary of a Convenient Vocabulary for the Semiotics of Human and Non-Human Assemblies', *Shaping Technology, Building Society. Studies in Sociotechnical Change*, edited by Wiebe E. Bijker and John Law, Cambridge, MA: MIT Press, pp. 259–64.

Albert, Gleb J. 2001, '"German October is Approaching". Internationalism, Activists, and the Soviet State in 1923', *Revolutionary Russia* 24, no. 2, pp. 111–42.

Albert, Gleb J. 2007, 'Ein Mann, ein Blatt. Franz Pfemfert und "Die Aktion" 1911–1932', *versa. Zeitschrift für Politik und Kunst* 7, pp. 48–62.

Alexander, Jeffrey C. 2006, *The Civil Sphere*, New York: Oxford University Press.

Alexandrov, Daniel A. 1995, 'The Historical Anthropology of Science in Russia', *Russian Studies in History* 34, no. 2, pp. 62–91.

Alsvaysruslandishe konferents fun yidishe kultur- un bildungstuer (eds.) 1931, *Resolyutsies*, Minsk: Tsentralfarlag.

Amelang, James Stephen 2009, 'Lifting the Curse. Or Why Early Modern Worker Autobiographers Did Not Write About Work', *The Idea of Work in Europe from Antiquity to Modern Times*, edited by Joseph Ehmer, Farnham, Surrey et al.: Ashgate, pp. 91–101.

Amiantov, Iurii Nikolaevich (ed.) 2010, *Bund Dokumenty i materialy. 1884–1921*, *Rossiiskaia politicheskaia entsiklopediia*, Moscow: ROSSPEN.

Anderson, Benedict 1983, *Imagined Communities. Reflections on the Origin and Spread of Nationalism*, London: Verso.

An-sky [Shloyme Zanvl Rappoport] 1927, 'Der yidisher khurbn fun Poyln, galitsye un bukovina fun tag-bukh 1914–1917', *Gezamelte shriftn*, Vol. IV, Warsaw, Vilius, New York: An-sky Publishing Company.

An-sky [Shloyme Zanvl Rappoport] 2002, *The Enemy at his Pleasure. A Journey Through the Pale of Settlement During World War I*, edited by Joachim Neugroschel, New York: Metropolitan Books.

Arbeter Ring, Yefim Yeshurin and Hertz Jacob Sh. (eds.) 1962, *Arbeter ring boyer und tuer*, New York: Arbeter ring boyer und tuer komitet.

Arndt, Agnes, Joachim C. Häberlen and Christiane Reinecke 2011, 'Europäische Geschichtsschreibung zwischen Theorie und Praxis', *Vergleichen, verflechten, verwirren? Europäische Geschichtsschreibung zwischen Theorie und Praxis*, edited by Agnes Andt, Joachim C. Häberlen and Christiane Reinecke, Göttingen: Vandenhoeck & Ruprecht, pp. 11–30.

Arnold 1922, 'A nesye mit Tshemodones. An episod fun dem amolikn umlegaln literatur-transport', *Arbeter luakh* 3, pp. 129–42.

Aronson, Grigori, Jacob S. Hertz et al. (eds.) 1960, *Di geshikhte fun Bund*, 5 volumes, New York: Unzer tsayt.

Aronson, Grigori 1962, *Rusish-yidishe inteligents. Klal-tuer, shrayber, politiker, tragishe geshtaltn*, Buenos Aires: Yidbukh.

Aronson, Irwin Michael 1990, *Troubled Waters: The Origins of the 1881 Anti-Jewish Pogroms in Russia*, Pittsburgh, PA: University of Pittsburgh Press.

Arroyo, Inka 2001, 'Autobiographik – Genre oder Modus der hebräischen Literatur', *Neuer Anbruch. Zur deutsch-jüdischen Kultur*, edited by Michael Brocke, Aubrey Pomerance, and Andrea Schatz, Berlin: Metropol, pp. 161–74.

Aschheim, Steven 1982, *Brothers and Strangers. The East European Jew in German and German Jewish Consciousness, 1800–1923*. Madison, WI: University of Wisconsin Press.

Asher, Robert 1976, 'Jewish Unions and the American Federation of Labor Power Structure 1903–1935', *American Jewish Historical Quarterly* 65, no. 3, pp. 215–27.

Assmann, Aleida 2007, *Geschichte im Gedächtnis. Von der individuellen Erfahrung zur öffentlichen Inszenierung*, Munich: C.H. Beck.

Avni, Haim 1973, *Argentina, 'The Promised Land'. Baron de Hirsch's Colonization Project in the Argentine Republic*, Jerusalem: Magnes Press, Hebrew University.

Avni, Haim 1983, *Argentina y la historia de la inmigración judía (1810–1950)*, Jerusalem: Ed. Univ. Magnes, AMIA.

Avni, Haim, Ignacio Klich and Efraim Zadoff 2007, 'Argentina', *Encyclopedia Judaica* 2, pp. 426–50.

Avrich, Paul 1984, *The Haymarket Tragedy*, Princeton, NJ: Princeton University Press.

Bade, Klaus J. 2003, *Migration in European History*, translated by Allison Brown, Oxford: Blackwell.

Baily, Samuel L. 1999, *Immigrants in the Land of Promise. Italians in Buenos Aires and New York City, 1870–1914*. Ithaca, London: Cornell University Press.

Baraldi, Claudio, Giancarlo Corsi and Elena Esposito 2008, GLU: *Glossar zu Niklas Luhmanns Theorie sozialer Systeme*, Frankfurt am Main: Suhrkamp.

Barkai, Avraham 2002, '*Wehr dich!': der Centralverein deutscher Staatsbürger jüdischen Glaubens (C.V.) 1893–1938*, Munich: C.H. Beck.

Barra, Francisco L. 1904, *La inmigración en la República Argentina. Informe rendido á las Secretarías de Relaciones Exteriores y de Fomento; Colonización é Industria de los Estados Unidos Mexicanos*, Buenos Aires: Compañía Sud-Americana de Billetes de Banco.

Basch, Françoise 1998, 'The Shirtwaist Strike in History and Myth', *The Diary of a Shirtwaist Striker*, Ithaca, NY: Cornell University Press, pp. 7–77.

Basch, Linda G., Nina Glick Schiller and Cristina S. Blanc 2006 [1995], *Nations Unbound: Translational Projects, Postcolonial Predicaments, and Deterritorialized Nation-States*, London: Routledge.

Bauman, Zygmunt 1987, 'Intellectuals in East-Central Europe: Continuity and Change', *East European Politics and Societies* 1, no. 2, pp. 162–86.

Bauman, Zygmunt 2000, *Modernity and the Holocaust*, Ithaca, NY: Cornell University Press.

Bauman, Zygmunt 2001, *Community. Seeking Safety in an Insecure World*, Cambridge: Polity.

Beito, David 2000, *From Mutual Aid to Welfare State. Fraternal Societies and Social Services, 1890–1967*, Chapel Hill, NC: University of North Carolina Press.

Belliger, Andréa and David J. Krieger 2006, 'Einführung in die Akteur-Netzwerk-Theorie', *ANThropolgy. Ein einführendes Handbuch zur Akteur-Netzwerk-Theorie*, edited by Andréa Belliger and David J. Krieger, Bielefeld: transcript, pp. 13–50.

Bemporad, Elissa 2013, *Becoming Soviet Jews: The Bolshevik Experiment in Minsk*, Bloomington, IN: Indiana University Press.

Bender, Daniel E. and Richard A. Greenwald (eds.) 2003, *Sweatshop USA: The American Sweatshop in Historical and Global Perspective*, New York: Routledge.

Bender, Daniel E. 2004a, *Sweated Work, Weak Bodies. Anti-Sweatshop Campaigns and Languages of Labor*, New Brunswick, NJ: Rutgers University Press.

Bender, Daniel E. 2004b, '"Too Much of Distasteful Masculinity". Historicizing Sexual Harassment in the Garment Sweatshop and Factory', *Journal of Women's History* 15, no. 4, pp. 91–116.

Benecke, Werner 2006, *Militär, Reform und Gesellschaft im Zarenreich. Die Wehrpflicht in Russland 1874–1914*, Paderborn: Ferdinand Schöningh.

Benjamin, Walter 2006 [1936], 'The Storyteller', *Selected Writings. Volume 3, 1935–1938*, edited by Howard Eiland and Michael W. Jennings, Cambridge, MA: Belknap, pp. 143–66.

Benjamin, Walter 2007 [1968], 'Theses on the Philosophy of History', *Illuminations*, translated by Harry Zohn, New York: Schocken, pp. 253–64.

Bennett, W. Lance 2005, 'Social Movements Beyond Borders: Understanding Two Eras of Transnational Activism', *Transnational Protest and Global Activism*, edited by Donatella della Porta and Sidney G. Tarrow, Lanham, MD: Rowman & Littlefield, pp. 203–26.

Berg, Walter Bruno 2002, 'Criollos y criollismo: Genese und Funktion historischer Begriffsbildung im Überschneidungsgebiet von Literatur- und Geschichtswissenschaft', *Literarische Begegnungen. Romanische Studien zur kulturellen Identität, Differenz und Alterität*, edited by Frank Leinen, Berlin: Erich Schmidt, pp. 273–86.

Bernheimer, Charles S. 1909, 'The Jewish Immigrant as an Industrial Worker', *Annals of the American Academy of Political and Social Science* 33, no. 2, pp. 175–82.

Bernstein, Eduard 1906, *Der Streik. Sein Wesen und sein Wirken*, Frankfurt am Main: Literarische Anstalt.

Bernstein, Herman and AJC (eds.) 1915, 'Events in 5674', *American Jewish Year Book* 16, Philadelphia: The Jewish Publication Society of America, pp. 128–275.

Berrol, Selma C. 1976, 'Education and Economic Mobility. The Jewish Experience in New York City, 1880–1920', *American Jewish Historical Quarterly* 65, no. 3, pp. 228–44.

Beyhaut, G.R. Cordes Conge, H. Gorostegui and S. Torrado 1961, *Inmigración y desarrollo económico*, Buenos Aires: Dep. de Sociología, Univ. de Buenos Aires.

Bigelmeyer, B. 1936a, 'A kval fun ibergegebnkeyt. Tsu Khmurners ershtn yortsayt', *Argentiner lebn* 4, p. 5.

Bigelmeyer, B. 1936b, '52 yor in der sotsyalistisher bavegung. Tsum 70-yoriken yubiley fun kh. Y. Blind', *Argentiner lebn* 7, p. 4.

Bilsky, Edgardo (ed.) 1987, *Bibliografía temática sobre judaísmo argentino. Vol. 4: El movimiento obrero judío en la Argentina*, Buenos Aires: Centro de Documentación e Información sobre Judaísmo Argentino 'Marc Turkow'.

Binyomen, Nadel 1995, 'Di bundishe prese in yidish', *Oksforder yidish* 3, pp. 633–46.

Biran, Yaad 2012, 'Fir teg fun bund oyf tlomatske-gas in varshe', *Lebns-fragn*, Tel Aviv 714–16, www.lebnsfragn.com/bin/articles.cgi?ID=1205 (last accessed 27 February 2017).

Birke, Peter 2007, *Wilde Streiks im Wirtschaftswunder. Arbeitskämpfe, Gewerkschaften und soziale Bewegungen in der Bundesrepublik und Dänemark*, Frankfurt am Main, New York: Campus-Verlag.

B. 1936, 'Kh' Y. Blind 70 yor alt', *Argentiner lebn* 5, p. 7.

Blatman, Daniel 1996, 'The Bund in Poland, 1935–1939', *POLIN* 9, pp. 58–82.

Blatman, Daniel 2003, *For Our Freedom and Yours. The Jewish Labour Bund in Poland 1939–1945*, London, Portland, OR: Vallentine Mitchell.

Blobaum, Robert E. (ed.) 2005, *Antisemitism and its Opponents in Modern Poland*, Ithaca, NY: Cornell University Press.

Blumenfield, Samuel M. 1968, 'Israel and Jewish Education in the Diaspora', *Journal of Jewish Education* 38, no. 4, pp. 25–30.

Bodnar, John 1987, *The Transplanted. A History of Immigrants in Urban America*, Bloomington, IN: Indiana University Press.

de Bollardière, Constance Pâris 2012, 'The Jewish Labor Committee and the Bundist

Movement in France, 1944–1949', presented at the workshop *Beyond Internal Paradigms: New Perspectives on the History of the Jewish Labor Bund*, Warsaw (June).

Bollenbeck, Georg 1976, *Zur Theorie und Geschichte der frühen Arbeiterlebenserinnerungen*, Kronberg: Scriptor-Verlag.

Boller, Paul F. Jr. and John George 1989, *They Never Said It: A Book of Fake Quotes, Misquotes, and Misleading Attributions*, New York: Oxford University Press.

Bonacich, Edna 1993, 'The Other Side of Ethnic Entrepeneurship. A Dialogue with Waldinger, Aldrich, Ward and Associates', *International Migration Review* 27, no. 3, pp. 685–92.

Le Bon, Gustave 2001 [1895], *The Crowd. A Study of the Popular Mind*, Kitchener, ON: Batoche.

Borochov, Ber 1984 [1932], *Class Struggle and the Jewish Nation. Selected Essays in Marxist Zionism*, edited with an introduction by Michael Cohen, New Brunswick and London: Transaction.

Borshchenko, I. 1959, *The Russian Trade Unions in 1907–1917*, Moscow: Profizdat Publishing House.

Botoshanski, Yankef [Jacob] 1936, 'In loyf fun tog. Bamerkungen', *Di prese*, Buenos Aires (20 July).

Bourdeiu, Pierre 1990 [1980], *The Logic of Practice*, translated by Richard Nice, Stanford, CA: Stanford University Press.

Boyer, Richard O. and Herbert M. Morais 1956, *A History of the American Labour Movement*, London: John Calder.

Brandes, Joseph 1976, 'From Sweatshop to Stability: Jewish Labor between Two World Wars', *YIVO Annual of Jewish Social Sciences* 16.

Brauch, Julia, Anna Lipphardt and Alexandra Nocke (eds.) 2008, *Jewish Topographies: Visions of Space, Traditions of Place*, Aldershot et al.: Ashgate.

Braun, Mayr 1946, 'Antshteyung un antviklung fun yidish-natsyonal arbeter-farband', *Yidish natsyonaler arbeter farband. 1910–1946. Geshikhte un dergreykhungen*, New York: General-eksekutive fun yidish-natsynonaln arbeter-farband, pp. 1–73.

Braun, Stefan 2008, 'Der Allgemeine Jüdische Arbeiterbund in Deutschland', *Kalonymos* 4, p. 15f.

Brecheisen, Claudia 1993, *Literatur des Holocaust: Identität und Judentum bei Jakov Lind, Edgar Hilsenrath und Jurek Becker*, PhD dissertation, University of Augsburg.

Brenner, Michael 1996, *The Renaissance of Jewish Culture in Weimar Germany*, New Haven and London: Yale University Press.

Brenner, Michael 2006, 'Ein jüdisches Jahrhundert? Jüdische Traditionen und Antisemitismus im 20. Jahrhundert', *Was heißt und zu welchem Ende studiert man Geschichte des 20. Jahrhunderts?*, edited by Norbert Frei, Göttingen: Wallstein, pp. 226–33.

Brinkmann, Tobias 2007, 'Managing Mass Migration. Jewish Philantropical Organizations and Jewish Mass Migration from Eastern Europe, 1868/69–1914', *Historisch Tijdschrift* 22, pp. 71–90.

Brinkmann, Tobias 2010a, 'From Immigrants to Supranational Transmigrants and Refugees: Jewish Migrants in New York and Berlin Before and After the Great War', *Comparative Studies of South Asia, Africa and the Middle East* 30, no. 1, pp. 47–57.

Brinkmann, Tobias 2010b, 'Taking the Global View: Reconsidering Migration History after 1800', *Neue Politische Literatur*, no. 2, pp. 213–32.

Broido, Eva 1931a, 'Dos sturmishe Lebn fun a revolutsyonern', *Naye folkstsaytung* 35 (6 February).

Broido, Eva 1931b, 'Shturmishe tsaytn', *Naye folkstsaytung* 36 (8 February).

Broido, Eva 1967 [1929], *Memoirs of a Revolutionary*, translated and edited by Vera Broido, Oxford: University of Oxford Press.

Brooks, Jeffrey 2003, *When Russia Learned to Read: Literacy and Popular Literature, 1861–1917*, Evanston, IL: Northwestern University Press.

Brown, Adam 2008, 'Traumatic Memory and Holocaust Testimony: Passing Judgement in Representations of Chaim Rumkowski', *Colloquy* 15, pp. 128–44.

Brubaker, Rogers 2005, 'The "Diaspora" Diaspora', *Ethnic and Racial Studies* 28, no. 1, pp. 1–19.

Brumberg, Abraham 2001, 'The Bund: History of a Schism', *Jewish Politics in Eastern Europe. The Bund at 100*, edited by Jack Jacobs, New York: New York University Press, pp. 81–9.

Brünzels, Sonja 1999, 'Reclaim the Streets. Karneval und Konfrontation', *UneFarce*, 3, 212.227.44.42/unefarce/n03/reclaim.htm (last acccessed 25 July 2013).

Budnitskii, Oleg V. 2006, *Rossiiskie evrei mezhdu krasnymi i belymi. 1917–1920*, Moscow: ROSSPEN.

'Bund' brentsh S.P. un S.L. klub 1907a, 'Der 10ter yehrlikher "yubileum" fun "bund"', *Di Rotshester tsaytungn* 1 (December), p. 1.

'Bund' brentsh S.P. un S.L. klub 1907b, 'Di shvue', *Di Rotshester tsaytung* 1 (December), p. 1.

'Bund' brentsh S.P. un S.L. klub 1907c, 'Tsehn yohr', *Di Rotshester tsaytung* 1 (December), p. 1, p. 3.

'Bund' brentsh S.P. un S.L. klub 1907d, 'Vos feyern mir? Vos vilen mir?', *Di Rotshester tsaytung* 1 (December), p. 2.

Bundishe grupe in Montevideo (ed.) 1937a, 'Unzere arbet oyfn shul-gebit. Opshatsungen un bamerkungen', *40 yor 'Bund'*, Montevideo: Bundishe grupe in Montevideo, pp. 38–41.

Bundishe grupe in Montevideo 1937b, 'Entusyastish durckhgefirt di akademye tsum 40-yorikn yuvl fun "bund" in B. Ayres', *40 yor 'Bund'*, Montevideo: Bundishe grupe in Montevideo, p. 54.

Bundisher Klub in Nyu York (ed.) 1932, *Ab. Kahan un der 'Bund' in Poyln*, New York: Bundisher Klub in Nyu York.

Bundisher Klub in Nyu York (ed.) 1935, *Der 'forverts' un der 'bund'*, New York: aroysgegebn fun Bundishn klub in NyuYork.

Bundisher Klub in Nyu York (ed.) 1938, *Zamlheft fun bundishn klub in Nyu York. Aroysgegebn lekhoved dem 15 yoriken yubiley*, New York: Bundisher Klub in Nyu York.

Bunzl, John 1975, *Klassenkampf in der Diaspora. Zur Geschichte der Jüdischen Arbeiterbewegung*, Vienna: Europaverlag.

Burbank, Jane 2004, *Russian Peasants Go to Court. Legal Culture in the Countryside, 1905–1917*, Bloomington, IN: Indiana University Press.

Burbank, Jane 2008, 'Securing Peasant Society: Constables and Courts in Rural Russia, 1905–1917', *Staats-Gewalt: Ausnahmezustand und Sicherheitsregimes*, edited by Alf Lüdtke and Michael Wildt, Göttingen: Wallstein, pp. 91–116.

Burnett, John 1974, *The Annals of Labour: Autobiographies of British Working-Class People, 1820–1920*, Bloomington, IN and London: Indiana University Press.

Byalostotski, B. 1932, 'Rikhtungen fun yidishizm', *Unzer shul*, New York, 2, no. 4, p. 8 ff.

Cahan, Ab. 1904, 'Faterland un "bund"', *Der fraynd fun bund. Gevidmet tsu di franyd fun 'bund', voz velen bezukhen dem ball in grand tsentral peles* (2 April), p. 1, p. 3.

Cahan, Ab. 1923, 'Forvort', *Fun mayn lebn*, Vol. 1, edited by Vladimir Medem, New York: Vladimir Medem Komite, [unpaginated].

Cahan, Ab. 1942, 'Kremer in Amerike', *Arkadi. Zamlbukh tsum ondenk fun Arkadi Kremer*, New York: Unzer tsayt, pp. 229–31.

Calhoun, Craig 1993, '"New Social Movements" of the Early Nineteenth Century', *Social Science History* 17, no. 3, pp. 385–427.

Callahan, Kevin J. 2010, *Demonstration Culture: European Socialism and the Second International, 1889–1914*, Leicester: Troubador.

Camarero, Hernán 2007, *A la conquista de la clase obrera. Los comunistas y el mundo del trabajo en la Argentina, 1920–1935*, Buenos Aires: Siglo XXI.

Canetti, Elias 1973 [1960], *Crowds and Power*, translated by Carol Stewart, New York: Continuum.

Carlsson, Chris (ed.) 2002, *Critical Mass. Bicycling's Defiant Celebration*, San Francisco: AK Press.

Carreras, Sandra, Horacio Tarcus and Jessica Zeller (eds.) 2008, *Los socialistas alemanes y la formación del movimiento obrero argentino. Antología del Vorwärts (1886–1901)*, Buenos Aires: Buenos Libros.

Ceplair, Larry 2007, *The Marxist and the Movies. A Biography of Paul Jarrico*, Lexington, KY: University Press of Kentucky.

Chace, William M. 2008, 'On the Margin. Irving Howe Reconsidered', *Common Knowledge* 14, no. 2, pp. 270–7.

Churchill, Ward 1997, *A Little Matter of Genocide: Holocaust and Denial in the Americas, 1492 to the Present*, San Francisco: City Lights.

Clasen, Claus-Peter 2008, *Streikgeschichten. Die Augsburger Textilarbeiterstreiks 1868–1934*, Augsburg: Wißner.

Clemens, Elisabeth S. 1996, 'Organizational Form as Frame. Collective Identity and Political Strategy in the American Labor Movement, 1880–192', *Comparative Perspectives on Social Movements. Political Opportunites, Mobilizing Structures, and Cultural Framings*, edited by Doug McAdam, John D. McCarthy, and Mayer N. Zald, Cambridge, MA, New York, Melbourne: Cambridge University Press, pp. 205–26.

Cohen, Aaron J. 2003, 'Oh, That! Myth, Memory, and World War I in the Russian Emigration and the Soviet Union', *Slavic Review* 62, no. 1, pp. 69–86.

Cohen, Jocelyn and Daniel Soyer (eds.) 2006a, *My Future Is in America: Autobiographies of Eastern European Jewish Immigrants*, New York: New York University Press.

Cohen, Jocelyn and Daniel Soyer (eds.) 2006b, 'Introduction. Yiddish Social Science and Jewish Immigrant Autobiography', *My Future Is in America: Autobiographies of Eastern European Jewish Immigrants*, edited by Jocelyn Cohen and Daniel Soyer, New York: New York University Press, pp. 1–17.

Cohen, Nathan 2008, 'The Yiddish Press and Yiddish Literature: A Fertile but Complex Relationship', *Modern Judaism* 28, no. 2, pp. 149–72.

Cohen, Robin and Shirin M. Rai 2000, 'Global Social Movements: Towards a Cosmopolitan Politics', *Global Social Movements*, edited by Robin Cohen and Shirin M. Rai, London, New York: Athlone Press, pp. 1–17.

Cohen, Stephen M. 1938, *American Modernity and Jewish Identity*, New York: Tavistock.

Cohler, Bertram J. 2009, 'Life writing in the shadow of the Shoah: fathers and sons in the memoirs of Elie Wiesel and Leon Weliczker Wells', *International Journal of Applied Psychoanalytic Studies* 7, no. 1 (17 December), pp. 40–57.

Collomp, Catherine 2005, 'The Jewish Labor Committee, American Labor, and the Rescue of European Socialists, 1934–1941', *International Labor and Working-Class History* 68, no. 1, pp. 112–33.

Conrad, Sebastian 2009, 'Double Marginalization: A Plea for a Transnational Perspective on German History', *Comparative and Transnational History: Central European Approaches and New Perspectives*, edited by Heinz-Gerhard Haupt and Jürgen Kocka, New York et al.: Berghahn, pp. 52–76.

Conrad, Sebastian 2010, *Globalisation and the Nation in Imperial Germany*, translated by Sorcha O'Hagan, Cambridge: Cambdrige University Press.

Conrad, Sebastian and Jürgen Osterhammel (eds.) 2004a, *Das Kaiserreich transnational*, Göttingen: Vandenhoeck & Ruprecht.

Conrad, Sebastian and Jürgen Osterhammel (eds.) 2004b, 'Einleitung', *Das Kaiserreich transnational*, edited by Sebastian Conrad and Jürgen Osterhammel, Göttingen: Vandenhoeck & Ruprecht.

Corney, Frederick C. 2004, *Telling October. Memory and the Making of the Bolshevik Revolution*, Ithaca, NY and London: Cornell University Press.

Corrsin, Stephen D. 1986, 'Polish Political Strategies and the "Jewish Question" During the Elections in Warsaw to the Russian State Dumas 1906–1912', *Proceedings of the Conference 'Poles and Jews: Myth and Reality in Historical Context'*, edited by John Micgiel, Robert Scott and H.B. Segel, New York: Institute on East Central Europe, Columbia University, pp. 140–67.

Corrsin, Stephen D. 1989, 'Polish Jewish Relations Before the First World War: The Case of State Duma Elections in Warsaw', *Gal-Ed* 11, pp. 46–53.

Cortés Conde, Roberto 2009, *The Political Economy of Argentina in the Twentieth Century*, Cambridge: Cambridge University Press.

Coser, Rose Laub 1999, *Women of Courage: Jewish and Italian Immigrant Women in New York*, Westport, CT: Greenwood Publishing Group.

Craftista Crafting Circle (ed.) 2009, *Craftista! Handarbeit als Aktivismus*, Wiesbaden: Mainz.

Creighton, Donald G. and John A. Macdonald 1955, *The Old Chieftan*, Toronto: Macmillan.

Cross, Truman B. 1971, 'Young Marx, Marxism: Viktor Chernov's Use of the Theses on Feuerbach', *Journal of the History of Ideas* 32, no. 4, pp. 600–6.

Daly, Jonathan W. 1998, *Autocracy under Siege. Security Police and Opposition in Russia. 1866–1905*, DeKalb, IL: Northern Illinois. University Press.

Daly, Jonathan W. 2004, *The Watchful State: Security Police and Opposition in Russia, 1906–1917*, DeKalb, IL: Northern Illinois University Press.

David-Fox, Michael 2006, 'Multiple Modernities vs. Neo-Traditionalism: On Recent Debates in Russian and Soviet History', *Jahrbücher für Geschichte Osteuropas* 54, pp. 535–55.

Davis-Kram, Harriet 1980, 'The Story of the Sisters of the Bund', *Contemporary Jewry* 5, no. 2, pp. 27–43.

Davis, William Watson 2009 [1913], *The Civil War and Reconstruction in Florida*, New York: Columbia University.

Dawidowicz, Lucy S. 1967, 'Introduction: The World of East European Jewry', *The Golden Tradition. Jewish Life and Thought in Eastern Europe*, edited by Lucy S. Dawidowicz, New York: Holt, Rinehart and Winston, pp. 5–90.

Debs, Eugene V. 2014 [2000], *Eugene V. Debs Reader: Socialism and the Class Struggle*, edited by William A. Pelz, London: Merlin.

Dekel-Chen, Jonathan 2005, *Farming the Red Land: Jewish Agricultural Colonization and Local Soviet Power, 1924–1941*, New Haven: Yale University Press.

DellaPergola, Sergio 1996, 'Between Science and Fiction. Notes on the Demography of the Holocaust', *Holocaust and Genocide Studies* 10, no. 1, pp. 34–51.

Delrio, Walter, Diana Lenton et al. 2010, 'Discussing Indigenous Genocide in Argentina: Past, Present, and Consequences of Argentinean State Policies toward Native Peoples', *Genocide Studies and Prevention* 5, no. 2, pp. 138–59.

Denz, Rebekka 2008, 'Der "Froyenvinkl". Die Frauenrubrik in der bundischen Tageszeitung "Naye folkstsaytung"', *PaRDeS. Zeitschrift der Vereinigung für Jüdische Studien e. V.* 14, pp. 96–124.

Denz, Rebekka 2009, *Bundistinnen. Frauen im Allgemeinen Jüdischen Arbeiterbund ('Bund') dargestellt anhand der jiddischen Biographiesammlung 'Doyres Bundistn'.* Pri ha-Pardes 5, Potsdam: Universitätsverlag Potsdam, opus.kobv.de/ubp/volltexte/2009/2788/ (last accessed 27 February 2017).

Depkat, Volker 2006, *Lebenswenden und Zeitenwenden. Deutsche Politiker und die Erfahrungen des 20. Jahrhunderts*, Munich: Oldenbourg.

Der avangard 1908, 'Vos vilen mir?', *Der avangard*, Buenos Aires 1, no. 1 (August), p. 1 f.

Der avangard 1909, 'Erklehrung', *Der avangard*, Buenos Aires 2, no. 2 (April), p. 1 f.

Der veker 1906, 'Fun der redaktsye', *Der veker*, Vilnius, 1 (3 January), p. 1.

Deutsch, Sandra McGee 2010, *Crossing Borders, Claiming a Nation: A History of Argentine Jewish Women, 1880–1955.* Durham, NC: Duke University Press.

Devoto, Fernando 2003, *Historia de la Inmigración en la Argentina*, Buenos Aires: Editorial Sudamericana.

Di shtime fun avangard 1909a, 'Fun redaktsye', *Di shtime fun avangard*, Buenos Aires 1, no. 1 (May), p. 1.

Di shtime fun avangard 1909b, 'Vikhtig fir arbeyter', *Di shtime fun avangard*, Buenos Aires 1, no. 2 (June), p. 22.

DiAntonio, Robert 1993, 'Introduction 1', *Tradition and Innovation. Reflections on Latin American Jewish Writing*, edited by Robert DiAntonio and Nora Glickman, Albany, NY: State University of New York Press, pp. 1–8.

Dikshteyn, S. 1905, *Fun vos eyner lebt*, Geneva: Drukerei fun Bund.

Dimitrov, Georg 1935, 'Ikh ken Telmans gurl nit fargesn!', *Der konfektsyon arbeter* 1, no. 2, p. 2.

Diner, Dan 1996, 'Gestaute Zeit – Massenvernichtung und jüdische Erzählstruktur', *Fünfzig Jahre danach: zur Nachgeschichte des Nationalsozialismus*, edited by Sigrid Weigel and Birgit R. Erdle, Zurich: vdf Hochschulverlag an der ETH Zürich, pp. 3–16.

Diner, Hasia 2001, *Hungering for America: Italian, Irish, and Jewish Foodways in the Age of Migration*, Cambridge, MA: Harvard University Press.

Diner, Hasia 2004, *The Jews of the United States, 1654 to 2000*, Berkeley, CA: University of California Press.

Dohrn, Verena 2008, *Jüdische Eliten im Russischen Reich. Aufklärung und Integration im 19. Jahrhundert*, Cologne: Böhlau.

Donaldson, Gordon 1975, *Fifteen Men. Canada's Prime Ministers from Macdonald to Trudeau*, 5th edition, Toronto: Doubleday.

Douglass, Paul H. 1919, 'Is the New Immigration More Unskilled Than the Old?', *Publications of the American Statistical Association* 16, no. 126, pp. 393–403.

Doyon, Louise M. 2006, *Perón y los trabajadores. Los orígenes del sindicalismo peronista, 1943–1955*, Buenos Aires: Siglo XXI.

Dubnow, Simon 1973 [1929], *History of the Jews. Volume 5: From the Congress of Vienna to the Emergence of Hitler*, translated by Moshe Spiegel, New York: Barnes.

Dubofsky, Melvyn 1968a, 'Success and Failure of Socialism in New York City, 1900–1918: A Case Study', *Labor History* 9, no. 3, pp. 361–75.

Dubofsky, Melvyn 1968b, *When Workers Organize. New York City in the Progressive Era*, Amherst, MA: University of Massachusetts Press.

Dücker, Burkhard 2007, *Rituale. Formen – Funktionen – Geschichte*, Stuttgart and Weimar: Metzler.

Dubofsky, Melvyn and Foster Rhea Dulles 2004 [1949], *Labor in America. A History*, 7th edition, Wheeling, IL: Harlan Davidson.

Dumont, René and Marcel Mazoyer 1973 [1969], *Socialisms and Development*, translated by Rupert Cunningham, London: Deutsch.

Dunlavy, Colleen and Thomas Welskopp 2007, 'Myths and Pecularities. Comparing US and German Capitalism', *Bulletin of the German Historical Institute, Washington DC* 41, pp. 33–64.

Duronio, Margaret A. and Eugene R. Tempel 1997, *Fund Raisers. Their Careers, Stories, Concerns, and Accomplishments*, San Francisco, CA: Jossey-Bass.

Dvinsker bundisher brentsh 75 arbeter ring 1939, *35-joriker yubiley-zshurnal. 1904–1939*, New York.

Dvorak, Stanislav 1979, untitled memoirs, *Vladimir Medem. The Life and the Soul of a Legendary Jewish Socialist*, edited by Samuel A Portnoy, New York: Ktav, pp. 550–8.

Eakin, Paul John 1999, *How Our Lives Become Stories: Making Selves*, Ithaca, NY: Cornell University Press.

Ebert, Christa 2004, 'Dichter-Ich versus Revolution. Autobiographische Revolutions-Berichte von Gippius, Cvetaeva, Bunin und Remizov', *Autobiographical Practices in Russia. Autobiographische Praktiken in Russland*, edited by Jochen Hellbeck and Klaus Heller, Göttingen: V & R unipress, pp. 197–222.

Eichenberg, Arianne 2004, *Zwischen Erfahrung und Erfindung. Jüdische Lebensentwürfe nach der Shoa*, Cologne, Weimar, Vienna: Böhlau.

Eisen, Arnold M. 1998, *Rethinking Modern Judaism: Ritual, Commandment, Community*, Chicago, IL: University of Chicago Press.

Eisenstadt, Shmuel N. 2000, 'Multiple Modernities', *Daedalus* 129, no. 1, pp. 1–29.

Elazar, Daniel J. 1983, 'Jewish Frontier Experiences in the Southern Hemisphere: The Cases of Argentina, Australia, and South Africa', *Modern Judaism* 3, no. 2, pp. 129–46.

Eley, Geoff 2002, *Forging Democracy. The History of the Left in Europe, 1850–2000*, Oxford: Oxford University Press.

Elkin, Judith Laikin 1980, *Jews of the Latin American Republics*, New York: University of North Carolina Press.
Embrick, David G. 2008, 'Activism', *International Encyclopedia of the Social Sciences*, Vol. 1, edited by William A. Darity Jr, Detroit: Thomson, p. 18.
Engels, Friedrich 2009 [1887], 'Preface to the American Edition', *The Condition of the Working Class in England*, Oxford: Oxford University Press, pp. 303–11.
Enstad, Nan 1999, *Ladies of Labor, Girls of Adventure. Working Women, Popular Culture, and Labor Politics at the Turn of the Twentieth Century*, New York, Chichester, West Sussex: Columbia University Press.
Entin, Yoel 1946, 'Di naye yidishe dertsyung (der onheyb fun di yidishe folks-shuln)', *Yidish natsyonaler arbeter farband. 1910–1946. Geshikhte un dergreykhungen*, New York: General-eksekutive fun yidish-natsynonaln arbeter-farband, pp. 145–97.
Entin, Yoel 1960a [1910], 'Di bildung fun yidishe sin un tekhter', *Gezamelte shriftn. Ershter teyl: yidishe dertsyung*, New York: Pinkhes Gingold farlag, pp. 10–14.
Entin, Yoel 1960b [1909], 'Vi zoln mir dertsyen undzere kinder do in land?', *Gezamelte shriftn. Ershter teyl: yidishe dertsyung*, New York: Pinkhes Gingold farlag, pp. 1–4.
Epple, Angelika 2012, 'The Global, the Transnational and the Subaltern: The Limits of History beyond the National Paradigm', *Beyond Methodological Nationalism: Research Methodologies for Cross-Border Studies*, edited by Anna Amelina, Devrimsel D. Nergiz, Thomas Faist and Nina Glick Schiller, New York: Routledge, pp. 155–75.
Epshteyn, Shakna 1927, *Der bund. Voz er iz geven un voz fun im iz gevorn*, New York: Yidishe sektsye vorkers (komunistisher) partey.
Epstein, Melech 1953, *Jewish Labor in the USA 1914–1952: An Industrial, Political and Cultural History of the Jewish Labor Movement*, Vol. 2, New York: H. Wolff.
ERF [Esther Frumkin] 1908, 'Di ershte yidishe sprakh-konferents', *Di naye tsayt* 4, pp. 89–104.
Eser, Ingo 2010, *'Volk, Staat, Gott!'. Die deutsche Minderheit in Polen und ihr Schulwesen 1918–1939*, Wiesbaden: Harrassowitz.
Estraikh, Gennady and Mikhail Krutikov (eds.) 2001, *Yiddish and the Left: Papers of the Third Mendel Friedman International Conference on Yiddish*, Oxford: European Humanities Research Centre of the University of Oxford.
Estraikh, G. [Gennadii] 2002, 'Itsik Fefer: A Yiddish Wunderkind of the Bolshevik Revolution', *Shofar* 20, no. 3, pp. 14–31.
Faist, Thomas 2004, 'The Border-Crossing Expansion of Social Space: Concepts, Questions and Topics', *Transnational Social Spaces: Agents, Networks, and Institutions*, edited by Thomas Faist and Eyüp Özveren, Aldershot: Ashgate, pp. 1–36.
Feiner, Shmuel 2002, *Haskalah and History. The Emergence of a Modern Jewish Historical Consciousness*, Oxford: The Littman Library of Jewish Civilization.
Ferziger, Adam S. 2005, *Exclusion and Hierarchy: Orthodoxy, Nonobservance, and the*

Emergence of Modern Jewish Identity, Philadelphia, PA: University of Pennsylvania Press.

Figes, Orlando and Boris Kolonitskii 1999, *Interpreting the Russian Revolution. The Language and Symbols of 1917*, New Haven and London: Yale University Press.

Fink, Leon (ed.) 2011, *Workers Across the Americas: The Transnational Turn in Labor History*, Oxford: Oxford University Press.

Finlayson, Geoffrey 1994, *Citizen, State and Social Welfare in Britain, 1830–1990*, Oxford: Clarendon Press.

Fishman, David 2009, 'Yiddish Schools in America and the Problem of Secular Jewish Identity', *Religion and Ethnicity. Jewish Identities in Evolution*, edited by Zvi Gitelman, New Brunswick, NJ and London: Rutgers University Press, pp. 69–89.

Fishman, Joshua A. 1965, *Yiddish in America: Socio-Linguistic Description and Analysis*, Bloomington, IN: Indiana University Press.

Fishman, Joshua A. 1981, 'Sociology of Yiddish', *Never Say Die! A Thousand Years of Yiddish in Jewish Life and Letters*, edited by Joshua A. Fishman, The Hague: Mouton.

Fitzpatrick, Sheila 1997, 'The Letter as a Work of Art. A Housing Claim in the Style of an Anketa', *Russian History* 24, pp. 189–93.

Foner, Philip S. 1977, *History of the Labor Movement in the United States, Vol. 2: From the Founding of the A.F. of L. to the Emergence of American Imperialism*, second printing, New York: International Publishers.

Foner, Philip S. 1986, *May Day: A Short History of the International Workers' Holiday, 1886–1986*, New York: International Publishers.

Ford, Aleksander 2006 [1936], *Children Must Laugh (Droga młodych/Mir kumen on)*, DVD, The National Center for Jewish Film, Brandeis University.

Frager, Ruth A. 1992, *Sweatshop Strife: Class, Ethnicity, and Gender in the Jewish Labour Movement of Toronto, 1900–1939*, Toronto: University of Toronto Press.

Frankel, Jonathan 1984, *Prophecy and Politics. Socialism, Nationalism, and the Russian Jews, 1862–1917*, Cambridge: Cambridge University Press, 1984.

Frankel, Jonathan 1997, 'The Roots of "Jewish Socialism" (1881–1892): From "Populism" to "Cosmopolitanism"?', *Essential Papers on Jews and the Left*, edited by Ezra Mendelsohn, New York: New York University Press, pp. 59–77.

Frankel, Jonathan 2009, 'Jewish Politics and the Russian Revolution of 1905', *Crisis, Revolution, and Russian Jews*, Cambridge: Cambridge University Press, pp. 57–71.

Freadman, Richard 2004, 'Generational Shifts in Post-Holocaust Australian Jewish Autobiography', *Life Writing* 1, no. 1, pp. 21–44.

Freadman, Richard 2007, *This Crazy Thing a Life: Australian Jewish Autobiography*. Crawley: University of Western Australia Press, 2007.

Freeberg, Ernest 2008, *Democravy's Prisoner. Eugene V. Debs, the Great War, and the Right to Dissent*, Cambridge, MA and London: Harvard University Press.

Freidenberg, Judith 2009, *The Invention of the Jewish Gaucho. Villa Clara and the Construction of Argentine Identity*, Austin: University of Texas Press.

Frerichs, Petra 1980, *Bürgerliche Autobiographie und proletarische Selbstdarstellung*, Frankfurt am Main: Haag + Herchen.

Frerichs, Regin 2008, *Im Fadenkreuz der Walfänger. Bordtagebuch einer Greenpeace-Aktivistin*. Stuttgart: Kosmos, 2008.

Fried, Albert (ed.) 1970, *Socialism in America. From the Shakers to the Third International. A Documentary History*, New York: Anchor Books.

Frost, Shimon 1998, *Schooling as a Socio-Political Expression. Jewish Education in Interwar Poland*, Jerusalem: Magnes Press, Hebrew University.

Frumkin, [Malke (Lifshitz)] (ed.) 1922, *Hirsh Lekert*, Moscow: Farlag fun Ts. K. rusl. komunistishn yugnt-farband.

Fry, Brian N. 2007, *Nativism and Immigration: Regulating the American Dream*, New York: LFB.

Gabaccia, Donna R. and Fraser M. Ottanelli 2001, *Italian Workers of the World: Labor, Migration and the Making of Multi-Ethnic Nations*, Urbana, IL and Chicago: University of Illinois Press.

Gallo, Ester 2009, 'In the Right Place at the Right Time? Reflections on Multi-Sited Ethnography in the Age of Migration', *Multi-Sited Ethnography: Theory, Praxis and Locality in Contemporary Research*, edited by Mark-Anthony Falzon, Farnham et al.: Ashgate, pp. 87–102.

Galpern, Martin 1909a, 'Dos lid fun der nayterin. Lidishe poem', *Der avangard*, Buenos Aires 2, no. 6, pp. 14–18.

Galpern, Martin 1909b, 'Dos lid fun der nayterin. Lidishe poem', *Der avangard*, Buenos Aires 2, no. 7, pp. 10–13.

Gartner, Lloyd P. 1998, 'The Great Jewish Migration – Its East European Background', *Tel Aviver Jahrbuch für Deutsche Geschichte* 27, pp. 107–33.

G-B 1907, 'Der ershte tsuzamenfar fun "Bund"', *Di hofnung*, Vilnius 14.

Gebert, Konstanty 2010, 'Poles Commemorate Warsaw Uprising in Marek Edelman's Style, With Silence', *The Jewish Daily Forward* (30 April), www.forward.com/articles/127434 (last accessed 28 February 2017).

Gechtman, Roni 1999, 'Socialist Mass Politics through Sport. The Bund's Morgenshtern in Poland, 1926–1939', *Journal of Sport History* 26, no. 2, pp. 326–52.

Gechtman, Roni 2005a, 'Conceptualizing National-Cultural Autonomy – From the Austro-Marxists to the Jewish Labor Bund', *Simon Dubnov Institute Yearbook* 4, pp. 17–49.

Gechtman, Roni 2005b, *Yidisher sotsializm. The Origin and Contexts of the Jewish Labor Bund's National Program*, PhD dissertation, New York University.

Gechtman, Roni 2012, 'Lifshits, Khaye Malke', *YIVO Encyclopedia of Jews in Eastern Europe*, www.yivoencyclopedia.org/article.aspx/Lifshits_Khaye_Malke (last accessed 28 February 2017).

Gelbard, Arye 1982, *Der jüdische Arbeiterbund im Revolutionsjahr 1917*, Vienna: Europaverlag.

Gellner, Ernest 1964, *Thought and Change*, London: Weidenfeld and Nicholson.

Geni, Pyetro 1936, 'Di rol fun der internatsyonaler arbetershaft in der shpanisher revolutsye', *Argentiner lebn* 7, p. 2.

Gerchunoff, Alberto 2003 [1910], *Parricide on the Pampa: A New Study and Translation of Los Gauchos Judíos*, edited and translated by Edna Aizenberg, Princeton, NJ: Markus Wiener.

Gerhard, Ute 2001, *Feminismus und Demokratie. Europäische Frauenbewegungen der 1920er Jahre*, Königstein/Taunus: Helmer.

Gerngroß, Marcus 2008, 'Terrorismus im Zarenreich mit Vorbildfunktion: Die "Narodnaya Woly"', *Sozialrevolutionärer Terrorismus. Theorie, Ideologie, Fallbeispiele*, edited by Alexander Straßner, Wiesbaden: vs, pp. 147–58.

Geyer, Dietrich 1962, *Lenin in der russischen Sozialdemokratie. Die Arbeiterbewegung im Zarenreich als Organisationsproblem der revolutionären Intelligenz 1890–1903*, Cologne and Graz: Böhlau.

Gilbert, Alan 1979, 'Social Theory and Revolutionary Activity in Marx', *The American Political Science Review* 73, no. 2, pp. 521–38.

Gilinski, Sh. 1971, 'Medem-sanatorye', *Medem-sanatorye*, edited by Khayim Solomon Kazdan, Tel Aviv: Hamenora, pp. 19–34.

Girtler, Roland 2006, *Abenteuer Grenze. Von Schmugglern und Schmugglerinnen, Ritualen und 'heiligen Räumen'*, Vienna: Lit.

Gitelman, Zvi 1972, *Jewish Nationality and Soviet Politics. The Jewish Sections of the CPSU, 1917–1930*, Princeton, NJ: Princeton University Press.

Gitelman, Zvi (ed.) 2003, *The Emergence of Modern Jewish Politics. Bund and Zionism in Eastern Europe*, Pittsburgh, PA: University of Pittsburgh Press.

Glazer, Nathan and Daniel P. Moynihan 1970, *Beyond the Melting Pot: The Negroes, Puerto Ricans, Jews, Italians, and Irish of New York City*, second printing, Cambridge, MA and London: MIT Press.

Glenn, Susanne A. 1990, *Daughters of the Shtetl. Life and Labor in the Immigrant Generation*, Ithaca, NY: Cornell University Press.

Godio, Julio 1985, *La Semana Trágica de enero de 1919*, Buenos Aires: Hyspamérica.

Gosudarstvennyi komitet po arkhivam i deloproizvodstvu Respubliki Belarus (ed.) 1997, *Bund v Belarusi. Dokumenty i materialy 1897–1921*, Minsk: BelNIIDAD.

Goetz, Thomas 2008, *Poetik des Nachrufs. Zur Kultur der Nekrologie und zur Nachrufszene auf dem Theater*, Vienna, Cologne, Weimar: Böhlau.

Goldfarb, A. 1967, 'Emanuel Novogrudski un Benyamin Tabatshinski', *Lebns-fragn*, Tel Aviv 188–9, p. 25.

Goldman, Y. 1905, 'Fun unzere organisatsyonen', *Der kemfer*, New York 1, no. 1 (3 November), p. 7.

Goldstein, Bernard 1949, *The Stars Bear Witness*, New York: Viking Press.

Goldstein, Jacob (ed.) 1998, *Jewish Socialists in the United States: The Cahan Debate, 1925–1926*, Brighton and Portland, OR: Sussex Academic Press.

Goldsztejn, Bernard 1948, 'Fighting in the Ghetto', *Jewish Labor Bund Bulletin* 4, p. 3.

Gompers, Samuel 1986, 'What Does Labor Want?', *The Samuel Gompers Papers*, edited by Stuart B. Kaufman and Peter J. Albert, Vol. 3, Urbana, IL: University of Illinois Press, pp. 390–2.

Gordon, Beverly 1998, *Bazaar and Fair Ladies. The History of the American Fundraising Fair*, Knoxville: University of Tennessee Press.

Gorelik, Aaron 1946, *Shturmedike yorn*, New York: IKUF.

Goren, Arthur A. 1970, *New York Jews and the Quest for Community. The Kehilla Experiment, 1908–1922*, New York and London: Columbia University Press.

Gorny, Yosef 2006, *Converging Alternatives. The Bund and the Zionist Labor-Movement*, Albany, NY: State University of New York Press.

Gottesman, Itzik Nakhmen 2003, *Defining the Yiddish Nation. The Jewish Folklorists of Poland*, Detroit: Wayne State University Press.

Goyens, Tom 2007, *Beer and Revolution. The German Anarchist Movement in New York City, 1880–1914*, Urbana, IL: University of Illinois Press.

Gramsci, Antonio 1971, *Selections from the Prison Notebooks*, translated by Quintin Hoare and Geoffrey Nowell-Smith, New York: International Publishers.

Green, Abigail 2010, *Moses Montefiore. Jewish Liberator, Imperial Hero*, Cambridge, MA and London: The Belknap Press of Harvard University Press.

Greenbaum, Avraham 1991, 'The Underground Jewish Press in Eastern Europe until 1917', *Qesher* 9, pp. 14e–19e.

Grinshteyn, Sheyne 1922, 'Di vilner geshehnishn fun Lekerts tsayt', *Hirsh Lekert. Tsum 20-tn yortsayt fun zayn kepung*, Moscow: Ruslendishe komunistishe partey, Ts. K. fun R.K.P., Ts. B. fun yidsektsye, pp. 17–21.

Gross, Naftali 1938, *Vladimir Medem. Di legende fun der Yidisher arbeter bavegung*, New York: Kinder ring bay dem bildungs komitet fun arbeter ring.

Guérin, Daniel 1979 [1976], *100 Years of Labor in the USA*, translated by Alan Adler, London: Ink Links.

Günter, Manuea 2002, *Überleben schreiben: Zur Autobiographik der Shoa*, Würzburg: Königshausen & Neumann.

Gusev, Viktor 2000, 'Bundïvskie organizatsii Ukraïni v 1905', *Zaporozhskie evreiskie chteniia* 4, pp. 98–101.

Gusev, Viktor 2006, 'V. Kossovskii i V. Medem protiv V. Lenina. Mogut li Evrei nazyvat'sia natsiei i imet' sobstvennuiu gosudarstvennost'?', *Materialy Trinadtsatoi Ezhegodnoi Mezhdunarodnoi Mezhdistsiplinarnoi konferentsii po iudaike*, edited by K. Iu. Burminstrov, Moscow: Inst. Slavianovedeniia RAN et al.

Guterman, Perets 1976, 'A muster fun oyfrikhtigkeyt', *Yid. Mentsh. Sotsysalist. I. Artuski ondenk-bukh*, edited by I. Artuski Bukh-Komitet, Tel Aviv: Lebn-fragn, pp. 76–9.

Haberer, Erich 1992, 'Cosmopolitianism, Antisemitism, and Populism: A Reappraisal of the Russian and Jewish Socialist Response to the Pogroms of 1881–1882', *Pogroms: Anti-Jewish Violence in Modern Russian History*, edited by John D. Klier and Shlomo Lambroza, Cambridge: Cambridge University Press, pp. 98–133.

Häfner, Claudia 2008, *Heimischwerdung am La Plata. Von der Deutschen Evangelischen La Plata Synode zur Iglesia Evnagélica del Río de la Plata*, Münster: Lit.

Häfner, Lutz 1994, *Die Partei der Linken Sozialrevolutionäre in der Russischen Revolution, 1917–1918*, Cologne, Vienna, Weimar: Böhlau.

Hahn, Alois 2000, *Konstruktionen des Selbst, der Welt und der Geschichte*, Frankfurt am Main: Suhrkamp.

Hahn, Sylvia 2012; *Historische Migrationsforschung*, Frankfurt am Main and New York: Campus.

Haimson, Leopold H. and Charles Tilly (eds.) 1989, *Strikes, Wars, and Revolutions in an International Perspektive. Strike Waves in the Late Nineteenth and Early Twentieth Centuries*, Cambridge: Cambridge University Press.

Halfin, Igal 2000, *From Darkness to Light. Class, Consciousness, and Salvation in Revolutionary Russia*, Pittsburgh, PA: University of Pittsburgh Press.

Halfin, Igal 2001, 'Looking into the Oppositionists' Souls', *Russian Review* 60, no. 3, pp. 316–39.

Halfin, Igal 2003, *Terror in My Soul: Communist Autobiographies on Trial*, Cambridge, MA: Harvard University Press.

Halperin, Samuel 1960, 'Ideology or Philanthropy? The Politics of Zionist Fund-Raising', *The Western Political Quarterly* 13, no. 4, pp. 950–73.

Hanagan, Michael P. 2004, 'An Agenda for Transnational Labor History', *International Review of Social History* 49, no. 3, pp. 455–74.

Hardt, Michael and Antonio Negri 2004, *Multitude. War and Democracy in the Age of Empire*, New York: Penguin.

Harshav, Benjamin 1990, *The Meaning of Yiddish*, Berkeley, CA: University of California Press.

Hartwich, Mateusz J. 2011, 'Wie schreibt man eine transnational orientierte Geschichte einer polnischen Provinz um 1956?', *Vergleichen, verflechten, verwirren? Europäische Geschichtsschreibung zwischen Theorie und Praxis*, edited by Agnes Andt, Joachim C. Häberlen and Christiane Reinecke, Göttingen: Vandenhoeck & Ruprecht, pp. 169–89.

Hart, Y. 1968, 'Bentsl Tsalevitsh', *Doyres bundistn*, edited by Jacob Sh. Hertz, 3, New York: Unzer tsayt, p. 71 f.

Harvey, David 1990, *The Condition of Postmodernity*, Malden, MA, Oxford, Victoria: Blackwell.

Haumann, Heiko 1997, '"Present-Day National Work" in the Shtetl: The Beginnings of Zionism in Galacia', *The First Zionist Congress in 1897: Causes, Significance, Topicality*, translated by Wayne van Dalsum and Vivan Kramer, Basel: Karger, pp. 74–8.

Haumann, Heiko 2002 [1990], *A History of East European Jews*, translated by James Patterson, New York and Budapest: Central European University Press.

Hebel, Udo J. (ed.) 2012, *Transnational American Studies*, Heidelberg: Winter.

Hellbeck, Jochen 1996, 'Fashioning the Stalinist Soul. The Diary of Stepan Podljubnyi', *Jahrbücher für Geschichte Osteuropas* 44, pp. 344–73.

Hellbeck, Jochen 2001, 'Working, Struggling, Becoming: Stalin-Era Autobiographical Texts', *Russ* 60, no. 3, pp. 340–59.

Hellbeck, Jochen and Klaus Heller (eds.) 2004, *Autobiographical Practices in Russia. Autobiographische Praktiken in Russland*, Göttingen: V & R unipress.

Herbeck, Ulrich 2009, *Das Feindbild vom 'jüdischen Bolschewiken': zur Geschichte des russischen Antisemitismus vor und während der Russischen Revolution*, Berlin: Metropol.

Hertz, Jacob Sholem 1946, *Di Geshikhte fun a yugnt. Der kleyner Bund – Yugnt-Bund Tsukunft in Poyln*, New York: Unzer tsayt.

Hertz, Jacob Sholem 1950, *50 yor arbeter-ring in yidishn lebn*, New York: Natsyonaln ekzekutiv-komitet fun Arbeter-ring.

Hertz, Jacob Sholem 1952, *Hirsh Lekert*, New York: Farlag Unzer tsayt.

Hertz, Jacob Sholem 1954, *Di yidishe sotsyalistishe bavegung in Amerike. 70 yor sotsyalistishe tetigkayt. 30 yor yidisher sotsyalistisher farband*, New York: Farlag der veker.

Hertz, Jacob Sholem (ed.) 1956, *Doyres bundistn*, Vol. 1, New York: Unzer tsayt.

Hertz, Jacob Sholem 1958, *Der Bund in bilder, 1897–1957*, New York: Unzer tsayt.

Hertz, Jacob Sholem 1962, 'Di ershte ruslender revolutsye', *Di geshikhte fun Bund*, Vol. 2, edited by Grigori Aronson and J. Sh. Hertz, New York: Unzer tsayt, pp. 7–482.

Hertz, Jacob Sholem 1968, *Doyres bundistn*, Vol. 3, New York: Unzer tsayt.

Hertz, Jacob Sholem 1969, 'The Bund's Nationality Program and Its Critics in the Russian, Polish and Austrian Socialist Movements', *YIVO Annual of Jewish Social Sciences* 14, pp. 53–67.

Herzberg, Julia 2007, 'Autobiographik als historische Quelle in "Ost" und "West"', *Vom Wir zum Ich. Individuum und Autobiographik im Zarenreich*, edited by Julia Herzberg Christoph Schmidt, Cologne: Böhlau, pp. 15–62.

Herzberg, Julia 2010, 'Onkel Vanjas Hütte. Leibeigenschaft in der bäuerlichen Autobiografik des Zarenreiches', *Jahrbücher für Geschichte Osteuropas* 58, pp. 24–51.

Herzberg, Julia 2013, *Gegenarchive: bäuerliche Autobiographik zwischen Zarenreich und Sowjetunion*, Bielefeld: Transcript.

Herzberg, Julia and Christoph Schmidt (eds.) 2007, *Vom Wir zum Ich. Individuum und Autobiographik im Zarenreich*, Cologne: Böhlau.

Hetmeier, Maria 1996, *Französische Arbeitermemoiren im 19 Jahrhundert: Zeugnisse einer anderen Kultur*, Münster: Lit.

Hilbrenner, Anke 2008, 'Gewalt als Sprache der Straße: Terrorismus und seine Räume im Zarenreich vor 1917', *Jenseits der Zarenmacht. Dimensionen des Politischen im Russischen Reich 1800–1917*, edited by Walter Sperling, *Historische Politikforschung* 16, Frankfurt am Main: Campus, pp. 409–32.

Hildermeier, Manfred 2000 [1978], *The Russian Socialist Revolutionary Party Before the First World War*, New York: St. Martin's Press.

Hingley, Ronald 1970, *The Russian Secret Police*, London: Hutchinson.

Hobsbawm, Eric J. 1959, *Primitive Rebels. Studies in Archaic Forms of Social Movements in the 19th and 20th Centuries*, Manchester: Manchester University Press.

Hobsbawm, Eric J. and George Rudé 1968, *Captain Swing*, New York: Pantheon Books.

Hödl, Klaus 1991, *'Vom Shtetl an die Lower East Side', Galizische Juden in New York*, Vienna et al.: Böhlau.

Hoerder, Dirk 2002, *Cultures in Contact. World Migrations in the Second Millennium*, Durham, NC: Duke University Press.

Hoffman, Benzion [Zivion] 1910, 'Der arbeter ring un zeyne kultur-oyfgabn', *Suvenir. Der tsenter yerlikher konvenshon gevidmet*, New York: Arbeter ring, pp. 167–87.

Hoffman, Benzion [Zivion] (ed.) 1941, *Toyznt yor Pinsk. Geshikhte fun der shtot, der yidisher yishuv, institutsyes, sotsyale bavegungen, perzenlekhkeytn, gezelshaftlekhe tuer, pinsk iber der velt*, New York: Pinsker brentsh 210 Arbeter-ring.

Hofmeester, Katrin 1990, 'The Jewish Workers' Movement in the Russian Empire', *The Formation of Labour Movements, 1870–1914: An International Perspective*, edited by Marcel van der Linden and Jürgen Rojahn, Leiden et al.: Brill, pp. 473–84.

Hofmeister, Alexis 2008a, 'Pogrom und Politik: Gewalt, Kommunikation und die Neuausrichtung jüdischer Erwartungshorizonte im Zarenreich', *Jenseits der Zarenmacht. Dimensionen des Politischen im Russischen Reich 1800–1917*, edited by Walter Sperling, *Historische Politikforschung* 16, Frankfurt am Main: Campus, pp. 375–407.

Hofmeister, Alexis 2008b, 'Vernunftjudentum: Die Figur des ostjüdischen Intellektuellen und der Geist der Aufklärung', *Orte eigener Vernunft. Europäische Aufklärung jenseits der Zentren*, edited by Alexander Kraus and Andreas Renner, Frankfurt am Main, New York: Campus, pp. 158–77.

Hofstadter, Richard 1956, *The Age of Reform, From Bryan to FDR*, New York: Knopf.

Holquist, Peter 2002, *Making War, Forging Revolution. Russia's Continuum of Crisis, 1914–1921*, Cambridge, MA: Harvard University Press.

Horn, Yosef 1936, 'Fun Bontshe Sheyg biz Hirsh Lekert. Tsum 39-tn yubiley fun "Bund"', *Argentiner lebn* 7, p. 3.

Horowitz, Brian 2009, *Jewish Philanthropy and Enlightenment in Late-Tsarist Russia*, Seattle, WA: University of Washington Press.

Horowitz, Irving Louis 1962, 'The Jewish Community of Buenos Aires', *Jewish Social Studies* 24, no. 4, pp. 195–222.

Horowitz, Joel and Sibila Seibert 1984, 'Ideologias sindicales y politicas estatales en la Argentina, 1930–1943', *Desarrollo Económico* 24, no. 94, pp. 275–96.

Howe, Irving 1976, *World of Our Fathers*, New York: Harcourt Brace Jovanovich.

Huber, Valeska 2012, 'Connecting Colonial Seas: The "International Colonisation" of Port Said and the Suez Canal During and After the First World War', *European Review of History* 19, no. 1, pp. 141–61.

Hunt, Scott A. and Robert D. Benford 2004, 'Collective Identity, Solidarity, and Commitment', *The Blackwell Companion to Social Movements*, edited by David A. Snow, Sarah Anne Soule and Hanspeter Kriesi, Malden, MA, Oxford, Victoria: Blackwell, pp. 433–58.

Hurevitsh, Yakob 1916, 'Vegen asimilatsye un shovinizm', *Der avangard*, Buenos Aires 1, second run, no. 11 (November), pp. 11–15.

Hyman, Paula E. 2000, 'Two Models of Modernization: Jewish Women in the German and Russian Empires', *Studies in Contemporary Jewry* XVI, pp. 39–53.

Ibsch, Elrud 2004, *Die Shoa erzählt: Zeugnis und Experiment in der Literatur*, Tübingen: Max Niemeyer.

Ipsen, Detlef 2002, 'Die Kultur der Orte. Ein Beitrag zur sozialen Strukturierung des städtischen Raumes', *Die Differenzierung des Städtischen*, edited by Martina Löw, Opladen: Leske + Budrich, pp. 233–45.

Irwin, Theodore 1940, *Inside the 'Christian Front'*, American Council of Public Affairs.

Jacobs, Jack 1993, *On Socialists and The Jewish Question After Marx*, New York: NYU Press.

Jacobs, Jack 1996, 'A friend in need: The Jewish Labor Committee and refugees from the German-speaking lands, 1933–1945', *YIVO Annual* 23, pp. 391–417.

Jacobs, Jack 2001, 'Creating a Bundist Counter-Culture. Morgnshtern and the Significance of Cultural Hegemony', *Jewish Politics in Eastern Europe. The Bund at 100*, edited by Jack Jacobs, New York: NYU Press, pp. 59–68.

Jacobs, Jack 2005, 'Bundist Anti-Zionism in Interwar Poland', *Tel Aviver Jahrbuch für deutsche Geschichte* 33, pp. 239–59.

Jacobs, Jack 2006, 'The Role of Women in the Bund', *Jewish Women. A Comprehensive Historical Encyclopedia*, edited by Paula E. Hyman, Jerusalem: Shalvi Publishing, jwa.org/encyclopedia/article/bund (last accessed 3 February 2019).

Jacobs, Jack 2007, 'Ab Cahan and the Polish Bund', presented at the conference *Abraham Cahan and the Forverts*, CUNY, New York, 15 April.

Jacobs, Jack 2009, *Bundist Counterculture in Interwar Poland*, Syracuse, NY: Syracuse University Press.

Jacobs, Jack 2010, 'Eulogy for Motl Zelmanowicz', www.bundism.net/info020 (last accessed 7 December 2010).

Jacobs, Jack 2013, 'The Bund in Vilna, 1918–1939', *POLIN* 25, pp. 263–92.

Jacobs, Jack and Gertrud Pickhan (eds.) 2013, 'New Research on the Bund', *East European Jewish Affairs* 43, no. 3.

Jacobs, James B. 2006, *Mobsters, Unions, and Feds: The Mafia and the American Labor Movement*, New York: New York University Press.

Jancke, Gabriele 2002, *Autobiographie als soziale Praxis. Beziehungskonzepte in Selbstzeugnissen des 15. und 16. Jahrhunderts im deutschsprachigen Raum*, Cologne, Weimar, Vienna: Böhlau.

Jenks, Jeremiah W. and Jett Lauck 1912, *The Immigration Problem*, New York: Funk & Wagnalls.

Joas, Hans 1996 [1992], *The Creativity of Action*, translated by Jeremy Gaines and Paul Keast, Cambridge: Polity.

Johnpoll, Bernard K. 1967, *The Politics of Futility. The General Jewish Workers Bund of Poland 1917–1943*, Ithaca, NY: Cornell University Press.

Johnson, Jeffrey A. 2008, *'They Are All Red Out Here'. Socialist Politics In the Pacific Northwest*, Norman, OK: University of Oklahoma Press.

Joseph, Samuel 1914, *Jewish Immigration to the United States from 1881 to 1910*, New York: Columbia University Press.

Judge, Edward H. 1992, *Easter in Kishinev. Anatomy of a Pogrom. Reappraisals in Jewish Social and Intellectual History*, New York: New York University Press.

Kadar, Marlene 1992, *Essays on Life Writing: From Genre to Critical Practice*, Toronto: University of Toronto Press.

Kadar, Naomi Prawer 2007, *Far di kinders vegn: Yiddish Periodicals for American Children, 1917–1950*, PhD dissertation, Columbia University.

Kangisser Cohen, Sharon 2010, 'Survivors of the Holocaust and Their Children', *Journal of Modern Jewish Studies* 9, no. 2, pp. 165–83.

Kantorovitsh-Gilinksi, Lyuba 1971, 'Der film "mir kumen on"', *Medem-sanatorye-bukh*, edited by Khayim Solomon Kazdan, Tel Aviv: Hamenora, pp. 174–8.

Kantorowicz, Ernst 1997, *The King's Two Bodies*, Princeton, NJ: Princeton University Press.

Kaplan Appel, Tamar 2005, 'Esther Frumkin', *Jewish Women. A Comprehensive Historical Encyclopedia*, Jewish Women's Archive, jwa.org/encyclopedia/article/frumkin-esther (last accessed 28 February 2017).

Kappeler, Andreas 2014 [1992], *The Russian Empire: A Multi-Ethnic History*, translated by Alfred Clayton, London: Routledge.

Karson, Marc 1958, *American Labor Unions and Politics, 1900–1918*, Carbondale, IL: Southern Illinois University Press.

Kastner, Jens 2007, *Transnationale Guerilla. Aktivismus, Kunst und die kommende Gemeinschaft*, Münster: Unrast.

Kats, Moshe 1946, 'Areynfir', *Shturmedike yorn, von Aaron Gorelik*, New York: IKUF pp. 7–11.

Katz, Daniel 2000, 'Race, Gender and Labor Education. ILGWU Locals 22 and 91, 1933–1937', *Labor's Heritage* 11, no. 1, pp. 4–19.

Katz, Daniel 2003, *A Union of Many Cultures. Yiddish Socialism and Interracial Organizing in International Ladies Garment Workers Union, 1913–1914*, PhD dissertation, Rutgers University.

Katz, Daniel 2011, *All Together Different: Yiddish Socialists, Garment Workers, and the Labor Roots of Multiculturalism*, New York: New York University Press.

Katz, Daniel 2016, 'The Key to Bernie Sanders's Appeal Isn't Socialism, It's Yiddish Socialism', *The Forward*, 14 February, www.forward.com/opinion/333489/the-key-to-bernie-sanderss-appeal-isnt-socialism-its-yiddish-socialism (last accessed 25 September 2019).

Katz, Jacob 1973, *Out of the Ghetto. The Social Background of Jewish Emancipation, 1770–1870*, Cambridge, MA: Harvard University Press.

Katz, Jacob 1987, *Toward Modernity: The European Jewish Model*, New York: Transaction Publishers.

Katz, Pinie 1927, 'Der bankrot fun yidishizm', *Nayvelt*, Buenos Aires 1, no. 5, pp. 18–20.

Kautsky, Karl 1906, 'Alte un naye revolutsyonen', *Der veker*, Vilnius 1 (3 January), p. 3f.

Kazdan, Khayim Solomon (ed.) 1932, 'Yidish un nokh "epes"', *Unzer shul*, New York 2, no. 4, pp. 3–8.

Kazdan, Khayim Solomon 1945, 'Der "bund" un der gedank vegn a yidish-veltlekher shul', *Unzer tsayt*, New York 7, pp. 39–41.

Kazdan, Khayim Solomon 1947, *Di geshikhte fun yidishn shulvezn in umophengikn Poyln*, Mexico: Geselshaft 'kultur un hilf'.

Kazdan, Khayim Solomon (ed.) 1952, *Lerer-Yizkher-Bukh*, New York: Komitet tsu faraeybikn dem ondenk fun di umgekumene lerer fun di TSYSHO shuln in Poyln.

Kazdan, Khayim Solomon 1956, *Fun kheder un 'shkoles' biz tsysho. Dos ruslendishe yidntum in gerangl far shul, sprakh, kultur*, Mexico: Shloyme Mendelson Fond.

Kazdan, Khayim Solomon 1962, *Mentshn fun gayst un mut*, Buenos Aires: Yidbukh.

Kazdan, Khayim Solomon 1971, *Medem-sanatorye-bukh*, Tel Aviv: Hamenora.

Kazin, Alfred 1979 [1949], *A Walker in the City*, Orlando, FL: Harcourt.

Kenneally, James J. 1973, 'Women and Trade Unions 1870–1920: The Quandary of the Reformer', *Labor History* 14, no. 1, pp. 42–55.

Kern, Thomas 2008, *Soziale Bewegungen. Ursachen, Wirkungen, Mechanismen*, Wiesbaden: VS.

Kessler-Harris, Alice 2003 [1982], *Out of Work. A History of Wage-Earning Women in the United States*, New York: Oxford University Press.

Keßler, Mario 1994, 'Parteiorganisation und nationale Frage – Lenin und der jüdische Arbeiterbund 1903–1914', *Lenin – Theorie und Praxis in historischer Perspektive*, edited by Theodor Bergmann, Mainz: Decaton, pp. 219–31.

Khagram, Sanjeev and Peggy Levitt 2008, 'Constructing Transnational Studies', *The*

Transnational Studies Reader: Intersections and Innovations, edited by Sanjeev Khagram and Peggy Levitt, New York and London: Routledge, pp. 1–18.

Khanin, N. 1938, *Berele*, New York: Kinder-Ring.

Kheifets, Viktor L. and Lazar Kheifets 2009, 'Die Komintern und Argentinien in den Jahren 1919–1922. Die Kommunistische Partei Argentiniens gegen die "argentinischen Lenins"', *International Newsletter of Communist Studies* 22, pp. 137–47.

King, Anthony 1969, 'Political Parties in Western Democracies: Some Sceptical Reflections', *Polity* 2, no. 2, pp. 111–41.

King, Francis (ed.) 2007, *The Narodniks in the Russian Revolution. Russia's Socialist-Revolutionaries in 1917*, London: Socialist History Society.

Kittner, Michael 2005, *Arbeitskampf. Geschichte, Recht, Gegenwart*, Munich: C.H. Beck.

Kłanska, Maria 1994, *Aus dem Schtetl in die Welt. Ostjüdische Autobiographien in deutscher Sprache, 1772–1938*, Cologne: Böhlau.

Kleinmann, Yvonne 2006, *Neue Orte – neue Menschen: Jüdische Lebensformen in St. Petersburg und Moskau im 19. Jahrhundert*, Göttingen: Vandenhoeck & Ruprecht.

Kleinschmidt, Harald 2003, *People on the Move. Attitudes Toward and Perceptions of Migration in Medieval and Modern Europe*, Westport, CT: Praeger.

Kleist, Olaf J. 2010, 'Grenzen der Erinnerung: Methoden des Vergangenheitsbezugs und ihre Implikationen für Migrationspolitik', *Migration und Erinnerung: Konzepte und Methoden der Forschung*, edited by Elisabeth Boesen and Fabienne Lentz, Berlin and Münster: Lit, pp. 223–55.

Klenner, Jost Phillipp 2009, 'Vom Titel, der nicht stirbt. Ernst Kantorowicz auf eine Formel gebracht', *Die Kunst der Geschichte. Historiographie, Ästhetik, Erzählung*, edited by Martin Baumeister, Moritz Föllmer and Philipp Müller, Göttingen: Vandenhoeck & Ruprecht, pp. 125–41.

Klier, John D. 1992, 'The Pogrom Paradigm in Russian History', *Pogroms: Anti-Jewish Violence in Modern Russian History*, edited by John D. Klier and Shlomo Lambroza, Cambridge: Cambridge University Press, pp. 13–38.

Klier, John D. 1996, 'Emigration Mania in Late Imperial Russia. Legend and Reality', *Patterns of Migration 1850–1914*, edited by Audrey Newman and Stephen W. Massil, London: Jewish Historical Society of England, pp. 21–30.

Klier, John D. 2002, 'Christians and Jews and the "Dialogue of Violence" in Late Imperial Russia', *Religious Violence between Christians and Jews. Medieval Roots, Modern Perspectives*, edited by Anna S. Abulafia, Houndmills: Palgrave, pp. 157–72.

Klier, John D. and Shlomo Lambroza (eds.) 1992, *Pogroms: Anti-Jewish Violence in Modern Russian History*, Cambridge: Cambridge University Press.

Kliger, Hannah 1998, 'Communication and Ethnic Identity in Jewish Community: The Role of Voluntary Association', *The Huddled Masses. Communication and Migration*, edited by Gary Gumpert and Susan J. Drucker, Cresskill, NJ: Hampton, pp. 221–39.

Kligsberg, Moshe 1974, *Di yidishe yugent-bavegung in Poyln tsvishen beyde velt-milkhomes. A sotsyologishe shtudye*, New York: YIVO.

Kling, Lazar 1917, 'Kooperatsyon un di sotsyalistishe bavegung', *Der avangard*, Buenos Aires 2, second run, no. 14 (February), pp. 55–60.

Knapheyt, Moshe (ed.) 1972, 'A blik oyf tsurik', *Yubeley shrift. 40 yor fun der 'geszelshaft far yidish-veltlekhe shuln in Argentine', 1932–1972*, Buenos Aires, p. 13 ff., p. 27.

Kobrin, Rebecca 2006, 'Rewriting the Diaspora: Images of Eastern Europe in the Bialystok Landsmanshaft Press, 1921–45', *Jewish Social Studies* 12, no. 3, pp. 1–38.

Kobrin, Rebecca 2010, *Jewish Białystok and Its Diaspora*, Bloomington, IN: Indiana University Press.

Kocka, Jürgen 1990, *Arbeitsverhältnisse und Arbeiterexistenzen. Grundlagen der Klassenbildung im 19. Jahrhundert*, Bonn: Dietz.

Koenker, Diane P. 2005, *Republic of Labor, Russian Printers and Soviet Socialism, 1918–1930*, Ithaca, NY and London: Cornell University Press.

Kohen, Yesir 1952, 'Bey aleksandern in kreyzl', *Arkadi. Zamlbukh tsum ondenk fun Arkadi Kremer*, New York: Unzer tsayt, p. 145 f.

Köhler, Bettina and Markus Wissen 2003, 'Globalizing Protest. Urban Conflicts and the Global Social Movements', *International Journal of Urban and Regional Research* 27, no. 4, pp. 942–51.

Kohn, Ahron 1909, 'Di bundisten un di amerikaner sotsyalistishe parteyn. An entfer tsu genosn Zivion', *Der yidishe arbeyter* (8 October).

Koller, Christian 2009, *Streikkultur. Performanzen und Diskurse des Arbeitskampfes im schweizerisch-österreichischen Vergleich (1860–1950)*, Vienna, Berlin, Münster: Lit.

Konrad, Helmut 1994, 'Arbeiterbewegung und bürgerliche Öffentlichkeit. Kultur und nationale Frage in der Habsburgermonarchie', *Geschichte und Gesellschaft* 20, pp. 506–18.

Kormann, Eva 2004, *Ich, Welt und Gott. Autobiographik im 17. Jahrhundert*, Cologne, Vienna, Weimar: Böhlau.

Kossovski, Vladimir 1942, 'Zubatov "likvidirt dem bund"', *Arkadi. Zamlbukh tsum ondenk fun Arkadi Kremer*, New York: Unzer tsayt, pp. 175–201.

Kozłowska, Magdalena 2014, '"In Sunshine and Joy"? The Story of Medem Sanatorium in Miedzeszyn', *East European Politics and Societies* 28, no. 1, pp. 49–62.

Kraut, Alan M. 1995, *Silent Travelers: Germs, Genes, and the 'Immigrant Menace'*, Baltimore, MD: Johns Hopkins University Press.

Kubik, Jan 1994, *The Power of Symbols Against the Symbols of Power. The Rise of Solidarity and the Fall of State Socialism in Poland*, Philadelphia, PA: Pennsylvania State University Press.

Kuhn, Axel 1982, 'Die proletarische Familie. Wie Arbeiter in ihren Lebenserinnerungen über den Ehealltag berichten', *Arbeiteralltag in Stadt und Land. Neue Wege der Geschichtsschreibung*, edited by Heiko Haumann, Berlin: Argument, pp. 89–119.

Kuhn, Rick 1998, 'Organizing Yiddish-Speaking Workers in Pre-World War Galicia: The Jewish Socialist Democratic Party', *Studies in Jewish Civilization* 9, pp. 37–63.

Kurski, Franz et al. (eds.) 1939, *Di yidishe sotsyalistsishe bavegung biz der grindung fun 'bund': Forshungen, zikhroynes, materialn*, Paris and Vilnius: YIVO.

Lainer-Vos, Dan 2012, *Sinews of the Nation: Constructing Irish and Zionist Bonds in the United States*, Cambridge: Polity Press.

Lambroza, Shlomo 1981, 'Jewish Self-Defence during the Russian Pogroms of 1903–1906', *The Jewish Journal of Sociology* 22, no. 2, pp. 123–33.

Lambroza, Shlomo 1992, 'The Pogroms of 1903–1906', *Pogroms: Anti-Jewish Violence in Modern Russian History*, edited by John D. Klier and Shlomo Lambroza, Cambridge: Cambridge University Press, pp. 195–247.

Lambroza, Shlomo and John D. Klier 1992, 'The Pogroms of 1991–1884', *Pogroms: Anti-Jewish Violence in Modern Russian History*, edited by John D. Klier and Shlomo Lambroza, Cambridge: Cambridge University Press, pp. 39–42.

Landesco, John 1968 [1929], *Organized Crime in Chicago. Pt. III of the Illinois Crime Survey*, Chicago, IL: University of Chicago Press.

Laslett, John H.M. 1967, 'Socialism and the American Labor Movement. Some New Reflections', *Labor History* 8, no. 2, pp. 136–55.

Latour, Bruno 1986, 'The powers of association', *Power, Action and Belief. A New Sociology of Knowledge?*, edited by John Law, London: Routledge & Kegan Paul, pp. 264–80.

Latour, Bruno 1993 [1991], *We Have Never Been Modern*, translated by Catherine Porter, New York: Harvard University Press.

Latour, Bruno 1999, *Pandora's Hope. Essays on the Reality of Science Studies*, Cambridge and London: Harvard University Press.

Latour, Bruno 2007 [2005], *Reassembling the Social. An Introduction to Actor-Network-Theory*, Oxford and New York: Oxford University Press.

Laubstein, Israel 1997, *Bund. Historia del Movimiento Obrero Judío*, Buenos Aires: Acervo.

Lederhendler, Eli 1989, *The Road to Modern Jewish Politics: Political Tradition and Political Reconstruction in the Jewish Community of Tsarist Russia*, Oxford: Oxford University Press.

Lederhendler, Eli 1997, *Jewish Responses to Modernity: New Voices in America and Eastern Europe*, New York: New York University Press.

Lederhendler, Eli 2009, *Jewish Immigrants and American Capitalism, 1880–1920: From Caste to Class*, Cambridge: Cambridge University Press.

Leff, Lisa Moses 2002, 'Jewish Solidarity in Nineteenth-Century France: The Evolution of a Concept', *Journal of Modern History* 74, no. 1, pp. 33–61.

Lehmann, Frauke and Norbert Meyerhöfer 2003, '"Wünsche mir, dass es irgendwann so kracht wie früher" – Der Revolutionäre 1. Mai als linksradikales Ritual', *Berlin, 1*.

Mai 2002. Politische Demonstrationsrituale, edited by Dieter Rucht, Opladen: Leske + Budrich, pp. 55–100.

Leiserson, William M. 1969 [1924], *Adjusting Immigrant and Industry*, New York: Arno.

Leivick, Hodem [Leivick Haplern] 1940, 'Di keytn fun meshiakh', *Ale verk fun H. Leyvik*, 2, New York: Posy-Shoulson Press, pp. 393–417.

Lejeune, Philipp 2005 [1975], *Der autobiographische Pakt*, second printing, Frankfurt am Main: Suhrkamp.

Lenin, Vladimir I. 1977a [1902], 'What Is to Be Done? Burning Questions of Our Movement', *Collected Works*, Vol. 5, Moscow: Progress Publishers, pp. 347–520.

Lenin, Vladimir I. 1977b [1913], 'Critical Remarks on the National Question', *Collected Works*, Vol. 20, Moscow: Progress Publishers, pp. 17–51.

Lens, Sidney 1949, *Left, Right and Center: Conflicting Forces in American Labor*, Hinsdale, IL: Regnery.

Léon, Abraham 1971 [1946], *The Jewish Question. A Marxist Interpretation*, translated by George Weissman, New York: Pathfinder.

Leonard, Oscar 1917, 'The East St. Louis Pogrom', *The Survey* 38, p. 331 ff.

Lesser, Jeffrey and Raanan Rein 2008, 'New Approaches to Ethnicity and Diaspora in Twentieth-Century Latin America', *Rethinking Jewish-Latin Americans*, edited by Jeffrey Lesser and Raanan Rein, Albequerque, NM: University of Mexico Press, pp. 23–40.

Lestchinsky, Jacob 1960, 'Jewish Migrations, 1840–1956', *The Jews. Their History, Culture and Religion*, edited by Louis Finkelstein, New York: The Jewish Publication Society of America, pp. 1536–96.

Levin, Nora 1977, *While Messiah Tarried. Jewish Socialist Movements, 1871–1917*, New York: Schocken.

Levine, Louis 1924, *The Women's Garment Workers: A History of the International Ladies' Garment Workers Union*, New York: Huebsch.

Levine, Robert M. 1993, *Tropical Diaspora: The Jewish Experience in Cuba*, Gainesville, FL: University Press of Florida.

Lewin, Boleslao 1971, *Cómo Fue La Inmigración Judía a La Argentina*, Buenos Aires: Plus Ultra.

Lewis, Daniel K. 2001, *The History of Argentina*, Westport, CT: Greenwood Press.

Libman, P. 1908, 'Tsu der taktik fun dem proletarishn kamf', *Der avangard*, Buenos Aires 1, no. 5 (December), pp. 4–11.

Libnyan, P. 1909, 'Rabbinismus Militans', *Der avangard*, Buenos Aires 2, no. 9, pp. 4–7.

Liebman, Arthur 1979, *Jews and the Left*, New York: John Wiley & Sons.

Liesin, A. 1904, 'Ahin erhoyb sikh vayt, mayn zeele', *Der fraynd fun bund. Gevidmet tsu di fraynd fun 'bund', voz velen bezukhen dem ball in grand tsentral peles* (2 April), p. 1.

Light, Ivan Hubert and Parminder Bhachu 1993, *Immigration and Entrepreneurship: Culture, Capital, and Ethnic Networks*, New Jersey: Transaction Publishers.

Lih, Lars T. 2006, *Lenin Rediscovered. What Is To Be Done? in Context*, Leiden: Brill.
Liliput 1909, 'Di S.L. P., di S.P. un der "Bund"', *Der arbeyter*.
Lindemann, Albert S. 1991, *The Jew Accused. Three Anti-Semitic Affairs (Dreyfus, Beilis, Frank), 1894–1915*, Cambridge and London: Cambridge University Press.
Linden, A. (ed.) 1910, *Die Judenpogrome in Russland. Herausgegeben im Auftrag des Zionistischen Hilfsfonds in London von der zur Erforschung der Pogrome eingesetzten Kommission*, two volumes, Cologne and Leipzig: Jüdischer Verlag.
van der Linden, Marcel 1999, 'Transnationalizing American Labor History', *The Journal of American History* 86, no. 3, pp. 1078–92.
van der Linden, Marcel 2003, *Transnational Labour History. Explorations*, Aldershot: Ashgate Publishing.
van der Linden, Marcel 2006, 'Transnationale Arbeitergeschichte', *Transnationale Geschichte: Themen, Tendenzen und Theorien*, edited by Gunilla-Friederike Budde, Sebastian Conrad and Oliver Janz, Göttingen: Vandenhoeck & Ruprecht, pp. 265–74.
Linfield, Harry S. 1933, *Jewish Migration. Jewish Migration as a Part of World Migration Movements, 1920–1930*, New York: Jewish Statistical Bureau.
Linfield, Harry S. 1945, 'Statistics of Jews', *American Jewish Year Book* 46, edited for the American Jewish Committee by Harry Schneiderman, pp. 490–519.
Lipphardt, Anna 2004, '"Vilne, Vilne, unzer heymshtot ...": Imagining Jewish Vilna in New York. The Zamlbukh Project of Vilner Branch 367 Arbeter Ring/Workmen's Circle', *Jüdische Kulturen im Neuen Europa. Wilna 1918–1939*, edited by Marina Dmitrieva and Heidemarie Petersen, Wiesbaden: Harrassowitz, pp. 85–97.
Lipphardt, Anna 2010, *Vilne. Die Juden aus Vilnius nach dem Holocaust. Eine transnationale Beziehungsgeschichte*, Paderborn, Munich, Vienna, Zurich: Ferdinand Schöningh.
Lipset, Seymour M. and Gary Marks 2000, *It Didn't Happen Here. Why Socialism Failed in the United States*, New York: Norton.
Litvak, A. 1908, 'Notitsn', *Der tog*, Vilnius 5 (October), p. 1.
Litvak, A. and I.B. Salutski 1917, 'Der ershter numer "arbeter shtime"', *Dos revolutsyonere rusland*, edited by I.B. Salutski and A. Litvak, New York: Yidishe sotsyalistishe federatsye in Amerike.
Liulevicius, Vejas G. 2000, *War Land on the Eastern Front. Culture, National Identity and German Occupation in World War I*, Cambridge: Cambridge University Press.
Ves Losada, Alfredo E. 1917, *Inmigración en la República Argentina. Breve estudio de caracter historico, consticional y estadistico*, PhD dissertation, Universidad nacional de La Plata. Facultad de ciencias jurídicas y sociales.
Lowenthal, Max 1950, *The Federal Bureau of Investigation*, New York: Sloane.
Löw, Martina 2016 [2000], *The Sociology of Space*, translated by Donald Goodwin, London: Palgrave MacMillan.
Löwy, Michael 1992, *Redemption and Utopia. Jewish Libertarian Thought in Central*

Europe: A Study in Elective Affinity, translated by Hope Heaney, Stanford, CA: Stanford University Press.

Lucassen, Jan and Leo Lucassen 2004, 'Alte Paradigmen und neue Perspektiven in der Migrationsgeschichte', *Über die trockene Grenze und Über das offene Meer: Binneneuropäische und transatlantische Migrationen im Vergleich*, edited by Mathias Beer and Dittmar Dahlmann, Essen: Klartext, pp. 17–44.

Luhmann, Niklas 1995 [1984], *Social Systems*, translated by John Bendarz, Jr with Dirk Baecker, Stanford, CA: Stanford University Press.

Luhmann, Niklas 2013 [2002], *Introduction to Systems Theory*, edited by Dirk Baecker and translated by Peter Gilgen, Cambridge: Polity.

Lumpkins, Charles L. 2008, *American Pogrom. The East St. Louis Race Riot and Black Politics*, Athens, OH: Ohio University Press.

Luxemburg, Rosa 1982 [1919], 'Die Maifeier im Zeichen des Wahlrechtskampfes', *Der 1. Mai. Kampftag der Arbeiterklasse*, Berlin: Verlag Neuer Kurs, pp. 17–20.

Mahla, Daniel 2010, 'Between Socialism and Jewish Tradition: Bundist Holiday Culture in Interwar Poland', *Studies in Contemporary Jewry* 24, pp. 177–92.

Malo, Markus 2009, *Behauptete Subjektivität. Eine Skizze zur deutschsprachigen jüdischen Autobiographik im 20. Jahrhundert*, Tübingen: Niemeyer.

Mannheim, Karl 1979 [1929], *Ideology and Utopia. An Introduction to the Sociology of Knowledge*, translated by Louis Wirth and Edward Shils, London and Henley: Routledge & Kegan Paul.

Manning, Patrick 2005, *Migration in World History*, New York: Routledge.

Manor, Ehud 2009, *Forward. The Jewish Daily Forward (Forverts) Newspaper. Immigrants, Socialism and Jewish Politics in New York, 1890–1917*, Brighton and Portland, OR: Sussex Academic Press.

Marcus, George E. 1995, 'Ethnography in/of the World System: The Emergence of Multi-Sited Ethnography', *Annual Review of Anthropology* 24 (1 January), pp. 95–117.

Margules, Lily M. 1999, *Memories, Memories ... From Vilna to New York with a Few Steps Along the Way, a Collection of Essays*, Anapolis, MD: ProStar Publications.

Marot, Helen 1910, 'A Woman's Strike. An Appreciation of the Shirtwaist Makers of New York', *Proceedings of the Academy of Political Science in the City of New York* 1, no. 1, pp. 119–28.

Marten-Finnis, Susanne 1999, *Sprachinseln*, Cologne, Weimar, Vienna: Böhlau.

Marten-Finnis, Susanne 2000, 'Wilna als Zentrum der jüdischen Parteiliteratur 1896 bis 1922', *Aschkenas* 10, no. 1, pp. 203–43.

Marten-Finnis, Susanne 2001, 'The Bundist Press: A Study of Political Change and the Persistence of Anachronistic Language During the Russian Period', *Jewish Politics in Eastern Europe. The Bund at 100*, edited by Jack Jacobs, New York: New York University Press, pp. 13–27.

Marten-Finnis, Susanne 2005, 'Translation as a Weapon for the Truth: The Bund's Policy of Multilingualism, 1902–1906', *POLIN* 18, pp. 337–51.

Marwell, Gerald and Pamela E. Oliver 1993, *The Critical Mass in Collective Action: A Micro-Social Theory*, Cambridge: Cambridge University Press.

Marx, Karl 1975 [1845], 'Theses on Feuerbach [Original version]', *Marx and Engels Collected Works*, Vol. 5, London: Lawrence & Wishart, pp. 3–5.

Marx, Karl and Friedrich Engels 2010 [1848], 'Manifesto of the Communist Party', *The Revolutions of 1848. Political Writings Volume 1*, London: Verso, pp. 62–98.

Mastrángelo, Mariana 2006, *Cultura Política en la Argentina. Los comunistas en la huelga de 1929 en San Francisco – Cordoba*, Buenos Aires: Imago Mundi – Facultad de Filosofía y Letras UBA.

Matshushita, Hiroshi 2006, 'El movimiento obrero socialista ante el avance del peronismo', *El pensiamento alternativo an la Argentina del siglo XX. Tomo II: Obrerismo, vanguardia, justicia social (1930–1960)*, edited by Hugo E. Biagni and Arturo A. Roig, Buenos Aires: Biblos, pp. 343–53.

Mayer, Arno J. 2002, *The Furies. Violence and Terror in the French and Russian Revolutions*, Princeton, NJ: Princeton University Press.

Mayer, Dovid 1947, 'Fun bundishn klub – biz der bundisher organisatsye in Nyu York', *Unzer tsayt*, New York 3–4, pp. 156–8.

Mayer, Dovid 1951, 'Der "bund" un Ab. Kahan', *Unzer tsayt*, New York 10, pp. 29–31.

Maynes, Mary J. 1995, *Taking the Hard Road. Life Courses in French and German Workers' Autobiographies in the Era of Industrialization*, Chapel Hill, NC: University of North Carolina Press.

Mayoraz, Sandrine 2013, 'The Jewish Labor Bund in Switzerland', *East European Jews in Switzerland*, edited by Tamar Lewinsky and Sandrine Mayoraz, Berlin: De Gruyter, pp. 54–76.

Mayoraz, Sandrine 2014, '"Wahrhaftige Festung des Bundes": der Allgemeine Jüdische Arbeiterverbund in Bern', *Wie über Wolken: jüdische Lebens- und Denkwelten in Stadt und Region Bern, 1200–2000*, Zurich: Chronos, pp. 223–40.

McAdam, Doug, John D. McCarthy and Mayer N. Zald 1988, 'Social Movements', *Handbook of Sociology*, edited by Neil J. Smelser, Newbury Park, Beverly Hills, London, New Delhi: Sage, pp. 695–737.

McAdam, Doug 1986, 'Recruitment to High-Risk Activism: The Case of Freedom Summer', *American Journal of Sociology* 92, no. 1, pp. 64–90.

McAdam, Doug and Richard W. Scott 2005, 'Organizations and Movements', *Social Movements and Organization Theory*, edited by Gerald Fredrick Davis, Doug McAdam, Richard W. Scott and Mayer N. Zald, Cambridge: Cambridge University Press, pp. 4–40.

McAdam, Doug, Sidney George Tarrow and Charles Tilly 2001, *Dynamics of Contention*, Cambridge: Cambridge University Press.

McClurg Mueller, Carol 1992, 'Building Social Movement Theory', *Frontiers in Social Movement Theory*, edited by Carol McClurg Mueller, New Haven and London: Yale University Press, pp. 3–25.

McGlothlin, Erin H. 2003, '"Im eigenen Hause" ... "vom eigenen Ich". Holocaust Autobiography and the Quest for "Heimat" and Self', *Erinnerte Shoa. Die Literatur des Überlebenden. The Shoa Remembered. Literature of Survivors*, edited by Walter Schmitz, Dresden: Thelem, pp. 91–119.

McKeown, Adam 2001, *Chinese Migrant Networks and Cultural Change: Peru, Chicago, Hawaii, 1900–1936*, Chicago, IL: University of Chicago Press.

McKeown, Adam 2004, 'Global Migration 1846–1940', *Journal of World History* 15, no. 2, pp. 155–89.

McKeown, Adam 2007, 'Periodizing Globalization', *History Workshop Journal* 63, no. 1, pp. 218–30.

McLuhan, Marshall and Quentin Fiore 1967, *The Medium Is the Message. An Inventory of Effects*, New York: Bantam.

Medem, Gina 1936, *Dos kind in der velt*, Buenos Aires: Kinder Bibliotek. Aroysgegebn funem Farband fun yidishe folks-shuln in Argentine.

Medem, Vladimir 1979, *The Life and the Soul of a Legendary Jewish Socialist*, translated and edited by Samuel A Portnoy, New York: Ktav.

Mehring, Franz 1906, 'A yor fun revolutsye', *Der veker*, Vilnius 7 (14 January), p. 2 f.

Melancon, Michael S. 2006, *The Lena Goldfields Massacre and the Crisis of the Late Tsarist State*, College Station, TX: Texas A&M University Press.

Melucci, Alberto 1988, 'Social Movements and the Democratization of Everyday Life', *Civil Society and the State*, edited by J. Keane, London: Verso, pp. 245–60.

Melucci, Alberto 2003 [1995], 'The Process of Collective Identity', *Social Movements and Culture*, edited by Hank Johnston and Bert Klandermans, Oxford: Routledge, pp. 41–63.

Mendel, Hersh 1989 [1959], *Memoirs of a Jewish Revolutionary*, translated by Robert Michaels, London: Pluto.

Mendelsohn, Ezra 1965, 'Worker Opposition in the Russian Jewish Socialist Movement, From the 1890s to 1903', *International Review of Social History* 10, pp. 268–82.

Mendelsohn, Ezra 1970, *Class Struggle in the Pale. The Formative Years of the Jewish Workers' Movement in Tsarist Russia*, Cambridge: Cambridge University Press.

Mendelsohn, Ezra 1976, 'The Russian Roots of the American Jewish Labor Movement', *YIVO Annual of Jewish Social Science* 16, pp. 150–77.

Mendelsohn, Ezra 1993, *On Modern Jewish Politics*, New York: Oxford University Press.

Merridale, Catherine 2002 [2000], *Nights of Stone. Death and Memory in Russia*, New York: Penguin.

Meyer, Michael A. 1995, *Response to Modernity: A History of the Reform Movement in Judaism*, Detroit: Wayne State University Press.

Meyer, Michael A. 2001, *Judaism Within Modernity: Essays on Jewish History and Religion*, Detroit: Wayne State University Press.

Michels, Tony 2000, 'Socialism and the Writing of American Jewish History: World of Our Fathers Revisited', *American Jewish History* 88, no. 4, pp. 521–46.

Michels, Tony 2005, *A Fire in Their Hearts. Yiddish Socialists in New York*, Cambridge, MA and London: Harvard University Press.

Michels, Tony 2009, 'Exporting Yiddish Socialism: New York's Role in the Russian Workers' Movement', *Jewish Social Studies* 16, no. 1, pp. 1–26.

Mikhed'ko, Vladimir 1998, 'Gomel'skii pogrom 1903 goda: Etnicheskii konflikt ili grazhdanhskiia voina?', *Evrei Belarusi*, no. 3–4, pp. 35–48.

Miller, Sally M. 1971, 'The Socialist Party and the Negro, 1901–20', *The Journal of Negro History* 56, no. 3, pp. 220–9.

Milman, Henry Hart 1836, *The History of the Jews. From the Earliest Period to the Present Time*, Vol. 3, New York: Harper & Brothers.

Milner, A. 1942, 'In vilner lerer-seminar', *Arkadi. Zamlbukh tsum ondenk fun Arkadi Kremer*, New York: Unzer tsayt, p. 254 f.

Minczeles, Henri 1995, *Histoire générale du Bund, un mouvement révolutionnaire juif*, Paris: Austral.

Mirelman, Victor A. 1990, *Jewish Buenos Aires. In Search of an Identity*, Detroit: Wayne State University Press.

Mirelman, Victor A. 2005, 'Buenos Aires Pogroms (1910, 1919)', *Antisemitism. A Historical Encyclopedia of Prejudice and Persecution*, Vol. 1, edited by Richard S. Levy, Santa Barbara, CA: ABC-CLIO, p. 88 f.

Mishinsky, Moshe 1969, 'Regional Factors in the Formation of the Jewish Labor Movement in Czarist Russia', *YIVO Annual of Jewish Social Sciences* 14, pp. 27–52.

Mitchell, Win 1966, 'John Barnes Nicholson: N.S.W. Southern Miners' Labour Members 1891–1917', *Labour History* 10, pp. 13–19.

Moch, Leslie Page 2003, *Moving Europeans: Migration in Western Europe Since 1650*, second edition, Bloomington, IN: Indiana University Press.

Möller, Silke 2001, *Zwischen Wissenschaft und 'Burschenherrlichkeit'. Studentische Sozialisation im deutschen Kaiserreich, 1871–1914*, Stuttgart: Steiner.

Moran, Gerard P. 2004, *Sending Out Ireland's Poor: Assisted Emigration to North America in the Nineteenth Century*, Dublin: Four Courts Press.

Morawska, Ewa 1996, *Insecure Prosperity. Small-Town Jews in Industrial America, 1890–1914*, Princeton, NJ: Princeton University Press.

Morris, Andrew J.F. 2009, *The Limits of Voluntarism. Charity and Welfare from the New Deal Through the Great Society*, Cambridge: Cambridge University Press.

Morrow, Raymond A. 2009, 'Norbert Elias and Figurational Sociology: The Comeback of the Century', *Contemporary Sociology* 38, 3, pp. 215–19.

Moseley, Marcus 2005, 'Jewish Autobiography: The Elusive Subject', *Jewish Quarterly Review* 95, no. 1, pp. 16–59.

Moseley, Marcus 2006, *Being for Myself Alone. Origins of Jewish Autobiography*, Stanford, CA: Stanford University Press.

Moss, Kenneth B. 2009, *Jewish Renaissance in the Russian Revolution*, Cambridge, MA and London: Harvard University Press.

Motolski, Elie 1945, '1-ter may 1903 in varshe. A bletl zikhroynes', *Unzer tsayt*, New York 5, pp. 36 f.

Moya, José C. 1998, *Cousins and Strangers: Spanish Immigrants in Buenos Aires, 1850–1930*, Berkeley and Los Angeles: University of California Press.

Moya, José C. 2004, 'The Positive Side of Stereotypes: Jewish Anarchists in Early-Twentieth-Century Buenos Aires', *Jewish History* 18, no. 1, pp. 19–48.

Moya, José C. 2006, 'A Continent of Immigrants. Postcolonial Shifts in the Western Hemisphere', *Hispanic American Historical Review* 86, no. 1, pp. 1–28.

Münchow, Ursula 1973, *Frühe deutsche Arbeiterautobiographie*, Berlin: Akademie-Verlag.

Münch, Richard 2010 [1988], *Understanding Modernity. Towards a new perspective going beyond Durkheim and Weber*, various translators, London and New York: Routledge.

Münz, Christoph 2004, '"Wohin die Sprache nicht reicht ..." Sprache und Sprachbilder zwischen Bilderverbot und Schweigegebot', *Verbot der Bilder – Gebot der Erinnerung. Mediale Repräsentation der Shoa*, edited by Bettina Bannash and Almuth Hammer, Frankfurt am Main and New York: Campus, pp. 146–65.

Murphy, Kevin 2005, *Revolution and Counterrevolution. Class Struggle in a Moscow Metal Factory*, New York: Berghahn.

Myers, Gustavus 1916 [1909], *Geschichte der großen amerikanischen Vermögen*, Vol. 1, Berlin: S. Fischer.

N.N. 1900, 'Di dekabristen', *Di arbeter shtime* 20, pp. 4–7.

N.N. 1901, 'Tsu der geshikhte fun der entviklung fun zshargonisher unlegaler politishe presse in russland', *Di arbeter shtime* 25, pp. 11–16.

N.N. 1902a, 'Girsh Lekert. Nekrolog', *Revoliutsionnaia Rossiia* 7 (Iun'), p. 1 f.

N.N. 1902b, 'Rundshoy', *Di tsukunft*, New York (July), p. 343.

N.N. 1902c, 'Tsu ondenkung fun dem 15 (28) yanuar 1886 yohr', *Di arbeter shtime* 26, pp. 3–8.

N.N. 1906a, 'Der organ fun der amerikanishe bundistn', *Der veker*, Vilnius 3 (9 January), p. 4 f.

N.N. 1906b, 'Vos is azoynt a revolutsye', *Der veker*, Vilnius 4 (10 January), p. 2 f.

N.N. 1907a, 'Der 25-ter September 1897–1907', *Di hofnung*, Vilnius 14 (October), p. 2.

N.N. 1907b, 'Di bundishe prese biz oktober 1905', *Di hofnung*, Vilnius 14, p. 5.

N.N. 1907c, 'Tsehn yor', *Di hofnung*, Vilnius 14 (October), p. 2.

N.N. 1908a, 'Durkh vemen kan sikh heren di folks-shtime in parlament', *Der avangard*, Buenos Aires, 1, no. 3 (October), p. 3 f.

N.N. 1908b, 'Kandidaten fun sotsyalistisher partey', *Der avangard*, Buenos Aires, 1, no. 3 (October), pp. 4–7.

N.N. 1908c, 'Oyfmerksam!', *Der avangard*, Buenos Aires 1, no. 1 (August), p. 18.

N.N. 1909a, [calendar], *Der avangard*, Buenos Aires, 2, no. 2 (April), p. 20.

N.N. 1909b, 'Der yidisher arbeyter farband', *Der avangard*, Buenos Aires 2, no. 7 (September), pp. 1–5.

N.N. 1909c, 'Di royte vokh', *Der avangard*, Buenos Aires 2, no. 4 (June), pp. 1–4.

N.N. 1910, 'Nokh di vahlen', *Der* 3, no. 3 (March), p. 1 f.

N.N. 1917, 'Der ershter may fun 1917', *Der avangard*, Buenos Aires 2, second run, no. 16–17, pp. 129–35.

N.N. 1919, 'Notitsn un komentaren. Nokh di wahlen', *Der avangard*, Buenos Aires, 1, third run, no. 16 (11 April), p. 2.

N.N. 1921a, 'Der ershte may amol', *Dos fraye vort*, Vilnius 15 (May), p. 2.

N.N. 1921b, 'Fun farlag', *Zikhroynes fun a yidishen sotsyalist, Bd. 1*, edited by Beynish Mikhalevitsh, Warsaw: Lebns-fragn.

N.N. 1922, *Arbeter Lualh* 3, Warsaw: Farlag Lebns-fragn.

N.N. 1924, 'Partey lebn', *Argentiner veker* 1, no. 3, p. 7.

N.N. 1927a, *30 yor bund, 1897–1927*, Riga: Bund in letland.

N.N. 1927b, 'Der mord fun Sako un Vantseti un di oyfgabe farn arbeter klas', *Der mebl arbeter* 14, p. 1.

N.N. 1928, *Byuletin tsum shalushim fun farshtorbenem khaver Beynish Mikhalevitsh* 1, no. 1 (November).

N.N. 1928b, 'Vi set oys di lage in ratnfarband', *Der mebl arbeter* 18, p. 2 f.

N.N. 1929, 'A vort tsu di eltern', *Undzer shul*, Buenos Aires, 1, p. 1 ff.

N.N. 1931, 'Oyfn yidishn kultur front', *Sotsyalistishe bleter*, Buenos Aires 2, no. 27, p. 5.

N.N. 1932, 'Der banket tsum opfarn fun kh. P. Vald', *Sotsyalistishe bleter*, Buenos Aires, 3, no. 39, p. 2.

N.N. 1935a, '7-ter november. 18 yor proletarishe ordnung', *Der konfektsyon arbeter* 2, no. 3, p. 2.

N.N. 1935b, 'Yedyem fun der sindikaler bavegung', *Der konfektsyon arbeter* 2, no. 3, p. 8.

N.N. 1936a, 'Der hertsiker gesegnungs-banket mit B. Shefnern in medem bibliotek baym yidish-sotsyalistishn farband', *Argentiner lebn* 6, p. 7.

N.N. 1936b, 'Dr. I.A. Merison [Obituary]', *Dos fraye vort*, Buenos Aires.

N.N. 1936c, 'Es ruft di yidish-veltlekhe shul in Poyln un Argentine', *Argentiner lebn* 1, no. 1, p. 1.

N.N. 1936d, 'Mir zaynen vider do', *Argentiner lebn* 1, no. 1, p: 1.

N.N. 1936e, 'Shabes dem 24-ten oktober, kh' Yitzkhok Blinds 70-yoriker yubiley', *Argentiner lebn* 6, p. 7.

N.N. 1937a, 'Di feyerung tsum 30-yorikn yubiley fun "avangard"', *Argentiner lebn* 13, p. 3.

N.N. 1937b, 'Mir viln lebn fun der arbet', *Byuletin fun heym shneyder un tazsheristn-fareyn* 1, no. 1, p. 1.

N.N. 1938, 'Tsu di leyener!', *Tsayt-fragn*, Buenos Aires 1, no. 1 (October), p. 1.

N.N. 1947a, 'Bageysterte manifestatsye far der yidish-veltlekher shul in Buenos-Ayres', *Unzer tsayt*, New York, 1–2, p. 47 ff.

N.N. 1947b, *Zigelboym-bukh*, New York: Unser tsayt.

N.N. 1948, 'From Our Movement. Poland', *The Jewish Labor Bund Bulletin* 1, no. 4, p. 7.

N.N. 1958, *Khmurner bukh*, New York: Unzer tsayt.

N.N. 1968, 'Farzamlung tsum ondenk fun E. Novogrudski un B. Tabasthinski', *Unzer tsayt*, New York, 8–9, p. 36.

N.N. 1971, 'Hakdome', *Khaym Finkelshtayn tsu zeyne 60 yor*, Montevideo, [unpaginated].

Naples, Nancy A. 2008, 'The Challenges and Possibilites of Transnational Feminist Praxis', *The Transnational Studies Reader: Intersections and Innovations*, edited by Sanjeev Khagram and Peggy Levitt, New York and London: Routledge, pp. 490–500.

Narsh, Galam 1917, 'Unzer prese. A bisel bibliografye', *Di arbeter shtime* 45, pp. 15–18.

Nathans, Benjamin 2004, *Beyond the Pale. The Jewish Encounter with Late Imperial Russia*, Berkeley, CA and London: University of California Press.

Nathaus, Klaus 2009, *Organisierte Gesellgikeit: Deutsche und britische Vereine im 19. und 20. Jahrhundert*, Göttingen: Vandenhoeck & Ruprecht.

Nath, Holger 1992, 'Yiddish as the Emerging National Language of Eastern European Jewry', *Sociolinguistica* 6, pp. 52–64.

Nicolaevsky, Boris I. 1934, *Aseff, the Spy, Russian Terrorist and Police Stool*, Garden City, NY: Doubleday, Doran & Company

Niger, Shmuel 1940, *In kamf far a nayer dertsyung. Di arbeter-ring-shuln, zeyer opshtam, antviklung, vuks un yitsiker tsushtand (1919–1939)*, New York: Arbeter-ring-bildungs-komitet.

Niger, Shmuel 1981, 'Vegn der natsionaler role fun yidish un der yidisher kultur', *Never Say Die!: A Thousand Years of Yiddish in Jewish Life and Letters*, edited by Joshua A. Fishman, The Hague: Mouton, pp. 129–39.

Nin, A. 1907, 'Der bleykhe strahl (Fun leben)', *Di hofnung*, Vilnius, 11 (4 September), p. 2 f.

Nishimura, Yuu 2013, 'On the Cultural Front: The Bund and the Yiddish Secular School Movement in Interwar Poland', *East European Jewish Affairs* 43, no. 3, pp. 265–81.

Noakh [Noakh Portnoy] 1936, 'Forvort', *In loyf fun yorn. Zikhroynes fun a yidishn arbeter*, edited by Layb [Laybetshke] Berman, Warsaw: Memuarn-komitet baym Dvinsker 'Bund' brentsh 75 fun arbeter-ring in Amerike, p. 5 f.

Noakh [Noakh Portnoy] 1941, 'Oyf unzer veg', *Unzer tsayt* 1, no. 1, pp. 3–5.

Nolan, Michael 1981, 'Political Communication Methods in Canadian Federal Election Campaign 1867–1925', *Canadian Journal of Communication* 7, no. 4, pp. 28–46.

Nora, Pierre 2001, 'General Introduction', *Rethinking France. Les Lieu de Mémoire, Vol. 1: The State*, London: University of Chicago Press, pp. vii–xxii.

North, Douglass 1990, *Institutions, Institutional Change, and Economic Performance. The Political Economy of Institutions and Decisions*, Cambridge: Cambridge University Press.
Novok, Hershl 1957, *Mayne yugnt yorn*, New York: Arbeter-ring bildungs-komitet.
Noyes, John Humphrey 1966, *History of American Socialisms*, New York: Dover.
Officer, Lawrence H. 2010, 'Dollar-Pound Exchange Rate From 1791', *MeasuringWorth*, www.measuringworth.com/exchangepound (last accessed 1 December 2010).
Oler, Leon 1973 [1957], 'Di "tsveyer" in poylishn "bund"', *Leon Oler. Zayn lebn un tetikeyt*, New York: Unzer tsayt, pp. 124–30.
Olgin, M[oshe] 1929, 'Di yidishe sprokh un di arbeter shul', *Undzer shul*, Buenos Aires 1, p. 12 ff.
Olgin, M[oshe] 1909, 'Fun der alter heym (brief)', *Der avangard*, Buenos Aires 2, no. 8, pp. 5–9.
Oliver, Pamela E. and Gerald Marwell 1988, 'The Paradox of Group Size in Collective Action: A Theory of Critical Mass II', *American Sociological Review* 53, no. 1, pp. 1–8.
Oliver, Pamela E. and Gerald Marwell 2001, 'Whatever Happened to Critical Mass Theory? A Retrospective and Assessment', *Sociological Theory* 19, no. 3, pp. 292–311.
Oltmer, Jochen 2009a, 'Einführung: Europäische Migrationsverhältnisse und Migrationsregime in der Neuzeit', *Geschichte und Gesellschaft* 35, no. 1, pp. 5–27.
Oltmer, Jochen 2009b, *Migration im 19. und 20. Jahrhundert*, Munich: Oldenbourg.
Oltmer, Jochen 2012, *Globale Migration: Geschichte und Gegenwart*, Munich: C.H. Beck.
Orla-Bukowska, Annamaria 2004, 'The Soviet Shtetl in the 1920s', *POLIN* 17, pp. 197–258.
Osterhammel, Jürgen 2001, *Geschichtswissenschaft jenseits des Nationalstaats: Studien zu Beziehungsgeschichte und Zivilisationsvergleich*, Bonn: Vandenhoeck & Ruprecht.
Osterhammel, Jürgen 2014, *The Transformation of the World. A Global History of the Nineteenth Century*, translated by Patrick Camiller, Princeton, NJ: Princeton University Press.
Ostheimer, Jochen 2008, *Zeichen der Zeit lesen. Erkenntnistheoretische Bedingungen einer praktisch-theologischen Gegenwartsanalyse*, Stuttgart: Kohlhammer.
Ott, Susan J. 2004, *Raring to Go. The ILGWU, Its History and the Educational Experiences of the Women Who Participated*, PhD dissertation, State University of New York at Buffalo.
Panettieri, José (ed.) 2000, *Argentina. Trabajadores entre dos guerras*, Buenos Aires: Eudeba, Universidad de Buenos Aires.
Panken, Jacob 1912, 'Report Submitted in Behalf of the Jewish Agitation Bureau to the Socialist Party National Convention', *Proceedings. National Convention of the Socialist Party, 1912*, edited by John Spargo, Chicago, IL: Socialist Party, p. 244 f.
Paretzki, Elie 1932, *Die Entstehung der jüdischen Arbeiterbewegung in Russland*, Riga: Verlag 'Jurist'.

Patel, Kiran Klaus 2004, 'Überlegungen zu einer transnationalen Geschichtswissenschaft', *ZfG* 52, no. 7, pp. 626–45.

Pavlevski, Sh. 1946, 'Bayshpiln fun eynheyt un kamf', *Unzer tsayt*, New York 8–9, p. 27f.

Peled, Yoav 1989, *Class and Ethnicity in the Pale. The Political Economy of Jewish Workers' Nationalism in Late Imperial Russia*, New York: St. Martin's Press.

Penkover, Monty N. 2004, 'The Kishinev Pogrom of 1903: A Turning Point in Jewish History', *Modern Judaism* 24, pp. 187–225.

Perlman, Selig 1922, *A History of Trade Unionism in the United States*, New York: Macmillan.

Perlman, Selig 1960, 'Jewish American Unionism, Its Births Pangs and Contribution to the General American Labor Movement', *Publication of the American Jewish Historial Society* 41, pp. 298–355.

Pernau, Margrit 2011, *Transnationale Geschichte*, Göttingen: Vandenhoeck & Ruprecht.

Pescher, Petra 2007, 'Identity, Immigration and Language Attrition', *Language Attrition*, edited by Barbara Köpke, Monika S. Schmid, Merel Keijzer and Susan Dostert, Amsterdam and Philadelphia, PA: John Benjamins, pp. 189–204.

P., F. 1907. 'Di opozitsye fun 1893', *Di hofnung*, Vilnius 14 (October), p. 4.

Pickhan, Gertrud 1994, 'Das NKVD-Dossier über Henryk Erlich und Wiktor Alter', *Berliner Jahrbuch für Osteuropäische Geschichte* 2, pp. 155–86.

Pickhan, Gertrud 2001a, *Gegen den Strom. Der Allgemeine Jüdische Arbeiterbund 'Bund' in Polen 1918–1939*, Munich: DVA.

Pickhan, Gertrud 2001b, '"Der Mensch in der Gesellschaft" Wiktor Alter (1890–1943) als Vordenker der Jüdischen Arbeiterbewegung in Polen', *Kollektivität Und Individualität: der Mensch im Östlichen Europa*, edited by Karsten Brüggemann and Thomas M. Bohn, Hamburg: Kovač, pp. 394–404.

Pickhan, Gertrud 2004, '"Wo sind die Frauen?" Zur Diskussion um Weiblichkeit, Männlichkeit und Jüdischkeit im Allgemeinen Jüdischen Arbeiterbund ("Bund") in Polen', *Zwischen den Kriegen. Nationen, Nationalismen und Geschlechterverhältnisse in Mittel- und Osteuropa, 1918–1939*, edited by Johanna Gehmacher, Elisabeth Harvey and Sophia Kemlein, Osnabrück: Fibre, pp. 187–99.

Pickhan, Gertrud 2009, 'Yiddishkayt and Class Consciousness. The Bund and Its Minority Concept', *East European Jewish Affairs* 39, 2, pp. 249–63.

Pickhan, Gertrud 2011, 'Vom Ereignis zum Mythos: die Revolution 1905 und die jüdische Linke in Osteuropa', *Revolution in Nordosteuropa*, edited by Detlef Henning, Wiesbaden: Harrassowitz, pp. 126–39.

Pinkus, Roberto 2008, *Villa Lynch era una fiesta*, Buenos Aires: De los cuatro vientos.

Pinson, Koppel S. 1945, 'Arkady Kremer, Vladimir Medem, and the Ideology of the Jewish Bund', *Jewish Social Studies* 7, no. 3, pp. 233–64.

Pipes, Richard 1974, *Russia Under the Old Regime*, New York: Collier Books.

Plotinsky, Anita H. 1995, 'From Generation to Generation: Transmitting the Jewish Philanthropic Tradition', *New Directions for Philantropic Fundraising* 7 [*Cultures of Giving. How Region and Religion Influence Philantropy*], pp. 117–31.

della Porta, Donatella and Sidney G. Tarrow (eds.) 2005, *Transnational Protest and Global Activism*, Lanham, MD: Rowman & Littlefield.

della Porta, Donatella, Hanspeter Kriesi and Dieter Rucht (eds.) 1999, *Social Movements in a Globalising World*, London: Macmillan.

della Porta, Donatella and Hanspeter Kriesi 1999, 'Social Movements in a Globalizing World: An Introduction', *Social Movements in a Globalizing World*, edited by Donatella della Porta, Hanspeter Kriesi and Dieter Rucht, London: Macmillan, pp. 3–22.

della Porta, Donatella and Sidney Tarrow 2008, 'Transnational Protest and Global Activism', *Social Movements: A Reader*, edited by Vincenzo Ruggiero, New York: Routledge, pp. 339–48.

Pratt, Norma F. 1981, 'Archival Resources and Writing Immigrant American History: The Bund Archives of the Jewish Labor Movement', *Journal of Library History* 16, no. 1, pp. 166–76.

Pries, Ludger 2008a, 'Transnational Societal Spaces: Which Unites of Analysism, Reference, and Measurement?', *Rethinking Transnationalism: the Meso-Link of Organisations*, edited by Ludger Pries, London: Routledge, pp. 1–20.

Pries, Ludger 2008b, *Die Transnationalisierung der sozialen Welt: Sozialräume jenseits von Nationalgesellschaften*, Frankfurt am Main: Suhrkamp.

Pries, Ludger 2010a '(Grenzüberschreitende) Migrantenorganisationen als Gegenstand der sozialwissenschaftlichen Forschung: Klassische Problemlagen und neuere Befunde', *Jenseits von 'Identität oder Integration'. Grenzen überspannende Migrantenorganisationen*, edited by Ludger Pries and Zeynep Sezgin, Wiesbaden: vs, pp. 15–60.

Pries, Ludger 2010b, *Transnationalisierung: Theorie und Empirie grenzüberschreitender Vergesellschaftung*, Wiesbaden: vs.

Program fun di arbeter ring shuln 1927, *Angenumen beym 6tn arbeter ring shul tsuzamefar, in filadelfye, PA*, New York: Bildungs department fun arbeter ring.

Quatember, Wolfgang 1988, *Erzählprosa im Umfeld der österreichischen Arbeiterbewegung. Von der Arbeiterlebenserinnerung zum tendenziösen Unterhaltungsroman*, Vienna, Zurich: Europaverlag.

Radt, Jenny 1935, *Die Juden in Polen*, Berlin: Schocken.

Rafes, Moisej G. 1920, *Dva goda revoliutsii na Ukraine: evoliutsiia i raskol Bunda*, Moscow: Gosudarstvennoe Izdatel'stvo.

Rafes, Moisej G. 1923, *Ocherki po istorii 'Bunda'*, Moscow: Moskovskii rabochii.

Rak, Elimelekh 1958, *Zikhroynes fun a yidishn handverker tuer*, Buenos Aires: Tsentralfarband fun poylishe yidn in Argentine.

Raschke, Joachim 1987, *Soziale Bewegungen. Ein Historisch-Systematischer Grundriss. Studienausgabe*, Frankfurt am Main: Campus.

Ravitch, Melech 1945, *Mayn leksikon*, 4 volumes, Montreal and Tel Aviv: A komitet, Veltrat far Yidish un Yidisher Kultur.
Reckwitz, Andreas 2006, *Das hybride Subjekt. Eine Theorie der Subjektkulturen von der bürgerlichen Moderne zur Postmoderne*, Weilerswist: Velbrück Wissenschaft.
Redaktsye 'lebns-fragn' 1919, *Unzer grus*, Warsaw.
Reichardt, Sven 2004, 'Praxeologie und Faschismus. Gewalt und Gemeinschaft als Elemente eines praxeologischen Faschismusbegriffs', *Doing Culture. Neue Positionen zum Verhältnis von Kultur und sozialer Praxis*, edited by Karl H. Hörning and Julia Reuter, Bielefeld: transcript, pp. 129–53.
Reiss, Matthias (ed.) 2007, *The Street as a Stage. Protest Marches and Public Rallies in the Nineteenth Century*, Oxford: GHI London, Oxford University Press.
Renan, Ernest 2000 [1892], 'What is a nation?', *Nation and Narration*, edited by Homi K. Bhabha, London and New York: Routledge, pp. 8–22.
República Argentina. Ministerio de Agricultura de la Nación 1920, *Ley de inmigración No. 817 y decretos reglamentarios*, Buenos Aires.
Riddell, John 1991, *Workers of the World and Oppressed Peoples Unite! Proceedings and Documents of the Second Congress*, Vol. 2, New York: Pathfinder.
Riis, Jacob 1996, 'How the Other Half Lives', *The Jewish East Side, 1881–1924*, edited by Milton Hindus, New Brunswick, NJ and London: Transaction, pp. 93–106.
Rischin, Moses 1977 [1962], *The Promised City. New York's Jews, 1870–1914*, Cambridge, MA and London: Harvard University Press.
Risse-Kappen, Thomas 1995, 'Bringing Transnational Relations Back In: Introduction', *Bringing Transnational Relations Back In: Non-State Actors, Domestic Structures, and International Institutions*, edited by Thomas Risse-Kappen, Cambridge University Press, pp. 3–33.
Ritzer, Georg 2007, *The Blackwell Encyclopedia of Sociology*, 11 volumes, Malden, MA, Oxford, Victoria: Blackwell.
Rockaway, Robert A. 2000, *But He Was Good to His Mother: The Lives and Crimes of Jewish Gangsters*, Jerusalem: Gefen.
Rogger, Hans 1966, 'The Beilis Case: Anti-Semitism and Politics in the Reign of Nicholas II', *Slavic Review* 25, no. 4, pp. 615–29.
Rogoff, Harry 1930, *An East Side Epic: The Life and Work of Meyer London*, New York: Vanguard Press.
Rojanski, Rachel 2007, 'Socialist Ideology, Traditional Rhetoric: Images of Women in American Yiddish Socialist Dailies, 1918–1922', *American Jewish History* 93, no. 3, pp. 329–48.
Rolf, Malte 2013, *Soviet Mass Festivals, 1917–1991*, translated by Cynthia Klohr, Pittsburgh, PA: University of Pittsburgh Press.
Rosenak, Michael 1987, *Commandments and Concerns. Jewish Religious Education in Secular Society*, Philadelphia, PA: Jewish Publication Society.

Rosenthal, Steven T. 2005, 'Long-Distance Nationalism', *The Cambridge Companion to American Judaism*, edited by Dana Evan Kaplan, New York: Cambridge University Press.

Roskies, David G. 1999, *The Jewish Search for a Usable Past*, Bloomington, IN: Indiana University Press.

Roßler, Gustav 2008, 'Kleine Gallerie neuer Dingbegriffe: Hybriden, Quasi-Objekte, Grenzobjekte, epistemische Dinge', *Bruno Latours Kollektive. Kontroversen zur Entgrenzung des Sozialen*, edited by Georg Kneer, Markus Schroer and Erhard Schüttpelz, Frankfurt am Main: Suhrkamp, pp. 76–107.

Rössler, Patrick 2005, *Inhaltsanalyse*, Konstanz: UTB.

Roth, Gerhard 1972, *Gramscis Philosophie der Praxis. Eine neue Deutung des Marxismus*, Düsseldorf: Patmos.

Rozen, Naythan 1943, 'Iberlebungen fun a "kleynem-bundist". Derinerungen fun Vilne, Vitebsk un Polotsk', *Unzer tsayt*, New York 12, pp. 29–33.

Rozshanski, Shmuel 1972, 'Mit 40 yor tsurik hot sikh dos angehoybn', *Yubeley shrift. 40 yor fun der 'geszelshaft far yidish-veltlekhe shuln in Argentine', 1932–1972*, edited by Moshe Knapheyt, Buenos Aires, p. 7f.

Rucht, Dieter 2005, 'The Transnationalization of Social Movements: Trends, Causes, Problems', *Transnational Protest and Global Activism*, edited by Donatella della Porta and Sidney G. Tarrow, Lanham, MD: Rowman & Littlefield, pp. 206–22.

Rutar, Sabine 2004, *Kultur – Nation – Milieu: Sozialdemokratie in Triest vor dem Ersten Weltkrieg*, Essen: Klartext.

Rutland, Suzanne D. 2001, *Edge of the Diaspora: Two Centuries of Jewish Settlement in Australia*, 2nd revised edition, New York: Holmes & Meier.

Rutz, Andreas 2002, 'Ego-Dokument oder Ich-Konstruktion? Selbstzeugnisse als Quellen zur Erforschung des frühneuzeitlichen Menschen', *zeitenblicke* 1, no. 2, www.zeitenblicke.de/2002/02/rutz/index.html (last accessed 1 March 2017).

Sachsenmaier, Dominic 2011, *Global Perspectives on Global History: Theories and Approaches in a Connected World*, Cambridge: Cambridge University Press.

Safran, Gabriella and Steven J. Zipperstein (eds.) 2006, *The Worlds of S. An-Sky: A Russian Jewish Intellectual at the Turn of the Century*, Stanford: Stanford University Press.

Salutski, I.B. 1913, 'Berikht vegen er thetigkayt, finansen und zushtand fun der federatsye', *Partey Byuleletin, aroysgegebn fun yidisher S.P. federatsyon fun Amerika*, Chicago 1, no. 1 (June), pp. 2–4.

Salutski, I.B. and A. Litvak (eds.) 1917, *Dos revolutsionere rusland*, New York: Yidishe sotsyalistishe federatsye in Amerike.

Salvatore, Nick 2007, *Eugene V. Debs. Citizen and Socialist*, second edition, Urbana, IL: University of Illinois Press, 2007.

Sander, Greif 1966, *Amerikas Gewerkschaften. Geschichte, Struktur, Probleme der Gewerkschaften in den USA*, Wiesbaden: Guido Pressler Verlag.

Saß, Anne-Christin 2012, *Berliner Luftmenschen. Osteuropäisch-jüdische Migranten in der Weimarer Republik*, Göttingen: Wallstein.

Schenkolewski-Kroll, Silvia 2001, 'El cooperativismo agrícola judío en la Argentina. Su funcíon socioeconómica y su identidad étnica. 1901–1948', *Judaica latinamericano* 4, pp. 47–61.

Schiller, Nina Glick 2010, 'A Global Perspective on Transnational Migration: Theorizing Migration without Methodological Nationalism', *Diaspora and Transnationalism: Concepts, Theories and Methods*, edited by Rainer Bauböck and Thomas Faist, Amsterdam: Amsterdam University Press, pp. 109–29.

Schiller, Nina Glick, Linda Basch and Szanton Blanc 1995, 'From Immigrant to Transmigrant: Theorizing Transnational Migration', *Anthropological Quarterly* 68, no. 1, pp. 48–63.

Schiller, Nina Glick and Ayse Çağlar 2009, 'Towards a Comparitive Theory of Locality in Migration Studies: Migrant Incorporation and City Scale', *Journal of Ethnic and Migration Studies* 35, no. 2, pp. 177–202.

Schimank, Uwe 2005, *Differenzierung und Integration der modernen Gesellschaft*, Wiesbaden: VS, 2005.

Schimank, Uwe 2007a, 'Die unmögliche Trennung von Natur und Gesellschaft – Bruno Latours Diagnose der Selbsttäuschung der Moderne', *Soziologische Gegenwartsdiagnosen 1*, edited by Uwe Schimank and Ute Volkmann, second printing, Wiesbaden: VS, pp. 157–69.

Schimank, Uwe 2007b, *Theorien gesellschaftlicher Differenzierung*, third printing, Wiesbaden: VS.

Schlögel, Karl 2002, *Petersburg. Das Laboratorium der Moderne, 1909–1921*, Munich and Vienna: Carl Hanser.

Schlögel, Karl 2012 [2008], *Moscow 1937*, translated by Rodney Livingstone, Cambridge: Polity.

Schlögel, Karl 2016 [2003], *In Space We Read Time: On the History of Civilization and Geopolitics*, translated by Gerrit Jackson, New York: Bard Graduate Center.

Schmidt, Christoph 2004, *Die entheiligte Utopie. Jüdische Ideen- und Sozialgeschichte am Dnepr (1750–1900)*, Cologne, Vienna, Weimar: Böhlau.

Schöck-Quinteros, Eva 2007, *Politische Netzwerkerinnen: Internationale Zusammenarbeit von Frauen, 1930–1960*, Berlin: Trafo-Verlag.

Schrader, Abby 2002, *Languages of the Lash. Corporal Punishment and Identity in Imperial Russia*, DeKalb, IL: Northern Illinois University Press.

Schrage, Dominik 2006, 'Von der Präsenzmasse zur statistischen Masse. Affekte und deskriptive Aspekte eines modernen Konzepts', *Die Macht der Menge. Über die Aktualität einer Denkfigur Spinozas*, edited by Gunnar Hindrichs, Heidelberg: Winter, pp. 93–112.

Schrag, Peter 2010, *Not Fit for Our Society: Nativism and Immigration*, Berkeley, CA: University of California Press.

Schroer, Markus 2008, 'Vermischen, Vermitteln, Vernetzen. Bruno Latours Soziologie der Gemenge und Gemische im Kontext', *Bruno Latours Kollektive. Kontroversen zur Entgrenzung des Sozialen*, edited by Georg Kneer, Markus Schroer and Erhard Schüttpelz, Frankfurt am Main: Suhrkamp, pp. 361–98.

Schuster, Frank M. 2004, *Zwischen allen Fronten. Osteuropäische Juden während des Ersten Weltkrieges (1914–1919)*, Cologne: Böhlau.

Schwarz, Jan 1998, 'Central Questions in Studying Autobiographies of Yiddish Writers', *Jewish Studies in a New Europe: Proceedings of the Fifth Congress of Jewish Studies in Copenhagen 1994, Under the Auspices of the European Association for Jewish Studies*, edited by Ulf Haxen, Hanne Trautner-Kromann and Karen L. Goldschmidt Salamon, Copenhagen: Reitzel, pp. 770–7.

Schwarz, Solomon M. 1951, *The Jews in the Soviet Union*, Syracuse, NY: Syracuse University Press.

Scott, James C. 1990, *Domination and the Arts of Resistance: Hidden Transcripts*, New Haven: Yale University Press.

Seaman, Bernard and Max D. Danish 1947, *The Story of the ILGWU*, New York: ILGWU.

Segler-Messner, Silke 2005, *Archive der Erinnerung. Literarische Zeugnisse des Überlebens nach der Shoa in Frankreich*, Cologne, Weimar, Vienna: Böhlau.

Seidman, Harold 1938, *Labor Czars: A History of Labor Racketeering*, New York: Liverlight.

Seligman, Edwin R.A. and Alvin Johnson (eds.) 1930, *Encyclopedia of the Social Sciences*, 15 volumes, New York: Macmillan.

Shabad, Zemakh 1916, *Vilner zamlbukh*, Vilnius: Rozental.

Shannon, David A. 1955, *The Socialist Party of America. A History*, New York: Macmillan.

Shapiro, Judah Joseph 1970, *The Friendly Society: A History of the Workmen's Circle*, New York: Media Judaica.

Shapiro, Robert Moses 1994, 'The Polish Kehilla Elections of 1936. A Revolution Reexamined', *POLIN* 8, pp. 206–26.

Shapiro, Shelby Alan 2009, *Words to the Wives: The Jewish Press, Immigrant Women, and Identity Construction, 1895–1925*, PhD dissertation, University of Maryland.

Shazar, Schneur Zalman 1967, 'Defenders of the City', *The Golden Tradition. Jewish Life and Thought in Eastern Europe*, edited by Lucy S. Dawidowicz, New York: Holt, Rinehart and Winston, pp. 383–8.

Shell-Weiss, Melanie 2009, *Coming to Miami: A Social History*, Gainesville, FL: University Press of Florida.

Shepard, Richard F. and Vicki Gold Levi 2000, *Live & Be Well: A Celebration of Yiddish Culture in America from the First Immigrants to the Second World War*, New Brunswick, NJ: Rutgers University Press.

Sherer, Emanuel [Szerer] 1960, 'Areynfir', *20 yor in avrshever 'bund'*, *1919–1939*, edited by Bernard Goldstein, New York: Unzer tsayt, pp. IX–XVI.

Sherwin, Bryon L. 2005, 'Thinking Judaism Through: Jewish Theology in America', *The Cambridge Companion to American Judaism*, edited by Dana Evan Kaplan, New York: Cambridge University Press, pp. 117–32.

Shneefal, S.K. 1910, 'Yidish, der yidisher arbeyter un di hoypt-oygabe fun arbeyter ring', *Der arbeter ring zamel bukh. Sovenir*, New York: Teshnte yehrlekhe konventshon konferents, pp. 129–35.

Shneer, David 2004, *Yiddish and the Creation of Soviet Jewish Culture 1918–1930*, New York: Cambridge University Press.

Shtakser, Inna 2009, 'Self-Defence as an Emotional Experience: The Anti-Jewish Pogroms of 1905–07 and Working Class Jewish Militants', *Revolutionary Russia* 22, no. 2, pp. 153–79.

Shtampfer, Shaul 1999, '"Is the Question the Answer?" East European Jews, Heder Education and Possible Antecedents of Contemporary Israeli and Jewish Life', *Studia Judaica* 8, pp. 239–54.

Shtayngart, Tsirl 1975, 'Di froyen in "bund"', *Unzer tsayt*, New York 3–4, pp. 19–22.

Shulman, Viktor 1951, 'Fun der "lebns-fragen" biz der "folkstsaytung"', 6 volumes, *Unzer shtime*, Paris 1443–8, p. 2 in each issue.

Shvarts, Solomon 1968, 'Vegn der "zubatovshine" in Minsk. An entfer tsu I. Sh. Herts', *Unzer tsayt* 1–2, pp. 26–32.

Silber, Michael K. 1992, 'The Emergence of Ultra-Orthodoxy: The Invention of a Tradition', *The Uses of Tradition: Jewish Continuity in the Modern Era*, edited by Jack Wertheimer, New York: Jewish Theological Seminary of America, pp. 23–84.

Sills, David L. and Robert K. Merton (eds.) 1968, *Encyclopedia of the Social Sciences*, 19 volumes, New York and London: Macmillan.

Silver, Ira 1998, 'Buying an Activist Identity: Reproducing Class through Social Movement Philanthropy', *Sociological Perspectives*, pp. 303–21.

Silver, Mitchell 1998, *Respecting the Wicked Child. A Philosophy of Secular Jewish Identity and Education*, Boston, MA: University of Massachusetts Press.

Simon, Rita J. 1997, *In the Golden Land. A Century of Russian and Soviet Jewish Immigration in America*, Westport, CT: Praeger.

Singer, Bernard 1996, 'The Jews, the Left and the State Duma Elections in Warsaw 1912: Selected Sources', *POLIN* 9, pp. 45–54.

Singer, Israel J. 1946, *Fun a velt voz iz nishto mer*, New York: Matones.

Singer, Israel J. 1971 [1946], *Of a World That Is No More*, translated by Joseph Singer, New York: Vanguard Press.

Slezkine, Yuri 2019 [2004], *The Jewish Century*, Princeton and Oxford: Princeton University Press.

Slucki, David 2008, 'Theorizing doikeit. Towards a History of the Melbourne Bund', *Australian Jewish Historical Society Journal* 19, 2, pp. 259–68.

Slucki, David 2009a, 'The Bund Abroad in the Postwar Jewish World', *Jewish Social Studies* 16, 1, pp. 111–44.
Slucki, David 2009b, *The Jewish Labor Bund after the Holocaust: A Comparative History*, PhD dissertation, Monash University, Melbourne.
Slucki, David 2010, 'Here-ness, There-ness, and Everywhere-ness: The Jewish Labour Bund and the Quetsion of Israel, 1944–1955', *Journal of Modern Jewish Studies* 9, 3, pp. 349–68.
Slucki, David 2012, *The International Jewish Labor Bund after 1945: Toward a Global History*, New Brunswick, NJ: Rutgers University Press.
Slutski, Yehuda (ed.) 1967, *Sefer zikaron le-kehilat Bobruisk u-veneteha. Yizker-bukh far Bobruisker kehilla un umgegnt*, Tel Aviv: Tabut ve-hinnuk [English: www.jewishgen.org/yizkor/bobruisk/Bysktoc1.html (last accessed 4 August 2010)].
Smelser, Neil J. and Paul B. Baltes (eds.) 2001, *International Encyclopedia of the Social and Behavioral Sciences*, 26 volumes, Amsterdam: Elsevier.
Smith, Sidonie and Julia Watson 2010, *Reading Autobiography: A Guide for Interpreting Life Narratives*, Minneapolis: University of Minnesota Press.
Sofer, Eugene F. 1982, *From Pale to Pampa: A Social History of the Jews of Buenos Aires*, New York: Holmes & Meier.
Solberg, Carl 1978, 'Mass Migrations in Argentina, 1870–1970', *Human Migration. Patterns and Policies*, edited by William H. McNeill and Ruth S. Adams, Bloomington, IN: Indiana University Press, pp. 146–70.
Sombart, Werner 1976 [1906], *Why Is There No Socialism In the United States?*, translated by P.M. Hocking and C.T. Husbands, London and Basingstoke: Macmillan.
Sorin, Gerald 1985, *The Prophetic Minority. American Jewish Immigrant Radicals, 1880–1920*, Bloomington, IN: Indiana University Press.
Sorin, Gerald 1992, *A Time for Building: The Third Migration 1880–1920. The Jewish People in America*, Vol. 3, Baltimore and London: Johns Hopkins University Press.
Southgate, M. Therese 1999, 'Anti-Slavery Picnic at Weymouth Landing, Massachusetts', *The Journal of the American Medical Association* 282, p. 7.
Soyer, Daniel 1997, *Jewish Immigrant Associations and American Identity in New York, 1880–1939*, Cambridge, MA: Harvard University Press.
Soyer, Daniel 1999, 'Documenting Immigrant Lives at an Immigrant Institution: Yivo's Autobiography Contest of 1942', *Jewish Social Studies* 5, no. 3, pp. 218–43.
Soyer, Daniel (ed.) 2005, *A Coat of Many Colors. Immigration, Globalism, and Reform in the New York City Garment Industry*, New York: Fordham University Press.
Sperling, Walter 2008, 'Jenseits von "Autokratie" und "Gesellschaft": Zur Einleitung', *Jenseits der Zarenmacht. Dimensionen des Politischen im Russischen Reich 1800–1917*, edited by Walter Sperling, Frankfurt am Main: Campus, pp. 7–40.
Stanislawski, Michael 2004, *Autobiographical Jews. Essays in Jewish Self-Fashioning*. Seattle, WA: University of Washington Press.

Steinberg, Mark D. 2002, *Proletarian Imagination. Self, Modernity and the Sacred in Russia, 1910–1925*, Ithaca, NY and London: Cornell University Press.

Stemberger, Günther 2006, *Jüdische Religion*, fifth printing, Munich: C.H. Beck.

Stolberg, Benjamin 1944, *Tailor's Progress. The Story of a Famous Union and the Men Who Made It*, Garden City, NY: Doubleday.

Sujecki, Janusz 1996, 'The Jews, the Left and the State Duma Elections in Warsaw in 1912', translated by Stephen D. Corrsin, *POLIN* 9, pp. 45–54.

Sulam, Y. 1928, 'Di martirer fun shikago', *Der mebl arbeter* 18, p. 4.

Suriano, Juan 2010, *Paradoxes of Utopia: Anarchist Culture and Politics in Buenos Aires, 1890–1910*, Oakland, CA: AK Press.

Svalov, A.N. (ed.) 2007, *Doklad Parizhskomu kongressu Vtorogo Internatsionala, 1900 god (Iz istorii sotsialisticheskogo dvizheniia v Rossii)*, Moscow: RGSU.

Svarch, Ariel 2010, 'Jewish Communist Culture and Identity in Buenos Aires. Ideas on Comparative Approaches', *Perush: An Online Journal of Jewish Scholarship and Interpretation* (UCLA) 2, no. 1, www.perush.cjs.ucla.edu/index.php/volume-2/jewish-urban-history-in-comparative-perspective-jewish-buenos-aires-and-jewish-los-angeles/-5-ariel-svarch-jewish-communist-culture-and-identity-in-buenos-aires-ideas-on-comparative-approaches (last accessed 1 March 2017).

Szajn, Israel 1983, 'Prasa Bundu w Polsce (1918–1939)', *Kwartalnik Historii Prasy Polskiej* 22, no. 2, pp. 91–100.

T. 1907, 'Vi azoy iz tsuzamengeshtelt un opgedrukt gevorn der ershter numer "arbeyter shtime"', *Di hofnung*, Vilnius 14, p. 3 f.

Tambiah, Stanley J. 2000, 'Transnational Movements, Diaspora, and Multiple Modernities', *Daedalus* 129, no. 1, pp. 163–94.

Tarcus, Horacio and Laura Ehrlich (eds.) 2007, 'Pedro Wald', *Diccionario Biográfico de la Izquierda Argentina de los Anarquistas a la "Nueva Izquierda", 1870–1976*, first edition, Buenos Aires: Emecé.

Tate, Avram, Haim Frumoiskii, S.I. Gozhanskii, Kaplinski et al. 1907, *Iz vospominanii starikh deiiatelei bunda*, RGASPI, Moscow, Fond 217, opis' 1 delo 310.

Taylor, Charles 1985, *Philosophical Papers*, Vol. 2, Cambridge: Cambridge University Press.

Taylor, Verta and Nella van Dyke 2004, '"Get Up, Stand Up": Tactical Repertoires of Social Movements', *The Blackwell Companion to Social Movements*, edited by David A. Snow, Sarah A. Soule and Hanspeter Kriesi, Malden, MA, and Oxford: Blackwell, pp. 262–93.

Taylor, Verta and Nancy E. Whittier 1992, 'Collective Identity in Social Movement Communities. The Lesbian Feminist Mobilization', *Frontiers in Social Movement Theory*, edited by Aldon D. Morris and Carol McClurg Mueller, New Haven and London: Yale University Press, pp. 104–29.

Tenenboym, Sh. 1968, 'Leyener fun der "folkstsaytung"', *Unzer tsayt*, New York 10, pp. 24–7.

Tenfelde, Klaus and Heinrich Volkmann (eds.) 1981, *Streik: Zur Geschichte Des Arbeitskampfes in Deutschland während Der Industrialisierung*, Munich: C.H. Beck.

Terman, Morris (ed.) 1913, *Di velt un di menshheyt. 12 forlezungen iber der entviklung fun natur un kultur mit 44 ilustratsyonen un 18 bilder*, New York: Edyukeyshonal komite fun arbeyter ring.

Thistlewaite, Frank 1960, 'Migration from Europe Overseas in the Nineteenth and Twentieth Centuries', *XI Congrès International des Sciences Historiques, Rapports V*, pp. 32–60.

Thompson, Edward P. 1964, *The Making of the English Working Class*, New York: Pantheon Books.

Tillotson, Shirley 2008, *Contributing Citizens. Modern Charitable Fundraising and the Making of the Welfare State, 1920–66*, Vancouver: UBC Press.

Tilly, Charles 1978, 'Migration in Modern European History', *Human Migration. Patterns and Policies*, edited by William H. McNeill and Ruth S. Adams, Bloomington, IN: Indiana University Press, pp. 48–72.

Tilly, Charles 1985a, 'The Complexity of Popular Collective Action', *New School for Social Research Working Paper Series* 8.

Tilly, Charles 1985b, 'Models and Realities of Popular Collective Action', *New School for Social Research Working Paper Series* 10.

Tobias, Henry J. 1965, 'The Bund and the First Congress of the RSDWP: An Addendum', *Russian Review* 24, no. 4, pp. 393–406.

Tobias, Henry J. 1972, *The Jewish Bund in Russia from its Origins to 1905*, Palo Alto, CA: Stanford University Press.

Tobias, Henry J. and Charles E. Woodhouse 1977, 'Political Reaction and Revolutionary Careers: The Jewish Bundists in Defeat 1907–1910', *Comparative Studies in Society and History* 19, no. 3, pp. 367–96.

Torbiner, Eran 2011, *Bunda'im*, documentary film, Tel Aviv.

Trachtenberg, Barry 2008, *The Revolutionary Roots of Modern Yiddish*, New York: Syracuse University Press.

Trębacz, Michał 2010, '"Rzadko kiedy żydowski dom łączył w sobie tyle światów i tyle wartości ...". Polsko-żydowska mozaika Rafała Lichtensteina – przyczynek do dziejów inteligencji wielokulturowej Łodz', *'Należę do polskiej szkoły historycznej'. Studia i szkice ofiarowane prof. Jakubowi Goldbergowi z okazji odnowienia doktoratu na Uniwersytecie Łódzkim*, edited by R. Stobiecki and J. Walicki, Lodz: Centrum Badań Żydowskich, Uniwersytet Łódzki, pp. 51–63.

Trębacz, Michał 2016, *Israel Lichtenstein. Biografia żydowskiego socjalisty*, Lodz: Instytut Pamięci Narodowej.

Trinchero, Héctor Hugo 2009, 'Las Masacres des Olvido. Napalpí y Rincón Bomba en la Genealogía del Genocido y el Racismo de Estado en la Argentina', *RUNA* 30, no. 1, pp. 45–60.

Troch, Harald 1991, *Rebellensonntag. Der 1. Mai zwischen Politik, Arbeiterkultur und Volksfest in Österreich (1890–1918)*, Vienna: Europaverlag.

Trotsky, Leon 2008 [1932], *The History of the Russian Revolution*, translated by Max Eastman, Chicago: Haymarket Books.

Trunk, Isaiah 1976, 'The Cultural Dimension of the American Jewish Labor Movement', *YIVO Annual of Jewish Social Sciences* 16, pp. 342–93.

Tsentralfarband fun die bundistishe organisatsyonen in Amerika 1905a, 'Der kemfer', *Der kemfer*, New York, 1, no. 1 (3 November 3), p. 1.

Tsentralfarband fun die bundistishe organisatsyonen in Amerika 1905b, 'Oyfruf', *Der kemfer*, New York 1, no. 1 (3 November 3), p. 1.

Tsherikover, Elias 1939, 'Yidn-revolutsyonern in rusland in die 60er un 70er yorn', *Historishe shriftn*, Vilnius 3, pp. 60–172.

Tsherikover, Elias 1961, *The Early Jewish Labor Movement in the United States*, New York: YIVO.

Tshernov, Viktor M. 1948, *Yidishe tuer in der partey sotsyalistn revolutsyonern. Biografishe eseyen*, New York: Grigori Gershuni brentsh 247 Arbeyter ring.

Tshukhinsi, B. (ed.) 1947, *Leo Glezer. Der kultur-tuer un frayhayt-kemfer*, Paris: Allgemeyne yidishe farteydikungs-komitet.

Tsuker, Golde 1972, 'Mit an eygemen tsugang tsum yidishn khinekh', *Yubeley shrift. 40 yor fun der 'geszelshaft far yidish-veltlekhe shuln in Argentine', 1932–1972*, edited by Moshe Knapheyt, Buenos Aires, p. 5 f.

Turner, Brian S. 2006, *The Cambridge Dictionary of Sociology*, Cambridge: Cambridge University Press.

Tussey, Jean Y. (ed.) 1970, *Eugene V. Debs Speaks*, New York: Pathfinder.

Tyrrell, Ian 2009, 'Reflections on the Transnational Turn in United States History: Theory and Practice', *Journal of Global History* 4, no. 3, pp. 453–74.

Uitermark, Justus 2004, 'Looking Forward by Looking Back: May Day Protests in London and the Strategic of the Urban', *Antipode* 36, no. 4, pp. 706–27.

Unfried, Berthold (ed.) 2008, *Transnationale Netzwerke im 20. Jahrhundert: historische Erkundungen zu Ideen und Praktiken, Individuen und Organisationen*, Leipzig: Akademische Verlagsanstalt.

Urales, Federico 1925, *Di fraye shule*, Buenos Aires: Idishe ratsyonalistishe gezelshaft.

Ury, Scott 2012, *Barricades and Banners: The Revolution of 1905 and the Transformation of Warsaw Jewry*, Stanford: Stanford University Press.

Vaihinger, Hans 1968 [1911], *The Philosophy of 'As If'*, transalted by C.K. Ogden, London: Routledge & Kegan Paul.

Vald, Pinie 1908a, 'Di geshikhte fun di yidishe sotsyal demokratishe arbeyter organisatsye in Argentine (avangard), Vol. 1', *Der avangard*, Buenos Aires 1, 1 (August), pp. 12–15.

Vald, Pinie 1908b, 'Di geshikhte fun di yidishe sotsyal demokratishe arbeyter organisatsye in Argentine (avangard), Vol. 2', *Der avangard*, Buenos Aires 1, 2 (September), pp. 21–3.

Vald, Pinie 1909a, 'Tsum yubileum', *Der avangard*, Buenos Aires 2, 1 (January), pp. 3–7.

Vald, Pinie 1909b, 'Der algemeyner shtreyk. Fun 1-ten biz dem 8ten may in argentina', *Der avangard*, Buenos Aires 2, 4 (June), pp. 14–18.

Vald, Pinie 1909c, 'Di oyfgabe fun der yidisher sotsyal-demokratisher arb. organisatsyon in argentina "avangard"', *Der avangard*, Buenos Aires 2, 6 (August), pp. 2–5.

Vald, Pinie 1917a, 'Natsyonal-kulturele oytonomye [Vol. 1]', *Der avangard*, Buenos Aires 2, second run, 14 (February), pp. 67–72.

Vald, Pinie 1917b, 'Natsyonal-kulturele oytonomye [Vol. 2]', *Der avangard*, Buenos Aires 2, second run, 15 (March), pp. 95–8.

Vald, Pinie 1929a, 'Mendl Maler', *Bletlekh [Hojas. Semblanzas de mi ambiente]*, Buenos Aires: Aroysgegebn fun yidishn literatn un zshurnalistn fareyn in Argentine, pp. 7–10.

Vald, Pinie 1929b, 'Stanislavski', *Bletlekh [Hojas. Semblanzas de mi ambiente]*, Buenos Aires: Aroysgegebn fun yidishn literatn un zshurnalistn fareyn in Argentine, pp. 23–32.

Vald, Pinie 1935, 'Yidish veltlekhe shul bavegung in Argentine', *Shul almanakh. Di Yidishe moderne shul oyf der velt*, Philadelphia: Central Committee of the Workmen's Circle Schools, pp. 320–29.

Vald, Pinie 1942, 'Yidishe sotsyalistishe und arbeter-bavegung in Argentine biz 1910', *Argetiner IWO shriftn* 2, pp. 96–126.

Vald, Pinie 1998 [1919], *Pesadilla. Novela-crónica de la semana trágica*, Rosario: Ameghino.

Valski, Stanislav 1908, 'Theorie und praktik fun anarkhismus', *Der avangard*, Buenos Aires 1, no. 2, pp. 9–12.

Valt, A. [Abraham Liessin] 1904, 'Hirsh Lekert un di Vilner may demonstratsyon in 1902', *Di tsukunft*, New York (July?), pp. 5–10.

Varone, Domingo 2004, *La Memoria Obrera. Testimonios*, second edition, Buenos Aires: Ediciones La Rosa Blindada, Cuadernos Marxistas.

Veidlinger, Jeffrey 2009, *Jewish Public Culture in the Late Russian Empire*, Bloomington IN: Indiana University Press.

Vierkandt, Alfred (eds.) 1931, *Handwörterbuch der Soziologie*, Stuttgart: Ferdinand Enke.

Vincent, David 1981, *Bread, Knowledge and Freedom. A Study of Nineteenth-Century Working Class Autobiography*, London: Europa-Publishers.

Visacovsky, Nerina 2005a, 'La educación judiá en Argentina, una multiplicidad de significados en movimiento: Del I.L. Peretz a Jabad Lubavitch', *Anuario de la sociedad argentina de historia en educación*, pp. 129–70.

Visacovsky, Nerina 2005b, 'Los judíos textiles de Villa Lynch y el I.L. Peretz. Síntesis de institución judía, club de barrio y centro cultural', Universidad Nacional de San Martín, www.unsam.edu.ar/escuelas/politica/centro_historia_politica/material/nerina .pdf (last accessed 23 April 2010).

Vivas Lencinas, Félix 1994, *Judíos en Argentina. Aspectos desconocidos de la inmigración*, Córdoba: Lerner.

Vogtmeier, Michael 1984, *Die proletarische Autobiographie 1903–1914. Studien zur Gattungs- und Funktionsgeschichte der Autobiographie*, Frankfurt am Main: Lang.

Voigt, Stefan 2009, *Institutionenökonomik*. second revised edition, Paderborn: Fink.

Volkov, Shulamit 2006, 'Jewish History. The Nationalism of Transnationalism', *Transnationale Geschichte: Themen, Tendenzen und Theorien*, edited by Gunilla-Friederike Budde, Sebastian Conrad and Oliver Janz, Göttingen: Vandenhoeck & Ruprecht, pp. 190–201.

Vural, Leyla F. 1994, *Unionism as a Way of Life. The Community Orientation of the International Ladie's Garment Workers' Union and the Amalgamated Clothink Workers of America*, PhD dissertation, Rutgers University.

Waldinger, Roger D. 1984, 'Immigrant Enterprise in the New York Garment Industry', *Social Problems* 32, no. 1, pp. 60–71.

Waldinger, Roger D. 1990, *Ethnic Entrepreneurs. Immigrant Business in Industrial Societies*, Newbury Park: Sage.

Walzer, Michael 1986, *Exodus and Revolution*, New York: Basic Books.

Warneken, Bernd Jürgen 1991, *Massenmedium Strasse: Zur Kulturgeschichte der Demonstration*, Frankfurt am Main: Campus.

Warnke, Nina 1996, 'Immigrant Popular Culture as Contested Sphere: Yiddish Music Halls, the Yiddish Press, and the Process of Americanization, 1900–1910', *Theatre Journal* 48, 3, pp. 321–35.

Wastl-Walter, D. 2001, 'Social Movements: Environmental Movements', *International Encyclopedia of the Social and Behavioral Sciences*, 26 volumes, edited by Neil J. Smelser and Paul B. Baltes, Amsterdam: Elsevier, pp. 14352–7.

Weber, Max 1978 [1922], 'Basic Sociological Terms', *Economy and Society*, edited by Guenter Roth and Claus Wittich, Berkeley, CA: University of California Press, pp. 3–62.

Web, Marek 2001, 'Between New York and Moscow: The Fate of the Bund Archives', *Jewish Politics in Eastern Europe: The Bund at 100*, edited by Jack Jacobs, New York: New York University Press, pp. 243–54.

Weeks, Theodore R. 1996, *Nation and State in Late Imperial Russia: Nationalism and Russification on the Western Frontier, 1863–1914*, DeKalb, IL: Northern Illinois. University Press.

Wehler, Hans-Ulrich 2006, 'Transnationale Geschichte – der neue Königsweg historischer Forschung?', *Transnationale Geschichte: Themen, Tendenzen und Theorien*, edited by Gunilla-Friederike Budde, Sebastian Conrad and Oliver Janz, Göttingen: Vandenhoeck & Ruprecht, pp. 161–74.

Weill, Claudie 2007, 'Biographies des socialistes juifs de l'empire russe', *Gesichter in der Menge. Kollektivbiographische Forschungen zur Geschichte der Arbeiterbewegung. Mouvement ouvrier, biographie collective, prosopographie*, edited by Bruno Groppo and Berthold Unfried, Vienna: Akademische Verlagsanstalt, pp. 95–104.

Weill, Simón 1936, *Población Israelita an la República Argentina. Conferencia pronunciada el 23 de Octubre de 1935 por el Hermano Ing. Simon Weill*, Buenos Aires: Bené Berith.

Weinreich, Uriel 1977, *Modern English-Yiddish, Yiddish-English Dictionary*, New York: Schocken.

Weinryb, Bernard D. 1946, 'The Adaptation of Jewish Labor Groups to American Life', *Jewish Social Studies* 8, pp. 219–44.

Weinstein, Ana E. and Eliahu Toker 2004, *La letra ídish en la tierra Argentina. Bibliografía de sus autores literarios*, Buenos Aires: Milá.

Weinstein, Bernard 1924, *Fertsig yohr in der yidisher arbeyter bavegung. Bletlekh erinerungen*, New York: Farlag 'veker'.

Weinstein, James 1967, *The Decline of Socialism in America, 1912–1925*, New York and London: Monthly Review Press.

Weissbach, Lee Shai 1988, 'The Jewish Communities of the United States on the Eve of Mass Migration. Some Comments on Geography and Bibliography', *American Jewish History* 78, no. 1, pp. 79–108.

Welskopp, Thomas 1994, *Arbeit und Macht im Hüttenwerk. Arbeits- und industrielle Beziehungen in der deutschen und amerikanischen Eisen- und Stahlindustrie von den 1860er bis zu den 1930er Jahren*, Bonn: Dietz.

Welskopp, Thomas 1998 'Klasse als Befindlichkeit? Vergleichende Arbeitergeschichte als kulturhistorische Herausforderung', *Archiv für Sozialgeschichte* 38, pp. 301–36.

Welskopp, Thomas 2000, *Das Banner der Brüderlichkeit. Die deutsche Sozialdemokratie vom Vormärz bis zum Sozialistengesetz*, Bonn: Dietz.

Welskopp, Thomas 2001, 'Die Dualität von Struktur und Handeln. Anthony Giddens' Strukturierungstheorie als "praxeologischer" Ansatz in der Geschichtswissenschaft', *Struktur und Ereignis*, edited by Andreas Suter and Manfred Hettling, Göttingen: Vandenhoeck & Ruprecht, pp. 99–119.

Welskopp, Thomas 2007, '"Die im Dunkeln sieht man nicht": Systematische Überlegungen zu Netzwerken der Organisierten Kriminalität am Beispiel der amerikanischen Alkoholsyndikate der Prohibitionszeit', *Unternehmerische Netzwerke: eine organisatorische Organisationsform mit Zukunft?*, edited by Hartmut Berghoff and Jörg Sydow, Stuttgart: Kohlhammer, pp. 291–317.

Welskopp, Thomas 2010, *Amerikas große Ernüchterung. Eine Kulturgeschichte der Prohibition*, Paderborn: Ferdinand Schöningh.

Welskopp, Thomas 2012, '"Wir nehmen unsere Angelegenheiten selbst in die Hände …":

Die deutsche Arbeiterbewegung vor 1863', *Katalog: Geschichte der Sozialdemokratie*, manuscript, pp. 2–23.

Welskopp, Thomas 2014, 'Sprache und Kommunikation in praxistheoretischen Geschichtsansätzen', *Unternehmen Praxisgeschichte*, Tübingen: Mohr Siebeck.

Werle, Isabel 2010, *Retrospektiven (üb)erlebten Tötens: autobiographische Zeugenschaft von Opfern und Tätern des Holocaust*, Hamburg: Kovač.

Williamson, Samuel H. 2020, 'Seven Ways to Compute the Relative Value of a U.S. Dollar Amount, 1790 to present', *MeasuringWorth*, www.measuringworth.com/uscompare/ (last accessed 11 October 2020).

Wiltfang, Greg and Doug McAdam 1991, 'Distinguishing Cost and Risk in Sanctuary Activism', *Social Forces* 69, pp. 987–1010.

Winsberg, Morton D. 1964, *Colonia Baron Hirsch, a Jewish Agricultural Colony in Argentina*, Gainesville, FL: University of Florida Press.

Wishnitzer, Mark 1948, *To Dwell in Safety. The Story of Jewish Migration since 1800*, Philadelphia, PA: Jewish Publication Society of America.

Wistrich, Robert S. 1976, *Revolutionary Jews from Marx to Trotsky*, London: Harrap.

Wolensky, Kenneth C., Nicole H. Wolensky and Robert P. Wolensky 2002, *Fighting the Union Label. The Women's Garment Industry and the ILGWU in Pennsylvania*, University Park, PA: Pennsylvania State University Press.

Wolff, Frank 2007, 'Heimat und Freiheit bei den Bundisten Vladimir Medem und Hersch Mendel', *Vom Wir zum Ich. Individuum und Autobiographik im Zarenreich*, edited by Julia Herzberg and Christoph Schmidt, Cologne: Böhlau, pp. 301–23.

Wolff, Frank 2009, 'Historiography on the General Jewish Labor Bund: Traditions, Tendencies and Expectations', *Medaon* 4, www.medaon.de/pdf/M_Wolff-4-2009.pdf (last accessed 19 February 2010).

Wolff, Frank 2012a, 'Eastern Europe Abroad. Exploring Actor-Network in Transnational Movements. The Case of the "Bund"', *International Review of Social History* 57, no. 2, pp. 229–55.

Wolff, Frank 2012b, 'From Cash Flow to Transnational Jewish Secularism: Practice and Effects of Bundist Revolutionary Fund-Raising between Eastern Europe, the United States and Argentina', presented at the BASEES Annual Conference, Fitzwilliam College, Cambridge University, 2 April.

Wolff, Frank 2013, 'Revolutionary Identity in the Process of Migration: The Commemorative Transnationalism of Bundist Culture', *East European Jewish Affairs* 43, no. 3, pp. 314–31.

Wolff, Frank 2014a, 'Global Walls and Global Movement: New Destinations in Jewish Migration, 1918–1939', *East European Jewish Affairs*, 44(3), pp. 187–204.

Wolff, Frank 2014b, 'Kollektive Identität als praktizierte Verheißung. Selbstzuschreibung und Gruppenkonstitution in der transnationalen sozialen Bewegung "Allgemeiner Jüdischer Arbeiterbund"', *Theoretische Ansätze und Konzepte der Forschung über soziale Bewegungen in den Geschichtswissenschaften*, edited by Helke Stadtland and Jürgen Mittag, Essen: Klartext, pp. 139–67.

Wolff, Frank 2017, 'Gangster, Sozialisten und Life Writing: die Zentralität der Ränder in der amerikanischen Geschichte', *Autobiographie zwischen Quelle und Text*, edited by Volker Depkat and Wolfram Pya, Berlin: Duncker & Humblot, pp. 105–21.

Wolff, Frank 2020, 'Beyond Genocide: Yiddish Culture, Bundist Networks, and How Refugee Agency Preserves Knowledge during Violence-Induced Migration', *Historical Social Research* (forthcoming).

Wolfson, Theresa 1950, 'Role of ILGWU in Stabilizing the Women's Garment Industry', *Industrial and Labor Relations Review* 4, no. 1, pp. 33–43.

Wood, Elizabeth A. 2005, *Performing Justice: Agitation Trials in Early Soviet Russia*, Ithaca, NY: Cornell University Press.

Woodhouse, Charles E. and Henry J. Tobias 1966, 'Primordial Ties and Political Process in Pre-Revolutionary Russia: The Case of the Jewish Bund', *Comparative Studies in Society and History* 8, no. 3, pp. 331–60.

Wright, Tony 1996 [1986], *Socialisms: Old and New*, second edition, New York: Routledge.

Yedlin, Marta 1982, 'Moisesville: un punto de partida', *Los Inmigrantes Judíos: Pioneros De La Argentina*, edited by Martha Wolff, Buenos Aires: M. Zago Ediciones, p. 12 f.

Yellowitz, Irwin 1976, 'American Jewish Labor: Historiographical Problems and Prospects', *American Jewish Historical Quarterly* 65, no. 3, pp. 203–14.

Yerushalmi, Yosef Hayim 1982, *Zakhor: Jewish History and Jewish Memory*, Seattle and London: University of Washington Press.

Yeshurin, Yefim 1964, *Arbeter ring in ranglenishn un dergreykhungen (1914–1964)*, New York: Aroysgegebn fun dem 'Natsyonaln sotsyaln klub' tsu zayn fuftsikstn yubl.

Y., V. 1939, 'Mir zaynen orem', *Gluboker shtime* 3.

Zadoff, Efraim 1994, *Historia de la educación judiá en Buenos Aires (1935–1957)*, Buenos Aires: Milá.

Zago, Manrique (ed.) 1982, *Los Inmigrantes Judíos: Pioneros De La Argentina*, Buenos Aires: M. Zago Ediciones.

Zaks, A. Sh. 1925, *Die geshikkhte fun arbeter ring. Tsveyter theil*, [New York]: Natsyonaler ekzekutiv-komitet fun Arbeter-ring.

Zelizer, Viviana A. 2017 [1997], *The Social Meaning of Money. Pin Money, Pay Checks, Poor Relief, and Other Currencies*, Princeton, NJ: Princeton University Press.

Zelmanovitsh, Efim Lozer 1948, 'Mayn baheft sikh mitn "bund"', *Historisher zamlbukh. Materialn un dokumentn tsutshayer tsu der geshikhte fun algemeyner yidisher arbeter-bund*, Warsaw: Ringen, pp. 49–53.

Zelmanowicz, Motl 1948, 'Tsum gevisn fon der velt', *Historisher Zamlbukh. Materialn un dokumentn tsutshayer tsu der geshikhte fun Algemeyner Yidisher Arbeter-Bund*, Varshe: Ringen, pp. 87–91.

Zelmanowicz, Motl 2009, *A Bundist Comments on History as It Was Being Made. The Post-Cold War Era*, translated by Barnett Zumoff, Philadelphia, PA: Xlibris.

Zimmerman, Joshua D. 2004, *Poles, Jews, and the Politics of Nationality. The Bund and the Polish Socialist Party in Late Tsarist Russia, 1892–1914*, PhD dissertation, University of Wisconsin.

Zimmermann, Moshe 2006, 'Die transnationale Holocaust-Erinnerung', *Transnationale Geschichte: Themen, Tendenzen und Theorien*, edited by Gunilla-Friederike Budde, Sebastian Conrad and Oliver Janz, Göttingen: Vandenhoeck & Ruprecht, pp. 202–16.

Zivion 1907, 'Di yidishe arbeyter in Paris', *Di hofnung*, Vilnius 14, p. 1.

Zivion 1909, 'Di bundisten un di S.L.P.', *Der arbeyter*.

Zivion 1917, '20 yor Bund un 5 yor federatsye', *Di tsukunft* 11, p. 629.

Zuckerman, Frederic S. 1996, *The Tsarist Secret Police in Russian Society. 1880–1917*, Basingstoke: Macmillan.

Index

Abramovitch, Raphael   156, 370, 378, 389
Acción Obrera   303
Agudat Hamorim   299–301
Alter, Viktor   83, 143, 393
Amalgamated Clothing Workers of America (ACWA)   291, 381
American Federation of Labor (AFL)   23–4, 291, 382
An-sky (Shloyfme Zanvl Rappoport)   118, 189, 402
Anarchism (anarchist, etc.)   43, 44, 47, 112, 114, 147, 154, 228, 284, 302–4, 306, 308, 311, 337–9, 396
Antek, Samuel   239
Arbeter emigratsye biro   304
Arbeter-ring   28, 141, 148, 156, 182, 197, 215, 216, 252, 257–68, 275, 278, 280–2, 293–6, 310–13, 318–35, 343, 357–60, 365–6, 380–2, 388–9, 395, 410
Arbeter-ring, Bundist branches   262, 265, 282
Arbeter-ring, Dvinsker Branch 75   267, 333, 365–6
Arbeter-ring, English-speaking branch   334
Arbeter-ring schools   353, 420
Arbeter shul organisatsye (Arbetershulorg)   339–43, 347
Asch, Sholem   305
Avangard (Group)   114–6, 121–2, 125, 162, 183, 205, 216, 227, 231, 235, 245–7, 254–8, 268–76, 296–9, 317, 337–58, 368, 370–6, 422
Aydlman, Fishl   192–3, 211, 215
Aysenshtot, Dovid   389
Azef, Evgeny F.   71, 89

Babits, Khaym   203
Bakunin, Mikhail   225
Baron, Julius   293, 328
Baskin, Joseph   252, 293, 381
Bauman, Zygmunt   47, 251
Bebel, August   126–7
Beer   63–4, 228, 396
Beilis Affair   240–1
Benjamin, Walter   43–4, 107, 124, 130
Berg, Ezra   392

Bergman, Israel   136, 143, 256, 289
Berlin   378, 379, 380, 384, 389, 394–5
Berman, Layb   71, 155–6, 160, 176, 182, 192, 250, 366
Bernstein, Eduard   379–80
Bershter Bund   82
Bialik, Chaim Nachman   305
Bialystok   212–13, 223, 410
Biblioteca popular nueva rusia   371
Biblioteca rusa   122, 225, 227, 269–71, 296–7
Bielsk   212–13
Birobidzhan   43, 274, 305, 347–9, 352
Birzshe   50, 58, 65–6, 95, 201–2, 223–9, 249, 295
Blekhman, Layb   42
Blind, Yitskhok   134
Blond, Dinah   238
Blum, Hillel   243
Blyumin-Kurski, M.   435
Bolsheviks   53, 128, 137–40, 166–7, 207, 210, 268, 272–3, 303
Bondarev, A.   269
Borochov schools   339–43, 346
Botoshansky, Jacob   351, 354–5, 357, 397, 399, 401, 406
Boym, Dovid   201
Buber, Martin   278
Bund anniversaries   67–8, 142, 241, 244, 274, 293, 370, 381, 391
Bund Archives   88, 161, 195, 196, 198, 325
Bund in Australia   149, 184, 195, 415, 419, 420
Bund in Belgium   144, 195, 414
Bund in France   195, 234, 389
Bund in Galicia   211–12, 271
Bund in Germany   394–5
Bund in Switzerland   110, 359–60
Bund in Uruguay   117, 244, 419
Bund Club in Buenos Aires   116, 376
Bund Club in Montevideo   376, 419
Bund Club in New York   142, 194, 204, 274–5, 363, 376–7, 383
Bund Club in Paris   69
Bund Clubs   69, 116, 142, 194, 204, 274–5, 363, 376–7, 383, 419
Byalon, Avrom   200

INDEX

Cahan, Abraham   241, 253–4, 257–8, 277, 286, 291, 360, 390, 392
Carasnik, Sam   86
Caspe, Abraham   136, 320, 360, 364–5
Centro Sionista   371
Chassidim (Chassidic, etc.)   44, 69, 402, 418
Chiaskelevitz, José   276
Chicago   242–3, 322
Collection lists   338, 341, 371–6, 403, 405
Colonies, Jewish   30–2, 305
Comité contra les pogromes en Polonia   372
Communism (Communists, etc.)   104, 112, 137–8, 140–1, 147, 154, 247, 263, 273–6, 302, 303–8, 311, 329, 331, 341–2, 345–8, 352–4, 375, 402–3
Communist Party, Argentina (Partido Comunista de la Argentina)   246, 273, 302, 306
Communist Party, Poland   146
Communist Party, Russia (RCP(b))   82, 104, 138, 207
Communist Party, USA   141, 242–3

DAIA/AMIA   346, 353, 420, 426
Daily Worker   242
De Leon, Daniel   23
Debs, Eugene V.   23–4, 28
Decembrists   114, 124, 128
Demonstrations   16, 48, 67–8, 223, 228, 240–7, 392
Der avangard   42, 73, 110–115, 117–19, 122, 131, 133, 237, 268–71, 297–9, 370
Der forverts (Forverts, etc.)   22, 29, 35, 46, 111, 136, 161, 202, 236–8, 250–1, 255–8, 275, 277–280, 282, 289–2, 357, 387, 390, 392, 395
Der kemfer   143, 253, 256, 289–90
Der mebl arbeter   303
Der sotsyaldemokrat   271
Der veker   111, 244, 252–3, 275, 288
Der yidisher arbeter   214
Di arbeter shtime   253
Di hofnung   115, 126–7, 137, 234, 253, 288
Di naye velt   257
Di shvue   36, 64, 109, 114, 244, 253, 402
Di tsukunft   126, 257, 318, 395
Dimitrov, Georgi   307

Doikayt   12, 16, 19–36, 121, 125, 139, 144, 147–8, 180, 217, 221, 240, 248, 258, 271, 280, 290, 323, 327–8, 349, 351, 398–407, 408, 412, 415–19
Donations   97, 131, 142, 187, 236, 242, 290, 298, 311, 338, 341, 344, 350, 361, 363–70, 371–2, 377, 381–90, 396–7, 401–6
Doyres bundistn   140, 171, 178, 189–93
Dubinsky, David   390
Dubkowski, Irshl   211
Duma elections of 1912   76, 200, 236

Edelman, Marek   1–2, 109, 349
Elections (electoral campaigns, etc.)   28, 75–7, 203, 204, 228–30, 237, 241, 369, 394
Emigration, flight   11, 30, 72, 110–11, 114, 13–3, 213–5, 222–8, 276, 295
Enlightenment (enlighteners, Maskilim, etc.)   44–5, 51, 61, 77–9, 105, 402
Entin, Joel   318
Epshteyn, A.   266, 269
Epshteyn, Shakhne   320
Epstein, José   352
Erlich, Henryk   135, 143, 389, 393–4

Farband fun yidishe folks shuln   347–8
Federación Obrera Regional Argentina (FORA)   303, 308
Federal Bureau of Investigation (FBI)   59
Feygenboym, Abraham   200
Feynberg, Israel   265–6
Feynsilber, Abraham   211
Folks shul rat (Alianza Israelita de Beneficencia y Educación)   337
Foreign Committee of the Bund, Geneva   90–91, 98, 124, 288, 290, 359–61, 364–5
Forenberg, Karl   359
Forois   363
Forverts Association   29, 141, 148, 257, 277
Forverts Building   29, 141, 279, 281, 381
Fox, Bertha   65–6, 94, 227
Fraynd fun bund   241, 251, 281–2, 359–61, 363–6
Friedman, Lena   294
Frumkin, Esther   138–40, 177

Gaucho Judío   32, 305
Gelberg, A.   380

Gelberg, Naftali 200
Gelibter, Philip 380
Gershuni, Grigory 89
Gezelshaft far yidishe veltlekhe shuln in argentine 239, 345
Goldberg, Manye 187–8, 195, 214
Goldfarb, Matis 352
Goldmintz, Hershl 346
Gomel 2, 21, 51, 66, 267
Gordin, Jacob 360
Grosman, Israel 250
Grosser, Bronislav 370
Gurevitsh, Moyshe 230, 237, 290

Haymarket Affair 242, 303
Hersh, Libman 80
Hertz, Jacob Sholem 190, 192, 200
Hester Market 225–6
Heym-shneyder un tasheristn fareyn 308, 311
Hilfs-komitet far di yidish-veltlekhe shuln in Poyln (Hilfs-komitet) 396–7, 404–6
Hilfs komitet farn bund in freyen rusland 372–5
Hilfsverein der deutschen Juden 378–9, 384
Hirschbein, Peretz 305
Holidays, Bundist/socialist 64, 124, 137–42, 242–4, 247
Holidays, Jewish 241–2, 350
Holocaust 12, 16, 61, 104, 127, 147, 184, 190, 234, 356, 358, 382, 414–16, 418–20
Holocaust autobiography 166–70, 174, 180–2, 195, 198, 204–5, 222
Horn, Yosef 132

Imprisonment (arrest, etc.) 59–61, 67, 71, 86, 90, 110, 126, 143, 171, 202, 244, 281, 424
International Jewish Labor Bund 12
International Ladies' Garment Workers' Union (ILGWU) 28, 141, 267, 291–4, 310, 365, 368, 381, 384
International Workers Order (IWO) 262, 275

Jewish Labor Committee (JLC) 368, 378, 381, 382–3, 391, 393
Jewish Renaissance 309, 408

Joint Distribution Committee (JDC) 378, 383
Justo, Augustin P. 247

Kanutsky, Guitl 302, 344–5, 351, 357
Kaplansky, Sh. 269
Kaplinski, Mikhel 71, 237
Kasen (kassy, trade union funds) 58, 80, 82, 259–60
Katz, Pinie 305–6, 309, 397
Kautsky, Karl 124, 126–7, 288
Kazin, Alfred 424
Khanin, Nokhem 65, 129, 244, 265–6, 381, 389
Khavershaft 12, 131, 172, 226, 264, 326, 356, 373, 386, 393, 424
Khazar mart 226
Khotin, Bela 332
Kleyner bund 93–7, 196, 267
Kling, Lazar 187–8
Kobe 145, 250
Kohn, A. 272–3, 373–5
Kossovski, Vladimir 143–5, 187
Kravchinsky, Sergey M. 129
Kremer, Arkadi 19, 187, 392–3
Kremer, Pati 392
Kruzhki (circles) 58, 63, 69, 78–9, 233, 312, 315, 322, 392
Kuybyshev, Valerian 138
Kushner, Mayr 293–4
Kuvelsman, Sh. 243–4, 247

La Protesta 302, 309, 337
Labour racketeering 85, 396
Language question in emigration 269–71, 296–7, 322
Language-based federations (language branches, agrupaciónes idiomáticos·) 246, 257, 334–5
Laubstein, Israel 117, 162, 217, 269, 276
Lebns-fragn 150, 162, 202–3, 210
Leiserson, William M. 226–7
Leivick, H. (Leivick Halpern) 327, 363
Lekert, Hirsh 90–3, 130, 140, 177, 263, 331
Lenin, Vladimir Ilyich Ulyanov 52–3, 81–2, 92
Leninism (Leninists, etc.) 63
Lestschinsky, Jakob 379, 394
Lestshinsky, Yosef (Khmurner) 134

INDEX 509

Levine, Benjamin   381–4, 389
Levin, Sholem   72, 85
Levin, Yankel   94
Lewintal, Simon   301–2, 308
Liber, Mark   368–9
Lichtenstein, Israel   186–7, 379, 394
Liessin, Abraham (Avrom Valt)   257, 260, 278, 282, 359
Lifshits, Yosef   66, 202, 225
Lincoln, Abraham   24
Lodz   223, 389
London, Meyer   29, 180, 241–2, 278, 360, 363, 390
Lower East Side, cultural life   141, 229, 236
Lower East Side, living conditions   22–3, 226, 238
Lower East Side, political life   26, 29, 37, 141, 241–2, 278, 290–3
Lublin   65, 202, 211
Lutik, Rakhel   328
Luxemburg, Rosa   67
Lviv   223

Mannheim, Karl   18, 41, 103, 209
Martov, Julius   378
Marx, Karl   19, 20, 44–5, 154, 225, 312
Marxism (Marxists, etc.)   3, 4, 15, 19, 44–5, 51–2, 80–1, 92, 107–8, 113, 124–5, 137, 141, 173, 259, 337, 339, 350
Mas, M.   269
May Day   49, 66, 67–8, 90–2, 223, 241, 242–7, 248–9, 287, 298, 308, 350
May Laws   60, 78
Mayer, Dovid   200–1, 275, 278, 381, 384, 388
Mecca Center   141, 233, 381
Medem, Gina   349
Medem, Vladimir   42, 45, 60, 70, 76, 89, 92–3, 132–3, 136, 150, 176, 182, 202–3, 213, 280, 293, 394
Medem Club   381–3, 388, 398
Medem Committee   384, 388
Medem Sanatorium   70, 314, 378–9, 383, 384–8
Medem vinkl   194
Mehring, Franz   124, 288
Memorik   16–18, 37, 104, 107–49, 151–2, 155–9, 161–7, 177–84, 185–6, 189–92, 209–10, 222, 263–4, 274, 307, 321, 356, 363, 390, 392, 395, 410–11, 414–16, 418

Mensheviks   156, 267, 378, 389
Merezhin, Avrom   138–9
Metaloviets, Hershl   176, 202, 273
Mikhalevitsh, Beynish   133, 135–6, 162, 186–7
Mill, Dzshon   81, 150
Mishpokhedikayt, mishpokhe   12, 22, 221, 223, 226, 250, 264, 360, 377
Mlotek, Yosef   333
Mogilev   294–5
Montevideo   21, 117, 123, 243, 244, 348, 350, 353, 376, 396, 399, 420–1
Motzkin, Leo   279
Mussolini, Benito   229, 247
Mutnikovitsh, Abraham (Gleb Mutnik)   73

Narodnaya Volya, Narodniks   43–5, 281
Natsyonaler sotsyaler klub (NSK)   262–5
Nayvelt   305–6
Necrology, obituaries   112–13, 129–31, 136, 145, 170, 192, 196
Niger, Shmuel   291, 313, 322, 329
Novidor   203
Novikov, Yoel   63–4, 69, 176
Novodvorsky, Sara   339, 354
Novogrudski, Emanuel   238, 377

Okhrana   59, 71–2, 201
Oler, Leon   16, 150–1, 157, 201
Olgin, Moshe   46, 340
Once (Buenos Aires)   34, 237, 299, 300, 341, 343
Opatoshu, Josef   363

Paris   30, 43, 69, 234, 240, 265, 267, 306, 314, 317, 362, 389, 394
Pat, Jacob   383, 389, 395
Pat, Yekum   145
Peretz, Isaac Leib   200, 337
Peretz School, Lavalle   277, 300, 350–1, 355–6, 397, 421
Peretz School, Villa Lynch   341, 349, 351–2
Peskin, Samuel   279, 359
Pine, Max   361
Plehve, Vyacheslav von   59, 89
Poale Zion (Poale Zionists, etc.)   79, 80, 88, 105, 148, 154, 262, 279, 302, 314, 318, 320, 323, 324, 330, 339, 340, 345–7, 348, 349–50, 351, 352, 354, 356, 372, 380, 394, 410

Polish Socialist Party (PPS)   71, 172, 203, 212–13, 267
Political picnics   227–33, 287, 338–9
Popular front   307–8, 422
Portnoy, Noakh   69, 143–5, 156–8, 187, 238, 370, 393
Prokor   339

Questionnaires   56, 61, 73, 75–6, 88, 95–7, 111, 158, 186–208, 210, 214, 262, 291, 301, 375

Rafes, Moshe   138–9
Regalsky, Mordekhai   345
Regenbogen, Shmuel Layb   293
Revolution of 1905   4–5, 36, 51, 82, 86–8, 94–5, 126–7, 268, 287, 298, 359–62, 419, 422
Revolution of 1917 (February)   4, 203, 246, 268, 282, 393
Revolution of 1917 (October)   2, 4, 104, 107, 116, 135, 137–40, 142, 175, 181, 202, 210, 231, 237, 246, 264, 268, 303, 418
Riis, Jacob   226
Rogoff, Hillel (Harry)   390
Rolland, Romain   307
Rollansky, Samuel (Shmuel)   276–7, 345–6, 350–1, 397, 399, 421
Roosevelt, Theodore   24
Rotshester tsaytung   135, 253–7
Rousseau, Jean-Jacques   154
Rozen, Maxim   273, 304
Rozen, Naythan   93–5
Rudovski, Y.   203
Russian Social Democratic Labour Party (RSDLP)   4, 126, 135, 210, 255, 257
Russo-Japanese War   93, 250

Sacco, Ferdinando Nicola   303
Salutsky, Yankef   257, 275, 282
Sanders, Bernie   2
Sholem Aleichem Schools   232, 322, 330, 338–42, 348, 349–52, 375, 399
Secondary Bundism   19, 28, 37, 111, 117–19, 122–3, 143, 148, 161–4, 246, 250–83, 291–3, 298, 300, 305, 308, 318–21, 322–33, 344, 341, 357–8, 362–7, 382, 388, 409, 411, 418–21
Self-defence (B.O., boevye otriady, kamf-druzshine)   51, 66, 84, 87–93, 157, 227, 364, 370, 371

Semana Trágica (Tragic Week)   116, 272
Shefner, Barukh   120, 134, 398–404, 405–6, 420, 422
Sheyner, Y.   269
Shirtwaist Strike   178, 256, 277, 292
Shtern, Berl   63, 212–13, 215–16
Shulman, Viktor   129, 202
Shvarts, Pinkhas   180
Siberia (exile, Katorga, etc.)   20, 57, 59–61, 84, 114, 166, 186, 202, 204, 236, 263, 377
Skutelski, Mendel   389
Smuggling   58, 72–4, 312, 364, 368
Social Democratic Party of Germany (SPD)   71, 124
Socialism, diluted   27, 248, 283, 295
Socialist Labor Party (SLP)   23, 267, 295
Socialist Party of America (SP)   23–4, 28–9, 241, 255, 257, 261–2, 282, 286–7, 294–5
Socialist Party of Argentina (Partido Socialista)   255, 258, 269–70, 286, 404
Socialist Revolutionaries (party)   43, 44, 52–3, 71, 89, 92–3, 203, 281, 392
Sotsyalistischer kinder-farband (SKIF)   79, 95–6, 203, 314–15
Soviet Union   137–9, 168, 170, 181, 245, 250, 303, 307, 309, 323, 349, 402, 408
Springfield Pogrom   242
Stolypin, Pyotr A.   127
Strikes   16–17, 24, 45–8, 50, 58, 60, 67, 80–4, 85–7, 94, 124, 178, 228, 240, 244–5, 249, 256, 274, 277, 284–311, 326–7, 350, 363, 403, 424
Switzerland   46, 50, 91, 98, 110, 125, 214
Syrkin, Nachman   279, 320
Szerer, Emanuel (Sherer)   145, 169

Tabachinsky, Benjamin   134, 345–6, 357, 391, 397, 405, 421
Tabatshnik, Khaym   211
Tailors' union   211, 309, 372, 401
Terrorism (Russia)   52, 59, 89, 92–3, 128–9, 331
Thälmann, Ernst   307
Thomas, Norman   29
Trade unions in Argentina   115, 193, 244, 295–311, 420
Trade unions in the US   24, 85, 198, 226–7, 252, 255, 262, 275, 284, 286, 290–1, 309–11, 382, 413

Tscherikover, Elias 324
Tselemenski, Yakob 201
Tsenter avangard 268–71, 272, 296
Tsentral farband fun di bundistishen organisatyonen in Amerika 290, 362, 365, 368–9
Tsentral hilfs-komite far di yidishe milkhomeleydende (Comité Central de Socorro a las Víctimas Israelitas de la Guerra) [Comité Central de Socorro] 370
Tsentrale veltlekhe yidishe shul-organisatsye (TSVYSHO) 346–51, 356, 380, 391, 398, 402, 405
Tsentrale yidishe kultur-organisatsye (TSYKO) 354–6
Tsentrale yidishe shul organisatsye (TSYSHO) 78–9, 120, 173, 295, 313, 314–17, 319, 344–6, 349–53, 358, 378–80, 381, 383, 388, 391, 394, 397, 405
Tsukerman, Noyekh 419

Union Israelita de Galitzia 403
Unión Sindical Argentina (US) 303
United Hebrew Trades (UHT) 141, 160, 290
Unzer tsayt 108, 111, 124, 143–9, 161, 169, 180–2, 217, 253, 388–9, 414
Uriburu, General José Félix 33, 116, 247, 345, 347, 397

Vaad Hakhinukh (VH) 336, 350–1
Vald, Pinie (Pedro) 134–5, 216, 224–5, 235–6, 269–71, 295, 344–6, 37, 369, 397–8, 401, 422–3
Vanzetti, Bartolomeo 303
Vasershtros, Alekher Zelig 202
Vasong, Moshe 211
Veber, M. 272–3, 372–5
Veterans Fond 389–90
Villa Crespo 341, 343
Vilnius 3, 21, 36, 63, 70, 80, 90–2, 95, 130, 210, 243–4, 253, 299, 382, 392, 410
Vilnius Opposition 269
Vladeck, Barukh Charney 278, 282, 291, 293, 381–2, 384
Vladimir Medem Centre (Buenos Aires) 353
Volkovitsh, Pinkhes 215

Wahl, Victor von 90–1
Warsaw 21, 66, 68–70, 95, 109, 132–3, 150, 169, 180, 200–2, 210, 225, 233, 351, 366, 389, 395–6
Warsaw ghetto 1–1, 5, 108, 147, 169, 180, 193, 216, 349, 415
Weber, Max 41, 224, 392
Weill, Simón 32–4
Weinstein, Bernard 290
Weizmann, Chaim 279
Wintshevsky, Morris 360
World Bund 144, 146, 165, 187–8, 195
World War I 4, 24, 29, 31, 34, 66, 83, 118, 132, 150, 154, 170, 201–3, 225, 243, 246, 255, 278, 299, 370
World War II 5, 12, 16, 77–8, 89, 111, 143, 148, 161, 165, 167–9, 176–9, 185–90, 216–18, 232, 238, 274, 311, 358, 370, 377, 382, 388, 393, 412, 415, 419

Yankelevitsh, Yankl 202
Yeshiva 88, 172–3, 187, 206–7, 212–13, 265
Yeshurin, Yefim 262–4
Yevsektsiya 82, 138–40, 177, 181, 207, 273, 304, 349
Yiddishland 299–306, 346
Yidish natsyonaler arbeter farband (Farband) 262, 318, 322–3, 324, 330, 380, 403
Yidishe agitatsye-byuro (Agitation Bureau) 251, 257–8, 265
Yidishe arbeter froy (YAF) 58, 96–7
Yidishe lerer organsatsye in argentine 301
Yidishe literarishe gezelshaft (Warsaw) 200
Yidishe ratsyonalistishe gezelshaft (Argentina) 303, 337–9
Yidisher arbeyterfarband far kegnzeytiger hilf 232
Yidisher kultur farband (IKUF) 275, 306, 397
Yidisher sotsyalistisher farband (YSF) 141, 160, 265–6, 274–6, 282
Yidisher sotsyalistisher farband in argentine (YSFA) 28, 117, 131, 194, 246–7, 276–7, 305, 308, 344, 350, 420–2
Yidishkayt 4, 12, 20, 37, 43, 58, 77–9, 81–4, 104–6, 107, 115, 116–21, 180, 207, 210, 238–40, 241, 260, 264, 268–71, 281, 284–311, 312–357, 368, 390, 395–6, 406, 408–9, 418–20

YIVO   95, 276, 277, 344, 350, 394, 421
YIVO 1942 autobiographical contest   158, 161, 183, 262, 276
Yudisher arbeyter farband   299
Yugnt bund 'tsukunft'   95–7, 186, 203, 211, 215, 314, 351

Zaks, A.S.   258, 260, 321
Zasulich, Vera   72
Zelenski   135
Zelmanovitsh, F. Loyzer   389
Zelmanovitsh, Motl   278
Zhitlowsky, Chaim   392
Zigelboym, Artur (Oskar)   83, 187
Zivion (Benzion Hofman)   69, 213–14, 234, 258, 273, 275, 278–9, 282, 318–21, 326, 357, 381, 390
Zshezshinski, Herman   211
Zubatov, Sergei V.   59, 71–2, 143, 171

www.ingramcontent.com/pod-product-compliance
Lightning Source LLC
Chambersburg PA
CBHW071327080526
44587CB00017B/2759